SEXUAL NATURE
SEXUAL CULTURE

CHICAGO SERIES ON SEXUALITY, HISTORY, AND SOCIETY

EDITED BY JOHN C. FOUT

SEXUAL NATURE
SEXUAL CULTURE

Edited by
PAUL R. ABRAMSON
STEVEN D. PINKERTON

THE UNIVERSITY OF CHICAGO PRESS
CHICAGO AND LONDON

PAUL R. ABRAMSON is professor of psychology at the University of California, Los Angeles. STEVEN D. PINKERTON is a teaching associate in psychology at the University of California, Los Angeles, and an associate research scientist at the Aerospace Corporation.

The University of Chicago Press, Chicago 60637
The University of Chicago Press, Ltd., London
©1995 by The University of Chicago
All rights reserved. Published 1995
Printed in the United States of America

04 03 02 01 00 99 98 97 96 95   1 2 3 4 5
ISBN: 0-226-00181-4 (cloth)
        0-226-00182-2 (paper)

Library of Congress Cataloging-in-Publication Data
Sexual nature, sexual culture / edited by Paul R. Abramson, Steven D.
  Pinkerton.
        p.   cm. — (Chicago series on sexuality, history, and society)
    Includes bibliographical references and index.
    1. Sex (Biology)   2. Sex.   I. Abramson, Paul R., 1949–
II. Pinkerton, Steven D.   III. Series.
QP251.S48283   1995
306.7—dc20   94-36662

Good night vanilla,
good night banana,
good night Annaka,
good night Sienna.
Daddy loves you.
(P.A.)

To my parents, Stan and Judy, who taught me
not only to ask questions, but to expect answers. (S.P.)

Contents

Preface

This volume is the culmination of a process initiated by Paul Abramson (UCLA) and Gilbert Herdt (University of Chicago) early in 1991, and developed and nurtured since with the additional assistance of Steven Pinkerton (also of UCLA). The basic impetus was to facilitate the conception and elucidation of broadly conceived theoretical perspectives on human sexuality, especially those that acknowledge the importance and implications of sexual pleasure in both reproductive and nonreproductive sexual behaviors.

The premise that sexual pleasure might offer a novel and fruitful vantage from which to view the diversity of human sexuality gained substantial momentum with the receipt of a grant from the Wenner-Gren Foundation for Anthropological Research. This grant provided the generous financial and organizational support required to underwrite a small multidisciplinary conference devoted to theoretical work on human sexuality, entitled "Theorizing Sexuality: Evolution, Culture, and Development." The conference was held March 19–27, 1993, at the Hotel do Gunicho in the picturesque coastal village of Cascais, Portugal, and was attended by a group of twenty-three scholars, drawn from such diverse fields as anthropology, endocrinology, psychology, sociology, primatology, and operations research. (A brief overview of the conference [Okami and Pendleton, 1994] is provided in the Appendix.)

All who have had the pleasure of attending a Wenner-Gren conference agree that it is a singular experience. Besides the preferential treatment participants receive and the unique locales typically selected, there are no conference presentations! Papers are written and distributed to conference participants months in advance. Hence, the "working" conference is freed for discussion and thoughtful criticism of the papers, and of other material germane to the field.

Since the papers are written prior to the meeting, and are thoroughly analyzed and criticized at the conference itself, the process of compiling them into an edited volume is somewhat simplified. Of course, conference papers do not spontaneously fashion themselves into a cohesive volume if simply left alone in a dark room. Substantial work and editing are necessary to achieve this objective. The final phase required to ensure fruition of the original premise was therefore undertaken by Paul Abramson and Steven Pinkerton, in cooperation with the University of Chicago Press. The end product, accordingly, is the culmination of all these efforts and sources of support.

Several considerations influenced the selection of the specific topics—and individuals—represented in the following chapters. In large part the composition of this volume was dictated by the protocol of the Weñner-Gren conference. As noted above, a select group of prominent researchers was assembled for a two-week period of cooperation and cohabitation, during which time various theoretical perspectives on human sexuality were developed, presented, and thoughtfully criticized. The small size of the group facilitated debate as well as cooperation. Diversity in training and outlook was also emphasized, so as to broaden the theoretical base. The limited size of the group and the emphasis on diversity over commonality necessarily produced a body of work that is selective and contrastive, rather than exhaustive and uniform. Nevertheless, the scope of the topics and perspectives represented herein, is, we believe, unparalleled in any extant publication.

Overview

Broadly speaking, the main objective of this volume is to highlight the mutual and interdependent contributions that nature and nurture render to an understanding of human sexual behavior. More specifically, it represents the development of transdisciplinary theoretical approaches towards the problem of assessing the relative importance of procreation and pleasure to human sexuality. This objective is collectively pursued from anthropological, biological, historical, psychological, and sociological vantage points. This volume presents not only a synthesis of existing data, but daring theoretical voyages as well. As such, it aims to articulate the substance of the pleasure/procreation distinction within human sexual behavior, and also to inform future investigations.

Though this topic—sex—is both highly familiar and widely engaging, its stature as an academic endeavor is paradoxically anemic. Historically, the field was dominated by physicians, whose primary concerns were the prevention, diagnosis, and treatment of sexual (and social) maladies. Scholarly and scientific interests were thus secondary to clinical concerns. Consequently, the study of human sexual behavior was co-opted by the "disease" practitioners (moral, physical, and psychological), hindering its assimilation into a broad scholarly—and transdisciplinary—tradition. Even Freud, who clearly recognized the necessity of healthy sexuality to psychological well-being, began his investigations into the sexual lives of his patients with the object of curing them of such psychosomatic maladies as hysteria. The medicalization of sexuality is further exemplified by the observation that psychoanalysis, a therapy in which the patient's sexual history is usually of paramount importance, can be practiced in the United States only by medically trained psychiatrists.

Social and political constraints that sought to stigmatize the study of human sexual behavior by characterizing it as an illegitimate intellectual enterprise strongly exacerbated the situation. Besides questioning the personal motives of sexual scholars and scientists, academia failed to offer the nurturing opportunities (e.g., designated professorships for the study of human sexuality), resources (e.g., grants and fellowships), and support (e.g., prospects for tenure, etc.) that would foster development in this field (Abramson, 1990). Furthermore, despite a growing number of introductory human sexuality courses in universities across the nation, the serious study of sexual matters remains an academic taboo, as witnessed by the scarcity of advanced, graduate-level courses and programs that focus on this important subject.

The precarious status of sex research is not merely a historical artifact. The *Journal of the History of Sexuality,* for example, did not open its door as a publication outlet—and thereby signify the emergence of a scholarly discipline—until 1990. Surely this subject matter (and the need for experts in this field) predated the last decade of the twentieth century. Even the oldest journals in the broader field of human sexual behavior, such as the *Journal of Sex Research,* the *Journal of Homosexuality,* and the *Archives of Sexual Behavior,* are of relatively recent origin: only one of these, the *Journal of Sex Research,* predates the 1970s, having first been published in 1965. This is not to deny or deprecate the important contributions of such eminent sexuality researchers as Havelock Ellis, Alfred Kinsey, William Masters, and Virginia Johnson (see Robinson, 1976), but only to suggest that, for sexuality studies, the arrival of the usual accoutrements of academic respectability has been greatly delayed.

Numerous other examples from disparate fields in the study of sexuality could also be cited to illustrate the piecemeal development of sexuality research. For instance, although the importance of cross-cultural research to our understanding of human sexuality predates Freud, Malinowski, and Mead, the anthropological imperative has faded over the past several decades. Around 1960, a now canonical conceptual split emerged between "sex" (biology) and "gender" (culture). Margaret Mead's much neglected paper, "Cultural Determinants of Human Sexuality," marked a watershed in discussion of the issues, with serious attention devoted to the theory and method of sexual investigation from an anthropological perspective. However, the last "unified" effort to engage social and biological scientists in a dialogue with anthropologists may very well have been a symposium chaired by Frank Beach in the mid-1960s (in which the anthropologists Gregory Bateson and William Davenport participated).

Much of the relevant work since the end of the 1960s has been concerned with gender, gendered relations, and the position of women in society. However, little of the work emanating from within the social and biological sciences has focused specifically on human sexual behavior and relationships. Kinship and marriage, for example, have generally been framed without reference to sexual behavior, or as though the idealized norms and institutional goals of society mirrored the experience and behavior of individuals. Furthermore, scant attention has been paid to the role and functions of aberrant or non-normative sexuality, including variability within and between individuals belonging to a common culture (e.g., life-span considerations), and differences across cultures and historical epochs. Finally, the multifield approach to the study of sexuality (linking prehistory, history, psychology, culture, language, biology, and evolution) has, to date, been concerned primarily with reproduction and reproductive fitness.

Sexuality as a *category* of social and biological study has also remained fuzzy and inconsistent within academia. Currently, we labor under the constricting influence of two conceptual dichotomies: sex/gender, which too harshly compartmentalizes the phenomena of interest into the illusory categories of "the biological" and "the cultural"; and the supposed conflict between essentialism and constructionism, which is often played out as a duel between cultural and biological interpretations of human sexuality. In fact, few serious scholars or scientists align themselves with the polar extremities of these dualities; most operate within the confines of an interactionist perspective, seeing a number of factors as influencing particular sexual phenomena. However, the precise nature of these interactionist approaches, and the place of current theory construction across various scientific fields, remains vague, somewhat contentious, and rather confusing.

Sexual Nature / Sexual Culture

The emphasis upon sexual reproduction (individual and group), in contrast to sexual pleasure, derives in part from the social ideology and Judeo-Christian heritage of Western societies. The preeminence of reproduction within Darwinian theory also tends to minimize appreciation of the role that sexual pleasure plays in human psychology, culture, and evolution (see Abramson and Pinkerton, 1995, for an expansive development of these issues). This emphasis, unfortunately, has also made it difficult to disentangle the diverse functions of human sexuality. Obviously, conclusions about our sexual heritage depend upon the questions we ask and the kinds of theories and data advanced to answer them. A clear bias towards reproductive interpretations of human sexuality is evident in much of the scientific discourse.

Recently, however, the social and biological sciences have begun in earnest to examine the complex, interacting dynamics that constitute the core of human sexuality. (No doubt this heightened awareness stems, in part, from concerns engendered by the current HIV/AIDS crisis.) The chapters presented herein reflect this new direction by considering both the "natural" and "cultural" properties of human sexuality, with particular concern for a reconsideration of the meanings of pleasure. A variety of disciplines is represented here

because the reconceptualization of sexual pleasure, and its relation to reproductive behavior, is a topic that clearly spans the artificial boundaries erected
by academicians.

To remain viable, a transdisciplinary approach to pleasure and reproductive
sexuality must engage at least three levels of analysis: the individual (developmental and adaptive-behavioral), the societal (historical and institutional), and
the cultural (representational and ideological). Thus, the chapters and topics
that make up this volume were selected to represent (in some measure) each
level of analysis, without compromising or unduly favoring a relevant vantage
point. At the individual level, for example, sexual behavior patterns (in humans
and other primates), biological systems, arousal, and private subjective states
of pleasure are considered throughout the volume. At the societal level, several
chapters examine historically situated institutions (such as family, church, etc.)
and their relations to sexuality and pleasure. And finally, at the cultural level,
the representation of categories (e.g., "homosexuality"), the collective experience of rituals, the shaping and control of sexuality by prescription and pro-
scription, and comparative approaches to sexual variability are also considered.

In addition to incorporating the three levels of analysis outlined above, the
chapters contained herein encompass four pivotal themes: *Evolutionary Origins, Biology and Behavior, Cultural Dimensions,* and *Quantitative Models
and Measurement.* The *Evolutionary Origins* chapters examine theories of selective fitness, attraction, desire, pleasure, and sexual function in human and
nonhuman primate evolution. The *Biology and Behavior* chapters raise questions about the genetic and hormonal origins (and expression) of sexual orientation, gender, and pleasure. The *Cultural Dimensions* chapters address the
role of pleasure in cultural practices, cultural representations of desire, the politics of sex, and the relation between pleasure and reproductive behavior in a
range of cultural contexts. Finally, the *Quantitative Models and Measurement*
chapters examine the manner in which data on human sexuality are obtained
and integrated into analytic models.

These particular themes have been selected for use as titles for the chapter
groupings because they are historically significant and ultimately essential to
a reconceptualization of human sexual behavior from the perspectives of both
pleasure and reproduction. Although other themes are certainly viable, it is
difficult to theorize about human sexual behavior in the absence of evolutionary models, biological mechanisms, cross-cultural comparisons, and quantitative data.

Lastly, although we have striven, at the Wenner-Gren conference and in this
volume, to optimize transdisciplinary models and dialogue in *each* chapter, this
goal has been implemented in disparate ways, often along essentially disciplinary lines. This is, perhaps, not surprising, since a widely heterogeneous group
of disciplines, methodologies, and theoretical heritages (each with cherished
language, concepts, and models) are represented within the chapters of this

volume. Crossing disciplinary borders, as one might imagine, is a daunting
task. At the very least, contributors to this volume sat at a table, for over sixty
hours, attempting to achieve this objective. Sometimes we were successful;
other times not (Okami and Pendleton, 1994). This is undoubtedly the nature
(or nurture?) of the beast. Some disciplinary borders are open; some are con-
tiguous; and some are contested. Consequently, although the individual chapters may be somewhat theoretically and disciplinarily circumscribed, the overall gestalt of the volume reflects our transdisciplinary objective.

The Chapters

Sexual nature and sexual culture are vast topics, seemingly relevant to almost
everything: children, mates, work, entertainment, religion, leisure, law,
dreams, rituals, and so on. It is therefore unsurprising that the present treatment
comes far short of exhausting its subject matter. As the reader will note, many
disciplines, perspectives, and topics are missing. Such deficiencies are unavoidable. And although an interactionist approach (described more fully in
the introduction) is evident in most chapters, the full weight of this perspective
is best gleaned from the volume as a whole. Taken collectively, the chapters
included herein—at the very least—provide solid evidence for interactionism
by making it difficult to dismiss either the biological or the cultural viewpoint.

   As noted above, this volume is organized around four centrally themed parts
or sections, each of which represents an aggregate concept of relevance to
current theories of human sexuality. Brief descriptions of the individual chapters included in these parts are provided below.

   The first part of the volume, *Evolutionary Origins,* consists of four chapters
that consider evolutionarily significant human and nonhuman primate sexual
behavior. The chapters are primarily theoretical, and address sexual issues that
are ultimately of relevance to human sexual expression, even when the osten-
sible focal point is nonhuman primates. Mary McDonald Pavelka's chapter argues for a cross-species perspective on primate sexuality and demonstrates
the utility of this approach by considering several focal topics, such as the
evolutionary significance of the "loss of estrus," the importance of nonreproductive sexuality, and the experience of sexual pleasure across primate species.
Frans de Waal's contribution is more narrowly focused. His description of the
sexual behavior of the bonobo (or "pygmy" chimpanzee) provides an alternative to restrictive conceptualizations of the function of sexual behavior in the
higher primates: while obviously critical to reproduction, sex is also instrumental for interpersonal exchanges such as reconciliation and reassurance,
thereby suggesting an evolutionary origin related to heterosexual bonding. The
evolution of primate sexuality is further explicated by Kim Wallen, who examines the multiplicative determinants of female sexual desire and the adaptive
function of pleasure. Donald Symons's chapter completes this part with a con-

sideration of the characteristics that constitute human female sexual attractiveness, viewed from an evolutionary psychological perspective.

The second part, *Crossroads: Biology and Behavior,* consists of three chapters. These chapters are more strongly data-based, though certainly not void of theoretical implications, from either a biologically deterministic or an interactionist perspective. The chapters in this part also fall more squarely within the traditional purview of biological approaches to human sexuality, i.e., hormones and genetics. The section begins with Jean Wilson's overview of the literature on hormones and human sexuality, with an emphasis on clinical abnormalities. In the following chapter, Heino Meyer-Bahlburg updates his earlier examination of possible hormonal influences on homosexuality (Meyer-Bahlburg, 1984). Finally, in a related piece, Angela Pattatucci and Dean Hamer present a broad overview of their search for—and discovery of—the location of a specific genetic factor influencing the prevalence of male homosexuality within particular pedigree lines.

The next part, *Cultural Dimensions,* is a diverse (and undoubtedly provocative) sampling of the sexual culture landscape. The chapters are united to the extent that they articulate the power of a culturalist perspective. In other respects the chapters are rather disparate; each provides a unique vantage point from which to conceptualize sexuality. Thus, the chapters in this part subtly form a collective gestalt.

In the first chapter, Alice Schlegel describes the cross-cultural variability exhibited in attitudes towards adolescent sexuality, with specific consideration of the communal ghotuls in Bastar, India. This is followed by a rather technical treatment by Robert Bailey and Robert Aunger of the cultural transmission dynamics of sexually transmitted diseases (STDs) and consequent subfertility levels of farmers and foragers in central Africa. David Greenberg then provides an analysis of the historical and cultural construction of homosexuality, especially as it relates to sexual pleasure. Donald Tuzin's chapter, in contrast, is a general, discursive analysis of anthropology's reluctance to embrace phenomenological sexuality as a legitimate area of inquiry.

The remaining chapters in this part are equally diverse. Lawrence Cohen's contribution describes in depth two unique groups of people, the castrated Hijras and the noncastrated Jankhas of India, and discusses the relevance of "third gender" conceptualizations to the discourse on sexuality. This is followed by an equally fascinating and informative account by Lenore Manderson of the sex industry in contemporary Thailand, and the contextual meaning of the pursuit of pleasure. In the final chapter of this part, Thomas Gregor explores the interrelationship between love and sexuality, both generally and within the context of a small Amazonian tribe, the Mehinaku of Brazil.

The volume concludes with the *Quantitative Models and Measurement* section, which addresses methodological issues in the study of human sexuality. Because most of what we know about sex is data-driven (as evidenced by the continued influence of the nearly fifty-year-old Kinsey reports), it seems obvious that we, as researchers, should also think deeply about how sexual data can be accurately collected and analyzed, and thereby how sexuality can be modeled or, conversely, obfuscated. The data themselves should also be closely scrutinized to determine just what they *mean*.

There are only two chapters in the final part. In the first, Edward Kaplan emphasizes the utility of mathematical descriptions of human sexual behavior, particularly as formalized in STD transmission models, and provides an overview of the modeling landscape. In the final chapter, Richard Berk, Paul Abramson, and Paul Okami address the fundamental question of whether people can accurately remember their own sexual activities. (To anticipate slightly, the answer, at least in this initial investigation, is no! People make errors of both omission and commission in recalling sexual episodes from even the very recent past.)

Final Note

While the diversity of topics, perspectives, and methods represented in this volume undoubtedly facilitates increased transdisciplinary understanding of the theoretical foundations of human sexuality, it is also likely to somewhat challenge the reader. Few of us are conversant in all the subjects discussed in this volume (e.g., evolution, genetics, endocrinology, history, anthropology, mathematics, etc.), or with the multifarious styles of presentation adopted by the authors, whether from the humanities or the sciences. This observation holds no less for the contributors to this volume than it does for the reader. Of course, as participants at the Wenner-Gren conference, the contributors had the luxury of conversing with one another to garner clarifications and further explanations. The reader, unfortunately, is denied such facilitative interactions. Nevertheless, we hope he or she will persevere—through both familiar territory and *terra incognita*—in order to attain the unity of understanding that, we believe, can be achieved only through a transdisciplinary approach to human sexuality.

Paul R. Abramson
Steven D. Pinkerton
Los Angeles

References

Abramson, P. R. 1990. Sexual science: Emerging discipline or oxymoron? *The Journal of Sex Research, 27,* 147–65.

Abramson, P. R., & Pinkerton, S. D. 1995. *With pleasure: thoughts on the nature of human sexuality.* Forthcoming, Oxford University Press.

terized by their factual regularity, such as the laws of classical thermodynamics, descriptions of planetary motions, and so on. Such laws must be distinguished from normative laws, which describe actions and phenomena that are merely frequent or widespread (Popper, 1962). Interestingly, it is the normative laws—particularly as they apply to human behavior—that typically evoke debate, vehemence, and confusion (Ohm's law seldom incites the masses, but premarital sex . . .). This is especially true, as just intimated, where human sexuality is concerned.

Nurture, formalized as culture, is no less problematic. Sir Edward Tylor's (1871) classic definition of culture is a case in point. In Tylor's hands nature is rendered obsolete by the emergence of culture, which he deemed a "complex whole" governing the generational transmission of knowledge, beliefs, laws, morals, and customs. The details of this process, however, remained vague, except to the extent that it was presumed hierarchical, in that nature was replaced by nurture.

This rather extreme position was modified in subsequent formulations in which culture *coexisted* with nature. Kroeber (1952) characterized culture as the patterns and values transmitted by "interconditioning of zygotes." Such terminology is obviously beholden to biological perspectives. Similarly, Lévi-Strauss (1963) contended that culture is best understood if treated "the same way as the geneticist . . . treat(s) the . . . concept of 'isolate.' What is called a 'culture' is a fragment of humanity . . . present(ing) significant discontinuities in relation to the rest of humanity" (p. 295). Though both of these definitions are biologically oriented, they continue to differentiate strongly between nature and nurture. Interactionism is conspicuously avoided. Furthermore, while nurture no longer dispenses with nature, it now seems to copy it as a loosely defined geneticist's model.

Contemporary cultural theorists propose an entirely different framework, one in which culture becomes interpretation. Clifford Geertz (1973) describes the modern approach thusly: "Believing, with Max Weber, that man is an animal suspended in webs of significance he himself has spun, I take culture to be those webs, and the analysis of it to be therefore not an experimental science in search of law but an interpretive one in search of meaning" (p. 5). This conceptualization of culture as interpretation is also evident in the writings of both Michel Foucault (1978) and Eve Sedgwick (1990). Utilizing a deconstructive perspective, their work challenges assumptions concerning both nature and nurture, particularly as they apply to sexuality. According to Foucault and Sedgwick, "natural" is merely a label in the nomenclature of culturally capricious categories. Thus, the valuation of one characteristic over another (e.g., heterosexuality over homosexuality) has no intrinsic validity. It is, instead, reflective of the process by which such characteristics are privileged within particular cultures. Neither characteristic is inherently privileged or "natural," and any designation as such necessarily reflects underlying cultural vagaries.

CHAPTER ONE

Introduction: Nature, Nurture, and In-Between

PAUL R. ABRAMSON AND STEVEN D. PINKERTON

The nature/nurture debate is antithetical to scientific enquiry. Ultimately the phenomena that confront science—and especially social science—are multiply determined. To harangue for priority, be it for nature or nurture, is analogous to claims for divine right, both being self-righteous and unquestionably tautological.

We invoke divinity here because the resolution of the nature/nurture debate often takes an act of apostasy. Either that, or scholarly retreat. Rarely, it seems, is an interactionist position embraced. Such a compromise, asserting that nature and nurture exert separate but often complementary influences that collectively and interactively determine behavior, is generally perceived as weak, imprecise, or specious.

We have overstated this point merely to confirm the obvious: Both nature *and* nurture matter. Even the actions of the genes themselves—those paragons of nature—necessarily unfold within particular proximal environments. Height, for example, is largely determined by heritable factors, but nutritional and other environmental influences are by no means insignificant. The interaction between nature and nurture is bidirectional. In the one direction, the environment constrains the expression of genetically determined predispositions, while in the other, expressed behaviors taken in toto define the breadth and extent of the personal and cultural environment in which further behaviors are manifested.

Nature and nurture are thus intricately intertwined as behavioral propensities and actualities. What is important, therefore, is not the current sway of the nature/nurture tug-of-war, but the attempt to understand the dynamics of both nature and nurture, individually and in concert, and to delineate the mechanisms and boundaries of their influences and interactions.

These objectives are easier to state than to satisfy, unfortunately. Simply defining "nature" and "nurture" is a daunting task in and of itself. There is much confusion in the historical usage of these terms, and the concepts themselves are often misunderstood or misapplied. Take *nature,* for instance. Generally, when the concept of nature is invoked, the existence of a lawlike relationship between phenomena, i.e., a natural law, is implicitly presumed. But what constitutes a natural law? According to Popper (1962), natural laws are charac-

1

Meyer-Bahlburg, H. F. L. 1984. Psychoendocrine research on sexual orientation. Current status and future options. *Progress in Brain Research, 61,* 375–98.

Okami, P., & Pendleton, L. 1994. Theorizing sexuality: Seeds of a transdisciplinary paradigm shift. *Current Anthropologist, 32,* 85–91.

Robinson, P. A. 1976. *The modernization of sex.* New York: Harper & Row.

With this much said, two conclusions are readily apparent. First, natural laws are conveniently disregarded when the term "natural" is utilized. Thus, "natural" is often a misnomer for "normative." Second, the concept of nurture (and its proxy, culture) is either multifaceted or chimerical, such that it manifests itself in different miens. These difficulties have undoubtedly undermined conceptual clarity, particularly where human sexuality is concerned.

Homosexuality provides a particularly cogent example. Some have argued that the past two thousand years of popular disgust and discomfort with homosexuality provides sufficient evidence to confirm the "unnaturalness" of homosexuality, which therefore constitutes a "sin against nature" (Bullough, 1982). The Bible, for example, is unequivocal on this point: "You shall not lie with a man as with a woman: that is an abomination" (Lev. 18:22). An antipathetic attitude towards homosexuality follows, quite naturally, from the procreational bias of the early Christian church, according to which marital intercourse between fertile individuals was the only legitimate expression of sexuality. Sex for pleasure, rather than procreation, was anathema (see Abramson and Pinkerton, 1995). Homosexuality, as perhaps the most conspicuous expression of nonprocreative sexuality, has been reviled and repressed in Christian and non-Christian nations alike, for thousands of years (Boswell, 1980).[1] Surely, billions of devout antihomosexuals, collectively spanning the millennia, can't be wrong? Or can they?

We wish to argue that they can and, in fact, often are. Unlike the objective and immutable natural laws, normative laws are the products of human societies and the collective psyche. They therefore cannot easily be disentangled from the subjective and temporally fluctuating value systems in which they are embedded. Hence, regardless of how many people believe that homosexuality is immoral, such judgments—and moralistic concerns in general—have only normative relevance; they have nothing whatsoever to say with regard to factual regularity, i.e., natural law.

Furthermore, normative laws are seldom free of political considerations. There are numerous reasons, economic as well as political, for pathologizing homosexuality (and nonreproductive sexuality more generally) since, for example, it potentially reduces the number of workers, constituents, etc. (Abramson and Pinkerton, 1995). We should therefore be cautious about accepting easy and ready damnations of nonreproductive lifestyles arising from purely normative considerations.

Unfortunately, the search for natural laws is itself frequently polluted by political contaminants. The discovery of a "homosexuality gene,"[2] for example, would be hailed by some gay and lesbian leaders as providing conclusive evidence that homosexuality is indeed "natural," thereby disarming those who would deny lesbians and gay men equal rights on that fallacious basis, or at the very least relocating the surrounding debate from the streets and classrooms to the courts. (The obvious question being: can a person legitimately be punished or discriminated against on the basis of an inborn and presumably immutable trait?)[3] On the other hand, such a finding would "biologize" the otherness of the homosexual category. The unfortunate repercussions of a biologic taxonomy could include renewed attempts to "cure" homosexuals, prenatal screening against carriers of the "homosexuality gene," and in a worst-case, holocaust-like scenario, the identification and systematic extermination of homosexuals.[4]

Notice that in the above extrapolations, the possession of a particular gene or genes (technically, we should be speaking here of particular alleles, or forms of the genes) is implicitly assumed to be both necessary and sufficient for the development of a homosexual orientation. However, both the necessity and sufficiency claimed here demand additional scrutiny, as does the entire notion of a "homosexual orientation." To begin, it is likely that homosexuality (tentatively defined here as sexual attraction towards same-sexed others) is multiply determined; even if for some people homosexuality arises as a direct consequence of genetic influences, it is doubtful that this is always the case. The anthropological and historical records clearly indicate the importance of cultural attitudes towards same-sex behaviors as proscriptive or facilitative influences.

Even if a "homosexuality gene" is not *necessary* for the development of homosexuality, it is often implicitly assumed that, if it existed, it would certainly be *sufficient,* in that possession of the gene would predetermine the sexual orientation of the carrier. This belief is indicative of a polar position in the nature/nurture debate. According to this view, environmental influences are insignificant—one either has the gene or not, and in the former instance a homosexual orientation is assured. This attitude further posits that orientation is fixed once the gene has expressed itself, owing to the assumed intransigence of sexual orientation with respect to the cultural environment.

At the opposite end of the nature/nurture continuum is the claim that homosexuality is a purely culturally or socially constructed phenomenon, in the sense that it relies for its independent existence on the social recognition and sanctions that surround it. From this perspective, homosexuality is neither functionally equivalent across cultures nor inherently meaningful beyond particular cultural abstractions. This latter point, incidentally, is a direct challenge to Plato's theory of ideas, in that it argues against the existence of an ideal form of homosexuality that is necessarily universal and monolithic. According to the constructivist view, there are only temporally and spatially limited behavioral interpretations, rather than an ideal form.

A wealth of evidence from the historical and cross-cultural records can be adduced in support of the constructionist viewpoint. In ancient Greece, for example, well-to-do male citizens often maintained sexual relationships with young boys in addition to prostitutes, concubines, and, of course, their wives (Dover, 1978; Greenberg, 1988; Halperin, Winkler, and Zeitlin, 1990; Tannahill, 1980; see also Greenberg, this volume). In contrast to contemporary Western expectations, their male-male contacts in no way decreased their social standing as solid, "heterosexual" citizens, provided that certain behavioral norms were respected (Foucault, 1985). Thus, there need be nothing pathological about same-sex relationships. In many cultures, even today, a man may assume the insertive role in anal intercourse without being branded a "homosexual" (Carrier, 1980). And in some cultures, ritual homosexual activity is a requisite part of male maturation (Herdt, 1984). Among the Sambia (a warrior-based culture in the highlands of Papua, New Guinea), for example, young boys are expected to actively engage in fellatio with older, "bachelor" boys as a means of ingesting the semen required to make them strong and courageous warriors (Herdt, 1987). Once married, however, all such same-sex activity is expected to cease. Adult homosexuality, though not entirely unknown, is nevertheless not acknowledged as such. Thus, although homosexuality *as a behavior* is widespread among Sambian males, homosexuality *as an identity* is nonexistent.

The above examples also point to the inadequacy of "homosexuality" as a meaningful construct, an inadequacy that will need to be addressed more fully by those positing strictly biological theories of sexual preference. How, for example, would a "homosexuality gene" assert its influence? Would it affect self-identity or just overt behaviors? Would it preclude attraction to oppositely gendered partners, or might such affinities be regulated by other, as yet undiscovered, genes?[5] More generally, what does it mean to claim that homosexuality is "genetic," "hard-wired," or "biologic"? All human behavior is ultimately biologic (arising, as it must, from the activity of the central nervous system), hence genetic at a trivial level of analysis (Bailey and Greenberg, 1993). But, just as clearly, cultural influences play a critical—albeit proximal rather than ultimate—role in shaping the manner in which behaviors are expressed. Nature and nurture are thus indissoluble codeterminants of complex behaviors such as homosexuality.

The question to be examined in the following section is how best to conceptualize the interplay of nature and nurture. After proposing an elementary model of nature/nurture interactions, we present our argument for the importance of the interactionist perspective in the study of human sexuality, first by discussing the explanatory power captured in the concept of "sexual pleasure," and then by examining how sexual pleasure interacts with interactionism.

A Simple Model of Nature/Nurture Interactions

As should be clear by now, we intend to argue that an interactionist approach, which considers both biological and cultural influences—not just singly, but in concert—is the only viable means by which we can hope to comprehend the complexities of human sexuality. Simply put, there can be no behavior without biology; but no less significantly, the behaviors of interest require a cultural milieu to give them meaning, much as a seed requires fertile soil to express its genetic potential. Thus we wish to argue for a mixed influence on sexual behavior, X parts nature and Y parts nurture. But how can the interaction of the separate influences best be understood? In this section we shall present a preliminary conceptualization of nature-nurture interactions.

In the model to be elaborated here, we shall identify each individual by his or her genotype, G. That is, G symbolizes the full complement of genes (comprising 46 chromosomes) that completely characterize an individual's genetic constitution. Identical (monozygotic) twins would have identical genotypes, of course, and in general there would be an overlap of approximately 50 percent in the genotypes of a parent and any one of his or her children.

Despite being genetically identical, monozygotic twins can be very different in personality and behavior. These differences are due to nurture, or more precisely, to differences in their unshared environments, where "environment" is meant to indicate the whole constellation of external influences on the behavior of interest, stretching back to the *in utero* environment and up to the present. A person's environment, E, is thus a history of the external stimuli to which he or she has been subjected. Given this definition, it is clear that no two people will ever share *exactly* the same environment. Even the environments of identical twins will be different—no matter how similarly they are treated by others—because of possibly minute historical differences, such as differing birth times. Despite such differences, certain aspects of the environment may be inconsequential with respect to the behaviors of interest, so we may on occasion speak of two environments being identical, although this is an obvious simplification.

The final element in the model being presented here is the behavior, or trait of interest, B. For example, B might be homosexuality or heterosexual promiscuity. The question is, how do G and E jointly determine B? In attempting to answer this we mean only to provide a conceptual framework in which to consider nature-nurture interactions, not to describe the biochemical mechanics of gene expression, or the manner by which environmental stimuli exert their multifarious influences.

In an ideal world of perfect information, for any behavior B, genotype G, and environment E, a definitive answer to the question, "Would a person with genotype G display behavior B, given exposure to environment E?" could be ascertained. This, in turn, would permit future behaviors to be predicted from knowledge of G and E. (This is the point at which an antideterministic furor normally arises in the nature/nurture debate. Few of us wish to believe that our behaviors are completely determined by anything but internal psychical forces. But remember that genetics and the environment jointly determine behavior. And unlike genetic effects, which are more likely to be stereotypical, the influence of environmental factors is largely unpredictable, and may even be chaotic, such that even the smallest change in the environment might have enormous behavioral consequences.)

At a more practical level, precise specification of the total environment E is all but impossible, hence it makes sense to consider E as symbolizing only that part of the environment thought to be influential with respect to the behavior in question. E might therefore represent "had a domineering mother," which according to psychoanalytic precepts is an environmental factor in the etiology of male homosexuality. We may then ask, "What is the probability that a person with genotype G would exhibit behavior B, given exposure to environment E?" In other words, we may attempt to evaluate the conditional probability P(B|G,E), i.e., "the probability of B given G and E."

This conceptualization allows us to restate the polar extremes in the nature/nurture controversy as follows: A "pure naturalist," i.e., one who completely discounts the influence of the environment, is one who believes that P(B|G,E) = P(B|G,E') for all environments E and E'. In other words, he or she believes that any one environment is as good as any other—only the genes matter. The "pure nurturalist" takes the opposite stance, symbolized by the equation P(B|G,E) = P(B|G',E), where G and G' are any two genotypes. The interactionist perspective, in contrast, denies the validity of both these equations for most, but not necessarily all, behaviors. (The complexity of human sexual behaviors suggests, however, that it would be an unlikely arena in which to discover exceptions to interactionism.)

Before pursuing the model further, we should emphasize that we are neither the first, nor the most eloquent, defenders of the interactionist approach to the study of human behavior. The nature/nurture debate has a long and ignominious history, with semantic and conceptual obfuscations and bickering on both sides. In the last few decades, however, an interactionist compromise has been endorsed by most of the principals involved (see, e.g., Lehrman, 1970). Thus, it is usually acknowledged that all behavior ultimately arises from the actions of genes and nerve cells, although the proximal expression of those behaviors often betrays strong environmental influences. Nevertheless, true interactionism, or what we will call here "strong interactionism" is seldom embraced. Strong interactionism does more than simply pay lip service to the truism that nature and nurture conjointly determine behavior, it explicitly acknowledges that interactions between the two are critical to the expression of many behaviors. One might imagine, for example, two strains of corn: Alpha corn, which thrives in environment A but withers and dies in environment B, and Beta corn that displays exactly the opposite survival pattern (statistically-minded readers will recognize this as a crossover interaction). In this example neither environment is inherently better or worse than the other. The value of a particular environment can be determined only with reference to the strain of corn to be grown in it. (A similar, though rather more complex, genotype-phenotype interaction is demonstrated by the *Achillea* plant—see Byne, 1994.)

The dividing line between weak and strong interactionism is an indistinct one in practice. The two types of interaction can, however, be illustrated within the theoretical framework proposed above (see also Haldane, 1946). To

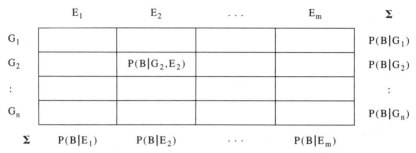

Figure 1.1 Conditional probabilities $P(B|G_i,E_j)$ of behavior B given genotype G_i and environment E_j. The column sums give the probabilities contingent only upon the environment, whereas the row sums are conditionalized exclusively on genetic influences. Notice that the sum of the row sums, and likewise the sum of the column sums, is unity; in other words, all possibilities are accounted for.

simplify the discussion somewhat, suppose that all possible genotypes may be found among G_1, G_2, . . . ,G_n, and similarly that E_1, E_2, . . . E_m exhausts the set of possible environments. The conditional probabilities $P(B|G_i,E_j)$ may then be arranged in a chart, as shown in figure 1.1. If any such behaviors are strictly genetically determined, such that one and only one set of genes leads to the behavior, and environmental influences are nil, a pattern such as that illustrated in figure 1.2(a) would emerge. If, in addition, interactions with the environment are allowed, then the weakly interactive pattern of figure 1.2(b) might be expected. In the example shown, environment E_2 is to be favored over either E_1 or E_3, and similarly for G_2 over G_1 and G_3.

Strong interactionism, on the other hand, yields a pattern in which the behavior is *jointly* determined by environment and genetics as shown in figure 1.2(c). In this case, as in figure 1.2(b), E_2 "dominates" both E_1 and E_3 in that the column sum (aggregate environmental influence) for E_2 exceeds that of either E_1 or E_3; likewise, G_2 dominates both G_1 and G_3. For weak interactionism the observation that $P(B|E_2)$ and $P(B|G_2)$ are both maximal is sufficient to conclude that $P(B|G_2, E_2)$ is also maximal. In contrast, this need not be the case for strong interactionism (compare parts b and c of figure 1.2).

Notice, however, that interactionism is not randomness (fig. 1.2(d), but instead displays significant effects of both E and G. This is an important point: the interactionist perspective acknowledges the influences of both nature and nurture, individually and conjointly, but in no way asserts that all influences are equivalent. Instead, it proposes that specific environmental factors, in conjunction with particular genotypes, lead to predispositions to certain behaviors.

The interactionist perspective also helps account for the persistence of both extreme points of view on the nature/nurture question. Both environmental and genetic main effects can be observed in figure 1.2(c) if one is willing to limit his or her examination to a single dimension. The true picture can be obtained,

	E_1	E_2	E_3	Σ
G_1	0	0	0	0
G_2	1/3	1/3	1/3	1
G_3	0	0	0	0
Σ	1/3	1/3	1/3	

(a)

	E_1	E_2	E_3	Σ
G_1	0	1/6	0	1/6
G_2	1/6	1/3	1/6	2/3
G_3	0	1/6	0	1/6
Σ	1/6	2/3	1/6	

(b)

	E_1	E_2	E_3	Σ
G_1	0	2/9	0	2/9
G_2	2/9	1/9	2/9	5/9
G_3	0	2/9	0	2/9
Σ	2/9	5/9	2/9	

(c)

	E_1	E_2	E_3	Σ
G_1	1/9	1/9	1/9	1/3
G_2	1/9	1/9	1/9	1/3
G_3	1/9	1/9	1/9	1/3
Σ	1/3	1/3	1/3	

(d)

Figure 1.2 Conditional probability patterns for (a) strict genetic determinism (one and only one set of genes leads to the target behavior while environmental influences are nil); (b) weak interactionism; (c) strong interactionism; and (d) true randomness.

we believe, only by enlarging the scope of inquiry to encompass both dimensions simultaneously. Failure to take into account either the genetic or environmental dimension results in a form of myopia not unlike that suffered by the two-dimensional creatures in Edwin Abbott's (1952) immortal *Flatland,* who, because they are unable to perceive the third dimension—hence to comprehend solid shapes—deny its very existence.

It is our belief that very few aspects of human sexual behavior display the genetic determinism of figure 1.2(a). Rather, the complexity and plasticity of human sexuality suggest that genotype-phenotype interactions are the rule. Thus, we believe that the vast majority of sexual behaviors require some form of culturally determined environmental activation to achieve full expression. Whether or not this is indeed the case for any particular behavior is, of course, open to empirical examination. We tentatively offer the above in the belief that research guided by a plausible model is more likely to bear fruit than that blinded by more glamorous and exclusionary possibilities.

Pleasure as an Explanatory Construct

Evolutionarily, there appear to be at least two stable, divergent strategies for regulating sexuality. The first is to directly control sexual functions and behaviors (including sexual arousal, proceptivity, and receptivity) through the actions of hormones (secondary to the central nervous system, of course). This solution to the reproduction problem is embraced by all but the highest orders of mammals: males and females are interested in sex, and copulation occurs, only when the female is in hormone-induced estrus. In primate species, sexual functioning is liberated from periodic hormonal tyranny, to a greater or lesser extent, with sexual freedom attaining its zenith in humans (see Pavelka, this volume, and Wallen, this volume).

Although circulatory hormones may exert small influences on the human sex drive, people are largely free to choose when, how, and with whom they have sex.[6] This in turn admits the possibility—indeed, we would argue, the *necessity*—of strong environmental influences. Significant regulation of sexual behaviors is necessitated by the critical role of reproduction in evolutionary processes. It therefore stands to reason that if direct biological control is diminished in humans, environmental influences should expand in a compensatory manner.

Human sexuality has myriad meanings, many of which are only remotely germane to reproduction. In contemporary Western cultures, for example, sex is primarily interpreted in either a reproductive or a pair-bonding context. However, as we have argued elsewhere, both of these functions are in some sense secondary to the concept of pleasure (Abramson and Pinkerton, 1995). The desire for pleasure is the principal motivator for penile-vaginal sexual intercourse, hence reproduction, and ultimately human evolution. An understanding of human reproduction is scarcely an understanding of human sexuality, and the missing conceptual key, we believe, is sexual pleasure.

Of course, the *ultimate* function of sex—human or otherwise—is the propagation of genes, and reproduction is therefore paramount. For humans, however, the proximal motivation for engaging in sex is usually the pursuit of pleasure rather than a conscious desire to procreate. The genetic call for reproduction is distal to everyday experience, whereas the desire for pleasure is a universal human imperative. In many instances, therefore, the explanatory power of pleasure—as a conceptual framework for analyzing human sexual behavior—far exceeds that of reproduction.

Furthermore, the genetically bound reproductive approach to human sexuality is frequently the wrong conceptual level at which to attempt a meaningful analysis. To understand a novel or misbehaving computer program, the skilled programmer typically examines the source code, written in a high-level language such as BASIC or Pascal, rather than poring over the pattern of ones and zeros that is the native tongue of the computer hardware itself, even though this "bit stream" constitutes the more fundamental level of operational analysis. Similarly, it is doubtful whether an analysis of reproduction and genetic transmission could ever adequately explicate the myriad meanings and rationales for sexual behavior. The concept of pleasure, though in some sense less basic than reproduction, seems much better suited to this particular task (Abramson and Pinkerton, 1995; see also Greenberg, this volume).

Interactionism and Human Sexuality

Like the concept of pleasure, the interactionist perspective also provides an additional vantage point, or level of analysis, from which to view human sexuality. The intricacies of human behavior arise from a complex interaction of genetic potentialities and internalized cultural influences. The end product, the human psyche, is not immediately dissolvable into separate components, but appears instead as a seamless whole, thereby obfuscating the analysis of individual behaviors.

It seems safe to assume that the interaction of biological and cultural forces within the psyche is highly nonlinear, perhaps even chaotic. Therefore, knowledge of the ingredients ("one part nature to two parts nurture") need not ensure an understanding of the recipe as a whole. The interactionist stance inherently recognizes these limitations of strictly biological or strictly cultural explications of complex behavioral phenomena. It seeks, instead, an additional level of analysis, one in which the component processes are integrated to form a single analyzable unit.

The interactionist perspective is perhaps nowhere more relevant than in the consideration of sexual pleasure (Abramson and Pinkerton, 1995). The visceral experience of pleasure is clearly biological in origin, but an individual's choice of sexual stimuli betrays obvious cultural biases.[7] Even female orgasm, with its indisputably physiological basis, is strongly influenced by cultural factors: a greater proportion of women tend to be orgasmic in sex-positive cultures where oral sex and greater attention to foreplay and female pleasure are encouraged, than in more sexually inhibited cultures (see, e.g., Davenport, 1977; Ford and Beach, 1951; Gladwin and Sarason, 1953; Marshall, 1971). Indeed, the biology of pleasure seems relatively more obscure than the sociology of pleasure.

It should also be remembered that humans, unlike corn or *Achillea* plants, can themselves significantly affect the environments in which they live. For example, parents, teachers, and peers may react to an effeminate boy in ways that increase the likelihood of homosexuality in adulthood. In a positive feedback loop, the attitudes of parents and others may cause the young boy to begin to see himself as a homosexual and to modify his behavior in such a manner that the perceptions of those around him are further reinforced. Carrier (1977, 1980) provides a concrete example of this dynamic. In traditional Mexican (mestizo) culture, it is considered *macho* for men and boys to assume the active (inserter) role in anal intercourse with other males, but not the passive (insertee) role, which is reserved for "homosexuals." Effeminate boys are identified as potential sexual partners at a very young age and are forced to assume the passive role in sexual encounters with older youths and adults. As Carrier (1980) notes, "it is a self-fulfilling prophecy of the society that effeminate males . . . are eventually, if not from the beginning, pushed toward exclusively homosexual behavior" (p. 110). Although the ultimate psychological effect of this coercion cannot be ascertained with certainty, it is clear that the adoption of a homosexual self-identity by effeminate males would facilitate a reconciliation of self-observed behavior with self-conception, and thereby attenuate cognitive and emotional dissonance.

Although we have concentrated primarily on homosexuality as an illustrative example, the psychosocial construction of sexual pleasure is evident in all aspects of human sexuality, from object choice (including animals, children, and fetishistic objects) to frequency of heterosexual intercourse. Historical, cultural, and psychological variables determine which sexual acts are pleasurable, and under what circumstances. Indeed, even the distinction between the sexual and the nonsexual is subject to cultural and historical variation.

All this, we believe, bears further witness to the intricate intertwining of the cultural and the biological in the experience of sexual pleasure, and substantiates the need for an interactionist approach to the complexities of human sexual behavior.

Notes

1. Homosexuality is not uniformly condemned by modern-day Christian denominations. According to the Lesbian & Gay Public Awareness Project (1991), the following organizations support full civil rights for lesbians and gay men: The National Council of Churches of Christ, the Union of American Hebrew Congregations, the Unitarian Universalist Association, the Society of Friends (Quakers), and the Universal Fellowship of Metropolitan Community Churches. (Our apologies to any organizations that have inadvertently been omitted.)

2. Dean Hamer and colleagues (Hamer, Hu, Magnuson, Hu, and Pattatucci, 1993; see also Pattatucci and Hamer, this volume) have recently reported finding a genetic link in at least some forms of male homosexuality. For a brief and highly readable account of the evidence supporting a strong "biological" influence in male homosexuality, see LeVay and Hamer (1994); a rebuttal is provided by Byne (1994).

3. Perhaps surprisingly, the answer is yes, as attested to by the frequently restricted reproductive rights of the developmentally disadvantaged (Abramson, Parker, and Weisberg, 1988).

4. Further social, political, and legal implications of the "biological" foundations of homosexuality are discussed by Bailey and Greenberg (1993).

5. Are there also genes for other non-normative sexual-object choices, such as animals or young children?

6. "People are largely free to choose. . . ." By this we mean only to stress humankind's relative freedom from hormonal tyranny. Many argue that people cannot "choose" their sexual orientation any more than they can choose their eye color. Never-

theless, just as some people elect to change the color of their eyes by the use of contact lens, some may also deny their inborn sexual preferences (if indeed they are inborn), or otherwise select a non-normative sexual object or activity. The who, what, when, why, and how of human sexuality are complexly determined by interacting psychological, social, and physical influences, not simply through the actions of circulating hormones.

7. Cognitive influences are also clearly in evidence. Why, for example, do some people prefer genital stimulation by persons of the same sex whereas others demand the opposite sex? Aren't the sensory signals impinging on the brain the same regardless of the gender of the person providing the stimulation? Cognitive evaluation of the sexual situation is thus critically important, for it is via this psychological process that the myriad influences of culture and the environment are actuated. (For a more extensive discussion of this point, see Abramson and Pinkerton [1995].)

References

Abbott, E. A. 1952. *Flatland.* New York: Dover.

Abramson, P. R., Parker, T., and Weisberg, S. R. 1988. Sexual expression of mentally retarded people: Educational and legal implications. *American Journal of Mental Retardation, 93,* 328–34.

Abramson, P. R. & Pinkerton, S. D. 1995. *With pleasure: thoughts on the nature of human sexuality.* Forthcoming, Oxford University Press.

Bailey, A. S. & Greenberg, J. M. 1993. Do biological explanations of homosexuality have moral, legal, or policy implications? *The Journal of Sex Research, 30,* 245–51.

Boswell, J. 1980. *Christianity, social tolerance, and homosexuality.* Chicago: University of Chicago Press.

Bullough, V. L. 1982. The sin against nature and homosexuality. In V. L. Bullough & J. Brundage, eds., *Sexual practices & the medieval church.* Buffalo: Prometheus Books.

Byne, W. 1994. The biological evidence challenged. *Scientific American, 270,* 50–55.

Carrier, J. M. 1977. Sex-role preference as an explanatory variable in homosexual behavior. *Archives of Sexual Behavior, 6,* 53–65.

Carrier, J. M. 1980. Homosexual behavior in cross-cultural perspective. In J. Marmor, ed., *Homosexual behavior: A modern reappraisal.* New York: Basic Books.

Davenport, W. H. 1977. Sex in cross-cultural perspective. In F. A. Beach, ed., *Human sexuality in four perspectives.* Baltimore: The Johns Hopkins University Press.

Dover, K. J. 1978. *Greek homosexuality.* Cambridge: Harvard University Press.

Ford, C. S. & Beach, F. A. 1951. *Patterns of sexual behavior.* New York: Harper & Row.

Foucault, M. 1978. *The history of sexuality.* New York: Pantheon.

Foucault, M. 1985. *The use of pleasure.* New York: Random House.

Geertz, C. 1973. *The interpretation of cultures.* New York: Basic Books.

Gladwin, T., & Sarason, S. B. 1953. *Truk: Man in paradise.* New York: Wenner-Gren Foundation for Anthropological Research.

Greenberg, D. F. 1988. *The construction of homosexuality.* Chicago: University of Chicago Press.

Haldane, J. B. S. 1946. The interaction of nature and nurture. *Annals of Eugenics, 13,* 197–205.

Halperin, D. M., Winkler, J. J., & Zeitlin, F. I. 1990. *Before sexuality.* Princeton: Princeton University Press.

Hamer, D. H., Hu, S., Magnuson, V. L., Hu, N., & Pattatucci, A. M. L. 1993. A linkage between DNA markers on the X chromosome and male sexual orientation. *Science, 261,* 321–27.

Herdt, G. H. 1984. *Ritualized homosexuality in Melanesia.* Berkeley: University of California Press.

Herdt, G. H. 1987. *The Sambia: Ritual and gender in New Guinea.* New York: Holt, Rinehart & Winston.

Kroeber, A. L. 1952. *The nature of culture.* Chicago: University of Chicago Press.

Lehrman, D. S. 1970. Semantic and conceptual issues on the nature-nurture problem. In L. R. Aronson, E. Tobach, D. S. Lehrman, and J. S. Rosenblatt, eds., *Development and evolution of behavior.* San Francisco: W. H. Freeman.

Lesbian & Gay Public Awareness Project. 1991. *Homophobia: What are we so afraid of?* (pamphlet). Los Angeles.

LeVay, S. 1993. *The sexual brain.* Cambridge: MIT Press.

LeVay, S., & Hamer, D. H. 1994. Evidence for a biological influence in male homosexuality. *Scientific American, 270,* 44–49.

Lévi-Strauss, C. 1963. *Structural anthropology.* New York: Basic Books.

Marshall, D. S. 1971. Sexual behavior on Mangaia. In D. S. Marshall & R. C. Suggs, eds., *Human sexual behavior.* New York: Basic Books.

Popper, K. R. 1962. *The open society and its enemies.* Princeton: Princeton University Press.

Sedgwick, E. K. 1990. *Epistemology of the closet.* Berkeley: University of California Press.

Tannahill, R. 1980. *Sex in history.* New York: Stein and Day.

Tylor, E. B. 1871. *Primitive cultures.* London.

PART ONE

Evolutionary Origins

CHAPTER TWO

Sexual Nature: What Can We Learn from a Cross-Species Perspective?

MARY S. McDONALD PAVELKA

Introduction

Humans are primates, and human sexuality is primate sexuality. Since the eighteenth-century work of Carolus Linnaeus it has been recognized that humans are animals, and in particular that we are strikingly similar in many ways to the other primates. Since the nineteenth-century work of Charles Darwin we have understood this similarity to be the result of the evolutionary process which produced all life forms. Both physically and behaviorally we carry the legacy of our evolutionary heritage.

Perhaps more than any other area of human behavior, sexuality spans the gap between what is normally perceived as biological and what is regarded as cultural (as discussed in the introduction to this volume). Underlying the great diversity of human beliefs and behaviors in the area of sex and sexuality are evolved biological and behavioral potentials, constraints, and hormonal regulators. Indeed, the evolutionary process gave rise to language and culture, which have rendered much of our experience unique in the animal kingdom. But our precultural evolutionary history is not so remote as to render us unique in all respects and isolated in the world of living things. Human sexuality is primate sexuality, and an understanding of human sexuality requires that we know something about our basic primate sexuality.

The objective of this chapter is to familiarize nonprimatologist readers with some aspects of primate sexuality that have relevance to issues of human sexuality. These include a consideration of issues such as the loss of estrus in humans, the perceived emancipation of human sexuality from hormonal regulation, nonreproductive sexuality such as sexual interactions with same-sex others, the question of whether sex is pleasurable in nonhuman primates, and the association between sex and aggression. Some aspects of the evolutionary approach to understanding primate sexuality are also discussed.

Loss of Estrus

One feature of human sexuality which has received much attention is the reported loss of estrus that took place over the course of human evolution. Much is made of the apparently "continuous" nature of women's sexuality when compared with that of other female primates. Obviously women do not engage in sexual activity "continuously" throughout their adult lives; however the sexual activity of women does appear to be considerably less periodic and circumscribed than it is in other primate females. Many primate species breed seasonally and engage in sexual behavior for only two or three months of the year.

Sexual activity in nonhuman primates is further circumscribed by estrus, a period of physiological and behavioral change during which most sexual activity takes place. The external manifestations of estrus vary widely across the primate order and might best be defined behaviorally as the period during which a female shows willingness and/or motivation to mate (Fedigan, 1992). For most of any female nonhuman primate's life, she shows no interest in sexual activity. In a twenty-year lifespan, most primate females are likely to spend less than twenty weeks during which they engage in sexual activity (Jolly, 1985). The nonhuman primate evidence suggests that the arousal of the male is dependent upon exposure to the physical and behavioral changes in the female (Rose et al., 1972; Vandenberg and Drickamer, 1974; Vandenberg and Post, 1976).

Human females exhibit no obvious period of estrus. They can and do engage in sexual behavior throughout the menstrual cycle, throughout the year, throughout pregnancy and lactation, and in the postreproductive portion of the lifespan. While there may be some subtle changes in behavior and pheromones at different points in the menstrual cycle of women, there are no obvious external changes to mark ovulation—no physical or behavioral changes directly comparable to the estrus period of some nonhuman primates. Although there are cultural taboos in some societies about interactions with women at certain times during the monthly cycle, or before and after parturition, human societies are not characterized by regular hormonally based behavioral cycles involving periods of sexual activity alternating with periods of complete sexual dormancy.

Three labels have been applied to this situation in women. Human females are said to have lost estrus, evolved concealed ovulation, or become continually sexually receptive. Although these three terms are often used more or less interchangeably, a brief discussion of their different connotations is warranted.

Loss of estrus, as described above, refers to the absence of clearly demarcated periods of physiological and behavioral change associated with sexual activity. Human females are generally said to show little or no cyclicity in sexual motivation (but see below) and to undergo no external changes such as swelling and reddening of the skin.

Concealed ovulation relates to loss of estrus in that the external physical changes as well as the behavioral alterations characteristic of estrus are believed to be indicative of internal endocrine events. The degree to which these external changes correlate with internal events (specifically ovulation) is highly variable, and at one level all primate behavior is said to be relatively emancipated from direct hormonal control; but female nonhuman primates mate and get pregnant only during estrus, so ovulation must occur at some point during estrus. In fact, estrus is widely believed to be a form of advertisement to let males know that a female is ready to conceive. Ovulation in human females is therefore concealed; there are no external indicators of this internal endocrine event. Furthermore, ovulation is concealed not only from others but from the woman herself. Great inter- and intra-individual variation in cycle length contribute to the need, in Western society at least, for rather sophisticated techniques for detecting ovulation. The difficulty that women themselves face in determining when ovulation occurs attests to the fact that, for most women, ovulation is indeed concealed.

The term "continual receptivity" is best understood in historical terms. The long-standing assumption that males are the initiators of sexual interaction, with females as passive recipients, is reflected in the terminology of animal courtship. The term "proceptivity" was introduced by Beach (1976) to refer to female sexual solicitation behaviors. Prior to that, only the terms "receptivity" and "attractiveness" were used. Receptivity refers to the acceptance by females of the advances of males. Attractiveness is a measure of the number of sexual invitations that a female receives. Estrus, the period in which females engage in sexual behavior, was conceived of in this passive terminology as the period in which females would *accept* the sexual initiations of males. Estrus was (and often still is) behaviorally defined as that period in which females are sexually *receptive*. The situation in human females, where no clearly demarcated estrus periods are seen, came to be known as *continual receptivity*. This term is misleading since no human female is continually sexually receptive. According to Frank Beach, "Any male who entertains this illusion must be a very old man with a short memory, or a very young man due for bitter disappointment" (1978, 114). Indeed, some have argued that for men not bonded to a particular woman, the situation might be more aptly termed "continuous nonreceptivity" (Alexander and Noonan, 1979). The underlying assumptions associated with the notion of continual receptivity, however inaccurate and/or biased, are actually fundamental to some of the explanations of estrus loss.

The apparent discontinuity in this basic biological feature of human versus nonhuman primate sexuality has led to numerous speculations about when and how and why this change took place in the course of human evolution. Most theories or speculative reconstructions of the evolution of the hominid line consider loss of estrus to be one of a number of critical adaptive changes essential to human evolution. In some scenarios the continual receptivity of the female is *the* critical feature. The most widespread and popular set of explanations for the evolution of loss of estrus see this change in female sexuality as being at the heart of the human male-female pair bond (Alexander and Noonan, 1979; Fisher, 1982; Lovejoy, 1981; Lancaster, 1975). Most assume that females need males and will use sex (their *continual receptivity* to male advances) to get them. A second set of explanations for the loss of estrus involves the notion that the presence of females in estrus led to intense competition and fighting among the males who desired them. Fox (1975) and others have argued that the loss of estrus evolved to reduce male competition and aggression and to promote more cooperation and cohesion in the social group.

Most of these attempts to understand the absence of estrus in human females emphasize the fact that the ovulatory cues are hidden from other group members, particularly males. A third set of explanations for loss of estrus focus on the concealment of ovulation from the female herself. Burley (1979) argues that concealed ovulation evolved after the initial evolution of intelligence and culture. Armed with increased intelligence, some hominid females came to understand the association between estrus, ovulation, copulation, and childbirth. Because of the pain and fear of childbirth, and the economic and social liabilities of children, these early hominid females practiced abstinence from intercourse near the time of ovulation in order to avoid pregnancy. Since natural selection could not favor such a practice, females who were less in tune with their ovulatory cycles and reproduced more would be favored. The fourth explanation, offered by Wilson (1980), is that loss of estrus is part of the overall tendency of hominids to be generalists as opposed to specialists. In human females, specializations that would advertise ovulation are lost, and sexual activity is more generalized, under less hormonal control.

In nonhuman primates, research has shown that attractivity, receptivity, and proceptivity, as behavioral patterns, correspond to, or are regulated by the levels of estrogen, progesterone, and androgen involved in the menstrual cycle (Johnson and Pheonix, 1976; Baum 1983). Specifically, estradiol may facilitate proceptivity and attractiveness, whereas progesterone may inhibit attractiveness. Underlying the interest in explaining the loss of estrus in humans is acceptance of the position that human females are free from hormonal control of sexual behavior and that we are distinct from the other primates in this regard. There is, however, evidence that human female sexual behavior remains somewhat periodic, and that it does correspond to hormonal activity. Despite the apparent absence of behavioral periodicity in the form of estrus states, it is generally agreed that the underlying menstrual cycle of primates is common to the human and nonhuman species within the order. The continuity across the human-nonhuman primate boundary in the menstrual cycle includes a basic similarity in hormonal fluctuations, and several researchers have explored the possibility of hormonally coincident behavioral fluctuations in women. Significant peaks in sexual activity have been found during the midcycle portion of the menstrual cycle (James, 1971a, b; Udry and Morris, 1968; Matteo and Rissman, 1984). Women taking the birth control pill, however, exhibit little variation in sexual behavior over the cycle, suggesting that the pill suppresses the normal hormonally mediated changes in sexual activity (Adams et al.,

1978). Baum et al. (1977) suggest that the hormonal modulation of human female sexual activity may be similar in many ways to that of monkeys.

The perceived distinction between the hormonal regulation of human and nonhuman primate sexuality is further broken down by the recognition that nonhuman primates, despite periodicity in interest, are themselves relatively emancipated from direct hormonal control of sexual behavior. Baum (1983) and others have argued that various social factors exert an overriding influence on the sexual activity of female nonhuman primates. Bonobos, for example, are one of our closest living relatives and perhaps the best model for early human behavior and biology. The bonobo is generally described as a very sexual species in which sexuality is often extensive and directly tied to social circumstances (see de Waal, this volume).

Furthermore, in many nonhuman primate species, ovulation is also concealed. Some species show no physical signs of estrus, and in most of those that do, the correspondence of external signs to internal endocrine events appears to be poor. Researchers of most primate species are regrettably unable to detect when ovulation occurs; the ability to do so would take us a long way toward refining measures of mating and reproductive success. Some baboon species, in which it is known that ovulation occurs two to three days prior to maximum swelling of the sexual skin (Shaikh et al., 1982) are the envious exception that proves the rule.

One aspect of human female reproductive biology which is almost certainly unique among the primates is menopause (Pavelka and Fedigan, 1991). With the depletion of the egg supply at age fifty, women who live out the species maximum lifespan spend fifty or more years in a postreproductive state. Nonhuman primate females normally do not outlive their egg supplies—they continue to reproduce to very near the end of their lifespans. Interestingly, the loss of reproductive function does not correspond to a loss of sexuality for females. For men the situation is quite different. Men produce new sperm throughout life, and many are able to reproduce into extreme old age. The form that reproductive senescence takes in men is highly variable and gradual, quite unlike the relatively abrupt cessation of menstrual cycling and reproductive function in virtually all women of middle age (see Flint, 1982). Men do however experience declines in sexuality. Hugh Barber characterized this sex difference in reproductive senescence for humans in colloquial terms: "It is a quirk of nature that women are not able to bear children after the menopause but can continue a very active sex life, whereas men are able to impregnate a woman throughout their lives but with advancing age have difficulty in completing the sex act" (1988, 236).

In the context of discussions about loss of estrus, it is often argued that men and women engage in sexual activity far more than they need to from a reproductive point of view. Reference to the nonreproductive nature of much of human sexuality is often used as a point of contrast between humans and other animals. Since much of human sexuality is far removed from reproduction, the evolutionary perspective that sheds light on nonhuman sexuality is sometimes felt to be inappropriate to understanding human sexuality. Again, the clarity of the distinction between human and nonhuman primates tends to be overblown. Nonhuman primates also engage in sexual activity far more than they need to from a reproductive point of view and thus much of their sexuality is nonreproductive.

Nonreproductive Sexuality in Nonhuman Primates: Same-Sex Sexual Interactions and Postconception Estrus.

The fact that the expression of sexuality in nonhuman primates is largely circumscribed by breeding seasons and estrus periods does not mean that sexuality is strictly reproductive in these animals. Nonreproductive sexual behavior occurs in most primate species and includes sexual interactions not close to ovulation, sexual interactions after conception, and sexual interactions with same-sexed others.

Sexual Interactions with Same-Sex Others

Sexual interactions with same-sexed others appears to be part of the normal behavioral repertoire of most animals (Beach, 1968; Chevalier-Skolnikoff, 1976), although its expression is variable both within and across species. Vasey and Chan (1992) reviewed the reports, mostly incidental, of homosexual behavior across the order primates and found that it had been observed in every major taxa with the exception of prosimians. It has been reported for several species of new world monkeys, old world monkeys, and lesser apes, and in all four great apes species. (Observations of seventeen species, (out of thirty identified) were made in the wild, thus dispelling the notion that this is an abnormality produced by the conditions of captivity.)

It could be argued that one major distinction between homosexuality in humans and isosexuality in nonhuman primates is that sexual interactions with same-sex others in nonhuman primates do not reflect the lifetime orientation of an individual. It is part of the normal sexual repertoire of all animals, expressed variously over the lifetime of an individual. In the Japanese macaques of the Arashiyama West colony, one female was known whose only consort relationships throughout her lifetime were with other females, and she did not ever reproduce. She represents a rare exception however to the general view that sexual interactions with both same- and opposite-sex others are part of the normal repertoire of nonhuman primate sexual behavior. It can be argued that this same behavioral tendency exists in humans, that the ability to achieve erotic fulfillment with both sexes is part of the sexual potential of all men and women. The current tendency in North American society to orient exclusively to a homo- *or* heterosexual identity is not a species-wide pattern and may be both culturally and historically quite specific.

Sexual interactions between individuals of the same sex appear to be as elaborate and enduring as are those between opposite-sex individuals. For example, Japanese monkeys, like many other primate species, exhibit a pattern of sociosexual behavior known as consorts. During the mating season, females who are in estrus form consort relationships with males which are quite unlike pair-bonds involving nonestrus females, or pair-bonds occurring outside of the mating season. Male-female consorts involve an exclusive attachment that is sexual in nature, but which affects many other social patterns. For a period of time, from a few days to a few weeks, the consort pair travel together, eat together, sleep together, support each other in conflict situations, and engage in repeated copulations. Female-female consorts involve the same kind of intense and enduring bond.

There is great variability in the expression of same-sex sexuality in nonhuman primates. For example, in Japanese macaques, female-female sexuality is much more common than is male-male. In mountain gorillas the reverse is true (Yamagiwa, 1987). In most species, same-sex sexual interactions occur considerably less frequently than do opposite-sex sexual interactions; however, in bonobos homosexual interactions are as frequent as are heterosexual ones (de Waal, 1987). Same-sex sexual interactions might even be more varied in expression than are opposite-sex ones, as across the many species in which this behavior occurs it has been observed to include genital-genital, oral-genital, anal-genital, anal-anal, and manual-genital contact. Sexual interactions between males and females are more likely to be genital-genital.

Explaining homosexual behavior in humans and other animals presents quite a challenge to the strict adaptationist. In and of itself homosexual behavior cannot increase the reproductive success of the actors, and from an extreme point of view it might be described as "biologically absurd" (Swanson, 1974). There have been attempts to explain this seemingly enigmatic behavior pattern within the context of current evolutionary thought. For example, female-female homosexuality might have evolved as a form of female-female mate competition in that it serves to prevent the other females from mating with males and conceiving offspring (Tyler, 1984; Srivastava et al., 1991) or as a means of population control (Kirsch and Rodman, 1982).

Several proximate or immediate functions for homosexual behavior have also been identified. In rhesus macaques female-female sexual bonds aid in the formation of female coalitions (Fairbanks and McGuire, 1977). In bonobos these interactions operate as a mechanism of tension reduction (de Waal, 1987, and this volume). The great variability in expression and in the proximate functions of homosexual behavior suggests that the occurrence and expression of this behavior is probably best understood within the context of the social organization of the group or species in which it appears.

Hyperselectionism

The desire to reconcile this obviously nonreproductive behavior with the reproduction mandate of natural selection highlights one problem with the evolutionary perspective. There is a tendency for some writers to be guilty of extreme adaptationism, assuming all aspects of behavior and biology to be the result of some direct selective forces. This Panglossian tendency (Gould and Lewontin, 1979) or hyperselectionism can reduce both the value and the credibility of the cross-species and evolutionary perspectives. In reviewing reports of and explanations for homosexuality in nonhuman primates, Vasey and Chan (1992) question the claim that current functions strongly imply past selection and adaptation. They argue that it is unnecessary to explain nonhuman primate homosexual behavior in adaptationist terms. Because this behavior forms part of the diverse sexual repertoire of the primates (Fedigan, 1992), the challenge is to explain the origins of the obvious plasticity in sexual expression, not the origins of any one form of expression, such as same-sex interactions. Hyperselectionism and strict adherence to the adaptationist program in an evolutionary approach are likely to interfere with the potential of this approach to shed light on our understanding of human sexuality.

Abramson and Pinkerton (1995) argue that strict selectionist interpretations of specific manifestations of sexual behavior are not necessary, and that a more general and parsimonious evolutionary model better explains the wide range of expression of human and nonhuman primate sexuality. The evolution of sexual pleasure would lead to sexual interactions of all kinds, and within this range of behavior there would be enough male-female reproductive contact to ensure the reproductive success of advantageous morphological and behavioral variations. This perspective assumes much less competition than do most sociobiological ones, which often include a consideration of the costs of sexual activity including the expenditure of energy and the distraction of the animal from food-getting and predator-avoidance activities.

Postconception Sexual Interactions in Nonhuman Primates

Another form of obviously nonreproductive sexuality in nonhuman primates is the widespread tendency for animals to engage in sexual interactions when conception is not possible, as when the female is already pregnant. If hormonal regulation were strict and fully efficient from a reproductive point of view, all indications of estrus, both behavioral and physical, would cease upon fertilization of the ovum. In fact, sexual activity during pregnancy has been reported for chimpanzees (Tutin and McGinnis, 1981; de Waal, 1982), gorillas (Harcourt et al., 1980), rhesus macaques (Bielert et al., 1976), stumptailed macaques (Slob and Nieuwenhuijsen, 1980), Japanese monkeys (Wolfe, 1984; Pavelka, 1993), and golden lion tamarins (Kleiman and Mack, 1977).

While some argue that this is evidence for the proximate explanation that these animals engage in sexual activity because it feels good (ex. de Waal, 1982), others seek an ultimate selection interpretation. Hrdy (1981), for example, argues that female promiscuity, including postconception estrus activity, can be ultimately explained as a mechanism by which females confuse paternity and thereby decrease the chances that their offspring will be injured by adult males and increase the chances that they will be protected by them. Female orgasm evolved as the proximate mechanism to motivate females to behave in this way.

Hrdy's provision for both a proximate and an ultimate explanation that work together to explain the animals' behavior adds considerably to the strength of the argument. One major stumbling block to accepting an evolutionary perspective on human behavior, indeed on nonhuman behavior for those of us who have spent considerable time watching nonhuman primates in social groups, is the issue of what motivates an individual to behave in certain ways. No one really thinks that humans, or other primates for that matter, actually make decisions because they consciously or unconsciously "want to get their genes into the next generation." A mediating proximate mechanism, either physiological or social, is often lacking in evolutionary explanations for behavior (see Symons, this volume).

Sex and Pleasure in a Cross-Species Perspective

Sexual pleasure is the obvious proximate mechanism that would explain the vast amount of sexual activity in human and nonhuman primates that is both reproductive and nonreproductive (Abramson and Pinkerton, 1995). Redressing the neglect of pleasure in anthropological studies of human sexuality is one of the main objectives of this volume. Although the significance of pleasure to our understanding of human sexuality is often overlooked, there is a widespread assumption that only human sexual activity is pleasurable. Even in nonhuman primates, where there is much sexual activity that is not reproductive and for which alternate social functions have been identified, researchers are disinclined to take that next step and talk about sexuality as pleasure. This is no doubt a function of the same discomfort which has directed the sidestepping of discussions of pleasure in traditional anthropological inquiry. Students learn early in their careers that the question of whether or not animals (or people) enjoy sex is not a concern addressed by a serious scholar.

Nonetheless, pleasure as a proximate mechanism has been recognized as a critical element to understanding the motivations of human and nonhuman primate sexuality. Central to this inquiry is the debate over whether or not female orgasm is an exclusively human experience. (While discussions of sexual pleasure often equate pleasure with orgasm, it should be kept in mind that pleasure can be experienced in the absence of orgasm, and this is very likely true for both human and nonhuman primates.) Since orgasm is an internal experience and sensation, we cannot ever expect to determine with certainty if our non-linguistic relatives share it. The best we can do is to look for evidence in non-human primates of the physical expressions which accompany the sensations described by humans. The behaviors of male nonhuman primates during ejaculation (muscle rigidity, perianal muscle contractions, a fixed stare) are generally accepted as sufficient evidence that ejaculation is accompanied by a pleasurable sensation, as we know it usually is in men. Demonstrating the presence of orgasm in nonhuman primate females is less straightforward. There is evidence that female nonhuman primates experience uterine contractions and heart-rate increases during sexual interactions that involve genital contact (Goldfoot et al., 1980) and in response to experimental stimulation (Burton, 1971; Allen and Lemmon, 1981). Several researchers have also described characteristic facial expressions observed in females during sexual encounters (Chevalier-Skolnikoff, 1974; de Waal, 1989).

Much of the debate over female orgasm is theoretical, with researchers arguing over whether or not it makes sense for female nonhuman primates to have orgasms from a selectionist point of view. The evidence offered above is interpreted accordingly. Many (ex. Ardrey, 1976) assume that female orgasm is uniquely human and that it evolved as part of the continuous receptivity that allowed females to get and hang on to their men. Symons (1979) argues that the evidence for the existence of orgasm in nonhuman primates is not convincing and that human female orgasm is simply a by-product of male orgasms (the clitoris and the penis begin as the same tissue in the embryo and thus share the capacity to precipitate orgasm). Hrdy's (1981) position is in direct contrast to Symon's. She argues that orgasm is not unique to women and that it evolved as a proximate mechanism to entice females to engage in behavior which confuses paternity.

Wolfe (1991) also rejects Symon's (1979) interpretation of the evidence for orgasm in nonhuman primates but does so by focusing on the genital anatomy of monkey, ape, and human females. She points out that, in monkeys and apes, the clitoris actually lies at or near the base of the vagina, a location that would insure direct and regular stimulation during intercourse. In human females the clitoris is situated away from the base of the vagina and this results in the indirect and often insufficient stimulation which is widely reported to result in a low frequency of orgasm during intercourse. Female orgasm during intercourse is thus an ancient primate characteristic that has been partially lost in the course of human evolution. Wolfe argues that this is a by-product of the changes in the skeleton during the evolution of bipedalism. Hominid females had to give birth to increasingly large-brained babies through a birth canal significantly narrowed by the reorganization of the pelvis and sacrum. Selection then favored the movement of the urinary meatus away from the vagina to protect it from trauma during childbirth; the placement of the clitoris away from the vagina in women is simply a by-product of this move.

Further support for the claim that nonhuman primates, particularly females, experience sexual pleasure and even orgasm, is found in the extensive observations that animals throughout the primate order engage in genital masturbation. In males, masturbation regularly leads to ejaculation and the associated indicators of orgasm. In females as well, manipulation of the genital area and clitoris by rubbing against materials in the environment or by manual stimulation sometimes results in contractions of the perianal area which are indicative of orgasm (Wolfe, 1991).

Sex and Aggression

In some aspects of human sexuality, the sex-as-pleasure perspective is remote, as in the association between sex and aggression. From the violent rape by a stranger, to acquaintance rape, to wife beating, to sadomasochistic sexual practices, to the widespread use of degradation and violence in pornography, it is clear that there is a strong link between two behavior patterns which at many levels seem distinct and incongruous.

The most widely accepted interpretations of sexual violence in humans are those which explain this behavioral connection in exclusively human terms, linking the behavior to aspects of human society and culture. The feminist perspective seeks to disassociate sex and violence and to explain sexual aggression as primarily an expression of, or reflection of, male desire to dominate and control women and their sexuality (Brownmiller, 1975; Dworkin, 1981, 1985; Sanday, 1981; Scully and Marolla, 1985). Rape, specifically, is not considered to be a sexual act, but a primarily aggressive and violent one which has more in common with nonsexual assaults than it does with consensual sex. The connection between sexuality and aggression in feminist perspectives on rape is seen to be a learned connection and a function of male-dominated patriarchal society. There is great overlap between some aspects of the feminist and social-learning theories of rape (see Check and Malamuth, 1985). Proponents of the social-learning theory of rape (Malamuth, 1980, 1984, 1986; Check, 1985; Zillmann, 1984) essentially see male sexual aggression toward women as stemming from the desensitizing effects of pornography, objectification of women in the mass media, and the acceptance and perpetuation of rape myths (i.e., women secretly want to be raped).

Considerable support can be found for many of the propositions of both the feminist and social-learning theories of rape (Ellis, 1989), and most adherents of these theories have been loath to consider any evolved component to this behavior, fearing the implications of a biologically deterministic view. However a full understanding of the connection between sex and aggression in human primates should take into account and attempt to understand the basis of the connection between sex and aggression in primates in general and then the conditions of its specific manifestation in humans.

If the connection between sex and aggression is a purely learned one that is grounded in patriarchal human society, then presumably a strong connection between the two would not be expected in nonhuman primate society. In fact, male aggression against females is widespread among primates, and much of it occurs in the context of mating. This has long been recognized by individual researchers, and the primatological literature is filled with passing reference to male aggression against females and to the substantial increase in aggressive male attacks received by females in estrus. Forced or attempted forced copulation with an obviously resistant female has not been observed for most nonhuman primates but it is now known to occur in orangutans (MacKinnon, 1974, 1979; Rijksen, 1975; Galdikas, 1981, 1985a, b; Mitani, 1985) and two cases have been reported in wild chimpanzees (Nadler, 1988). Other species in which male sexual aggression against females has been observed include spider monkeys, baboons, macaques, chimpanzees, and mountain gorillas (Smuts and Smuts, 1993).

Parental Investment: The Sociobiological Explanation

The evolutionary explanations which have been offered for the connection between sex and aggression are constructed within the framework of Darwinian sexual selection theory. Sexual selection was reformulated as parental investment theory by Trivers (1972) to explain sex differences in behavior. Underlying this sociobiological perspective is the view that males and females have a fundamental conflict of interest with regard to reproduction and that much of their behavior, particularly their sexual behavior, can be understood as a function of this reproductive conflict. According to the theory, males and females, with their very different roles in reproduction, employ very different strategies for maximizing reproductive success. Because females produce only a single large egg each month (compared to the millions of sperm produced with each ejaculation) and because females have the job of gestating and lactating offspring, they are seen as having, from the moment of conception, a greater investment in each individual offspring. They are also limited in their total number of offspring produced, as compared with the total number of offspring which any male could potentially sire. Males invest very little in the production of each offspring, and thus have little to lose should any particular offspring not survive. The strategy that should be employed by most males, then, is to abandon the female and newly created offspring shortly after conception and attempt to gain sexual access to as many fertile females as possible. Females, on the other hand, have invested more than the male from the moment of conception, and always have more to lose should the offspring not survive. Females thus employ a very different reproductive strategy. They are, for example, much more discriminating in their choice of mates, as they have so much more invested in each offspring. It is predicted that females might choose

SEXUAL NATURE: A CROSS-SPECIES PERSPECTIVE

males who have given some indication that they will "stick around" and share in some of the costs of ensuring the survival of the offspring.

Triver's theory of parental investment has been extremely influential, and its ideas dominate current evolutionary thought on sexuality and sex roles in reproduction. It is not, however, without critics. Many researchers (ex. Fedigan, 1992; Ruse, 1979) have pointed out that the theory is inherently sexist, constructing male and female strategies such that females are at a disadvantage from the outset, a disadvantage which they are continually (and mostly unsuccessfully) trying to overcome. The prediction that males should be indiscriminate and promiscuous and females should be choosy and monogamous certainly strikes a cord of similarity with cultural stereotypes. Critics argue that the theory is more a heavily value-laden biological justification for social behavior patterns that are unacceptable to women than it is an explanation for well-documented behavior patterns. More specific criticisms involve the basic construction of the theory and some of the assumptions on which it rests. For example, by choosing the term *parental* investment, which by definition cannot begin until an animal is a parent, the theory effectively cuts out the often very large amount of time and energy invested by males in getting to the point of conception. Much of the theory hinges on the different investment by males and females "from the outset," but the difference itself depends heavily on how the "outset" is defined. Another assumption on which the theory rests heavily is that there is much greater variation in reproductive success among males than there is among females. Some males may be very successful and others not at all—the stakes and payoffs of male reproductive striving are much higher than they are for females—and male behavior is interpreted in this context. However, without any way to measure the reproductive success of males, this remains an unproven assumption. When all is said and done, the contribution of offspring to the next generation by individual males may vary no more or less than does the contribution of individual females.

In spite of all this, the theory has a great deal of empirical support. Animals, maybe even humans, do behave in many ways that are consistent with the predictions of the theory. Moreover, widespread behavior patterns that are otherwise extremely difficult to comprehend, such as infanticide by adult males (Hrdy, 1979; Hrdy and Hausfater, 1985) and sexual aggression against females (Smuts and Smuts, 1993), have been convincingly argued as male reproductive strategies.

Both Ellis (1989) and Smuts (1992), drawing on the extensive evidence that sex and aggression are connected in a wide range of animals and in particular in the primates (Smuts and Smuts, 1993), have found the parental investment perspective to provide a good, and least partial, explanatory framework for rape and other forms of male aggression against women. Smuts and Smuts (1993) argue that males may be using sexual coercion to increase access to mates, and they thus interpret male sexual aggression as a male reproductive

strategy. Ellis (1989) cites evidence from studies of human rape which supports a male reproductive strategy explanation. For example, forced copulations carry a significant risk of impregnation, rape victims are primarily of
reproductive age, rape is vigorously resisted (especially when the offender is
not someone the victim would have chosen to have sex with), and rapists, especially those who assault strangers, are less likely than other males to attract
voluntary partners.

Biological Determinism?

The hypothesis that sexual coercion is a male reproductive strategy includes
the prediction that the manifestation of sexual aggression will differ in different groups, as successful female strategies, or counterstrategies, are taken into
account. Additionally, this evolutionary perspective on male aggression is not
one of biological reductionism. While some sociobiologists (and most of the
popular media) are guilty of sensationalism and biological reductionism, biological or genetic determinism is not the basis of evolutionary perspectives. A
colleague who saw me photocopying articles on rape in nonhuman species
asked me how I dealt with the "obvious implication that rape in humans is
inevitable and unavoidable." This kind of misunderstanding of the value of an
evolutionary perspective is widespread, despite the painstaking efforts of many
members of the primatological community to emphasize that the expression
of behaviors is obviously highly varied and that environmental factors play a
substantial role in most if not all behavioral expression. Critics of the evolutionary perspective on male aggression against women have tended to depict
it as an all-or-none proposition, one which ignores the learning, situational,
and social structural factors that influence rape probabilities (Ellis, 1989). In
fact most evolutionary theorists have emphasized these factors, none of which
preclude the involvement of evolutionary ones. Smuts, in her review of male
violence against women worldwide stressed that "far from being an immutable
feature of human nature, male aggression toward women varies dramatically
depending on circumstances" (1992, 24). No knowledgeable evolutionary the-
orist would argue that men (and women) are not responsible for their choices
and their behavior—quite the contrary. Furthermore, few if any current evolutionary theorists are guilty of the naturalistic fallacy, the illogical move from
describing what *is* to arguing for what *should be.* Evolutionary explanations of
a behavior's adaptiveness in the past, particularly those without a proximate
mechanism, do not reveal the range of current or future expression. It is pure
fallacy to confuse hypotheses about what is in nature (including adaptive stories about what should be from a strictly selection point of view) with value
judgments about what ought to be regarded as normal and right in human life.

  There is counterevidence to the suggestion that male aggression increases
male reproductive success. Bercovitch et al. (1987) reported a negative correla-

tion between male aggression toward females and male success at achieving intromissions, which can be interpreted as evidence that selection does not favor male aggression as a reproductive strategy, at least in this species. But note that evidence that male aggression does not increase male reproductive success may lead to the rejection of the interpretation of this behavior as an evolved male reproductive strategy, but it does not discount the reality of the connection between the behaviors in a wide cross-species perspective.

While not trying to make an evolutionary argument, Zillmann (1984) provides what could be seen as the proximate mechanism for the evolutionary, feminist, or social-learning perspectives on the connection between sexuality and aggression. He has developed an excitation-transfer paradigm which emphasizes underlying autonomic and adrenal commonalties in both sexual and aggressive behavior. The interdependencies in sexual and aggressive response are said to result from "insufficient differentiation in the autonomic response components together with the somewhat archaic stimulus control of excitatory reactions" (1984, viii). In other words, the physiological basis of sexual excitement is very similar to the physiological basis of aggressive excitement. In humans, then, the feelings produced by these very similar physiological states would have to be interpreted by the individual through the use of a host of environmental variables.

Conclusions

Understanding any behavior pattern in the cross-species context provides an important source of information for those interested in the manifestation of the behavior in any one species. As biological animals, human beings have certain evolved potentials, limitations, and tendencies affecting their behavior, and a full understanding of human sexuality cannot be gained from an exclusively cultural point of view. In spite of misunderstanding and misapplication of evolutionary explanations, in this area of human behavior perhaps more than any other, the cross-species and evolutionary perspective is critical to informed theory-building.

Biological approaches to understanding behavior have come a long way since the days when behavior was conceived of as *either* instinctive (rigidly programmed, inescapable, inevitable) *or* purely learned. This false dichotomy (Fedigan, 1992) has long been recognized (see the Introduction, this volume). Even the sociobiological search for adaptive explanations to account for the evolutionary history of a behavior—an exercise which dominated the field from the mid-1970s to the mid-1980s—has been replaced with a recognition of the great range of expression in behavior and the need to understand the immediate physiological and social conditions under which behaviors occur. Animals have become "adaptive decision-makers" (de Waal, personal communication), with individuals behaving in accord with a host of complex variables including the individual personality and choices of the actor. The cross-species evolutionary approach to human behavior is not one which discounts the obvious roles played by language, culture, ideology, and self-reflection in human behavioral expression.

In terms of human sexuality, we have much to gain from an appreciation of our evolved primate tendencies, whether these be shared or uniquely human. Shared mammalian hormonal fluctuations of the menstrual cycle may influence the sexual behavior of individuals. Menopause renders women unable to reproduce halfway through the maximum lifespan, an evolved constraint which is unique to our species. Exclusive heterosexuality in humans is clearly not an evolved limitation or constraint. The cross-species perspective reveals that sexual expression in primates is flexible and diverse, including same-sex sexuality as part of the normal repertoire of behavior for most animals. Sexual expression beyond the demands of reproduction, including sexual activity during pregnancy and lactation, is also the norm in many primate societies. Our physiological capacity to experience orgasm (both male and female) is probably shared by the monkeys and apes, although the experiential components which are tied to language and conceptual thought are most likely uniquely human. The human female difficulty in experiencing orgasm during intercourse may also be evolved—as a by-product of rearrangements in genital anatomy during the evolution of bipedalism. The cross-species capacity for orgasm, extensive nonreproductive sexuality, and masturbation in primates all support the interpretation that sexual pleasure is an evolved feature of primate sexuality. On the darker side, the association between sex and violence which is cause for much concern in human social life is also not uniquely ours. An understanding of the underlying biological connection between sex and aggression will be necessary if we are to fully understand—and influence—the expression of behavior in humans.

References

Abramson, P. R., and Pinkerton, S. D. 1995. With pleasure: thoughts on the nature of human sexuality. New York: Oxford University Press.

Adams, D. B., Gould, A. R., and Burt, A. D. 1978. Rise in female-initiated sexual activity at ovulation and its suppression by oral contraceptives. New England Journal of Medicine 299:1145–50.

Alexander, R. D., and Noonan, K. M. 1979. Concealment of ovulation, parental care, and human social evolution. In Evolutionary Biology and Human Social Behavior. N. A. Chagnon and J. W. Irons, eds. Massachusetts: Duxbury Press.

Allen, M. L., and Lemmon, W. B. 1981. Orgasm in female primates. American Journal of Primatology 1:5–15.

Ardrey, R. 1976. The Hunting Hypothesis. New York: Athenaeum.

Barber, H. R. K. 1988. Perimenopausal and Geriatric Gynecology. New York: Macmillan.

Baum, M. J. 1983. Hormonal modulation of sexuality in female primates. Bioscience 33:578–82.

Baum, M. J., Everitt, B. J., Herbert, J., and Keverne, E. B. 1977. Hormonal basis of proceptivity and receptivity in female primates. Archives of Sexual Behavior 6:173–92.

Beach, F. A. 1968. Factors involved in the control of mounting behavior by female mammals. In Perspectives in Reproduction and Sexual Behavior. M. Diamond, ed. Bloomington: Indiana University Press, pp. 83–131.

Beach, F. A. 1976. Sexual attractivity, proceptivity, and receptivity in female mammals. Hormones and Behavior 7:105–38.

Beach, F. A. 1978. Human sexuality and evolution. In Human Evolution: Biosocial Perspectives. S. L. Washburn and E. R. McCown, eds. Menlo Park: Benjamin Cummings.

Beilert, C., Czaja, J. A., Eisele, S., Sheffler, G., Robinson, J. A., and Goy, R. W. 1976. Mating in the rhesus monkey (Macaca mulatta) after conception and its relationship to estriol and progesterone levels throughout pregnancy. Journal of Reproduction and Fertility 46:179–87.

Bercovitch, F. B., Sladky, K. K., Roy, M. M., and Goy, R. W. 1987. Intersexual aggression and male sexual activity in captive rhesus macaques. Aggressive Behavior 13:375–79.

Brownmiller, S. 1975. Against Our Will: Men, Women, and Rape. New York: Simon and Schuster.

Burley, N. 1979. The evolution of concealed ovulation. The American Naturalist 114(6):835–58.

Burton, F. D. 1971. Sexual climax in female Macaca mulatta. In Proceedings of the Third International Congress of Primatology. Basel: Karger.

Check, J. V. P. 1985. Hostility toward women: Some theoretical considerations. In Violence in Intimate Relationships. G. W. Russel, ed. Jamaica, N.Y.: Spectrum.

Check, J. V. P., and Malamuth, N. M. 1985. An empirical assessment of some feminist hypotheses about rape. International Journal of Women's Studies 8:414–23.

Chevalier-Skolnikoff, S. 1974. Male-female, female-female, and male-male sexual behavior in the stumptail monkey, with special attention to the female orgasm. Archives of Sexual Behavior 3:95–116.

Chevalier-Skolnikoff, S. 1976. Homosexual behavior in a laboratory group of stumptailed monkeys (Macaca arctoides): Forms, contexts, and possible social functions. Archives of Sexual Behavior 5(6):511–27.

de Waal, F. B. M. 1982. Chimpanzee Politics. Baltimore and London: John Hopkins University Press.

de Waal, F. B. M. 1987. Tension regulation and non-reproductive functions of sex in captive bonobos (Pan paniscus). National Geographic Research 3(3):318–38.

de Waal, F. B. M. 1989. Peacekeeping Among Primates. Cambridge: Harvard University Press.

Dworkin, A. 1981. Pornography: Men Possessing Women. New York: Perigee.

Dworkin, A. 1985. Against the male flood: Censorship, pornography, and equality. Harvard Women's Law Journal 8:1–29.

Ellis, L. 1989. Theories of Rape: Inquiries into the Causes of Sexual Aggression. New York: Hemisphere.

Fairbanks, L. A., and McGuire, M. T. 1977. Sex and aggression during rhesus monkey group formation. Aggressive behavior 3: 241–49.

Fedigan, L. M. 1992. Primate Paradigms: Sex Roles and Social Bonds. Chicago: University of Chicago Press.

Fisher, H. 1982. The Sex Contract: The Evolution of Human Behavior. New York: Quill Press.

Flint, M. 1982. Anthropological perspectives of the menopause and middle age. Maturitas 4:173–80.

Fox, R. 1975. Primate kin and human kinship. In Biosocial Anthropology. R. Fox, ed. London: Malaby Press.

Galdikas, B. M. F. 1981. Orangutan reproduction in the wild. In Reproductive Biology of the Great Apes. C. E. Graham, ed. New York: Academic Press.

Galdikas, B. M. F. 1985a. Adult male sociality and reproductive tactics among orangutans at Tanjung Putiny. Folia Primatologica 45:9–24.

Galdikas, B. M. F. 1985b. Subadult male orangutan sociality and reproductive behavior at Tanjung Putiny. American Journal of Primatology 8:87–99.

Goldfoot, D. A., Westerborg-Van Loon, H., Groeneveld, W., and Slob, A. K. 1980. Behavioral and physiological evidence of sexual climax in female stumptailed macaques (*Macaca arctoides*). Science 208:1477–78.

Gould, S. J., and Lewontin, R. C. 1979. The spandrels of San Marco and the Panglossian paradigm: a critique of the adaptationist program. Proceedings of the Royal Society of London B 205:581–98.

Harcourt, A. H., Fossey, D., Stewart, K. J., and Watts, D. P. 1980. Reproduction in wild gorillas and some comparisons with chimpanzees. Journal of Reproduction and Fertility, Supplement 28:59–70.

Hrdy, S. B. 1979. Infanticide among animals: A review, classification, and examination of the implications for the reproductive strategies of females. Ethology and Sociobiology 1:13–40.

Hrdy, S. B. 1981. The Woman that Never Evolved. Cambridge: Harvard University Press.

Hrdy, S. B., and Hausfater, G. 1985. Comparative and evolutionary perspectives on infanticide: An introduction and overview. In Infanticide: Comparative and Evolutionary Perspectives. G. Hausfater and S. B. Hrdy, eds. Hawthorne, N.Y.: Aldine.

James, W. H. 1971a. The distribution of coitus within the human intermenstruam. Journal of Biosocial Science 3:159–71.

James, W. H. 1971b. Coital rates and the pill. Nature 234:555–56.

Johnson, D. F., and Pheonix, C. H. 1976. Hormonal control of female sexual attractiveness, proceptivity, and receptivity in rhesus monkeys. Journal of Comparative and Physiological Psychology 90(5):473–83.

Jolly, A. 1985. The Evolution of Primate Behavior. New York: Macmillan.

Kirsch, J. A. W., and Rodman, J. E. 1982. Selection and sexuality: The Darwinian view of homosexuality. In Homosexuality: Social, Psychological, and Biological Issues. W. Paul, J. D. Weinrich, J. C. Gonsiorek, M. E. Hotvedt, eds. Beverly Hills: Sage, pp. 183–95.

Kleiman, D. G., and Mack, D. S. 1977. A peak in sexual activity during pregnancy in the golden lion tamarin (*Leontopithecus rosalia*). Journal of Mammalogy 58:657–60.

Lancaster, J. B. 1975. Primate Behavior and the Emergence of Human Culture. New York: Holt, Rinehart, and Winston.

Lovejoy, C. O. 1981. The origin of man. Science 211:341–50.

MacKinnon, J. 1974. The behavior and ecology of wild orangutans, *Pongo pygmaeus*. Animal Behavior 22:3–74.

MacKinnon, J. 1979. Reproductive behavior in a wild orangutan population. *In* The Great Apes. D. A. Hamburg, and E. R. McCown, eds. Menlo Park: Benjamin/Cummings, pp. 257–74.

Malamuth, N. M. 1980. Testing hypotheses regarding rape: Exposure to sexual violence, sex differences, and the "normality" of rapists. Journal of Research in Personality 14:121–74.

Malamuth, N. M. 1984. Aggression against women: Cultural and individual causes. *In* Pornography and Sexual Aggression. N. M. Malamuth and E. Donnerstein, eds. New York: Academic Press, pp. 19–52.

Malamuth, N. M. 1986. Prediction of naturalistic sexual aggression. Journal of Personality and Social Psychology 50:953–962 .

Matteo, S. and Rissman, E. F. 1984. Increased sexual activity during the midcycle portion of the human menstrual cycle. Hormones and Behavior 18:249–55.

Mitani, J. C. 1985. Mating behavior of male orangutans in Kutai Game Reserve, Indonesia. Animal Behavior 33:392–404.

Nadler, R. D. 1988. Sexual aggression in the great apes. Annals of the New York Academy of Science.

Pavelka, M. S. M. 1993. Monkeys of the Mesquite: The Social Life of the South Texas Snow Monkey. Dubuque: Kendall/Hunt.

Pavelka, M. S. M., and Fedigan, L. M. 1991. Menopause: A comparative life history perspective. Yearbook of Physical Anthropology 34:13–38.

Rijksen, H. D. 1975. Social structure in a wild orangutan population in Sumatra. *In* Contemporary Primatology. J. Kondo, M. Kawai and A. Ehara, eds. Basel: Karger, pp. 373–79.

Rose, R. M., Gordon, T. P., and Bernstein, I. S. 1972. Plasma testosterone levels in the male rhesus: influences of sexual and social stimuli. Science 178:643–45.

Ruse, M. 1979. Sociobiology: Sense or Nonsense? Boston: D. Reidel.

Sanday, P. 1981. The socio-cultural context of rape: A cross-cultural study. Journal of Social Issues 37:5–27.

Scully, D., and Marolla, J. 1985. "Riding the bull at Gilley's": Convicted rapists describe the rewards of rape. Social Problems 32:251–63.

Shaikh, A. A., Celaya, C. L., Gomez, I., and Shaikh, S. A. 1982. Temporal relationships of hormonal peaks to ovulation and sex skin deturgescence in the baboon. Primates 23:444–52.

Slob, A. K., and Nieuwenhijensen, K. 1980. Heterosexual interactions of pairs of laboratory-housed stumptailed macaques (*Macaca arctoides*) under continuous observation with closed-circuit video recording. International Journal of Primatology 1:63–80.

Smuts, B. 1992. Male aggression against women: An evolutionary perspective. Human Nature 3(1):1–44.

Smuts, B., and Smuts, R. 1993. Male aggression and sexual coercion of females in nonhuman primates and other mammals: Evidence and theoretical implications. *In* Advances in the Study of Behavior, vol. 22. P. J. B. Slater, M. Milinski, J. S. Rosenblatt, and C. T. Snowdon, eds. Academic Press, pp. 1–61.

Srivastava, A., Borries, C., and Sommer. 1991. Homosexual mounting in free-ranging female Hanuman langurs (*Presbytis entellus*). Archives of Sexual Behavior 20(5):487–512.

Swanson, H. D. 1974. Human Reproduction: Biology and Social Change. New York: Oxford University Press.

Symons, D. 1979. The Evolution of Human Sexuality. New York: University of Oxford Press.

Trivers, R. L. 1972. Parental investment and sexual selection. *In* Sexual Selection and the Descent of Man: 1871–1971. B. Campbell ed. Chicago: Aldine.

Tutin, C. E. G., and P. R. McGinnis. 1981. Sexuality of the chimpanzees in the wild. *In* Reproductive Biology of the Great Apes: Comparative and Biomedical Perspectives. C. E. Graham, ed. New York: Academic Press, pp. 239–64.

Tyler, P. A. 1984. Homosexual behaviour in animals. *In* The Psychology of Sexual Diversity. K. Howells, ed. London: Basil Blackwell.

Udry, J. R., and Morris, N. M. 1968. Distribution of coitus in the menstrual cycle. Nature 220:593–96.

Vandenberg, J. G., and Drickamer, L. C. 1974. Reproductive coordination among free-ranging rhesus monkeys. Physiology and Behavior 13:373–76.

Vandenberg, J. G., and Post, W. 1976. Endocrine coordination in rhesus monkeys: female responses to the male. Physiology and Behavior 17:979–84.

Vasey, P., and Chan, L. 1992. Homosexual behavior in alloprimates: Definition, survey and evolutionary interpretations. Paper presented at the Canadian Association for Physical Anthropology meetings, Edmonton.

Wilson, P. 1980. Man the Promising Primate: The Conditions of Human Evolution. New Haven: Yale University Press.

Wolfe, L. D. 1984. Japanese macaque female sexual behavior: A comparison of Arashiyama East and West. *In* Female Primates: Studies by Women Primatologists. M. F. Small, ed. New York: Alan R. Liss, pp. 141–57.

Wolfe, L. D. 1991. Evolution and female primate sexual behavior. *In* Understanding Behavior: What Primate Studies Tell Us About Human Behavior. J. D. Loy and C. B. Peters, eds. New York: Oxford University Press, pp. 121–51.

Yamagiwa, J. 1987. Intra- and inter-group interactions of all male groups of Virunga mountain gorillas (*Gorilla gorilla beringei*). Primates 28(1):1–30.

Zillmann, D. 1984. Connections between Sex and Aggression. Hillsdale, NJ: Lawrence Erlbaum Associates.

CHAPTER THREE

Sex as an Alternative to Aggression in the Bonobo

FRANS B. M. DE WAAL

Introduction

If, as both Christian doctrine and biology would have it, the purpose of sex is reproduction, why do millions of human couples engage in it on a daily or weekly basis even though the average family-size in industrialized nations has dropped to only one or two children? Perhaps they do so simply because it makes them feel good, almost like an addiction. Yet this possibility raises the question: Why does it make people feel so good? After all, most other animals restrict their mating to a particular season or a couple of days in their ovulatory cycles; they do not seem to feel any need for nonreproductive sex. Are we the only ones with such sexual appetites, or are there other species like us?

There is one, and it can hardly be coincidental that it is, together with the chimpanzee (*Pan troglodytes*), our nearest relative. Known as the bonobo (*Pan paniscus*), or pygmy chimpanzee, the creature was discovered only in the 1920s (see Coolidge, 1984, and de Waal, 1989), and has recently become a hot topic of debate among primatologists. Whereas the chimpanzee shows little variation in the sexual act, bonobos behave as if they have read the Kama Sutra, performing every position and variation one can imagine. Yet, their rate of reproduction in the wild is approximately the same as that of the chimpanzee, with single births to a female at intervals of five to six years. So, bonobos share with us both a rich sexuality and a partial divorce of sex from reproduction.

In biology, sexual behavior generally is investigated from the perspective of reproduction. Although the nonreproductive use of the same behavior is common to many species, this use is considered of secondary importance. From an evolutionary perspective, the primary function of sexual behavior, that is, the function most directly relevant for natural selection, is its capacity of producing a zygote. But if fertile and infertile partner combinations engage in sexual behavior with equal intensity and equal frequency, as is the case in the bonobo, it would seem that the reproductive function has decreased in relative importance.

Before a partial divorce between sexual behavior and its fertilization function is accepted, two conditions must be met. First, sexual contact in infertile partner combinations—such as individuals of the same sex or adults and juveniles—should not be a mere substitute for heterosexual contact between adults. In other words, given a choice, the animals should not necessarily give priority to the second type of contact. The frequent isosexual mounts that Yamagiwa (1987) observed within an all-male band of wild gorillas (*Gorilla gorilla beringei*) probably are examples of redirected sex. The dominant silverback males of this band treated the younger males as a "harem," competing over ownership in the same way known of bisexual units. Yamagiwa suggested that the formation of this special male band may have been related to an increased male/female ratio in the population, i.e., a relative lack of females.

Second, infertile sexual contact would be considered deviant behavior unless such contact is functionally integrated into the natural social life of the species. To give an extreme example: a sexual motor pattern that is observed exclusively in individuals reared in isolation would not meet the requirement because it is not possible that sexual behavior evolved under this condition. In short, it would be accepted that sexual motor patterns serve functions other than fertilization if their infertile use occurs both by choice and in a naturally adaptive context. Both criteria must be kept in mind, as the current study concerns captive bonobos.

The following descriptions are given from an unusual perspective, because my main research focus is not primate sex per se but rather aggression and aggression-control. Many primate species have evolved special reassurance gestures that maintain peaceful relationships. Calming behavior occurs in response to social tensions (i.e., when there exists a high probability of interindividual conflict) and in the aftermath of fights. Reunions between former opponents following aggression, known as *reconciliations,* are characterized by kissing and embracing in the chimpanzee (de Waal & van Roosmalen, 1979), whereas these contacts often involve genital stimulation in its congener, the bonobo (de Waal, 1987).

Neither the exchange of sexual signals outside the copulatory context nor nonreproductive mounting are absolutely restricted to the bonobo. Wickler (1967) proposed the label "sociosexual behavior" to cover the wider employment of sexual patterns. For example, de Waal and Ren (1988) reported a significant increase in "hold-bottom" gestures among stumptail macaques (*Macaca arctoides*) during reconciliations following fights. These monkeys even may show their so-called "orgasm face" during postconflict reunions: a particular facial expression demonstrably associated with physiological signs of sexual climax, such as increased heart rate and uterine contractions (Goldfoot et al., 1980). Normally, these behavior patterns are part of copulations in this species (Nieuwenhuijsen, 1985). The bonobo goes further than the stumptail macaque, and most other primates, however, in that complete sexual sequences are used for nonreproductive purposes rather than mere sexual gestures or perfunctory mounts. (See Pavelka, this volume, for a related discussion.)

Sociosexual Behavior

Traditionally, face-to-face copulation has been seen as reflecting the dignity
and sensibility that separate civilized humans from subhumans. It was believed, for example, that preliterate people would benefit from education about
this mode of intercourse, hence the term "missionary position." The position
was elevated to a cultural innovation of great significance, one which, according to Hockett and Archer (1963, 34), fundamentally changed the relationship between men and women: "Our guess is that it changed, for the adult
female, the relative roles of the adult male and of the infant, since after the
innovation there is a much closer similarity for her between her reception of
an infant and of a lover. This may have helped to spread the "tender emotions"
of mammalian mother-infant relations to other interpersonal relationships
within the band, ultimately with such further consequences as the Oedipus
complex." Wescott (1963, 92) took this idea a step further: "It seems not only
that the adult male becomes, in face-to-face copulation, a surrogate suckling
to the adult female by virtue of his position; but also that the adult female
becomes a surrogate suckling to the adult male by virtue of her behavior, which
is that of soliciting and receiving a life-giving liquid from an adult bodily pro-
tuberance."

Not surprisingly, given the entirely cultural interpretation often given to
face-to-face copulation, Tratz and Heck (1954) carefully wrapped their findings in Latin when first reporting that chimpanzees mate *more canum* (like
dogs) and bonobos *more hominum* (like people). Published in the German
language, their study as well as other early observations of bonobo behavior
(Rempe, 1961; Kirchshofer, 1962) were ignored by the scientific establishment, however. The bonobo's humanlike sexuality needed to be rediscovered,
in the 1970s, before it became widely accepted as a species characteristic. This
rediscovery was based on studies of both captive bonobos and fieldwork by a
Japanese team at Wamba and a Euro-American team at Lomako Forest, both
in Zaire (Hübsch, 1970; Jordan, 1977; Savage and Bakeman, 1978; Savage-
Rumbaugh and Wilkerson, 1978; Kano, 1980; Kuroda, 1980, 1984;
Thompson-Handler et al., 1984; Dahl, 1985, 1986, 1987; Blount, 1990).

My own study concerned the world's largest captive collection of bonobos,
at the San Diego Zoological Garden. Ten of these rare apes were kept in three
separate subgroups. One subgroup included an adult male/female pair and an
adolescent male. Another subgroup consisted of a mother-infant pair and an
adolescent male. The third subgroup included four juveniles, two of each sex.
The first two subgroups were merged in the course of the study, allowing the
observation of interactions between adult females and between a fully adult
male and adolescent males. I observed the apes for nearly 300 hours, standing
in front of their enclosure. Oral accounts of the bonobos' social behavior were

recorded either on an audiorecorder or on the audio channel of a videorecorder. Video was added at moments of great social activity, such as at feeding time or during the introduction of new group members.

From these observations, and the studies mentioned before, the following conclusions can be drawn regarding the bonobo's sexual peculiarities.

Extended Receptivity

The period of sexual receptivity of bonobo females is dramatically extended compared to the chimpanzee, and most other primates. Whereas the chimpanzee has a menstrual cycle of approximately 35 days, the bonobo's is closer to 45 days, and the period of genital tumescence encompasses a greater proportion of the cycle than in the chimpanzee (Furuichi, 1987; Dahl et al., 1991). In captivity, low-ranking bonobo females may copulate throughout most of the cycle, but females in the wild or high-ranking captive females (i.e., females with greater control over when and where to engage in sexual intercourse) are most receptive during the phase of maximum swelling (Dahl, 1987; de Waal, 1987; Furuichi, 1992). Also, the rhythm of male thrusting—perhaps a measure of sexual arousal—is higher during matings with tumescent than with detumescent females (de Waal, 1987).

Variable Mounting Positions

Because the clitoris and vulva are ventrally oriented, the female's genital anatomy seems adapted for face-to-face copulation, a frequently adopted position (fig. 3.1). Table 3.1 provides the distribution of six behavior patterns over 42 dyadic directions among the San Diego bonobos (2 directions per pair of individuals) and the combined frequency of sociosexual interaction per dyadic direction per hour of observation. Dyadic directions have been arranged according to the rate with which sociosexual behavior was initiated (the actor is defined as the individual making the first invitational gesture or approach, even if that individual is not the more sexually active partner).

By far the most common pattern was the *ventro-ventral mount,* observed in no fewer than 33 different dyadic directions. There is no dyadic category in which this behavior did not occur, except for the one female-female relationship among juveniles. Characteristic are genital rubbing movements between females mounted in a ventro-ventral position, one female carrying the other (fig. 3.2). This carrying posture—with one female being lifted off the ground while she clings to her partner much like an infant clings to its mother—allows both females to make sideways rubbing movements. The females rub their clitori together with an average of 2.5 lateral moves per second; this is approximately the same rhythm as that of a thrusting male (de Waal, 1987). The pattern is now widely known as *GG-rubbing*; an abbreviation of genito-genital

Table 3.1 Frequency of six sociosexual interaction patterns among different partner categories of bonobos at the San Diego Zoo.

Initiator	Partner	Mounting Ventro-ventral	Ventro-dorsal	Opposite	Oral and Manual Genital massage	Oral sex	Mouth-kiss	Total	Per Hour
Adol. Male	Infant	49	65					114	1.64
Adol. Male	Female *	63	18					81	1.17
Infant	Adol. Male	47	2	3			1	53	0.76
Male	Adol. Male	5	7		23		1	36	0.64
Female	Female	37		4			1	42	0.63
Adol. Male	Female *	33	1					34	0.51
Male	Infant	19	8					27	0.49
Infant	Male	15	5					20	0.36
Female	Female	10	1	11			1	23	0.34
Juv. Male	Juv. Male		9			3	14	26	0.32
Adol. Male	Female *	25	8		1			34	0.31
Male	Adol. Male	11	7	1	10		2	31	0.28
Juv. Male	Juv. Male	7	1		1	5	6	20	0.25
Adol. Male	Adol. Male	12	3					15	0.22
Adol. Male	Male	2	8		1			11	0.20
Adol. Male	Infant	16	4	1				21	0.19
Male	Female *	9						9	0.16
Male	Female *	17						17	0.15
Juv. Female	Juv. Male				1	4	3	8	0.10
Female	Infant	4	2					6	0.09
Female	Adol. Male *	2	3					5	0.07
Infant	Adol. Male	8						8	0.07
Adol. Male	Male	3		2		1	2	8	0.07
Juv. Male	Juv. Male	2				3		5	0.06
Female	Male *	2	1					3	0.05
Adol. Male	Female *	5			1			6	0.05
Female	Adol. Male *	3						3	0.04
Juv. Female	Juv. Male	3						3	0.04
Juv. Male	Juv. Female						3	3	0.04
Juv. Female	Juv. Male						3	3	0.04
Juv. Male	Juv. Female	1				1	1	3	0.04
Juv. Male	Juv. Female	1					2	3	0.04
Infant	Female		1	1				2	0.03
Adol. Male	Adol. Male	2						2	0.03
Female	Infant	3						3	0.03
Female	Adol. Male *	2	1					3	0.02
Female	Adol. Male *	1					1	2	0.02
Female	Male *		1		1			2	0.02
Juv. Male	Juv. Female						1	1	0.01
Juv. Female	Juv. Female						1	1	0.01
Infant	Female	1						1	0.01
Juv. Female	Juv. Female							0	0.00
Total		420	156	23	39	17	43	698	

Note: Adults are indicated as Male and Female; adolescents as Adol.; juveniles as Juv., and the two-year-old female infant as Infant. Each of 42 directions between individuals is represented separately. Dyadic directions are ordered according to the rate of sociosexual contacts initiated per hour of observation (observation time is not the same for all dyads). Asterisks mark potentially fertile partner combinations.

Figure 3.1 Ventro-ventral copulation between an adolescent male and adult female, while the female's infant daughter looks on (infants often try to squeeze themselves between adults so as to "participate" in the intercourse). Photo by the author.

rubbing first proposed by Kuroda (1980). It has been observed by all students of bonobo behavior, and is unique to the species.

Another rare mounting pattern occurred between adult females, with the partners facing in opposite directions. While one female lies on her back, the other stands over her, with her back turned, rubbing her genitals against her recumbent partner's. A similar posture occurs between males, with both males standing quadrupedally back-to-back, rubbing their scrota together.

In contrast, the posture during so-called *mutual penis rubbing* resembles that of a heterosexual mating, with one male (usually the younger) passively on his back, the other male thrusting on him. Because both males have an erection and because intromission does not occur, their penises rub together. Attempts to achieve anal intromission were not observed, and ejaculation never resulted. Kano (1989) further describes *penis fencing:* a rare behavior, thus far observed only in the wild, in which two males hang face to face from a branch while rubbing their erect penises together as if crossing swords.

A frequent posture involving the female infant was one in which she climbed on the belly of an adolescent male and pressed her vulva against his genitals, whereupon the male, either in a sitting or a recumbent position, made a series

Figure 3.2 Two adult females during GG-rubbing, both with extensive baring of the teeth at the climax. The bottom female also squeals. Notice the eye-contact. Photo by the author.

of pelvic thrusts (fig. 3.3). On other occasions, the infant presented for a ventro-dorsal mount. Mounts with this infant never resulted in intromission or ejaculation. As can be gathered from table 3.1, sociosexual contacts of adults and adolescents with the infant were frequently initiated by the infant herself (i.e., 32.9 percent of the time).

Ventro-dorsal mounting positions are typical of most primates. Chimpanzees, for instance, mate in this position almost exclusively (McGinnis, 1973; Savage-Rumbaugh and Wilkerson, 1978; personal observation). The low frequency of ventro-dorsal relative to ventro-ventral mounts in the San Diego colony may not be general for the bonobo; according to most reports on other populations, both captive and wild, the ventro-dorsal mounting position is the more common one, employed between 62 and 74 percent of the time (Jordan, 1977; Kano, 1980; Thompson-Handler et al., 1984). The important point, though, is that thus far all investigators have reported the regular use of both positions, which means that both can be considered species-typical.

Other Acts of Stimulation

Two oral sociosexual patterns occurred almost exclusively in the group of juveniles (83.3 percent; table 3.1). The first is *mouth-mouth kissing,* i.e., one part-

Figure 3.3   A 7-year-old adolescent male is mounted ventro-ventrally by a 2-year-old infant. The infant presses her vulva against the male's erect penis (no intromission occurs) while he performs a series of upward pelvic thrusts. Photo by the author.

ner places his or her open mouth over that of the other. In about one-quarter of the instances this involved extensive tongue-tongue contact (fig. 3.4). The second pattern is *fellatio,* i.e., one partner taking the penis of another in the mouth. These two sociosexual patterns frequently occurred in the context of rough-and-tumble play. A bout of chasing and wrestling would be interrupted by sociosexual games in which all four juveniles might participate, some of them mounting, others engaging in the just-described oral patterns. Play would resume within a few minutes.

The sixth sociosexual behavior pattern is *manual massage* of another individual's genitals. The large majority of instances (84.6 percent) was directed by the adult male to one of the adolescent males. The younger male, with back straight and legs apart, would present his erect penis to the adult male, who would loosely close his hand around the shaft, making caressing up-and-down movements (fig. 3.5).

This pattern is the social equivalent of *masturbation,* which the bonobos also showed. Neither genital massage nor masturbation was observed to produce ejaculation. Of the 39 observed masturbations, none were performed by the adult male, 58.9 percent were performed by the two adolescent males, 23.1

Figure 3.4 Mouth-to-mouth kissing, with tongue interaction, between two juvenile males. Photo by the author.

percent by the two adult females, and 17.9 percent by immatures. Another form of self-stimulation was nipple-caressing, i.e., an individual stimulating one or both nipples with rapid movements of the thumb(s). This behavior may have served a self-reassurance function as it occurred often after frustrating events, such as when begging for food had been unsuccessful or an aggressive rebuff had been received. The behavior was observed in five different individuals of both sexes, but 82.8 percent of the 99 instances concerned a single adolescent male (fig. 6).

Pleasure

To what extent these sociosexual patterns are accompanied by pleasure is of course impossible to determine through mere observation, but if the sounds and facial expressions of this species are any indication, we estimate these

Figure 3.5 A 8-year-old adolescent male presents his erect penis to the adult male (left) following an aggressive incident between them. The adult male performs a genital massage. Photo by the author.

contacts to be gratifying. Females frequently bared their teeth during sex (fig. 2), particularly towards the end of the interaction (at its climax), an expression interpreted as an *Orgasmusgesicht* by Becker (1984) and as a *pleasure grin* by de Waal (1988). Wide baring of the teeth also occurred during solitary masturbation, or during excitement over new play objects or food. Furthermore, females often uttered characteristic screams or squeals before or during copulation (Savage-Rumbaugh and Wilkerson, 1978; de Waal, 1988).

Partner Choice

Assuming that the two adolescent males were fertile (both were capable of semen production), 12 dyadic directions concern potentially fertile partner combinations (table 1). The mean ($\pm$ SE) hourly rate of sociosexual initiatives

Figure 3.6 At times of stress or insecurity some individuals would self-caress their nipples with rapid movements of the thumbs, here shown by an adolescent male. Photo by the author.

in these directions was 0.22 ± 0.10, compared to 0.23 ± 0.06 in fertile directions. The difference between these two means is nonsignificant (t-test, t = 0.16, df = 40, P > 0.05). If the analysis is limited to mounting behavior or if the data are combined for both directions per dyad, the same conclusion applies, that is, fertile and infertile partner combinations show virtually identical rates of sociosexual behavior.

Another way of summarizing the data is to calculate the rate of sociosexual initiatives dependent on two factors: (a) relative age of the partner and (b) sex combination. Four age classes were distinguished: adult (10 years and older); adolescent (7–9 years); juvenile (3–6 years); and infant (0–3 years). Partners can belong to the same age class as actors or to an older or a younger class. Three intersex directions were distinguished: male toward female; female toward male; and same-sex combinations. This analysis indicated a relatively high level of heterosexual initiatives toward older partners by both males and females. Males more often initiated contact with younger partners of the opposite sex than did females. Heterosexual contacts were relatively uncommon between partners of the same age class. Isosexual initiatives (interactions between partners of the same sex), finally, were mainly directed at partners of the actor's own or a younger age class. See de Waal (1990) for a more detailed presentation.

Partner choice was not unlimited at the San Diego Zoo, however. The two juvenile females, for example, exhibited relatively low rates of sexual initiative, yet might have been more active in the presence of adults. All that can be concluded is that given the conditions under which these bonobos lived—allowing all individuals a choice of partner sex and most individuals a choice of several partner age classes—no evidence was found that potentially fertile partner combinations engaged in sociosexual behavior more often than infertile combinations.

Moreover, it must be emphasized that heterosexual intercourse between sexually mature individuals is only potentially fertile: first, because not every copulation involves ejaculation, and second because females are fertile only during a few days of their menstrual cycle. As an external sign of receptivity, they develop a conspicuous genital swelling, but this is an unreliable indicator of fertility; the swelling phase far exceeds the period of ovulation, and swellings also may be shown by pregnant or lactating, hence noncycling, females (Dahl, 1986).

Whereas it is virtually impossible to know with certainty which copulations involve an ejaculating male with an ovulating female, it is not difficult to distinguish, on the basis of behavior, infertile mounts. These are mounts without intromission; mounts broken off well before the male partner slowed down for the final, deeper thrusts indicative of ejaculation; and/or mounts involving a female with detumescent genitals. Because the dominant male tended to interfere with heterosexual intercourse of the adolescent males and because the females mated throughout all cycle phases (cf. Savage-Rumbaugh and Wilkerson, 1978; Thompson-Handler et al., 1984; Dahl, 1987), fertilization could be excluded for a considerable number of mounts in partner combinations marked as potentially fertile in table 3.1.

Lest the rich variety of sexual patterns and the bonobo's evident bisexuality leaves the impression of a pathologically oversexed species, I must add, based on hundreds of hours of watching bonobos, that their sexual activity is rather casual and relaxed; it appears a completely natural part of their group life. Also, even though the bonobo is a serious contender for the title of sex champion of the primate world, including the prize for the longest penis—a distinction thus far erroneously reserved for *Homo sapiens* (e.g., Morris, 1967)—its sexiness should also not be exaggerated. With the average copulation lasting 13 seconds at the San Diego Zoo (de Waal, 1987) and 15 seconds in the wild (Kano, 1992), sexual contact among bonobos is rather quick by human standards. Thus, instead of an endless orgy, we see a social life peppered by brief moments of sexual activity.

Recently, I observed a colony of chimpanzees at the Yerkes Primate Center in a study modeled after the bonobo study. The rate of sociosexual behavior by

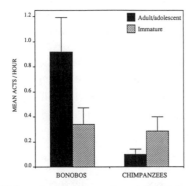

Figure 3.7   Mean (+ SEM) number of sociosexual acts initiated per hour per individual for the San Diego bonobos and an outdoor colony of chimpanzees at the Yerkes Regional Primate Research Center's Field Station, separately for (a) adults and adolescents (black) and (b) younger individuals (hatched).

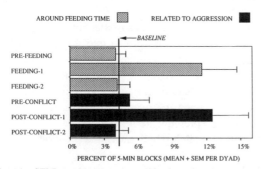

Figure 3.8   Mean (+ SEM) rate per partner combination of sociosexual and affiliative interactions, excluding grooming, in the San Diego Zoo bonobo colony. The rate is the percentage of 5-minute blocks in which the behavior occurred. Hatched: three 15-min periods around feeding time (before the introduction of food and immediately following food provisioning). Black: three 15-min periods relating to spontaneous aggressive incidents in the absence of food (before aggression occurred, and immediately following aggression). The baseline concerns all remaining observation time. From de Waal (1987).

adult and adolescent chimpanzees was significantly lower than that by the same age category in bonobos (fig. 3.7; t-test, $t = 5.23$, $df = 16$, $P = 0.0001$). This difference existed despite a greater partner choice for the chimpanzees, which lived in a group of 19 individuals. Rates of sociosexual behavior of immatures were similar in the two species.

Context of Sociosexual Behavior

Seven conditions were distinguished in my continuous records of bonobo behavior:

Pre-feeding	15 min prior to feeding time
Feeding-1	first 15 min of the feeding session
Feeding-2	second 15 min block following feeding
Pre-conflict	15 min prior to an aggressive conflict unrelated to food
Post-conflict-1	first 15 min following aggressive conflict
Post-conflict-2	second 15 min block following aggressive conflict
Baseline	all remaining observation time

Hourly behavioral rates under these conditions were compared for each pair of individuals. The following changes occurred in a significant majority of dyads (de Waal, 1987):

1. An increase in aggression following food provisioning.
2. A decrease in social grooming following food provisioning.
3. An increase in nongrooming contact, including sociosexual behavior, following both food provisioning and aggressive incidents unrelated to food (fig. 3.8).

Hence, food provisioning stimulated the bonobos' affiliative and sociosexual behavior (with the exception of grooming behavior, which was suppressed). In theory, this effect could have been caused either directly, by the presence of food (excitement over food is transformed into sexual arousal), or indirectly, in response to the competitive atmosphere inevitably created by an attractive resource (as reflected in the observed aggression increase). The second hypothesis is better supported, because affiliative and sociosexual behavior also increased following aggression that was not food-related. In other words, the presence of food was no prerequisite for sociosexual behavior, and the causal factor most elegantly explaining both measured increases was tension among individuals.

Typically, the bonobos would become very active upon introduction of food, engaging in aggressive competition but also inviting one another for sociosexual contact. These contacts appeared to reduce the tension and to allow for food sharing. Thus, it could be demonstrated that subordinate group members more often removed food from the hands of dominant possessors following a sociosexual contact than without such prior contact (de Waal, 1987). The interaction could even take the form of an exchange, e.g., a female presents to a male who is holding a large bundle of branches with leaves and takes the entire bundle out of his hands following sexual intercourse. On other occasions, sociosexual behavior was used as a reconciliation. The majority of instances of genital massage, for instance, followed aggressive incidents in which the adult male had chased one of the adolescent males. After a couple of minutes, the younger male would return to the aggressor to present his genitals.

In short, the bonobo's sociosexual behavior serves important tension-regulating functions. These functions explain why the behavior occurs with high frequency in all possible partner combinations, because tensions are obviously not limited to male-female combinations. It is instructive to compare these observations with the behavior of chimpanzees. This species regulates social tension by means of nongenital contact forms; in various studies of captive chimpanzees, mounting and mating never even ranked among the ten most common modes of reconciliation (de Waal and van Roosmalen, 1979; de Waal, 1992).

Discussion

Chimpanzees and bonobos are particularly relevant to our understanding of human social evolution since humans are estimated to have diverged from these two species a "mere" 8 million years ago, compared to 30 million years, or more, for the split between humans and most other primates (Sibley and Ahlquist, 1984; Marks, 1992; Goodman, 1992).

It is rather surprising how much humankind's two closest relatives differ with regard to the use of sociosexual behavior. From my extensive observations of chimpanzees, I believe that most sexual activity in this species either serves reproduction directly or serves as a preparation for reproductive sex. Thus, juvenile male chimpanzees are attracted to females in estrus, and pubertal females begin to explore sexual contact with older males as soon as their genital swellings develop (van der Weel, 1978; de Waal, 1982; Goodall, 1986). Such intergenerational experiences undoubtedly contribute to the development of adequate sexual skills.

The incorporation of sexual elements into reassurance behavior is rather limited in chimpanzees. Like almost all primates, they present their anogenital region in a gesture of submission or appeasement, often followed by a genital inspection by the recipient. Furthermore, chimpanzees show mouth-to-mouth kissing, and adult males of the species may mount one another during or following aggressive incidents (de Waal and van Hooff, 1981). These contacts lack the intensity and arousal obvious during kissing and isosexual mounts among bonobos, however. Thus, neither GG-rubbing between females nor tongue-kissing have ever been reported for the chimpanzee. All in all, bonobos seem to do with a variety of sociosexual behavior patterns what chimpanzees do with embracing and relatively "platonic" kissing. It is a difference in degree, yet an important one.

This difference cannot be explained as a product of the conditions at the San Diego Zoo. Although a few of my observations have not been reported by others (such as the use of mounting postures during reconciliation), this omission probably is due to the detail in which captive animals can be studied, rather than to fundamental differences with wild conspecifics. The Japanese team of field workers in particular has reported a remarkable variety of sociosexual behavior patterns in wild bonobos; their largely qualitative descriptions and interpretations are consistent with my quantitative data. Furthermore, that attractive food induces sexual activity rather than competition, has been observed not only in zoos or at the Japanese field site, where humans provide food, but also at a site at which food provisioning is totally absent. In Lomako Forest, also in Zaire, Thompson-Handler et al. (1984) saw wild bonobos engage in sex when they entered trees loaded with ripe figs, or when one amongst them had captured a prey animal, such as a small forest duiker. The flurry of sexual contacts would last for five to ten minutes, after which the apes would settle down to consume the food.

Occasionally, the role of sex in relation to food is taken one step further, a step that brings bonobos very close to humans indeed. It has been speculated by anthropologists, such as Lovejoy (1981) and Fisher (1983), that the reason for the partial separation between sex and reproduction in our species is that sex serves to cement mutually profitable relationships between men and women. The human female's capacity to mate throughout her cycle, and her strong sex drive, make it possible to exchange sex for male commitment and paternal care, thus tying men and women together in the nuclear family. Instead of a conscious strategy, this is of course thought of as an arrangement favored by natural selection for the simple reason that it allows women to raise more offspring than they would be able to raise on their own. Bonobo behavior seems to fit important elements of this model: female bonobos show extended receptivity and use sex to obtain male favors. Thus, a female who does not dominate a particular male still has sex as a source of leverage.

At the San Diego Zoo, I observed that if Loretta was in a sexually attractive state, she would not hesitate to approach the adult male, Vernon, if he had food. She would present herself to Vernon, mate with him, and make high-pitched food calls while taking over his entire bundle of branches and leaves. She would hardly give the male a chance to pull out a branch for himself, sometimes grabbing the food out of his hands in the midst of intercourse. This was quite a contrast with periods in which Loretta had no genital swelling; then she would wait until Vernon was ready to share (de Waal, 1989). Kuroda (1984, 317) reports similar exchanges at Wamba: "A young female approached a male, who was eating sugar cane. They copulated in short order, whereupon she took one of the two canes held by him and left." In another case, "a young female persistently presented to a male possessor, who ignored her at first, but then copulated with her and shared his sugar cane."

It is no wonder that Mori (1984, p. 277) concluded on the basis of his observations of the bonobos at Wamba: "Coexistence of plural males and females without agonistic competition in mating could be guaranteed by changing the character of sexual behavior into affiliative behavior in which all individuals can participate, and by decreasing the reproductive meaning."

Previously, I have argued that the most logical pathway via which sexual behavior evolved into a general reassurance and appeasement mechanism in the bonobo is that this mechanism was first established in the adult male-female relationship (the original functional context of all sexual behavior), after which it was adopted by other age and sex combinations. In other words, the widespread application of sexual behavior in the bonobo's social life has its origin in an early emphasis on heterosexual bonding (de Waal, 1987). Field research supports this view in that male-female relationships seem closer and more tolerant in bonobos than in chimpanzees. Chimpanzee foraging parties typically consist either of adult males (sometimes accompanied by females in estrus) or mother-offspring units, whereas bonobos tend toward larger, mixed-sex parties (Badrian and Badrian, 1984; Badrian and Malenky, 1984; Kano and Mulavwa, 1984; Wrangham, 1986). This possible evolutionary background of bonobos' sexuality is relevant to human sexuality, both because of the shared biological ancestry and because of the characteristic heterosexual bonding of the human species.

Humans go further in the latter respect than bonobos, however. Despite the quid pro quo between the sexes, there are no indications that bonobos form humanlike nuclear families with permanent bonds between a male and one or several females; in the bonobo, the burden of raising offspring appears to rest entirely on the female's shoulders. In fact, nuclear families are probably incompatible with the widespread use of sex found in bonobos. If we speculate that our ancestors started out with a sex life similar to that of bonobos, the evolution of the family must have brought dramatic change.* The integrity of this social unit requires all sorts of protective moral restrictions and taboos that, among other things, assure males that they are caring for their own, not someone else's, offspring. Thus, although our species is characterized by an extraordinary interest in sex, there are no human societies in which people publicly engage in it with the "freedom" characteristic of bonobos. A sense of shame and a desire for domestic privacy, which have no place in bonobo society, are typical human concepts related to the evolution and cultural bolstering of the family unit.

Sex does probably serve peacemaking and bonding functions *within* the human family, however, as when a couple seals a reconciliation by making love. In addition, it is obvious that no degree of moralizing can make sex disappear from every nonfamily realm of human society. The bonobo's behavioral peculi-

---

*During the conference from which this volume resulted, some participants indulged in speculation along the lines that "there is a bonobo in all of us." This may well be true, but we should remember that this ape is not on its way to becoming human any more than humans are on their way to becoming apelike. We share a common ancestor, i.e., are separate branches on the same evolutionary tree. If hominids did indeed know the pansexuality of the bonobo, this would suggest that our common ancestor showed such behavior as well. If so, we would need to explain why it disappeared in the chimpanzee (which shares the same ancestor) and why in modern humans male-female relations became the basis of exclusive reproductive units within the social system.

arities may help us understand why that is, and as such have serious implications for models of human evolution.

Acknowledgments

The bonobo study was made possible by the San Diego Zoological Society and a grant from the National Geographic Society. The study and writing of this paper were further supported by National Institutes of Health grants to the Wisconsin Regional Primate Research Center (RR-00167) and the Yerkes Regional Primate Research Center (RR-00165), the latter also supporting the collection of comparative data on chimpanzees at the Yerkes Field Station. The author thanks Katherine Offutt for assistance with data analysis, Frank Kiernan for printing the photographs, and the conference participants for discussion of an earlier version of the manuscript.

References

Badrian, A., and Badrian, N. 1984. Social organization of *Pan paniscus* in the Lomako Forest, Zaire. In R. Susman (Ed.), *The Pygmy Chimpanzee.* New York: Plenum Press, pp. 325–46.

Badrian, N., and Malenky, R. 1984. Feeding ecology of *Pan paniscus* in the Lomako Forest, Zaire. In R. Susman (Ed.), *The Pygmy Chimpanzee.* New York: Plenum Press, pp. 275–99.

Becker, C. 1984. *Orang-Utans und Bonobos im Spiel.* Munich: Profil Verlag.

Blount, B. G. 1990. Issues in bonobo (*Pan paniscus*) sexual behavior. *American Anthropologist* 92: 702–14.

Coolidge, H. J. 1984. Historical remarks bearing on the discovery of *Pan paniscus.* In R. Susman (Ed.), *The Pygmy Chimpanzee.* New York: Plenum Press, pp. ix–xiii.

Dahl, J. F. 1985. The external genitalia of female pygmy chimpanzees. *Anatomical Record* 211: 24–28.

Dahl, J. F. 1986. Cyclic perineal swelling during the intermenstrual intervals of captive female pygmy chimpanzees (*Pan paniscus*). *Journal of Human Evolution* 15: 369–85.

Dahl, J. F. 1987. Sexual initiation in captive group of pygmy chimpanzees (*Pan paniscus*). *Primate Report* 16: 43–53.

Dahl, J. F., Nadler, R. D., and Collins, D. C. 1991. Monitoring the ovarian cycles of *Pan troglodytes* and *P. paniscus:* A comparative approach. *American Journal of Primatology* 24: 195–209.

Fisher, H. 1983. *The Sex Contract: The Evolution of Human Behavior.* New York: Quill.

Furuichi, T. 1987. Sexual swellings, receptivity, and grouping of wild pygmy chimpanzee females at Wamba, Zaire. *Primates* 28: 309–18.

Furuichi, T. 1992. The prolonged estrus of females and factors influencing mating in a wild group of bonobos (*Pan paniscus*) in Wamba, Zaire. In *Topics in Primatology: Vol. 2, Behavior, Ecology, and Conservation.* Itoigawa, N., Sugiyama, Y., Sackett, G. P., and Thompson, R. K. R. (Eds.). Tokyo: University of Tokyo Press, pp. 179–90.

Goldfoot, D. A., Westerborg-van Loon, H., Groeneveld, W., and Slob, A. K. 1980. Behavioral and physiological evidence of sexual climax in the female stump-tailed macaque (*Macaca arctoides*). *Science* 208: 1477–79.

Goodall, J. 1986. *The Chimpanzees of Gombe: Patterns of Behavior.* Cambridge: The Belknap Press of Harvard University Press.

Goodman, M. 1992. Hominoid evolution at the DNA level and the position of humans in a phylogenetic classification. In *Topics in Primatology: Vol. 1, Human Origins.* Nishida, T., W. C. McGrew, P. Marler, M. Pickford, and F. B. M. de Waal (Eds.). Tokyo: University of Tokyo Press, pp. 331–46.

Hockett, C. F., and Archer, R. 1963. The human revolution. *Current Anthropology* 5: 135–68.

Hübsch, I. 1970. Einiges zum Verhalten der Zwergschimpansen (*Pan paniscus*) und der Schimpanzen (*Pan troglodytes*) im Frankfurter Zoo. *Zoologische Garten* 38: 107–32.

Jordan, C. 1977. *Das Verhalten Zoolebender Zwergschimpansen.* Ph.D. dissertation, Goethe University, Frankfurt.

Kano, T. 1980. Social behavior of wild pygmy chimpanzees (*Pan paniscus*) of Wamba: A preliminary report. *Journal of Human Evolution* 9: 243–60.

Kano, T. 1989. The sexual behavior of pygmy chimpanzees. In P. G. Heltne and L. A. Marquardt (Eds.), Understanding Chimpanzees. Cambridge: Harvard University Press, pp. 176–83.

Kano, T. 1992. *The Last Ape: Pygmy Chimpanzee Behavior and Ecology.* Stanford: Stanford University Press.

Kano, T., and Mulavwa, M. 1984. Feeding ecology of the pygmy chimpanzees (*Pan paniscus*) of Wamba. In R. Susman (Ed.), *The Pygmy Chimpanzee.* New York: Plenum Press, pp. 233–74.

Kirchshofer, R. 1962. Beobachtungen bei der Geburt eines Zwergschimpansen (*Pan paniscus,* Schwarz 1929) und einige Bemerkungen zum Paarungsverhalten. *Zeitschrift für Tierpsychologie* 19: 597–606.

Kuroda, S. 1980. Social behavior of the pygmy chimpanzees. *Primates* 21: 181–97.

Kuroda, S. 1984. Interaction over food among pygmy chimpanzees. In R. Susman (Ed.), *The Pygmy Chimpanzee.* New York: Plenum Press, pp. 301–24.

Lovejoy, C. O. 1981. The origin of man. *Science* 211: 341–50.

Marks, J. 1992. Genetic relationships among the apes and humans. *Current Opinion in Genetics and Development* 2: 883–89.

McGinnis, P. 1973. *Patterns of Sexual Behavior in a Community of Free-living Chimpanzees.* Ph.D. dissertation, Cambridge University.

Mori, A. 1984. An ethological study of pygmy chimpanzees in Wamba, Zaire: A comparison with chimpanzees. *Primates* 25: 255–78.

Morris, D. 1967. *The Naked Ape.* London: Jonathan Cape.

Nieuwenhuijsen, K. 1985. *Geslachtshormonen en Gedrag bij de Beermakaak (Macaca arctoides).* Ph.D. Dissertation, Erasmus University, Rotterdam.

Rempe, U. 1961. Einige beobachtungen an Bonobos (*Pan paniscus,* Schwarz, 1929). *Zeitschrift für Wissenschaftliche Zoologie* 165: 81–87.

Savage, S., and Bakeman, R. 1978. Sexual morphology and behavior in *Pan paniscus. Proceedings of the 6th International Congress of Primatology.* New York: Academic Press, pp. 613–16.

Savage-Rumbaugh, S., and Wilkerson, B. 1978. Socio-sexual behavior in *Pan paniscus* and *Pan troglodytes:* A comparative study. *Journal of Human Evolution* 7: 327–44.

Sibley, C., and Alhquist, J. 1984. The phylogeny of the Hominoid primates, as indicated by DNA-DNA hybridization. *Journal of Molecular Evolution* 20: 2–15.

Thompson-Handler, N., Malenky, R., and Badrian, N. 1984. Sexual behavior of *Pan paniscus* under natural conditions in the Lomako Forest, Equateur, Zaire. R. Susman, (Ed.). *The Pygmy Chimpanzee*. New York: Plenum, pp. 347–68.

Tratz, E., and Heck, H. 1954. Der afrikanische Anthropoide "Bonobo," eine neue Menschenaffengattung. *Säugetierkundige Mitteilungen* 2: 97–101.

de Waal, F. B. M. 1982. *Chimpanzee Politics*. London: Jonathan Cape.

de Waal, F. B. M. 1987. Tension regulation and nonreproductive functions of sex among captive bonobos (*Pan paniscus*). *National Geographic Research* 3: 318–35.

de Waal, F. B. M. 1988. The communicative repertoire of captive bonobos (*Pan paniscus*), compared to that of chimpanzees. *Behaviour* 106: 183–251.

de Waal, F. B. M. 1989. *Peacemaking among Primates*. Cambridge: Harvard University Press.

de Waal, F. B. M. 1990. Sociosexual behavior used for tension regulation in all age and sex combinations among bonobos. In *Pedophilia: Biosocial Dimensions*, J. R. Feierman (Ed.). New York: Springer, pp. 378–93.

de Waal, F. B. M. 1992. Appeasement, celebration, and food sharing in the two *Pan* species. In *Topics in Primatology: Vol. 1, Human Origins*. T. Nishida, W. C. McGrew, P. Marler, M. Pickford and F. B. M. de Waal (Eds.). Tokyo: University of Tokyo Press, pp. 37–50.

de Waal, F. B. M., and Ren, R. 1988. Comparison of the reconciliation behavior of stumptail and rhesus macaques. *Ethology* 78: 129–42.

de Waal, F. B. M., and van Hooff, J. A. R. A. M. 1981. Side-directed communication and agonistic interactions in chimpanzees. *Behaviour* 77: 164–98.

de Waal, F. B. M., and van Roosmalen, A. 1979. Reconciliation and consolation among chimpanzees. *Behavioral Ecology and Sociobiology* 5: 55–66.

van der Weel, M. 1978. Sexuele interacties en relaties tussen chimpansees. Unpublished Research Report, University of Utrecht.

Wescott, R. W. 1968 (1963). In A. Montagu (Ed.). *Culture: Man's Adaptive Dimension*. Oxford: Oxford University Press, pp. 91–93.

Wickler, W. 1969 [1967]. Socio-sexual signals and their intra-specific imitation among primates. In D. Morris (Ed.). *Primate Ethology*. Garden City: Anchor Books, pp. 89–189.

Wrangham, R. 1986. Ecology and social relationships in two species of chimpanzee. In D. Rubenstein and R. Wrangham (Eds.), *Ecological Aspects of Social Evolution: Birds and Mammals*. Princeton: Princeton University Press, pp. 352–78.

Yamagiwa, J. 1987. Intra- and inter-group interactions in an all-male group of Virunga mountain gorillas (*Gorilla gorilla beringei*). *Primates* 28: 1–30.

CHAPTER FOUR

The Evolution of Female Sexual Desire

KIM WALLEN

Our understanding of the relative contributions made by male and female mammals to mating has radically changed during the last fifty years. Until recently females were commonly viewed as sexually passive participants (Beach, 1947, 1967), whose primary function in mating was to attract males (Michael and Keverne, 1968; Keverne, 1976) and to accommodate male sexual initiation (Beach, 1947, 1967). The minority view, that females actively initiated sexual activity (Goy and Resko, 1972), did not gain currency until the publication of Beach's article on attractivity, proceptivity, and receptivity (Beach, 1976), which focused attention on the active nature of female sexual behavior. In the continuing reexamination of male and female sexual behavior, the notion of the sexually passive female is, one hopes, dead, as convincing evidence of female sexual initiation has now been reported in a range of mammalian species (Beach, 1976; Erskine, 1989; Pavelka, this volume; Wallen, 1990). Thus, even those who argued in the past that primate sexual behavior was primarily modulated by changes in female attractivity, now acknowledge the importance of female behavior (Michael and Zumpe, 1993). However, while males and females are both active initiators of sexual activity, the mechanisms underlying male and female sexual behavior are not completely comparable. The following explores the role of sexual desire in mammalian sexual behavior, with particular focus on the occurrence of sexual desire in mammalian females.

The earlier view of the sexually passive female partly resulted from the consistency with which the active components of male sexual behavior are evident across various environments, while the female contribution to mating is often obscured by the specific testing situation (Wallen, 1990). Furthermore, the most striking aspect of female sexual behavior in many nonprimate species is the female's acceptance and accommodation of the male's attempts to mount and achieve intromission through the reflexive arching of her back (lordosis). Only when the full context of sexual behavior is included, or when the testing environment is specially modified to increase female control, is active female initiation of mating apparent (Wallen, 1990; Pavelka, this volume; McClintock, 1981, 1987). The ease in identifying male behaviors resulted in early investigation of the motivational mechanisms influencing male behavior. For example, male sexual behavior in mammals was thought to require both sexual desire and sexual reward, since fertilization using intravaginal ejaculation requires that males be sufficiently aroused for penile erection and willing to insert his penis into the female's vagina. The male must also thrust long enough to release the ejaculatory reflex. Thus males must be motivated to engage in sexual behavior and persistent enough to complete the behavioral sequence—something assured by hormonally mediated sexual desire and ejaculation or orgasm as a powerful incentive (Kagan, 1955). Although exactly the same mechanisms should also pertain to female sexual behavior, since both males and females are under comparable selective pressure for effective reproductive behavior, it is not clear that this is actually the case.

Since the motivation to engage in sexual behavior can obviously influence an individual's potential reproductive success, female and male sexual behavior should depend upon similar motivational mechanisms. However, females do not actively thrust and ejaculate in mammalian copulation and their physical ability to mate is regulated, in many species, by hormonally regulated reflexive mechanisms ensuring female responsiveness (Wallen, 1990). Thus the exact role of female sexual motivation in modulating female sexual behavior is unclear. The resolution of this issue lies in understanding the role gonadal hormones play in regulating the female's ability to mate and her interest in mating.

In most mammals a female's ovarian condition accurately and precisely predicts the likelihood and timing of reproductive behavior. This is because reflexive aspects of female sexual behavior which regulate the female's ability to mate are strictly regulated by ovarian hormones (Wallen, 1990). In contrast, in humans and other primate species, copulation and female hormonal condition are loosely coupled, with hormonal condition providing little prediction of the occurrence of mating behavior under many circumstances. The reasons for this remarkable species difference has been the subject of much speculation and in part stem from the disappearance in all primates, except prosimians (Doyle, 1974), of hormonal regulation of the physical capacity to engage in sex, making it possible for primate females to mate at any time with or without hormonal stimulation (Miller, 1931; Wallen, 1990). Understanding the evolution of this difference requires investigating the constraints that internal fertilization imposes on mammals and that differentially influence the character and regulation of male and female sexual behavior. (See Pavelka, this volume, for a related discussion.)

Constraints Imposed by System of Fertilization

Successful reproduction requires combining male and female gametes during a limited period of viability. This requirement produces a narrow window when both males and females produce viable gametes making temporal and spatial coordination crucial. External fertilization, by allowing sequential gamete release, minimizes the behavioral coordination required for successful reproduction. Even cases requiring simultaneous gamete release do not require physical contact between males and females, only that they be in close proximity. When gametes can be released sequentially, males and females sometimes do not even have to be present simultaneously, as in some salamanders, where males drop spermatophores and leave a pheromone trail which females follow, collecting the packets with a special genital adaptation (Elia, 1988).

The limited behavioral coordination required for external fertilization makes possible the regulation of reproduction through highly stereotyped mechanisms such as pheromones and visual or auditory releasers to cause synchronous release of gametes, leaving little to volitional control in either males or females. The well-known example of a male *Bombyx* moth copulating with a piece of filter paper infiltrated with the female sex pheromone is testimony to the rigid and reflexive control possible in externally fertilizing species (Izard, 1983). This degree of external regulation assures strict coordination between male and female fertility, something particularly crucial in species with short life-spans and short gamete cycles. However, external fertilization has inherent drawbacks. The nutrition available to the developing embryo is limited to that present in the egg at fertilization, and fertilized gametes are at greater risk of predation and environmental damage. Nutritional constraints limit the size and complexity of offspring, and vulnerability to environmental loss leads to production of massive numbers of gametes to produce much smaller numbers of surviving offspring. In addition, the heavy reliance upon reflexes and external coordination of reproductive behavior can lead to shedding gametes in conditions unsuitable for reproduction, as in the case of homing salmon spawning in ancestral waters as a result of environmental cues even though local conditions can no longer support hatchlings. Internal fertilization solves many of these problems, but imposes new behavioral requirements resulting in the diverse set of solutions that are the focus of this chapter. Consider first the advantages provided by internal fertilization.

Internal fertilization shields gametes from predation and environmental damage and, when combined with gestation, provides the developing embryo with a nutrient source that changes in response to fetal growth, allowing the development of larger and more complex offspring. In addition, because the female reproductive tract can maintain viable sperm beyond the immediate post-insemination period, the time from insemination to fertilization can be dramatically longer than with external fertilization. In species with sperm storage capacity, such as some insects, a single insemination can last for the female's lifetime, completely uncoupling insemination and fertilization. Even in females without sperm storage capability, sperm ejaculated into the female reproductive tract before egg release can fertilize the egg when it is released several days later. In addition, the capability of carrying the developing embryo allows internal fertilizing species to escape local food shortages and habitat degradation without sacrificing their current reproductive output. Thus internal fertilization avoids many of the challenges produced by external fertilization, but adds new and important behavioral constraints. In particular, while the temporal synchrony of gamete release may be relaxed in internally-fertilizing species, there is now a more stringent requirement for behavioral synchrony, as mating requires the concurrent participation of both the male and female. Furthermore, internal fertilization using peno-vaginal intromission, as is the case with all mammals, presents new behavioral challenges to successful reproduction.

Behavioral Adaptations Required for Mammalian Sexual Behavior

Ejaculation into a female's vagina requires several complementary behavioral adaptations. First, the male must be attracted to a female and sufficiently aroused to produce an erection rigid enough for vaginal penetration. The male must also be interested in copulating and willing to penetrate the female's vagina with his penis. The minimum behavior required of the female is to be attracted to the male and allow vaginal penetration. Because a brief intromission is rarely sufficient to produce fertilization, the male must thrust sufficiently to trigger the ejaculation of sperm and the female must facilitate this by allowing intromission and thrusting. Thus, for the male, several psychological and behavioral mechanisms are required to trigger the reflexive components of erection and ejaculation. Complementary mechanisms are required in females but take a quite different form. After initial mate selection and the initiation of copulation, females are theoretically required only to behaviorally accommodate the male's intromission and ejaculation. In practice, it is not this simple, and females often regulate the timing and pacing of the sexual interaction, in addition to responding, at least in rats, to the male's behavior (Erskine, 1989). Just as males and females differ in their reproductive investment, leading to different reproductive strategies (Trivers, 1972; Symons, 1980), they also differ in their behavioral requirements for fertile copulation. In many cases, behavioral and physiological adaptations have evolved that appear to reduce female voluntary control of mating and maximize female cooperation during copulation.

For example, females of several mammalian species exhibit adaptations that prevent copulation except when they are fertile, or assure copulation by physically immobilizing them when males initiate sexual activity. These mechanisms make it unnecessary, unlike the case in males, for females to be sexually motivated during copulation itself. Instead, the clear motivational requirement across mammalian females is increased attraction to males when they are fertile, to facilitate finding a mate. In contrast, most primate species do not exhibit these copulatory regulating mechanisms and mating is apparently completely under voluntary control. The source of this disparity across species may be key to understanding the role sexual behavior plays in the social structure of a species.

The answer lies in the specific mechanisms which females have evolved to ensure that matings are fertile. Obviously one way to assure fertile copulation is to allow mating only when the female can become pregnant through mechanisms strictly regulated by the same hormones that produce fertility. The existence of such mechanisms influences the apparent role of motivational systems in regulating female sexual behavior.

Vaginal Barriers, Immobilization, and Male Attractiveness

Many nonprimates and some primates have physical and behavioral mechanisms that strictly limit mating. In some species, the female's vagina is sealed by a membrane that disappears for a short time under the influence of elevated preovulatory estrogens (Young, 1937 [guinea pig]; Doyle, 1974 [prosimians]). Similarly, the vaginal opening in rodent species normally points towards the ground, making intromission impossible without lordosis, which elevates and rotates the pelvis, making the vagina accessible to the male (Diakow, 1974; Pfaff et al., 1978). Since the release of the lordosis reflex is completely controlled by ovarian hormones under natural conditions (Pfaff, 1980), mating is not possible outside of the female's fertile period. In addition to these physical barriers, there are several behavioral mechanisms that maximize female participation in copulation by immobilizing her just prior to and during copulation, preventing her from terminating mating. The stimulation necessary to produce immobilization varies across species. The most striking case is in pigs, where placing a boar's saliva on the snout of an estrous sow produces an immobilization response so strong that a human can sit astride her without producing an escape response (Izard, 1983). Thus close proximity between a sexually potent boar and a fertile sow is sufficient to make her sexually responsive to the male. In hamsters, rats, mice, and guinea pigs, the arching of the back and the rotation of the pelvis during lordosis is also associated with immobilization ranging in duration from seconds to minutes (Komisaruk, 1974). In fact the release of lordosis, at least in rats, requires immobilization (Komisaruk, 1974). In addition, vaginal stimulation both potentiates the release of lordosis and increases the duration and strength of the immobilization (Diakow, 1974; Komisaruk, 1974). Thus, during lordosis, the female withdrawal response is inhibited and she is physically unable to break off the sexual interaction, which ensures that the male will be able to intromit and thrust.

The hamster strikingly illustrates the interaction between male characteristics and female response. Estrous female hamsters will approach and stand next to an intact male, displaying lordosis for several minutes, seemingly soliciting mating. However, what appears to be female sexual initiation apparently is a combination of attraction to a male hamster and induction of lordosis triggered by a combination of male odor and ultrasonic vocalization (Beach et al., 1976). If the male is caged in a solid plexiglass cage, or the estrous females are deafened, preference for the intact male disappears and the females cease to display lordosis. Thus hamsters have evolved a mechanism involving female attraction to males and responsiveness to male behavior that guarantees mating.

The existence of these diverse mechanisms, which limit mating to periods of fertility and assure female participation in copulation, is an unexplained puzzle. Possibly they reflect that males and females are normally separated in these species and are often aggressive towards each other outside of breeding. Such a condition makes it necessary that any female response to male mating attempts avoids any indication of aggression. Complete female immobility during copulation would be likely to convey a nonaggressive demeanor, reducing male caution in interacting with the female. While females must be attracted to males, the existence of immobilizing mechanisms suggests that these females may not actually be motivated towards copulation itself, since such motivation would seem to make immobilization unnecessary. In this regard, it is unclear whether female rodents find intromissions and ejaculation rewarding or aversive or some combination of both (Erskine, 1989; Oldenburger, Everitt, and de Jonge, 1992). Extensive data in rodents show females selecting sexually active males in a choice apparatus (Edwards and Pfeiffle, 1983; Dudley and Moss, 1985) or actively pursuing males in an artificial burrow system (McClintock, 1981, 1987), suggesting female sexual desire. Actually, these data are more parsimoniously interpreted as a demonstration of female attraction to males, not necessarily of a specific interest in mating. Furthermore, the finding that when females control access to males they return more rapidly to the male after a mount without an intromission than after an intromission, could be interpreted as evidence of the aversive nature of intromissions to females, although it could also simply reflect female pacing of copulation (Erskine, 1989). In addition, lordosis in female rats produces a strong analgesia, lending further support to the notion that intromission may be painful or aversive (Komisaruk, 1974). In contrast, female rats can be conditioned to prefer a place where they received intromissions from a male (Oldenburger, Everitt, and de Jonge, 1992), providing evidence that females are interested in mating per se. Resolution of whether females are primarily attracted to males, or both attracted and interested in mating, requires evidence that intromissions are reinforcing to females, as is the case with males (Sheffield, Wulff, and Backer, 1951; Kagan, 1955). Without such studies, the possibility remains that rodent females are attracted to males but do not really desire mating. In fact, estrogen-treated female rats increase their approaches to male rats, before they are capable of showing lordosis (Edwards and Pfeiffle, 1983) suggesting that estrogen primarily increases attraction to males. Thus in nonprimate females coordination of sexual behavior with fertility relies upon physical barriers, immobiliz-

ing mechanisms, hormonally regulated attraction to males, and possibly female sexual desire. Regulation of sexual behavior with fertility in nonhuman
primates differs significantly from that just described in other mammalian females.

Voluntary Sex and Female Desire

Except in prosimian females, physical barriers to sexual activity have disappeared in nonhuman primates. While some prosimian species retain vaginal
membranes strictly limiting sexual activity to the fertile period (Doyle, 1974;
Hrdy and Whitten, 1987), these do not appear in simians, apes, or humans.
Thus I exclude prosimians when I refer to nonhuman primates, though from an
evolutionary standpoint the fact that prosimians have female physical barriers
makes their sexual behavior particularly interesting. Unfortunately, there are
too few quantitative studies of prosimian sexual behavior to draw meaningful
conclusions. In other primate species physical barriers have disappeared. Although female monkeys may present their genitals to a male, this is not analogous to lordosis in a rat, since it is not obligatory for intercourse to occur. A
characteristic that all primates beyond prosimians seem to share is that males
can force females to mate, something not possible in other mammalian species
(Miller, 1931; Wallen, 1990; Pavelka, this volume). Even though the disappearance of physical barriers to sexual behavior emancipated sexual activity from
hormonal control, such forced mating rarely occurs in primates other than
humans.

The regulation of mating through hormonally mediated reflexes and physical barriers limits sexual behavior to reproduction. In contrast, sexual behavior
in primates can, and does, occur in a wide variety of contexts, most of which
have little to do with reproduction (Wallen, 1990). This sexual flexibility became possible with the evolution of voluntary, rather than reflexive, control of
sexual behavior. However, strictly voluntary sexual activity uncouples sexual
behavior from fertility, particularly in females with long gamete cycles, and
mating no longer guarantees the possibility of fertilization. Thus females with
completely voluntary sexuality would be at a selective disadvantage to females
possessing a mechanism coupling mating and fertility. This selective disadvantage would produce strong selection for strict coupling between mating and
fertility, resulting in the disappearance of random maters. However, in females
with long gamete cycles, like primate females, nonreproductive mating, if not
costly, is without evolutionary consequence as long as fertile mating also occurs. Thus a solution to the problem presented by voluntary control is to allow
mating to occur at any time the female chooses, but increase the probability
she will initiate mating during the fertile period. In other words, females could
mate at any time in their ovarian cycle but would be most likely to mate when
fertile. This circumstance is achieved in primates by having the hormones that

regulate fertility also produce heightened female sexual desire. Thus although most primate females can engage in sex without regard to fertility, they are also most likely to engage in sex when fertile (Wallen, 1990). (For an exception, see de Waal's description of the bonobo, this volume).

This has meant that the occurrence of copulatory behavior per se does not really indicate the relationship between the female's ovarian state and her sexual motivation. Understanding the relationship between female sexual motivation and sexual intercourse is important for understanding the role ovarian hormones play in regulating primate sexual behavior. For this purpose I will focus on rhesus monkeys and humans, because we know the most about these primates in a variety of contexts where we also know the underlying hormonal changes. However, the relations described here are likely to be found in other primates as well, though they may not apply to prosimians.

Rhesus Social Context and the Regulation of Sexual Behavior

It has been known for more than twenty-five years that the pattern of sexual behavior displayed by rhesus females varies as a function of social context. Rhesus females in complex social groups display a brief but intense period of sexual activity in each nonpregnant ovarian cycle (Carpenter, 1942). In contrast, when rhesus are observed as male-female pairs (pair-test) in confined areas they quite often mate throughout the female's cycle, though mating is more likely at midcycle than at other times. Figure 4.1 illustrates these relationships using data from two laboratory studies, one of pair-tests in a small area (Goy, 1979) and the other from a group test in a large area (Wallen et al., 1984). The pair-test data illustrate the common finding that mating occurs in some pairs throughout the female's cycle, but that there is an increased probability of mating around ovulation. In contrast, mating in a social group is much more limited and is essentially restricted to the period of fertility. The specific group used here consisted of nine adult females and a single male, which probably increased competition between females, enhancing the degree of coupling between the female's cycle and mating. However, very similar patterns of mating are seen when there are many more males and females in the group (Wilson, Gordon, and Collins, 1982).

The results from these different testing situations clearly illustrate that social context influences the relationship between female hormonal changes and mating behavior. In a simple pair-test context, the female's hormonal state has less influence on the occurrence of sexual behavior than in a multifemale group. Two principles account for this effect of social context. First, female rhesus, unlike rodent females, or even prosimian females, are physically capable of mating at any time in their cycle and have no strict physical barriers preventing copulation. Second, female interest in males and interest in mating vary with female hormonal state and are increased at the time of ovulation by the same

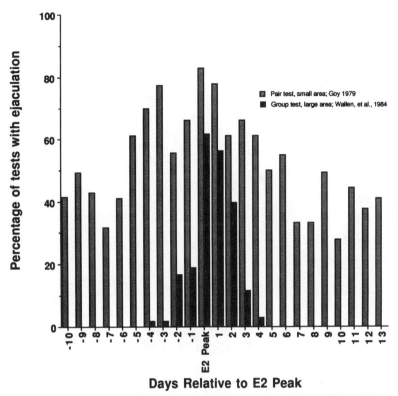

Figure 4.1   The occurrence of ejaculation in relation to the female's estradiol peak in rhesus monkeys studied in two different social conditions. Hatched bars represent data from male-female pairs tested in a 2m × 3m area (Goy, 1979). Solid bars represent data from a single male tested with nine females in a 15m × 15m area (Wallen et al., 1984). Both show a midcycle peak in mating but differ in the probability of mating during early follicular and luteal tests.

hormones that trigger ovulation. Figure 4.2 illustrates female approaches to the male and the frequency of her attempts to initiate copulation (*solicits*) in a multifemale group. These data support the idea that female rhesus sexual motivation varies systematically with her ovarian cycle.

In multifemale groups females rarely approach males, and when they do it is strongly related to the stage of their ovarian cycle. About five days prior to the midcycle estradiol peak, thus about six days prior to ovulation, females start approaching and following males. This approaching precedes by several days the actual start of male mounting behavior (Wallen et al., 1984). Approaching a male only indicates increased female interest in the male, since female attempts to initiate copulation increase after female approaches are al-

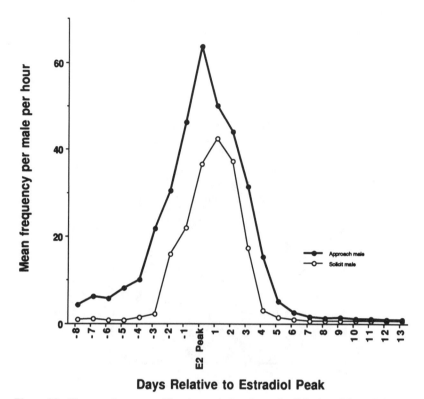

Days Relative to Estradiol Peak

Figure 4.2   The mean frequency of female approach and sexual solicitation of the male in relation to the female's midcycle estradiol peak in a social group consisting of nine intact females and
one adult male. Female approaching is significantly elevated earlier in the cycle than is sexual soliciting.

ready elevated. As the female nears ovulation, she dramatically increases her
attempts to initiate copulation by standing in front of the male, presenting her
genitals, slapping the ground to get his attention, and sometimes grabbing the
male's leg and pulling his pelvis toward her genitals. The frequency of these
sexual solicitations increases rapidly, peaking on the day of ovulation and then
falling rapidly during the next two days. Changes in both female approaches
to males and female initiation of copulation are completely eliminated by suppression of ovarian function (Wallen et al., 1986). Thus it appears that female
rhesus experience a marked increase in attraction to males and in sexual desire
around the time of ovulation, which are not present at other times in the cycle.
Since female hormonal cycles are exactly the same in both group and pair-
tests, why doesn't this hormonally mediated increase in sexual desire produce
the same pattern of restricted mating when females are paired with a single
male? One conclusion is that only in a group context does female sexual desire

become a particularly important determinant of sexual behavior. Put another way, sexual behavior in a pair-test does not require very high levels of female sexual motivation and therefore is less affected by changes in female sexual desire. This less restricted pattern of mating in pair-tests also suggests that the willingness of a female rhesus to participate in sex doesn't vary greatly with her hormonal state; she will readily respond to male sexual initiation at any point in her cycle. What does vary is the amount of effort a female is willing to expend to initiate sex. In the limited environment typically employed in pair-test studies, selecting and courting a partner requires little effort, and there are few behavioral alternatives to sex. Under these conditions rhesus females mate during a much greater portion of their ovarian cycle than is seen in multi-female groups.

The view that female rhesus are generally receptive to sex throughout their menstrual cycle but are interested in initiating sex only around ovulation is quite different from what we have seen in nonprimate species, where sex is always limited to the ovulatory portion of the female's cycle. The distinction between a female being receptive to sex and her willingness to initiate sex is not commonly made by researchers studying rhesus sexual behavior, or humans for that matter. This distinction is probably important, as several laboratories have reported that rhesus females rarely react negatively to rhesus male sexual initiation, even in the confines of small testing cages, leading several investigators to conclude that rhesus female sexual receptivity is not under ovarian hormonal control (Johnson and Phoenix, 1976; Wallen and Goy, 1977; Keverne, 1983). This apparent constant female receptivity does not result from males forcing the females to mate, despite the fact that male rhesus are larger than the females. When we compared the sexual behavior of pairs of rhesus in a small 2m × 3m cage and in a much larger 15m × 15m compound (Wallen, 1982), tested under both spatial conditions on the same day, we found that female hormonal state was a more important determinant of sexual behavior in the large than in the small space. In a striking aspect of this study, we observed a female who had just mated in the small area essentially ignore the male in the large area. He neither pursued her, nor did she avoid him, they just went about their individual business in the compound, whereas just an hour previously (or an hour later, depending upon the testing order) they actively mated in the small cage. Only 18 instances of females reacting negatively to the males were recorded in 60 tests, and these were unrelated to the female's cycle, being as likely to occur near ovulation as in the luteal phase (Wallen, 1982). Although males initiated most of the mating in the small area, it was clear that the females willingly responded to the males' initiation and did not attempt to stop the sexual interaction. This provided support for the notion that female arousability is not influenced by hormones, only her interest in mating. This is similar to humans, where female sexual desire is clearly related to ovarian hormones (Adams, Gold, and Burt, 1978; Sherwin, Gelfand, and Brender,

1985; Stanislaw and Rice, 1988), but arousability to erotic stimuli is generally reported not to vary in relation to hormonal state (Abramson, Repczynski, and Merrill, 1976; Griffith and Walker, 1975; Hoon, Bruce, and Kinchloe, 1982; Slob, Ernste, and van der Werff ten Bosch, 1990).

What mechanism produces this tight coupling between female ovarian condition and sexual behavior in the group setting, but not in pair-tests? The answer is the principle that when sex requires effort or involves risk it only occurs when sexual motivation is high. The corollary is that sex in a social group is risky for a rhesus female. Midcycle females are the target for aggression by other females, whether or not the other females are near midcycle (Wallen and Winston, 1984; Walker, Wilson, and Gordon, 1983). A female who suddenly abandons her female grooming partners to follow and pursue a male is the target of female agonism (Wallen and Winston, 1984). The degree of risk for individual females varies with their social rank and, as would be expected, the sexual behavior of high-ranking females is less strongly correlated with hormonal condition than it is in low-ranking females (Wallen, 1990). In addition, a female faces other social risks from males who may rebuff her attempts to initiate sex, usually with threats, rarely with attacks (Carpenter, 1942; Smuts and Smuts, 1993). Thus a female in a social group needs to be highly sexually motivated to attempt to overcome potential social risks and initiate mating. Though females may be willing to mate at any time in their cycle, they initiate mating in a social group only when strongly motivated. Why might this have evolved?

Social Structure and Female Sexual Desire

Rhesus society is organized along matrilines, with females staying in their natal group for life and males migrating in adulthood (Lindburg, 1969, 1971). This organization means that females live in a complex social matrix with historical continuity, whereas males break their matrilineal ties and must be integrated into a new social context. One consequence of this male pattern is that males are much less likely to receive aid and support in social conflicts than is the case for females who have their matriline to support them. Thus, in contrast to what is typically reported for pair-tests, male rhesus in social groups do little initiating of sexual behavior (Wallen et al., 1984) and instead wait for females to initiate sexual activity. Even when females attempt to initiate mating, males often don't respond immediately but instead leave the female as soon as she approaches (personal observation). This pattern of female approach and male departure, with the female following, is typically repeated several times before the male responds sexually to the female. In this social structure, the evolution of female sexual desire was critical to successful mating. The social risk to a male who attempts to initiate sex with an uninterested female in a rhesus group can be great; thus the male strategy is to wait for the female to indicate her unequivocal interest. Under such circumstances, females for whom sexual desire is coupled to fertility have a selective advantage over females with no hormonally regulated sexual desire.

The findings from pair-tests are also in accord with this view. Though female sexual desire is not as critical in a situation divorced from its evolutionary context, an ovulatory increase in mating is still evident, suggesting that female desire still functions to increase the probability of mating even against a background of relatively constant sexual activity. Some have found it difficult to identify changes in female behavior associated with midcycle hormonal increases (Michael and Zumpe, 1993) leading them to argue that the midcycle increase in mating in pair-tests reflects increased female attractiveness due to a vaginal pheromone which causes the male to increase his initiation (Keverne, 1976, 1983; Michael and Zumpe, 1993). However, this cannot be the case. First, it is well established that the putative vaginal pheromone peaks midluteally after the increase in behavior (Goldfoot et al., 1976; Michael and Bonsall, 1977). Second, removing the sense of smell of male rhesus does not eliminate the midcycle increase in sexual behavior (Goldfoot et al., 1978). It has been suggested that male rhesus continue to show cyclic changes in sexual behavior following anosmia because they remember from one cycle to the next the female's pattern of sexual response (Michael and Zumpe, 1993). This explanation seems highly unlikely as it does not explain what would motivate a male rhesus to increase and decrease his mating behavior to match the pattern shown in a previous ovarian cycle. Furthermore, if the pair-test is modified so that the female has to perform an operant to gain access to the male or the male is tethered so that only the female can initiate mating, she increases her effort at the same part of her cycle that increased mating occurs (Keverne, 1976; Pomerantz and Goy, 1983). It is not necessary to speculate about possible olfactory cues as regulators of rhesus sexual behavior when obvious behavioral mechanisms account for the changes in sexual behavior of rhesus monkeys across the different social contexts studied.

Hormonal Influences on the Sexual Behavior of Women

Hormonal influences in rhesus females have evolved to solve the specific problem of mating in a social group. The same principles have relevance to human sexual behavior. Like rhesus females, women are physically capable of mating at any time in their cycle. This physical capability has confused the occurrence of sexual intercourse with the occurrence of female sexual motivation, one reason why intercourse frequency correlates poorly with female ovarian cycles in humans (Wallen and Lovejoy, 1993). The notion is widespread that women are continuously receptive, because they are always capable of engaging in intercourse. Women certainly are not continuously receptive, being quite selective in their sexual behavior. Beach (1971) suggested that women are "continu-

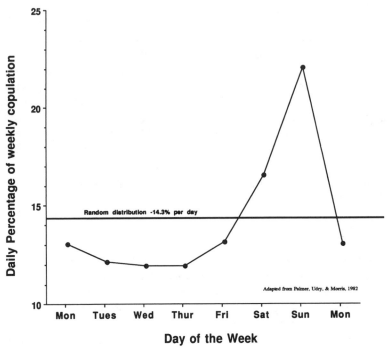

Figure 4.3 The distribution of copulation (N = 1941) in relation to day of the week for 78 women (adapted from Palmer, Udry, and Morris, 1982). The daily percentage differed from a random distribution on Saturday and Sunday.

ously copulable," an awkward phrase that conveys the distinction between the psychological condition of being willing to engage in sex, or receptivity, and the physical condition of being able to engage in sex. The question remains, however, whether sexual behavior in humans is similarly influenced by both social context and hormones, as it is in rhesus. Figure 4.3 illustrates one example of the influence of social context on human sexual behavior.

As seen in this figure social structure has a strong influence on human sexual behavior. Sexual intercourse is not randomly distributed throughout the week, but shows a striking increase on Saturdays and Sundays in comparison to the other days of the week (Palmer, Udry, and Morris, 1982). Interestingly, the peak on Sunday is significantly higher than on any other day, and is primarily accounted for by more intercourse throughout the day than on the other days of the week. Thus, not surprisingly, the construction of a work schedule directly influences the occurrence of sexual behavior. As with rhesus, this social influence occurs because the physical ability to have sex is emancipated from hor-

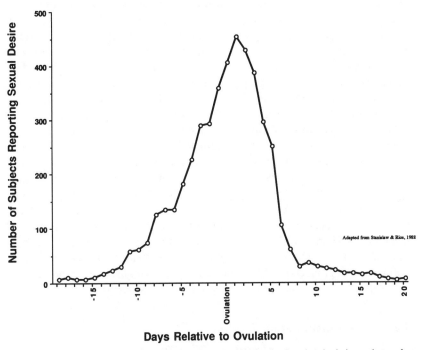

Figure 4.4 The number of women reporting sexual desire for the first time in their ovarian cycle in relation to the presumed time of ovulation as determined by a basal body temperature shift (adapted from Stanislaw and Rice, 1988).

monal control. In contrast, sexual desire is not similarly emancipated; many pieces of evidence suggest that it is coupled to hormonal state in women. Figure 4 illustrates one of the most striking examples of the relationship between sexual desire and the menstrual cycle. The incidence of women reporting sexual desire increases dramatically across the ovarian cycle, peaking during the period of maximal fertility and then declining rapidly during the luteal phase (Stanislaw and Rice, 1988).

If the units were removed from the Y-axis of figure 4.4, it would easily transpose over figure 4.2, suggesting our primate heritage. Similarly, when we consider female initiation of sexual behavior we find a midcycle peak in women who are not taking hormonal contraceptives and are employing permanent and reliable contraception, which eliminates fear of pregnancy, an important regulator of human sexual behavior (Adams, Gold, and Burt, 1978; Tsui, de Silva, and Marinshaw, 1991). Further evidence comes from studies of women who have had their ovaries removed prior to menopause. These women, even though they still have intact adrenals, report an almost complete disappearance of sexual desire that is reinstated only with hormonal therapy (Sherwin and Gelfand, 1988). There is, however, much confusion about how pronounced these influences are and exactly when they occur in the female's cycle. This confusion has two main sources. First, female cycles in humans are not treated in a standardized manner. Unlike studies in nonhuman primates where the norm is to use a hormonal marker to align cycles and then look at cycles day by day, human researchers use a variety of methods both for aligning cycles and for dividing the cycle into phases. Thus it is very difficult to determine in many studies exactly where the critical event of ovulation occurs across the study's subjects. The second source of confusion comes from expecting hormonal influences to exert rigid control over female behavior, as is the case in many nonprimate females. Human sexual behavior, like that of nonhuman primates, is an interaction between social context and hormonally mediated motivational systems because the ability to engage in sex is not under hormonal control (see Meyer-Bahlburg, this volume). Just as the day of the week dramatically effects the pattern of sexual behavior, so do other factors such as choice of contraceptive (Adams, Gold, and Burt, 1978) and fear of pregnancy (Tsui, de Silva, and Marinshaw, 1991). The evolution of female sexual desire regulated by the same hormones that produce fertility is the mechanism that guarantees reproduction while allowing sexual activity to occur in a variety of social contexts.

The Role of Female Sexual Pleasure

It is not likely that sexual behavior in mammalian males would be sustained without the strong reinforcement of sexual arousal and orgasm. While orgasm is considered as the primary reinforcer of male sexual behavior, arousal itself may be as important in motivating males to mate. Nearly fifty years ago it was demonstrated that sexually naive male rats would learn a T maze using copulation without ejaculation as the reinforcer (Sheffield, Wulff, and Backer, 1951). In humans, testimony to the rewarding properties of arousal itself is found in the existence of a massive industry where males pay substantial amounts of money to view naked women in a context where orgasm is unlikely. Though arousal is rewarding, orgasm is an equally powerful incentive in males, where it is a potent reinforcer in learning by rats (Kagan, 1955) and in men as evidenced by the prevalence of prostitution and massage parlors, where male ejaculation is the principal purpose. The strength of male motivation to seek arousal and orgasm is seen in the flourishing sex industry supported by males even in the face of social disapproval, risk of disease or injury, and substantial expense (Abramson and Pinkerton,1995)

The role of arousal and orgasm in female sexual behavior is less clear. Although sexual arousal must be as important for females as for males, studies using copulation as a reinforcer have not been done in female rodents. However, female rats in estrus show a conditioned preference for a place associated with intromission from a male rat (Oldenburger, Everitt, and de Jonge, 1992). In women, as previously described, arousal to erotic materials does not vary with the female's cycle, and responsivity to erotic stimuli does not differ between males and females (Rubinsky et al., 1987). However, the arousal-seeking behavior of women, as opposed to their arousal response when provided with sexual stimuli, has not been investigated. Thus while arousal to sexual stimuli is similar in men and women, it is not clear that women are willing to expend as much effort or take as many risks as do males to find sexually arousing stimuli. The small size of the female-focused sex industry suggests that seeking sexually arousal is less common in women. However, social disapproval of public expressions of female sexual interest could also limit female participation as consumers of sexually stimulating materials. It is unlikely that social sanctions fully account for this difference, since the male-focused sex industry is socially stigmatized, often is illegal, involves substantial risk and cost, yet still finds massive demand. It is more likely that the size of the female-focused sex industry reflects the small size of the potential market, not social suppression of female sexuality. However, the importance of arousal-seeking in the sexual behavior of females requires further investigation. The importance of orgasm as a regulator of female sexual behavior is also unclear.

Although all mammalian males show analogous behavior that produces ejaculation, there is no convincing evidence that something akin to orgasm occurs in all mammalian females other than primates. The evidence in non-human primates, while sketchy, suggests that females of several nonhuman primate species are capable of physiological responses analogous to those recorded in women during orgasm (Allen and Lemmon, 1981) with the most complete evidence reported for the stump-tailed macaque during both female-female and heterosexual sexual interactions (Goldfoot et al., 1980; Slob, Groeneveld, and van der Werff ten Bosch, 1986). In humans, many women routinely experience orgasm, but it is equally clear that reaching orgasm is a less certain event in women than in men, with a substantial percentage of women reporting never having experienced orgasm (Kinsey et al., 1953). Although treatment of female anorgasmia is a significant emphasis in sex therapy, for many women orgasm may not be as important as other aspects of sexual behavior. For example, several studies report that women consider affection and communication as more important than orgasm in sexual relationships (Tiefer, 1991). Similarly, a survey of 267 undergraduate women and 178 undergraduate men found that 90 percent of the women, as opposed to 46 percent of the men, stated that they could be sexually satisfied without orgasm (Edwards, unpublished). Similarly, females do not seem to seek orgasm with the intensity and single-mindedness of males. This is most clearly seen in the striking sex difference in masturbation, where significantly fewer females ever masturbate, and those who do, masturbate significantly less frequently than males (Leitenberg, Detzer, and Srebnik, 1993; Oliver and Hyde, 1993). In this regard, the survey referred to above found that only 57 percent of the women had ever masturbated as opposed to 94 percent of the men (Edwards, unpublished). Similarly, Leitenberg et al. (1993) found that 45 percent of 175 women and 81 percent of 105 males ever reported masturbating. Since the primary function of masturbation is to produce orgasm, these data suggest that women are not as motivated to seek orgasm as are males. While it has been argued that differential socialization between males and females accounts for this difference (Leitenberg, Detzer, and Srebnik, 1993; Oliver and Hyde, 1993) this seems unlikely. First, masturbation is a private event, making it difficult to observe. Second, the evidence for social suppression is stronger for male masturbation than for female masturbation. Third, evidence suggests that negative socialization has little effect on masturbation, at least in males. Male masturbation is strongly stigmatized, having been regarded as deviant sexual behavior (Clark and Tift, 1966). Furthermore, biblical prohibitions against onanism apply only to males, and warnings against "self-pollution" have historically been part of a boy's sexual training but not that of girls. Historically, males have faced parental, religious, and mental-health injunctions against masturbation, yet most males masturbate (see Abramson and Pinkerton, 1995, for an extended discussion). In contrast, since the early 1970s female masturbation has been encouraged in female sexuality and is an integral part of many female sex therapies (Barbach, 1975; Heiman, 1976). Thus the lower incidence of female masturbation found today is unlikely to result from social suppression of female sexuality but instead reflects women's more intermittent interest in seeking orgasm.

The view that women do not feel driven as frequently as males to seek sexual arousal and orgasm certainly does not mean that they do not experience intense sexual desire. In fact this behavioral sex difference would be expected if sexual desire is regulated by gonadal hormones in both males and females and is explained by the different pattern of hormonal stimulation experienced by the sexes. Sexual desire in males is strongly coupled to testosterone, but arousability is not. Hypogonadal males, who have castrate levels of testosterone, readily become aroused to sexually explicit stimuli (Kwan et al., 1976; Bancroft et al., 1974), yet they do not report the erections as pleasurable and they do not seek opportunities to become aroused. Similarly, females are capable of becoming aroused independently of their hormonal condition, and arousability typically has not been found to vary with the female's menstrual cycle (Abramson, Repczynski, and Merrill, 1976; Griffith and Walker, 1975; Hoon, Bruce, and Kinchloe, 1982; but see: Slob, Ernste, and van der Werff ten Bosch, 1990). However, female sexual desire clearly varies with ovarian activity. Thus the difference in arousal- and orgasm-seeking behavior between males and females probably reflects the different periodicity and duration of sexual desire in the sexes. Males experience relatively constant hormonal stimulation producing constant sexual desire, and their sexuality often is expressed in a more compulsive and driven manner. Females, in contrast, experience cyclic periods of hormonal stimulation associated with a short, but intense, period of sexual desire. This results in less frequent arousal and orgasm-seeking across the ovarian cycle. Thus peak sexual desire does not differ between men and women; what differs is how consistently they experience intense sexual desire.

This difference in the constancy of intense sexual desire probably affects the daily behavior of men and women. The female pattern of cyclic increases in sexual desire produces periods of low sexual desire allowing dispassionate assessment of social interactions uncolored by sexual interest. This, in turn, lets females exert more choice and selectivity in sexual interactions than is the case for males. In contrast, the relatively constant high level of sexual interest experienced by males provides a markedly different context for social relationships. This difference in the way in which males and females experience sexual desire must influence the way in which males and females view the role of sex in daily life.

The disappearance of female physical barriers to sexual behavior allowed sexual behavior in most primate species to be routinely used in nonreproductive contexts. The evolution of female sexual desire tightly coupled to fertility was necessary to assure female reproduction. This set of circumstances expanded the integration of sexual activity into other than reproductive contexts while liberating females from the constant sexual desire that makes it difficult for males to divorce social interactions from sexual ones.

Acknowledgments

Catherine Tardivel is thanked for first pointing out the importance of female immobilizing mechanisms in understanding the evolution of sexual behavior and for her kind permission to pursue this idea. Dr. Dario Maestripieri is thanked for discussions of this chapter and for his insight into the evolutionary significance of coupling sexual desire to ovarian hormone changes. Dr. Kurt Wallen is thanked for helpful discussions that improved the focus of this chapter. Dr. David Edwards is thanked for allowing me to present his unpublished survey data. Dr. Michael D. Zeiler is thanked for discussions concerning the reinforcing properties of sexual arousal. The preparation of this chapter was supported in part by Grant RR-00165 awarded by the National Center for Research Resources to the Yerkes Regional Primate Research Center and by RSDA award K02 MH01062. The research reported here was supported by NSF grants: BNS 81-17627, BNS 84-18060, BNS 86-07295 and BNS 89-19888.

References

Abramson, P. R. and Pinkerton, S. D. 1995. *With pleasure: thoughts on the nature of human sexuality.* New York: Oxford University Press.

Abramson, P. R., Repczynski, C. A., and Merrill, L. R. 1976. The menstrual cycle and response to erotic literature. *J. Consul. Clin. Psychol. 44*:1018–1019.

Adams, D. B., Gold, A. R., Burt, A. D. 1978. Rise in female-initiated sexual activity at ovulation and its suppression by oral contraceptives. *N. Engl. J. Med. 299*:1145–1150.

Allen, M. L. and Lemmon, W. B. 1981. Orgasm in female primates. *Am. J. Primatol. 1*: 15–34.

Bancroft, J., Tennent, T. G., Loucas, K., and Cass, J. 1974. Control of deviant sexual behaviour by drugs: behavioural effects of oestrogens and antiandrogens. *Br. J. Psychiatry 125*:310–319.

Barbach, L. G. 1975. *For yourself: The fulfillment of female sexuality.* New York, Anchor Press.

Beach, F. A. 1947. Evolutionary changes in the physiological control of mating behavior in mammals. *Psych. Rev. 54*:297–315.

Beach, F. A. 1967. Cerebral and hormonal control of reflexive mechanisms involved in copulatory behavior. *Physiol. Rev. 47*:289–316.

Beach, F. A. 1971. Human sexuality and evolution. In *Reproductive behavior,* ed. W. Montagna and W. A. Sadler, New York, Plenum Press.

Beach, F. A. 1976. Sexual attractivity, proceptivity, and receptivity in female mammals. *Horm. Behav. 7*:105–138.

Beach, F. A., Stern, B., Carmichael, M., and Ranson, E. 1976. Comparisons of sexual receptivity and proceptivity in female hamsters. *Behav. Biol. 18*:473–487.

Carpenter, C. R. 1942. Sexual behavior of free ranging rhesus monkeys (*Macaca mulatta*). I. Specimens, procedures, and behavioral characteristics of estrus. *J. Comp. Psychol. 33*:113–142.

Clark, J. P. and Tift, L. L. 1966. Polygraph and interview validation of self-reported deviant behavior. *Am. Sociol. Rev. 31*:516–521.

Diakow, C. 1974. Motion picture analysis of rat mating behavior. *J. Comp. Physiol. Psychol. 88*:704–712.

Doyle, G. A. 1974. Behavior of prosimians. In *Behavior of nonhuman primates,* vol. 4, ed. A. M. Schrier and F. Stollnitz. New York: Academic Press.

Dudley, C. A. and R. L. Moss. 1985. LHRH and mating behavior: Sexual receptivity versus sexual preference. *Pharmacol. Biochem. Behavio. 22*:967–972.

Edwards, D. A. and Pfeiffle, J. K. 1983. Hormonal control of receptivity, proceptivity and sexual motivation. *Physiol. Behav. 30*:437–443.

Elia, I. 1988. *The female animal,* New York, Henry Holt.

Erskine, M. S. 1989. Solicitation behavior in the estrous female rat: A review. *Horm. Behav. 23*:473–502.

Goldfoot, D. A., Goy, R. W., Kravetz, M. A., Freeman, S. K. 1976. Lack of effect of vaginal lavages and aliphatic acids on ejaculatory responses in rhesus monkeys: behavioral and chemical analyses. *Horm. Behav. 7*:1–27.

Goldfoot, D. A., Westerborg-van Loon, H., Groenveld, W., and Slob, A. K. 1980. Behavioral and physiological evidence of sexual climax in the female stump-tailed macaque (*Macaca arctoides*). *Science 208*:1477–1479.

Goldfoot, D. A., Essock-Vitale, S. M., Asa, C. S., Thornton, J. E., and Leshner, A. I. 1978. Anosmia in male rhesus does not alter copulatory activity with cycling females. *Science 199*:1095–1096.

Goy, R. W. 1979. Sexual compatibility in rhesus monkeys: Predicting sexual behavior of oppositely sexed pairs of adults. In: *Sex, hormones, and behavior.* Ciba Foundation Symposium. Amsterdam: Elsevier/North Holland.

Goy, R. W. and Resko, J. A. 1972. Gonadal hormones and behavior of normal and pseu-
dohermaphroditic-nonhuman female primates. *Rec. Prog. horm. Res. 28*:707–733.

Griffith, M. and Walker, C. E. 1975. Menstrual cycle phases and personality variables
as related to response to erotic stimuli. *Arch. Sex. Beh. 4*:599–603.

Heiman, J. 1976. *Becoming orgasmic: A sexual growth program for women.* New Jer-
sey, Prentice-Hall.

Hoon, P. W., Bruce, K., and Kinchloe, B. 1982. Does the menstrual cycle play a role in
sexual arousal? *Psychophysiology 19*:21–27.

Hrdy, S. B. and Whitten, P. L. 1987. Patterning of sexual activity. In *Primate societies,*
ed. B. Smuts, *et al.,* Chicago, The University of Chicago Press.

Izard, M. K. 1983. Pheromones and reproduction in domestic animals, In *Pheromones
and reproduction in mammals*, ed. J. G. Vandenberg, Academic Press, New York.

Johnson, D. F. and Phoenix, C. H. 1976. Hormonal control of female sexual attractiveness, proceptivity, and receptivity in rhesus monkeys. *J. Comp. Physiol. Psychol.
90*: 473–483.

Kagan, J. 1955. Differential reward value of incomplete and complete sexual behavior.
J. Comp. Physiol. Psychol. 48:59–65.

Keverne, E. B. 1976. Sexual receptivity and attractiveness in female rhesus monkeys.
Advan. Study Behav. 7:155–200.

Keverne, E. B. 1983. Chemical communication in primate reproduction, In *Pheromones and reproduction in mammals,* ed. J. G. Vandenberg, Academic Press, New
York.

Kinsey, A. C., Pomeroy, W. B., Martin, C. E., and Gebhard, P. H. 1953. *Sexual behavior
in the human female.* Philadelphia, W. B. Saunders and Co.

Komisaruk, B. R. 1974. Neural and hormonal interactions in the reproductive behavior
of female rats. In *Reproductive behavior,* ed. W. Montagna and W. A. Sadler, New
York: Plenum Press.

Kwan, M., Greenleaf, W. J., Mann, J., Crapo, L., and Davidson, J. M. 1983. The nature
of androgen action on male sexuality: A combined laboratory self-report study on
hypogonadal men. *J. Clin. endocrinol. Metab. 57*:557–562.

Leitenberg, H., Detzer, M. J., and Srebnik, D. 1993. Gender differences in masturbation
and the relation of masturbation experience in preadolescence and/or early adolescence to sexual behavior and sexual adjustment in young adulthood. *Arch. Sex.
Behav. 22*:87–98.

Lindburg, D. G. 1969. Rhesus monkeys: Mating season mobility of adult males. *Science 166*:1176–1178.

Lindburg, D. G. 1971. The rhesus monkey in North India: an ecological and behavioral
study. *Primate Behavior 2*:1–106.

McClintock, M. K. 1981. Simplicity from complexity: A naturalistic approach to behavior and neuroendocrine function. In *New directions for methodology of social and
behavioral science. vol. 8,* ed. I. Silverman, San Francisco, Jossey-Bass.

McClintock, M. K. 1987. A functional approach to the behavioral endocrinology of
rodents. In *Psychobiology of reproductive behaviors, an evolutionary perspective*,
ed. D. Crews. Englewood Cliffs, NJ, Prentice-Hall.

Michael, R. P. and Bonsall, R. W. 1977. Chemical signals and primate behaviour. In
Chemical signals in vertebrates, ed. M. M. Mozell, New York, Plenum.

Michael, R. P. and Keverne, E. B. 1968. Pheromones and the communication of sexual
status in primates. *Nature (London) 218*: 746–749.

Michael, R P. and Zumpe, D. 1993. A review of hormonal factors influencing the sexual and aggressive behavior of macaques. *Am. J. Primatol. 30*:213–241.

Miller, G. S. 1931. The primate basis for human sexual behavior. *Q. Rev. Biol. 6*: 379–410.

Oldenburger, W. P., Everitt, B. J., and de Jonge, F. H. 1992. Conditioned place preference induced by sexual interaction in female rats. *Horm. Behav. 26*:204–213.

Oliver, M. B., and Hyde, J. S. 1993. Gender differences in sexuality: A meta-analysis. *Psych. bull. 114*:29–51.

Palmer, J. D., Udry, J. R., and Morris, N. M. 1982. Diurnal and weekly, but no lunar rhythms in human copulation. *Hum. Biol. 54*:111–121.

Pfaff, D. W. 1980. *Estrogens and brain function.* New York, Springer-Verlag.

Pfaff, D. W., Diakow, C., Montgomery, M., Jenkins, F. A. 1978. X-ray cinematographic analysis of lordosis in female rats. *J. Comp. Physiol. Psychol. 92*:937–941.

Pomerantz, S. M. and Goy, R. W. 1983. Proceptive behavior of female rhesus monkeys during tests with tethered males. *Horm. Behav. 17*:237–248.

Rubinsky, H. J., Eckerman, D. A., Rubinsky, E. W., and Hoover, C. R. 1987. Early-phase physiological response patterns to psychosexual stimuli: comparison of male and female patterns. *Arch. Sex. Behav. 16*:45–56.

Sheffield, F. D., Wulff, J. J., and Backer, R. 1951. Reward of copulation without sex drive reduction. *J. Comp. Physiol. Psychol. 44*:3–8.

Sherwin, B. B. and Gelfand, M. M. 1988. The role of androgen in the maintenance of sexual functioning in oophorectomized women. *Psychosom. Med. 49*:397–409.

Sherwin, B. B., Gelfand, M. M., and Brender, W. 1985. Androgen enhances sexual motivation in females: A prospective, crossover study of sex steroid administration in surgical menopause. *Psychosom. Med. 47*(2):339–351.

Slob, A. K., Ernste, M., and van der Werff ten Bosch, J. J. 1990. Menstrual cycle phase and sexual arousability in women. *Arch. Sex. Behav. 20*:567–577.

Slob, A. K., Groeneveld, W. H., and van der Werff ten Bosch, J. J. 1988. Physiological changes during copulation in male and female stumptail macaques (*Macaca aretoids*). *Physiology and Behavior 38*:891–895.

Smuts, B. B. and Smuts, R. W. 1993. Male aggression and sexual coercion of females in nonhuman primates and other mammals: Evidence and theoretical implications. *Advances in the Study of Behavior 22*:1–63.

Stanislaw, H. and Rice, F. J. 1988. Correlation between sexual desire and menstrual cycle characteristics. *Arch. Sex. Behav. 17*:499–508.

Symons, D. 1980. Précis of *The evolution of human sexuality. Behav. Brain Sci. 3*: 171–214.

Tiefer, L. 1991. Historical, scientific, clinical, and feminist criticisms of "the human sexual response cycle" model. *Ann. Rev. Sex. Res. Volume II*:1–23.

Trivers, R. L. 1972. Parental investment and sexual selection. In *Sexual selection and the descent of man, 1871–1971,* ed. B. Campbell, Chicago, Aldine.

Tsui, A. O., de Silva, S. V., and Marinshaw, R. 1991. Pregnancy avoidance and coital behavior. *Demography 28*:101–117.

Walker, M. L., Wilson, M. E., Gordon, T. P. 1983. Female rhesus monkey aggression during the menstrual cycle. *Anim. Behav. 31*(4):1047–1054.

Wallen, K. 1982. Influence of female hormonal state on rhesus sexual behavior varies with space for social interaction. *Science 217*:375–376.

Wallen, K. 1990. Desire and ability: hormones and the regulation of female sexual behavior. *Neurosci Biobehav Rev 14*:233–241.

Wallen, K. and Goy, R. W. 1977. Effects of estradiol benzoate, estrone, and propionates of testosterone or dihydrotestosterone on sexual and related behaviors of ovariectomized rhesus monkeys. *Horm. Behav. 9*:228–248.

Wallen, K. and Lovejoy, J. 1993. Sexual behavior: Endocrine function and therapy. In *Hormonally induced changes in mind and brain,* New York, Academic Press.

Wallen, K. and Winston, L. A. 1984. Social complexity and hormonal influences on sexual behavior in rhesus monkeys (*Macaca mulatta*). *Physiol. Behav. 32*:143–162.

Wallen, K., Winston, L. A., Gaventa, S., Davis-DaSilva, M., and Collins, D. C. 1984. Periovulatory changes in female sexual behavior and patterns of ovarian steroid secretion in group-living rhesus monkeys. *Horm. Behav. 18*:431–450.

Wallen, K., Mann, D. R., Davis-DaSilva, M., Gaventa, S., Lovejoy, J. C., Collins, D. C. 1986. Chronic gonadotropin-releasing hormone agonist treatment suppresses ovulation and sexual behavior in group-living female rhesus monkeys. *Physiol. Behav. 36*:369–375.

Wilson, M. E., Gordon, T. P., Collins, D. C. 1982. Variation in ovarian steroids associated with the annual mating period in female rhesus (*Macaca mulatta*). *Biol. Reprod. 27*(3):530–539.

Young, W. C. 1937. The vaginal smear picture, sexual receptivity, and the time of ovulation in the guinea pig. *Antat. Rec. 67*(3):305–325.

CHAPTER FIVE

Beauty Is in the Adaptations of the Beholder: The Evolutionary Psychology of Human Female Sexual Attractiveness

DONALD SYMONS

She's beautiful and therefore to be woo'd . . .
—William Shakespeare

Geneticist Theodosius Dobzhansky once observed that nothing in biology makes sense except in light of evolution. This necessarily includes pleasure, since pleasure, like all experiences, is the product of brain mechanisms, and brain mechanisms are the products of evolution by natural selection. The question is not so much whether this view of pleasure is *correct*—as there is no known or suspected scientific alternative to it—but whether it is *useful*. I will argue that it *is* useful, that Darwin's theory of evolution by natural selection can help us to make sense of sexual pleasure. I will use sexual *attraction/attractiveness* as an index of sexual pleasure. That is, I will assume that if X perceives A as more sexually attractive than B, then X typically would experience more pleasure (and would anticipate experiencing more pleasure) from copulating with A than with B.

Although the determinants of male and female sexual attractiveness are equally susceptible to a selectionist analysis, in this essay I will consider only the latter, for the following reasons. First, our theoretical understanding of the determinants of female sexual attractiveness is better developed. For example, there is a reasonably rigorous selectionist argument relating female age cues and male sexual attraction (see below), but the theory relating male age cues and female sexual attraction is murkier and the expectations are less clear cut (Kenrick and Keefe, 1992). Second, female sexual attractiveness depends more on easily observed, described, and quantified physical features and less on abstract attributes such as status and prowess (Symons, 1979; Jackson, 1992). And third, there are much better data on female sexual attractiveness (see Jackson 1992 for a review of the literature on physical appearance and attractiveness in both sexes).

We take for granted that small differences in things like skin texture and facial hair can have large effects on women's sexual attractiveness, but *why* this should be so is not obvious. By way of contrast, consider how we assess an array of apples and choose which one we want to eat. Apples vary in several dimensions—sweetness, juiciness, flavor—that determine the amount of pleasure we experience when we eat them. In choosing which apple to eat we use particular visual, tactual, and olfactory cues because we have learned that these cues reliably predict variations in the gustatory sensations that occur during eating. We have come to care about an apple's firmness, for example, only because firmness has, in our experience, been a reasonably reliable predictor of sweetness and juiciness. But there seems to be no such mapping between the specific visually perceived physical characteristics that determine female sexual attractiveness and the nature or quality of the tactual sensations that occur during a sexual interaction.

Imagine that you are a heterosexual man who is fortunate enough to be able to choose among an array of potential sexual partners. No doubt they vary in many dimensions that you consider to be sexually relevant. Do they like to do the same things in bed (or wherever) that you do? How sensitive would they be to your desires and responses? How much do they enjoy sex? How skilled are they in this or that aspect of lovemaking? How well would your bodies fit together? What is remarkable about the visually perceived physical characteristics that determine female sexual attractiveness is that they predict none of these things.

How, then, can one account for perceptions of female sexual attractiveness? Is there any perspective from which they make sense? I will try to show that there is one, and only one: the primary determinants of female sexual attractiveness are predicted in straightforward fashion from the perspective of the *adaptationist program*. I will argue that human males evolved psychological mechanisms that selectively detect and respond to certain specific characteristics (such as smooth skin and bilateral symmetry) of women's bodies. These universal mechanisms were shaped by natural selection to have the specific forms that they do because these forms produced reproductively functional behavior in the environments and conditions in which our ancestors evolved. My goal is to demonstrate that the psychological mechanisms in human males that underpin the experience of sexual attraction have functional designs.

The Adaptationist Program in Biology

The goal of the adaptationist program, according to George Williams (1985), is to recognize certain features of the organism as components of some special problem-solving machinery. These problem-solving mechanisms are called "adaptations." The identification and description of adaptations has always been the core of biological study, because that is how organisms are partitioned into nonarbitrary, scientifically useful, functional components. The nature and scope of the adaptationist program can be characterized briefly as follows.

1. The adaptationist program long preceded Darwin. As Ernst Mayr (1983)

has pointed out, "The adaptationist question, 'What is the function of a given structure or organ?' has been for centuries the basis for every advance in physiology" (p. 328). William Harvey's discovery that the heart is a pump, for example, was a signal contribution to the adaptationist program. In fact, adaptationism pervades every level of biological inquiry—molecular, cellular, tissue, organ, and whole organism—because at every level descriptions of relevant phenomena almost always are (at least implicitly) *functional* descriptions.

Darwin's contribution to the adaptationist program was to provide the first and only scientifically coherent account of the origin and maintenance of adaptations: evolution by natural selection. He argued that in nature species evolve by a process analogous to selective breeding, or *artificial selection,* wherein organisms are modified in the course of successive generations to suit human purposes. In artificial selection the breeder capitalizes on naturally occurring variation and allows only those individuals with desired characteristics (such as running fast or producing abundant milk) to reproduce. Since offspring tend to resemble their parents more than they resemble a random member of their species, the result is the evolution of domesticated breeds that manifest in exaggerated form whatever qualities the breeder has selected for. By this simple process a wolf can be transformed into a Pekinese in what is, on a geological time scale, the blink of an eye.

Darwin discovered that a similar process occurs in nature. In essence, evolution by natural selection couples random variation in the hereditary material (mutation) with systematic nonrandom replication of the variants. It is this process that produces and maintains hearts, eyes, edge-detecting cells in the mammalian visual cortex—all of the complex machinery of life. In fact, natural selection can be viewed more as a theory of adaptation than as a theory of evolution. For one thing, there are other causes of evolutionary change besides natural selection (e.g., genetic drift), but there are no other causes of adaptation. For another, natural selection eliminates the vast majority of novel genetic variants (because they are deleterious), hence its primary effect is not to cause evolutionary change but to prevent it—i.e., to maintain the status quo.

2. The overwhelming majority of arbitrarily demarcated traits of organisms are not adaptations but mere by-products of adaptations. Bone is white and blood is red, but whiteness and redness are not, in themselves, adaptations. Bone was selected for its structural properties, not its color, and the redness of blood is an incidental by-product of the chemical natures of oxygen and hemoglobin. To propose that a particular anatomical, physiological, or psychological trait is an adaptation is not merely to propose that the trait evolved: it is to propose that the trait per se was *designed* by natural selection to serve some function. Design can be suggested by comparative studies of evolutionary convergences and divergences (Darwin, 1859; Curio, 1973; Mayr, 1983) and demonstrated by "engineering" analyses, wherein design is recognized in the precision, economy, efficiency, constancy, and complexity with which ef-

fects are achieved (Darwin, 1859; Williams, 1966, 1985; Curio, 1973; Dawkins, 1986; Thornhill, 1990).

3. Because it is logically impossible to describe an adaptation, in functional terms, without describing the environmental features to which the adaptation is adapted, specific assumptions about the past are implicit in every description of an adaptation, whether or not that description explicitly mentions adaptation, function, evolution, natural selection, ancestral populations, or past environments. The features of past environments to which the adaptation is adapted may or may not exist in the present.

4. The theory of evolution by natural selection does not imply that every imaginable adaptation can evolve. There are many kinds of constraint on the evolution of adaptations. Natural selection is constrained, for example, by physical laws, by the necessity for all of an organism's adaptations to work together as an integrated whole, and by the phylogenetic history of each lineage. Complex adaptations can arise only via incremental modifications of pre-existing designs, wherein every step is an adaptive improvement. Williams (1992) notes that the neck skeletons of mice, humans, and giraffes are marvels of mechanical engineering, superbly adapted to the divergent ways of life of these species, yet each has seven vertebrae. The only plausible explanation is descent from a common ancestor with seven cervical vertebrae. "That ancestor must have reached a threshold of specialization (e.g., of cervical contributions to the brachial plexus) that would make any mutant individual with six or eight cervical vertebrae functionally defective in serious ways. Any that might have been formed were consistently eliminated by natural selection" (Williams, 1992, 7).

5. Despite these and other kinds of constraints, adaptations regularly manage to exhibit phenomenal complexity and precision. We are often awestruck by natural examples of camouflage and mimicry—the astonishingly detailed resemblance of a stick insect to a stick, for example—probably because in such cases we have a clear standard for recognizing design (i.e., we can visually compare insect and stick). But there is no reason to suppose that the resemblance of a stick insect to a stick, or of a leafy sea dragon to seaweed, represents anything special in the way of good design. Most organs of extreme perfection and complication, in Darwin's words, may fail to elicit spontaneous awe simply because we don't have immediately available in our mind's eye a standard of optimal design to compare them to.

6. Individual and population variation notwithstanding, within a sexually reproducing species *complex* adaptations are of essentially uniform design. That is why it is possible to have textbooks on *human* anatomy and *human* physiology. We manifestly do not need a different textbook for each person, tribe, or population. This within-species uniformity of design is an ineluctable concomitant of sexual processes. Here, in brief, is why (see Tooby and Cosmides, 1990a for the full story).

Every complex adaptation, such as a heart or an eye, comprises many components and subcomponents, which must articulate precisely with one another if the adaptation is to perform its function. Even a relatively small structural perturbation will usually compromise or destroy the functional integrity of a complex adaptation, just as a small random alteration to a component of a car's engine can prevent the engine from running. The ontogenetic development of a complex adaptation requires the combined action of a large number of co-adapted genes, each of which must be present in an individual's genome if the individual is to develop that adaptation. Any mutant allele (alternative form of a gene) that significantly perturbs the ontogeny of a complex adaptation will be eliminated from the species' gene pool by natural selection.

In a sexually reproducing species, genomes are chopped up, shuffled, dealt out, and recombined every generation by sexual processes (meiosis, crossing-over, fertilization, recombination), hence each genome is a unique and evanescent sampling of the species' gene pool. An individual can acquire, by mutation, a unique beneficial allele, but there is no way in which the *entire set* of genes required to construct a complex adaptation could be assembled in the genome of only one individual—or in the genomes of only one subset of individuals—within a sexually reproducing species. Even if, by some miracle of simultaneous mutation, the entire set of genes required to construct a novel complex adaptation did materialize in a single genome, that set could not be passed on to future generations intact, because the genes could not stick together as a discrete group over the course of successive generations. They would be dispersed throughout the species' gene pool by sexual processes, never to be reassembled in a single genome. Therefore, in order for a complex adaptation to exist, all of the genes (Y chromosome excepted) required to construct it must be present in the genomes of all individuals of the species. Hence, all of a species' complex adaptations must be of essentially uniform design.

This conclusion is not invalidated by the fact that species comprise fundamentally different types, or "morphs"—such as caterpillar/butterfly, tadpole/frog, and male/female—which exhibit complex adaptations that are morph-typical rather than species-typical. Morphs within a species differ from one another phenotypically for the same reason that cell types within a body differ from one another, though they contain identical genes: different sets of genes are activated in different morphs. Among humans, there are only two known kinds of morph: sex and age. (Although there are no textbooks on *Swedish* anatomy or *Yanomamo* physiology, there *are* textbooks on *human female* anatomy and on *human fetal* physiology.) The human uterus, for example, is a complex adaptation that is manifested phenotypically only in the female morph, yet the entire set of genes required to construct a uterus exists in the genomes of male as well as female individuals.

None of this is to deny the existence of population-typical (as opposed to species-typical) adaptations to local environmental conditions, but these are likely to be simple adaptations, based on a very small number of genes, that are manifested phenotypically in *quantitative* (body height, amount of melanin, etc.) rather than in *qualitative* population differences. If one human population had been reproductively isolated from all other populations long enough to have evolved a unique, complex, population-specific adaptation, we would observe outbreeding depression (or even infertility) when members of that population interbred with members of other populations, because hybrid offspring would not possess all of the genes required to construct the population-specific adaptation. There is, however, no evidence among humans for outbreeding depression.

7. Adaptations do not spring into being fully formed; they have ontogenies, which require continuous interaction among genes, gene products, and specific features of the internal and external environments that were sufficiently stable over evolutionary time to become incorporated into developmental programs. For example, infant and juvenile rhesus monkeys develop species-typical fighting skills in part by play-fighting with one another (Symons, 1978), and the existence of playmates in the environment is as thoroughly incorporated into rhesus developmental programs as are the nutrients and antibodies in mother's milk. When certain features of the internal or external environments are absent or altered, the normal development of an adaptation may be perturbed. For example, if infant rhesus monkeys are raised experimentally in an impoverished visual environment that lacks edges, they will not develop species-typical edge-detecting cells in their visual cortexes.

8. Even when an adaptation develops normally, it may not function normally in an environment different from that in which it evolved—its *environment of evolutionary adaptedness,* or EEA. The EEA is not a particular time or place, but a set of environmental parameters relevant to the ontogeny and functioning of a given adaptation. For example, the human visual system contains adaptations designed to maintain perceptual color constancies despite almost continuous variation in the frequencies of light reflected from object surfaces. That is why we do not perceive objects to change color every time a cloud obscures the sun or to be different colors at midday than they were in the morning. These color-constancy mechanisms were shaped by natural selection in an environment in which the light source was the sun. When the light source is the artificial spectrum of a sodium vapor lamp the mechanisms do not maintain color constancies (which is why it can be hard to recognize your car in certain parking lots at night).

In sum, to propose that a trait is an adaptation is to propose that it was designed by natural selection in past environments to serve some function. The function of an adaptation is to promote, in some specific way, the survival of the genes that directed its construction. This does not imply that a given adaptation promoted reproduction in every instance in past environments (only that it did so on balance) or ever promotes reproduction in current environments, nor does it imply that the measurement of reproductive differentials in current environments plays a significant role in the adaptationist program (Thornhill, 1990; Tooby and Cosmides, 1990b, 1992; Symons, 1992a).

The Adaptationist Program and Human Psychology

Every coherent theory of human behavior (including the most radical empiricist, environmentalist, and cultural constructionist ones) assumes, at least implicitly, the existence of some sort of structured species-typical psychological machinery. After all, nothing comes from nothing. The only known or suspected scientific account of the origin and maintenance of such machinery is evolution by natural selection. Psychological research that is explicitly informed by the knowledge that human psychological adaptations were shaped over vast periods of time to solve the recurrent information-processing problems that our ancestors faced has come to be called "evolutionary psychology" (Tooby, 1985; Cosmides and Tooby, 1987; Symons, 1987b, 1992a; Daly and Wilson, 1988; Barkow, 1989; Tooby and Cosmides, 1989, 1990b, 1992; Barkow, Cosmides and Tooby, 1992; DeKay and Buss, 1992).

Because our hunter-gatherer ancestors were faced with many different kinds of information-processing problems—finding food, choosing mates, selecting habitats, and so forth—each of which required its own distinctive solution, the human brain must comprise a large number of complex mechanisms specialized for solving diverse problems in different domains. It is no more likely that some sort of general-purpose brain mechanism could have solved all of the information-processing problems that our ancestors faced than it is that some sort of general-purpose organ could have solved all the physiological problems. The psychological mechanisms underpinning food choice, for example, are exceedingly unlikely to be identical to those underpinning mate choice, if only because the criteria that determine "food value" are utterly different from those that determine "mate value." In short, there is no such thing as a general problem solver because there is no such thing as a general problem.

Evolutionary psychology is sometimes thought to be more speculative than other kinds of psychological inquiry because evolutionary psychological hypotheses are grounded in explicit assumptions about past selection pressures and the human EEA, which cannot be observed "directly." But this view of evolutionary psychology is erroneous. As noted above, *every* coherent theory of human behavior necessarily implies the existence of some sort of structured species-typical psychological machinery, hence *every* such theory necessarily implies the prior existence of (a) processes that produced the machinery and (b) environments in which the production occurred. Evolutionary psychology thus is not more *speculative* in these respects, but rather more *explicit*. Its hypotheses are explicitly inspired and guided by evolutionary theory and by hypotheses about the human EEA gleaned from various sources, including the historical, ethnographic, archeological, fossil, and geological records. But an evolutionary psychologist's hypothesis that such-and-such a psychological mechanism exists is subject to exactly the same evidentiary standards and testing procedures that *all* psychological hypotheses are subject to. Every psychological hypothesis—whatever its source of inspiration, and whether or not its assumptions about historical processes and past environments are made explicit—must stand or fall on its own merits, in competition with other psychological hypotheses (see Cosmides and Tooby, 1987; Symons, 1987b; Tooby and Cosmides, 1989, 1992).

Psychological Adaptations Underpinning the Human Male's Experience of Sexual Attraction

Since natural selection is the only known or suspected evolutionary process capable of producing and maintaining complex design, one might suspect that adaptationism has informed research on sexual attraction at least for the last century or so. Surprisingly, however, this has not been the case. Although hypotheses about the determinants of attractiveness have existed for millennia, and in recent years a substantial empirical literature on this topic has accumulated, few investigators have been guided by any theory, and fewer still by evolutionary theory. For example, since antiquity various students of facial attractiveness have searched for general "aesthetic" principles (such as the golden section) that govern aesthetic feeling in every domain, including faces (Alley and Hildebrandt, 1988; Jackson, 1992, 4). To the evolutionary psychologist, however, this search is doomed, because humans have been designed to assess different kinds of objects for different purposes according to different criteria.

In the remainder of this essay I will elaborate the following view of human male sexual attraction. During the course of human evolutionary history one of the adaptive problems that our male ancestors regularly and predictably faced was mate choice. Sexual attraction may not have been the only basis of mate choice (Barkow, 1989), but certainly it was an important one (Symons, 1979; Buss, 1989, 1994; Townsend, 1989, 1993; Townsend and Levy, 1990a, 1990b; Jackson, 1992, 5; Wiederman and Allgeier, 1992; Wiederman, 1993). Potential mates necessarily varied in *mate value*—i.e., in the degree to which each would promote the reproductive success of the males who mated with them—just as potential food varied in food value and potential habitats varied in habitat value. Female mate value was determined by a number of variables, and information about some of them was reliably available in specific observable characteristics of female bodies. Selection thus produced psychological mechanisms of sexual attraction specialized to extract and to process this information: male sexual attraction was designed to vary in intensity directly with perceived cues of female mate value.

In the human EEA the following probably were the most important determinants of female mate value: (1) The closely related variables of age, hormonal status, parity, and fecundity. Obviously, these could not have been *directly* observed by ancestral males, since it is impossible to directly observe things like age, estrogen levels, ovulation, a gestating embryo, a woman's reproductive history, or a woman's reproductive future. What ancestral males could have observed are specific characteristics of female bodies that were reliable cues or indices of these variables. I will argue that selection favored males equipped with psychological mechanisms that perceived cues of *nubility* as maximally sexually attractive (other things equal). A nubile female is one who is just beginning ovulatory menstrual cycles and who has not yet become pregnant. (2) The closely related variables of health and design quality. Good health comprises a number of attributes, including relative freedom from parasites and infectious diseases, resistance to such diseases, and freedom from physiological anomalies and pathologies. Good design overlaps with good health insofar as cues of health are also cues of design quality, but it consists of other things as well, such as bilateral symmetry and masticatory efficiency. On average, a healthy and well-designed female would have had higher mate value *whether or not* variation in health and design quality resulted from genetic variation (i.e., whether or not any given aspect of health or design quality was heritable). Males thus would have been selected to be sexually attracted by cues of good health, good design, and developmental stability.

In this essay I will focus on the determinants of female sexual attractiveness, not on actual matings, because the former more clearly illuminate the design of the psychological machinery underpinning male sexual attraction. Who men actually mate with depends on many things (such as opportunity and risk) in addition to sexual attraction. Few fifty-year-old American men will ever mate, short-term or long-term, with a twenty-year-old woman, but as Townsend (1992) points out, *Playboy* magazine does not need to publish a special edition for older men featuring photographs of older women.

Age, Hormonal Status, Parity, and Fecundity

That adult human female sexual attractiveness declines systematically with observable cues of increasing age is a theme that runs through the ethnographic and historical records, folk tales, great literature, less-than-great literature, movies, plays, soap operas, jokes, and everyday experience. It accounts for a large portion of the billions of dollars spent annually throughout the world on makeup, cosmetic surgery, diets, and exercise. It is so deeply ingrained in the human condition that ethnographers—with rare exceptions, such as Jankowiak (1993)—take it for granted, and merely allude to it in passing in the course of making some other point (see Symons, 1979, for examples). Social scientists have documented the existence of this phenomenon (Alley, 1988; Jackson, 1992, 65–66), and yet, to my knowledge, there has never been a single study—adaptationist or otherwise—that has attempted to systematically map the relationships between observable age cues and female sexual attractiveness.

These relationships are not expected to be identical in every species but rather to vary systematically with species-typical mating patterns. In humans, these relationships are significantly affected by the fact that females conceal, rather than advertise, ovulation (see Pavelka, this volume). In *The Evolution of Human Sexuality* (Symons, 1979) I argued that if selection had designed human male psychological mechanisms of sexual attraction to evaluate females primarily as potential wives, males would be most strongly sexually attracted by observable characteristics of female bodies that reliably indexed nubility during the course of human evolutionary history. Studies of living natural-fertility preliterate peoples provide information about the age at which females became nubile in the human EEA. The best available long-term demographic data on a preliterate people living in undisturbed aboriginal conditions come from various studies of the Yanomamo of southern Venezuela and northern Brazil (Neel and Weiss, 1975; Melancon, 1982; Early and Peters, 1990; Chagnon, 1992). Among Yanomamo females, menarche occurs at an average age of 12.4 years, cohabitation begins sometime within the next two years, first live births occur at an average age of 16.8 years (hence first conceptions typically occur at about 16 years of age), peak fertility occurs between 20 and 24 years of age, and last births occur at an average age of 39.9 years (Early and Peters, 1990). Undoubtedly there was both intra- and inter-population variation in the ages of menarche, nubility, and menopause in ancestral populations, just as there is in current populations; in the EEA nubility probably occurred between 15 and 18 years of age.

Here, in brief, is my adaptationist argument, slightly beefed up over the years (see Symons, 1979, 1987a, 1989, 1992b). The data on living natural-fertility preliterate peoples strongly implies that for tens of thousands of years, at least, women almost always were married by the time they were nubile, the biological father of a woman's child was very likely to be her husband, and women typically began their reproductive careers at nubility, could rear no more than one child every three or four years, and nursed each child intensively for a period of years.

An ancestral male who married a nubile (or somewhat younger) female would have had maximum opportunity to sire her offspring during her most fecund years and, more important, would not have had to invest in children that had been sired by other men or to incur the various costs involved in ongoing conflict with the mother over how she allocates her parental effort among his and other men's children. Also, a nubile woman, compared to a woman even a few years older, would not have been investing her time and energy in other men's children, would have had more living relatives to invest in her and her children (Chagnon, 1988), and would have been more likely to survive until a newly conceived child was old enough to survive on its own.

On the other hand, I argued, if selection had designed male psychological mechanisms of sexual attraction primarily to evaluate females as potential short-term sexual partners, males would be most strongly sexually attracted by observable features of female bodies that, in the EEA, reliably indexed maximum fecundity. A maximally fecund woman—i.e., a woman who is most likely to ovulate if she is cycling, to conceive if she is inseminated, to bear a healthy infant if she is impregnated, and to survive childbirth—would have been in her early twenties. Since the empirical evidence seemed to me to indicate unambiguously that human males are, in fact, more strongly sexually attracted by features of female bodies that, in the EEA, indexed nubility than by features that indexed maximum fecundity, I concluded that the male psychological machinery of sexual attraction was designed more as a wife detector than as a short-term mate detector.

Recently, however, Margie Profet (personal communication) has noted a flaw in this reasoning. She points out that in ancestral populations women spent almost all of their reproductive years pregnant or lactating. Among the Yanomamo, for example, the average female reproductive period, from first conception to weaning the last child, is 26 years, from 16 to 42 years of age, including 6 years of pregnancy and 18 years of lactation (Early and Peters, 1990). The average Yanomamo woman thus is pregnant or nursing for 24 of those 26 years, or 92 percent of her reproductive life. Since round-the-clock nursing on demand effectively suppresses ovulation, ancestral parous women would have ovulated very infrequently. Consider the following ballpark calculation. Between ages 17 (first birth) and 39 (last conception), the average Yanomamo woman is nonpregnant and nonlactating for 2 years, during which she ovulates 26 times, if every cycle is ovulatory. Assuming 3 days of fecundity per cycle, she is capable of conceiving on 78 of 8,030 days between ages 17 and 39, or 1 percent of the time. (Some ovulatory cycles are likely to occur late in each lactation period, when the nursing child is beginning to suckle less intensively, but, on the other hand, not every cycle during the nonpregnant/ nonlactating phases will actually be ovulatory; hence this ballpark estimate of 1 percent seems reasonable.) In short, only about one in a hundred random copulations with the average parous Yanomamo woman can even *potentially* result in conception.

Thus, in the human EEA a nubile nullipara would have been more fecund, on average, than a parous woman in her early twenties in the sense that the nullipara would have been more likely to be cycling—and, hence, ovulating— at any given time (and human females do not advertise ovulation via estrus). *In this sense,* nubility cues *were* fecundity cues in the human EEA. Profet therefore concludes that selection would have favored maximum sexual attraction to nubility cues for *either* long- *or* short-term matings.

Phenotypic features such as skin texture, muscle tone, stretch marks, breast shape, and facial configuration that reliably indexed female age and parity in the EEA can be expected to be important determinants of female sexual attractiveness. Because female mate value declines throughout adulthood, sexual attractiveness can be expected to decline in tandem (Williams, 1975; Symons, 1979). I predict that wherever women manipulate age and parity cues in order to enhance their sexual attractiveness, they will attempt to mimic or enhance nubility cues (e.g., through makeup, clothing, cosmetic surgery, diets, and exercise).

The hypothesis that human males are most strongly sexually attracted by nubility cues is subject to many independent tests, because it implies that every typical pregnancy- and lactation-induced change in women's bodies that could have been reliably detected by ancestral males should tend to reduce female sexual attractiveness (other things equal). Two of the best documented determinants of female sexual attractiveness—low waist-to-hip ratio and lighter-than-average skin color—appear to conform to this prediction.

Waist-to-Hip Ratio

Among human females waist-to-hip ratio (WHR) is a reliable index of age, hormonal status, parity, fecundity, and health. As outlined by Singh (1993a, 1993b, 1994, n.d.), before puberty girls and boys have similar WHRs, but at puberty a girl's WHR decreases, because her pelvis widens and she deposits fat primarily on her hips and thighs. This is "reproductive fat," utilized almost exclusively during late pregnancy and lactation when fetal growth and milk production require large amounts of energy. Free (unbound, biologically active) estrogen lowers WHR, free testosterone increases it, resulting in a bimodal distribution of WHRs with little overlap between the sexes: healthy premenopausal women typically have WHRs between .67 and .80, healthy men between .80 and .95 (Singh, n.d.). Among premenopausal women WHR and free testosterone levels are highly positively correlated, independent of body weight (Singh, n.d.).

An increase in WHR can be an early sign of pregnancy. Clapp et al. (1988) found that body fat increased linearly during the first fifteen weeks of pregnancy and that "Abdominal and suprailiac skinfold thicknesses increased much faster than the other four folds measured. The two former measures represented only 30% of the total before conception, but accounted for 65% of the increase observed at 15 weeks. Thus, fat deposition in early pregnancy was site specific, being localized primarily to the pelvic girdle region" (p. 1458).

WHR obviously increases dramatically and transiently later in pregnancy, but some of this increase is permanent, so that WHR tends to increase with each successive pregnancy (Singh, n.d.). In the absence of pregnancies, WHR still increases with age, but much more slowly, so that a 22-year-old nullipara has essentially the same WHR that she had at 17 (Singh, n.d.). During menopause, female WHR rises almost to that of the male. Thus, in the human EEA average female WHR was lowest at nubility and rose thereafter with increasing age and successive pregnancies.

Singh (1993a, 1993b, n.d.) reviews the substantial body of evidence that female WHR is an accurate index of reproductive endocrinological status and fecundity. Women with lower WHRs become pregnant more easily than do women with higher WHRs. In a recent study of 500 women, aged 20 to 42, presenting for artificial donor insemination, Zaadstra et al. (1993) found that WHR was strongly negatively associated with the probability of conception per insemination cycle, both before and after controlling for age, fatness, reasons for artificial insemination, cycle length, cycle regularity, smoking, and parity. Zaadstra et al. also found that increasing age was significantly related to lower fecundity, and that very lean and obese women were less likely to conceive.

WHR also indexes certain aspects of health. For example, a bloated abdomen—and consequent high WHR—often is a sign of parasite infection. Singh (1993a, 1993b, n.d.) reviews the large number of studies demonstrating that a high female WHR is a better predictor of menstrual irregularity, hirsutism (heavy, abnormal hair distribution), elevated plasma triglycerides, diabetes, hypertension, heart attack, stroke, gallbladder disease, and cancer (endometrial, ovarian, and breast) than is total body fat or other anthropometric measures. Although not all of these diseases occurred with sufficient frequency in the human EEA to have exerted a selection pressure on male sexual psychology, some probably did. Folsom et al. (1993) report that mortality rates among older women were elevated in both the leanest and the most obese women, and that WHR was strongly and positively associated with mortality in a dose-response manner. "In summary, WHR, independent of overall body fat and weight, is a powerful predictor of endocrinological aberration [and] risk for various diseases . . ." (Singh n.d.).

Because WHR reliably indexes many aspects of female mate value, males can be expected to have evolved psychological mechanisms specialized to extract and to process information about WHR: other things equal, female sexual attractiveness can be expected to vary inversely with WHR. Singh (1993a, 1993b, 1994, n.d.) found that subjects of both sexes, and of various ages, socioeconomic statuses, ethnicities, and occupations rated female figures (line drawings) with the lowest WHRs (.6 or .7, depending on the study) as most attractive. Singh notes that although *Playboy* centerfold models and Miss America winners have tended to become slimmer over last thirty to sixty years, WHRs have remained essentially constant, in the .68 to .72 range. He proposes that a male sexual preference for a low female WHR will be found to be universal, and that wherever women attempt to enhance their sexual attractiveness through manipulation of WHR the manipulation will decrease apparent WHR (e.g., through such devices as wide belts, corsets, girdles, and bustles). Since high levels of free estrogen decrease female WHR, Profet (personal communication) hypothesizes that women may have slightly lower WHRs and be perceived as slightly more sexually attractive near ovulation than at menses.

Skin Color

In the human EEA female skin color (on the lightness-darkness dimension) may have indexed age, hormonal status, parity, fecundity, and health. Humans are born with light skin, compared to their parents, and darken during childhood. At puberty, however, both sexes lighten, but girls lighten more, becoming significantly lighter than boys (see Frost, 1988, 1989, 1990). Female skin is lightest at nubility. (Female skin color also fluctuates slightly with the menstrual cycle, being lightest near ovulation [van den Berghe and Frost, 1986].)

During pregnancy up to 90 percent of women experience hyperpigmentation, a mild, generalized darkening of the skin that is accentuated in normally hyperpigmented regions such as freckles, the areolae of the breasts, perineal skin, genitals, anal region, armpits, linea alba (which becomes the linea nigra), and inner thighs (McKenzie, 1971; Winton, 1981, 1982; Wong and Ellis, 1984). Hyperpigmentation begins early in pregnancy, progresses throughout gestation, and usually decreases, but does not disappear completely, after parturition. The regions that are normally hyperpigmented remain darkened. In addition, 50 percent to 75 percent of pregnant women experience melasma (sometimes called "the mask of pregnancy"), a bilateral, blotchy, irregular hyperpigmentation of the face, usually beginning in the second half of pregnancy (McKenzie, 1971; Hellreich, 1974; Wade et al., 1978; Winton, 1981, 1982; Wong and Ellis, 1984; Sodhi and Sausker, 1988). Melasma usually disappears within a year of delivery, but one study showed persistence in 30 percent of the cases after ten years (Wong and Ellis, 1984). In nonpregnant women, melasma can be caused by mild ovarian dysfunction (Perez et al., 1983) and by thyroid disorders (Lutfi et al., 1985), hence light skin may also be a cue of endocrinological health and fecundity. I have not been able to find data on hair-color changes with pregnancy, but there is substantial anecdotal evidence that hair too often darkens permanently after full-term pregnancies. In the human EEA, a healthy post-pubescent female's skin (and probably hair) color thus would have been lightest when her WHR was lowest: at nubility.

In the human EEA, skin (and hair) color within local populations may typically have been sufficiently homogeneous that lightness was a reliable cue of nubility and endocrinological health. In their survey of the ethnographic record, van den Berghe and Frost (1986) found that wherever there was reliable information, men were reported to prefer women with relatively light skin. This preference almost certainly is worthless as a fecundity detector in a modern industrialized society comprising many racial groups that vary markedly in skin color (see below). A species-typical male preference for hair that is lighter than the local post-pubescent female average may account for the attractiveness of blonds in most modern Western societies (Alley and Hildebrandt, 1988).

Other Pregnancy-Induced Phenotypic Changes

During pregnancy maternal bone formation rates are elevated, which may cause permanent facial lengthening (Behrents, 1990). Furthermore, a growth hormone (hGH-V) is expressed in the placenta and secreted into the maternal bloodstream in large amounts, which may cause a "coarsening" of facial features (Baumann et al., 1991). Women who gestate male fetuses may undergo additional facial remodeling owing to the testosterone that is produced in the fetal testes and secreted into the maternal bloodstream (Profet, personal communication). Many women also experience an increase in the lengths of their hands and feet during pregnancy.

In addition to hyperpigmentation and melasma, a variety of dermatoses regularly occur during pregnancy (see McKenzie, 1971; Hellreich, 1974; Wade et al., 1978; Winton, 1981, 1982; Wong and Ellis, 1984; Sodhi and Sausker, 1988), including the following: (1) Vascular spiders—small, flat, or slightly raised, faintly pulsating, dilated capillaries and arterioles—which appear in 67 percent of whites and 11 percent of blacks during the second to fifth months of gestation, most commonly in the face (especially around the eyes), neck, throat, and arms. About 75 percent spontaneously fade by the seventh week after parturition, but they rarely disappear completely. (Vascular spiders can also be caused by liver disease.) (2) Varicosities, which often appear in the third month of pregnancy, most commonly in the legs. They tend to regress after parturition but often not completely. (3) Stretch marks, which develop in about 90 percent of pregnant women during the sixth and seventh months of gestation, primarily on the abdomen, breasts, upper arms, lower back, buttocks, thighs, and groin. They gradually fade after parturition but do not disappear completely. (Stretch marks also occur in Cushing's syndrome.) (4) Hirsutism, sometimes accompanied by acne, which generally starts early in pregnancy and is most pronounced on the face, but the arms, legs, and back may also be involved. Most of the excess fine hair disappears within six months after parturition, but coarse and bristly hair remains. (5) Edema of the eyelids (resulting from increased capillary permeability), which occurs in about 50 percent of pregnant women, and may also involve the face, hands, and feet. (6) Small skin-growths (molluscum fibrosum), especially involving the sides of the face, neck, axillae, feet, and upper trunk, which arise in the second half of pregnancy, and often disappear after parturition. (7) Marginal gingivitis, which occurs in about 80 percent of pregnant women between the second and fourth months. The gingival margins become dark red and swollen. These gum changes persist through pregnancy, and may not recede until one or two months after parturition. I predict that all such pregnancy-induced phenotypic changes systematically reduce female sexual attractiveness, both during and after pregnancy.

Implications about Past Selection Pressures and the EEA

In the human EEA a twenty-five-year-old nullipara almost certainly would have been sterile, or, at least, highly subfertile. Thus, the apparent tendency of pregnancy- and lactation-induced changes in women's bodies to systematically reduce sexual attractiveness implies that female sterility not associated with some externally visible cue (such as a high WHR) was not sufficiently common during the course of human evolutionary history to have constituted a significant selection pressure on male sexual psychology. If female sterility not associated with an externally visible cue had been common, selection would have favored males who perceived twenty-five-year-old parous women as *more* sexually attractive than twenty-five-year-old nulliparas. Current human populations with extremely high rates of female sterility caused by sexually transmitted diseases (see Bailey and Aunger, this volume) therefore are probably evolutionary novelties. Among the Yanomamo, female sterility is extremely rare (Neel and Weiss [1975] and Melancon [1982] each report a single case), and 94 percent of Yanomamo women have given birth to at least one child by the time they are twenty years old (Melancon, 1982).

The human male's sexual preference for observable characteristics of female bodies that reliably indexed nubility in the EEA is the product of a specific selective history, not of a mysterious physical or biological law that applies to animal species in general. Dominant male rhesus monkeys, for example, who often have the opportunity to choose among several estrous females, are more likely to mate with an older, parous female than with a three-year-old nullipara who is in estrus for the first time. The adaptationist explanation is clear: rhesus females advertise rather than conceal ovulation (i.e., they have estrous periods); rhesus consortships are short-term rather than long-term, so a consorting male is not acquiring future reproductive interests; a rhesus male who mates with an older female does not have to invest in her extant offspring; and an older rhesus female is far more likely than a three-year-old to conceive, to carry an infant to term, and to bear a healthy infant that survives its first year.

The ethnographic and historical records of human sexual and marital practices indicate that nowhere have human mating patterns remotely resembled those of rhesus monkeys or chimpanzees (Brown, 1991). Nevertheless, one might ask: isn't the assumption that ancestral human mating patterns resembled those of known humans, rather than those of rhesus monkeys or chimpanzees, still just untestable speculation about an inherently unobservable past? Without the invention of a time machine, can we actually acquire direct evidence about ancestral human mating patterns? The answer is yes, we càn: those patterns are instantiated in the designs of human adaptations. As Randy Thornhill (personal communication) puts it, the adaptations constitute a kind of reverse time machine, transporting the past to us. They are windows through which we can observe adaptively significant features of ancestral environments.

If human male sexual psychology was, like rhesus or chimpanzee male psychology, adapted to an environment in which ovulation was advertised during estrous periods and matings consisted of brief consortships, human males would perceive physical characteristics typical of a female in her early to mid-twenties in the EEA—including a higher WHR (than that of a nubile female), less smooth skin, coarser facial features, stretch marks, more pendulous breasts, and darker nipples—as more sexually attractive than nubility cues. If human male psychology was adapted to an environment in which ovulation was advertised *and* there were long-term mateships, the above physical characteristics would be perceived as most attractive for short-term estrous matings, nubility cues for long-term matings.

Health and Design Quality

Skin Condition

Many aspects of female health and fecundity are indexed by skin condition. Skin lesions can be caused by autoimmune disorders, benign or malignant tumors, and fungal, viral, bacterial, and parasite infections. Skin eruptions can be caused by sweating disorders, which may be of endocrine origin, and by allergies. Skin growths can be malignant or especially prone to malignancy. And acne and hirsutism in women of reproductive age are highly predictive of ovulatory dysfunction. In a prospective study of 139 reproductive-age women presenting with a complaint of acne, Steinberger et al. (1981) found that 90 percent had plasma testosterone levels above the normal mean, and 57 percent had some degree of ovulatory dysfunction. Testosterone levels were directly related to the severity of menstrual cycle disturbance, the highest levels occurring in patients with amenorrhea. In 97 percent of the patients masculine-type hair growth was observed on the face, chest, abdomen, sacrum, perianal area, or upper inner thighs. In a subsequent study, the same relationship between acne/hirsutism and testosterone levels was found in an unselected population of women presenting with a variety of dermatologic complaints (Held et al., 1984). The highest mean serum testosterone level was observed in the group of patients with both acne and hirsutism. The authors conclude: "Since hyperandrogenism is associated with ovarian dysfunction . . . the presence of acne should alert the physician to the possibility of a disorder with systemic and reproductive consequences" (Held et al., 1984, 225).

As skin condition appears to reliably index several aspects of female mate value, human males, universally, can be expected to be most strongly sexually attracted by female skin that is free of lesions, eruptions, warts, moles, cysts, tumors, acne, and hirsutism. Also, wherever women modify their skin to increase their sexual attractiveness they can be expected to enhance or mimic indices of health and fecundity and to eliminate or conceal indices of disease and hyperandrogenism. I would expect such embellishments as tattoos and scarification (which may signify group membership or status) to either be neutral with respect to these goals or actually to promote them (for example, by concealing or obscuring lesions).

Composite Faces

The relationship between design quality (as distinct from health) and attractiveness has been studied most extensively in the face. More than a century ago, Francis Galton (1883) developed a technique for making a "composite portrait" by superimposing photographic negatives of many individual faces on a single photographic plate; the resulting print in essence averaged the information in the constituent faces. To his surprise, Galton discovered that the composites were more attractive than their constituents. I hypothesized (Symons, 1979) that humans evolved psychological mechanisms of attractiveness perception that operate in a manner analogous to composite portraiture: the mechanisms (unconsciously) average—presumably with appropriate age-corrections—the faces each individual observes, and thereby generate a male and a female template of facial attractiveness. Deviations from a template, in this view, reduce attractiveness.

My adaptationist rationale for this hypothesis was that for any given phenotypic feature the local population's central tendency often approximates the naturally selected optimal design, hence selection is expected to have favored the ability to detect and prefer the central tendency. In this way, radically different local phenotypic optima, in our highly polytypic species, could be detected by the same species-typical psychological mechanisms. Thornhill and Gangestad (1993) propose that selection favored a preference for average features because such features index a high level of heterozygosity, which is positively correlated with pathogen resistance.

The hypothesis that local male and female composites are templates of facial attractiveness was tested by Langlois and Roggman (1990), who used a computer program to digitize and mathematically average photographs of faces, thus generating much more sophisticated male and female composites than Galton did. Adults then rated the attractiveness of the individual component faces and the computer-generated composites. The composites were rated as

more attractive than almost any component face, and the more faces that contributed to a composite (up to thirty-two), the more attractive it became.

Langlois and Roggman's methodology obviously could not elucidate every
determinant of facial attractiveness. For one thing, the effects of age were not
assessed (all photographs were of university students). For another thing, the
effects of health, as evidenced in skin texture, were not assessed, because
blemishes and other skin irregularities were eliminated in the computer processing (for both the individual photographs and the composites). Benson and
Perrett (1992) demonstrated that smooth skin texture does indeed contribute
significantly to perceived attractiveness: when photographs of individual faces
were given, via computer processing, the same smooth unblemished skin that
composites inevitably possess, their attractiveness was enhanced significantly.

One finding of Langlois and Roggman, which they themselves did not pursue, is that a few individual faces in their sample were rated as more attractive
than any composite. Initially, I guessed that the university women whose faces
constituted Langlois and Roggman's female composite might simply have been
too old, and that a composite of 16- to 17-year-olds might turn out to be the
most attractive female face. But more recent research indicates that this guess
almost certainly was wrong, and that approximating the composite is not the
whole story; that is, composite faces are attractive, but the most attractive faces
are not composites (Alley and Cunningham, 1991).

Johnston and Franklin (1993) developed a computer program that allows a
user to "evolve" on a computer screen—by a process of random variation and
selective retention—his or her ideal face (within the limits set by the system's
somewhat cartoon-like representations of faces). Twenty male and twenty female subjects used this program to evolve their ideal beautiful female face.
Johnston and Franklin then computer-generated a composite of these forty
faces (the "beautiful composite") as well as a composite of the faces of their
female subjects (the "subject composite"), whose average age was twenty. In
most dimensions the beautiful composite and the subject composite did not
differ significantly, but the beautiful composite had a significantly shorter
lower face (the nasion to chin proportion was typical of an 11- or 12-year-old
girl), fuller lips in the vertical dimension (female lip fullness peaks at age 14
in Western populations [Farkas, 1981]), and a smaller mouth. However, the
beautiful composite definitely appears to be a sexually mature woman, not a
barely pubescent girl.

Johnston and Franklin then asked independent judges to rate the attractiveness of each of the forty beautiful faces and the subject composite. On
average, the beautiful faces were judged to be about as attractive as the composite, which supports previous findings that composites are indeed attractive.
But when Johnston and Franklin altered the highest-rated beautiful face to give
it the same vertical proportions as the subject composite (i.e., the lower face

was lengthened), the altered version was judged to be significantly less attractive.

Perrett, May and Yoshikawa (1994) obtained very similar results using computer-generated composites of (Caucasian) female faces. They found that a composite of the fifteen most attractive faces in a sample of sixty United Kingdom females (aged 20–30) was rated as more attractive than a composite of the entire sample. Furthermore, the attractive composite became even more attractive when the computer exaggerated the differences between it and the sample composite by .5. (However, *all* of the composites, even that comprising the fifteen *least* attractive faces, were rated as more attractive than most of the individual faces [Perrett, personal communication].) Japanese and English subjects rated the composites in exactly the same way (Perrett, personal communication).

The composite of the fifteen highest-rated faces, compared with the sample composite, was found to have higher cheekbones, larger eyes relative to face size (but not in absolute dimensions), a thinner jaw, and shorter distances between nose and mouth and between mouth and chin. When the same experiment was conducted in Japan, using female Japanese faces and Japanese raters, the same results—except for cheekbones—were obtained, and the results were replicated using United Kingdom raters. The findings of Perrett, May and Yoshikawa (1994) are quite similar to those of Cunningham (1986).

All of the research cited above found that a relatively short lower face and gracile jaw are perceived as attractive. During adulthood there is a generalized vertical elongation of female facial structures (Behrents, 1990). Furthermore, high levels of serum testosterone appear to promote bone growth in the lower face, as evidenced by pubertal males, who, on average, develop significantly longer lower faces and more robust jaws than females do (Merow and Broadbent, 1990). It is also possible that the placenta-expressed growth hormone (hGH-V), which is secreted into the pregnant woman's bloodstream in large amounts during the last half of pregnancy, promotes growth in the lower face. Thus, among post-pubescent females, a relatively short lower face, gracile jaw, and full lips may index youth, a relatively low testosterone/estrogen ratio (Johnston and Franklin, 1993) and nullipara status—at least within populations that are relatively homogeneous phenotypically.

Many women use cosmetics to make their eyes look larger. This may enhance attractiveness by making the lower face look smaller by comparison (just as shoulder pads make a woman's waist look smaller). If this hypothesis is correct, women with the shortest lower faces and most gracile jaws should benefit least from using eye makeup in this way.

Most recent studies have found that "high" or "prominent" female cheekbones are perceived as attractive (Cunningham, 1986; Perrett, May and Yoshikawa, 1994; Grammer and Thornhill, in press). Indeed, "high cheekbones are a classic feature of femininity, much emphasized by beauty analysts" (Enlow, 1990:8). Enlow notes that the entire nasal region and lower forehead (supra-orbital ridge/glabella) is more protuberant in men than in women, which he attributes to men's larger body size, greater aerobic capacity, and consequent larger airway, beginning with the nose and nasopharynx. According to Enlow, because women, on average, have less protrusive noses and lower foreheads than men do, women's cheekbones typically *look* more prominent than men's, even though they are neither larger nor higher (in fact, the zygomatic promi-nences [cheekbones] are significantly larger, on average, in males [Merow and Broadbent, 1990]). A relatively gracile jaw also seems to me to contribute to the impression that a woman has high cheekbones. According to Nakdimen (1984), the phenomenon of "high cheekbones" has a different origin in men than it does in women: "High cheekbones in men are a rather severe, bony feature, owing to the relative prominence of the zygomatic bone itself and the contrasting relative leanness of the area from the bone to the nasolabial fold. In women, the proportion of the hard and soft tissue components of the contour known as high cheekbones is reversed. The zygomatic bone itself is propor-tionately smaller, while the soft tissue overlying the bone and extending to the nasolabial fold is relatively ample" (p. 501).

I propose that women who are perceived as having high cheekbones in fact have comparatively less protrusive supraorbital ridge/glabellas and compara-tively gracile jaws. High cheekbones in women may be yet another index of a low testosterone/estrogen ratio and youth. If this hypothesis is correct, one might predict that the most attractive women will, on average, have relatively gracile versions of every sexually dimorphic feature of the skull, whether or not the feature actually contributes to the perception of attractiveness. For ex-ample, adult males have significantly larger mastoid processes than females do (Merow and Broadbent, 1990), hence the most attractive female faces may have smaller mastoids, on average, than the least attractive faces do. (In human females, mastoid size does correlate positively, though modestly, with supraor-bital ridge/glabella size and with mental eminence [the bony projection on the chin] size [Walker, personal communication].)

Several features of female bodies—such as WHR, skin color, presence or absence of acne and hirsutism, length of the lower face, and presence or ab-sence of high cheekbones—may make independent, additive contributions to sexual attractiveness, if each is detected by a different psychological mecha-nism, and yet covary significantly, if each indexes the same or similar endocri-nological states. If so, this may help to explain why women of the same age, lacking obvious deformities or diseases, can vary so much in sexual attrac-tiveness.

I now propose the following modification of my hypothesis (Symons, 1979) concerning the attractiveness of composites: in any given human population the composite of the faces of each age/sex class constitutes a template of attractiveness for that class, *unless* another psychological mechanism instantiates the rule, "prefer such-and-such a deviation from the composite." In other words, the composite constitutes a sort of "attractiveness default" position. Even when some other mechanism is operating, the composite-generating mechanism nonetheless serves as a reference or anchor point. When no additional mechanism is operating, deviations from the composite diminish sexual attractiveness. This almost certainly includes deviations from perfect bilateral symmetry (if a composite comprises a sufficient number of faces, it will be perfectly bilaterally symmetrical).

Fluctuating Asymmetry

The externally visible human body has been designed by selection to be bilaterally symmetrical. "Fluctuating asymmetry"—which refers to small random deviations from perfect bilateral symmetry—has been studied in many animal species because it indexes (a) the capacity to resist genetic and environmental stresses that can perturb development (Palmer and Strobeck, 1986; Parsons, 1992) and (b) degree of heterozygosity, which is associated with enhanced pathogen resistance (Thornhill and Gangestad, 1993). In many animal species fluctuating asymmetry has been found to correlate positively with parasite load and negatively with growth rate, survival, success in intrasexual competition, mating success, and fecundity (Møller, 1992b, 1992c; Thornhill, 1992b, 1992c). In humans, fluctuating asymmetry in various bilateral morphological structures has been found to correlate positively with morbidity and developmental anomalies and negatively with heterozygosity (Livshits and Kobyliansky, 1991). Mate preferences for low fluctuating asymmetry and for characteristics correlated with low fluctuating asymmetry have been demonstrated in a number of insect and bird species (Møller, 1992a, 1993; Thornhill, 1992a).

Obvious deviations from bilateral symmetry, like all obvious developmental anomalies, unquestionably reduce human female sexual attractiveness, but the effects of relatively small amounts of fluctuating asymmetry are only beginning to be studied. The evolutionary psychological prediction is clear: There will be no such thing as having too little fluctuating asymmetry because in the EEA there was no such thing as being too well designed, too developmentally stable, or too healthy. Furthermore, since fluctuating asymmetry tends to increase with age (Alley, 1988), low fluctuating asymmetry also may index youth. In an experiment by Grammer and Thornhill (in press), in which male subjects rated the attractiveness of computer-generated images of women's faces, fluctuating asymmetry and attractiveness were found to be negatively correlated (also see Thornhill and Gangestad, 1993; Gangestad, Thornhill and Yeo, 1994).

Because fluctuating asymmetry in breast size is large compared with other morphological characteristics (Møller and Soler, n.d.) and relatively easy to assess visually, it may play an especially important role in sexual attraction. (Extreme asymmetry in breast size is associated with lactation failure due to insufficient glandular development in *both* breasts [Neifert, Seacat, and Jobe, 1985].) Where breasts are normally left uncovered, men apparently do not "eroticize" them (i.e., the sight of breasts is not in itself sexually arousing), but this does not mean that breasts are irrelevant to sexual *attractiveness*. After all, faces are not usually eroticized, and yet facial structure is an important determinant of female sexual attractiveness. Discussions of breast attractiveness, at least in the United States, tend to focus on the question of size (see Jackson, 1992, 158), but absolute size probably is of secondary importance. I predict that the most important determinants of breast sexual attractiveness are: (a) presence rather than absence (indicating a pubescent or post-pubescent female); (b) firm rather than pendulous (indicating a young nullipara); and (c) low fluctuating asymmetry in size and shape (indicating health and design quality).

Masticatory Efficiency

Another aspect of design quality is masticatory efficiency. Carello et al. (1989:246–47) write that "craniofacial morphology is modeled under a field of forces that operate on hard and soft tissue. . . . Normal growth is promoted by the mechanical forces of mastication, the hydrodynamic forces of breathing and swallowing, and the visco-elastic forces of changing muscular tonus and contractile state in chewing, speaking, or expressing emotions. The joint action of these growth directing forces, however, can be upset by deforming forces originating from malocclusions or from growth anomalies. Impeding or misdirecting forces warp the field . . . making it functionally less effective. . . . When the face is functioning (chewing, breathing, etc.) as it was designed to, that should be apparent in the morphological consequences of the design." Carello et al. asked subjects to rate the attractiveness of line drawings (made from photographs) of women's faces seen in profile. The experimenters also determined how closely each face approximated the orthodontic ideal of masticatory efficiency, using X rays of hard tissue. They found that "The closer a face is to its functional/structural ideal, the more attractive it is" (p. 247). The experimenters did not attempt to determine what cues the subjects used to assess attractiveness. It would be interesting to determine whether the attractiveness of faces seen in profile (where symmetry cues are absent) correlates negatively with fluctuating asymmetry. (I'm betting that it does.)

Conclusions, Evolutionarily Novel Environments, and Research Implications

To suppose that the determinants of male sexual attraction are arbitrary, capricious, whimsical, or nonutilitarian is to libel the evolutionary process that produced stick insects and retinal neurons capable of responding to a single photon. The central theme of this essay is that these determinants are thoroughly utilitarian and, for the most part, easily identified by adaptationist analysis. During the course of human evolutionary history one of the adaptive problems that our male ancestors regularly faced was mate choice. Female mate value was determined by a number of variables—including age, hormonal status, parity, fecundity, health, design quality, and developmental stability—and information about these variables was reliably available in specific characteristics of female bodies. Natural selection thus produced a number of psychological mechanisms specialized to extract and process this information. The intensity of male sexual attraction was designed to vary directly with indices of female mate value. For example, if the relationship between female skin texture and the intensity of male sexual attraction were arbitrary, in some human communities men would perceive wrinkles as sexually attractive, in others as unattractive, and in most as having no systematic effect whatever on attractiveness. In such circumstances, any genetic mutation that promoted the development of an innate preference for unwrinkled female skin would tend to increase the fitnesses of its bearers and would spread through the population's gene pool in the course of successive generations. The view of sexual attraction sketched in this essay is fundamentally incompatible with every theory in which the determinants of male sexual attraction are assumed to be arbitrary or capricious, including the following.

An adaptationist analysis of male sexual attraction is incompatible with the "standard social science model" of human psychology, in which human behavior is assumed to be the product of a few general-purpose psychological mechanisms (see Tooby and Cosmides, 1992). Most anthropologists, for example, assume that sexual attraction is "culturally determined." This implies that sexual attraction is merely one by-product of some sort of (vague and undescribed) general-purpose "capacity-for-culture" mechanism, which, according to this view, underlies the myriad phenomena of culture (religion, pottery styles, kinship systems, language, etc.). If the standard social science model were correct, the determinants of male sexual attraction would be unpredictable. (Whereas if the evolutionary psychological model is correct, the determinants of male sexual attraction are predictable via a relatively straightforward calculus.) In the final analysis, to claim that male sexual attraction is culturally determined is to deny its existence as a distinct psychological phenomenon (see Symons, 1987a, 1987b, 1992a). Similarly, the ecumenical bromide that sexual attraction is codetermined by "biology" and "culture" begs all the relevant psychological questions: What is the nature of the psychological machinery that underpins the human male's experience of sexual attraction? What kind of information does this machinery accept as input? How does it process this information to generate output (i.e., the experience of sexual attraction or the willingness to expend effort in mate acquisition)?

The fact that some determinants of human female sexual attractiveness vary through time and across cultures by no means constitutes evidence that male sexual attraction is the product of general-purpose psychological mechanisms. Such variation may result primarily from the following factors. First, *Homo sapiens* is a highly polytypic species. A species-typical male psychological mechanism that instantiates the rule "prefer a skin color somewhat lighter than the local female average" obviously will yield dramatically different absolute ideals in Norway and Nigeria. Similarly, if humans universally prefer cleanliness in a sexual partner (which makes adaptive sense, given the relationship between cleanliness and health), absolute standards of cleanliness nonetheless will vary enormously because different human communities have very different opportunities for bathing and other hygienic practices.

Second, human males may have psychological adaptations designed to facultatively adjust certain determinants of sexual attraction to local conditions. Such adaptations may account for temporal and cross-cultural variation in the amount of female body fat that males perceive as maximally sexually attractive. I would not expect males anywhere to perceive very thin females as maximally attractive, because, as discussed above, thinness is a cue of reduced fecundity. Despite frequent claims that males in Western societies perceive thin females as maximally sexually attractive, studies have consistently shown that Western males typically prefer female bodies that are average in weight and height (Jackson, 1992, 176; Singh, 1993a, 1993b, 1994, n.d.) (although this may apply primarily to females who are relatively young). Nor would I expect males anywhere to perceive obese females as maximally attractive; although such females probably existed rarely, if ever, in the human EEA, and hence could not have exerted much of a selection pressure on male sexual psychology, they have relatively high WHRs (Singh, n.d.).

However, females with identical WHRs can still vary substantially in total body fat, and the maximally attractive amount of total body fat does appear to vary through time and across cultures (see Anderson et al., 1992, and Smuts, 1992, for references to the evolution-minded literature on this topic). Since our hunter/gatherer ancestors must have faced periodic food shortages, and one function of body fat is to serve as an energetic buffer against starvation, one might expect human males to prefer relatively plump females for any given WHR. In most times and places this probably was the case, but it is not the case in modern industrialized societies. One possible explanation is that males are adapted to detect and respond to population-specific correlates of female health and age. Throughout most of human evolutionary history, total female body fat and health almost certainly were positively correlated (Symons, 1987a), but in modern industrialized societies the relationship is reversed, since upper-class women are typically thinner and healthier than lower-class women. Hence, in modern industrialized societies males may perceive (presumably by some sort of specialized association process) fatter females as being less healthy than average-weight females, for any given WHR. Also, throughout most of human evolutionary history adult humans did not tend to gain weight with age (Eaton et al., 1988), but in modern industrialized societies they do, hence in such societies males may perceive fatter females as being older than average-weight females, for any given WHR. Indeed, Singh (n.d.) found that line drawings of overweight female figures are perceived as significantly less healthy and significantly older than similar figures of normal weight for every WHR tested. In sum, I predict that no more than a tiny fraction of the total variance in human female sexual attractiveness results from the operation of a general-purpose male psychological mechanism that instantiates a rule such as: "Be sexually attracted by whatever characteristics you perceive other males being attracted by."

The adaptationist analysis of male sexual attraction presented in this essay also is incompatible with one version of "sexual selection" theory, first sketched by Darwin (1871). According to this theory, when enough individuals of one sex come to prefer, for whatever reason, a functionally arbitrary trait exhibited by some individuals of the other sex, preference and trait become linked through positive feedback in a runaway coevolutionary "explosion," in which both preference and trait become progressively exaggerated (for lucid and accessible accounts of this [hypothetical] process, see Dawkins, 1986, and Cronin, 1991). Darwin believed that most human "racial" differences evolved in this way. If so, one would predict that (a) geographic phenotypic variation does not primarily reflect adaptation to local environmental conditions, and (b) members of each racial group innately prefer the (presumptively) nonadaptive phenotypic features that distinguish their group from others. The first prediction almost certainly is wrong. For example, geographic variation in body form and limb length proportions among living humans and fossil hominids appears to be highly consistent with thermoregulatory principles (Ruff, 1993). I know of no evidence supporting the second prediction.

Finally, the adaptationist analysis presented in this essay is incompatible with the view that certain female traits are sexually attractive because they either (a) resemble those of neonates (e.g., Cunningham, 1986) or (b) contrast with those of adult males (e.g., Frost, 1988, 1989, 1990). Although superficially "evolutionary," such views actually are nonadaptationist. As neonates have relatively little mate value, it is hard to imagine why selection would have favored male sexual attraction to neonatal features, and I know of no evidence that it did. For example, if selection favored a preference for female skin that is lighter than the local adult female average, then the most attractive female skin color will be closer to that of a neonate than will the average skin color (because neonates have very light skin). But this is not evidence that selection favored male sexual attraction to neonatal traits. The mate choice problem faced by ancestral males did not entail comparing women with neonates; it entailed comparing women with *one another*. Neither did it entail comparing women with men. Male secondary sexual characteristics are caused by high levels of androgens, especially testosterone, and I have argued that, in women, phenotypic features indicating high levels of androgens decrease sexual attractiveness because hyperandrogenism is associated with reduced fecundity. Thus, it should not be surprising that very attractive women are perceived as being more feminine than less attractive women (Jackson, 1992, 73); but this does not mean that selection uniformly favored male sexual attraction to "hyper-feminine" versions of every sexually dimorphic trait. Ancestral women were shorter, on average, than ancestral men, yet selection does not seem to have favored a male sexual preference for the shortest women.

Sexual Attractiveness in Modern Industrialized Societies

In modern industrialized societies the close coupling of female age and reproduction that persisted throughout the vast majority of human evolutionary history has broken down, largely because contraceptive technology allows women to postpone or forego reproduction. In such societies many women thus retain a relatively nubile appearance far longer than preliterate women do or than ancestral women did. My colleague Napoleon Chagnon, who has studied the Yanomamo in southern Venezuela for the last thirty years (Chagnon, 1992), reports (personal communication) that Yanomamo men of all ages state unequivocally that women are most attractive, as sexual partners and as wives, when they are *moko dude*. The Yanomamo word *moko* when used with respect to fruit means that the fruit is edible; when used with respect to a woman, it typically means that the woman is fertile. *Moko dude* when used with respect to fruit means that the fruit is perfectly ripe; when used with respect to a woman, it means that the woman is nubile, approximately fifteen to seventeen years old. Nothing in my reading of the ethnographic record suggests that Yanomamo men are atypical in this respect (see Symons, 1979).

Among natural-fertility preliterate peoples, such as the Yanomamo, a 25-year-old woman typically will have borne and nursed two to four children and been exposed to the elements of nature every day of her life, and the effects of gestation, lactation, and a rigorous physical existence will be manifested clearly in almost every feature of her body. During my lectures on sexual attractiveness I sometimes show a series of Chagnon's slides of Yanomamo girls and women ranging in age from eleven to the mid-forties. In my experience, after seeing these slides everyone in the audience intuitively understands why Yanomamo men are most strongly sexually attracted to *moko dudes*.

The relationship between female age and sexual attractiveness among natural-fertility preliterate peoples highlights the vacuity of the commonly voiced claim that Western men are sexually attracted to young women (and to older women who retain a relatively youthful appearance) because ours is a "youth culture." Between 1953 and 1990 the average age of a *Playboy* centerfold model was 21.3 years (Bogaert et al., 1993), but if the Yanomamo had "skin" magazines, there would be *no* centerfolds as old as twenty-one (Chagnon, personal communication). In fact, during the period from 1953 to 1990 the average age of *Playboy* centerfolds increased (Bogaert et al., 1993). This may be because in recent years many women have begun to exercise more (Bogaert et al., 1993) and sunbathe less, thus retaining a relatively nubile appearance into their twenties. In addition, during the last forty years there has been a general trend among women to postpone marriage and first reproduction, so that there is a larger pool of nulliparas in their early to mid-twenties today than there was during *Playboy*'s early years.

Another evolutionarily novel feature of most modern industrialized societies is that they comprise individuals of extremely heterogeneous phenotypes. The human psychological machinery of sexual attraction almost certainly was not designed to deal with substantial racial variation, because our hunter-gatherer ancestors lived in relatively homogeneous local populations. Nevertheless, the better one understands this machinery the more accurately one should be able to predict cross-racial perceptions of attractiveness. If species-typical psychological mechanisms generate composites of observed phenotypes, as outlined above, men would not be expected to exhibit any innate preference for the phenotypic features that distinguish their own racial group. A male of European ancestry, for example, who is adopted at birth by an Asian family, raised in Asia, and exposed only to Asians is expected to perceive female attractiveness in the same way that his neighbors do, because he and they will have observed approximately the same array of females.

One question for future research is whether there is a "critical period" during ontogeny for template generation, as there is for language acquisition, or whether the template is updated throughout life. I discussed this question briefly in *The Evolution of Human Sexuality* (Symons, 1979), and speculated, on the basis of anecdotal reports by male ethnographers, that the template is updated throughout life. Since then, I have informally interviewed a number of male anthropologists and biologists who have lived for extended periods of time among non-Western peoples, isolated from other Westerners. They uniformly report that the longer they were in the field the more they were attracted to the racially distinctive features of the people among whom they lived.

If two heretofore geographically isolated racial groups, A and B, come into contact for the first time, group A men would not be expected to assess group B women in precisely the same way that group B men do, although there should be substantial concordance. For example, all the men should perceive unblemished skin and low fluctuating asymmetry as attractive, but if A and B differ dramatically in skin color, perceptions of the ideal female skin color are expected to differ between the groups (because each man will perceive as maximally attractive a color somewhat lighter than the adult female average in his natal group). Given the multiplicity of psychological mechanisms that underpin sexual attraction, group A men may perceive group B women as being less attractive than group A women in some respects and more attractive in others.

This phenomenon is strikingly illustrated in Wagatsuma's (1967) classic discussion of the perception of skin color in Japan: "Long before any sustained contact with either Caucasoid Europeans or dark-skinned Africans or Indians, the Japanese valued 'white' [female] skin as beautiful and deprecated 'black' skin as ugly. Their spontaneous responses to the white skin of Caucasoid Europeans and the black skin of Negroid people were an extension of the values deeply embedded in Japanese concepts of beauty" (p. 407). When Japanese men first encountered Western women they were attracted by the lightness of the women's skin but *not* by other phenotypic characteristics that typically distinguish Western from Japanese women, such as eye color, hair color, facial hairiness (Japanese women shaved their faces), and skin characteristics other than color. Wagatsuma writes: "Linked with concerns for the skin's whiteness are desires that it also be smooth with a close, firm texture, a shiny quality, and no wrinkles, furrows, spots, or flecks" (p. 418). In these respects the skin of most Western women—at least older women—was perceived as less attractive than that of most Japanese women. In sum, cross-racial perceptions of sexual attractiveness, which so often are assumed to result from racism and beliefs about racial superiority/inferiority, might profitably be reconsidered as the output of species-typical perceptual machinery processing a greater range of phenotypic information than it was designed to process.

Another evolutionarily novel feature of many current human environments that may affect attractiveness perception is the ubiquity of mirrors. During the course of human evolutionary history our ancestors undoubtedly saw their reflections in still water from time to time, but they could not have been regularly exposed to clear, stable images of their own faces, as we are. Mirrors may affect attractiveness perception (particularly of same-sex individuals) in evolutionarily unprecedented ways, and may even be responsible for some positive assortative mating (Symons, 1992b).

Finally, most people in modern industrialized societies—unlike our hunter-gatherer ancestors—are regularly exposed, through the mass media, to images of extremely attractive individuals (who have been culled from a pool of hundreds of millions, and then made up and photographed to maximize their attractiveness). It is entirely possible that during the course of evolutionary history the average person never saw a single individual as attractive as those that we see every day on magazine covers, in movies, and on TV. The perceptual "illusion" that our social world is populated by a high proportion of extremely attractive people may affect our everyday perceptions of attractiveness.

Furthermore, the mass media probably play an important role in changing our perceptions of attractiveness, but *not,* as is often imagined, in arbitrary or capricious ways. For example, because relatively full female lips are perceived as attractive, many models and actresses have their lips injected with collagen. Consequently, we are regularly exposed to images of female faces with artificially-enhanced lips, our template of the "average" female face gradually becomes fuller-lipped, our standard of "ideal" lip fullness is therefore ratcheted up, and we come to perceive as attractive lips that formerly would have appeared a bit too puffy. This short-term "runaway" process is not arbitrary because (a) the initial cosmetic change had to be in the direction of fuller, rather than narrower, lips in order to enhance attractiveness, and (b) the process was driven at every stage by an innate preference for fuller-than-average lips. Actresses, models, publishers, editors, photographers, producers, directors, plastic surgeons, heads of modeling agencies, makeup artists, and casting agents did not conspire to make us perceive fuller lips as attractive. The role of the mass media in this process is simply to disseminate images of women that the public perceives, at any given time, as maximally attractive.

Research Implications

The view of female sexual attractiveness presented in this essay provides a preliminary framework for future research. There is much to be learned about the selection pressures that shaped the machinery of sexual attraction and almost everything to be learned about the machinery itself. Future research will need to include more phenotypic features, to be more cross-cultural, and to employ more realistic stimuli than line drawings, computer-generated representations, and photographs. (The fact that we perceive certain highly exaggerated features—such as a tiny WHR and enormous breasts—as attractive in a sexy cartoon woman, when we probably would perceive these features as deformities in a real woman, should give us pause for thought.) Female sexual attractiveness is determined by many variables, but how these are weighted and how they interact with one another is unknown. Also unknown is how the intensity of attraction varies with trait variation. It is one thing to propose that the optimal amount of fluctuating asymmetry is zero, but quite another to map the relationships between facial attractiveness and various kinds of deviation from perfect symmetry. From the perspective of the adaptationist program, however, testable hypotheses almost suggest themselves. For example, it is unlikely that all deviations of a given "amount" from perfect symmetry will reduce sexual attractiveness to the same extent. A deviation resulting from a developmental anomaly in hard tissue can be expected to reduce sexual attractiveness far more than the same amount of deviation in, say, nose form, which may result from a minor mishap and indicate little about design quality or developmental stability.

Van den Berghe and Frost (1986) proposed that the human male's sexual preference for lighter-than-average skin has led, in every class-stratified society, to upper classes becoming lighter skinned than lower classes. This is because attractive women tend to marry up (Jackson, 1992, 135), lighter women are, other things equal, more attractive, and skin color is heritable. The result, after a few generations of light-skinned female hypergyny, is class differences in average skin color. If this analysis is correct, hypotheses about heritable determinants of female sexual attractiveness could be tested by comparing women of different social classes across an array of class-stratified societies. If, for example, men universally prefer relatively gracile jaws (and jaw robusticity is heritable), then upper-class women in every class-stratified society should, on average, have more gracile jaws than lower-class women do. In addition, comparing upper- and lower-class women across an array of class-stratified societies might turn up heretofore unsuspected determinants of male sexual attraction.

A good theory of male sexual attraction should explain not only why some phenotypic features play an important role in determining female sexual attractiveness, but also why other features that could *do not*. I predict, for example, that being a few inches above or below the average body height or a few pounds above or below the average body weight will have relatively little effect on female sexual attractiveness (compared, say, to small variations in WHR, facial hair, and acne) because minor variations in these features are unlikely to have been important determinants of female mate value in the EEA.

A good theory also should shed light on individual differences, within local populations, in male perceptions of female sexual attractiveness. Some differences are predicted in a straightforward fashion by the view of sexual attraction sketched in this essay. For example, each male's "template" female face will be slightly different from that of every other male, because each male will have seen a different array of female faces during his lifetime; i.e., the informational input to the composite-generating mechanism will be slightly different for each male. (Because most males are exposed disproportionately to the faces of their own female kin, each male's template is likely to deviate slightly from the population composite in the direction of kin-typical features [Symons, 1987a]; some positive assortative mating may occur as a by-product of this phenomenon [Symons, 1992b].) Also, males vary greatly in mate value, and certain aspects of male sexual psychology may be facultatively affected by this variation. With respect to any motivational system, it makes adaptive sense for one's reach (desire) always to exceed one's grasp, *but not by too much* (Symons, 1985). Perhaps all males perceive female attractiveness in roughly the same way, but the lower a male's mate value, the greater the *range* of females he finds sexually arousing. For example, as a man's mate value declines with age he probably does not gradually come to prefer a WHR of .8 to a .7, and then a .9 to a .8; but he may come to find females with higher WHRs more sexually arousing than he did when his own mate value was higher and he could afford to be choosier.

A mature evolutionary psychology of sexual attraction will have to take account of *supernormal stimuli* and *asymmetrical fitness distributions*. Supernormal stimuli probably are common by-products of perceptual mechanisms. For example, if ringed plovers are presented with a normal plover egg, which is light brown with darker brown spots, and an experimental egg with a clear white ground and black spots, they prefer the latter (Tinbergen, 1969). A plausible explanation is that (a) plovers use contrast in egg detection, (b) the experimental eggs provide supernormal contrast, and (c) among ancestral plovers a simple contrast-detecting psychological mechanism was adaptive (because there were no black-and-white eggs around to confuse with plover eggs). A possible human analog is men's sexual preference for very low WHRs. A female WHR of .6—which is within the human female range, but extremely uncommon—is perceived as more attractive than a WHR of .7 (Singh, 1994). There is no reason to suppose that a .6 WHR indexes greater fecundity than a .7 WHR does (although it may). Perhaps in the human EEA there was no such thing as a woman with too low a WHR (or, at least, such women were very rare), selection favored a simple psychological mechanism instantiating the rule "lower is better," and the maximally attractive WHR thus is supernormally low. As WHR declines, at some point it obviously will deviate far enough from the norm to be perceived as a deformity, but the maximally attractive WHR nonetheless may well be below the functional optimum.

Alternatively, male attraction to very low female WHRs may result from an asymmetrical fitness distribution in the human EEA. Asymmetrical fitness distributions occur when a unit of deviation from the optimum in one direction depresses fitness more than does a unit of deviation in the other (Williams, 1992). Extreme examples have been referred to as the *cliff-edge effect*: the grass may be most nutritious right at the edge of a steep cliff, but the cow that always tries to graze there is unlikely to have the highest lifetime reproductive success in the herd (Williams, 1992, personal communication). Asymmetrical fitness distributions in the human EEA may account for many aspects of male sexual attraction. For example, males may be attracted to very low female WHRs because the fitness penalty for choosing a mate with a WHR one unit above the optimum was much greater than that for choosing a mate with a WHR one unit below the optimum. Similarly, men may prefer women with relatively short lower faces and gracile jaws *not* because ancestral women with these features were more fecund than women who were average in these respects, but because the fitness penalty for choosing a mate with a longer-than-average lower face and a more-robust-than-average jaw was relatively large.

If in the EEA the optimal female mate was just beginning ovulatory menstrual cycles, selection would have penalized an error in the too-old and too-pregnant direction much more strongly than it penalized an error of the same magnitude in the too-young and not-quite-fecund direction. As mentioned above, if the Yanomamo had "skin" magazines they would not feature any centerfold models as old as twenty-one, but they would feature some fourteen-year-olds (Chagnon, personal communication). In fact, about 90 percent of Yanomamo females are copulating with sexually mature males by the time they are fourteen years old (Chagnon, personal communication).

When male mating psychology is better understood, even the notion of a single, unitary continuum of "sexual attraction" may turn out to be too simple. Margaret Mead wrote in *Male and Female* that everywhere girls are permanently clothed before boys, and that a little girl will be taught to cross her legs, or to tuck her heels under her, or to sit with her legs parallel. This is because "Older boys and men find little girls of four and five definitely female and attractive, and that attractiveness must be masked and guarded just as the male eye must be protected from the attractiveness of their older sisters and mothers" (Mead, 1967, 105). During the course of human evolutionary history men may often have been betrothed and even married to prepubescent girls, as often occurs among living preliterate peoples. Male mating psychology may turn out to include sentiments, which are elicited by very young females, that are not exactly sexual, but not exactly not sexual either, sentiments for which there are no specific words in the English language. (It would be interesting to know whether such words exist in any language.)

I noted in the introduction that we care about an apple's firmness only because we have learned that firmness is a reasonably reliable predictor of certain gustatory sensations, such as sweetness. Sweetness, however, is *innately* pleasurable. This is because in the EEA the "food value" of fruit varied directly with its sugar content (not its firmness), hence natural selection favored individuals who experienced the sensation engendered by sugar on the tongue as pleasurable. Characteristics of human female bodies such as low WHR, unblemished skin, and low fluctuating asymmetry are analogous to the sweetness, rather than to the firmness, of apples. That is, males are attracted by these characteristics not because they predict anything about the tactual sensations that occur during sexual activity but because in the EEA they reliably indexed high female mate value, and, therefore, natural selection favored males who *innately* experienced them as pleasurable.

Ultimately, the hypothesis that beauty is in the adaptations of the beholder may not explain every aspect of female sexual attractiveness. But as George Williams once remarked in a similar context, I believe that it is the light and the way.

Acknowledgments

I thank Donald Brown, David Buss, Napoleon Chagnon, Peggy La Cerra, Margie Profet, Devendra Singh, Randy Thornhill, and John Tooby for their careful readings of various drafts of this essay and for their many helpful suggestions. I am especially indebted to Margie Profet for editing two drafts and for her preternaturally keen adaptationist eye.

References

Alley, Thomas R. 1988. The effects of growth and aging on facial aesthetics. Pp. 51–62 in Thomas R. Alley, ed., *Social and Applied Aspects of Perceiving Faces*. Hillsdale, N.J.: Lawrence Erlbaum.

Alley, Thomas R., and Cunningham, Michael R. 1991. Averaged faces are attractive, but very attractive faces are not average. *Psychological Science* 2:123–25.

Alley, Thomas R., and Hildebrandt, Katherine A. 1988. Determinants and consequences of facial aesthetics. Pp. 101–40 in Thomas R. Alley, ed., *Social and Applied Aspects of Perceiving Faces*. Hillsdale, N.J.: Lawrence Erlbaum.

Anderson, Judith L., Crawford, Charles B., Nadeau, Joanne, and Lindberg, Tracy. 1992. Was the Duchess of Windsor right? A cross-cultural review of the socioecology of ideal of female body shape. *Ethology and Sociobiology* 13:197–227.

Barkow, Jerome H. 1989. *Darwin, Sex, and Status*. Toronto: University of Toronto Press.

Barkow, Jerome H., Cosmides, Leda, and Tooby, John, eds. 1992. *The Adapted Mind: Evolutionary Psychology and the Generation of Culture*. New York: Oxford University Press.

Baumann, Gerhard, Davila, Norma, Shaw, Melissa A., Ray, Jharna, Liebhaber, Stephen A., and Cooke, Nancy E. 1991. Binding of human growth hormone (GH)-variant (placental GH) to GH-binding proteins in human plasma. *Journal of Clinical Endocrinology and Metabolism* 73:1175–79.

Behrents, Rolf G. 1990. Adult facial growth. Pp. 423–43 in Donald H. Enlow, ed., *Facial Growth* (3d ed.). Philadelphia: W. B. Saunders.

Benson, Philip, and Perrett, David. 1992. Face to face with the perfect image. *New Scientist* 22 Feb.: 32–35.

Bogaert, Anthony F., Turkovich, Deborah A., and Hafer, Carolyn L. 1993. A content analysis of *Playboy* centrefolds from 1953 through 1990: Changes in explicitness, objectification, and model's age. *The Journal of Sex Research* 30:135–39.

Brown, Donald E. 1991. *Human Universals*. Philadelphia: Temple University Press.

Buss, David M. 1989. Sex differences in human mate preferences: Evolutionary hypotheses tested in 37 cultures. *Behavioral and Brain Sciences* 12:1–14.

Buss, David M. 1994. *The Evolution of Desire: Strategies of Human Mating*. New York: Basic Books.

Carello, Claudia, Grosofsky, Alexis, Shaw, Robert E., Pittenger, John B., and Mark, Leonard S. 1989. Attractiveness of facial profiles is a function of distance from archetype. *Ecological Psychology* 1:227–51.

Chagnon, Napoleon A. 1988. Male Yanomamo manipulations of kinship classifications of female kin for reproductive advantage. In Laura Betzig, Monique Borgerhoff Mulder, and Paul Turke, eds., *Human Reproductive Behavior: A Darwinian Perspective*. Cambridge: Cambridge University Press.

Chagnon, Napoleon A. 1992. *Yanomamo* (4th ed.). Fort Worth, Texas: Harcourt Brace Jovanovich.

Clapp, James F. III, Seaward, Brian L., Sleamaker, Robert H., and Hiser, John. 1988. Maternal physiologic adaptations to early human pregnancy. *Am. J. Obstet. Gynecol.* 159:1456–60.

Cosmides, Leda, and Tooby, John 1987. From evolution to behavior: Evolutionary psychology as the missing link. Pp. 277–306 in J. Dupre, ed., *The Latest on the Best: Essays on Evolution and Optimality.* Cambridge, Mass.: MIT Press.

Cronin, Helena. 1991. *The Ant and the Peacock.* Cambridge: Cambridge University Press.

Cunningham, Michael R. 1986. Measuring the physical in physical attractiveness: Quasiexperiments on the sociobiology of female facial beauty. *Journal of Social and Personality Psychology* 50:925–935.

Curio, E. 1973. Towards a methodology of teleonomy. *Experientia* 29:1045–58.

Daly, Martin, and Wilson, Margo. 1988. *Homicide.* New York: Aldine de Gruyter.

Darwin, Charles. 1859. *On the Origin of Species by Means of Natural Selection, or the Preservation of Favoured Races in the Struggle for Life.* London: Watts and Co.

Darwin, Charles. 1871. *The Descent of Man and Selection in Relation to Sex.* London: Murray.

Dawkins, Richard. 1986. *The Blind Watchmaker.* New York: W. W. Norton.

DeKay, W. Todd, and Buss, David M. 1992. Human nature, individual differences, and the importance of context: Perspectives from evolutionary psychology. *Current Directions in Psychological Science* 184–89.

Early, John D., and Peters, John F. 1990. *The Population Dynamics of the Mucajai Yanomama.* San Diego: Academic Press.

Eaton, S. Boyd, Shostak, Marjorie, and Konner, Melvin. 1988. *The Paleolithic Prescription.* New York: Harper & Row.

Enlow, Donald H. 1990. Faces. Pp. 1–24 in Donald H. Enlow, ed., *Facial Growth* (3d ed.). Philadelphia: W. B. Saunders.

Farkas, L. G. 1981. *Anthropometry of the Head and Face in Medicine.* New York: Elsevier.

Folsom, Aaron R., Kaye, Susan A., Sellers, Thomas A., Hong, Ching-Ping, Cerhan, James R., Potter, John D., and Prineas, Ronald J. 1993. Body fat distribution and 5-year risk of death in older women. *JAMA* 269:483–87.

Frost, Peter. 1988. Human skin color: A possible relationship between its sexual dimorphism and its social perception. *Perspectives in Biology and Medicine* 32:38–58.

Frost, Peter. 1989. Human skin color: The sexual differentiation of its social perception. *The Mankind Quarterly* 30:3–16.

Frost, Peter. 1990. Fair women, dark men: The forgotten roots of colour prejudice. *History of European Ideas* 12:669–79.

Galton, Francis. 1883. *Inquiries into Human Faculty and Its Development.* London: Macmillan.

Gangestad, Steven W., Thornhill, Randy, and Yeo, Ronald A. 1994. Facial attractiveness, developmental stability, and fluctuating asymmetry. *Ethology and Sociobiology.*

Grammer, Karl, and Thornhill, Randy. In press. Human facial attractiveness and sexual selection: The roles of averageness and symmetry. *Journal of Comparative Psychology.*

Held, Beverly L., Nader, Shahla, Rodriguez-Rigau, Luis J., Smith, Keith D., and Steinberger, Emil. 1984. Acne and hyperandrogenism. *Journal of the American Academy of Dermatology* 10:223–26.

Hellreich, Philip D. 1974. The skin changes of pregnancy. *Cutis* 13:82–86.

Jackson, Linda A. 1992. *Physical Appearance and Gender: Sociobiological and Sociocultural Perspectives.* Albany: State University of New York Press.

Jankowiak, William R. 1993. *Sex, Death, and Hierarchy in a Chinese City: An Anthropological Account.* New York: Columbia University Press.

Johnston, Victor S., and Franklin, Melissa. 1993. Is beauty in the eye of the beholder? *Ethology and Sociobiology* 14:183–99.

Kenrick, Douglas T., and Keefe, Richard C. 1992. Age preferences in mates reflect sex differences in human reproductive strategies. *Behavioral and Brain Sciences* 15:75–91.

Langlois, Judith H., and Roggman, Lori A. 1990. Attractive faces are only average. *Psychological Science* 1:115–21.

Livshits, G., and Kobyliansky, E. 1991. Fluctuating asymmetry as a possible measure of developmental homeostasis in humans: A review. *Human Biology* 63:441–66.

Lutfi, Ruben J. Fridmanis, Miguel, Misiunas, Alejandro L., Pafume, Oscar, Gonzalez, Enrique A., Villemur, Jorge A., Mazzini, Miguel A., and Niepomniszcze, Hugo. 1985. Association of melasma with thyroid autoimmunity and other thyroidal abnormalities and their relationship to the origin of the melasma. *Journal of Clinical Endocrinology and Metabolism* 61:28–31.

Mayr, Ernst. 1983. How to carry out the adaptationist program? *The American Naturalist* 121:324–34.

McKenzie, A. W. 1971. Skin disorders in pregnancy. *The Practitioner* 206:773–80.

Mead, Margaret. 1967. *Male and Female: A Study of the Sexes in a Changing World.* New York: William Morrow.

Melancon, Thomas F. 1982. Marriage and Reproduction Among the Yanomamo Indians of Venezuela. Ph.D. thesis, The Pennsylvania State University.

Merow, William W., and Broadbent, B. Holly, Jr. 1990. Cephalometrics. Pp. 346–95 in Donald H. Enlow, ed., *Facial Growth* (3d ed.). Philadelphia: W. B. Saunders.

Møller, Anders Pape. 1992a. Female swallow preference for symmetrical male sexual ornaments. *Nature* 357:238–40.

Møller, Anders Pape. 1992b. Patterns of fluctuating asymmetry in weapons: Evidence for reliable signalling of quality in beetle horns and bird spurs. *Proceedings of the Royal Society of London B* 248:199–206.

Møller, Anders Pape. 1992c. Parasites differentially increase the degree of fluctuating asymmetry in secondary sexual characters. *Journal of Evolutionary Biology* 5:691–99.

Møller, Anders Pape. 1993. Patterns of fluctuating asymmetry in sexual ornaments predict female choice. *Journal of Evolutionary Biology.* 6:481–91.

Møller, A. P., and Soler, M. N.d. Breast asymmetry and human reproductive success.

Nakdimen, Kenneth Alan. 1984. The physiognomic basis of sexual stereotyping. *American Journal of Psychiatry* 141:499–503.

Neel, James V., and Weiss, Kenneth M. 1975. The genetic structure of a tribal population, the Yanomama Indians. *American Journal of Physical Anthropology* 42:25–51.

Neifert, Marianne R., Seacat, Joy M., and Jobe, William E. 1985. Lactation failure due to insufficient glandular development of the breast. *Pediatrics* 76:823–28.

Palmer, Richard A., and Strobeck, C. 1986. Fluctuating asymmetry: Measurement, analysis, patterns. *Annual Review of Ecology and Systematics* 17:391–421.

Parsons, P. A. 1992. Fluctuating asymmetry: A biological monitor of environmental and genomic stress. *Heredity* 68:361–64.

Perez, Maritza, Sanchez, Jorge L., and Aguilo, Francisco. 1983. Endocrinologic profile of patients with idiopathic melasma. *Journal of Investigative Dermatology* 81: 543–45.

Perrett, D. I., May, K. A., and Yoshikawa, S. 1994. Facial shape and judgements of female attractiveness. *Nature* 368:239–42.

Ruff, Christopher B. 1993. Climatic adaptation and hominid evolution: The thermoregulatory imperative. *Evolutionary Anthropology* 2:53–60.

Singh, Devendra. 1993a. Adaptive significance of female physical attractiveness: Role of waist-to-hip ratio. *Journal of Personality and Social Psychology* 65:293–307.

Singh, Devendra. 1993b. Body shape and women's attractiveness: The critical role of waist-to-hip ratio. *Human Nature* 4:297–321.

Singh, Devendra. 1994. Is thin really beautiful and good? Relationship between waist-to-hip ratio (WHR) and female attractiveness. *Person. individ. Diff.* 16:123–32.

Singh, Devendra. N.d. Waist-to-hip ratio: Indicator of female health, fecundity and physical attractiveness.

Smuts, R. W. 1992. Fat, sex, class, adaptive flexibility, and cultural change. *Ethology and Sociobiology* 13:523–42.

Sodhi, Vimal K., and Sausker, William F. 1988. Dermatoses of pregnancy. *American Family Physician* 37:131–38.

Steinberger, E., Rodriguez-Rigau, L. J., Smith, K. D., and Held, B. 1981. The menstrual cycle and plasma testosterone levels in women with acne. *Journal of the American Academy of Dermatology* 4:54–58.

Symons, Donald. 1978. *Play and Aggression: A Study of Rhesus Monkeys.* New York: Columbia University Press.

Symons, Donald. 1979. *The Evolution of Human Sexuality.* New York: Oxford University Press.

Symons, Donald. 1985. Darwinism and contemporary marriage. Pp. 133–55 in Kingsley Davis, ed., *Contemporary Marriage: Comparative Perspectives on a Changing Institution.* New York: Russell Sage.

Symons, Donald. 1987a. An evolutionary approach: Can Darwin's view of life shed light on human sexuality? Pp. 91–125 in J. H. Geer and W. O'Donohue, eds., *Theories of Human Sexuality.* New York: Plenum.

Symons, Donald. 1987b. If we're all Darwinians, what's the fuss about? Pp. 121–46 in Charles Crawford, Martin Smith, and Dennis Krebs, eds., *Sociobiology and Psychology: Ideas, Issues, and Applications.* Hillsdale, N.J.: Lawrence Erlbaum.

Symons, Donald. 1989. The psychology of human mate preferences. *Behavioral and Brain Sciences* 12:34–35.

Symons, Donald. 1992a. On the use and misuse of Darwinism in the study of human behavior. Pp. 137–59 in Jerome H. Barkow, Leda Cosmides, and John Tooby, eds., *The Adapted Mind: Evolutionary Psychology and the Generation of Culture.* New York: Oxford University Press.

Symons, Donald. 1992b. What do men want? *Behavioral and Brain Sciences* 15:113–14.

Thornhill, Randy. 1990. The study of adaptation. Pp. 31–62 in M. Bekoff and D. Jamieson, eds., *Interpretation and Explanation in the Study of Animal Behavior* (vol. 2). Boulder, Colo.: West View Press.

Thornhill, Randy. 1992a. Female preference for the pheromone of males with low fluctuating asymmetry in the Japanese scorpionfly (*Panorpa japonica*: Mecoptera). *Behavioral Ecology* 3:277–83.

Thornhill, Randy. 1992b. Fluctuating asymmetry and the mating system of the Japanese scorpionfly (*Panorpa japonica*). *Animal Behaviour* 44:867–79.

Thornhill, Randy. 1992c. Fluctuating asymmetry, interspecific aggression, and male mating tactics in two species of Japanese scorpionflies. *Behavioral Ecology and Sociobiology* 30:357–63.

Thornhill, Randy, and Gangestad, Steven W. 1993. Human facial beauty: Averageness, symmetry and parasite resistance. *Human Nature* 4:237–69.

Tinbergen, N. 1969. *The Study of Instinct.* New York: Oxford University Press.

Tooby, John. 1985. The emergence of evolutionary psychology. Pp. 1–6 in D. Pines, ed., *Emerging Syntheses in Science.* Santa Fe: Santa Fe Institute.

Tooby, John, and Cosmides, Leda. 1989. Evolutionary psychology and the generation of culture, part I: Theoretical considerations. *Ethology and Sociobiology* 10:29–49.

Tooby, John, and Cosmides, Leda. 1990a. On the universality of human nature and the uniqueness of the individual: The role of genetics and adaptation. *Journal of Personality* 58:17–67.

Tooby, John, and Cosmides, Leda. 1990b. The past explains the present: Emotional adaptations and the structure of ancestral environments. *Ethology and Sociobiology* 11:375–424.

Tooby, John, and Cosmides, Leda. 1992. The psychological foundations of culture. Pp. 19–136 in Jerome H. Barkow, Leda Cosmides, and John Tooby, eds., *The Adapted Mind: Evolutionary Psychology and the Generation of Culture.* New York: Oxford University Press.

Townsend, John Marshall. 1989. Mate selection criteria: A pilot study. *Ethology and Sociobiology* 10:241–53.

Townsend, John Marshall. 1992. Measuring the magnitude of sex differences. *Behavioral and Brain Sciences* 15:115–16.

Townsend, John Marshall. 1993. Sexuality and partner selection: Sex differences among college students. *Ethology and Sociobiology* 14:305–30.

Townsend, John Marshall, and Levy, G. D. 1990a. Effects of potential partners' costume and physical attractiveness on sexuality and partner selection. *Journal of Psychology* 124:371–89.

Townsend, John Marshall, and Levy, G. D. 1990b. Effects of potential partners' physical attractiveness and socioeconomic status on sexuality and partner selection. *Archives of Sexual Behavior* 19:149–64.

van den Berghe, Pierre, L., and Frost, Peter. 1986. Skin color preference, sexual dimorphism and sexual selection: A case of gene culture co-evolution? *Ethnic and Racial Studies* 9:87–113.

Wade, Thomas R., Wade, Sylvia L. and Jones, Henry, E. 1978. Skin changes and diseases associated with pregnancy. *Obsterics and Gynecology* 52:233–42.

Wagatsuma, Hiroshi. 1967. The social perception of skin color in Japan. *Daedalus* 96:407–43.

Wiederman, Michael W. 1993. Evolved gender differences in mate preferences: Evidence from personal advertisements. *Ethology and Sociobiology* 14:331–52.

Wiederman, Michael W., and Allgeier, Elizabeth Rice. 1992. Gender differences in mate selection criteria: Sociobiological or socioeconomic explanation? *Ethology and Sociobiology* 13:115–24.

Williams, George C. 1966. *Adaptation and Natural Selection*. Princeton: Princeton University Press.

Williams, George C. 1975. *Sex and Evolution*. Princeton: Princeton University Press.

Williams, George C. 1985. A defense of reductionism in evolutionary biology. *Oxford Surveys in Evolutionary Biology* 2:1–27.

Williams, George C. 1992. *Natural Selection: Domains, Levels, and Challenges*. New York: Oxford University Press.

Winton, George B. 1981. Dermatoses of pregnancy. *Journal of the Association of Military Dermatologists* 7:20–27.

Winton, George B. 1982. Dermatoses of pregnancy. *Journal of the American Academy of Dermatology* 6:977–98.

Wong, Reynold C., and Ellis, Charles N. 1984. Physiologic skin changes in pregnancy. *Journal of the American Academy of Dermatology* 10:929–43.

Zaadstra, Boukje M., Seidell, Jacob C., Van Noord, Paul A. H., te Velde, Egbert R., Habbema, J. Dik F., Vrieswijk, Baukje, and Karbaat. 1993. Fat and female fecundity: Prospective study of effect of body fat distribution on conception rates. *British Medical Journal* 306:484–87.

PART TWO

Crossroads: Biology and Behavior

CHAPTER SIX

Sex Hormones and Sexual Behavior

JEAN D. WILSON

In most animal species virtually every aspect of reproduction is under the control of steroid hormones from the gonads (ovaries and testes; several of the more technical terms used in this chapter are defined in the notes). Such functions include the formation of the male and female phenotypes during embryogenesis, sexual maturation and the onset of gametogenesis at the time of puberty, and the acquisition of specific behaviors such as sex drive (libido), the capacity for intercourse (potentia), and patterned behaviors. Patterned behaviors encompass gender identity and gender role as well as diverse behaviors such as mating songs in birds, the drive for dominance (musth in elephants), and ritual mating behaviors in many species. These actions of steroid hormones are due to effects in the central nervous system and in peripheral tissues. Some effects of steroid hormones in the brain cause permanent anatomical and functional changes, whereas others require continued exposure to the hormones.

In the human, gonadal hormones are also responsible for phenotypic differentiation during embryogenesis, sexual and reproductive maturation at puberty, and, in part, development of libido and potentia. The extent to which gonadal hormones are involved in the development of patterned behavior in men and women is not so clear. It is difficult to devise appropriately controlled experiments to establish the significance of hormonal factors in human behavior, and most studies of the role of hormones in human sexual behavior have utilized subjects with pathological states such as the hypogonadal or postmenopausal state or abnormalities of human sexual development, the so-called intersex states. Such studies, imperfect though they are, raise fundamental questions about the relative roles of psychological, social, and biological forces in human sexual behavior.

Effect of Hormones on the Sexual Behavior of Animals

The influence of gonadal hormones on behavior in animals is well documented. Many aspects of the problem are beyond the scope of the present discussion, but several features deserve emphasis:

A somewhat different version of this chapter has been published in Clinical Neuroendocrinology (Besser GM, Martini L, eds), Vol 2, Chap 1, copyright © 1992 by Academic Press, Inc., and is used here with permission of the publisher.

First, diverse sexually dimorphic behavior patterns are regulated by gonadal steroids, ranging from the songs and mating rituals of birds to copulatory patterns in mammals. For example, male and female rodents differ in the predominant type of sexual postures they assume during coitus as well as the sexual partner they pursue (see the Pavelka and Wallen chapters in this volume). These behaviors can be reversed by appropriate hormonal manipulation. If testosterone is given to rats soon after birth, the female is made anovulatory. Likewise, male rats that are castrated during the neonatal period have sexual responses as adults to estrogen and progesterone like those of females.

Although androgens and estrogens are formed in both males and females (both hormones probably play physiological roles in both sexes), in general androgens (and androgen metabolites) dictate male behavior patterns, and estrogens (and to a certain extent progesterone) dictate female behavior patterns.

These hormones act in the central nervous system mainly via the same molecular mechanisms that operate in peripheral tissues. Pathological states that impair either hormone formation or the machinery of hormone action block hormone effects in the central nervous system as well as in peripheral tissues. Steroid hormones also have effects in the central nervous system not mediated by the known receptor mechanisms (e.g., effects on cell permeability).

In the male rodent the surge of testosterone secretion during the neonatal period plays a vital role in virilizing the hypothalamus, namely, in inducing a tonic pattern of gonadotropin[1] release as compared to the cyclic patterns in females. (This action of testosterone in the central nervous system may be mediated by testosterone metabolites.) A neonatal surge in testosterone secretion also occurs in the human male infant and could conceivably play a similar role.

Two general types of effects of gonadal steroids on behavior can be delineated. In the terminology of Phoenix and colleagues (Phoenix et al., 1959, 1967), these phenomena are termed organizational and concurrent. Organizational effects are those that require the presence of the steroid at a specific time of development, that appear to result in a permanent effect on function or behavior, and that persist (to a greater or lesser degree) even after the steroid is no longer present. Such organizational effects may take place during the neonatal surge of testosterone production and may be accompanied by permanent changes in anatomical development and organization of the brain. Concurrent effects require the continued presence of the steroid for the full manifestation of the effects, e.g., the mounting response of the female rodent when in estrus. Although the delineation of these phenomena is of conceptual importance, there is considerable overlap between them in the sense that "organizational" effects may be silent in the absence of the proper hormonal milieu. Furthermore, some concurrent phenomena such as the typical male behavior involved in intromission and ejaculatory thrusting may persist for a variable period in the castrated animal.

The behavioral effects of steroid hormones are due to complicated interaction between peripheral and central actions of the hormones. For example, the paradigm of sexual behavior in the mammal that has been best explored is the mounting reflex of the female rat. When the female in estrus is mounted by a male, she extends the hind legs, elevates the rump, and dorsiflexes the vertebral column. These actions involve not only sensory input from the rump but a well-defined neural arc that includes motor and sensory components and specific estrogen-dependent nuclei in the central nervous system. While the central nervous system plays a vital role in the hormone-mediated control of sexual behavior in animals, individual components of behavior may be influenced to different degrees by central versus peripheral actions of the hormones. Even under defined laboratory conditions, it is difficult to devise experimental conditions that allow quantification of the relative contribution of each to a given action.

Animal species differ in the extent to which hormones exert a permanent organizational effect on behavior and on gonadotropin production. For example, organizational effects in primates appear to be less clear-cut than in rodents; when estrogens are given in appropriate amounts to male rhesus monkeys of any age a positive release of luteinizing hormone (similar to that of the normal ovulatory surge in females) can be induced. This suggests that hormones play a less permanent role in mediating this central nervous system function in the primate (see Wallen, this volume, for related issues).

Even when hormones are involved in specific aspects of behavior, stereotyping can also play a role. For example, development of the normal male song pattern in some bird species requires both the action of androgen and exposure of the developing male to a mature male of the same species. In this case the hormone acts both directly and by influencing learning patterns.

In summary, the role of gonadal steroids in sexual behavior involves, at a minimum, direct effects on the central nervous system, development of the genital tracts in the two sexes, reflex, sensory, and motor aspects of neurosensory arcs, and integration of the various neural subsystems that constitute the behavioral process.

Control of Libido and Potentia

The investigation of behavior patterns in the human is more complex at every level. For the purposes of this discussion, we shall use the terms *libido* for the instinctual sexual drive and *potentia* for the ability to perform and complete sexual intercourse. These functions are not generally considered to be sexually dimorphic, but they are influenced by gonadal hormones. The simplest question is whether copulation is possible in humans in the absence of gonadal steroids. In the males of most species, mating capacity is maintained for a variable period after orchidectomy[2] and then followed by progressive failure, whereas ovariectomy[3] of female animals causes immediate complete abolition of female mating behavior. In the human, prepubertal castration of boys uniformly prevents the development of normal male behavior, and orchidectomy in the adult has sequelae similar to those in animals, i.e., castration of adult men causes a decline in sexual behavior with only occasional castrated subjects capable of normal sexual activity after two years. Furthermore, physiological androgen replacement therapy in such patients causes a rapid and reliable restoration of male sexual activity. Thus, the hormonal control of male sexual behavior is similar in man and animals.

However, removal of ovarian secretions by ovariectomy or via the natural menopause does not have a consistent effect on sexual activity in women, in contrast to the situation in animals. The usual interpretation is that once sexual patterns are fixed in women, sexual drive is endocrine independent. This interpretation may be incorrect since removal of the human ovaries does not impair formation of sex steroids by the adrenal glands. Furthermore, adrenalectomy[4] and hypophysectomy[5] in previously castrated women are reported to cause a profound decrease in sexual desire. Consequently, it is possible that the sexual life of the human female is as hormone dependent as that of animals. Adrenal androgen (ablated either by hypophysectomy or adrenalectomy) could have a direct effect on sexual desire in women, or adrenal androgen can act as a prohormone[6] for estrogen synthesis in peripheral tissues and supply sufficient estrogen for maintenance of sexual drive in the absence of the ovaries. (Whether hormones are involved in the genesis of normal sexual drive at female puberty is also unclear, some evidence suggesting a role for adrenal androgens in the process.)

A similar problem of interpretation exists as to exactly which hormones regulate male sexual behavior. Occasional castrate males of all species sustain a capacity and drive for intercourse for long periods. In the castrate male considerable estrogen and small amounts of testosterone are formed in peripheral tissues from adrenal androgen, and in some animal species estradiol[7] enhances the effect of androgen on male sexual drive. Thus, the small amounts of testosterone and/or estrogens formed via this mechanism may be enough to sustain libido and potentia in some adult male castrates. In other words, libido and potentia would be preserved only in those castrated men able to produce sufficient hormones by the adrenals and/or peripheral tissues.

In summary, testicular secretions clearly play an important role in the male sexual drive of humans and animals, whereas ovarian secretions appear to be more important in influencing the female sexual behavior of animals. As in the rhesus monkey, there does not appear to be a permanent imprinting by steroid hormones on gonadotropin secretion in the human. For example, the normal tonic pattern of gonadotropin secretion in adult men can be altered to the cyclic pattern characteristic of the female by administration to men of ovarian steroids so as to mimic the pattern of secretion of the normal ovary. This finding, together with the fact that gonadal steroids may not be required to maintain sexual libido in women, suggests that the effects of hormones on central nervous system functions—both behavioral and nonbehavioral—are different in the human than in lower animals.

Gender Identification in the Human

In contrast to sexual drive—which is not usually considered to be sexually dimorphic—sexual behavior relating to identification is fundamentally different in males and females. For the present purposes the two important concepts are *gender identity* and *gender role*. *Gender identity* is defined as the unified and persistent experience of oneself as male, female, or ambivalent. *Gender role* is composed of the actions, activities, and behaviors that indicate to others the degree to which one perceives oneself as male, female, or ambivalent. The factors that constitute gender role are obviously influenced by a multitude of cultural and social variables, since actions and activities of the two sexes vary in different societies. Consequently, the patterns by which one identifies oneself as male or female vary. Some aspects of dimorphic behavior are beyond the scope of the present discussion: sexual orientation (whether sexual object choice is heterosexual, homosexual, or bisexual) and parenting (the desire and capacity for the care of children). Knowledge of endocrine influences on both processes is sparse (see Meyer-Bahlburg, this volume, for endocrine influences on sexual orientation).

Vagueness in the definition and understanding of gender identity and gender role reflects the fact that it is difficult to quantify these parameters in any meaningful way and more difficult to devise means of investigating their provenance. Appropriately controlled experiments that would allow rigorous definition of the determinants of sexual identification and behavior cannot be performed in humans. As a consequence, a major emphasis in the study of human sexual behavior has been the analysis of gender role and behavior in subjects with histories of endocrine abnormalities, particularly studies of patients with abnormalities of sexual development. To understand the limitations in the usefulness of these pathological states for the analysis of human behavior it is necessary first to consider briefly the pathophysiology of abnormal sexual development.

Abnormal Sexual Development

Derangements of any of the three primary processes involved in sexual differentiation can cause abnormal sexual development. Disorders of chromosomal, gonadal, and phenotypic sex occur in the human (table 6.1). Such abnormalities can arise from environmental insult, as in the ingestion of a virilizing drug; aberrations of the sex chromosomes, as in 45,X gonadal dysgenesis;[8] developmental birth defects of multifactorial etiology, as in most cases of hypospadias;[9] or hereditary disorders resulting from single-gene mutations, as in the

Table 6.1 Occurrence of Ambiguous Genitalia and Changes in Gender Role in Abnormalities of Sexual Development

Type of disorder	Disorder	Ambiguity of external genitalia	Reported change in gender role
Chromosomal sex	Klinefelter syndrome	None	
	XX male	None	
	Gonadal dysgenesis	None	
	Mixed gonadal dysgenesis	Common	Occasional female to male
	True hermaphroditism	Occasional	Unusual
Gonadal sex	Pure gonadal dysgenesis	Occasional	
	Absent testis syndrome	None	
Phenotypic sex	Female pseudo-hermaphroditism		
	Congenital adrenal hyperplasia	Common in females	Unusual
	Nonadrenal female pseudohermaphroditism	Common in females	Unusual
	Developmental disorders of the müllerian duct	None	
	Male pseudohermaphroditism		
	Abnormalities of androgen synthesis	Common	Occasional female to male
	Abnormalities of androgen action		
	5α-Reductase deficiency	Common	Female to male
	Defects of the androgen receptor		
	Testicular feminization	None	
	Reifenstein syndrome	Common	Rare
	Male infertility	None	
	Persistent müllerian duct syndrome	None	
	Sporadic hypospadias	Occasional	Rare

testicular feminization syndrome.[10] The pathogenesis, clinical spectrum, endocrine pathology, and functional derangements that accompany these disorders have been reviewed extensively and will not be considered here. However, several aspects of abnormal sexual development are relevant to the analysis of human sexual behavior.

First, there is considerable variation in the phenotypic defects that occur in the various types of abnormal sexual development. For example, men with the 47,XXY Klinefelter syndrome[11] or with the XX male syndrome[12] develop as men (albeit infertile because of azoospermia) and express endocrine abnormalities only later in life. Likewise, subjects with 45,X gonadal dysgenesis or the syndrome of pure gonadal dysgenesis develop a female phenotype, and most patients with true hermaphroditism have unambiguous male or female pheno-types. Thus, many patients with abnormalities of sexual development end up with unequivocal male or female anatomical development. This is the conse-quence either of the fact that the formation of testicular hormones was suffi-cient to induce a male phenotype or that the failure of production of testicular hormones is complete enough to result in formation of a female phenotype. If hormones are involved in the formation of gender identity, the endocrine pat-tern in most individuals with abnormal sexual development would correspond with the anatomical development and hence with the sex assignment at birth.

Second, disorders that appear phenotypically similar can result from differ-ent mechanisms. For example, some patients with errors in chromosomal sex, such as mixed gonadal dysgenesis, have phenotypes similar to those of patients with abnormalities of phenotypic sex, such as 5α-reductase deficiency.[13] Since different disorders differ in their pathophysiology, it is essential that the diag-nosis be established before any valid interpretation can be drawn as to behav-ioral consequences of a given abnormality.

Third, ambiguity of genital development (and hence confusion as to appro-priate gender assignment at birth or in subsequent life) occurs in only a few disorders: (1) The testes do not produce sufficient hormones to virilize the male embryo—either because of developmental abnormality of the testes (as in mixed gonadal dysgenesis or true hermaphroditism) or because of a heredi-tary defect in one of the enzymes required for testosterone biosynthesis. (2) Sufficient testosterone is synthesized by the testes, but due to an inherited ab-normality that affects the molecular machinery of androgen action (frequently the receptor protein or 5α-reductase enzyme) the hormone cannot act to viril-ize the embryo normally. (3) Overproduction of androgen occurs in the female embryo, as in congenital adrenal hyperplasia[14] due to deficiency of the 21-hydroxylase enzyme.

If hormones are involved directly or indirectly in development of gender identity, one would predict that gender identity would be most imperfect in patients with ambiguous genitalia. However, even if this were true, gender identity would not be expected to be influenced in every patient. All defects that cause ambiguous genitalia vary in severity among affected individuals and consequently result in variable degrees of genital abnormality. For example, the external phenotypes of males with abnormalities of the androgen receptor or of females with 21-hydroxylase deficiency can span an entire spectrum from male to ambiguous to female. One would not expect abnormalities of gender identity in those individuals with minor or no defects in genital development.

Fourth, even when the degree of ambiguity of the external genitalia is simi-lar, disorders can have different times of onset and different long-term endo-crine consequences. For example, disorders of androgen synthesis and/or ac-tion influence embryonic development beginning at the end of the first trimester, whereas adrenal function—and hence adrenal virilization in 21-

hydroxylase deficiency—does not begin until later in embryogenesis. Furthermore, adult males with 17β-hydroxysteroid dehydrogenase deficiency, mixed gonadal dysgenesis, or 5α-reductase deficiency may have a normal endocrine profile for a postpubertal man despite the profound defect in androgen action during embryogenesis, whereas the testicular lesions in the Klinefelter syndrome and in the XX male become progressively severe so that plasma testosterone values, although initially normal, decline with age. Behavioral consequences might or might not occur in these disorders, depending on when in development gonadal steroids exert an effect on gender identity.

Thus, abnormalities of sexual development differ in their influence on the sexual phenotypes, their effects on hormone patterns at various times of life, their times of manifestation during life, and their ultimate metabolic consequences. Any interpretation as to possible behavioral consequences of a specific disorder has to take these various factors into account. Since various abnormalities have different effects on the anatomic and functional phenotypes, different behavioral consequences would be predicted in different disorders if hormones are involved in the genesis of human sexual behavior. For these reasons, it is necessary to be especially cautious in interpreting any negative result, specifically one that fails to support an effect of hormones on gender development.

Behavioral Studies in Patients with Abnormalities of Sexual Development

While different forms of abnormal sexual development have been lumped together in many reports, detailed studies have been performed in six groups of patients with specific diagnoses:

1. Females exposed to excess androgens as a result of congenital adrenal hyperplasia develop a variable degree of virilization of the external genitalia. Gender identity is usually female despite the presence of virilization and despite the fact that in some studies effects can be delineated on certain aspects of gender role behavior, generally a tomboyishness and characteristic male energy expenditure.
2. Children and animals who are exposed to exogenous estrogen or progesterone during gestation usually have appropriate male or female phenotypes. These agents, at best, have minor effects on sexually dimorphic behavior and no discernible effect on gender identity.
3. Genetic males with profound androgen resistance and the syndrome of testicular feminization develop a female phenotype. Such patients have testes and male testosterone levels but cannot respond to androgen and consequently differentiate as phenotypic women. Gender identity and gender role in such patients are unequivocally female in accord with anatomy and sex

assignment, and such patients when tested rank high in all femininity quotients.

4. Men with partial androgen resistance usually differentiate as phenotypic males but with severe hypospadias; their gender role and behavior appear to be concordant with the male phenotype and the male sex of rearing.

5. True hermaphrodites have both ovaries and testes and may have male, female, or ambiguous phenotypes. In such individuals gender identity and role usually correspond to the sex of rearing.

6. Women with gonadal dysgenesis have female phenotypes and generally have normal female gender role behavior and gender identity. Since such subjects are believed to be profoundly estrogen deficient throughout life, it has been inferred that gonadal estrogen plays at best a minor role in the evolution of female gender identity.

The general conclusion from these various studies has been that gender role and identity usually differentiate in conformity with the sex of assignment and rearing. In other words, gender role and identity correspond to the predominant anatomical development and hence to the predominant prenatal hormonal milieu. This conformity can withstand various perturbations that include: (1) contradictory hormonal patterns in which a girl virilizes or a boy feminizes at puberty, (2) tomboyish energy expenditure in girls, and (3) imperfect development of the secondary sexual characteristics at puberty. The conclusion that gender identity usually corresponds to sex assignment has been drawn by workers in different countries studying different types of patients. Despite inherent weaknesses in design in all such studies, and despite the fact that none of the disorders constitutes a perfect experiment, the unanimity of opinion in this regard is impressive.

The problem, however, is that the phenomenon is open to diametrically opposite interpretations. One view—most eloquently formulated by John Money and his coworkers—is that sex assignment at birth influences parental attitudes and the way in which infants are treated, and that these social forces are paramount in determining human gender identity and role, so powerfully as to be irreversible after a few years of rearing. According to this formulation, any effect of hormones in development of gender identity in the human is secondary, indeed probably minor. This interpretation was dominant for many years. Nevertheless, a different interpretation is possible. Gonadal steroids could be primary determinants of gender development, but since they also determine anatomical development, and hence sex assignment and the sex of rearing, gender identity and anatomical sex would almost invariably be the same. It would thus be expected that phenotypic sex (sex assignment) and gender role and identity usually correspond. In such a view, it is impossible to determine the extent to which psychological and social versus endocrine determinants are

more important, because the psychological and social forces generally correspond with the anatomical and endocrine factors.

Apparent Reversal of Gender Identity

From the first, a minority view has held that both biological determinants and
psychological factors influence gender identity. Indeed, occasional instances
have been reported over the years in which individual patients with abnormal
sexual development have undergone a change in gender role and gender behavior at some time after the critical period when gender identity is usually considered to be irreversibly fixed. The majority of these instances were described
before the means of making specific diagnoses of the etiology of abnormal
sexual development were available. It is not possible, in retrospect, to determine the diagnoses in most such reports. Nevertheless in analyzing these reports two facts seem clear: (1) the majority of patients in whom gender identity
does not differentiate in conformity with gender assignment have ambiguous
genitalia at birth; i.e., they are usually genetic males in whom male development is incomplete, resulting in a female sex assignment at birth; and (2) the
decision to change gender role at puberty is most commonly to shift from female to male. In other words, the shift is usually from a misassigned gender in
biological/hormonal terms to the correct one; only rarely does a shift occur
from the correct biological sex. The reverse sequence, a shift from male to
female gender role, has been reported in subjects with abnormal sexual development but is quite rare.

A change in gender role and assignment at puberty has been documented
during the past two decades in two specific types of male pseudohermaphroditism, namely, patients with 5α-reductase deficiency and subjects with a hereditary defect in testosterone synthesis due to deficiency of 17β-hydroxysteroid
dehydrogenase. A similar phenomenon has also been described in rare subjects
with ambiguous genitalia due to mixed gonadal dysgenesis. It has been implied
(but not established) that such individuals may have undergone a change in
gender identity as well as a change in gender role and assignment, i.e., that a
true reversal of gender identity can take place at the time of expected puberty.

These reports have reactivated the question as to the role of biological (endocrine) versus psychosocial factors in determining gender identity. Indeed, the
suggestion has been made that androgen action on the brain *in utero,* during
the neonatal period, and at puberty plays an important role in the determination
of male gender identity and that, under certain circumstances, it can override
female sex assignment and female sex of rearing. Interesting as these observations may be, they are also open to several problems of interpretation:

First, no prospective studies have been performed, so that it is impossible to
ascertain whether the gender identity prior to puberty in such subjects was in

fact unambiguously female. Apparent gender reversal is a prominent feature only of those forms of abnormal sexual development in which genital ambiguity is pronounced (table 6.1). Many individuals with ambiguous genitalia are aware of their abnormalities from an early age and consequently are unclear as to their exact gender role prior to puberty. In such individuals a change in gender role behavior could be a resolution of an uncertain gender identity rather than a true change in gender identity.

Second, many patients in whom gender role behavior has changed from female to male at puberty have been raised in cultures in which the sexes have fairly rigid stereotypes as to sexual role and in which the traditional female roles centering on home and family life are difficult, if not impossible, for women with phallic enlargements and shallow vaginas. Consequently, in such an environment cultural forces serve to reinforce any biological forces involved in a change from a female to a male role. It is particularly difficult to perform prospective studies of sexual behavior in these communities.

Third, even if it were established that the changes in gender role behavior in such patients were due to an actual change in gender identity and that gender identity and role behavior are determined solely, or predominantly, by endocrine or biological forces rather than psychosocial factors, it would still not be clear whether the changes are due to effects on the central nervous system or the peripheral target tissues. The development of a functional penis might influence behavioral patterns independent of the central nervous system. Any effects of gonadal steroids on human behavior could be mediated largely, if not exclusively, by their effects on peripheral tissues. These actions could include such diverse phenomena as tomboyish behavior, which might result from androgen actions on muscle growth, as well as adoption of a male gender role due to virilization of the genitalia.

Finally, if it were true, however, that androgens can override female gender identity—by whatever mechanism—it is interesting that the disorders in which reversal apparently occurs (5α-reductase deficiency, defects in testosterone synthesis, and possibly mixed gonadal dysgenesis) are those in which the neonatal surge in testosterone synthesis is probably normal, suggesting the possibility that the neonatal phase of male sexual life might be of importance in influencing development of male gender identity.

In summary, it is impossible on the basis of the evidence at hand to be certain of the extent to which biological factors interact with psychosocial forces to determine sexual behavior of humans, and it is equally impossible to know whether any biological factors involved act directly on the central nervous system. It seems safe to assume that the truth lies somewhere between the extremes of the anthropocentric and zoocentric schools, namely, that both biological and psychosocial factors play a role in determining the sexual behavior of humans (see Introduction, this volume, for a relevant model). Interesting though the quantitative issues may be, definitive studies are difficult because of inherent limitations in techniques available for analysis of human behavior.

Conclusion

In all species, including the human, steroid hormones are involved in the conversion of the sexually indifferent embryo into the male phenotype, in sexual and reproductive maturation of males and females during postnatal life, and, in the male at least, in the development of a basic sexual drive at the time of sexual maturation. In animals gonadal steroids also play a critical role in the development of the specific actions that characterize male and female reproductive behavior, and a portion of hormone action in this regard is due to direct effects on the central nervous system. Cultural imprinting also plays a role in sex-specific behavior in some animal species. The steroid hormones act predominantly via a specific receptor protein to exert effects in diverse tissues such as external genitalia and brain.

There are differences in the extent to which gonadal steroids influence the behavior of man and animals, however. The most clear-cut examples of such differences appear to be the lack of documentation of an effect of ovarian hormones on libido in women and the lack of a permanent imprinting of androgens on the hypothalamic control of gonadotropin production in men. It is also not established whether gonadal hormones have any direct effect on the development of gender identity and gender role in the human (i.e., outside the role in anatomical development of the sexual phenotypes). Whether biological or cultural forces predominate in influencing gender identity and behavior in the human or whether both forces are critical is one of the unresolved problems of human biology. It seems likely that both types of forces are involved, namely, that both androgens and cultural factors play roles in the development of characteristic male behavior. The relative contribution of the two types of forces and the extent to which any effect of androgen is exerted directly upon the central nervous system or indirectly via effects on peripheral sensory input are unresolved. Indeed, it seems unlikely that these issues—either qualitative or quantitative—can be elucidated in the foreseeable future.

Notes

1. Gonadotropin: any of several hormones produced in the pituitary gland that act on the testes or ovaries.
2. Orchidectomy: surgical removal of one or both of the testes.
3. Ovariectomy: surgical removal of an ovary.
4. Adrenalectomy: excision of one or both adrenal glands.
5. Hypophysectomy: surgical removal or destruction of the pituitary gland.
6. Prohormone: a precursor to a particular hormone.
7. Estradiol: one of the (primarily) female sex hormones produced by the ovary.
8. 45,X gonadal dysgenesis: abnormal gonadal development caused by a chromo-

somal abnormality (a form of Turner syndrome) in which there is only one sex chromosome (X). The vast majority of 45,X individuals are phenotypical females, although occasionally a phenotypic male is afflicted.

9. Hypospadia: surgically-correctable congenital abnormality in men in which the urethra is on the underside of the penis.

10. Testicular feminization syndrome (complete androgen insensitivity): a congenital condition due to defects in the androgen receptor that causes feminization of the external genitalia in genetic males (see also Meyer-Bahlburg, this volume).

11. 47,XXY Klinefelter syndrome: a genetic disorder in which there are three sex chromosomes (XXY). Individuals with this disorder are chromosomally male, but have small testes, enlarged breasts, and an absence of facial and body hair.

12. XX male syndrome: a rare chromosomal abnormality in which a phenotypic male possesses the XX sex chromosomes characteristic of genetic females (typically, some portion of male [Y] chromosomal material can also be identified in the XX male genome).

13. 5-alpha reductase deficiency: a hereditary disorder causing pseudohermaphroditism in genetic males due to an inability to convert testosterone to dihydrotestosterone. Afflicted individuals are typically born with ambiguous external genitalia, but exhibit increased masculine differentiation (their voices deepen, their penises grow, their testes descend, and so on) at puberty.

14. Congenital adrenal hyperplasia (CAH): a hormonal disorder caused by 21-hydroxylase enzyme deficiency that results in exposure to excess fetal androgen in genetic females. The excess androgen causes varying degrees of masculinization (pseudohermaphroditism), particularly of the external genitalia (see also Meyer-Bahlburg, this volume).

Selected Reading

Beach FA (1948). "Hormones and Behavior," Harper (Hoeber), New York.

Beach FA (1977). In: "Human Sexuality in Four Perspectives" (Beach FA, ed), Johns Hopkins University Press, Baltimore, pp 247–67.

Bremer J (1959). "Asexualization," Macmillan, New York.

Davidson JM, Camargo CA, Smith ER (1979). J Clin Endocrinol Metab 48:955–58.

Griffin JE, Wilson JD (1989). In: "The Metabolic Basis of Inherited Disease" (Scriver CR, Beaudet AL, Sly WS, Valle D, eds), 6th Ed, McGraw-Hill, New York, pp 1919–44.

McEwen BS (1980). Mol Cell Endocrinol 18:151–64.

Money J (1977). In: "Handbook of Sexology" (Money J, Musaph H, eds), Elsevier, Amsterdam, pp 47–79.

Money J, Ehrhardt AA (1972). "Man and Woman, Boy and Girl," Johns Hopkins University Press, Baltimore.

Phoenix CH, Goy RW, Gerall AA, Young WC (1959). Endocrinology 65:369–82.

Phoenix CH, Goy RW, Young WC (1967). In: "Neuroendocrinology" (Martini L, Ganong WF, eds), Vol II, Academic Press, New York, pp 163–96.

Salmimies P, Cockott G, Pirke KM, Vogt HJ, Schill WB (1982). Arch Sex Behav 11:345–53.

Sherwin BB (1988). Psychobiology 16: 416–25.

Udry JR, Billy JOG, Morris NM, Groff TR, Raj MH (1985). Fertil Steril 43:90–94.

Whalen RE (1977). In: "Human Sexuality in Four Perspectives" (Beach FA, ed), Johns Hopkins University Press, Baltimore, pp 215–46.

Wilson JD (1982). In: "Clinical Neuroendocrinology" (Besser GM, Martini L, eds), Vol I, Chap 1, Academic Press, New York, pp 1–29.

CHAPTER SEVEN

Psychoneuroendocrinology and Sexual Pleasure: The Aspect of Sexual Orientation

HEINO F. L. MEYER-BAHLBURG

Sexual Pleasure in Sexology

There is a dearth of literature on "sexual pleasure." "Sexual pleasure" or similar terms are not even listed in the indices of leading sexological textbooks such as the one by Bancroft (1989), nor in the publications of such senior sexologists as Money (e.g., 1980), nor in sexological treatises such as Tennov's (1979) book on passionate love. Pleasure simply has not been the focus of much research in sexology, especially not its psychobiological side.

Ironically, the area of sexual dysfunctions is where "sexual pleasure" plays a significant role and where "pleasuring" (partner or self) has become a standard term. "Sexual pleasure" or sex as an "enjoyable" or "pleasurable" experience are terms that are often included in the assessment of sexual dysfunctions for both clinical and research purposes. Yet, the primary dependent variables in psychobiological sex research, even in psychobiological research on sexual dysfunctions, has been the frequency of sexual activities and the prevalence of classical dysfunctions, and maybe of such negative emotions during sex as anxiety, aversion, and avoidance; pleasure seems to have gotten the short end of the stick, so to speak, even in my own research.

A likely reason for this is that psychobiological, and especially psychoendocrine, research in sexology has been strongly oriented toward animal models where pleasure is not part of the usual equation. A good example is the exquisite composite picture of the anatomical, neurophysiological, and neurochemical organization of hormone-dependent sexual behavior in the female rat, as provided by Schwartz-Giblin et al. (1989). Moreover, even where pleasure and related terms are included in the assessment of human sexuality, such terms are usually left undefined, as if we can assume that every participant understands these terms in the same way. If one looks more closely, "pleasure" often appears to be used synonymously with "nondysfunction." Given the large variety of dysfunctional disorders and states, it again seems likely that pleasure has quite divergent meanings or connotations. What provides pleasure during sexual activity is probably as variable as what motivates people to seek sex. In fact, sexual motivation is often equated with seeking sexual pleasure. Specific aspects of sexual pleasure are probably associated with each stage of the mating sequence and the sexual response cycle, as are specific aspects of sexual motivation. Consequently, the sex hormones and neurotransmitters involved are likely to play specific roles associated with these various stage-related aspects of sexual pleasure, but specifics are not known.

"Pleasuring" as used in the clinical sex dysfunction literature refers mostly to body caresses, but clinically one gets the impression that there are many diverse aspects of sexuality from which people draw pleasure, ranging from the awareness of attraction and beauty to the excitement of flirtation and courtship to the experience of orgasm and subsequent relaxation, interwoven with all the nonsexual aspects of sexual motivation (Schmidt, 1983). It would be astonishing if these various aspects of "sexual pleasure" were not associated with differential predictors, including biological predictors, but the necessary footwork for conceptual clarification and operationalization has not yet been done.

There is much evidence for the induction of sexual motivation (pleasure-seeking) by hormone administration in individuals with low sex-hormone levels (Bancroft, 1988). On the other hand, the absence or inhibition of sexual motivation/pleasure-seeking ("hypoactive sexual desire," in DSM-III-R) is a well-established phenomenon in sexually mature adults with normal adult sex-hormone levels. Motivation for sexual activity can apparently also be induced in prepubertal and adult individuals with low sex-hormone levels. Thus, adolescent or adult sex-hormone levels are neither necessary nor sufficient for the development of some degree of sexual motivation and sexual enjoyment. Furthermore, when postchildhood sex-hormone levels are established, they interact in their effects on sexual behavior with the individual's social and sexual (that is, culturally mediated) history (e.g., Udry, 1988).

One important aspect of both sexual pleasure and sexual motivation is the individual's selective erotic attraction or erotic responsiveness to certain types of potential sexual partners. Partners other than those the individual is usually attracted to may not evoke as much arousal; they may even incur avoidance or aversion. Sexual orientation, or being predominantly erotically responsive to men, to women, or to both men and women, is one of the major aspects of selective attraction. The research on biological factors in the development of sexual orientation is the focus of this chapter.

Sexual Orientation and Psychosexual Differentiation

Recent publications on putative psychobiological explanations of homosexual development have received an unusual degree of interest. Is this a sign of marked progress? Is a consensus emerging as to *the* psychobiological theory of sexual orientation?

About ten years ago I conducted a detailed review of the psychoendocrinology of sexual orientation (Meyer-Bahlburg, 1984). My purpose here is to take stock of developments in this field since then. The psychoendocrine approach to sexual orientation has moved virtually exclusively to the prenatal hormone theory (Meyer-Bahlburg, 1993). Already at the time of the 1984 review, the consensus was that there is no difference in systemic sex-hormone levels between homosexual and heterosexual men, and possibly a minor difference indicating slightly higher androgen levels in lesbian women as compared to heterosexual women. The few additional studies on men since that time have not changed the earlier conclusions (Meyer-Bahlburg, 1990/91a). Two additional studies in women (Downey et al., 1987; Dancey, 1990) did not yield any differences in sex-hormone levels between lesbian and heterosexual women, but a new study (Balen et al., 1993) of untreated female-to-male transsexuals who usually are sexually attracted to women confirmed an earlier finding of increased rates of polycystic ovary syndrome which is typically associated with increased androgen levels.

The prenatal hormone theory of sexual orientation is essentially one aspect of the prenatal hormone theory of psychosexual differentiation in general. In this view, an individual's homosexual orientation constitutes an aspect of cross-gender behavior, i.e., behavior that is more typical of the other gender than of the person's own. Empirically, this notion has found partial support in the demonstration of neuropsychological differences between homosexual and heterosexual men that to some extent are similar to those found between the sexes (Gladue et al., 1990; McCormick & Witelson, 1991). However the results are often inconsistent, and many critics have presented plausible (although not compelling) arguments in favor of determinants other than the prenatal sex hormones. The prenatal hormone theory in its various versions (e.g., Dörner, 1989) follows closely the best-studied animal models in this area, mostly rodents such as the rat and the guinea pig, and to a much lesser extent a primate, the rhesus monkey. A decisive role of pre- or perinatal sex hormones in the development of sex-typical repertoires of both reproductive and nonreproductive behaviors has been demonstrated in many mammalian species (Gerall, et al., 1992), and more recent studies have shown the prenatal/perinatal hormone-dependence of the development of an apparent sexual preference (under laboratory conditions) in several species of lower mammals (for a critical review, see Adkins-Regan, 1988).

Parenthetically, I should point out that these are not the only possible animal models for psychosexual differentiation. There are animal models of psychosexual differentiation which depend more on pubertal than on prenatal hormones, for instance, the pig (Ford, 1983; Ford & D'Occhio, 1989). There are other animal models of sexual orientation that do not seem to imply any primary effects of pre- or postnatal sex hormones, for instance, the conditioning model of the rat (Rasmussen, 1955), or the isosexually reared ram (Perkins & Fitzgerald, 1992). The latter model may be of particular interest in the recent rekindling of attention to findings of increased numbers of same-sex siblings in families of homosexual individuals (Blanchard & Sheridan, 1992a,b; Blanchard & Zucker, in press; Blanchard et al., in press). Yet, little attention has been paid to these alternative models, and most of the recent empirical work has been devoted to the prenatal hormone hypothesis. (See Pattatucci & Hamer, this volume, for their research on the genetics of male homosexuality.)

Sexual Differentiation

To quite an extent, the principles governing the sexual differentiation of brain and behavior as distilled from animal models and human research seem to overlap with the principles regulating genital differentiation. In regard to the latter, there is general agreement on the following.

1. The genital anlagen are the same for both sexes.
2. Sexual differentiation of the anlagen depends on the pre- or perinatal hormonal milieu.
3. The critical factors here are the testicular hormone production, metabolic enzymes, and the receptor sensitivity of target tissues.
4. At least three hormones are involved in prenatal genital differentiation: testosterone, its metabolite dihydrotestosterone, and Müllerian inhibiting hormone.
5. Hormone-dependent differentiation takes place during a critical period relatively early during prenatal or perinatal development.

The corresponding principles for sexual differentiation of the brain are as follows:

1. The brain anlagen, as far as sex-dimorphic nuclei are concerned, seem to be the same for both sexes. That is, where sexually dimorphic brain structures have been identified, they seem to be associated with hormone exposure rather than directly with the sex chromosomes. However, a caveat is in order. The identification of sex-dimorphic areas in the brain has only begun in nonhuman mammals and is at an even more rudimentary stage in human research.
2. In rodent models, sexual differentiation of the brain nuclei depends on the prenatal and/or perinatal hormonal milieu. With regard to humans, the same statement would be premature, given the extremely limited data base (see Swaab et al., 1992; Byne & Parsons, 1993). Rhesus monkeys, whose endocrine development has many similarities to that of humans, show strong behavioral effects of prenatal hormones. In males of this species, Eisler et al. (1993) demonstrated that gonadal testosterone production during the first half-year of infancy contributes to the development of aspects of sexual motivation expressed in adulthood. This finding suggests that the well-

documented testosterone peak in human males during the first half-year of infancy may exert significant behavioral effects.

3. The critical factors in the differentiation of the brain are testicular hormone production, metabolic enzymes, and probably the receptor sensitivity of target tissues.

4. Several hormones seem to be involved in the sexual differentiation of the brain. More specifically, and unlike the situation in genital differentiation, there seems to be an androgen pathway and an estrogen pathway (McEwen, 1983) regulating both neuronal development and selective neuronal death.

5. Hormone-dependent differentiation takes place during a sensitive period early in development. This has been well established for lower mammals and to some extent also for the rhesus monkey, at least with regard to the timing of early sex-hormone exposure and its impact on sex-dimorphic behavior as a functional indicator of brain effects. Data on humans are suggestive but not conclusive.

6. "Organizational" effects of sex hormones during the early development are followed by "activational" effects from puberty on (although pubertal hormones may also have organizational effects of their own; Arnold & Breedlove, 1985). This principle is well established for a number of nonhuman mammals. Whether it really strictly applies to human sex-dimorphic brain development and behavior has not been satisfactorily shown.

Of potentially great importance for human behavior are more recent findings in animal research that demonstrate the transient appearance of sex-hormone receptors in the cortex during early development (e.g., McEwen, 1987) and the association of brain asymmetries with early sex-hormone exposure (e.g., Holman & Hutchison, 1991). These observations may point to the basis for sex differences in brain lateralization and neurocognitive functions, and for related differences between homo- and hetero-sexual individuals.

Strategies in Human Research

Given the ethical limits to systematic experimentation for research purposes in human beings, human investigation is limited to a number of less direct research strategies (Meyer-Bahlburg, 1992). Seven approaches to studying hormone-dependent psychosexual differentiation are available.

1. Persons with prenatal endocrine abnormalities, that is, prenatal sex-hormone disorders or sex-hormone receptor disorders (see Wilson, this volume, for an overview).

2. Offspring of sex-hormone treated pregnancies.

3. Individuals whose sex-hormone levels in cord blood have been determined at the time of birth.

4. Persons whose sex-hormone levels and amniotic fluid were assessed at the time of amniocentesis.

5. People whose mothers' sex hormones were measured at the time of pregnancy and are presumed to reflect in some way a significant aspect of the hormonal milieu of the fetus.
6. People whose mothers were exposed to marked stress during pregnancy which, on the basis of experimental animal studies, is hypothesized to have interfered with the normal prenatal hormonal milieu.
7. As an alternative to the approaches above, one can select people for specific behavioral characteristics and inquire whether they show any indications of a prenatal hormonal milieu that differs in the expected direction from those of other individuals not sharing the same behavioral characteristics.

Approaches 3, 4, and 5 have not yet been applied to the study of sexual orientation and will be disregarded in the subsequent discussion. All of these approaches are beset with major methodological problems (Meyer-Bahlburg, 1992), and none of them permit a strict causal analysis of hormonal influences. In the best case, these strategies deliver data that are compatible with the prenatal hormone hypothesis but do not prove it.

Results on Sexual Orientation

At the time of the 1984 review, most of the evidence linking prenatal hormone variations to variations in human sexual orientation came from studies of persons with endocrine disorders involving major variations in the fetal production or utilization of androgens. The syndromes of prenatal androgen excess in genetic females and the syndromes of androgen insensitivity in genetic males continue to be the most important examples (see also Wilson, this volume).

The classical form of Congenital Adrenal Hyperplasia (CAH), a result of a deficiency of the enzyme 21-hydroxylase, is the most prevalent syndrome of fetal androgen excess in genetic females (Speiser & New, 1990). CAH women are born with varying degrees of external genital ambiguity, but their ovaries, fallopian tubes, and uteri are normal. In 1968, Ehrhardt, Evers and Money described an increase of bisexual and homosexual orientation among a sample of CAH. This finding has now been replicated with improved methodology on three samples (Money et al., 1984; Dittmann et al., 1992; Zucker et al., 1992). The data lead to two conclusions. One concerns the finding of increased bi- and homo-sexuality. It suggests that high prenatal levels of circulating androgens in women contribute to the development of a nonheterosexual orientation. The demonstration of Dittmann et al. (1992) that the more severe (salt-wasting) form of the syndrome shows considerably stronger behavioral effects suggests a dose-response relationship, but the underlying mechanism has yet to be worked out. A second conclusion needs to be drawn from the fact that the majority of CAH patients seem to be heterosexual, in spite of their—often severe—prenatal androgen exposure. This fact implies that prenatal androgens may contribute to, but do not fully determine, the development of sexual orientation.

Genetic males with complete androgen insensitivity (originally known as testicular feminization) have normal testes and make at least normal amounts of testosterone (T) and its 5-alpha-reduced metabolite dihydrotestosterone (DHT), but they are unable to respond to either, due to defects in the androgen receptor. At birth, the external genitalia look feminine, and consequently these infants are raised as girls. Two early studies (Masica et al., 1971; Lewis & Money, 1983) found such persons to be erotically attracted to men. Of course, the feminine psychosexual differentiation of these persons may be attributed to social-rearing effects as well as to androgen insensitivity. Unfortunately, no further studies of such women by independent investigators have been reported.

Genetic males with partial androgen insensitivity who produce normal amounts of androgens but respond with only partial genital masculinization usually become erotically attracted to females, as had been shown by Money and Ogunro (1974). Again, this study still remains to be replicated. Most such persons are raised as males, but at least some of those raised female also develop sexual attractions to other females and may even undergo gender change later, as described in an instructive case report by Gooren and Cohen-Kettenis (1991).

Androgen insensitivity syndromes are usually assumed to reflect generalized genetic defects of the androgen receptors, i.e., the receptor defect is not confined to specific tissues. Recent findings, however, have raised the possibility of CNS-specific androgen-receptor defects. LaSpada et al. (1991, 1992) have demonstrated that spinal bulbar muscular atrophy, a progressive degenerative disorder of the spinal motor neurons, is based on a genetic abnormality of the androgen receptor that is apparently manifested primarily in the central nervous system. If one tries to interpret homosexuality in men, at least in those with a history of atypical gender-role behavior, in the context of psychosexual differentiation, an androgen-receptor defect that manifests itself primarily in the brain would constitute a mechanism suitable to explain the presence of behavioral undermasculinization in combination with full somatic masculinization. A first search for corresponding variations in the androgen receptor gene of homosexual men by Macke et al. (1993) has, however, not been successful.

Genetic males with 5-alpha-reductase deficiency (Imperato-McGinley et al., 1974, 1979) secrete normal amounts of testosterone but cannot convert it into dihydrotestosterone. Consequently, their external genitalia look female at birth, and they are apparently raised as girls. They virilize strongly in response to pubertal increases in circulating testosterone. If they remain untreated, they tend to develop sexual feelings towards women, and many seem to adopt a male gender role in later adolescence or adulthood. A similar life course has been described for individuals with 17-beta-hydroxysteroid-dehydrogenase deficiency (Rösler & Kohn, 1983). The behavioral methodology of these studies is highly problematic, however (Herdt & Davidson, 1988; Meyer-Bahlburg, 1982), and does not permit a clarification of whether and to what extent hormonal and nonhormonal factors contribute to the psychosexual development of these persons. Replication studies are urgently needed.

In summary, the evidence from human intersex research has remained very limited, and only with regard to the CAH syndrome in women can we be reasonably confident that the existing data hold up with replication. Limited as they are, however, the data present a coherent picture. In combination, the evidence continues to suggest that, in either genetic males or females (i.e., independently of chromosomal sex), prenatal exposure to androgens and their utilization seems to "facilitate" (Money, 1988), but certainly not to determine, the development of erotic attraction to females as postulated by the prenatal hormone theory. The data on partial androgen insensitivity indicate that, in genetic males, the putative androgen effects are already noticeable with only modest degrees of prenatal androgen exposure, while the CAH data demonstrate that, in genetic females, prenatal exposure to even high levels of androgens is not necessarily associated with marked bi- or homo-sexuality. It appears, however, that complete nonresponsiveness to androgens is associated with the development of erotic attraction to males.

One potentially confounding factor in the study of intersex patients is the visible status of the external genitalia. When Money's team (Money et al., 1986; Money & Norman, 1987) demonstrated the increased prevalence of "gender transpositions" (including both gender identity change and sexual orientation) in female-assigned as compared to male-assigned pseudohermaphrodites, a history of prolonged ambiguity of external genital status after birth was a statistically significant predictor of gender transposition. At this stage of our knowledge, it is an open question whether responses of the social environment to an ambiguous genital status or its effects on the body-image of a young child are sufficient to bring about gender transpositions. The latter possibility is strongly suggested by the phenomenon of cross-gender identity or transsexualism in persons with no known somatic intersexuality, but the cause(s) of its development are also not well understood. On the other hand, as Goy et al. (1988) clearly demonstrated, prenatal sex-hormone manipulation can be timed so that hormone effects on behavior are induced in the absence of effects on genital development. This demonstration underlines the plausibility of a direct effect of prenatal hormones on the brain and behavior of the human primate.

Also, estrogens need to be considered in the context of the prenatal hormone theory of sexual orientation. As mentioned earlier, animal research has indicated that some effects of prenatal and perinatal androgens on the central nervous system, e.g., on gonadotropin regulation and copulatory behavior of rats, are at least partially mediated by estrogens; these are derived from testosterone by aromatization inside the target cells. To induce such effects by exogenous estrogen administration, one has to employ pharmacologic doses of steroidal estrogens or a nonsteroidal estrogen such as diethylstilbestrol; both are able to bypass mechanisms that ordinarily inactivate estradiol before it reaches the fetal brain. My 1984 report contained preliminary data showing increased bisexuality in women with a history of prenatal exposure to DES that had been administered to their pregnant mothers. In the meantime, that first report has been fully published (Ehrhardt et al., 1990). Subsequent studies by our team replicated the initial results on two additional samples with independent control groups, and on a subsample of DES-exposed women compared to their unexposed sisters (Meyer-Bahlburg et al., in press). Although the effect sizes were quite modest, these data suggest that estrogen-mediated developmental effects on sexual orientation may have to be taken into consideration and lend support to a prenatal hormone theory that implicates both androgens and estrogens in the development of sexual orientation. As we have discussed in detail in the two publications listed, however, even successfully replicated studies of this kind cannot by themselves exclude competing hypotheses about the actual mechanisms involved.

If one wants to generalize the prenatal hormone theory of sexual orientation from patients with known prenatal hormone abnormalities to the general population, one needs to search for indications of a difference in the prenatal hormonal milieu between homosexuals and heterosexuals. Here the evidence is insufficient. Homosexuals usually do not have somatic symptoms of intersexuality, and the fact that their adult sex-hormone levels are in the normal range also does not suggest prenatal hormone abnormalities. Likewise, an investigation of the androgen receptor gene on the X chromosome in a sample of nonintersex homosexual brother pairs did not show any molecular abnormalities that would indicate abnormalities of the androgen receptor (Hamer, 1993a, 1993b; Macke et al., 1993; see also Pattatucci & Hamer, this volume).

As indicated above, it is entirely conceivable that prenatal sex hormones affect the developing brain at a time other than when genital differentiation takes place. Thus, functional signs of such hormone exposure are of great interest. One such functional sign of pre- or perinatal sex hormone variations may be the positive estrogen feedback effect on luteinizing hormone (LH) demonstrated in rodent research. In the mature female, rising estrogen levels typically trigger an LH surge associated with ovulation, but in rodents who have been pre- or perinatally exposed to androgens, the LH surge is blocked. Due to pre- or perinatal exposure to their own androgens, genetic males usually do not show this phenomenon unless they have been castrated very early in development.

In the search for corresponding functional signs of intersexuality in human homosexuals, Dörner and his team have found that homosexual and transsexual men are more likely to react to estrogen administration with a delayed increase of luteinizing hormone (LH) (Dörner, 1988; Dörner & Döcke, 1987). The authors interpreted the delayed LH response as an effect of positive estrogen feedback and a sign of deficient prenatal androgenization.

It can be argued, however, that the delayed LH response does not meet usually accepted criteria of a positive estrogen feedback effect, and is a mere rebound phenomenon (e.g., Gooren, 1986a, b). Also, unlike rodents, nonhuman primates such as rhesus monkeys do not show a marked effect of prenatal androgen levels on their pattern of LH regulation; instead, the positive estrogen feedback effect on LH depends on systemic androgen levels at the time. Finally, attempts at replicating the findings of Dörner's team by other laboratories brought conflicting results (Gladue et al., 1984; Gooren, 1986a; Gooren et al., 1984; Hendricks et al., 1989; Seyler et al., 1978). Studies of other features of gonadotropin regulation, such as pulse frequency and amplitude, also yielded mixed results (Spijkstra et al., 1988).

Therefore, other explanations of Dörner's LH rebound findings must be considered. For example, the LH rebound effect could be due to increased rates of testicular impairment resulting from a high rate of sexually transmitted diseases in homosexuals (Hendricks et al., 1989), especially if the samples, as in the case of some of Dörner's studies, are recruited in STD clinics. Such an interpretation is plausible since men (regardless of sexual orientation) who show a marked LH rebound after estrogen administration also have a decreased testicular capacity to release testosterone after priming with human chorionic gonadotropin (Gooren, 1986a). In view of these arguments, the LH rebound effect is not widely accepted as a sign of prenatal hypoandrogenization, although a consensus has not yet been achieved. This controversy will be increasingly difficult to settle during the current HIV epidemic, when the study of LH regulation in human homosexuals has been complicated by findings of lowered T and elevated LH levels in homosexual men who have advanced stages of HIV disease (Croxson et al., 1989; see also Grinspoon & Bilezikian, 1992).

Assuming for a moment that a definitive functional indicator of a particular prenatal hormonal milieu had been found in homosexuals, how could neuroendocrine intersexuality develop without genital intersexuality? One mechanism, in males, might be a brain-specific genetically based androgen-receptor defect, as discussed earlier. Other mechanisms may involve the timing of prenatal hormone effects and stress. As pointed out before, detailed developmental studies in animals have shown that the sex-hormone-dependent differentiation of the genitals has a different time course than the sexual differentiation of the brain (Goy et al., 1988). Other animal experiments have indicated that drugs or severe stress can influence the prenatal hormonal milieu, and can affect brain and behavior, without signs of genital abnormalities (e.g., Ward, 1992).

Therefore, several researchers have looked for effects of prenatal stress in humans. The results have been inconsistent. Dörner's group (Dörner et al.,

1991) has summarized several of their studies that suggest a prenatal stress interpretation for human homosexuality, but these studies suffer from problems of sampling and assessment, and alternative psychosocial interpretations of the findings appear plausible, especially with regard to an association of prenatal stress with postnatal stress conditions and ensuing psychosocial effects on the developing child and the mother-child relationship. Of two prenatal-stress studies in the U.S., one has been positive (Ellis et al., 1988), and the other, methodologically very carefully done, has been negative (Bailey, 1989).

Psychosocial stress tends to involve the endocrine system, especially its hypothalamic-pituitary-adrenal axis. With this fact in mind, Dörner and co-workers (1991) have formulated a new version of the prenatal hormone theory of homosexual orientation by combining the prenatal stress hypothesis with a genetic vulnerability to hormonal stress effects; the genetic vulnerability is based on deficiencies of enzymes involved in steroid synthesis. The authors developed this theory when they found the cortisol (F) precursor 21-deoxycortisol (21-DOF) to be significantly increased after ACTH stimulation in homosexual males and females as compared to heterosexual controls; a similar increase was found in the mothers of homosexual men. In female-to-male transsexuals, 21-DOF was increased significantly already before ACTH stimulation and even more after. The 21-DOF increase is compatible with insufficient availability of the enzyme 21-hydroxylase in the biochemical pathway for the synthesis of cortisol. More severe forms of this enzyme deficiency are the cause of CAH. Dörner and coworkers (1991) concluded, therefore, from their data that "heterozygous and homozygous forms, respectively, of 21-hydroxylase deficiency represent a genetic predisposition to androgen-dependent development of homosexuality and transsexualism in females." This theory would also be compatible with the findings mentioned earlier of an increased prevalence of polycystic ovary syndrome in female-to-male transsexuals. For genetic males, Dörner et al. suggested that testicular androgen deficiency "may be induced by prenatal stress and/or maternal or fetal genetic alterations." In addition, the authors found increased basal levels of dehydroepiandrosterone in male-to-female transsexuals as compared to normal males (and in one homosexual male who did not show the 21-DOF increase), and concluded that "partial 3β-ol hydroxysteroid dehydrogenase deficiency" may be "a predisposing factor for the development of male-to-female transsexualism." (Transsexuals are of interest here because at least half of these persons have a history of predominantly to exclusively homosexual orientation relative to their original gender.) This bold and complex theory and the data it is based on are in urgent need of independent testing and replication. Even if replication should be successful, there is at least one significant problem: the theory by itself fails to explain why the majority of women with classical CAH (which is due to 21-hydroxylase deficiency in its homozygous form) do not develop homosexuality or transsexualism.

In summary, it is too early to conclude definitively that there is a contribution of pre- or perinatal sex-hormone levels to the development of homosexuality in general, except perhaps in persons with clear-cut physical signs of intersexuality. Also, there are other potential avenues to a psychoendocrine explanation of homosexuality (Meyer-Bahlburg, 1984) which have not yet been exhausted.

Neuroanatomic studies

During the last three decades, a variety of sex-hormone-dependent structural sex differences, ranging from dendritic branching patterns of neurons to the size of nerve cell nuclei, have been determined in the brain of several avian and mammalian species (Allen et al., 1989; Tobet & Fox, 1992). More recently, structural sex differences have also been reported for the human brain, in terms of both large brain structures and specific cell nuclei (Allen et al., 1989; LeVay, 1991, 1993; Swaab et al., 1992). The available data must be considered tentative at best, however, given that for most of these findings replications by independent laboratories have not yet been attempted or have failed.

In line with the fact that the psychobiological theory of sexual orientation constitutes a specific application of the general psychobiological theory of psychosexual differentiation, several researchers have searched for differences in sex-dimorphic structures between homosexual and heterosexual individuals. Swaab and Hofman (1990) performed a morphometric analysis of the human hypothalamus and determined that the volume of the suprachiasmatic nucleus (SCN) in a sample of homosexual men was 1.7 times as large as that of a reference group of male subjects and contained 2.1 times as many cells; however, the sex difference they had noted previously had pertained only to the shape of the SCN, not its volume or cell number. Nonetheless, the observation of a similarly enlarged SCN in a woman with Prader-Willi syndrome whose features include a congenital luteinizing hormone-releasing hormone deficiency in which sex-hormone levels are very low, suggests that the interaction with sex hormones at some stage of development of the SCN might be involved. In general, the SCN is involved in the regulation of physiological rhythms; the specific role it may have for sexual orientation is unknown. A nearby nucleus, called the Sexually Dimorphic Nucleus (SDN), for which Swaab and coworkers have previously reported a marked sex difference in volume and cell number did not yield differences between homosexual men and controls. Working independently of Swaab's team, LeVay (1991) reported that one of two sex-dimorphic interstitial nuclei of the anterior hypothalamus (INAH 3), out of a total of 4 INAH's, was more than twice as large in heterosexual men as in women and also more than twice as large in heterosexual men as in homosexual men; using the same samples, LeVay could not replicate the sex-dimorphism of the SDN described by Swaab and Hofman.

A third paper was published by Allen and Gorski (1992), who found a larger brain structure which was dimorphic for both sex and sexual orientation.

In this case, however, the homosexual men did not fit in a continuum with heterosexual men and women at the two poles, but surpassed both groups: The anterior commissure (AC) in homosexual men was 18 percent larger in its midsagittal area than in heterosexual women and 34 percent larger than in heterosexual men. The AC is thought to be related to cognitive function and cerebral lateralization but not reproductive function; it is of interest in this context that there are several (inconsistent) reports of increased rates of non-right-handed men in homosexuals in the literature. The authors interpret their AC finding, somewhat vaguely, as supporting the hypothesis that factors operating early in development differentiate sexually dimorphic structures and functions of the brain in a global fashion.

It is important to keep in mind that the findings of brain structural differences between homosexuals and heterosexuals have to be considered even more tentative than the respective findings of differences between the sexes. None of the findings on sexual orientation have yet been replicated by independent laboratories, and the published studies differ markedly in the neuroanatomic techniques employed and in important characteristics of the persons whose brains were analyzed, such as age at death and AIDS status.

Conclusion

Over the last ten years, the prenatal hormone theory of sexual orientation has become somewhat more firmly established for intersex patients, but no progress has been made in establishing its validity for nonintersex people who diverge in sexual orientation, apart from some indirect support from findings—often inconsistent—in the neuropsychologic area. The fact that, at the same time, more evidence is being accumulated for heritability of sexual orientation in nonintersex individuals, both in nontwin relatives (Pillard & Weinrich, 1986; Bailey & Pillard, 1991; Bailey & Benishay, 1993; Bailey et al., 1993; Buhrich et al., 1991; Hamer et al., 1993a; Hamer & Copeland, 1994) and in twins (Kallmann, 1952a, b; Heston & Shields, 1968; Eckert et al., 1986; Bailey & Pillard, 1991; Buhrich et al., 1991; King & McDonald, 1992; Bailey et al., 1993; Whitam et al., 1993) demands the identification of potential proximal mechanisms. There is little evidence that it is going to be the prenatal sex hormonal milieu which is providing this basis in the nonintersex cases, unless the new findings by Dörner's team can be confirmed; the manner in which pregnancy stress would conform to the genetic data is also not easy to see.

One way out of this dilemma is to postulate sex-dimorphic temperament (and, later in development, personality factors) as the basis for the development of a particular sexual orientation, as Byne and Parsons (1993) have recently argued. Sex-dimorphic temperament, in turn, can be influenced by prenatal hormones as well as by other biological and nonbiological factors, independently of sex hormones. In animal research, however, it has become clear that such seemingly temperamental characteristics as rough-and-tumble juvenile play behavior are dependent on prenatal hormones in a different way than sexual behavior. Also, we have to assume that at least in some individuals similar mechanisms may be at work in their ontogenesis of homosexuality or heterosexuality, as in the development of paraphilias for which sex-hormone based animal models do not exist at all. We conclude that we have far to go before there will be a general consensus on the diverse factors that contribute to the development of sexual orientation.

References

Adkins-Regan, E. (1988). Sex hormones and sexual orientation in animals. *Psychobiology, 16,* 335–47.

Allen, L. S., & Gorski, R. A. (1992). Sexual orientation and the size of the anterior commissure in the human brain. *Proceedings of the National Academy of Sciences of the United States of America, 89,* 7199–7202.

Allen, L. S., Hines, M., Shryne, J. E., & Gorski, R. A. (1989). Two sexually dimorphic cell groups in the human brain. *Journal of the Neurological Sciences, 9,* 497–506.

Arnold, A. P., & Breedlove, S. M. (1985). Organizational and activational effects of sex steroids on brain and behavior: A reanalysis. *Hormones and Behavior, 19,* 469–98.

Bailey, J. M. (1989). A test of the maternal stress hypothesis for human male homosexuality. Doctoral dissertation, University of Texas at Austin.

Bailey, J. M., & Benishay, D. S. (1993). Familial aggregation of female sexual orientation. *American Journal of Psychiatry, 150,* 272–77.

Bailey, J. M., & Pillard, R. C. (1991). A genetic study of male sexual orientation. *Archives of General Psychiatry, 48,* 1089–96.

Bailey, J. M., Pillard, R. C., Neale, M. C., & Agyei, Y. (1993). Heritable factors influence sexual orientation in women. *Archives of General Psychiatry, 50,* 217–223.

Balen, A. H., Schachter, M. E., Montgomery, D., Reid, R. W., & Jacobs, H. S. (1993). Polycystic ovaries are a common finding in untreated female to male transsexuals. *Clinical Endocrinology* (Oxford), *38,* 325–29.

Bancroft, J. (1988). Sexual desire and the brain. *Sexual and Marital Therapy, 3,* 11–27.

Bancroft, J. (1989). *Human sexuality and its problems* (2d ed.). Edinburgh: Churchill Livingstone.

Blanchard, R., & Sheridan, P. M. (1992a). Sibship size, sibling sex ratio, birth order, and parental age in homosexual and nonhomosexual gender dysphorics. *The Journal of Nervous and Mental Disease, 180,* 40–47.

Blanchard, R., & Sheridan, P. M. (1992b). Proportion of unmarried siblings of homosexual and non homosexual gender-dysphoric patients. *Canadian Journal of Psychiatry, 37,* 163–67.

Blanchard, R., Zucker, K. J., Bradley, S. J., & Hume, C. S. (in press). Birth order and sibling sex ratio in homosexual male adolescents and probably prehomosexual feminine boys. *Developmental Psychology.*

Blanchard, R., & Zucker, K. J. (in press). Reanalysis of Bell, Weinberg, and Hammersmith's data on birth order, sibling sex ratio, and parental age in male homosexuals. *American Journal of Psychiatry.*

Buhrich, N., Bailey, J. M., & Martin, N. G. (1991). Sexual orientation, sexual identity, and sex-dimorphic behaviors in male twins. *Behavior Genetics, 21,* 75–96.

Byne, W., & Parsons, B. (1993). Human sexual orientation. The biologic theories re-appraised. *Archives of General Psychiatry, 50,* 228–39.

Croxson, T. S., Chapman, W. E., Miller, L. K., Levit, C. D., Senie, R., & Zumoff, B. (1989). Changes in the hypothalamic-pituitary-gonadal axis in human immunodeficiency virus-infected homosexual men. *Journal of Clinical Endocrinology and Metabolism, 68,* 317–21.

Dancey, C. P. (1990). Sexual orientation in women: An investigation of hormonal and personality variables. *Biological Psychology, 30,* 251–64.

Dittmann, R. W., Kappes, M. E., & Kappes, M. H. (1992). Sexual behavior in adolescent and adult females with congenital adrenal hyperplasia. *Psychoneuroendocrinology, 17,* 153–70.

Dörner, G. (1988). Neuroendocrine response to estrogen and brain differentiation in heterosexuals, homosexuals, and transsexuals. *Archives of Sexual Behavior, 17,* 57–75.

Dörner, G. (1989). Hormone-dependent brain development and neuroendocrine prophylaxis. *Experimental and Clinical Endocrinology, 94,* 4–22.

Dörner, G., Döcke, F., Götz, F., Rohde, W., Stahl, F., & Tönjes, R. (1987). Sexual differentiation of gonadotrophin secretion, sexual orientation and gender role behavior. *Journal of Steroid Biochemistry, 27,* 1081–87.

Dörner, G., Poppe, I., Stahl, F., Kölzsch, J., & Uebelhack, R. (1991). Gene- and environment-dependent neuroendocrine etiogenesis of homosexuality and transsexualism. *Experimental and Clinical Endocrinology, 98,* 141–50.

Downey, J., Ehrhardt, A. A., Schiffman, M., Dyrenfurth, I., & Becker, J. (1987). Sex hormones in lesbian and heterosexual women. *Hormones and Behavior 21,* 347–57.

Eckert, E. D., Bouchard, T. J., Bohlen, J., & Heston, L. L. (1986). Homosexuality in monozygotic twins reared apart. *British Journal of Psychiatry, 148,* 421–25.

Ehrhardt, A. A., Evers, K., & Money, J. (1968). Influence of androgen and some aspects of sexually dimorphic behavior in women with the late-treated adrenogenital syndrome. *Johns Hopkins Medical Journal, 123,* 115–22.

Ehrhardt, A. A., & Meyer-Bahlburg, H. F. L. (1990). Influence of in utero exposure to hormones on mood and behavior in adulthood (abstract). *Neuroendocrinology Letters, 12,* 216.

Ehrhardt, A. A., Meyer-Bahlburg, H. F. L., Rosen, L. R., Feldman, J. F., Veridiano, N. P., Zimmerman, I., & McEwen, B. S. (1985). Sexual orientation after prenatal exposure to exogenous estrogen. *Archives of Sexual Behavior, 14,* 57–77.

Eisler, J. A., Tannenbaum, P. L., Mann, D. R., & Wallen, K. (1993). Neonatal testicular suppression with a GnRH agonist in rhesus monkeys: Effects on adult endocrine function and behavior. *Hormones and Behavior, 27,* 551–67.

Ellis, L., Ames, M. A., Peckham, W., & Burke, D. (1988). Sexual orientation of human offspring may be altered by severe maternal stress during pregnancy. *Journal of Sex Research, 25,* 152–57.

Ford, J. J. (1983). Postnatal differentiation of sexual preference in male pigs. *Hormones and Behavior, 17,* 152–62.

Ford, J. J., & D'Occhio, M. J. (1989). Differentiation of sexual behavior in cattle, sheep and swine. *Journal of Animal Science, 67,* 1816–23.

Friedman, R. C. (1988). *Male homosexuality. A contemporary psychoanalytic perspective.* New Haven: Yale University Press.

Gerall, A. A., Moltz, H., & Ward, I. L. (Eds.). (1992). *Handbook of behavioral neurobiology: Vol. 11. Sexual differentiation.* New York: Plenum Press.

Gladue, B. A., Green, R., & Hellman, R. E. (1984). Neuroendocrine response to estrogen and sexual orientation. *Science, 225,* 1496–99.

Gladue, B. A., Beatty, W. W., Larson, J., & Staton, R. D. (1990). Sexual orientation and spatial ability in men and women. *Psychobiology, 18,* 101–8.

Gooren, L. (1986a). The neuroendocrine response of luteinizing hormone to estrogen administration in heterosexual, homosexual, and transsexual subjects. *Journal of Clinical Endocrinology and Metabolism, 63,* 583–88.

Gooren, L. (1986b). The neuroendocrine response of luteinizing hormone to estrogen administration in the human is not sex specific but dependent on the hormonal environment. *Journal of Clinical Endocrinology and Metabolism, 63,* 589–93.

Gooren, L., & Cohen-Kettenis, P. T. (1991). Development of male gender identity/role and a sexual orientation towards women in a 46,XY subject with an incomplete form of the androgen insensitivity syndrome. *Archives of Sexual Behavior, 20,* 459–70.

Gooren, L. J. G., Rao, B. R., van Kessel, H., & Harmsen-Louman, W. (1984). Estrogen positive feedback on LH secretion in transsexuality. *Psychoneuroendocrinology, 9,* 249–59.

Goy, R. W., Bercovitch, F. B., & McBrair, M. C. (1988). Behavioral masculinization is independent of genital masculinization in prenatally androgenized female rhesus macaques. *Hormones and Behavior, 22,* 552–71.

Goy, R. W., & McEwen, B. S. (1980). *Sexual differentiation of the brain.* Cambridge: MIT Press.

Grinspoon, S. K., & Bilezikian, J. P. (1992). HIV disease and the endocrine system. *The New England Journal of Medicine, 327,* 1360–65.

Hamer, D. H., & Copeland, P. (1994). *The science of desire. The search for the gay gene and the biology of behavior.* New York: Simon & Schuster.

Hamer, D. H., Hu, S., Magnuson, V. L., Hu, N., & Pattatucci, A. M. L. (1993a). A linkage between DNA markers on the X chromosome and male sexual orientation. *Science, 261,* 321–27.

Hamer, D. H., Hu, S., Magnuson, V. L., Hu, N., & Pattatucci, A. M. L. (1993b). Molecular genetic studies of sexual orientation. Paper presented at the International Academy of Sex Research, 19th Annual Meeting, Pacific Grove, Calif., June 27–July 1, 1993. ABSTRACTS, p. 31.

Hendricks, S. E., Graber, B., & Rodriguez-Sierra, J. F. (1989). Neuroendocrine responses to exogenous estrogen: No differences between heterosexual and homosexual men. *Psychoneuroendocrinology, 14,* 177–85.

Herdt, G. H., & Davidson, J. (1988). The Sambia "turnim-man": Sociocultural and clinical aspects of gender formation in male pseudohermaphrodites with 5-alpha-reductase deficiency in Papua New Guinea. *Archives of Sexual Behavior 17,* 33–56.

Heston, L. L., & Shields, J. (1968). Homosexuality in twins. A family study and a registry study. *Archives of General Psychiatry, 18,* 149–60.

Holman, S. D., & Hutchison, J. B. (1991). Lateralized action of androgen on development of behavior and brain sex differences. *Brain Research Bulletin, 27,* 261–65.

Imperato-McGinley, J., Guerrero, L., Gautier, T., & Peterson, R. E. (1974). Steroid 5α-reductase deficiency in man: An inherited form of male pseudohermaphroditism. *Science, 186,* 1213–15.

Imperato-McGinley, J., Peterson, R. E., Gautier, T., & Sturla, E. (1979). Androgens and the evolution of male-gender identity among male pseudohermaphrodites with 5α-reductase deficiency. *New England Journal of Medicine, 300,* 1233–37.

Kallmann, F. J. (1952a). Comparative twin study on the genetic aspects of male homosexuality. *The Journal of Nervous and Mental Disease, 115,* 283–98.

Kallmann, F. J. (1952b). Twin and sibship study of overt male homosexuality. *American Journal of Human Anatomy, 4,* 136–46.

King, M., & McDonald, E. (1992). Homosexuals who are twins. A study of 46 probands. *British Journal of Psychiatry, 160,* 407–9.

La Spada, A. R., Wilson, E. M., Lubahn, D. B., Harding, A. E., & Fischbeck, K. H. (1991). Androgen receptor gene mutations in X-linked spinal and bulbar muscular atrophy. *Nature, 352,* 77–79.

La Spada, A. R., Roling, D. B., Harding, A. E., Warner, C. L., Spiegel, R., Hausmanowa-Petrusewicz, I., Yee, W-C., & Fischbeck, K. H. (1992). Meiotic stability and genotype-phenotype correlation of the trinucleotide repeat in X-linked spinal and bulbar muscular atrophy. *Nature Genetics, 2,* 301–4.

LeVay, S. (1991). A difference in hypothalamic structure between heterosexual and homosexual men. *Science, 253,* 1034–37.

LeVay, S. (1993). *The sexual brain.* Cambridge: MIT Press.

Lewis, V. G., & Money, J. (1983). Gender-identity/role: G-I/R Part A: XY (androgen-insensitivity) syndrome and XX (Rokitansky) syndrome of vaginal atresia compared. In L. Dennerstein & G. D. Burrows (Eds). *Handbook of psychosomatic obstetrics and gynaecology* (p. 51). Amsterdam, New York, Oxford: Elsevier Biomedical Press.

Macke, J. P., Hu, N., Hu, S., Bailey, M., King, V. L., Brown, T., Hamer, D., & Nathans, J. (1993). Sequence variation in the androgen receptor gene is not a common determinant of male sexual orientation. *American Journal of Human Genetics, 53,* 844–52.

Masica, D. N., Money, J., & Ehrhardt, A. A. (1971). Fetal feminization and female gender identity in the testicular feminizing syndrome of androgen insensitivity. *Archives of Sexual Behavior, 1,* 131–42.

McCormick, C. M., & Witelson, S. F. (1991). A cognitive profile of homosexual men compared to heterosexual men and women. *Psychoneuroendocrinology, 16,* 459–73.

McEwen, B. S. (1983). Gonadal steroid influences on brain development and sexual differentiation. In R. O. Greep (Ed.), *Reproductive Physiology IV* (pp. 99–145). Baltimore: University Park Press.

McEwen, B. S. (1987). Steroid hormones and brain development: Some guidelines for understanding actions of pseudohormones and other toxic agents. *Environmental Health Perspectives, 74,* 177–84.

Meyer-Bahlburg, H. F. L. (1982). Hormones and psychosexual differentiation: Implications for the management of intersexuality, homosexuality, and transsexuality. *Clinical Endocrinology and Metabolism, 11,* 681–701.

Meyer-Bahlburg, H. F. L. (1984). Psychoendocrine research on sexual orientation. Current status and future options. *Progress in Brain Research, 61,* 375–98.

Meyer-Bahlburg, H. F. L. (1990/1991a). Can homosexuality in adolescents be treated by sex hormones? *Journal of Child and Adolescent Psychopharmacology, 1,* 231–35.

Meyer-Bahlburg, H. F. L. (1990/1991b). Will prenatal hormone treatment prevent homosexuality? *Journal of Child and Adolescent Psychopharmacology, 1,* 279–83.

Meyer-Bahlburg, H. F. L. (1992). Möglichkeiten und Grenzen Psychoendokrinologischer Erklärungsansätze für die menschliche Geschlechtertypik (Potential and limits of psychoendocrine approaches to human gender typology). In: K. F. Wessel and H. A. G. Bosinski (Eds.), *Interdisziplinäre Aspekte der Geschlechterverhältnisse in einer sich wandelnden Zeit.* Berliner Studien zur Wissenschaftsphilosophie & Humanontogenetik, vol. 1. Bielefeld: Kleine Verlag, pp. 103–20.

Meyer-Bahlburg, H. F. L. (1993). Psychobiologic research on homosexuality. *Child and Adolescent Psychiatric Clinics of North America, 2*(3), 489–500.

Meyer-Bahlburg, H. F. L., Ehrhardt, A. A., Rosen, L. R., Gruen, R. S., Veridiano, N. P., Vann, F. H., & Neuwalder, H. F. (in press). Prenatal estrogen and the development of homosexual orientation. *Developmental Psychology.*

Money, J. (1980). *Love and love sickness. The science of sex, gender difference, and pair-bonding.* Baltimore: The Johns Hopkins University Press.

Money, J. (1988). *Gay, straight, and in-between. The sexology of erotic orientation.* New York: Oxford University Press.

Money, J., Devore, H., & Norman, B. F. (1986). Gender identity and gender transposition: Longitudinal outcome study of 32 male hermaphrodites assigned as girls. *Journal of Sex and Marital Therapy, 12,* 165–81.

Money, J., & Ehrhardt, A. A. (1972). *Man and woman. Boy and girl.* Baltimore, London: The Johns Hopkins University Press.

Money, J., & Norman, B. F. (1987). Gender identity and gender transposition: Longitudinal outcome study of 24 male hermaphrodites assigned as boys. *Journal of Sex and Marital Therapy, 13,* 75–92.

Money, J., & Ogunro, C. (1974). Behavioral sexology: Ten cases of genetic male intersexuality with impaired prenatal and pubertal androgenization. *Archives of Sexual Behavior, 3,* 181–205.

Money, J., Schwartz, M., & Lewis, V. G. (1984). Adult erotosexual status and fetal hormonal masculinization and demasculinization: 46XX congenital virilizing adrenal hyperplasia (CVAH) and 46XY androgen insensitivity syndrome (AIS) compared. *Psychoneuroendocrinology, 9,* 405–15.

Perkins, A., & Fitzgerald, J. A. (1992). Luteinizing hormone, testosterone, and behavioral response of male-oriented rams to estrous ewes and rams. *Journal of Animal Science, 70,* 1787–94.

Pillard, R. C., & Weinrich, J. D. (1986). Evidence of familial nature of male homosexuality. *Archives of General Psychiatry, 43,* 808–12.

Rasmussen, E. W. (1955). Experimental homosexual behavior in male albino rats. *Acta Psychologica, XI,* 303–34.

Remafedi, G., Resnick, M., Blum, R., & Harris, L. (1992). Demography of sexual orientation in adolescents. *Pediatrics, 89,* 714–21.

Rösler, A., & Kohn, G. (1983). Male pseudohermaphroditism due to 17β-hydroxysteroid dehydrogenase deficiency: Studies on the natural history of the defect and effect of androgens on gender role. *Journal of Steroid Biochemistry, 19,* 663–74.

Schmidt, G. (1983). Motivationale Grundlagen sexuellen Verhaltens. In H. Thomä (Ed.), *Psychologie der Motive* (pp. 70–109). Vol. 2 of the series Motivation und Emotion, of Enzyklopädie der Psychologie. Göttingen: Verlag für Psychologie, Dr. C. J. Hogrefe.

Schwartz-Giblin, S., McEwen, B. S., & Pfaff, D. W. (1989). Mechanisms of female reproductive behavior. In F. R. Brush & S. Levine (Eds.), *Psychoendocrinology* (pp. 41–104). San Diego: Academic Press.

Seyler, L. E., Canalis, E., Spare, S., & Reichlin, S. (1978). Abnormal gonadotropin secretary responses to LRH in transsexual women after diethylstilbestrol priming. *Journal of Clinical Endocrinology and Metabolism, 47,* 176–83.

Sherwin, B. B. (1988). A comparative analysis of the role of androgen in human male and female sexual behavior: Behavioral specificity, critical thresholds, and sensitivity. *Psychobiology, 16,* 416–25.

Speiser, P. W., & New, M. I. (1990). An update of congenital adrenal hyperplasia. In F. Lifshitz (Ed.), *Pediatric endocrinology. A clinical guide. (Second Edition)* (p. 307). New York: Marcel Dekker.

Spijkstra, J. J., Spinder, T., Gooren, L. J. G. (1988). Short-term patterns of pulsatile luteinizing hormone secretion do not differ between male-to-female transsexuals and heterosexual men. *Psychoneuroendocrinology, 13,* 279–83.

Swaab, D. F., Gooren, L. J. G., & Hofman, M. A. (1992). The human hypothalamus in relation to gender and sexual orientation. *Progress in Brain Research, 93,* 205–19.

Swaab, D. F., & Hofman, M. A. (1990). An enlarged suprachiasmatic nucleus in homosexual men. *Brain Research, 537,* 141–48.

Tennov, D. (1979). *Love and limerence. The experience of being in love.* New York: Stein and Day.

Tobet, S. A., & Fox, T. O. (1992). Sex differences in neuronal morphology influenced hormonally throughout life. In A. A. Gerall, H. Moltz, I. L. Ward (Eds.), *Handbook of behavioral neurobiology: Vol. 11. Sexual differentiation* (p. 41). New York: Plenum.

Trautman, P. D., Meyer-Bahlburg, H. F. L., Postelnek, J., & New, M. I. (in press). The effects of early prenatal dexamethasone on the cognitive and behavioral development of young children: Results of a pilot study. *Psychoneuroendocrinology.*

Udry, J. R. (1988). Biological predispositions and social control in adolescent sexual behavior. *American Sociological Review, 53,* 709–22.

Ward, I. L. (1992). Sexual behavior. The product of perinatal hormonal and prepubertal social factors. In A. A. Gerall, H. Moltz, I. L. Ward (Eds.), *Handbook of behavioral neurobiology: Vol. 11. Sexual differentiation* (p. 157). New York: Plenum.

Whitam, F. L., Diamond, M., & Martin, J. (1993). Homosexual orientation in twins: A report on 61 pairs and three triplet sets. *Archives of Sexual Behavior, 22,* 187–206.

Zucker, K. J., Bradley, S. J., & Oliver, G., Hood, J. E., Blake, J., & Fleming, S. (1992). Psychosexual assessment of women with congenital adrenal hyperplasia: Preliminary analyses. In Abstracts of the 18th Annual Meeting, International Academy of Sex Research, Prague, CSSR (unpaginated).

CHAPTER EIGHT

The Genetics of Sexual Orientation:
From Fruit Flies to Humans

ANGELA M. L. PATTATUCCI AND DEAN H. HAMER

There are two proximate motivations for human sexuality: reproduction and pleasure. While the evolutionary necessity for reproduction is obvious, the role of pleasure is more elusive. How are sex and pleasure linked in the human brain? Why are certain forms and expressions of sexuality enjoyable to some individuals but distasteful to others? Are some types of sexuality "natural" and others "unnatural," or are these meaningless distinctions?

To answer these questions completely would require a thorough understanding of both the brain chemistry and evolutionary pathways that underlie human sexual desire and activity. A useful starting place is the study of the mechanisms responsible for individual differences in one particular dimension of human sexuality, namely, sexual orientation. In what follows, we outline the approach that our laboratory is using to study genetic sources of variation in sexual orientation and how such research may ultimately lead to a deeper understanding of human evolution and behavior.

In the early nineteenth century persons engaging in same-sex love were named *inverts,* which literally means to turn upside down or inside out(1). The terms in common usage today, *homosexual* and *lesbian,* were not coined until after the 1850s(2). This act of naming implied that homosexuals were different from "normal" people and thus constituted a medical abnormality in need of scientific study and cure. Over the years since this naming event, homosexuality has been extensively studied, and so-called "therapies" were developed that have ranged from the threat of bodily injury to brain surgery(3). These interventions were carried out with the biomedical establishment's self-proclaimed goal of helping the homosexual to readjust to the presumed normal state of heterosexuality.

It is within this context that the nature versus nurture debates regarding sexual orientation emerged and have been vigorously fought (see the Introduction, this volume, for a related discussion). Many proponents of the nature side of the argument take an essentialist stance, basically saying that homosexuality is innate—that people are born homosexual. The nurture side is a social constructionist position, arguing that certain social conditions produce homosexuality in cultures. Interestingly, both opinions have historically viewed individuals as passive; they are either controlled by their biology or by the social environment in which they grow.

Julia Penelope provides some thoughtful insight on this debate.

> I don't understand why so many of the popular theorists of our day describe essentialism and social construction as necessarily opposing accounts of sexual identity. . . . It seems to me that the "debate" between essentialists and social constructionists is nothing more than an academic brouhaha contrived to advance the now academically respectable discipline of Lesbian and gay studies. The two points of view are not mutually exclusive, although they are presented that way, nor should it be necessary to dismiss Lesbians like myself as "abnormal" in order to preserve not only one's theory, but one's stake in such a fabricated dispute. (4)

Decades of study by the medical community have not only consistently failed to demonstrate that homosexuality is a pathology(5–6) but, confounding the position of the social constructionists, have also failed to show that homosexuality is a preference, exhibiting plasticity, and thus subject to reversal(3). This apparent failure caused a replacement of the term "sexual preference," popular in the 1970s, by the designation "sexual orientation," which implies a more fixed state of being. Coincident with this evolution of terms has been a movement to account for sexual orientation, and human behavior in general, by explanations that are, at least in part, biological. However, the social constructionist view certainly has not disappeared. Instead it has evolved to embrace the current position that human behavior is so complex that it is impossible to separate out individual contributing components and reliably ascribe them to specific groups(7–9). Proponents of this stance seem to be setting a criterion requiring that any biological factor implicated in the expression of homosexuality in *some* individuals must be found and determined to act in an identical manner in *all* homosexuals. Such an unrealistic view is not shared by most of those involved in biological research on human or animal behavior (see Meyer-Bahlburg, this volume).

The concept that sexual orientation may have a biological component is certainly not new. For example, the early twentieth century sexologist Magnus Hirschfeld considered marriage of homosexuals to be extremely undesirable. He believed that homoeroticism was a means by which nature disposed of degenerate stock, asserting that the children of homosexuals were mentally inferior and a threat to racial hygiene(3). So influential were Hirschfeld's views that large numbers of lesbians and gay men were said to have belonged to his *Wissenschaftlich-humanitäres Kommittee* (Scientific Humanitarian Committee) and to have made impassioned declarations that they were born neither female nor male, but members of a "third sex"(10).

The first systematic studies of sexual orientation in the United States were the surveys conducted by Kinsey and colleagues(11–12). These studies, encompassing the sexual histories of about 20,000 individuals, suggested that homosexuality crosses the boundaries of family, social and economic class, as well as educational and geographic backgrounds, with rates that are, for the most part, comparable. Because it seemed unlikely that individuals with such diverse histories could have faced similar rearing environments, biological explanations for sexual orientation began to be seriously considered.

Initial Studies Potentially Linking Biology and Sexual Orientation

It was probably in response to the report of Kinsey and colleagues that Kallman initiated twin studies on male homosexuals(13–14). Kallman reported a surprising concordance rate of 100 percent for 37 monozygotic (identical) twins compared to a 15 percent rate for 26 dizygotic (fraternal) twins. Although criticized for its methodological shortcomings(15), Kallman's study stood virtually alone among only a few case studies(16–22), until systematic investigations focusing on the familial nature of homosexuality were initiated by J. Michael Bailey and Richard Pillard (23–29). Separate twin studies on female and male homosexuals performed by Bailey, Pillard, and colleagues have yielded similar results. For females, a concordance rate of 48 percent was found in monozygotic twins, compared to a 16 percent rate in dizygotic twins and a 6 percent rate in adoptive sisters(29). When considering male homosexuality among twins, the concordance rate was 52 percent for monozygotic twins, 22 percent for dizygotic twins, and 11 percent for adopted brothers of non-twin homosexuals(28). From these data, Bailey and Pillard proposed heritability constants of about 50 percent for both female and male homosexuality. Additionally, the data suggest that biological factors contributing to the expression of homosexuality, if they exist, may be at least partly different for females and males.

An accurate assessment of sexual orientation in some females may be complicated by nonbiological factors(10, 30–31). For example, the quote below suggests that a woman naming herself a lesbian on a questionnaire or in an interview may not define that term in a manner congruent with that of the researcher.

> The lesbian personality manifests itself in independence of spirit, in willingness to take responsibility for oneself, to think for oneself, not to take "authorities" and their dictum on trust. It usually includes erotic attraction to women, although we know there have been *many* women of lesbian personality who *never* had sexual relations with one another. Even where an erotic relationship exists the sensually sexual may be far from predominant. What is strongly a part of the lesbian personality is loyalty to and love of other women. . . . The important point is that the lesbian has sought wholeness within herself, not requiring in the old romantic sense, to be "completed" by an opposite. (32) (Emphasis ours)

Coincident with the twin studies suggesting a familial nature for homosexuality have been brain anatomy studies (see Meyer-Bahlburg, this volume, for a related discussion). To date, there have been three reported differences in the brain anatomy of male homosexuals as compared to heterosexuals: the third interstitial nucleus of the anterior hypothalamus (INAH-3)(34), a region of undetermined function in humans but which lies in an area reported to regulate sexual behavior in rats; the anterior commissure(33), a bundle of neuronal fibers connecting the right and left hemispheres of the cerebral cortex; and the suprachiasmatic nucleus(35), a region of the hypothalamus thought to control circadian rhythm. All three studies have been criticized on methodological grounds, most notably for small sample size, for the fact that many of the homosexual subjects died of complications associated with AIDS, and because only alleged or presumed sexual-orientation information was available for the subjects. Nevertheless, the data presented were statistically significant for the subjects studied, and certainly justify further investigation. Probably the most important element missing at this point is not whether a correlation exists between brain anatomy and sexual orientation, but whether a causal relationship can be established between the reported anatomical differences and sexual orientation.

Complementing the twin and brain anatomy studies have been investigations linking endocrinology and behavior (see the Meyer-Bahlburg, Wallen, and Wilson chapters, this volume). It has been demonstrated in avian, reptilian, and a number of mammalian species that the presence of steroid hormones during particular stages of early neonatal and/or fetal development exerts a strong influence on the probability that certain sex-specific behaviors will be exhibited at later ages (36–38). These comparative findings from diverse organisms support a hypothesis that biological mechanisms are involved in the development and subsequent expression of sexual behavior. However, due to ethical considerations, it has not been possible to perform analogous experiments on humans to determine the degree, if any, to which hormones present early in development influence adult sexual behavior. Studies with the goal of addressing this question have been restricted mainly to assessing gender identity and hormone levels in transsexuals, homosexuals, and persons with various forms of hermaphroditism. Unfortunately, these investigations have, for the most part, yielded confusing and often conflicting results (39).

Further complicating studies aimed at identifying biological components associated with sex-specific behavior is the fact that these behaviors are not islands unto themselves, but occur within certain contexts. Because it had been demonstrated that changing the hormonal environment at prescribed times during early development could have striking effects on adult sex-specific behavior, it was important to ask if changing the context in which the sex-specific behavior develops or occurs could also alter behavioral patterns. The most compelling evidence supporting this notion comes from studies performed on rhesus monkeys.

In rhesus monkeys, sex rehearsal play, undistinguished with respect to sex, begins in young infancy. At about 6 months, sex-specific behavior is established and predominant, with females characteristically adopting a presenting position on all fours, and males mounting from behind. This sex rehearsal play persists until the onset of puberty. Monkeys raised in isolation fail to achieve this positioning and consequently do not reproduce(40–41). Isosexually reared monkeys perform their rehearsal play homosexually(42). When placed in a heterosexual environment at adulthood, these monkeys are said to be bisexually capable. However, the isosexually reared females and males appear to be more at ease in homosexual, compared to heterosexual partnerships, flexibly change from mounting to presenting positions, and, in the case of males mounting males, achieve intromission(43–44). Given these findings, Goldfoot and colleagues come to the following conclusion.

> In our view, the results do suggest a model of behavioral development that includes the joint actions of prenatal endocrine and postnatal social processes to yield expression of dimorphic behavior "tailored" to the social environment in which it developed(42).

The possibility that sexually dimorphic behavior is the outcome of combined influences of biology and social context seems intuitively obvious (see the Introduction, this volume, for a related discussion). The critical question is whether it is possible to identify specific biological factors that have potential influences on sexual behavior, without disturbing the contexts in which the behaviors typically occur and without the need for extensive surgical alterations or atypical endocrinological manipulations. Thus, while past experiments have provided substantial evidence supporting a link between biology and behavior, it is now time to move to the next level: the identification and characterization of particular biological factors contributing to an overall behavioral pattern. With this in mind, our laboratory has chosen a genetic approach for the study of sexual orientation both in humans and, as a simple model system, the fruit fly *Drosophila melanogaster.*

Drosophila melanogaster as a Simple Model System for Studying Sexual Orientation

For a number of reasons, Drosophila is a promising organism in which to study the genetics of sexual orientation. Most important, Drosophila is a versatile organism that lends itself well to genetic, molecular, and developmental investigations. Its anatomy has been well characterized and there exists a large body of data on the neurogenetics of Drosophila. Important for a study of the genetics of sexual orientation is that courtship behavioral patterns in both female and male Drosophila are stereotypical. As humans, we tend to frown upon and resist our behavior being characterized as stereotypical. This may be due to the notion that stereotypical behavior seems contrary to individuality, on which Western society places a high premium. However, for a scientist engaged in a genetic study of sexual orientation, stereotypical behavior is actually desirable, because it significantly reduces the number of variables under consideration.

Courtship displays performed by sexually mature Drosophila males toward virgin females are sustained and elaborate. When sexually mature female and male pairs are observed in a small chamber for ten minutes, the male will spend more than 50 percent of the time courting the female(45). A courtship bout may persist for several minutes and characteristically begins with the male closely following a moving female, occasionally tapping her abdomen with a foreleg. Subsequently, the male will extend and rapidly vibrate one or both wings to produce a courtship "song," typically followed by extending his proboscis to "lick" the female's genitals. At this point, the male will curl his abdomen and thrust his genitalia toward those of the female in a copulation attempt. These behaviors are performed with the goal of stimulating the sexually mature, virgin female to open her vaginal plates and copulate with the male(46).

Sexually mature males will also aggressively court immature males. The initial frequency of this homosexual courtship by mature males approaches that observed toward virgin females in heterosexual courtship(47–49). The use of genetic tools to create female/male sex mosaics has suggested that male tissue in specific regions of the brain and thoracic ganglion is necessary for a sexually mature male to court both virgin females and immature males(50–53).

Visual and chemical components have been shown to contribute to the courtship of young males, and, coupled with these, there is a strong sensory element to the successful courtship of virgin females(54). As young males reach sexual maturity, they characteristically begin producing anti-aphrodisiac compounds and display courtship rejection behaviors toward other males(55–57). Together, these tend to inhibit homosexual courtship among adult males. Additionally, homosexual courtship tends to decrease with the amount of experience that mature males have in courting bouts with young males(58–59). Interestingly, mature males courted when they were young mate more readily than control males that were isolated until maturity(60). Taken together, these data suggest that homosexual courtship in *Drosophila melanogaster* may perform a function similar to the sex rehearsal play among sexually immature rhesus monkeys mentioned earlier.

Not surprisingly, a subset of the genes involved in the Drosophila sex determination pathway, as well as genes involved in learning, olfaction, and the production of pheromones, all have some influence on courtship behavior(54). However, the most striking departure from the stereotypical array of Drosophila courtship behaviors is observed in a strain of flies called *fruitless* (*fru*), which carry a small chromosomal inversion on the right arm of the third chromosome(61–63). Males that are homozygous for this chromosomal inversion (*fru/fru*) both aggressively court other males and elicit vigorous courtship from wild-type (strains established from flies captured in the wild) and other *fruitless*-bearing males.

A simple explanation for this phenomenon would be that males homozygous for the *fruitless* trait fail to reach sexual maturity and thus remain sexually "attractive" to males throughout adulthood. However, the fact that *fruitless*-bearing males actively court wild-type females and males, as well as *fru/fru* males, indicates that they are sexually mature. In fact, when groups of males homozygous for the *fruitless* trait are placed together, they line up, mouthparts-to-genitals-to-mouthparts, forming striking courtship chains, with each fly courting the one directly in front while being simultaneously courted from another behind(63). This behavior has not been reported as a characteristic of wild-type *Drosophila melanogaster.*

A number of chemical compounds, believed to act as pheromones (both aphrodisiacs and inhibitors), have been identified and studied in Drosophila(64–67). A simple explanation for the ability of *fruitless*-bearing males to elicit courtship from other males would be that *fruitless* males are producing pheromonal combinations similar to those of other sexually attractive flies. However, pheromonal profiles of males homozygous for the *fruitless* trait suggest that they are unique compared to other sexually attractive flies, such as wild-type immature males and females, or sexually mature females. Unlike the other flies, males bearing the *fruitless* trait are reported to produce reduced quantities of a compound believed to inhibit courtship, while also synthesizing large quantities of another proposed inhibitor(57). To account for this apparent paradox, it has been suggested that the aphrodisiac or inhibitory properties of pheromones may be concentration dependent(68). Thus, it has been speculated that the combination of below average concentrations of one inhibitory pheromone and above average concentrations of another, now capable of acting as an aphrodisiac, result in the sexual attractiveness of *fru/fru* males(54).

Despite no obvious defects in their reproductive tracts or sperm production, *fru/fru* males are sterile. The sterility is caused by a failure of *fruitless*-bearing males to curl their abdomen in copulation attempts, making them behaviorally sterile(62). Other aspects of the stereotypical courtship pattern are exhibited by *fruitless* males. However, there appears to be a significant increase in the amount of genital licking performed by *fru/fru* males in courtship directed toward both males and females compared to that displayed by wild-type males toward virgin females.

Mammals such as rodents and monkeys are known to have pleasure centers in their brains. In the case of fruit flies, whether they have pleasure centers and experience pleasure is an open question, one which would be extremely difficult to determine experimentally. Thus, at this point, one can only speculate regarding whether aspects of Drosophila courtship are "pleasurable" for the fly.

Genetically, the *fruitless* trait has been linked to a small chromosomal inversion on the right arm of the third chromosome. Genetic manipulations performed in this region of the chromosome have suggested that the active and passive aspects of the fruitless phenotype may be associated with separate inversion breakpoints(63). It has been reported that the factor(s) causing *fruitless* males to be attractive to other males may be associated with the inversion breakpoint proximal to the centromere, while the factor(s) involved in the active courtship of other males, failure to curl the abdomen, and absence of a sexually dimorphic muscle of unknown function characteristically present in wild-type males, are apparently associated with the inversion breakpoint distal to the centromere(63–69). This suggests a possibility that more than one gene may be involved in the male-specific *fruitless* behavioral array.

Of particular interest is the fact that the fruitless phenotype is only expressed in males. Females homozygous for the *fruitless* chromosomal inversion are indistinguishable from wild-type females in their behavior and readily mate with males. Our present efforts are directed toward a further genetic characterization and molecular cloning of the two breakpoints associated with the *fruitless* chromosomal inversion with the goal of identifying the gene(s) responsible for the sexual orientation of the *fruitless* males.

Genetic Studies on Sexual Orientation in Humans

Of course, human sexuality is far more complex than the stereotypical behavior of the fruit fly. Therefore, our initial goal in humans is modest: to determine whether or not there is *any* genetic influence on sexual orientation. Because we consider this an open question, we wanted to use techniques of sufficient power to either confirm or disprove the existence of such genes. The human genome-mapping initiative provides the necessary reagents for such a rigorous test.

There are two main components to our human genetic analysis. These are the collection and examination of family pedigrees and the study of linkage patterns. A pedigree analysis is founded on the principle that, if a trait is genetically influenced, it will tend to aggregate in families. Thus, by studying the degree and patterns of familial aggregation, inferences can be made regarding the possible number of genes involved in the expression of a trait and how those genes may act.

The 23 pairs of chromosomes comprising the human genome have been divided and classified as autosomes (22 pairs) and a single pair of sex chromosomes. When examining the genetic contribution for a given trait, three primary modes of inheritance are initially considered: recessive, dominant, and sex-linked. If a trait is an autosomal recessive, the proband (specific individual being studied in a family pedigree) must inherit a version of the gene under consideration, known as an allele, from both parents. The alleles contributed by each parent need not be absolutely identical; however, for the trait to be viewed as an autosomal recessive, the two alleles must be incapable of conferring expression of the trait when in single copy, and able to do so when two copies are present, either in homoallelic (the same alleles) or heteroallelic (different alleles) combination. To illustrate, if the incidence of homosexuality in a family is due, at least in part, to the recessive effects of a certain autosomal gene, one would expect to find increased rates of homosexuality in the siblings of a homosexual proband, but not in the parents or necessarily in distant relatives. An exception to this prediction would be in the rare circumstance of a consanguineous (of the same blood relation) marriage, in which case increased rates could also be seen in distant relatives.

In the case of a dominant inheritance pattern, a particular allele of a gene in single copy is sufficient to contribute to the expression of a trait. Offspring could receive this allele from either parent. However, given that homosexual men have fewer children, on average, than lesbians, a dominant allele might be seen as preferentially passed to offspring through their mothers in family pedigrees. Regardless of whether there may be a sex-specific selection for passage of a dominant allele, family pedigrees should reveal the appearance of homosexuality in each generation. Furthermore, the rate of homosexuality in parents should be approximately the same as in their children.

Sex-linked traits are the third primary mode of inheritance, and are characterized by genetic linkage to either the X or Y chromosomes. This mechanism has unique qualities with respect to the previous two examples because, although there are exceptions (see Wilson chapter, this volume), individuals assigned as male in our society typically have an XY chromosome constitution which renders them hemizygous for the X chromosome. Thus, a recessive allele of a gene on the X chromosome can exhibit what phenotypically appear to be dominant effects in males because it is the only copy present in the genome. Conversely, the phenotypic effects observed in males would, under most circumstances, be observed in a female only if she carries two copies of the recessive allele in her genome, one on each of her two X chromosomes. Examples of human sex-linked traits are hemophilia and red-green color blindness. Although both of these traits occur in females, they are far more prevalent in males.

If a gene which in some way contributes to the expression of homosexuality in both sexes is located on the X chromosome, then an elevated rate in males compared to females would be expected, due to male hemizygosity. Additionally, the rate of homosexuality among male relatives on the maternal side of the family should be elevated compared to those appearing in the paternal lineage. This is because a male receives his single X chromosome solely from his mother and never from his father. Combined with the ability of a female to "carry" an X-linked allele without being homosexual herself, a very strong bias toward male homosexuality on the maternal side could emerge for a sex-linked allele when family pedigrees are examined.

An additional complexity is that some traits are sex-limited, meaning that they are expressed exclusively or preferentially in one sex. The homosexual courtship phenotype previously mentioned for the *fruitless* trait in Drosophila is an example of one that is sex-limited. Baldness is an example of a sex-limited trait in humans. Recent studies comparing rates of homosexuality among monozygotic, dizygotic, and non-related sibling pairs have suggested that genetic contributions to the expression of homosexuality in females and males may be at least partially independent(28–29). One way to explain elevated rates of homosexuality among siblings of the same, but not of the opposite, sex is if the genetic factors contributing to its expression are sex-limited. In this case, female homosexuality would be primarily transmitted through heterosexual fathers and male homosexuality through heterosexual mothers.

The previous examples of recessive, dominant, and sex-linked traits reflect the simple case in which a single gene contributes to the expression of homosexuality. However, this circumstance is improbable given the complexity of human behavior. A somewhat more realistic view is that homosexuality, when considered in terms of a genetic trait, is either *oligogenic* (involving a few genes) or *polygenic* (involving many genes). In either of these cases, one would expect to observe a complex pattern of inheritance that is intermediate between the previously discussed single-gene examples in family pedigrees.

Given the rather extensive variability and complexity of human behavior, one might predict that when environmental influences are taken into consideration together with traits that are oligogenic or polygenic, identifying individual components would be practically impossible. This would more than likely be true if all homosexuals on the planet were viewed simultaneously, and attempts were made to generate a single unifying hypothesis, in part based upon genetics, that would account for each person's homosexuality. However, if a more realistic stance is adopted that operates from the assumption that for some individuals genetics plays a slight or nonexistent role in their sexual orientation, while for others genetics may have an intermediate influence, and for still others genetics may play a major role, then it seems promising that by studying families in which there is a clustering of homosexuality, opportunities to identify possible modes of inheritance and isolate individual genetic components might emerge. In fact, by studying sibling pairs sharing a common trait, it is possible to select for genes that are relatively rare in the population and for which environmental factors exert a strong influence on the trait's expression.

In his book, *Tchaikovsky: The Quest for the Inner Man,* Alexander Poznansky provides a historical example of familial aggregation of homosexuality. Poznansky reports that Tchaikovsky was a homosexual who engaged in a life-long struggle for self-acceptance. Typical of the era, Tchaikovsky came from

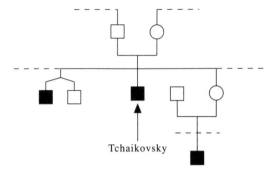

Tchaikovsky

Figure 8.1 Abbreviated Pedigree of the Tchaikovsky Family.

a large family (at least by today's standards), and Poznansky identifies at least two other family members who were also homosexuals. One of these was his younger brother, a fraternal twin whose co-twin was apparently heterosexual. The other was his nephew, the son of an apparently heterosexual sister, who at some point became the intimate of Tchaikovsky(70).

The pedigree in figure 8.1, where squares designate males, circles females, and homosexuals are represented by darkened figures, indicates that homosexuality in the Tchaikovsky family is consistent with some of the expectations for sex-linked transmission of male sexual orientation. However, great caution must be exercised in overinterpreting the pattern in any single pedigree. Lack of information on other family members can cause undue focus on those members for whom information is available, consequently causing a bias toward certain explanations over others. Furthermore, no single family history can prove that a pattern exists. To detect such patterns, it is essential to analyze a large number of pedigrees.

With this idea in mind, we have initiated a systematic study of the family pedigrees of homosexual women and men. Information is collected on relatives up to grandparents, down to nieces and nephews, and out to first cousins. Whenever possible, the proband's assessment is confirmed by direct interview with at least one other family member. In our study, male probands were primarily recruited through the HIV outpatient clinic at the National Institutes of Health and female probands through various homophile organizations. In order to minimize ascertainment bias, probands were recruited without prior knowledge of this aspect of the study. We have uncovered a number of different pedigree patterns that are potentially of interest.

The pedigree in figure 8.2 shows a clustering of both female and male homosexuality appearing in a single generation. Because there is no reported homosexuality in past generations, it is difficult to project a mode of transmission for this pattern, although an autosomal recessive gene affecting both genders is one possibility. Complicating a pedigree analysis of this type is the fact that

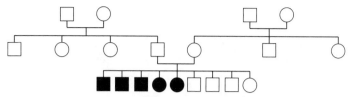

Figure 8.2 Single-generation clustering of female and male homosexuality among first-degree relatives.

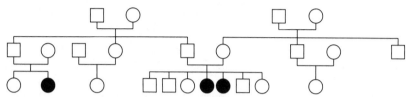

Figure 8.3 Single-generation clustering of female homosexuality among first- and third-degree relatives.

homosexuality was a silent or "closeted" orientation in past generations much more so than it is today, making the reliability of information concerning heterosexuality dubious at best. However, this phenomenon means that, if anything, homosexuality will tend to be underrepresented in family pedigrees rather than overrepresented, and information regarding homosexuality in past generations can be considered quite reliable.

Although we have obtained other pedigrees that exhibit the previously shown pattern, far more representative are ones where the clustering is exclusively or predominantly restricted to one gender. The pedigree in figure 8.3 is one such example. In this family, there is a clustering of lesbianism, presumably coming from the father's side of the family. Our analysis thus far has indicated that female homosexual (or bisexual) probands are more likely to have a homosexual sister and/or female homosexual cousins from a paternal uncle than they are male homosexual relatives. This again is a difficult pedigree pattern to interpret in terms of a single factor influencing homosexuality in females. However, minimally the relatively large number of pedigrees that we have collected exhibiting this pattern would suggest that genetic factors contributing to the expression of homosexuality in females may be sex-limited.

From a genetic perspective, the most interpretable pattern that we have found in our pedigree analysis is diagrammed in figure 8.4. Notice the similarity between this pedigree and the one previously diagrammed for the Tchaikovsky family. We have obtained several family pedigrees of this type showing an absence of female homosexuality while exhibiting a clustering of male homosexuality that segregates in a manner consistent with sex-linkage transmitted through the maternal lineage. Similar to what was suggested for female

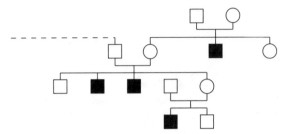

Figure 8.4   Multi-generation clustering of male homosexuality among first- and second-degree relatives.

homosexuality above, the elevated rates of homosexuality among male siblings and relatives support a hypothesis that factors contributing to the expression of homosexuality may be in part sex-limited. That putative human sexual-orientation genes may be sex-limited in their expression is quite interesting when considered in the context of the *fruitless* trait in Drosophila, which affects the sexual orientation of males but not females, is also sex-limited.

We would like to emphasize that even though our pedigree analysis has identified familial clustering patterns of homosexuality that are consistent with genetic contribution, alternative hypotheses can always be imagined. For this reason, a pedigree analysis cannot stand on its own. The only definitive way to demonstrate a genetic contribution to the expression of homosexuality in individuals is to isolate a gene. The search for such a gene is seemingly complicated by the fact that we really have no clear idea of how this putative sexual-orientation gene would function in the human body. For example, would a sexual-orientation gene act prenatally or perinatally, as might be suggested from hormonal studies? (See Meyer-Bahlburg, this volume.) Would this putative gene's action be restricted to the regions of the brain reported to exhibit dimorphism between heterosexual and homosexual men? For what type of protein would such a gene code?

Fortunately, geneticists have developed a powerful technique called *linkage analysis* that enables one to search for a gene even though there is little information available about how, where, and in what capacity it may function. Linkage analysis is based upon two fundamental principles. First, if a trait is genetically influenced, then related individuals who share the trait should share the gene more often than expected by chance alone. Second, genes that are close in proximity on the same chromosome are usually co-inherited. Thus, linkage analysis can be used to initiate a search for putative sexual-orientation-linked genes by looking for common genetic markers in related homosexual individuals.

To be successful, a linkage analysis requires the availability of a large number of genetic markers. Fortunately, many geneticists are collectively working on establishing genomic markers. To date, over 3,000 polymorphic DNA fragments have been identified that span the entire human genome, and this number is steadily increasing.

Equally important for the success of a linkage analysis seeking to identify a putative sexual-orientation gene is the identification and recruitment of suitable families. Our pedigree studies have shown an excess of inheritance through the maternal lineage in some families where there is a clustering of male homosexuality. From a genetic point of view, this pattern can be explained in terms of sex-linkage, and suggests that the most promising families with which to begin a linkage analysis are those where there are two or more male homosexual relatives. An experimental design focusing on analysis of sibling pairs has several theoretical and practical advantages(71–77). The most notable among these is that sib-pair analysis is capable of detecting a single linked genetic locus even if additional genes or environmental conditions are required to express the trait. Other benefits include: (1) it is nonparametric and independent of gene penetrance and frequency; (2) for traits displaying limited familiality, greater precision can be attained by studying siblings rather than more distant relatives; (3) individuals who have or will have a homosexual orientation but choose to identify themselves as heterosexual ("false negatives") are irrelevant to the analysis because they are not studied; (4) individuals who have a heterosexual orientation but choose to identify themselves as homosexual ("false positives") are expected to be rare due to negative social stigma associated with homosexuality; (5) analyzing sib-pairs is more refractory to errors in genotyping and to mistakes or alterations in phenotype than are large pedigree methods; and (6) it is more practical to obtain the cooperation of nuclear sib-pair families than of multigenerational families.

Our efforts are currently focused on the X chromosome. We feel that this is a sound approach because the X chromosome has been densely mapped with respect to genetic markers, and evolutionary considerations suggest that genes involved in sexual differentiation might be preferentially clustered on the X chromosome. Our preliminary findings have shown genetic linkage between DNA markers on X28, a subtelomeric region of the long arm of the X chromosome, and sexual orientation in male sib-pairs(78). This analysis revealed a correlation between male homosexual orientation and the inheritance of polymorphic markers on the X chromosome in approximately 64 percent of the sib-pairs tested, resulting in a multipoint LOD score of 4.0 ($P = 10^{-5}$). This represents a statistical confidence level of greater than 99 percent that at least one subtype of male sexual orientation is genetically influenced.

We would like to emphasize that sexual orientation is complex. It is probably the result of numerous genetic, physiological, and environmental factors interacting together. Therefore, it is our view that no single factor, be it genetic, physiological, or environmental, *determines* a given person's sexual orientation. Rather, we believe that certain factors may *contribute* to the overall development of an individual's sexual orientation (see Introduction, this volume, for a related discussion). Given this level of apparent complexity, it may seem that the identification of any single factor would be extremely difficult. However, the sib-pair experimental design represents a powerful tool for the identification of putative genetic contributors to sexual orientation. Once one is found, elucidating the roles of other genetic, physiological, and environmental factors should be facilitated.

Given that this is a volume with a primary focus on pleasure and sexuality, an obvious question is whether any putative sexual-orientation-linked genes will be associated with the pleasure response. Stated another way, might there be genetic selectivity associated with whom particular individuals seek to experience sexual pleasure?

From a biological perspective, pleasure is ultimately the result of a chemical reaction taking place in the brain. Most neuropsychiatric research suggests that sexual pleasure derives from excitation of the dopaminergic pathway, mediated through stimuli conducted through the peripheral and central nervous systems to the medial forebrain bundle of the brain(79–81). Although these questions have not yet been studied in detail, we consider it plausible that the pleasure associated with emotional attraction to another person, courtship, love, lust, and the sexual act itself may proceed through this or a related pathway. We presume that, in evolution, neural pathways have developed that couple sex and all of its precedents to an excitation of the dopaminergic pathway such that sexual activity, and therefore reproduction, is encouraged, ultimately passing those genes involved in this process onto the subsequent generations. This may be the evolutionary reason why sex is pleasurable. Variations at any step in these undoubtedly complex pathways could contribute to diversity in sexual orientation. Whether these variations occur directly in the pleasure-producing part of the pathway or, perhaps more likely, in the complex cortical functions that ultimately lead to pleasure is a question that can be answered only by identifying and cloning the relevant sexual orientation related genes.

Conclusions

Whenever an area of inquiry garners as much attention as reports on searches for biological contributions to sexual orientation have, it is not surprising that some people become uneasy. Richard Nisbett has identified three main areas of concern regarding biological approaches to behavior and the sister field of evolutionary psychology.

> The first is that very broad claims are often made on the basis of little that most social psychologists [and those in related fields] would regard as evidence. The second is plain old-fashioned turf protection. Evolutionary psychologists [and behavioral geneticists] seem to be mowing much of the same grass that social psychologists have long regarded as their own, and the ques-

tion naturally arises as to who is going to own the intellectual territory here. The third concern is about values. Outsiders often think that [behavioral geneticists and] evolutionary psychologists like to believe that certain behavior patterns are fixed or hard-wired. Social psychologists like to believe in flexibility in general, and they certainly don't want to believe in fixedness of the kind of behaviors that [behavioral geneticists and] evolutionary psychologists discuss most frequently, such as aggression and behavior related to gender roles. (82)

The above quote would seem to bring us full circle to the nature/nurture, essentialist/social-constructionist issues we alluded to at the beginning. However, as the quote from Julia Penelope indicated, essentialism and social construction are not mutually exclusive concepts. Too often in these debates perspective is lost and extreme views are adopted in their place (see Introduction, this volume). For example, hearing references to possible genetic contributions to a complex phenomenon such as sexual orientation, people often adopt the drastic position that those of us working in the field see humans as robot-like automatons, with our behavior strictly determined by genes in a way that is inflexible and immune to social, environmental, and cultural influences. We would argue that a majority of us do not share this view and fully acknowledge that context plays an enormous role in the expression of human behavior. Our goal is not to deny the flexibility and variability of human behavior, but to identify putative genetic factors that are part of an intricate network of psychological mechanisms that facilitate our adaptability in various personal and social contexts.

We as humans do not seem to have a problem accepting that male tissue is required in the brain and thoracic ganglion for Drosophila males to exhibit the typical array of male courtship behaviors. We also do not seem to have difficulty accepting that alterations in the level and availability of estrogen and testosterone during early development can have striking affects on adult behavior in many mammalian species. However, we sometimes maintain a chauvinistic, romanticized view of our own species. We like to think of ourselves as above or more highly evolved than other species on this planet. But the very term "evolved" implies common starting materials among species. Molecular biology studies have revealed that many molecules once thought unique to a certain species are in fact highly conserved among species and perform similar functions; steroid hormones in mammals are a case in point. Why then is it so far-fetched to accept that biological mechanisms may contribute to human behavioral patterns? A main difference between humans and other species, as we see it, is that the cerebral cortex is highly developed in humans and apparently capable of overriding many behaviors that are considered to be biologically driven in other species. However, it does not necessarily follow that genetic and biological contributions to behavior are absent in humans. It means that they may play a more subtle role.

References

1. Downing, C., 1991. *Myths and Mysteries of Same-Sex Love.* New York: Continuum.
2. Herzer, M., 1985/1986. Kertbeny and Nameless Love. *Journal of Homosexuality* 12: 1–26.
3. Murphy, T. F., 1992. Redirecting Sexual Orientation: Techniques and Justifications. *The Journal of Sex Research* 29(4): 501–23.
4. Penelope, J., 1992. Does It Take One to Know One? In: *Call Me Lesbian: Lesbian Lives, Lesbian Theory.* Freedom, Calif.: The Crossing Press.
5. Hooker, E., 1957. The Adjustment of the Male Overt Homosexual. *Journal of Projective Techniques* 21: 18–31.
6. Hooker, E., 1958. Male Homosexuality in the Rorschach. *Journal of Projective Techniques* 23: 278–81.
7. Hubbard, R., 1990. The Political Nature of Human Nature. In: D. L. Rhode (ed.), *Theoretical Perspectives on Sexual Difference.* New Haven: Yale University Press.
8. Kitcher, P., 1985. *Vaulting Ambition: Sociobiology and the Quest for Human Nature.* Cambridge: The MIT Press.
9. Fausto-Sterling, A., 1992. *Myths of Gender,* 2nd ed. New York: Basic Books.
10. Faderman, L., 1981. *Surpassing the Love of Men: Romantic Friendship and Love Between Women from the Renaissance to the Present.* New York: William Morrow.
11. Kinsey, A. C., W. B. Pomeroy and C. E. Martin, 1948. *Sexual Behavior in the Human Male.* Philadelphia: W. B. Saunders.
12. Kinsey, A. C., W. B. Pomeroy, C. E. Martin and P. H. Gebhard, 1953. *Sexual Behavior in the Human Female.* Philadelphia: W. B. Saunders.
13. Kallmann, F. J., 1952. Comparative Twin Study on the Genetic Aspects of Male Homosexuality. *Journal of Nervous Mental Disease* 115: 283–98.
14. Kallmann, F. J., 1952. Twin and Sibship Study of Overt Male Homosexuality. *American Journal of Human Genetics* 4: 136–46.
15. Rosenthal, D., 1970. *Genetic Theory and Abnormal Behavior.* New York: McGraw-Hill.
16. Rainer, J. D., A. Mesnikoff, L. C. Kolb and A. Carr, 1960. Homosexuality and Heterosexuality in Identical Twins. *Psychosomatic Medicine* 4: 251–59.
17. Pardes, H., J. Stinberg and R. C. Simons, 1967. A Rare Case of Overt and Mutual Homosexuality in Female Identical Twins. *Psychiatric Quarterly* 41: 108–133.
18. Heston, L. L. and J. Shields, 1968. Homosexuality in Twins: A Family Study and Registry Study. *Archives of General Psychiatry* 18: 149–160.
19. Perkins, M. W., 1973. Homosexuality in Female Monozygotic Twins. *Behavior Genetics* 3: 387–88.
20. Myers, M. F., 1982. Homosexuality, Sexual Dysfunction and Incest in Male Identical Twins. *Canadian Journal of Psychiatry* 27: 144–47.
21. Eckert, E. D., T. J. Borchard, J. Bohlen and L. L. Heston, 1986. Homosexuality in Monozygotic Twins Reared Apart. *British Journal of Psychiatry* 148: 421–25.
22. King, M. and E. McDonald, 1992. Homosexuals Who Are Twins: A Study of 46 Probands. *British Journal of Psychiatry* 160: 407–9.
23. Pillard, R. C. and J. D. Weinrich, 1986. Evidence of Familial Nature of Male Homosexuality. *Archives of General Psychiatry* 43: 808–12.

24. Pillard, R. C., J. I. Poumadere and R. A. Carretta, 1981. Is Homosexuality Familial? A Review, Some Data, and A Suggestion. *Archives of Sexual Behavior* 10: 465–75.
25. Bailey, J. M. and D. S. Benishay, 1993. Familial Aggregation of Female Sexual Orientation. *American Journal of Psychiatry* 150: 272–77.
26. Buhrich, N. J., J. M. Bailey and N. G. Martin, 1991. Sexual Orientation, Sexual Identity, and Sex-Dimorphic Behavior in Male Twins. *Behavior Genetics* 21: 75–96.
27. Bailey, J. M., L. Willerman and C. Parks, 1991. A Test of the Maternal Stress theory of Human Male Homosexuality. *Archives of Sexual Behavior* 20: 277–93.
28. Bailey, J. M. and R. C. Pillard, 1991. A Genetic Study of Male Sexual Orientation. *Archives of General Psychiatry* 48: 1089–96.
29. Bailey, J. M., R. C. Pillard, M. C. Neale and Y. Agyei, 1993. Heritable Factors Influence Sexual Orientation in Women. *Archives of General Psychiatry* 50: 217–23.
30. Kitzinger, C., 1987. *The Social Construction of Lesbianism.* London: Sage.
31. Hoagland, S. L., 1988. *Lesbian Ethics: Toward New Value.* Palo Alto, Calif.: Institute of Lesbian Studies.
32. Gidlow, E., 1977. Lesbianism as a Liberating Force. *Heresies* 1(2): 94–95.
33. Allen, L. S. and R. A. Gorski, 1992. Sexual Orientation and the Size of the Anterior Commissure in the Human Brain. *Proceedings of the National Academy of Sciences* 89: 7199–7202.
34. LeVay, S., 1991. A Difference in Hypothalamic Structure Between Heterosexual and Homosexual Men. *Science* 253: 1034–37.
35. Swaab, D. F. and M. A. Hofman, 1990. An Enlarged Suprachiasmatic Nucleus in Homosexual Men. *Brain Research* 537: 141–48.
36. Goy, R. W. and D. A. Goldfoot, 1973. Hormonal Influences on Sexually Dimorphic Behavior. In: Greep, R. O. and E. B. Astwood (eds.), *Handbook of Psychology-Endocrinology II.* Washington, D. C.: American Physiological Society.
37. Dörner, G., 1987. Sexual Dimorphism of the Brain: Model for Hormone-Dependent Brain Organization. In: Genazzani, A. R., A. Volpe and F. Facchinetti (eds.), *Gynecological Endocrinology: The Proceedings of the First International Congress on Gynecological Endocrinology.* Carnforth, U.K. and Park Ridge, N. J.: Parthenon.
38. Gorski, R. A., 1985. Gonadal Hormones as Putative Neurotrophic Substances. In: Cotman, C. W. (ed.), *Synaptic Plasticity.* New York: Guilford Press.
39. Unger, R., 1993. Alternative Conceptions of Sex (and Sex Differences). In: Haug, M., R. Walen, Cl. Aron and K. L. Olsen (eds.), The Development of Sex Similarities and Differences in Behavior. Dordrecht: Kluwer Academic Publishing.
40. Goy, R. W. and K. Wallen, 1979. Experimental Variables Influencing Play, Foot-Clasp Mounting and Adult Sexual Competence in Male Rhesus Monkeys. *Psychoneuroendocrinology* 4: 1–12.
41. Phoenix, C. H. and K. C. Chambers, 1982. Moderate Social Restriction During Infancy Reduces Sexual Receptivity in Adult Female Rhesus Macaques. *Behavioral and Neural Biology* 36: 259–65.
42. Goldfoot, D. A., K. Wallen, D. A. Neff, M. C. McBrair and R. W. Goy, 1984. Social Influences on the Display of Sexually Dimorphic Behavior in Rhesus Monkeys: Isosexual Rearing. *Archives of Sexual Behavior* 13: 395–412.

43. Goldfoot, D. A. and K. Wallen, 1978. Development of Gender Role Behaviors in Heterosexual and Isosexual Groups of Infant Rhesus Monkeys. In: Chivers, D. J. and J. Herbert (eds.), *Recent Advances in Primatology, Vol. 1, Behaviour.* London: Academic Press.

44. Goldfoot, D. A. and D. A. Neff, 1987. On Measuring Behavioral Sex Differences in Social Contexts: Perspectives from Primatology. In: Reinisch, J. M., L. A. Rosenblum and S. A. Sanders (eds.), *Masculinity/Femininity: Basic Perspectives.* New York: Oxford University Press.

45. Tompkins, L. and S. P. McRobert, 1989. Regulation of Behavioral and Pheromonal Aspects of Sex Determination by the *Sex lethal* Gene. *Genetics* 123: 535–41.

46. Ewing, A. W., 1983. Functional Aspects of Drosophila Courtship. *Biological Reviews* 58: 275–92.

47. Cook, R. and A. Cook, 1975. The Attractiveness to Males of Female *Drosophila melanogaster:* Effects of Mating, Age and Diet. *Animal Behavior* 23: 521–26.

48. McRobert, S. P. and L. Tompkins, 1983. Courtship of Young Males Is Ubiquitous in *Drosophila melanogaster. Behavior Genetics* 13: 517–23.

49. Curcillo, P. and L. Tompkins, 1987. The Ontogeny of Sex Appeal in *Drosophila melanogaster* males. *Behavior Genetics* 17: 81–86.

50. Hall, J. C., 1977. Portions of the Central Nervous System Controlling Reproductive Behavior in male *Drosophila melanogaster. Behavior Genetics* 7: 291–312.

51. Hall, J. C., 1979. Control of Male Reproductive Behavior by the Central Nervous System of Drosophila: Dissection of a Courtship Pathway by Genetic Mosaics. *Genetics* 92: 437–57.

52. Schilcher, F. and J. C. Hall, 1979. Neural Topography of Courtship Song in Sex Mosaics of *Drosophila melanogaster. Journal of Comparative Physiology* 129: 85–95.

53. Napolitano, L. and L. Tompkins, 1989. Neural Control of Homosexual Courtship in *Drosophila melanogaster. Journal of Neurogenetics* 6: 87–94.

54. Tompkins, L., 1989. Homosexual Courtship in Drosophila. In: Carew, T. J. and D. B. Kelly (eds.), *Perspectives in Neural Systems and Behavior.* New York: Liss.

55. Tompkins L. and J. C. Hall, 1980. Courtship-Stimulating Volatile Compounds from Normal and Mutant Drosophila. *Journal of Insect Physiology* 26: 689–97.

56. Tompkins, L., R. W. Siegel, D. A. Gailey and J. C. Hall, 1983. Conditioned Courtship in Drosophila and Its Mediation by Association of Chemical Cues. *Behavior Genetics* 13: 565–78.

57. Jallon, J-M., 1984. A Few Chemical Words Exchanged by Drosophila During Courtship and Mating. *Behavior Genetics* 14: 441–78.

58. Gailey, D. A., F. R. Jackson and R. W. Siegel, 1982. Male Courtship in *Drosophila melanogaster:* The Conditioned Response to Immature Males. *Genetics* 102: 771–782.

59. Zawistowski, S. and R. C. Richmond, 1985. Experience-Mediated Courtship Reduction and Competition for Mates by Male *Drosophila melanogaster. Behavior Genetics* 15: 561–69.

60. McRobert, S. P. and L. Tompkins, 1988. Two Consequences of Homosexual Courtship Performed by *Drosophila melanogaster* and *Drosophila simulans* Males. *Evolution* 42: 1093–97.

61. Gill, K. S., 1963. A Mutation Causing Abnormal Courtship and Mating Behavior in Male *Drosophila melanogaster. American Zoologist* 3: 507.

62. Hall, J. C., 1978. Courtship Among Males Due to a Male-Sterile Mutation in *Drosophila melanogaster. Behavior Genetics* 8: 125–41.

63. Gailey, D. A. and J. C. Hall, 1989. Behavior and Cytogenetics of *fruitless* in *Drosophila melanogaster:* Different Courtship Defects Caused by Separate, Closely Linked Lesions. *Genetics* 121: 773–85.

64. Jackson, L. L., M. T. Arnold and G. J. Blomquist, 1981. Surface Lipids of *Drosophila melanogaster:* Comparison of the Lipids from Female and Male Wild-Type and Sex-Linked *yellow* Mutant. *Insect Biochemistry* 11: 87–91.

65. Antony, C. and J-M Jallon, 1982. The Chemical Basis for Sex Recognition in *Drosophila melanogaster. Journal of Insect Physiology* 28: 873–80.

66. Pechine, J. M., C. Antony and J-M Jallon, 1988. Precise Characterization of Cuticular Compounds in Young Drosophila by Mass Spectrophotometry. *Journal of Chemical Ecology* 14: 1071–85.

67. Schaner, A. M., P. D. Dixon, K. J. Graham and L. L. Jackson, 1989. Courtship-Stimulating Pheromones of Young Male *Drosophila melanogaster. Journal of Insect Physiology* 35: 341–46.

68. Rodriguez, V. and O. Siddiqi, 1978. Genetic Analysis of Chemosensory Pathway. *Proceedings of the Indian Academy of Sciences* 87: 147–60.

69. Gailey, D. A., B. J. Taylor and J. C. Hall, 1991. Elements of the *fruitless* Locus Regulate Development of the Muscle of Lawrence, a Male-Specific Structure in the Abdomen of *Drosophila melanogaster* Adults. *Development* 113: 879–90.

70. Poznansky, A., 1991. *Tchaikovsky: The Quest for the Inner Man.* New York: Schirmer Books.

71. Suarez, B. K., J. Rice and T. Reich, 1978. The Generalized Sib-Pair IBD Distribution: Its Use in the Detection of Linkage. *Annals of Human Genetics* 42: 87–94.

72. Thomson, 1986. Determining the Mode of Inheritance of RFLP-Associated Diseases Using the Affected Sib-Pair Method. *American Journal of Human Genetics* 39: 207–21.

73. Bishop, D. T. and J. A. Williamson, 1990. The Power of Identity-By-State Methods for Linkage Analysis. *American Journal of Human Genetics* 46: 254–65.

74. Risch, N., 1990. Linkage Strategies for Genetically Complex Traits. II. The Power of Affected Relative Pairs. *American Journal of Human Genetics* 46: 229–41.

75. Risch, N., 1990. Linkage Strategies for Genetically Complex Traits. III. The Effect of Marker Polymorphisms on Analysis of Affected Relative Pairs. *American Journal of Human Genetics* 46: 242–53.

76. Freije, D., C. Helms, M. S. Watson, H. Donis-Keller, 1992. Identification of a Second Pseudoautosomal Region Near the Xq and Yq Telomeres. *Science* 258: 1784–87.

77. Ward, P. J., 1993. Some Developments of the Affected-Pedigree-Member Method of Linkage Analysis. *American Journal of Human Genetics* 52: 1200–1215.

78. Hamer, D. H., S. Hu, V. L. Magnuson, N. Hu and A. M. L. Pattatucci, 1993. A Linkage Between DNA Markers on the X-Chromosome and Male Sexual Orientation. *Science* 261:321.

79. Benassi-Benelli, A., F. Ferrari and B. Pellegrini-Quarantotti, 1979. Penile Erection

Induced by Apomorphine and N-*n*-propyl-norapomorphine in rats. *Arch Int. Pharmacodyn. Ther.,* 242: 241–45.

80. Serra, G. and G. L. Gessa, 1984. Role of Brain Monoamines and Peptides in the Regulation of Male Sexual Behavior. In: Shah, N. S. and A. G. Donald (eds.), *Psychoneuroendocrine Dysfunction.* Plenum: New York.

81. Olds, J. and P. Milner, 1954. Positive Reinforcement Produced by Electrical Stimulation of the Septal and Other Regions of the Rat Brain. *J. of Comparative and Physiological Psychology* 47: 419–27.

82. Nisbett, R. E., 1990. Evolutionary Psychology, Biology, and Cultural Evolution. *Motivation and Emotion* 14: 255–63.

PART THREE

Cultural Dimensions

CHAPTER NINE

The Cultural Management of Adolescent Sexuality

ALICE SCHLEGEL

Adolescent sexuality is a matter of broad social concern. The sexual games of children before puberty have few if any practical consequences, and the sexuality of married adults serves the goals of family and society; it is the reproductively capable but unmarried young whose sexuality is the most problematic, as their impulses are strong but not safely channelled. These lusty but unmated young people are the subject of this paper.

The very fact of adolescence is defined by reproductivity. As a social stage intervening between childhood and adulthood, social adolescence is virtually universal for both sexes. The beginning of this stage is tied to physical markers indicating the biological transition into reproductive capacity. Girls usually move out of childhood at or shortly after menarche.[1] It is curious that first ejaculation, as distinguishable an event as first menstruation, does not precipitate social movement for boys as menarche does for girls. Nevertheless, boys become social adolescents about the time when their bodies show the beginning of adult development, although the criterion for transition in some places may be the successful demonstration of a skill such as the first kill of a large animal.

The biological events of puberty cluster within the short span of a couple of years and produce the secondary sex characteristics that are the unambiguous signals of reproductive capability. While these signals are universally observed and made use of to mark the beginning of adolescence, the end of this social stage is marked by social rather than biological reproductive capacity. In most societies, marriage or the birth of the first child after marriage is the turning point into adulthood. In some cases, marriage follows soon after the assumption of adult status; for example, the Hopi Indian boy (*tiyo*) became a man (*taka*) after his initiation into one of the ceremonial fraternities, and he married shortly thereafter (although the Hopi girl [*mana*] became a woman [*wuhti*] upon marriage). Very commonly, adulthood is attained when bachelors and maidens become benedicts and matrons.

The problem of adolescent sexuality would not arise if all persons were married upon reaching puberty, the point at which desire can have the socially serious consequence of producing a new kinsperson for at least the girl's family. Marriage is widely seen as the license to reproduce, and in fact most human reproduction occurs within marriage. If young people are biologically capable of reproducing, why are they not given social license to do so? On the contrary, they must wait some time: commonly, one to three years for girls, two to ten years for boys.[2] Boys generally have a longer adolescence than girls, as a long delay in girls' marriages is the norm only when dowry payment or paid employment of unmarried females make it attractive to the parents of daughters to delay their marriages.

While the lower mammals apparently begin to reproduce as soon as they are biologically ready (see Wallen, this volume), the males of our nearest relatives, the higher primates—monkeys and apes—also experience a social adolescence (see Pavelka and de Waal chapters, this volume). While young males may occasionally have sexual intercourse with females, they do not reach adult mating frequency until several years after puberty, when they attain full body size. Lancaster (1979) proposes that this is because females choose to mate with the mature males, who have proven their ability to survive and may therefore be genetically superior to the high number of males who die during adolescence (72 percent in one study of toque macaques).

Human males do not experience the same high mortality rate during adolescence; nevertheless, there are some similarities in the mating habits of humans and primates, along with some important differences. A major difference is that in most human groups young people do not have freedom of choice of a partner as do primates. Marriage, the human mating system within which most reproduction occurs, is always constrained by considerations other than attraction and availability; cultural restrictions or social pressures serve to allocate marriage partners in all kinds of societies, even where parents do not have the authority to choose or veto a child's spouse. However, I propose that there is a kind of female choice that operates in human as in primate mating, although in humans the choice is usually made or directed by the parents of a girl rather than the potential bride herself (see Wallen, this volume, for a related discussion). When we consider that most brides are girls in their middle to late teens, it is not surprising that they are so much under family control. (This is especially true for first marriage; in subsequent marriages of mature people, those to be married usually have a greater voice in mate selection.)

The parents of a girl, and perhaps other kin, are just as concerned with finding her a socially attractive husband as the primate female is concerned with finding a genetically fit impregnator. I am not pushing a sociobiological argument here, although the case could be made that socially attractive males are more likely to support their children and enhance their social and reproductive status than are socially unattractive males, thereby increasing the inclusive fitness of the girl's kin through her offspring (see Symons, this volume, for an alternative perspective). Whatever the final cause, mine is a proximate-cause argument. In my view, the "cause" of delayed marriage for boys is the need for a period of assessment, when boys are sorted out as to their attractiveness as sons-in-law. Even in the simpler societies, where boys by puberty have the skills they need to support their families—that is, where there is no need for a longer period of training, as there is in more technologically advanced societies—boys do not marry until at least their late teens. Boys' marriages may be delayed even longer when extended training or education is required, or in some (but by no means all) bridewealth-giving societies where it may take time to accumulate the bridewealth.

It hardly seems fair that boys, whose sexual urges are so strong in the teenage years, should be forced to delay for so long the freedom of sexual intercourse that is one of the attractions of marriage. The remainder of this paper is concerned with the sexual activities that are and are not permitted to adolescents and how permissiveness and repression are related to broader familial and social concerns.

I shall focus on three kinds of concerns that families and societies may have about lusty but unmated young people. The first, which has received the widest attention, is heterosexual activity and the consequences of illegitimate pregnancy. The second, receiving attention more recently, is homosexual activity and social attitudes toward it. Finally, I will pay some attention to the question of sibling incest, a long-lived theme in psychological anthropology, and how this potential problem is handled.

The Value on Virginity in Adolescence

Many theories have been constructed to explain why some societies expect unmarried girls to remain virgins and some do not, from those relating the suppression of adolescent sexuality to fear of sex, to those linking it to the development of the state (for discussion and references, see Schlegel and Barry 1991). Virginity is a concern primarily of the girl's family, which bears the consequences when she bears a child. In short, virginity is valued in those societies in which bastardy has serious deleterious outcomes for families. Therefore, it is to familial costs that we shall look to interpret the value on virginity.

While families are more concerned with the virginity of girls than of boys (boys do not become pregnant), boys' heterosexual activity is often suppressed along with that of girls. This is because the most common sexual partner for an adolescent boy is an adolescent girl. One reason is female choice: women are not likely to find most adolescent boys to be desirable sexual partners, as boys rarely achieve full growth before their very late teens or early twenties. Consequently, boys rarely have access to adult women unless prostitutes are available and, even then, adolescents rarely have the means to pay prostitutes, whether in cash or the other goods or favors that are the currency of sex.

In cultures where wife-sharing or other forms of legitimate sexual access outside of marriage are condoned, even if husbands do not demand exclusive rights to their wives' sexuality, it is unlikely that adolescent boys would be the recipients of married men's generosity, as they would have little with which to reciprocate. The situation changes somewhat in class societies, in which high-status families preserve the virginity of their daughters but may wink at their sons' seductions of lower-class girls whose families are less able to guard them or feel less compelled to do so. Thus, while our concern here is the virginity of girls, we note that boys' heterosexual experience is drastically reduced when girls' sexuality is suppressed.

If an unwelcome pregnancy is the major reason that families do not allow their daughters sexual freedom, then their fears should diminish when the like-lihood of pregnancy is low. Whiting, Burbank, and Ratner (1986), in a study using the Standard Cross-Cultural Sample, have shown that the prescription of virginity is significantly less when maidenhood, as they call that period be-tween puberty and marriage, is short. They explain this by the greatly reduced probability of pregnancy within a year or two of menarche, a phenomenon known as adolescent sub-fecundity.

Nevertheless, early marriage is not the only explanation for tolerance. Southeast Asia is known from historical records to have been a region of later marriage of girls, their age being late teens or early twenties; yet, before the introduction of Islam and outside of its range, this region has been documented as one of sexual permissiveness since at least the sixteenth century (see Reid 1988). It is probable that the widespread and legitimate use of abortion, appar-ently a quite safe procedure among these medically sophisticated peoples, made an unwanted pregnancy a nuisance rather than a family tragedy.

However, the Southeast Asian elite, non-Islamic as well as Islamic, guarded the chastity of their daughters. In this they were like the elite—nobility, gentry, or merely prosperous—in a large number of societies that did not require vir-ginity of lower-status girls. Examples that come to mind include not only states but also chiefdoms, like the Samoans of Polynesia or the Omaha of the North American Great Plains.

A cross-cultural study using the same sample (Schlegel 1991) revealed that while pregnancy is a concern, it is not an equal concern everywhere. It is not uncommon in permissive societies for girls to be married to their boyfriends if they become pregnant. In some cases, like that of the Ijo of Nigeria (Hollos and Leis 1986), the "bastard" child will be left with the girls' parents when she marries and joins her husband, who is pleased that his bride has proven her fertility even if with another man.

This study showed that a value on virginity is most likely to occur when the families of daughters give property at their marriages, in the form of dowry, indirect dowry, or extensive gift exchange.[3] (The minimal gift exchange of lower-status families in Southeast Asia and elsewhere involves very little prop-erty.) Contrary to the common belief that virginity is a widespread concern in bridewealth-giving societies, on the assumption that when men give goods for a wife they expect to receive a virgin, the number of such societies that value virginity is actually less than the number that do not. Families may not be so motivated to guard the virginity of their daughters when they pay to get a bride as when they pay to give one!

My interpretation of this association between virginity and forms of marriage transaction is that families who give property with daughters are, in effect, buying a son-in-law. With dowry this is quite clear: dowry is used to marry a daughter up by exchanging wealth for higher social position; to marry her to a social equal, when the bride's dowry is matched against the groom's settlement (a kind of male dowry) or his anticipated inheritance; or to bring in a client son-in-law who will be loyal to the family that provided him with his household goods and family connections. (This latter form seems particularly suited to mercantile families that might need to turn to sons-in-law to manage the family business when sons are lacking or unsuitable.)

In gift exchanges, the goods ensure that the intermarrying families are social equals in that they own equivalent amounts of goods or can come up with them from kin or subjects. Thus, a transaction that is of no economic benefit to either side serves another kind of purpose, that of ensuring equivalent status. It is probably no accident that elaborate exchanges of gifts are most commonly found where rank is finely graded and may be ambiguous, as in Polynesia and some parts of Southeast Asia. In such societies, wealth, as a measure of economic and political support, is the clearest way of indicating status equivalency. When gifts are exchanged, families of girls and boys alike know that they are not acquiring affines of a lower status.

If family social status is maintained or improved through the marriages of daughters, a paternity claim on a daughter's child by an unwelcome male would be a family disaster or at least a waste of its asset. Since the surest way to prevent pregnancy is to prevent intercourse, property-giving families guard their daughters against would-be social climbers, who might seek upward mobility for themselves and their children by seducing the daughters of the rich or powerful.

When upward mobility through seduction is a possibility, and a man is not killed or severely injured as a result—the castration of Abelard at the hands of Heloise's brothers must have been a clear warning to other would-be seducers—we can expect to see a cultural emphasis on seduction, as both a theme and as an act attempted and bragged or lied about by boys and even men. It is not just the lure of the forbidden, since boys in permissive societies like Samoa are just as concerned with seduction as are the Don Juans of restrictive ones like Spain. In Spain the lower-ranking seducer, if he survived attempts at revenge, would see his children inherit some of his wife's goods. In Samoa, it was the lower-status girls who were in theory seducible, their marriages being frequently by elopement and unaccompanied by much in the way of goods exchanged. High-ranking girls, however, were able to transmit family titles to their children, and considerable wealth followed their marriage in an elaborate exchange of gifts. It was these girls whose virginity was guarded— and whose seduction was the most prized, as the elopement of a *taupou,* or "village princess," was a lifelong coup for the lucky boy, his family, and his village, to which the young couple fled. One might say that boys practiced their seduction skills on girls of their own rank, particularly on virgins, in hopes of their big chance with a *taupou,* which of course never came for most of them.

My claim, therefore, is that several factors can explain the value on virginity. Short maidenhood is one; the acquisition of a desirable son-in-law through the giving or exchange of property is another. It is likely that there are others, such as the emulation of higher-status people or conversion to a new religion, particularly when the new religion is that of higher-status people. The surveillance of an adolescent girl is a burden to her family, which must begin to socialize her in childhood and monitor her behavior until she is married. This, I aver, is not a burden families are willing to assume unless they profit from doing so.

Adolescent Homosexual Activity

In recent years there has been an explosion of historical and ethnographic studies of homosexuality. Unfortunately, this growing literature on individual societies and time periods has not been accompanied by much comparative research, and we are unable to identify cross-cultural factors concomitant with either the attitude toward or the frequency of homosexual acts (see Greenberg, this volume, for a related discussion). Broude and Greene's (1980) code on sexual attitudes and practices, using the Standard Cross-Cultural Sample, does include codings for attitudes toward homosexuality (42 societies) and frequency of homosexuality (70 societies), so the raw material for a comparative study is available. Schlegel and Barry (1991) coded attitudes toward homosexual activity among adolescents, with information on 57 societies for boys, 44 for girls. For many of our questions, we found more societies with information on boys than on girls, and the descriptions of boys' activities were fuller.

We were unable to find correlations between attitudes toward adolescent homosexual activity and attitudes toward heterosexual activity, indicating that a society may be permissive toward one form but restrictive toward the other. None of the features of parent-child relations that we measured showed an association with attitudes toward homosexual acts, nor did any of the features associated with strong male bonding. What we did find held no surprises: permissiveness or restrictiveness toward boys and girls are correlated; and attitudes toward male homosexual behavior in adolescence are correlated with attitudes toward such behavior in adults.

What I report here, then, is based primarily on a reading of the ethnographies. With the exception of some of the Melanesian societies that institutionalize homosexual activity, and other societies that have tolerated or encouraged private homosexual relations between adolescents and older youths or men, homosexual activity is fairly widely regarded as childish behavior that will be abandoned when adolescents marry and have free access to heterosexual intercourse. In other words, except for those with a homosexual orientation, homosexual activity is generally a substitute for heterosexual activity that is either prohibited or not very accessible.

Many cultures tolerate physical expressions of affection between same-sex adolescents even though these are not approved among adults; I have seen Philippine Bontoc boys sit in public with arms and legs draped over one another, whereas adult men in the same setting sat upright and dignified, not touching. When and how such casual intimacy extends into specifically erotic stimulation is a question that has not been much addressed by anthropologists. One observer, Constance Cronin (personal communication 1992), tells me that she has observed rural Sicilian girls climbing into bed together, in full view of anyone in the room, where they kiss and snuggle under the covers, giggling and whispering. Who knows if hands wander? This is a common occurrence, taken for granted as a normal part of Sicilian adolescent life.

An example of tolerated but not encouraged homosexual activity among adolescents and unmarried youth is the blind eye that Nyakyusa fathers turn to their sons' sexual play. While this African society tolerates premarital intercourse for both sexes, girls can be coy and diffident about accepting boys' advances, and female sexual partners are not readily available. The boys move into boys' villages, next to the parental village, upon reaching puberty, and they spend much of their time in one another's company. When a boy is lucky enough to find a girlfriend, they practice interfemoral intercourse so that she will not get pregnant. When boys make do with one another, interestingly, they also practice interfemoral intercourse. There is no indication in the literature on this kind of casual homosexual activity of dominance and submission among adolescent same-sex partners; the relationship seems to be characterized by mutuality rather than by power. (In fact, homosexual activity within a same-sex group may promote social cohesiveness—see the discussion below on permissive societies, and de Waal, this volume, on bonobos.)

When homosexual relations are institutionalized, there appears to be more of a power differential (see also Creed 1982). This can be very mild and have the character of a mentor-protégé relationship, as among the Kiman of Melanesia, where preadolescent boys fellated the adolescents who were their mentors. The "mummy" and "baby" friendships of South African Lesotho girls (Gay 1986) are similar. However, the power dimension may be stronger when the inseminator is an adult man or, more commonly, an unmarried youth in his twenties, and the inseminated is a preadolescent or early-adolescent boy. This kind of man-boy homosexual relationship is known historically among ancient Greeks, pre-Roman Germanics, Ottoman Turks, African Azande, and a number of other peoples where marriage and easy access to women were denied to all or certain classes of young men (see Greenberg 1988). Posner (1992) has pointed out that the desired junior male sexual partner was the pre- or early-adolescent boy. These boys, as yet without masculine facial hair and muscular development, are, according to Posner, the closest to females that unmarried youths can find and still be able to develop romantic or companionable friendships, which they could not do with female prostitutes.

In his emphasis on the economics of the sexual search, Posner (1992) overlooks the power dimension. I propose that when male dominance over women is expressed and symbolized through sexual penetration, dominance of men over other men can be expressed in the same way. Thus, machismo's disgust with homosexuality is compatible with male-male sodomy or fellatio, the penetrator disdaining his partner and not identifying himself as homosexual. (For the Mexican case, see Taylor 1986.) The young adolescent boy partner in such societies, however, is exempted from disdain since he has not attained manhood.

The Avoidance of Sibling Incest

Almost all peoples disapprove of sibling incest, although their fear of it may not reach the extreme form taken by those who practice sister-brother avoidance. Whatever the response to incest, from mild disapproval to killing or ostracizing the incestuous pair, it is generally negative. (For variations in the direction and intensity of the incest taboo, see Schlegel 1972; Taggart 1992.)

It is important to separate the incest taboo, which is a cultural construction, from the avoidance of close mating, which is a behavioral trait that humans apparently share with all other two-sexed species. There is some slippage, i.e., observations of incestuous matings have been made for many animals, and there is plenty of evidence of parent-child and sibling incest among humans. Nevertheless, very little human reproduction is the result of these incestuous acts. Whatever the genetic advantages of bisexual reproduction may be in dispersing the genes, humans seem to behave like other two-sexed species. The incest taboo is a cultural aid to a behavior pattern that finds its proximate cause in, possibly, psychological mechanisms that inhibit desire or its expression.

In a review of the patterns of association that the cross-cultural study of adolescence revealed, it became clear that there is a general kind of human social organization that is similar to the social organization of many primate species. What primatologists call the "female assembly," the "male cohort," and the "bachelor band" can be seen over and over in human societies. The primate female assembly, composed of females of all ages plus juvenile males, has its counterpart in the tendency of women and girls to associate often and freely, including in their groups the women's little sons. Among males, however, there is not this free and frequent association between elders and adolescents. Men (that is, the married males plus whichever other males are considered to be social adults) tend to cluster separately from adolescent boys, unless labor or training activities bring them together. In their leisure time, boys are found in age-segregated peer groups much more often than girls, and boys are in the company of men much less often than girls are in the company of women. While this pattern is obvious in sexually segregated societies and those in which male and female social roles differ markedly, it can be seen even in modern industrial societies, where girls spend more time with mothers than boys do with either parent.

Whatever other social functions this kind of gender separation serves, it does shorten the time that opposite-sex adolescent siblings are together. Even where the sister-brother is the strongest cross-sex social bond, as is the case in many matrilineal societies, there may be sibling avoidance in some form. Among the matrilineal Hopi, sisters and brothers are expected to help and interact with one another, and the brother is an honored guest in his sister's home. Nevertheless, I was told that adolescent girls are advised by their mothers not to be alone in the house with a sexually mature brother, because men, even brothers, are unable to control their sexual impulses around a nubile girl.

There are a few historical cases in which sibling incest has not been totally avoided: with one known exception (see below), sibling marriage is limited to royal or chiefly families. Its purpose is to consolidate political and spiritual power. (For information on sibling marriage, see Goggin and Sturtevant 1964.) Obviously, when siblings can marry, the same kind of socialization for incest avoidance cannot occur. Siblings may still be separated before their marriage in societies in which the genders are generally segregated; in fact, such separation may actually increase the likelihood of sexual attraction between them when they do marry, as one theory of incest avoidance holds that early intimacy depresses sexual interest or at least inhibits its expression (Bischof 1975; Parker 1976). The royal and chiefly marriages of siblings can be understood as overriding the incest taboo for dynastic or politically strategic reasons. It is more difficult to understand the sibling marriages of ordinary people, as among the Greeks of northern Egypt under the Roman Empire. We know very little about such marriages, except that some apparently did occur; we have no information on adolescent sexual socialization in a society that tolerated sexual relations among such close kin.

Pleasure in the Service of Power

The discussion so far makes it clear that adolescent sexuality is highly constrained even in sexually permissive societies. Apart from the avoidance of close kin, which humans share with other two-sexed species, adolescents are prohibited or discouraged from sexual relations with adults, except in the cases of institutionalized man-boy homosexual activity. Girls tend to marry young in most societies, so it is boys who most often suffer from a lack of heterosexual partners. (As we have seen, there is evidence for situational homosexual activity in several societies; the actual number of these societies is probably much greater than the evidence indicates.)

All human sexuality is culturally and socially constrained, and adolescents, being junior and dependent, are more restricted than adults in this as in other aspects of their lives. Nevertheless, some societies constrain more than others. In this section, I shall address some of the ways that the sexuality of adolescents is manipulated to serve others' social goals.

The most direct restricters of adolescents' sexuality are their parents. If premarital pregnancies are unwelcome, girls are socialized to preserve their virginity and monitored to make certain that they do so. The surest way of avoiding pregnancy is to prevent any contact with boys and men, and this is done through the segregation of adolescent girls. It is sometimes overlooked that sexual segregation serves the ends of the parents of boys as well as girls. There is no reason to assume that adolescent boys in non-Western societies are any less vulnerable to falling in love, to experiencing that mixture of passion and personal attraction, than teenagers in societies that elevate romantic love to a cultural theme (see Gregor, this volume, for a related discussion). It is easier to prevent unruly passions than to control them, and boys do not fall in love with girls they have never seen. From the point of view of the family, it is safer to allow boys to indulge in homosexual games than to risk upsetting strategic marriage plans.

Even in sexually permissive societies, elders usually control the young through control over their future sexual lives, i.e., marriage. Although girls may be available to adolescent boys in theory, they are not always so in practice. As I pointed out for the Nyakyusa, it may take some time and effort to win the consent of a girl, who will of course consider her own interests before she accepts the attentions of any particular boy. If there is a large difference in age of marriage, older adolescent boys and youths may have to make do with very young adolescent girls rather than their more mature and desirable age-mates, who are already married. To an adolescent boy, the prospect of marriage's pleasures must be very appealing.

Adolescents rarely have access to the resources they need to get married. They are dependent on their families not only for present support but also for help in getting a spouse. This is obvious when the form of marriage transaction is bridewealth or indirect dowry or gift exchange, as the groom's family must come up with goods for the transaction. When the girl's family pays, in dowry-giving societies, potential grooms are, in effect, on display for their marriage-ability, or more precisely, their desirability as sons-in-law. The same could be said for societies in which brideservice is given; the youth must prove himself to his in-laws if he wants to get or keep a wife. The prospect of unconstrained sexual expression that future marriage promises is a powerful incentive to accept subordination in the present.

What about the few places where adolescents have virtually total sexual freedom, where sexual relations are a normal part of everyday life for everyone? These teenage paradises are those communities that have adolescent houses where the young people retire after the day's work to frolic and sleep, generally in couples. One such society is the Muria, a tribe in the former princely state of Bastar, in central India. The following description (Schlegel and Barry 1991:108) of their adolescent house, the *ghotul,* is summarized from Elwin (1968), who was there from 1935 to 1942.

> During the afternoon, girls sweep and clean the yard. The adolescents are responsible to the village for keeping the building and its compound clean and will be fined if it is left untended. At sunset, boys come to start the fire, the only light for the evening's activities.
>
> After the evening meal taken at home, the boys straggle into the *ghotul* carrying their sleeping mats. The smaller boys bring firewood, and they may be called on to massage the legs of the older boys if they are tired. Meanwhile, the girls are assembling somewhere outside, and they enter as a group. A troop of girls from another hamlet may be visiting. Some girls sit with the boys, others sit together and talk, and fatigued boys and girls nap in quiet corners.
>
> For an hour or two the mood is very informal. People gather in groups to talk; someone will tell a story or pose riddles; plans for a dancing expedition to another *ghotul* may be made or duties at a village wedding allocated; or there may be dancing. Sometimes boys sing taunting songs to the girls, who reply in kind.
>
> By about 10 o'clock, the girls collect around the girl leader, who allots to each her sleeping partner. Every girl then goes up to a boy, often but not necessarily this partner, to comb his long hair and massage his back and arms. This, of course, brings them into close contact with one another, and the boys often call out sexy remarks about themselves or others.
>
> When the massages are finished, it is bedtime. Girls visiting from another *ghotul* are now expected to leave. (If any visiting girl is discovered by her own *ghotul* boys to have remained the night, they get very angry and she is punished with a heavy fine.) The younger children go to sleep in a row. The adolescents pair off, two on a mat. Extra boys share a mat. Elwin notes that there are more often extra boys than girls. This is possibly because menstruating girls do not go to the *ghotul.* Those who intend to have intercourse may retire to a small hut on the compound. Soon all is quiet. Everyone arises before dawn, for they should be at home and working when their parents arise.
>
> While girls are expected to have intercourse at least some of the time, forcing the girl is extremely offensive and can result in a heavy fine. In some *ghotuls,* couples are paired off and expected to remain faithful to one another, although it is unlikely that one's "*ghotul* husband" or "*ghotul* wife" will be one's eventual spouse. In others, there is a rule against sleeping together too often, which the boy and girl leaders enforce.

One might imagine that the novelty of changing partners would contribute to the excitement and adventure of the *ghotul,* but it has its price. There is jealousy when a favored partner is required by group pressure to pair off with another, and the marriage of a beloved to someone else—since *ghotul* partners are rarely affianced to each other—can be emotionally devastating. Even here, constraints on erotic expression exist, and the Muria say that they welcome marriage with its privacy and the freedom to express themselves emotionally as well as sexually. The description of the Muria *ghotul* is the fullest in the literature on adolescent dormitories, but they all seem to be under the authority of group leaders, and social pressures on their participants are as strong as peer-group pressures under other conditions.

We can ask whose social ends are being served in the control over *ghotul* sexuality. The group leaders must sense their power over the erotic experiences of their peers, but the source of their power is the approval of the peers who selected them for this task. Sexual control is very likely a group process in which all control each and thereby create a sense of group identity. Sharing sexual partners, like sharing food or any other good, creates attachments (see Gregor, this volume).[4] By preventing emotional intimacy, the peer group saves itself from splintering into couples. The eroticism of the peer group is that of the excitement and risk of new partners, saving for marriage the deeper satisfactions brought by the eroticism of sexual love.

While not all permissive societies have adolescent dormitories, there are indications that the process of peer-group control over the sexual activities of group members is a common phenomenon. In the Trobriand Island of Melanesia, boys tried to prevent the girls of their village from having liaisons with boys from other villages, while girls seemed to have tried to keep boyfriends in both their native village and in other villages within walking distance. In this they were abetted by other girls (Malinowski 1932). Presumably, the same boys who took offense at their local girlfriends' infidelity also had girlfriends in other villages. This multiplicity of sexual attachments, and the spirit of adventure and gamesmanship in which it was carried out, prevented close pairing off.

Among the East African Kikuyu, it was the adolescent girls rather than the boys who had multiple sexual partners, as boys did not engage in socially approved sexual relations until after circumcision at about age 18. At this time the youths passed into the warrior age-grade. They moved into bachelor huts, where the young adolescent girls visited them. Youths and girls were expected to rotate partners; not to do so would have been selfish and unsociable (Worthman 1986). Considering the very strong male bonding among young age-mates in age-grading societies, it is likely that this rotation was promoted in order to prevent the formation of romantic couples.

Discussion

The management of adolescent sexuality, like the management of all sexuality, serves social ends. Adolescent sexuality is the sexuality of the unmarried; adult sexuality for most people in most places, certainly in tribal and traditional societies, is the sexuality of the married.

Adolescent Sexuality: "Nature" Constrained[5]

Hormonal activity creates the powerful sexual urges that accompany the bodily changes of puberty (see Wilson, this volume). "Nature" designs us to begin our sexual lives at biological adolescence, but "culture" intervenes with a social adolescence that does not include unconstrained sexuality. It is one of the ironies of human society that girls, whose sexual impulses may not be as strong in adolescence as they later become, are married young, whereas boys, whose bodies are flooded with androgens, usually must wait out a longer social adolescence before marriage brings them sexual intercourse with regularity.

We have seen some of the ways adolescent sexuality is controlled, and for what reasons. It may be in the interests of families, who wish to choose their in-laws, to prohibit the sexuality of daughters who might become pregnant. Chastity of adolescent girls imposes chastity on adolescent boys or at least reduces their opportunities. As we have seen, homosexual activity may be permitted.

Control is also exerted by peers, especially in sexually permissive societies. It has often been observed that in extended families expressions of affection and sexual interest between husband and wife are suppressed when they are in the company of others. This can be interpreted as an attempt to dampen the pull that love and sex have on the husband, in a patrilocal setting, or on the wife, in a matrilocal one, toward the spouse and away from the kin that form the household's core. The sexual bond threatens the solidarity of the kin group, as the married pair are tempted to consider their own well-being in distinction to the interests of the household. The same principle applies to the peer group, which retains its cohesiveness at the expense of attachment between lovers, or at least in tension with it. Adolescent promiscuity in permissive societies cannot therefore be simply taken as evidence for nature unfettered, but rather must be seen in light of the resistance of the peer group to the formation of loving couples among its members.

Married Sexuality: "Nature" Transformed

Marriage limits the number of legitimate sexual partners to one or several, but it lifts the restrictions on the free expression of sexuality within the marriage bed. It provides the prospect of a long-term, if not permanent, relationship that is conducive to the letting down of one's guard and the formation of bonds of trust and common interest. If adolescent sexuality is nature constrained, married sexuality is nature transformed, domesticated to serve the ends of family and society but also to lay the basis for close emotional ties (see Gregor, this volume). Eroticism takes on new dimensions when sexual stimulation is accompanied by the comforting sensuality of the familiar body.[6]

If the problem of adolescent sexuality for adults is the wayward passions that can upset the family's marriage plans or introduce an unwanted bastard, the problem for adolescents themselves is the frustration of desire. Constrained by their families in restrictive societies and by peers in permissive ones, they look to marriage as the step toward adulthood that brings the freedom of sexual gratification. Desire makes them docile, willing to subordinate themselves to those who control their marital destinies, without whose help they would not marry at all.

However, there have been times when some adolescents and youths have rejected marriage. To refuse to marry can be a subversive act, for in doing so one denies dependency on those who make marriage possible. Unmarried persons are liable to be suspected of an undomesticated sexuality ready to burst through the constraints that surround it. It is probably no historical accident that early Christian youths and maidens who chose to remain virgins faced resistance from their parents, while at a later time, after the establishment of monasteries and nunneries that assured tight clerical control of their chaste members, the celibate life was one of social honor. (Nevertheless, the Beguines and Beghards of late medieval Flanders, in their associations of celibate laypersons, were looked on with much suspicion by the Church, as they were not in orders under its control.) More explicitly defiant were the female silkworkers of nineteenth-century China who refused marriage, and only the remittance of most of their wages to their parents made it possible for them to maintain their celibate lives (Topley 1975).

We can say with Foucault (1990:81): "Where there is desire, the power relation is already present." Celibate morality usually speaks of chastity as loosening the hold of the flesh over the spirit; it is not so often made explicit that the denial of desire is also the denial of power to those who constrain or transform sexuality and who hold the necessary means for its expression.[7]

Conclusion

A discussion of adolescent sexuality probes into the most fundamental issues of human sexuality. We examined the incest taboo and the separation of adolescent girls and boys in the family. I propose that this is both a response to the taboo and a feature of human social organization comparable to social mechanisms in other species that depress close inbreeding. In a review of the value placed on virginity, parental control over adolescent sexuality was seen as a device for ensuring parental control over marriage choice, particularly when family property is a marker of social status and power in class and rank societies. The discussion of adolescent homosexual activity raises the issue of bisexuality: if many adolescents engage in homosexual play, even if their preference might be for a partner of the opposite sex, just how "unnatural" are "unnatural acts"?

A theme running through this chapter has been the tension between pleasure and power. This is made most explicit when sexuality is directly associated with power. When men's power over women (or other men and boys) is manifested through sexual penetration, the use of their bodies is a graphic statement of dominance. A more complex association between pleasure and power exists in the institutionalization of sexual expression. Desire becomes an instrument of power in the hands of those who control its fulfillment. To deny desire is to remove this instrument.

Sexuality also makes any division between "nature" and "culture" problematic (see Introduction, this volume). It may be currently fashionable to speak of the "cultural construction of ____ [the reader can fill in the blank]"; but this presupposes culture creating something *de novo,* which is clearly not the case with sexuality (which is assured by our anatomy), or it raises the image of culture working to modify a constant given by nature. Sexuality does not lend itself to either of these kinds of constructions. It is undeniable that cultures define the sexually permissible and attractive in various manners and interpret sexuality in a variety of ways—from evil to good to dangerous, or some combination of these (see Symons, this volume, for a different perspective).[8] Nevertheless, as Freud taught us, human sexuality is learned in the human family, in the emotional bonds between mother and child and between mother and her mate. Is this nature or culture? Any attempt to force sexuality into either of these constructs is doomed to frustration.[9] Anthropology's gift to the study of human sexuality is this recognition of the truly holistic character of sexuality, a faceted mirror whose biological, psychological, and cultural dimensions reflect one another.

Notes

Much of the data for this paper come from Schlegel and Barry (1991) and from Schlegel (1972).

1. There are some exceptions; for example, among some Australian Aboriginal peoples, girls enter social adolescence at the first signs of puberty and are often married before first menstruation.

2. In our study of adolescence (Schlegel and Barry 1991), we were unable to find cross-cultural information on age of puberty for boys, although there is considerable data on girls. Length of adolescence for boys, therefore, is not as well established as it is for girls across cultures.

3. Dowry is the gift of the girl's family to the new conjugal couple. It may be controlled jointly or by either spouse. It is not the mirror image of bridewealth, as it goes to the couple and not to one set of parents. Indirect dowry is the gift from the groom's

family to the bride, either directly or through her father (i.e., a combination of bride-wealth and dowry). This form is common in the Semitic and Muslim world-areas. Gift exchange is the exchange of equivalent amounts of goods between the bride's and groom's families. For a fuller description and discussion, see Schlegel and Eloul (1988).

4. There are numerous examples of strongly bonded groups whose members share sexual partners: African age-grade mates, American biker gangs, and American college fraternity brothers are just a few. In the case of the *ghotul,* the bonding seems to be among girls as well as boys, in contrast to these examples of male-bonded groups.

5. The quotation marks around *nature* indicate that I use this word in a metaphorical sense, for I question the separation of nature and culture in human behavior (see also the Introduction to this volume). This view will be explicated further in this chapter.

6. In almost all societies, marriage is the culturally approved and expected state for most or all adults. The exceptions are the widowed elderly, religious celibates, the severely physically or mentally disabled, slaves in many societies, "bachelor uncles" and "spinster aunts" who remain in the household, and members of the underclass too poor to marry. Until recent times, the divorced person was considered anomalous, even in societies that permitted divorce. It was assumed that, unless elderly, the individual would remarry. There was often pressure to do so, for the divorced man or woman was a potential loose cannon, a sexual threat to married couples. Increasingly over the last fifty years, a new definition of adulthood is emerging which does not necessarily include marriage as a criterion for this status.

7. It may be that the obsession with children's masturbation that gripped the minds of parents and educators in the nineteenth century was due to the fear that if children learned that they could give themselves pleasure, they would have taken the first step toward independence. The historical context of this obsession is a time in which economic dependence upon parents was loosening as industrial capitalism and colonialism combined to open up economic opportunities to those whose families could not or would not provide them with property. The rigid socialization of the nineteenth century could have been an attempt to impose through discipline and shaming the control that was being lost through an expanding economy.

8. It is one of the disappointments of Foucault's massive study of sexuality (Foucault 1990 and subsequent volumes) that his case material rarely goes beyond the descriptive. Although he compared Greek, Roman, and early Christian attitudes toward sexuality, he did not seek to explain the historical changes or even to ground the views of the different periods in their historically specific economic, political, or social contexts.

9. Thoughtful sociobiologists are aware of this. It is generally accepted that cross-sex pair-bonds, and close ties of the child to its mother and to the male with whom the mother is pair-bonded, are as much a characteristic of *homo sapiens* as the social patterns of animals are characteristic of their species. (For a discussion of why the male with whom the woman bonds is usually her reproductive partner rather than her brother or another male, see the discussion in Schlegel and Barry [1991].)

Bibliography

Bischof, Norbert. 1975. A Systems Approach Toward the Functional Connections of Attachment and Fear. *Child Development* 46:801–17.

Broude, Gwen J., and Sarah J. Greene. 1980. Cross-Cultural Codes on Twenty Sexual Attitudes and Practices. In *Cross-Cultural Samples and Codes,* ed. Herbert Barry III and Alice Schlegel, 313–34. Pittsburgh: University of Pittsburgh Press.

Creed, Gerald W. 1982. Sexual Subordination: Institutionalized Homosexuality and Social Control in Melanesia. *Ethnology* 21:157–76.

Elwin, Verrier. 1968. *The Kingdom of the Young.* Bombay: Oxford University Press.

Foucault, Michel. 1990. *The History of Sexuality. Vol. I: An Introduction.* New York: Vintage Books.

Gay, Judith. 1986. "Mummies" and "Babies" and Friends and Lovers in Lesotho. In *Anthropology and Homosexual Behavior,* ed. Evelyn Blackwood, 97–116. New York: Haworth Press.

Goggin, John M., and William C. Sturtevant. 1964. The Calusa: A Stratified Non-Agricultural Society (With Notes on Sibling Marriage). In *Explorations in Cultural Anthropology: Essays in Honor of George Peter Murdock,* ed. Ward H. Goodenough, 179–219. San Francisco: McGraw-Hill.

Greenberg, David F., 1988. *The Construction of Homosexuality.* Chicago: University of Chicago Press.

Hollos, Marida, and Philip E. Leis. 1986. *Becoming Nigerian in Ijo Society.* New Brunswick: Rutgers University Press.

Lancaster, Jane B. 1979. Sex and Gender in Evolutionary Perspective. In *Human Sexuality: A Comparative and Developmental Perspective,* ed. Herant A. Katchadourian, 51–80. Berkeley: University of California Press.

Malinowski, Bronislaw. 1932. *The Sexual Life of Savages in Northwestern Melanesia.* London: Routledge and Kegan Paul.

Parker, Seymour. 1976. The Precultural Bases of the Incest Taboo: Toward a Biosocial Theory. *American Anthropologist* 78:285–305.

Posner, Richard A. 1992. *Sex and Reason.* Cambridge: Harvard University Press.

Reid, Anthony. 1988. *The Lands Below the Winds. Southeast Asia in the Age of Commerce 1450–1680, vol. 1.* New Haven: Yale University Press.

Schlegel, Alice. 1972. *Male Dominance and Female Autonomy.* New Haven: Human Relations Area Files Press.

———, 1991. Status, Property, and the Value on Virginity. *American Ethnologist* 18:719–34.

Schlegel, Alice, and Rohn Eloul. 1988. Marriage Transactions: Labor, Property, and Status. *American Anthropologist* 90:291–309.

Schlegel, Alice, and Herbert Barry III. 1991. *Adolescence: An Anthropological Inquiry.* New York: Free Press.

Taggart, James M. 1992. Gender Segregation and Cultural Constructions of Sexuality in Two Hispanic Societies. *American Ethnologist* 19:75–96.

Taylor, Clark L. 1986. Mexican Male Homosexual Interactions in Public Contexts. In *Anthropology and Homosexual Behavior,* ed. Evelyn Blackwood. New York: Haworth Press.

Topley, Marjorie. 1975. Marriage Resistance in Rural Kwangtung. In *Women in Chinese Society,* ed. Margery Wolf and Roxane Witke, 67–88. Stanford: Stanford University Press.

Whiting, John W. M., Victoria K. Burbank, and Mitchell S. Ratner. 1986. The Duration of Maidenhood across Cultures. In *School-Age Pregnancy and Parenthood: Bio-*

social Dimensions, ed. Jane B. Lancaster and Beatrix A. Hamburg, 273–302. New York: Aldine De Gruyter.

Worthman, Carol M. 1986. Development Dysynchrony as Normal Experience: Kikuyu Adolescents. In *School-Age Pregnancy and Parenthood: Biosocial Dimensions,* ed. Jane B. Lancaster and Beatrix A. Hamburg, 95–112. New York: Aldine De Gruyter.

CHAPTER TEN

Sexuality, Infertility and Sexually Transmitted Disease among Farmers and Foragers in Central Africa

Robert C. Bailey and Robert V. Aunger

Many areas in Africa are known to have among the highest, if not the highest, levels of fertility in the world, with total fertility rate (TFR) in many countries averaging 6.5–8.0. Despite such overall high fertility, numerous populations in sub-Saharan Africa actually experience very low fertility (Page and Coale, 1972); this is true in spite of the virtual absence of intentional practices to lower reproduction. Subfertility is nowhere in Africa more prevalent than in the rural areas of the central part of the continent, the part covered by moist tropical forest. Belsey (1976) has documented what he calls the "infertility belt" spanning a broad zone from Nigeria and Cameroon eastward through Zaire to Uganda, with 25–40% of women completing their reproductive careers without bearing a child. Within this belt are high-fertility populations neighboring and surrounding low-fertility populations with high frequencies of infertile women. Thus, infertility appears not to be uniformly distributed across the African infertility belt, but to occur in isolated pockets, which often follow ethnic lines (Frank, 1983; Caldwell and Caldwell, 1983). Such non-uniform geographic distribution of high-infertility populations suggests that, whatever the underlying causes, a substantial part of the explanation for the infertility must lie in cultural practices.

Every author who has ever investigated low fertility in sub-Saharan Africa has attributed the high rates of infertility to sexually transmitted diseases (STDs), especially gonorrhea (*Neisseria gonorrhea*), which cause adhesions, scarring, occlusions, and other permanent damage to women's Fallopian tubes. Tubal occlusion may result from a single episode of infection by gonorrhea or chlamydia (*Chlamydia trachomatis*), with risk of occlusion increasing with each repeated infection. Although infection occurs occasionally in only one Fallopian tube, bilateral infection is usual, so that bilateral occlusion and infertility appear to be the normal sequellae of repeated infection. Once scarring and occlusion have occurred, pharmacological treatment does not improve reproductive performance. Male sterility may also result from STDs causing blockage of sperm ducts, or from disorders in sperm production resulting in semen that contains too few sperm and/or abnormal sperm (Romaniuk, 1967; Voas, 1981; Belsey, 1976; Caldwell and Caldwell, 1983; Page, 1989).

Romaniuk (1968) estimated the frequency of STD in the central African country of Zaire, using hospital records and medical surveys. He reported that 35–45% of women in the province of Equateur were infertile according to demographic survey undertaken by the Belgian colonial administration during 1955–57. From simultaneous medical surveys in the same area, up to 29.4% of adults showed clinical signs of syphilis and 38.3% clinical signs of gonorrhea. Arya et al. (1973) conducted a major study in rural Uganda involving medical examination of 270 men and 343 women from randomly selected households in a district of high infertility. Twenty-three percent of men reported a past history of genital sores, 75% of polygynous men and 56% of monogamous men reported previous urethral discharge. Clinical exams uncovered 12% of men exhibiting urethral discharge at the time of the study; 10% had gonorrhea. Among women, 23% were without a live birth, and 18% were detected to have gonorrhea. In Cameroon, Merle and Puech-Lestrade reported that 43% of 1,566 infertile women at hospitals showed gonococcal symptoms, 19% with anatomical signs. Other studies showing typically high frequencies of clinically discovered STDs in low-fertility areas include Allard (1955), Sydes (1988), and those reviewed in Retel-Laurentin (1974:55–62).

How long STDs have been widely prevalent in central Africa is not clearly established, but all evidence points to their widespread presence since at least the later part of the last century. Some historians and demographers believe gonorrhea and syphilis were introduced into central Africa by Arab traders seeking ivory and slaves during the second half of the nineteenth century. It seems likely that gonorrhea was present, at least at low frequencies, for millennia, since Chinese writings as early as 2637 B.C., as well as the unmistakable references in the Bible to gonorrhea, attest to its widespread existence for many centuries (Blau, 1961; Fiumara, 1971). However, it seems probable that infertility was not so prevalent until the disruptive effects of the rubber trade imposed by the Belgians around the turn of the century produced the social disorganization conducive to the spread of venereal disease (Voas, 1981). Caldwell and Caldwell (1983) believed that infertility rates increased during the first part of the twentieth century. Extrapolating backward from prevalence figures for the recent past, they conclude that STDs began making inroads in about 1880, when Arabs and Europeans began having significant disruptive effects on the social relations and cultural beliefs of central African families. Indicating that STDs had already had significant impacts on fertility before the 1880s is the German explorer Schweinfurth's notation in 1870 of the childlessness of pygmy populations in what is now northeast Zaire, and there are missionary accounts of having to treat numerous "cases of immorality" before 1900 (Ransford, 1983). The fact that central Africans today have terms designating and describing syphilis and gonorrhea in their indigenous languages (in addition to the French, Swahili, and English terms) suggests a considerable antiquity for the presence of STDs in these populations.

"African Sexuality" and the Transmission of STDs

Social and sexual arrangements among sub-Saharan Africans have been viewed by many as distinct from those in any other geographic region of the world and, in large part, as responsible for the high prevalence of STDs in these populations. In much of sub-Saharan Africa, social arrangements are considered as geared toward maximizing women's exposure to pregnancy through early sexual activity, universal early marriage, levirate and ease of re-marriage, polygyny, and little censure of extramarital relations. Inability to reproduce is often associated with social discrimination and may result in women being subject to divorce. These and other characteristics of sub-Saharan African social and sexual relations have been outlined explicitly by Caldwell and Caldwell (1989). They argue, for example, that there is little reference made to virginity as a desirable aspect of a woman at marriage in African cultures; rather, proven fertility is often valued. Premarital sexual activity is not necessarily discouraged; coitus interruptus is a means of birth control during premarital sex in many areas; and there is a widespread existence of long-term "parallel"relationships and lack of moral censure of illegitimacy. Sex in Africa, even between spouses, is often conceived of in commercial terms of men buying sexual favors. A separate category of women who provide sexual favors on demand to a wide variety of men on a short-term basis (formal prostitution) is limited largely to urban settings and truckstop situations. In rural areas, many women engage in liaisons with exchange of "gifts," especially women between marriages and infertile women. Between postpartum taboo periods and long-term separation of spouses due to work-related migration, opportunities for extramarital sex can be frequent and may often be taken advantage of. Caldwell and Caldwell (1989), citing the work of many others before, depict Africans as "reproduction-oriented," having a "non-religious" attitude toward sexual relations—feelings of guilt or remorse are minimal and they tend not to attach other kinds of meaning to the sexual act.

Romaniuk (1967), referring to demographic trends in Zaire, noted "a general procreative ethos" that manifests itself in early and universal marriage for women, premarital unions, ease of divorce (especially in cases of infertility), ease of remarriage, and tolerance for illegitimacy. Rural Africans see fertility as an intimate component of general health and well-being. Unlike many people in developed countries, Africans generally have a greater fear of sterility than of excess fertility. Against these beliefs and practices must be put, however, the occasional practice of abortion, pervasive sexual taboos during certain times of the sexual cycle or during certain periods between conceptions, and spousal separations.

Caldwell et al. (1989) and Romaniuk (1967) both emphasize the importance of understanding these patterns of "African sexuality" to predict the epidemiology of STD on that continent. Certainly, having knowledge of the general terrain on which variation between populations and individuals may operate will be useful. However, to truly understand how and whether these cultural beliefs and practices translate into STD transmission and frequency, studies that link variation in fertility and infertility with variation in sexual attitudes and behaviors are necessary. Such studies are few, because demographers, who are most likely to measure fertility differences, seldom collect information about attitudes and beliefs, while other social scientists (e.g., anthropologists) are in a position to be informed about sexual behaviors and beliefs, but seldom collect appropriate demographic information.

The purpose of this chapter is to report the findings of a study undertaken in northeast Zaire among four different tribal groups of village-living, slash-and-burn farmers with varying levels of completed fertility. The study was designed to determine the varying levels of fertility and infertility and to investigate the attitudes and practices associated with that variation. For comparative purposes, I will also include demographic data from a population of seminomadic foraging people, called Efe, who live in association with one of the four farming groups.[1]

The Study Populations

The four different cultural groups studied (Lese, Mamvu, Budu, and Bila) live in the Ituri Forest in northeastern Zaire. The Ituri is an area of approximately 24,300 square miles of tropical rain forest situated between 0 and 3 degrees N latitude and 27 and 30 degrees E longitude. Before 1930, people in the Ituri were distributed more or less evenly throughout the forest as segmented patrilineal clans residing in small, isolated villages. Between 1920 and 1950, the Belgian colonial administration created chiefdoms, imposed peaceful relations between clans, constructed roads, and coerced people to move their villages and gardens to the roadsides, where most remain today. Except in a few large towns on the edge of the Ituri, most people live in villages with 10 to 150 residents. They practice a mixed subsistence economy, engaging in slash-and-burn horticulture, some growing a few cash crops, and most doing some hunting for meat, seasonal fishing, and foraging for wild yams and honey in the forest.

All four cultural groups are similar in their residence and marriage patterns. Residence is mainly patrilocal, with women marrying out of their natal clan and residing virilocally in villages composed mostly of men related to one another. The ideal marriage is achieved through payment of bridewealth, but sister-exchange is also practiced. All four groups are polygynous, with from 15% to 30% of men having two or more wives (no men in our sample had more than four wives). Girls reach menarche late by Western standards, normally between 15 and 16 years of age. A special public ceremony usually marks the occasion of a girl's first menstrual period, and sexual activity may commence at that time. Although girls are eligible for marriage at men-arche, first marriage occurs generally, but not always, two or more years there-after.

The Bila and Budu are Bantu-speaking, while the Mamvu and Lese speak a tonal Central Sudanic dialect. The Mamvu and Lese are more isolated than the two other groups; commercial markets are less accessible; dispensaries and medical services are less available; schools are virtually absent; and conse-quently cultural and economic influences on these two groups by the govern-ment and commercialization have been less. The Bila live along the major commercial highway connecting eastern Zaire to Kisangani, a major city and commercial port serving traffic on the Zaire River. Consequently, the Bila have the greatest access to markets, the most diversified economy, the best access to medical care, and the most contact with truckers and other possible outside sources of STD. The Budu are in an area with numerous coffee plantations and so have access to outside markets. They tend to be commercially minded, and place the highest value on formal education; most boys and many girls attain six years of schooling in contrast to just one to three years for those in other groups.

Associated with each of these groups of farmers is one of four different tribal groups of Bambuti: the Mbuti, Tswa, and two different groups of Efe. The Efe are associated with the Lese and Mamvu; Mbuti with the Bila; and the Tswa (Sua) with the Budu. The Bambuti are seminomadic and subsist by hunting and foraging forest resources (meat, honey, fruits, nuts, tubers, insects, and mushrooms) which they consume themselves or trade to their farming neighbors. In return for these forest products and for their labor in the farmers' gardens, the Bambuti receive agricultural foods (mainly bananas, cassava, pea-nuts, rice, and squashes) cloth, pots, ax blades, salt, and other material items not available in the forest. Relations between Bambuti and farmers extend be-yond economics to include all aspects of ritual and social life. Sexual relations between farmer men and Bambuti women may be frequent and widespread. Intermarriage can occur between all these groups, but it is especially common between the Lese and Efe, with 14% of Efe women married to Lese men (Bai-ley, 1988). Farmer women virtually never engage in sex with Bambuti men, and of thousands of farmer marriages, we know of just one between a farmer woman and an Mbuti. As with the farmers, residence by Bambuti is mainly patrilocal-virilocal. Payment of brideprice, however, is not common; sister-exchange is the ideal means of marriage, although this ideal is achieved in only 30% of cases (Bailey, 1988). Bambuti girls reach menarche slightly later, on average, than farmer girls. Sexual relations may begin around the time of men-arche; first marriage tends to be later than among the farmers. Bambuti are generally not integrated into the economy or politics of Zaire; they more often barter than handle currency; they seldom have any schooling; and they tend not to visit the few dispensaries or take advantage of sources of Western medicine.

Data Collection

Pregnancy and birth histories of all women over the age of 16 were collected between February 1987 and August 1987 in several villages within the boundaries of each of four ethnic groups. Interviews were conducted in the presence of others, usually spouses, siblings, children, and others familiar with the subject. These observers served to correct or corroborate the informants' responses. Since social embarrassment is associated only with infertility, underreporting of births was unlikely. The sex ratio of reported offspring was 102.2:100 (M:F), indicating no bias in sex of births reported. Women's ages were only imperfectly calculated, based on important local events of known date and birth orders of various pairings of individuals. Ages at death of children were calculated by asking whether certain developmental milestones had been passed (e.g., walking, talking, deciduous tooth loss, etc.) For further explanation of demographic methods, see Howell (1979) and Bailey (1991).

Reliable information concerning sexual histories, experience with STDs, attitudes about marriage and sexual activity could not be collected from women by a male anthropologist. However, men seemed uninhibited about disclosing such personal information. A total of 105 men were interviewed using a prepared questionnaire designed to elicit information about recent sexual activity, history of STD infection, source of medication, and attitudes about premarital sexual activity.

Levels of Fertility and Infertility in the Ituri

Desire for large families is widespread in rural Africa, such that childlessness is at best a heartfelt tragedy and at worst a reason for ostracism and lack of community support. This section describes the low levels of fertility and high levels of infertility among five different tribal groups in the Ituri Forest. First, we describe the fertility of the Efe, a population of Bambuti foragers who live in association with the Lese. Then we turn to the Lese, to describe their age-specific fertility rates. We show that their fertility levels have remained low, but for them, unlike the Efe, fertility and infertility have changed over the last several decades. Looking at the completed family sizes of the other three groups indicates that, although there is variation among the groups in fertility and infertility, all these populations exhibit subfertility, and they show the same pattern of variable infertility over the last sixty years.

Modern forms of contraception are unknown to the majority of individuals in these groups, and there are no or very few sources. Based on interviews and ethnographic experience over twelve years, we consider it very unlikely that even a handful of births have been prevented through the use of modern contraceptives. There is knowledge of indigenous forms of contraception, but there is little evidence that they are used, except under rare and dire circumstances.

Table 10.1   Results from reproductive histories of 89 postmenopausal Efe women showing the mean number of live births per woman and the cumulative proportion of childhood mortality by age class.

Live Births			Deaths by Age Class			
Male	Female		0-1	0-4	0-9	0-14
119	109		32	40	48	51
2.56			.140	.175	.211	.224

Abortifacients are also known, but they seem to be little used, and their efficacy is unknown.

Efe Fertility

We first examine a summary of the results from reproductive interviews with 89 postmenopausal Efe Bambuti forager women (shown in table 10.1). These women had a total of 228 live births and an average completed fertility of just 2.56 live births per woman. Mortality of infants was 14%, and childhood mortality in the first five years of life was 17.5%. Just over 22% of children died before reaching the age of 15.

A look at the frequency distribution of women according to their completed fertility (see figure 10.1) reveals considerable variance in fertility, with two women having nine children, but 90% of women having born six or fewer children. Most dramatic is the high number of women with no live births at all—28% of postmenopausal Efe women were childless—and 18% of the women had just one live birth.

These data from the women who had completed their fertility show that Efe have lower fertility than expected of an African population living largely by hunting and gathering. For example, Howell (1979) found that the !Kung San in the Kalahari Desert, Botswana, had a completed fertility of 4.7 live births, and the Hadza, a foraging people in Tanzania near Lake Eyasi, have a completed fertility of approximately 6.0 live births (Blurton-Jones et al., 1992). We would predict such foraging societies to have low completed fertility due to high levels of energy expenditure, seasonal changes in nutritional status, and high frequencies of infant suckling, all of which are known to be proximate mechanisms causing reduced ovulatory function (Bentley, 1985; Ellison, Peacock and Lager, 1986; Ellison, 1991). However, these behavioral and ecological variables are unlikely to cause total completed fertility rates as low as seen here among the Efe women. Nor should the proximate ecological and behavioral mechanisms causing reduction in ovulatory cycles cause a pattern of Efe primary and secondary sterility in which 46% of women had one or no live births.

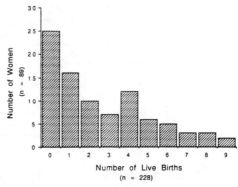

Figure 10.1   The distribution of 228 live births by 89 postmenopausal Efe women. The mean number of live births per woman is 2.56, and 28% of women have no live births.

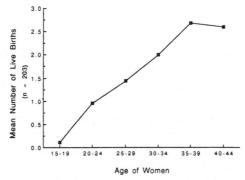

Figure 10.2   The parity distribution of 117 Efe women of reproductive age. The fertility of these reproductive women is consistent with the completed fertility of postmenopausal women.

It is possible, however, that these older women are underreporting births. The infant and child mortality rates, low relative to many other African populations, might lead us to suspect that women are omitting from their reproductive histories children who died young. However, they do not seem to be under-reporting one sex in favor of another, as indicated by the almost exactly 105:100 sex ratio of the reported live births.

One possible way to detect underreporting by older women is to check their fertility histories against those of the younger women—those that are still of reproductive age. The parity distributions of the women still in their reproductive careers are shown in figure 10.2. They are consistent with those of the postmenopausal women. Parity peaks at 2.6 live births among women aged 35–45, and the proportions that are infertile are between 26% and 33%, not significantly different from the 28% primary sterility of the 89 postmenopausal Efe women. Additionally, the mortality of children born to women still in their reproductive years is 14.8%, which is only slightly higher than and not signifi-

Table 10.2 Results from reproductive histories of 119 postmenopausal Lese women showing the mean number of live births per woman and the cumulative proportion of childhood mortality by age class.

Live Births			Deaths by Age Class			
Male	Female		0-1	0-4	0-9	0-14
139	140		50	67	71	76
2.34			.179	.240	.254	.269

cantly different from the 14% of children born to the older women. These results indicate that the fertility and mortality schedules of Efe have remained stable over the lifetimes of the oldest living people. The Efe have low fertility with a high incidence of primary and secondary sterility, and this has been so at least since the 1930s, when the older living women entered their reproductive years.

Lese Fertility

The number of live births and the proportions of infants and children that died of 119 postmenopausal Lese women are shown in table 10.2. The completed fertility of the Lese women is lower than that of the Efe. The 119 Lese women reported a total of 279 live births, or a mean of 2.35 births each. The mortality rates are higher than for the Efe, with nearly 18% infant mortality and 24% mortality of children up to age five.[2] These are lower mortality rates than most other rural African populations.

The distribution of live births among the 119 Lese women is shown in figure 10.3. There is a greater range in Lese fertility than in the Efe, with one woman giving birth to 15 infants. However, 94% of women had 6 live births or fewer. Most striking is the high incidence of primary sterility—37% of Lese women had no live births.

Are the fertility schedules of the younger, currently reproductive women similar to those of the postmenopausal women? Figure 10.4 shows the parity distributions of 166 Lese women over the age of 15 by five-year cohorts. If the fertility of Lese women were consistent over the sixty or so reproductive years represented, the mean fertility of each five-year age group should increase up to age 45 and then remain more or less constant across the older cohorts. This is not the case. Mean parity rises until, at ages 35–50, women have between 3.33 and 3.10 live births. Thereafter, mean parity declines. Clearly the women who are younger than 50 (i.e., born after 1933) are reproducing at higher rates than those who are older. Much of the difference in fertility between women born before 1933 and those born after is attributable to differences in primary sterility (see figure 10.5). Twenty percent of women between 25 and 50 are childless, whereas 37% of those older than 50 are childless. Infant and child-

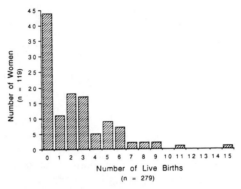

Figure 10.3 The distribution of 279 live births by 119 postmenopausal Lese women. The mean number of live births per woman is 2.35, and 37% of women have no live births.

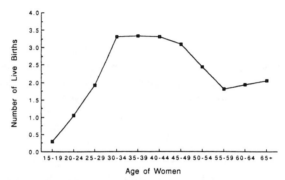

Figure 10.4 The parity distribution of 166 Lese women. Women over 50 have lower completed fertility than younger women, suggesting changing conditions in the early 1950s when the younger women were entering reproductive age.

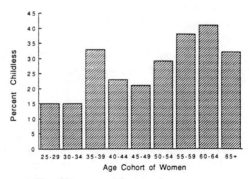

Figure 10.5 Primary sterility of Lese women by age cohort.

Table 10.3 Completed fertility and primary sterility of postmenopausal women in four tribal groups in the Ituri Forest.

Tribe	Number of Women	Mean No. Live Births	Percent Childless
Lese	119	2.35	37
Mamvu	105	1.89	44
Bila	117	3.36	37
Buda	113	3.04	34

hood mortality levels (not shown) are slightly higher in later years, but essentially remain constant.

Other Ituri Agriculturalists

Table 10.3 summarizes the results of reproductive interviews with postmenopausal women from three agricultural groups—the Mamvu, Bila, and Budu—with the Lese data for comparison. Across all four populations there are similarly high proportions of women who are infertile, ranging from 34% of the Budu to 44% of the Mamvu. Although all of the four populations clearly suffer from subfertility, there is variation between them in mean completed parity. The mean number of live births per woman ranges from 1.89 for the Mamvu to 3.36 for the Bila. All of this variation cannot be attributed to primary sterility, since, for example, the Lese and Bila both have 37% of women with no live births, yet the Bila complete their reproductive careers with 43% more children on average.

The historical pattern of subfertility and primary sterility has been consistent across all four of these tribal groups. Figure 10.6 shows the age-specific parity distributions of the Lese and the other three groups combined. The women from the tribes other than the Lese attain higher fertility by age 49, but like the Lese, the fertility of women born before 1933 drops significantly, and women over 55 from all four groups have the same low level of completed fertility. Among the non-Lese women, those in the 45–49 age cohort have a completed fertility of 4.7 live births; whereas those over 55 years of age average just 2.1.

As shown in figure 10.7, the other tribes also show the same pattern as the Lese of significantly higher levels of primary sterility among women 50 years and older. Thirty-eight percent of the postmenopausal women have never born a child, as opposed to 19% of the women under 50. It is worth noting, however, that for all four tribal groups there is one cohort of younger women with high levels of primary sterility, and that is among women who were 35–39 in 1987. These are women who were born 1952–57 and became sexually active 1967–72, a period when northeast Zaire was in the midst of continuous unrest due to the Simba Rebellion.

To summarize the demographic data, despite some variation in the levels of

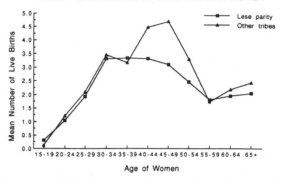

Figure 10.6 The age-specific fertility of women in three tribal groups compared to Lese women. As with the Lese, women over 50 in the other tribal groups have lower completed fertility than younger women.

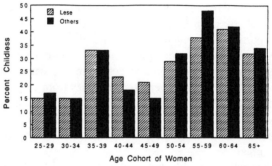

Figure 10.7 Primary sterility of women in three tribal groups by age cohort compared to Lese women. The pattern of primary sterility is similar for all tribal groups. Women aged 35–39 during the 1987 study entered reproductive maturity around the time of the tumultuous Simba Rebellion.

both completed fertility and primary sterility among the four different agricultural tribal groups in the Ituri, all four can be characterized as low-fertility, high-infertility populations consistent with the pervasive subfertility pattern common in the African infertility belt. This is also true of the Efe, a population of Bambuti foragers living a nomadic lifestyle. Very striking is the consistency across the four agricultural groups with respect to their history of infertility, as revealed by the reproductive histories of the living women. Fertility and infertility levels have not remained constant over the last sixty years. Except for the cohort of women born 1952–57, the mean parity of women still in their reproductive years is higher than that of women who have passed menopause. Those women born before 1933 have significantly lower completed fertility and significantly higher rates of childlessness than younger women. The same historical pattern is not true of the Efe women: the fertility schedules of the currently reproductive women is consistent with those of the postmenopausal

Table 10.4   Numbers of men interviewed in 1987 by tribal group and age class.

Tribe	<20	20–24	25–29	Age Category 30–39	40–49	50+	Total
Budu	1	2	6	8	3	7	27
Bila	3	2	6	5	1	6	23
Mamvu	0	2	1	6	7	6	22
Lese	3	1	9	6	3	11	33
Total	7	7	22	25	14	30	105

women. What may account for the differences between the agriculturalists and the Efe will be discussed in a later section of this chapter.

Sexual Histories and Experience with STD

In order to investigate differences between ethnic groups in their sexual attitudes and behaviors, a series of questions were asked during interviews with 105 adult male members of the four different tribal groups. The questions were designed to elicit information about the men's sexual histories, their knowledge of and experiences with STDs, and their attitudes about premarital and extramarital sexual relationships. The purpose was to detect differences between men that might be associated with variation across groups in levels of subfertility and infertility. In the final analysis, there were few significant differences between the groups with respect to the variables examined. This lack of variability in responses provides insights into the links between the sexuality of these central African peoples and infertility. This section will review the responses to questions concerning, first, the men's sexual histories; second, their experience with STDs; third, access to and use of STD cures; and last, their attitudes about virginity, premarital sex, and postpartum sexual abstinence.

The age distribution of the subject men within each tribal group is shown in table 10.4. The mean age of the entire sample in 1987 was 48.1 (SD = 14.1) years and there were no significant differences between groups in mean age. Most men were married or cohabiting with a woman; 19 of the 105 (18%) were single at the time of the interview, and of those 13 (68%) were below the age of 30.

Sexual Histories

The men were asked several questions to elicit information about their sexual histories from the time they began sexual activity. They were asked how many different sexual partners they had had prior to marriage. The mean for the entire sample was 10.4 (SD = 8.2), with no significant differences between the four groups. This figure may well be lower than the true number of premarital sexual contacts, since just one of the 86 married men interviewed had never had sexual relations with a woman before marriage, but many men responded they had slept with "more than they could possibly count." Men were also asked to estimate their age at first marriage (marriage defined as cohabiting with the same woman for more than one year). The mean estimated age at first marriage was 19.9 (SD = 2.4) years. This seems highly unlikely since males in these populations do not become reproductively mature until age 16–19; young men of that age seldom have the resources (e.g., house, garden, bride-wealth) sufficient to attract or support a woman; and the youngest age at marriage I (Robert Bailey) have ever known for any man during twelve years of working in the area is 19 years. I would estimate a more accurate mean age at first marriage for men to be 22–25 years.

When men were asked to count the number of women who had moved into their household prior to their first marriage, the mean number was just .34 (SD = .92). These being tribal groups with virilocal marital residence, the data suggest that men have numerous sexual contacts with women before marriage, but they seldom cohabit with a particular woman until they are prepared to make a substantial commitment. Another way to interpret the data is that once a woman has been invited into the household, there is a good chance she will stay for more than one year.

Yet marriages are seldom permanent. When asked how many women they had lived with for more than a year, the men responded an average of 3.03 (SD = 3.15). One older man, who had three wives at the time of the interview, had lived with a total of 14 women for more than a year, while others had been with the same woman for many decades. As we would expect, the number of women men had lived with for more than a year varied significantly with their age (r^2 = .13; p = .0002). These data seem consistent with the perception of central Africans as having high rates of marital dissolution.

Two questions were designed to determine the degree of promiscuity among the sampled men. First, men were asked to disclose how many different women, other than their spouse, they had had intercourse with during the previous week. The mean for the entire sample (n = 103) was .16 (SD = .52). Eighty-eight percent of the men reported having had no extramarital sexual contact in the previous week; 10% reported having had one. There was no significant effect of either age or tribal group. This turned out not to be a particularly revealing question, the time period of one week being so brief that the values were low and variability small.

More revealing was the second question, "How many different women other than your spouse have you had intercourse with during the last year." The results from the interviews with 102 men by age category are shown in Table 10.5. The mean number of extramarital sexual partners for the entire sample of 102 men is 2.8 (SD = 4.5) (see Gregor, this volume, for the same question with a different sample). There is no difference between men by tribal affiliation, but there is significant variation in the responses by age (ANOVA;

Table 10.5 Numbers of women other than spouses with whom men of different age groups reported having sexual contact within the last year.

Age	N	Mean	SD
<30	34	5.15	6.4
30–39	24	2.46	3.1
40–49	14	2.00	2.2
50+	30	.80	1.6
Total	102	2.80	4.5

p < .001) with a very large and highly significant difference between men under age 30 (mean = 5.1 sexual partners per year) and men over 50 (mean = .8 sexual partners per year). This age effect is not particularly surprising, since we expect younger men to be more sexually active than men over 50. Nevertheless, nearly one extramarital sexual partner during the past year can hardly be considered sexually inactive or nonpromiscuous, and over five such partners, even for 20–30 year-old men, could certainly be considered active. And these differences are not accounted for by marital status. There was no difference in the number of sexual partners of single men (mean = 3.4 sexual partners) versus married men (mean = 2.9 sexual partners) (two-tailed test; t = −.48; p = .63). Indeed, if you consider that married men are having intercourse with their wives in addition to their other sexual partners, married men are actually sexually active with more women than single men. Since it has been shown that married men in the Ituri (Bailey, 1991; Wrangham and Ross, 1983) as elsewhere (Betzig, 1986) have greater wealth than same-age single men, these results are consistent with the notion that Ituri women are attracted to men with greater wealth.[3]

The sexual histories of Ituri men as elicited during these interviews seem consistent with "African sexuality" as presented by Caldwell and Caldwell. Men seem to begin sexual activity soon after reproductive maturity and to have many sexual partners prior to their first marriage. They have seemingly high rates of marital dissolution, and have numerous extramarital partners. Younger men report many more sexual partners, as perhaps befits their stage of life, but men continue to be sexually active even quite late in life, and according to the data marriage seems to have no inhibiting effect on these activities.

Experience with STDs

Several questions were targeted to garner information about the men's history of STD infection, their knowledge of different STDs and their transmission, and the means of obtaining curative relief. First, men were asked if they knew of any disease(s) they could "catch" by having intercourse with a woman. The nonvenereal illnesses mentioned by the 105 respondents included hernia, diarrhea, leprosy, and epilepsy. Many men mentioned "kasende," the local Swahili term for syphilis, and all but three men either mentioned one of the local terms for gonorrhea ("suffice," "suffici," "boba") or described the symptoms accurately. In a separate question, the men were asked to describe the symptoms of gonorrhea. Many men mentioned that it was difficult or impossible to detect gonorrhea in a woman; the only obvious symptom being "a foul odor emanating from her genitals." In reference to men, nearly every man responded, "it hurts to pee," or "your penis exudes pus," while many also mentioned sores on the penis and stomach pain. Other responses included sores around the mouth, sores all over the body, weight loss, hair loss, foul body odor, swollen lymph nodes, and hernia. While a few of these responses are off the mark, it is clear that men in these populations are very familiar with gonorrhea and aware that it is transmitted sexually.

When asked how they first learned about gonorrhea, most of the men said they were informed as adolescents before they became sexually active. They were most frequently told by an older male sibling or by older boys in their clan. Only two men learned of gonorrhea for the first time from their father and very few learned of it from an older adult male. Two men learned of it for the first time the painful way—when they contracted it. When asked if they could tell if another man had the disease, most responded that they could because either the infected man would have stains on his trousers, or he would walk in a way that divulged his great discomfort.

Several questions were designed to discover the prevalence of gonorrhea in the population. Each man was asked if he knew of any other man in the vicinity who currently had an active case of gonorrhea. Most men knew of at least one person nearby who had gonorrhea; some named three or four. The total pool of men from which each man was choosing varied between populations, but ranged between 20 and 35. Only among the Bila did the majority of men not know another person with an active case of the disease. This suggests that gonorrhea was highly prevalent at the time of the interviews (February–August, 1987), except possibly among the Bila—the group with the highest fertility and, as we shall see, fewest reported cases of gonorrhea and best access to antibiotics.

Each man was asked if he had ever had a STD himself. If he had, he was asked to review each case, how old he was at the time, where he was, what cure(s) he had obtained, and where he had obtained the cures. Only four cases of syphilis were reported by the 105 men.[4] Gonorrhea, on the other hand, was much more prevalent. Only between 8% (Mamvu) and 12% (Lese) of men reported never having had gonorrhea. Across the whole sample of 105 men, a mean of 1.19 (SD = 1.29) cases were reported per man interviewed. There were no significant differences between the four tribal groups in number of cases reported per man. Surprisingly, age category had no effect on number of cases reported. Men below age thirty reported having had gonorrhea as many times in their life as older men, despite their having had less time to be exposed to the disease. There are several possible explanations for this. There may be a limit to the number of cases a man will report, either because he has a limited memory, or because he believes the interviewer may disapprove beyond a certain number. An alternative explanation is that younger men are currently experiencing a higher incidence of gonorrhea than their elders did. This is consistent with our earlier finding that the men below age thirty have had exposure to significantly more sexual partners during the previous year than older men, although we do not know how sexually active the older men were when they were under age thirty themselves.

Access to and Use of STD Cures

The greatest differences between the four tribal groups turned out to be related to their access to and use of medical care, both indigenous and Western. Every man was asked when he last visited a source of Western medicine (i.e., a dispensary), what the distance to that source was, his reason for going there, when he last took antibiotics for any reason, where he obtained them, why he took them, and, finally, when he last had a case of gonorrhea, if he obtained treatment with indigenous medicine.

Men who had contracted gonorrhea reported obtaining treatment with antibiotics in 68% of the cases. In 24% of such cases they obtained treatment from indigenous medicines, and in 8% they reported obtaining some other treatment or no treatment whatsoever. The Lese men were the most likely to seek and obtain treatment with indigenous medicines (45% of cases); whereas the Bila seem to have abandoned indigenous forms of treatment altogether—none of the 18 Bila men interviewed reported obtaining indigenous medicine to cure their gonorrhea. This is consistent with the finding that the Bila have the shortest time since last use of antibiotics and the shortest time since last visit to a dispensary. Bila also have the second shortest distance to travel to the nearest dispensary. In fact, they are able to reach the nearest dispensary much more easily than other groups since they live on a main truck route and can quite easily obtain a ride for the 14 kilometers to a dispensary. Whether abandoning indigenous medicines is the effect of visiting dispensaries and obtaining antibiotics more often, or whether it is the cause of turning to Western sources of medicine is not clear. That the dispensary is more accessible to the Bila, and that they tend to have a greater variety of sources of income to pay for medicines, hints toward ease of access to Western medicine as causing the loss of indigenous systems. However, surely other historical forces have converged to affect the loss of a practice that, judging by other central African groups, was recently socially very significant.

The most commonly reported reason for a man's last visit to a dispensary was treatment of STD (21%), followed by general aches and pains (15.5%) and then stomach problems (14%). The illnesses for which the last antibiotic

Table 10.6 Responses by men of four tribal groups to questions concerning STD experience and use of indigenous and Western medicine (mean values).

Variable	Budu	Bila	Tribal Group Mamvu	Lese	Total
# lifetime STD episodes	1.30	0.83	1.41	1.21	1.19
# times treated with indigenous medicine	0.35	0.00	0.15	0.45	0.28
# times treated with antibiotics	1.04	0.56	0.62	0.87	0.81
Months since last antibiotic treatment	26.3	21.4	53.8	65.5	42.2
Distance to last dispensary (Km)	8.1	14.0	29.3	42.3	23.5

was used followed a very similar pattern of response: treatment of STD (24% of cases), aches and pains (19%), and stomach problems (9.5%).

The two groups with the lowest completed fertility and highest incidence of infertility (the Mamvu and Lese) are those that have the poorest access to antibiotics (see table 10.6). These two groups are the farthest from a dispensary, traveled the farthest to get their last antibiotic treatment, and have gone significantly longer since their last antibiotic treatment, despite there being no significant difference between groups in the frequency with which they have contracted gonorrhea. The Lese rely on indigenous medicine more often than the men in other groups. The Lese used indigenous medicine 37% of the times they contracted gonorrhea. According to the men, indigenous medicines were quite effective at alleviating the symptoms of gonorrhea; however, their efficacy at actually curing cases was questionable. Many informants reported recurrence of symptoms weeks or months after initial treatment by indigenous sources, and many admitted they had little faith in their effectiveness but used them because they alleviated pain, were accessible, and were inexpensive or free. Since the Lese reside in the most remote locality and are the poorest and most traditional of the groups, it is not surprising that they rely on their own medicines to a relatively greater degree.

The data on incidence of STD and use of medicine suggest that men in the four groups contract gonorrhea equally frequently, but the Bila and Budu have greater access to Western sources of medicine. They are closer to dispensaries and they go less time between uses of antibiotics. We infer from this that, although Budu and Bila contract gonorrhea as often as others, they seek and receive an effective cure more quickly. The Budu and Bila also reside in the least remote localities, have higher incomes, get to towns more easily and frequently, and thus have contact with women outside their tribal group. This may mean that Budu and Bila women are not as exposed to gonorrheal infection as frequently as women in the other two groups—men get gonorrhea as frequently, but they get it from women outside the population and they receive the cure more quickly and by more effective means.

Attitudes and Beliefs about Sex

A number of questions were designed to discover possible differences between tribal groups with respect to men's attitudes about women's premarital sexual contacts. This was considered important because men often influence, or attempt to influence, the sexual activities of their daughters, their sisters, and their female clan relatives (Paige and Paige, 1981; also Schlegel, this volume). If men tend to be more protective of young women, or attempt to "guard" or restrain women within their clan more than do men in other groups, then such guardianship could translate into lower levels of promiscuity by young women and, consequently, lower levels of primary sterility. Thus, the expectation was that the group(s) that put the greatest value on premarital chastity and guarded their female relatives most assiduously would have the lowest level of infertility.

Men were asked how they felt about a woman having sexual contact with a man prior to marriage. There was no significant variation in responses across the four groups. The great majority of men responded that there was no problem with premarital sex. The most frequent response was, "It is up to her." This response was most frequent despite the nearly universal unsolicited caveat that frequent premarital sex might mean that the young woman could catch a venereal disease and become incapable of having children.

Thinking that men may have a different attitude about their daughters' sexual activity than just any woman's, we also asked how they felt about their daughter having sexual relations before marriage. Overall, men were slightly less indifferent, but not significantly so, to female premarital sex when their daughter was in question. In this there was highly significant variation across the four groups (ANOVA; $F = 8.74$; $p < .001$), with the Budu expressing significantly greater protectiveness toward their daughters than men in the other groups. In general, Budu men seemed to put a higher premium on sexual abstinence of young women, especially members of their own family. The most frequent reason given was schooling—if a girl became pregnant before she finished secondary school, she would have to terminate her education. The Budu put much higher value on education than the other four groups. Women in this tribal group are well known throughout eastern Zaire as excellent traders (*commerçants*) and as very commercially minded. It is recognized that a secondary education is helpful in this regard, not only because it improves literacy and accounting abilities, but because it exposes young people to experiences outside the local village setting.

Men were also asked the following question: "If a young man came to you and asked to sleep with your daughter, what would be your response?" Some men responded, "I would absolutely refuse." However, they were in the minority. Most answered that it was up to the daughter; the father would ask the daughter, and if she answered favorably, he would allow it. A significant number of men said they would charge the suitor money; if he wanted to sleep with his daughter, the suitor would have to pay first. Others were concerned that the daughter sleep with only one suitor at a time, lest conflict between suitors or between the father's family and several suitors' families ensue. The overall tenor of the responses was that fathers felt unable to prevent their daughters from sleeping with anyone they chose, so most of their efforts would be directed toward, at very least, avoiding social conflict and preferably profiting socially or monetarily through the daughter's sexual liaisons. In a few cases among the Lese and Mamvu, men stated forthrightly that they would actively encourage a daughter to sleep with a man in order to extract money from the suitor. Such cases are not uncommon during the period when a girl has just reached menarche and is sequestered in the puberty hut. During this time, most commonly among the Lese and Mamvu, suitors pay the father or a male relative of the girl to enter and spend the night in the puberty hut.

It is difficult to interpret the interview data concerning sexual attitudes. Despite their recognition that early sexual activity by their female relatives can lead to sterility caused by a STD, these central African men seem not to place high value on premarital chastity. Women are expected to engage in premarital sex and in some cases even encouraged to do so. In one group, the Budu, there was a strong expression of concern for early sexual activity by female relatives, and infertility levels in this group were the lowest (34%), although still high compared to most other populations in the world. In general, the men seemed desirous of having some control over their daughters' sexual lives, not necessarily to restrict sexual activity but to direct it in ways that might increase their own or their family's status or wealth (see Schlegel, this volume).

Discussion

The interviews with 105 men from agricultural villages in the Ituri Forest indicate that their sexual and marital histories as well as their attitudes about premarital sexual contacts are consistent with the "pro-natalist" attitudes that Caldwell and Caldwell identify as representative of "African sexuality." Early onset of sexual relations, premarital promiscuity, nearly universal marriage, high rates of marital dissolution combined with frequent remarriage (or cohabitation), frequent extramarital sexual contacts, little censure of extramarital relations, lack of moral censure of illegitimacy—all these are practices that enhance exposure to multiple sexual partners and maximize women's exposure to pregnancy. Beside frequent nursing causing lactational amenorrhea, the practices that might moderate the effects of such "pro-natalist" behaviors are abortion, spousal separation, and sexual taboos, the first two of which are minimal in the four groups studied. While postpartum sexual taboos are prominent in these populations, none extend beyond one year—a period most probably shorter than lactational amenorrhea—and most of the men report having ways (usually by employing indigenous medicines) to circumvent the taboos. Thus the behaviors and attitudes of the people in these four natural-fertility tribal groups seem well geared toward maximal fertility.

The demographic analyses of the reproductive histories of the women revealed that, contrary to the expected outcome of such a "procreative ethos," all four of these groups have low fertility, with TFRs of women ranging from just 1.89 by the Mamvu to 3.36 by the Bila. Clearly, these low levels of completed fertility are the result primarily of high rates of primary and secondary sterility, with 34–44% of women finishing their reproductive careers with no live births and another 10–20% with just one. Such high rates of sterility are consistent with, if a little higher than, many parts of the infertility belt across central Africa and are caused by STDs, especially gonorrhea and possibly chlamydia (Romaniuk, 1967; Belsey, 1976; Frank, 1983; Caldwell and Caldwell, 1983; Larsen, 1989; Pennington and Harpending, 1991).[5]

The historical patterns in changes in levels of fertility and infertility revealed by the demographic analyses point to the pervasiveness among the four different groups of the "procreative ethos." The fertility of women born before 1933 was significantly lower and the levels of primary infertility were significantly higher than they were for women born after 1933. What was the cause of these changes in fertility and infertility? Probably not a change in sexual behavior. The most likely cause was the widespread installation of medical dispensaries by the Belgians during the late 1940s and early 1950s when these women were reaching reproductive maturity and beginning sexual activity. At that time, in addition to making antibiotics and other Western medicines available, the Belgians instituted biannual mandatory clinical examinations of every male, and a system of paid informants in every *localité* to disclose persons complaining of the symptoms of gonorrhea or syphilis. Those discovered to have the symptoms were forced to be treated along with their sexual partner. While these policies and practices did not eradicate STDs, they appear to have had a significant salutary effect.

The introduction and use of antibiotics among the Ituri being the most likely explanation for their rise in fertility and drop in infertility is consistent with other demographic studies of historical changes in fertility in other areas of central Africa. Caldwell and Caldwell (1983), Romaniuk (1968) and Sala-Diakanda et al. (1981) all document dramatic reductions in childlessness among diverse populations across central Africa between 1945 and 1960, and they attribute the reductions to the introduction of Western medical treatment by the colonial administration. "It is hard to avoid the conclusion that we are dealing with an infection or contagious disease that began its inroads as soon as the populations were unsettled from about 1880, and was increasingly successfully combated between 1945 and 1960 . . . the period when the Belgian administration was extending health services, and for the first time began using penicillin" (Caldwell and Caldwell, 1983:11).

That the reductions in infertility were caused by the introduction of antibiotics to these village-farmer populations is further supported by the analysis of Efe forager reproductive histories showing no such reductions. The parity distributions of older Efe women were consistent with those of the younger women—there was no downward shift in the level of childlessness among women born after 1933, as there was for the farmers. This is what should be expected, since the Efe are much less likely than farmers to present at dispensaries and to use Western medicines. Moreover, they were never well integrated into the workforce at plantations, among road crews, or in other Belgian commercial operations that provided surveillance of STD symptoms and regular medical care.

The results from the interviews with the 105 Ituri men revealed essentially no differences between the four tribal groups in their sexual behavior or their attitudes about sexual relations. The variation between the groups in fertility and childlessness cannot be attributed to differences in sexual behavior, at least judging by the men's reports. The men in the four groups did not differ significantly in their sexual histories or in the incidence of gonorrhea. One tribal group, the Budu, did seem to place greater value on their daughters' premarital chastity, but it did not translate into any difference in childlessness. Where the groups did differ significantly was in their access to and use of dispensaries and antibiotics. The Bila and Budu are closer to dispensaries and have means other than walking of getting to them. They visit dispensaries more often, and they have taken antibiotics much more recently.

The Sad Irony of Sexual Behavior and Disease

There is a sad irony to the juxtaposition of the demographic data, revealing such low fertility and high rates of infertility, with a suite of behaviors that seem designed to maximize completed lifetime fertility. The irony, of course, is that just those behavioral patterns that increase women's exposure to pregnancy also provide frequent opportunity for exposure to the fertility-reducing effects, not to mention the life-threatening effects, of STDs.

The pro-natalist attitudes and practices that form the "African sexuality" have provided STDs with an advantageous, if not ideal, social environment in which to proliferate at the expense of the reproductive fitness of their hosts. The extent to which central Africans are changing their sexual attitudes and beliefs in response to this threat to their fitness is open to question, but it does not appear to be great at this time. Indeed, the finding that younger men are more promiscuous and have contracted gonorrhea more times per year of sexual activity than older men would suggest otherwise. The more acculturated groups, those living near main roads and with greater access to markets and towns (the Budu and Bila) do seem to be having greater reproductive success, but there is no indication that this is due to any significant change in their attitudes or sexual behavior. Rather these groups alleviate the fitness-reducing consequences of STDs, not through behaviors that promote avoidance but simply by gaining access to antibiotics. When the supply or access to effective curatives is disrupted, as it was during the Simba Rebellion, the people seem willing to suffer the consequences rather than change their sexual behavior.

Sexual Desire from an Evolutionary Perspective

Why do people in the Ituri persist in their promiscuous attitudes and behaviors even in the face of such great loss in fertility and, by extension, in their own sense of social and psychological well-being? This poses a significant problem, not only for those concerned with population and health policy in central Africa, but also for those sex researchers who approach human sexuality from an evolutionary perspective. For some, evolutionary theory leads to the expectation that "human behavior will be adaptive, that is, designed to promote maximum reproductive success (RS) through available descendent and non-descendent relatives" (Betzig and Turke, 1985:79). Yet if central Africans (and others) were acting adaptively, they would be practicing sexual behaviors that avoid or minimize transmission of sex-related diseases, since those diseases clearly lower reproductive success. One possible explanation for the persistence of behaviors that reduce reproductive success is that the people continue to practice high-risk behaviors simply because they do not make the connections between the behavior, the transmission of the disease, and the long-term effects of the disease. Yet we know from our interviews with the Ituri men that they do make these connections. Indeed, almost without exception, the men expressed unsolicited knowledge of how early and frequent sex by women can lead to infection with gonorrhea and ultimate sterility. It is difficult to believe that if fathers, brothers, and sons are acutely aware of these connections, mothers, sisters, and daughters do not also have them in mind.

An alternative explanation consistent with an evolutionary view of human behavior is that humans are not well equipped psychologically to alter their sexual behavior in response to diseases not present during most of human evolution. The psychological mechanisms that guide present-day humans' decisions about with whom and how often they have sex were designed by means of natural selection under conditions different from those of today. Thus, as evolutionary psychologists (Barkow, Cosmides and Tooby, 1992; Cosmides and Tooby, 1987; Symons, 1989) believe, we should not expect all human behavior to be adaptive nor "designed to promote reproductive success" under current conditions. Rather, the psychological mechanisms guiding reproductive decisions evolved in an environment of evolutionary adaptedness (EEA)—

"the Pleistocene environment in which the overwhelming majority of human evolution occurred" (Symons, 1992)—where STDs, if present at all, were of low prevalence and most likely less virulent (Caldwell and Caldwell, 1983). (See Symons, this volume, for an overview of related issues.)

While the human organism seems poorly designed to detect sexually transmitted diseases, it appears very well designed both psychologically and physically to actively seek sexual contact. Indeed, many of the physical and behavioral characteristics that make humans different from other animals are related to our apparent need to seek pleasure through sexual contact (Abramson and Pinkerton, 1995). Alexander and Noonan (1979) have listed thirty characteristics that make humans different from other organisms. Among them are features that have been cited by one or more researchers as designed primarily or in part to enhance sexual pleasure. They include relative hairlessness, concealed ovulation, lack of female estrus, greater prominence of female orgasm, and extreme flexibility in rates of forming and dissolving coalitions. In addition, there are other human characteristics that may have been designed by natural selection to enhance sexual pleasure. Among them are large penises, permanently enlarged breasts, female capacity for multiple orgasms, and enhancement of tactile sensitivity of certain body parts ("erogenous zones"). One can quibble as to whether any one of these features is truly an adaptation for enhancing sexual pleasure, or one might like to add still other features, but one conclusion is inescapable: natural selection has endowed us with a strong desire for sex and, compared to other animals, an extraordinary capacity for orgasmic pleasure. No wonder, with the possible exception of bonobos (see de-Waal, this volume), no animal enjoys sex with the same intensity or with the same frequency as humans.

An outcome of our remarkable capacity for sexual pleasure and desire for sexual contact is an apparent inability or unwillingness to detect and avoid the pathogens transmitted by the frequent sexual activities we seek. While we have the cognitive processes that enable us to be conscious of the risks associated with sexual contacts, the evolved psychological mechanisms driving our sexual desires may be overcome only under extreme conditions (e.g., in the face of a life-threatening epidemic—see, however, Pinkerton and Abramson, 1992).

This view of human sexual behavior and the mechanisms driving it suggests that certain strategies will be more effective than others for reducing the incidence of STDs in Africa as well as in other human populations. If humans are so well designed to seek sexual pleasure, it seems unlikely that promoting sexual abstinence will be highly effective for restricting the transmission of STDs. A more effective strategy will be to promote and make available technologies designed to protect people from transmission of disease during sexual acts (e.g., condoms or vaccines). In addition, such primary preventative technologies must also be complemented with widespread availability of secondary measures (e.g., antibiotics) designed to either cure or arrest development and transmission of diseases once they are contracted. Health practitioners and policy makers in most countries seem to be well aware of the relative efficacy of promoting abstinence versus preventive technologies and cures. However, in most areas of central Africa as well as in other parts of the developing world, the personnel and resources necessary for implementing such strategies—even if the technologies are available—are woefully inadequate. In an age of ever more virulent strains of STDs (e.g., HIV/AIDS) being transmitted among ever larger populations, implementing effective preventive and curative strategies will be a formidable challenge.

Notes

This paper was first prepared for the conference "Theorizing Sexuality: Evolution, Culture, and Development," which was held in Cascais, Portugal, in March, 1993. We are grateful to Paul Abramson and Gilbert Herdt for organizing, and to the Wenner Gren Foundation for Anthropological Research for sponsoring, that conference. We thank Gillian Bentley, Edward Kaplan, Nadine Peacock, and Jocelyn Peccei for their comments; the National Science Foundation, the National Geographic Society, the Swan Fund, and the UCLA Academic Senate for supporting the research; and especially the many people of the Ituri Forest who generously participated in these studies.

1. The Efe (pronounced "ef-fay") is one of four tribal groups comprising the Bambuti ("ba-mm-boo-tee") of northeastern Zaire. Collectively, the Bambuti are known to most Westerners as "pygmies." However, the Efe and Bambuti prefer to be known by their various tribal names.

2. Lese children may be more susceptible than Efe to parasitic infections associated with their more sedentary existence. Additionally, Bailey et al. (1992) have shown that Lese experience dramatic seasonal fluctuations in nutritional status, whereas Efe, by virtue of their nomadic lifestyle, are able to move to areas with more plentiful food and are thereby buffered from seasonal fluctuations in the food supply.

3. Whether men are able to marry because they have greater wealth, or whether married men are wealthier because they have one or more wives to help them acquire wealth, remains an open question. Additionally, no one would suggest that particular women are attracted to particular men purely on the basis of wealth.

4. Syphilis is caused by *Treponema pallidum*. In the Ituri, as in much of Africa, yaws is prevalent and endemic syphilis may be present. These diseases are transmitted nonvenereally but are caused by *Treponema,* either serologically or morphologically indistinguishable from *T. pallidum.* Measuring the prevalence of venereal syphilis is therefore difficult. All three (yaws, endemic syphilis, and venereal syphilis) cause cross-immunity, and since yaws and endemic syphilis are childhood diseases, venereal syphilis does not become prevalent in areas where other *Treponema* prevail (Pennington and Harpending, 1991).

5. While the high rates of infertility are surely caused by the high prevalence of venereal disease, this cannot fully account for the low fertility of these populations. For example, even if we ignore those women who are childless, the mean parity of Lese women over forty years of age is only 3.8, and only 8 of 119 women have more than

six live births. In addition, despite similar levels of primary sterility, Lese and Budu women have very different levels of completed fertility. Some of this is probably caused by secondary sterility, women suffering the deleterious effects of gonorrhea on their reproductive tracts after one or more births. However, other factors are surely at work: high work-loads, breastfeeding patterns, and nutritional status all have influences on fecundity and fertility. For example, Ellison, Peacock and Lager (1986) found that 44–52% of Lese women's monthly cycles are anovulatory, and as Lese women lose weight during periodic seasonal food shortages, their ovarian function is impaired, causing pronounced seasonal reduction of births (Bailey et al., 1992).

References

Abramson, P. R. & Pinkerton, S. D. (1995). With pleasure: Thoughts on the nature of human sexuality. New York: Oxford University Press.

Alexander, R. D. and K. M. Noonan (1979). "Concealment of ovulation, parental care, and human social evolution." In N. A. Chagnon and W. Irons (eds.), Evolutionary Biology and Human Social Behavior: An Anthropological Perspective. N. Scituate, Mass.: Duxbury Press.

Allard, R. (1955). "Contribution gynécologique a l'étude de la sterilité chez les Mongo de Befale." Annales de la Société Belge de Médecine Tropicale 35(6): 630–48.

Arya, O. P., H. Nsanzumuhire and S. R. Taber (1973). "Clinical, cultural, and demographic aspects of gonorrhoea in a rural community in Uganda." Bulletin of the World Health Organization 49:587–595.

Bailey, R. C. (1988). "The significance of hypergyny for understanding subsistence behaviour among contemporary hunters and gatherers." In B. V. Kennedy and G. M. LeMoine (eds.), Diet and Subsistence: Current Archaeological Perspectives. Calgary: Univ. of Calgary, pp. 57–65.

Bailey, R. C. (1991). The Behavioral Ecology of Efe Pygmy Men in the Ituri Forest, Zaire. Ann Arbor: Museum of Anthropology, University of Michigan.

Bailey, R. C., M. Jenike, P. Ellison, G. Bentley, A. Harrigan and N. Peacock (1992). "The ecology of birth seasonality among agriculturalists in central Africa." Journal of Biosocial Science 24:393–412.

Barkow, J. H., L. Cosmides, J. Tooby (1992). The Adapted Mind: Evolutionary Psychology and the Generation of Culture. New York: Oxford University Press.

Belsey, M. A. (1976). "The epidemiology of infertility: a review with particular reference to sub-Saharan Africa." Bulletin of the World Health Organization 54:319–341.

Bentley, G. R. (1985). "Hunter-gatherer energetics and fertility: A reassessment of the !Kung San." Human Ecology 13:79–109.

Betzig, L. L. (1986). Despotism and Differential Reproduction: A Darwinian View of History. Hawthorne, NY: Aldine.

Blau, S. (1961). "The venereal diseases." In A. Ellis and A. Abarbanel (eds.), The Encyclopedia of Sexual Behavior, Vol. II. New York: Hawthorne Books.

Blurton-Jones, N. G., L. Smith, J. F. O'Connell, K. Hawkes, and C. L. Kamuzora (1992). "Demography of the Hadza, an increasing and high density population of savanna foragers." American Journal of Physical Anthropology 89:159–181.

Caldwell, J. and P. Caldwell (1983). "The demographic evidence for the incidence and course of abnormally low fertility in tropical Africa." World Health Statistics Quarterly 36:2–34.

Caldwell, J. and P. Caldwell (1989). "High fertility in sub-Saharan Africa." Scientific American 262:118–31.

Caldwell, J. C., P. Caldwell and P. Quiggin (1989). "The social context of AIDS in sub-Saharan Africa." Population and Development Review 15(2): 185–234.

Cosmides, L. and J. Tooby (1987). "From evolution to behavior: evolutionary psychology as the missing link." In J. Dupre (ed.) The Latest on the Best: Essays on Evolution and Optimality (pp. 277–306). Cambridge: MIT Press.

Ellison, P. T. (1991). "Reproductive ecology and human fertility." In G. W. Lasker and C. G. N. Mascie-Taylor (eds.), Applications of Biological Anthropology to Human Affairs. Cambridge: Cambridge University Press, pp. 14–54.

Ellison, P. T., N. R. Peacock and C. Lager (1986). "Salivary progesterone and luteal function in two low-fertility populations of northeast Zaire." Human Biology 58: 473.

Fiumara, N. J. (1971). "Gonococcal pharyngitis." Medical Aspects of Human Sexuality 12:194–209.

Frank, O. (1983). "Infertility in sub-Saharan Africa: Estimates and implications." Population and Development Review 9:137–45.

Gray, R. H. (1977). "Biological factors other than nutrition and lactation which may influence natural fertility: A review." In H. M. and Jane Menken Leridon (eds.), Natural Fertility: Patterns and Determinants of Natural Fertility. Liege: Ordina Editions, pp. 217–51.

Howell, N. (1979). Demography of the Dobe !Kung. New York: Academic Press.

Larsen, U. (1989). "A comparative study of the levels and the differentials of sterility in Cameroon, Kenya, and Sudan." In R. J. Lesthaeghe (ed.), Reproduction and Social Organization in Sub-Saharan Africa. Berkeley: University of California Press, pp. 67–211.

Lesthaeghe, R. and F. Eelens (1989). "The components of sub-Saharan reproductive regimes and their social and cultural determinants: Empirical evidence." In R. Lesthaeghe (ed.), Reproduction and Social Organization in Sub-Saharan Africa. Berkeley: University of California Press, pp. 60–121.

Page, H. J. and A. J. Coale (1972). "Fertility and child mortality south of the Sahara." In S. H. Ominde and C. N. Ejiogu (eds.), Population Growth and Economic Development in Africa. London: Heinemann, pp. 51–69.

Paige, K. E. and J. M. Paige (1981). The Politics of Reproductive Ritual. Berkeley: University of California Press.

Pennington, R. and H. Harpending (1991). "Infertility in Herero pastoralists of southern Africa." American Journal of Human Biology 3:135–53.

Pinkerton, S. D. and P. R. Abramson (1992). "Is risky sex rational?" The Journal of Sex Research 29:561–68.

Promislow, D. and P. Harvey (1990). "Living fast and dying young: A comparative analysis of life-history variation among mammals." Journal of the Zoological Society of London 220:417–37.

Ransford, O. (1983). Bid the sickness cease: Disease in the History of Black Africa. London: J. Murray.

Retel-Laurentin, A. (1974). "Sub-fertility in black Africa—the case of the Nzakara in Central African Republic." In B. K. Adadevoh (ed.), Sub-fertility and Infertility in Africa. Ibadan, Nigeria: Caxton Press, pp. 69–80.

Romaniuk, A. (1968). "The demography of the Democratic Republic of the Congo." In

W. Brass and A. Coale (eds.), The Demography of Tropical Africa. Princeton: Princeton University Press, pp. 241–341.

Romaniuk, A. (1967). La fécondité des populations congolaises. Paris: Payot.

Sala-Diakanda, M., N. A. Pitshandenge, D. Tabutin and E. Vilquin (1981). "Fertility and child-spacing in western Zaire." In H. J. Page and R. Lesthaeghe (eds.), Child-Spacing in Tropical Africa: Traditions and Change. London: Academic Press, pp. 287–99.

Sydes, K. A. (1988). Infertility among the Efe and Lese: Screening for Gonorrhea and Chlamydia among Two Low Fertility Populations in the Ituri Rain Forest. Undergraduate Honors Thesis, Department of Anthropology, UCLA, Los Angeles.

Symons, D. (1989). "A critique of Darwinian anthropology." Ethology and Sociobiology 10:131–44.

Symons, D. (1992). "On the use and misuse of Darwinism in the study of human behavior." In J. H. Barkow, L. Cosmides and J. Tooby (eds.), The Adapted Mind. New York: Oxford University Press, pp. 137–59.

Turke, P. W. and L. L. Betzig (1985). "Those who can do: Wealth, status and reproductive success on Ifaluk." Ethology and Sociobiology 6: 79–87.

Voas, D. (1981). "Subfertility and disruption in the Congo Basin." In African Historical Demography II. Edinburgh: Centre of African Studies, University of Edinburgh, pp. 777–802.

Wrangham, R. W. and E. A. M. Ross (1983). "Individual differences in activities, family size, and food production among Lese horticulturalists of northeast Zaire." Paper presented at the 82nd Annual Meeting of the American Anthropological Association, Chicago.

CHAPTER ELEVEN

The Pleasures of Homosexuality

DAVID F. GREENBERG

Introduction

Historical, sociological, and anthropological research on homosexuality has demonstrated variability in patterns of homosexual behavior (Ford and Beach, 1951:125–43; Bullough, 1976; Greenberg, 1988). These differences have been understood as demonstrating that social or cultural factors influence, shape or create homosexual desire and expression in humans. At the same time, evidence has been accumulating that is consistent with a genetic, hormonal, or neuroanatomical explanation of sexual orientation (see Pattatuci and Hamer, this volume, and references cited therein; also see Ruse, 1981; Ellis and Ames, 1987; Weinrich, 1987; Puterbaugh, 1990; LeVay, 1993; Whitam, Diamond and Martin, 1993).

Much of the biological research has been contested on methodological grounds, or because findings could not be replicated (Meyer-Bahlberg, 1977, 1979, 1984, and this volume; Futuyma and Risch, 1983/84; Hoult, 1983/84; Ricketts, 1984; Doell and Longino, 1988; Byne and Parson, 1993; Paul, 1993). As a result, the relative importance of biological and cultural or social factors, and the ways they might interact with one another in influencing homosexual behavioral patterns, remain obscure (see Introduction, this volume).

One dimension of homosexuality that has not thus far figured in discussions of these issues is its pleasurability. Indeed, few subjects have been more neglected in the historical and social-science literature on homosexuality than pleasure. Anthropologists have documented cross-cultural variability in the frequency of same-sex erotic *behavior,* in the systems used to classify sexual acts and actors, and in the relationship between gender identity and homoerotic interest and behavior. They have speculated about the social functions homosexuality serves, but have given very little attention to the question of what it is about their homosexual experiences that participants find personally gratifying.

Likewise, sociologists and historians have studied homosexual identities, communities, social movements, and subcultures. Psychologists have focused on questions of etiology and treatment and, more recently, on the stages in gay identity formation and "coming out." But the phenomenology of homosexual experience, within which an analysis of pleasure might take place, has largely been ignored. Books on homosexuality written by social or behavioral scientists usually fail even to mention the subject of pleasure.

Why this neglect? Several factors will have surely contributed, among them fear that the study of pleasure will arouse suspicions of prurient interests, and the belief that the role of pleasure in homosexuality is sufficiently obvious as to be banal.[1] Peripheral nerve endings in the erotogenic zones of the human body provide pleasurable sensations when stimulated by physical contact. This setup undoubtedly confers an evolutionary advantage by providing positive reinforcement to penile-vaginal intercourse, and by strengthening romantic or affectional attachments to a sexual partner. These attachments might increase the number of offspring an individual has and, by preserving a relationship between a father and a mother, increase their children's chances for survival. Through natural selection, this pleasure-producing mechanism would have been incorporated in the human makeup. The inability of these peripheral nerves to discriminate between stimuli originating with same-sex partners and those originating with opposite-sex partners has as its consequence the physical pleasurability of homosexual sexual contact.

Historical and contemporary evidence, however, makes clear that the subjective experience of pleasure is not wholly determined by physiological mechanisms. Consider the protagonist in Martial XI.43:

> You shout at me with bitter words when I'm lying on my boy,
> wife, and tell me you have an ass, too.
> How often Juno said the same to the lustful Thunderer
> when he was lying beside great Ganymede.
> Hercules bent Hylas over when he laid his bow aside:
> You don't think Megara had a butt?
> Daphne fled and tortured Phoebus, but the
> Oebalian boy put those fires out.
> Although Briseis often turned on her side,
> his smooth friend was nearer to Achilles.
> So stop giving a masculine name to your thing, wife:
> just consider that you've got two cunts.[2]
>
>   (trans. J. P. Otte)

In a purely physiological sense, the male anus surely does not differ from the female in its capacity to stimulate a penis to orgasm, and the bodily sensations of the orgasm do not depend on the sex of the partner who has been penetrated. The protagonist of the poem, however, has a preference that will shape his experience of anal intercourse. It cannot be based on the bodily sensations associated with sexual contact.[3]

A similar analysis can be applied to other possible combinations of partners. There is no anatomical difference between the mouths of male and female humans, yet in the contemporary Western world, most men who enjoy being fellated will prefer a fellator of one sex over the other. Women, too, will usually care whether the tongue performing cunnilingus on them is attached to a male or female person. The meaning someone attaches to a sexual encounter will play an important role in determining whether that encounter will be experienced as pleasurable. This meaning is not determined by the nerve endings that produce sensations of bodily pleasure but by many other factors, including the sex of the partner (see Abramson and Pinkerton, 1995).[4]

The origin of these meanings is not fully understood. To a certain extent they are individual, personal, and idiosyncratic. Yet differences in sexual meanings can also vary systematically within a society—by class, sex, ethnicity, and religion, for example. Cultures and subcultures supply possible meanings to a society's members, and the range of meanings offered varies from one society to another. These meanings will designate certain individuals but not others as acceptable partners. They will specify certain motives for engaging in sexual activity as permissible, and others as impermissible. They may stipulate the feelings and emotions that sexual experiences should evoke. Social structure will facilitate or discourage certain activities, thereby encouraging or limiting an individual's prospects of realizing sexual goals or experiencing certain types of sexual events. It does these things differentially: people who are differently located in the social structure may have distinct chances for having specific kinds of experiences. Thus an understanding of the role of pleasure in homosexual expression cannot be restricted to genes, hormones, or anatomy alone. These observations will be illustrated with materials derived from contemporary anthropological research and from earlier periods of history.

It is true here, as for any historical study of homosexuality, that the sources available to us must be used with caution. For most societies, documentary evidence is available only for a small and highly atypical fraction of the population, and is the product of conventions of representation dictating the kinds of experience that may be described in writing, or in particular genres, and what can be said about those experiences. For these reasons, we know about the pleasures of homosexuality largely as they are represented in texts. The experiences of pleasure themselves are largely unrecoverable.

I

There are societies and settings in which one, and perhaps both, of the partners in a homosexual interaction participate for reasons other than the physical pleasure they might derive from the experience. Consider those societies—primarily Melanesian in the modern world—where sexual contacts between males figure in male initiation. The boys who are being transformed into men through their homosexual contacts do not seek out those contacts. Their initial participation is coerced by the older men in circumstances that allow the boys little choice. At first the boys fear the sexual contact, worrying that they might become pregnant. However, many come to like it. Sambian boys of New Guinea enjoy being fellators, are excited by the experience, even enthusiastic about it. Same-sex erotic contacts become a part of their fantasies and desires. But their desires and fantasies are irrelevant to the ideology that legitimates the initiation and do not explain the boys' initial involvement, which is not elective (Herdt, 1981:282, 319; 1984; Greenberg, 1988:26–40).

The degree to which the boys' older inseminators derive pleasure from these sexual contacts also varies. Some are enthusiastic pederasts; others abandon the practice as soon as the norms of their culture permit. Prior to that time, participation, which is universal, is again unrelated to personal pleasure.[5]

One may wonder about the extent to which the existence of such rituals can be explained by their pleasurability. The fact that most New Guinea peoples do not have such rituals implies that the physical pleasure derived from a sexual encounter cannot alone explain it. Other cultural or social-structural factors must determine why some peoples initiate their youths in this way rather than in some other way. Nevertheless, the sexual pleasure derived from these pederastic rituals may explain why it is that the initiation takes a certain form when these cultural or social-structural factors are present.

Similarities between features of pederasty in contemporary New Guinea and classical Greece have often been noted (and their significance debated). Lack of concern for, or awareness of, the boy's pleasure has been considered one of these. Xenophon comments in relation to ancient Greek male prostitution that "the boy does not share in the man's pleasure in intercourse, as a woman does; cold sober, he looks upon the other drunk with sexual desire" (*Banquet* 8.21, quoted in Dover, 1978: 52).[6] That the Greeks did not always conform to this norm is evident from depictions on vases of bearded men supplying genital stimulation to their youthful partners (Dover, 1978: 204; Keuls, 1985); from Plato's observation that "in a weaker or wine-filled moment," two male lovers "may take part in the physical pleasures which many consider bliss" (*Phaedrus* 256c–e); and from the lines in Theognis, a poet of Megara in the sixth century B.C., that compare the boy to a horse that impatiently seeks a good rider (B1249–51).

A partial parallel may be found in the butch-femme lesbian bar subculture that flourished in American cities in the 1940s and 1950s. It was the responsibility of the "stone butch" to provide sexual pleasure to her femme partner; she herself was not to be touched sexually and sometimes did not undress fully; her gratification came from the response she evoked in her partner, or from a spontaneous physical response not evoked by physical stimulation from her partner.[7] Though this rule may sometimes have been broken, gossip among the femmes served as an effective deterrent. (Kennedy and Davis, 1993: 192, 196, 204–9).

In slave societies, masters may use their slaves for sexual purposes without regard to any preference or pleasure on the part of the slave. Either this exploitation will not be prohibited, or there may be a prohibition that is widely ignored. In ancient Greece and Rome this exploitation took homosexual as well as heterosexual forms: masters sometimes forced themselves on their male slaves. We have no testimony about those relations from the slaves themselves.

Pleasure is equally irrelevant to the victim of a homosexual rape. The inclusion of a provision dealing with male homosexual rape in the Assyrian Law Code suggests that it was common enough in that ancient Mesopotamian society to be a matter of public concern (Pritchard, 1955:181; Greenberg, 1988:125). Ancient Roman law actually authorized the victim or the victim's agent to rape a thief or adulterer. The Roman poet Catullus boasts of having carried out such a rape:

> O, a ridiculous thing, Cato, really laughable,
> fit for your ears and your wit!
> Have a good laugh at Catullus, I beg you;
> the thing really is ridiculous and laughable.
> I just now caught some little snot banging my
> girl, and I cut him down with my
> rigid . . . well, it wasn't my sword.
> (Catullus 56, trans. J. P. Otte)

To the Romans, oral rape was the most degrading form of homosexual rape. In one of the poems collected in the *Priapea,* the phallic god Priapus cautions:

> I'm warning: a youth I'll split open; a girl I'll force to fuck.
> A bearded thief will get a third penalty.
> (*Priapea* 13, my translation)

The Greeks and Romans were well aware that some men liked to take a receptive role in anal intercourse despite the stigma.[8] Some Latin verses even suggest that thieves stole in the hope of being caught and anally raped:

> A soft smooth queer comes here to steal,
> Because he badly wants to feel
> The punishment he knows applies
> To garden thieves—I'll close my eyes.
> (*Priapea* 64, trans. Parker, 1988:147)

In another poem, Priapus wonders:

> Why do so many thieves enter my yard,
> When if they're caught, I thrust it up them hard?
> The figs here are no better than next door;
> The grapes, compared with Arete's are poor.
>
> . . . .
> . . . It seems the treatment rude
> Is what attracts them: so I must conclude.
> (*Priapea* 51, trans. Parker, 1988:147)

This, however, is surely as much a fantasy as the contemporary fiction that heterosexual women enjoy being raped.

One might suppose that the role of pleasure will be greater for the rapist, but the nature of this pleasure cannot be taken for granted. It has been argued in recent years that heterosexual rape is motivated not by sexual pleasure but by the desire to dominate and humiliate. The argument has surely been taken too far; it naively assumes that one motive must exclude the other. Obviously, it needn't. To the extent that one can distinguish different sources of pleasure in rape, the mix of pleasures stemming from domination and from more narrowly defined sexual experience is likely to vary from one individual to another.[9] One sees in this poem of Catullus an instance in which domination is the most significant component of pleasure:

> Aurelius, Father of Appetites,
> not only of these now, but however many there were or are or will be hence
> in other years, you're dying to have my love's ass. And not in secret! You're
> with him always, you joke together, you stick to his side and try everything
> you can . . . in vain! For I'll get you first, in your treacherous plots, and
> make you suck my cock.
> If you were content to just do what you're doing,
> I'd be silent. But as it is, I grieve because
> my boy is learning to hunger and thirst himself.
> So cut it out, while your modesty's intact [*dum licet pudico*],
> lest you come to an end . . . with my dick in your mouth.
>   (Catullus 21, trans. J. P. Otte).

It may well be that Catullus would enjoy being fellated simply because it would give him physical pleasure, but that is incidental to his humiliating a rival. It is the *symbolic* rather than the physical aspect of sex that is most important here.

One contemporary setting in which homosexual rapes take place is prison. Rape in men's prisons has long been understood as a way to reconcile traditional male norms of domination with the restriction and subordination to staff that are inherent in the prison setting. By raping another inmate, the rapist gains a sense of potency that would be achieved in other ways outside prison. Prison rapists typically do not think of themselves as being homosexual, and many lack homosexual experience prior to their imprisonment (Wooden and Parker, 1982). All this may be true, but it does not follow that they derive no pleasure from raping. That may or may not be true.

The role of pleasure in homosexual prostitution will surely be variable as well. Some male prostitutes seem to be motivated largely by the prospect of financial gain. In a study of juvenile delinquents in Tennessee, Reiss (1961; see also Harris, 1973) discovered some teenage hustlers who allowed older men to fellate them in return for money. During the encounters the youths closed their eyes and imagined that they were with their girlfriends. In other instances, sexual gratification may be part of the attraction of prostitution, limited, perhaps, by the need to accept customers one has not chosen and to accommodate their particular demands (Pittman, 1971).

II

Institutional practices, cultural definitions, and structural constraints present in a society can limit an individual's ability to pursue a sexual relationship—whether for pleasure or any other source of gratification—and can profoundly shape the character of that relationship. Where marriages are arranged, for example, pleasure may at best be an accidental by-product of the marriage, or may be sought outside it.[10] Thus Demosthenes said about Greek men, "We have *hetairai* for our pleasure, concubines for our daily needs, and wives to give us legitimate children and look after the housekeeping" (*In Nearam* 122, quoted in Tannahill, 1980:100).[11]

Questions of marital power are relevant to the ability of one spouse to pursue an extramarital affair. The wives of Athenian citizens were in no position to interfere with their husbands' affairs, or to have such affairs themselves.[12] Spartan wives may have had greater freedom in this respect.

A second constraint is the imperative of collecting or producing subsistence necessities. Where virtually all waking hours must be devoted to sustaining life, there will be little time and energy available to pursue pleasure for its own sake. In the early civilizations, a high standard of living for a minority was made possible through the coerced extraction of surplus from the bulk of the population, which labored long and hard, and had little time for anything else.[13]

It is in these early civilizations that the pursuit of sexual pleasure for its own sake came to be valued by the court aristocracy and was made the subject of art and literature produced for elite audiences. The Indian *Kama Sutra* and its equivalents in China, Greece, and Rome instructed readers on the techniques of erotic love, including methods of enhancing sexual pleasure (Davies, 1984:207).[14]

All these handbooks take for granted a lifestyle of affluence and leisure, with servants and attendants at beck and call. Though the manuals give most of their attention to heterosexual pleasure, they never ignore homosexual pleasure as a secondary possibility. Where the pursuit of pleasure is emphasized, the sex of the partner is unlikely to be of primary importance, and typologies of sexual actors tend not to be based on sexual orientation in the modern sense.

As the populations of ancient societies grew, and the surplus available to elites rose, brothels multiplied, providing men who could pay with male and female sexual partners.[15] Competition for customers presumably gave the prostitutes an incentive to provide a pleasurable experience. Lucretius (1986:79) tells us that female prostitutes moved their hips in "sinuous wave-movements" to avoid pregnancy "and at the same time to make the sex itself more pleasing to men." His observation that "wives don't need any of these movements" may explain why there were so many prostitutes (*De Rerum Natura,* 1268–76).

With few exceptions, popular Greek culture of the classical age raised no objection to the pursuit of pleasure, or sex for pleasure. Some philosophers saw pleasure as "the restoration of a natural balance" which remedied bodily deficiencies (Gosling and Taylor, 1982:1–2).[16] To abstain from the pursuit of pleasure was to act contrary to nature.

This acceptance of pleasure was, however, subject to important qualifications. One of the most important was conformity to gender and status roles proscribing male submission. The receptive role was widely regarded as unfitting to an adult male citizen because it entailed subordination. To those who held a subordinate social status, though, it was appropriate. Seneca the Elder observed that "submission is infamous for a free man; in a slave, an absolute duty to the master; to the freedman, it remains a moral duty of compliance" (*Controversiae* 4, *Praef.* 10, quoted in Boswell, 1980:78). A child, too, could acceptably submit to an adult; and as the passages quoted from Xenophon, Ovid, and Catullus might suggest, many Greek and Roman men chose youths as their same-sex partners.

Some philosophical writings, however, differentiated between pleasures of the body and those of the soul. Pleasures of the body were pernicious because they tended to disturb or enslave the soul, preventing it from attaining its good (Plato, *Gorgias* 493a,e–494f, 499d; Gosling and Taylor, 1982:79–83). The wise man avoided them because there were better ways of spending one's time. Intellectual pleasures were superior to the pleasures of the flesh (Plato, *Phaedo* 64d–66c; Aristotle, *Nicomachean Ethics* X.5.12.71, 6.13.23; Brundage, 1987:19). Even bodily pleasures, however, could be justified by an appropriate nonsensual benefit: "total submission to the wishes of another is not dishonorable if done for self-improvement. It is creditable to grant any favor in any circumstances for the sake of becoming a better person" (Plato, *Symposium* 184c, quoted in Dover, 1978:82–83).

We cannot suppose that the philosophers' distrust of pleasure was shared by ordinary citizens. However, physicians advised parents to be calm and unexcited during intercourse to avoid transmitting unfavorable character traits to their offspring (Foucault, 1988:1257–27). It was believed that the loss of too much seminal fluid would impair the health. Some considered the excessive enjoyment of food and sex to be unmanly (Gosling and Taylor, 1982:13). Greeks who devoted too much time and energy to chasing boys were considered wild and uncivilized (Bremmer, 1988), while Romans of the second century A.D. regarded sexual intercourse "as one of the many aspects of their lives that they could bring under their control through sense and breeding" (Brown, 1988:19).

The advice of the Athenian orator Isocrates (1990:133–35) to Nicocles points to a political source for this concern:

> Govern yourself no less than your subjects, and consider it the highest achievement of kingship if you are a slave to no pleasure but rule more firmly over your desires than over your people (*To Nicocles* 29).

A school exercise from Gaul in which a father admonishes his son, "One who gives counsel to others must know how to rule himself" (Brown, 1988:22), shows that Romans shared this concern. A member of the Greek or Roman upper class could not be, or appear to be, a slave to the appetites. He could not exemplify the traditional virtues of *dignitas* and *gravitas* and at the same time live the life of a voluptuary. For the sake of larger responsibilities, it was necessary to moderate the pursuit of pleasure. Cicero (1958: 441, 461) wrote,

> Nature itself is prodigal of youthful passions; and if they do find a vent so as not to shatter anyone's life, nor to ruin anyone's home, they are generally regarded as easy to put up with: we tolerate them. . . . let youth be allowed greater freedom; let not pleasures always be forbidden; . . . Lastly, when he has listened to the voice of pleasure and given some time to love-affairs and these empty desires of youth, let him at length turn to the interests of home life, to activity at the bar and in public affairs (*Pro Caelio* 12:28, 18:42).

A man who was excessively devoted to carnal pleasure could not be counted on to give political leadership. These concerns are manifest in Euripides' *Antiope*. In a surviving fragment, one character cautions that a man who neglects his estate to devote himself to music is "useless to his family, his friends, and his city. . . . Inborn qualities are lost when a man is worsted by the delights of pleasure" (quoted in Dover, 1978:74).

The militaristic character of classical Greek and Roman society shaped these views as well. It was feared that someone who made pleasures of the body his highest good would be unwilling or unable to endure the hardships of a military campaign.[17] The fear of homosexual pleasure reemerged in the nineteenth and twentieth centuries during periods of nationalistic militarization (Mosse, 1985). Modern European stereotypes of the Orient linked its economic and political stagnation with a tropical, languid sensuality that included homosexual indulgence (Burton, 1886).

These considerations help us to understand a feature of Greek and Roman pederastic poetry that might otherwise seem odd: the pleasures of the body are almost never mentioned. Love poetry praises the boy's beauty, expresses longing, desire, frustration and jealousy, and laments his physical maturation. But tactile pleasures, especially those of orgasm, are slighted. Indeed, the only corporeal pleasures specifically mentioned are those of kissing boys and looking at their beautiful bodies.[18] The public representation of pederasty had to

emphasize love for the boy and concern for his education, not the carnal pleasures of the older partner.[19]

All these concerns fed into the philosophers' devaluation of sexual pleasure.[20] To preserve the equanimity conducive to philosophical reflection, some
philosophers opted for celibacy, at least for themselves—they never thought
that the entire population should abstain from sexual activity. The Roman Stoic
Musonius Rufus, for example, recognized that most people would marry, and,
in an age where companionate marriage was developing, he advocated marital
egalitarianism. He rejected all expressions of lust, even within marriage, as
threatening to mutual respect. Sexual activity whose purpose was anything
other than procreation was to be avoided (Lutz, 1947).

I have discussed elsewhere the social and political developments within the
Roman Empire that gave such views currency (Greenberg, 1988:184–241).
Christianity both perpetuated and transformed Stoic suspicion of sex. Saint
Paul called on Christians to avoid "revelry and drunkenness, . . . debauchery
and licentiousness" (Romans 13:13). With the Kingdom of God at hand, dis-
tracting obligations had to be given a low priority: "Put on the Lord Jesus
Christ, and make no provision for the flesh, to gratify its desires" (Romans
13:14).

Leading figures of the early Church, who went far beyond Paul's strictures,[21]
saw lust as a potential threat not to philosophical contemplation but to the
salvation of the soul. Sexual abstinence was a strategy for getting to heaven,
for hastening the arrival of the Messianic era (Brown, 1988:31–32). According
to Saint Gregory of Nyssa (1967: 48) "Corruption has its beginning in birth and
those who refrain from procreation through virginity themselves bring about a
cancellation of death by preventing it from advancing further because of them."
In fact, it was not merely sexual *activity* that was to be curbed: desire itself had
to be suppressed.[22] The more one loved the flesh, the less one loved the spirit.[23]
The pleasure of sexual activity, which the Church fathers readily acknowledged, made total abstention imperative; sexual pleasure, once experienced,
would be hard to resist.[24]

The early Christian opposition toward sexual relations between males,
which was radical, consistent, and uncompromising, could have followed directly from this repudiation of sensual pleasure. The patristic writings themselves, however, do not make this connection. They denounce male effeminacy,
and condemn carnal relations with males as infertile and sinful, without entirely rejecting pleasure. Indeed, as the Church became institutionalized, it begrudgingly came to terms with pleasure. Thus Saint John Chrysostom, one of
the most virulent polemicists against male homosexual relations, granted that
God allows "legitimate [sexual] pleasure," but not the illegitimate kind: "Sins
against nature . . . are more difficult and less rewarding, so much so that they
cannot even claim to provide pleasure, since real pleasure is only in accord

with nature" (*In Epistolam ad Romanos,* Homily 4, quoted in Boswell, 1980:360).

The triumph of Christianity, the collapse of the Roman Empire, and the rise of a feudal social world, brought an end to the civilizations that accepted—even if at times ambivalently—sexual activity between males. The celebration of sexuality in public festivities ended, and cult prostitution, both male and female, was suppressed.

The distinction John Chrysostom made between permitted and prohibited sources of sexual pleasure was embraced by virtually all Roman Catholic writers through the Middle Ages. Saint Thomas Aquinas, for example, maintained that it was not sinful to experience pleasure during marital intercourse (*Summa Theologiae* 1a–2ae.q.32.a.4 ad 2) provided the *aims* of intercourse were acceptable. Acceptable aims included procreation, preventing a spouse from sinning, and paying the "marital debt." Intercourse *for* pleasure, or with a partner in a prohibited category (someone of the same sex, or a nonhuman animal), or in the wrong bodily orifice, however, was contrary to natural law, and sinful. Some Christian writers compared the experiencing of excessive pleasure in marital intercourse to adultery (Brundage, 1987:285–87).[25]

The Renaissance saw only very limited concessions to sexual pleasure. As feudalism waned, the household, organized on the basis of cooperation between family members, became an important economic unit. This development may explain why some sixteenth- and seventeenth-century Catholic moralists allowed married couples to engage in foreplay, and permitted women who had not achieved orgasm during intercourse to masturbate afterwards (Gardella, 1985; Hurteau, 1993). John Major, a Scottish theologian of the first half of the sixteenth century, argued that because finding "consolation" was a legitimate purpose of marriage, "it is difficult to prove that a man sins in knowing his own wife for the sake of having pleasure." Such Catholic humanists as Erasmus and Vives proposed the elevation of marital sexuality to the status of celibacy (Noonan, 1965:311; Todd, 1980; Leites, 1986:80). But others within the Church attacked this view, and the Council of Trent repudiated it. As a result, the Church never accepted sexual pleasure as a good in its own right.[26] Obviously, there was no place here for same-sex eroticism, whether sought for pleasure or for any other purpose.

From the fall of Rome to the High Middle Ages, the texts through which we learn of sexual relations between persons of the same sex (mostly men) were largely written from the official point of view of Roman Catholicism. This viewpoint was not interested in the thoughts and feelings of practitioners.[27] The love poetry between males that comes down to us from the Middle Ages expresses love without referring to carnal pleasure. Official repression of homoerotic expression made it dangerous to acknowledge the physical expression of same-sex love.

One of the earliest documents to discuss homoerotic sexual pleasure explicitly is the *Hermaphrodites* of Artus, a work of fiction that depicts an imaginary island inhabited only by men whose highest good is pleasure, and who engage in sexual relations with one another. Published in 1605, *Hermaphrodites* marks a transition from the medieval conceptualization of sodomy as a discrete act, undertaken volitionally, to the early modern conceptualization of the sodomite as a type of person, one whose unbridled egoism, expressed sexually and in many other ways, made him an enemy of organized society and religion (Stone, 1992).[28] This reconceptualization may have owed something to the weakening of organized Christianity in the face of the strengthening of the secular state and the growth of a capitalist market economy, which raised fears of the potential dangers to society of unlimited self-seeking.

Although the notion that sexual pleasure has a valuable place within a marriage can be traced to early modern Catholic writings, it became more important in English and colonial American Puritanism, which—unlike the Roman Catholic Church—did not have to defend the superiority of clerical celibacy. Puritan writers valued the contribution that erotic pleasure could make to a happy married life (E. Morgan, 1942; Leites, 1986; but see Verduin, 1983).

The trend may have been due to the transformation of marriage itself. Instead of being arranged, marriages were increasingly made by freely contracting individuals, based on romantic love. Sex could strengthen and preserve that love, and also serve as a vehicle for expressing it. With the cooperative household serving as the central social unit of the New England colonial economy, investing the relationship between spouses with romantic and erotic feelings was a means to the buttressing of a pivotal social institution.

Yet many factors—fear of social disorder (including threat to the stability of families), the desirability of restricting consumption on the part of the laboring classes in a mercantile economy, the persistent influence of older Christian teachings—continued to make sexual pleasure suspect unless it took place within a marriage, and was moderate in both frequency and intensity. Masturbation fears intensified in the eighteenth and nineteenth centuries, and marriage handbooks advised married couples not to have intercourse too often. Physicians worried that excessive sexual pleasure could cause an astonishing range of medical problems.[29]

It is probably for these reasons that the European homophile movement of the nineteenth century failed to insist on the positive value of sexual pleasure in human life. Its leading spokesmen argued for the repeal of irrational criminal legislation and against etiological theories of homosexual orientation based on seduction or learning. They combed the past for illustrious men and women who loved others of their own sex. But with sexual expression of all kinds still quite suspect and in some countries illegal, the pioneer liberationists did not say much about their sexual experiences when they wrote for audiences that were predominantly heterosexual. Edward Carpenter (1909:13), a pioneer in the English homosexual rights movement, defensively maintained that "the defect of the male Uranian, or Urning, is *not* sensuality—but rather *sentimentality*" (emphasis in original).[30]

In the twentieth century, urbanization, which reduced the number of children middle-class couples could use productively or afford, the greater availability of contraception, the discovery of antibiotics that could cure venereal disease, and the growth of moral relativism, weakened the older strictures against sexual pleasure. Positive views of sexual pleasure began to appear in marital advice books. They informed the teachings of the various Protestant denominations and, to a certain extent, even of the Catholic Church, which could not wholly ignore changes in popular morality (D. S. Smith, 1973; Gordon, 1978; Gardella, 1985; Ehrenrich, Hess and Jacobs, 1986; D'Emilio and Freedman, 1988; Flandrin, 1991:89–97).

The shift in sensibilities is evident in the writings of Sigmund Freud, who held that excessive repression of the sexual drive could lead to neurosis. Sexual pleasure, not necessarily with a spouse, and not necessarily for the purpose of procreation, was beneficial to one's mental health. These ideas circulated widely after the First World War, and helped liberalize sexual attitudes. Yet in prioritizing heterosexual genital intercourse in adulthood, Freud implicitly devalued other forms of sexual expression and pleasure.

This new acceptance of sexual pleasure in heterosexual marriages gradually expanded to include premarital sexual intercourse, for instance, among engaged couples. Yet prior to the mid-sixties few defended extramarital or homosexual relations publicly. As early as the mid-fifties, when automation was expected to reduce the manpower needs of production, Herbert Marcuse (1955) developed a Freudian Marxist vision of a society that abolished surplus sexual repression. He heralded the release of libido that did not need to be dignified by procreation or love, and that could be expressed homosexually. But it was not until the sixties that Marcuse's ideas gained a popular following. The sixties saw the growth of a young unmarried adult population in a state of prolonged adolescence, increased availability of contraception, the development of a consumer ethos based on mass prosperity and leisure, the weakening of traditional authority (brought about by the expansion of higher education, as well as the civil rights and the antiwar movement), and a rapid expansion in premarital heterosexual experience. These developments facilitated the expansion and greater visibility of the lesbian and gay male subcultures that had been gradually taking shape in North American cities over a period of decades; and in the case of Europe, over a period of centuries (D'Emilio, 1983; Greenberg, 1988; Faderman, 1991; Epstein, 1993; Kennedy and Davis, 1993).

The sexual mores of the gay male subculture differed from those that prevailed in classical antiquity in a number of ways. First, those who were central to these subcultures identified themselves as homosexual or gay. In antiquity, homoerotic interest did not become the basis of a personal or collective identity so long as a man took a role defined as active. Second, male homoerotic interests shifted from being predominantly pederastic (a pattern that persisted through the Renaissance) to predominantly androphilic—that is, to a preference for adult partners. This shift is plausibly attributed to the sharper social differentiation between children and adults brought about in the course of capitalist development, and to the growth of an ideology of democratic egalitarianism that accompanied the decline of estate society.[31]

Third, oral sex was becoming more popular, perhaps because of improved hygiene. There was a definite demand for fellatio in antiquity, but fellators were hard to find because the act was considered demeaning to the fellator. Female prostitutes made customers who wanted fellatio pay higher fees.[32] Martial IX.67 (1987:332–33), for example, tells us:

> Last night the soft charms of an exquisite whore
>   Fulfilled every whim of my mind,
> Till, with fucking grown weary, I begged something more,
>   One bliss that still lingered behind.
> My prayer was accepted; the rose in the rear
>   Was opened to me in a minute;
> One rose still remained, which I asked of my dear,—
>   'Twas her mouth and the tongue that lay in it.
> She promised at once, what I asked her to do;
>   Yet her lips were unsullied by me,
> They'll not, my old friend, remain virgins for you,
>   Whose penchant exceeds e'en her fee.

As far as we can tell, anal intercourse remained the most common form of homosexual contact from late antiquity through the Renaissance.[33] It is not easy to chart the shift in favor of oral sex, but Ulrichs, writing in late nineteenth-century Germany, contended that in his day anal intercourse was rare (Kennedy, 1988:74–75). Even if one discounts this contention as an exaggeration intended to calm squeamish heterosexual readers, there is little doubt that a major shift occurred. Remarkably, John Fout (1993) has found that oral sex was virtually unknown in small German towns as late as 1933–45. In recent years, fear of AIDS has again made oral sex and mutual masturbation more popular (Callen, 1992).[34]

III

Gay and lesbian social worlds of the twentieth century have offered multiple pleasures. There are the pleasures of homo*sociality*—which are presumably similar to the pleasures derived from socializing within other groups—and the pleasures (and disappointments) associated with the *pursuit* of sexual partners.[35] There are also the pleasures that outsiders derive from gay institutions and culture, or from sexual relations with gays.

As important as these pleasures are to an understanding of contemporary social life, we leave them aside to focus on the pleasures gays themselves find in same-sex relations. Although it seems unlikely that there is anything particularly distinctive about the corporeal experiences of erotic contact between same-sex partners, much lesbian literature has commented on the enhanced pleasures to be had from a partner who is familiar with female anatomy and its responses. This could also be true of men.[36]

Possibly better than any other author, Plato has captured the distinctive power of sexual union to achieve a transcendence of the boundaries of the self. In his *Symposium* (Plato, 1989), Aristophanes argues in a speech that treats homoerotic and hetero-erotic love on the same footing, that love is an attempt to restore a primeval unity that had been artificially broken by Zeus:

> And so when a person meets the half that is his very own . . . the two are struck . . . by a sense of belonging to one another, and by desire, and they don't want to be separated from one another, even for a moment (Plato, 192B–C).

What the lover wants is "to come together and melt together with the one he loves, so that one person emerged from two" (192E). This passage highlights a potential meaning of a sexual experience that transcends the corporeal and that the term "pleasure" can hardly capture.[37] Psychoanalysts of the object-relations school link the adult experience of merging or boundary-crossing with one's sexual partner to the infant's experience of union with its mother (Balint, 1965:116; Gregor, this volume; Kernberg, 1977).[38]

This experience is, however, only potentially available. People do not always seek, or experience, transcendence or union with their partners. Some want nothing more than physical gratification or release from arousal, without emotional entanglements. To the Roman poet Horace, virtually any human outlet would do when he was aroused:

> When parched thy throat, dost thou insist on wine?
> Or starving, all but choicest game and fish decline?
> And when thy member swells, and for thy lust
> A serving girl stands there, in whom to thrust—
> Or a boy slave, would'st rather burst? Not me!
> I like to have it quick and trouble-free.
> (*Satires* I.2,114–19, trans. Parker, 1988:51)

It was slavery that made sexual partners of either sex so readily available to Roman men; citizen youths were supposed to play "hard to get." In modern times, casual sex[39] with same-sex partners without substantial emotional involvement has been available, accepted within much of the gay male community, and to varying degrees has been a feature of the gay male experience.[40] Though individuals who place "personals ads" are not necessarily representative of all lesbians and gay men, the sex differences in contents of the ads in gay publications are nevertheless quite striking: lesbians mostly seek romance,

Table 11.1   Number of Partners Ever by Race and Sex

Number of Partners	White Male	Black Male	White Female	Black Female
1	0%	0%	3%	5%
2	0	0	9	5
3–4	1	2	15	14
5–9	2	4	31	30
10–14	3	5	16	9
15–24	3	6	10	16
25–49	8	6	8	11
50–99	9	18	5	8
100–249	15	15	1	2
250–499	17	11	1	2
500–999	15	14	0	0
1000 or more	28	19	0	0
N	(574)	(111)	(227)	(664)

Source: Bell and Weinberg (1978:308).

while gay men tend to designate body parts or types, and highly specific sexual roles or performance.[41]

Further data, though now somewhat dated, come to us from Bell and Weinberg's (1978) survey of San Francisco-area homosexual men and women. The contrast between men and women respondents in the number of partners they have ever had (table 11.1), in the number of partners for whom they had some affection (table 11.2), and in the proportion of partners with whom the respondent had sex only once (table 11.3) is remarkable.[42]

These differences are relevant to our discussion in two respects. First, when one's partner is someone whom one has never met before, for whom one feels no affection or love, and whom one never expects to see again, the subjective experience of a sexual encounter is likely to be different from what it is when one likes or loves one's partner and is in an ongoing relationship with that partner.[43] Second, when a substantial proportion of the members of a group spend much time seeking casual sex, that group develops a subculture of sexuality focused on the pursuit of partners and on the sensual dimension of sex. Such a sexual subculture has developed in the Western world among gay men and, to a more modest extent, among lesbians.[44]

The divergence between the sexual cultures of lesbian and gay men has its roots in the social conditions under which distinct lesbian and gay male social worlds emerged.[45] Male homosexual networks in the larger cities of England and Europe became visible in the early modern era (Murray and Gerard, 1987; Greenberg, 1988). This development made it easier to find same-sex partners.

At a time when sodomy was a capital offense almost everywhere in Europe, it was imperative to avoid being identified publicly as a sodomite. Intense stigma perpetuated this imperative even when legal penalties were reduced or

Table 11.2 Affection for Partners by Race and Sex

Proportion for Whom Respondent Had Some Affection	White Male	Black Male	White Female	Black Female
None	2%	2%	1%	3%
Half or less	71	66	18	36
More than half	27	32	81	61

Source: Bell and Weinberg (1978:309).

Table 11.3 "Sex with Partner Only Once" by Race and Sex

Proportion of Partners with Whom R Had Sex Only Once	White Male	Black Male	White Female	Black Female
None	1%	4%	38%	1%
Half or Less	29	59	51	55
More than half	70	38	12	5

Source: Bell and Weinberg (1978:309).

repealed. Urbanization and the rise of market economies made it possible for men to meet one another in taverns and inns with limited risk of public exposure or arrest. Though in a few instances men were able to achieve long-term, stable, intimate relationships with one another, the great majority could not. Most men with strong homoerotic interests suppressed them, or expressed them in transitory couplings or short-lived relationships. They led dual lives, keeping their homosexual desires and experiences a closely guarded secret.[46]

The secretiveness required of the early male homosexual communities gave rise to a subculture in which selves were self-consciously presented dramaturgically and theatrically. This subculture sensitized participants to distinctions between an interior reality that could not be revealed and an appearance that was unconnected to that reality (Sontag, 1969:275–92; Newton, 1972). The limited possibilities for establishing long-term relationships based on a complementary division of labor or child care (as in the typical heterosexual marriage), increased the salience of sexual desire and experience as an element of that reality, making homosexual men more oriented than other men toward the sexual dimension of life.

At least publicly, our culture values sincerity—that is, a correspondence between inner feeling and outward representation.[47] To heterosexuals who value sincerity in the conduct of people's lives, the theatrical style of gay self-presentation, exemplified by Oscar Wilde's public persona, has often seemed frivolous and decadent. Some homosexuals have shared this view. David McReynolds, an antiwar activist who later revealed his homosexuality, wrote in the *Village Voice* in the early sixties that the gay subculture was one in which "sex is substituted for real personal values." He described the subculture as "brittle" and "cold," and contended that it had produced "nothing of value" (quoted in Bronski, 1984:199).

Some advocates of decriminalizing sexual relations between persons of the same sex argued that those features of male homosexual life they found distasteful—such as depersonalized sexual encounters with strangers in public places—were consequences of its illegality and stigmatization, and would disappear once sodomy laws were repealed.

Thus far experience has not borne out this prediction. Decriminalization, along with a limited degree of destigmatization, did not lead to a decline in casual sex.[48] Indeed, commercial establishments that facilitated casual sex grew in number during the seventies. For some men, pursuit of sexual pleasure with multiple partners became a way of affirming a gay identity. Techniques for intensifying that pleasure—sex gadgets and paraphernalia, drugs—became part of the gay male subculture, promoted by its commercialization (Altman, 1982; Lauritsen, 1993).

Even when not accompanied by a theatrical presentation of self, the pursuit of depersonalized sexual contacts probably shares with that pursuit a lack of engagement with deep levels of the self.[49] This lack of engagement may be objectionable to those who do not object to homosexual relations themselves, or to pleasure in itself (Boyers, 1980). It runs counter to the modern middle-class linkage of sex and romantic love. Those who believe that people's sexual experiences should reflect who they are, and that sexual expression should entail a genuine engagement with a partner who is uniquely valued for who he or she is in a "deep" sense—a sense that goes beyond the sensual—may regard disengaged sex as unfulfilling, at least in the long run.

This concern with the unique partner is related to a historical heritage of heterosexual marriage, with its concern for the transmission of property along "blood lines," a concern that was given religious sanction by the Christian repudiation of polygamy. In the modern era, however, it has been sustained by romantic individualism, which has sometimes run into conflict with older institutional restrictions on partner choice such as monogamous marriage and prohibitions against adultery.[50]

For some men, the degree of participation in "the fast life" of bars, baths, discos, and casual sex is limited by its potential incompatibility with important life-goals. One man interviewed by McWhirter and Mattison (1984:161) observed:

> I think I would have gone further in school, but when I came out I really got caught up in the "gay life." It was so much fun. I was out every night with my newfound friends, getting to bed at four, five or six each morning, having wonderful and wild sex, going to great parties. I was carried away by it all and couldn't see any reason to continue with school. I dropped out.

For many, however, involvement in this round of activities is not all-encompassing, and can be maintained without jeopardy to school or work (Murray, 1992). Moreover, there is little reason to think that participation damages one's ability to engage himself more profoundly. Though most of Bell and Weinberg's male respondents had numerous partners for whom they felt no affection, hardly any had never felt affection for their partners and almost 40% were in stable, quasi-marital relationships (Bell and Weinberg, 1978:132–35).

Some spokesmen for gay liberation repudiated the standards by which heterosexual critics—and some homosexuals—had judged the emergent gay subculture flawed. New Leftist Carl Wittman (1972) argued that "Traditional marriage is a rotten oppressive institution . . . fraught with role playing . . . which smothers both people, denies needs, and places impossible demands on both people." Gay liberationists, he said, were trying to get away from "exclusiveness" and "promises about the future."

In recent years, fear of AIDS has led many gay men to abandon the hedonistic pursuit of anonymous sex. "It used to be that sex was like brushing your teeth," but now "sex is careful, not carefree." Many gay men are spending more time at home or with friends in nonsexual social activities (Gorman, 1992; Levine, 1992).[51] On the other hand, the establishment of J/O ("jack-off") clubs, and the many efforts being made to eroticize "safe sex" techniques, show that hedonism is not being abandoned wholesale. It is rather being reshaped to avoid new risks.

Interviews with gay male couples carried out by McWhirter and Mattison (1984) in the late seventies show that the importance of sex and of variety in partners vary with stages in the life-cycle and in a relationship. In the early stages of a relationship there was typically a high degree of sexual activity, yet sex "was not the principal reason for entry into their relationships" (p. 35). Sex was accompanied by emotions of love, feelings of togetherness and merging:

"When I was married, I really got into sex with my wife, but [his homosexual relationship] is different. I didn't want to *be* her, just please her. With Jim . . . I wanted his eyes to be my eyes, and his legs to be my legs." (p. 36)

In this instance, the bodily similarity of the two men seems to have contributed to the feelings of merging that Aristophanes identified as being central to the experience of sexual union. On the other hand, some authors suggest that sexual arousal is heightened by barriers or tension, and conclude that similarity can reduce sexual interest.[52] In any event, sex was surely important in creating a bond between these two men; it helped to break down barriers to the expression of intimate feelings (p. 37).

With time, familiarity led to the loss of erotic passion for one another,[53] and most of the men in the study sought casual sexual contacts with other men, purely for the sake of sex, without ending their commitments to their long-term partners. Though some couples continued to have satisfying sexual experiences together, other sensual pleasures, derived from cuddling, kissing, and holding one another, were important (p. 95), as were shared traditions, hobbies, and holidays. Defining fidelity in terms of emotional commitment rather than sexual exclusiveness, these extrasexual satisfactions held the couples together for many years.

The historical trajectory of sexual pleasure for lesbians has been quite different. During the eighteenth and nineteenth centuries, while male homosexual communities were gradually forming—first in Europe, then in the United States—it was becoming economically more difficult for women to live independently of men. Middle-class women were being excluded from major sectors of the economy, and channeled into gender-stereotyped jobs or housework. Respectable women were barred from premarital or extramarital sexual experience.

These constraints limited women's capacities to enter into lesbian relationships, or to form more extended networks and communities, except for a small number of women with particular backgrounds—actresses and singers, authors, those in marriages of convenience to homosexual husbands, those who attended college or worked in the professions, and the independently wealthy. Where middle- and upper-class women did form couples, they were able to live together without interference because stereotypes of women as asexual shielded those in "romantic friendships" from suspicions of sexual involvement. Lack of documentation makes it difficult to be confident about the role of sexuality in these relationships, but in many instances it may have been quite limited (Sahli, 1979; Smith-Rosenberg, 1979; Faderman, 1981:190–238; 1991:1–36).

Perhaps to protect girls from pregnancy and from acquiring a reputation as licentious, they have been discouraged from talking or thinking about sex. Girls' peer culture has been less oriented toward sex than boys', and has consequently not been as important a source of information about sexual possibilities. Many girls have lacked even the vocabulary that would enable them to communicate effectively with one another about sex.[54] They may not even be aware of their own sexual desires or states of arousal unless they are responding to someone else's sexual initiative (Nichols, 1987).

Girls raised in a society whose culture dictates that the sexual initiative should be reserved to men do not necessarily lose their inhibitions by being or becoming lesbian. Assumptions that women are supposed to respond to someone else's initiative can carry over into a lesbian relationship. When both partners are hesitant about taking the initiative, much of the time neither one will do so. Sex in this circumstance will inevitably play a limited role in their relationship. In fact, lesbian couples interact sexually less often than gay male couples or heterosexual couples, and have a more limited range of techniques.

Some lesbians say they prefer nongenital physical contact (hugging, cuddling) to genital sex (Blumstein and Schwartz, 1985:195–97). From 1955, when it was founded, until 1968, the Daughters of Bilitis—the leading lesbian political organization, whose members mostly had middle-class backgrounds—never discussed sex in peer counseling sessions; the subject did not come up (Lyon, 1980; Kennedy and Davis, 1993:224).

When the modern lesbian movement emerged in the seventies, female sexuality was becoming more widely recognized and accepted within the middle class, a development that one would expect to lead to a heightened eroticization of lesbian life. However, the movement emerged in part from a feminist movement that was strongly critical of many manifestations of male heterosexual sexual culture—pornography, rape, child-molesting—as oppressive to women. Robin Morgan (1977:180) spoke for many feminist women when she wrote that for gay males:

> the emphasis on genital sexuality, objectification, promiscuity, emotional non-involvement . . . was the *male style* . . . we as women, placed greater trust in love, sensuality, humor, tenderness, commitment. (Emphasis in original)

For many lesbians, rejection of male sexual culture implied a rejection of sexual expression itself. Genital sexuality and orgasm were downplayed in favor of a more diffuse sensuousness and emotional intimacy (Katz, 1972; Nichols, 1987; Faderman, 1991:231). Some opted for celibacy.

The working-class lesbian bar subculture that developed in the early and middle decades of this century was less constrained by considerations of respectability than the middle- and upper-class lesbian friendship circles that met in private homes. It formed at a time when marriage manuals were telling husbands that it was important to satisfy their wives sexually. The butch lesbians who imported this instruction into their relationships with femmes assumed responsibility for satisfying them, while denying themselves the same gratification. Although serial monogamy was the norm within the subculture, many participants had discreet casual outside affairs and one-night stands from time to time. Sex was an important component of relationships, yet themes of sexual pleasure were not culturally elaborated. Sex toys, dildos, and pornography, for example, were not used, and there was very little group sex (Kennedy and Davis, 1993).

"Sex radicals" of the 1980s criticized the feminist critique of sex, announced their interest in flavors of sex other than vanilla, and defended pornography and sadomasochism.[55] Many were lesbians. The emergence of a young generation of lesbians less tied to feminist issues of the seventies has created a constituency for a more explicitly sexual subculture. Some lesbians now purchase sex toys. Lesbian writers publish pornographic fiction, and filmmakers make porn films, sometimes featuring sadomasochistic themes. Lesbian clubs in New York now screen porn films and stage live shows featuring striptease dancers.

A few establishments have opened darkened backrooms featuring anonymous lesbian sex (Byron, 1985; Sundahl, 1985; Smyth, 1990; Faderman, 1991: 249–68; Minkowitz, 1992; Stein, 1992).[56]

IV

Twenty years ago, in the early days of gay liberation, some activists could argue that gay liberation was subversive of the capitalist social order. The latter, they argued, was built on the patriarchal family, which confined and restricted sensual and sexual expression, and oppressed women. The transformation of heterosexual eroticism within the last generation largely undercuts that argument.

Where heterosexual relations are charged with social functions, such as increasing the size of the population, cementing alliances between kinship groups (relevant to "primitive societies" and to feudal aristocracies), and socializing the young, pleasure as a specific feature of heterosexuality will be underplayed.[57] Contemporary industrial societies do not depend on heterosexual relations for the performance of critical social functions to nearly the same extent as in the recent past. We no longer want to promote population growth; and we rely heavily on schools to socialize the young.

Nor is stability in heterosexual relations as important as it once was. The welfare state and an expanding market for female labor have made it easier for women to support themselves. Heterosexual relations are, in consequence, much less restricted to stable, life-long marriages than used to be the case.

Adjustment to these changes takes time. Conservative moralists deplore premarital and extramarital sex, and easy divorce, but they are a reality. Moreover, their concerns have not been shared by some segments on the left. Figures as politically diverse as Herbert Marcuse (1955) and Christopher Lasch (1978) worried that a permissive, pleasure-oriented society would fail to build the ego strength and character needed to achieve standards of self-discipline that originated in an earlier century.[58] If sexual partners are available to anyone who wants them, without commitment or anticipation of a shared future, then individual character structures may develop in a manner that renders us unable to delay gratification or to establish empathetic bonds with others. The fact that many gay men have found their lovers through casual sexual encounters suggests that this concern is baseless, but even if it were true, what would Marcuse and Lasch have us do about it? Their explanations, which attribute these changes to structural arrangements in modern society, suggest that little could be done.

That does not mean these concerns will disappear from the minds of those raised on an ethic of self-denial. But this ethic, with roots in an economy based on hard work and scarcity, has already weakened in major strata of the population at large under the impact of affluence and consumerism. Nowadays, the ability to play and to enjoy oneself is considered part of psychological normalcy. In sexual matters, religious figures have lost some of the authority they once commanded. Sexually-oriented advertising bombards us from every direction. High school students now regard sexual expression as a birthright. To prevent the transmission of disease, condoms are now dispensed freely on college campuses and in some high schools. Spouses in celibate marriages are no longer the heroes they were to early Christian ascetics; we think they're weird, candidates for therapy. Droves of patients complain to therapists about their loss of sexual drive. Books offering instruction on methods for maximizing sexual pleasure are available to anyone who can read or look at pictures. Pornographic videos can be rented at neighborhood stores; many couples use them to enhance their own sexual activity.

Romance has certainly not disappeared; it is still widely sought—by both gays and straights. But its connection with sex has weakened. Many no longer expect all their sexual experiences to entail romance or love. And it is widely realized that love and marriage do not always endure for a lifetime. These changes in heterosexual culture have, of course, not influenced the entire population uniformly. Some still think that love is an essential prerequisite to sex, and their capacity to cause trouble to those who think differently is substantial. Culture conflict on the basis of differences in sexual culture will continue. The role of pleasure will figure prominently in this conflict.

Notes

I have learned much from participants in the Columbia University Seminar on Homosexualities, and about Roman sexual culture from John Patrick Otte. I am indebted to Paul Abramson, Barry Adam, Kathleen Dunleavy, Wayne R. Dynes, Gilbert Elbaz, Janet Halley, Iona Mara-Drita, Laurence Senelik, Edward Stein, Sherry Turkle, and Stephen O. Murray for helpful comments on an earlier draft.

1. An older psychiatric literature on homosexuality does treat pleasure, but in a manner that is shaped by its uncritical acceptance of the notion that homosexuality is necessarily pathological. In this literature, gratification from homosexuality is only an inauthentic or substitute pleasure. The focus here becomes the etiology and treatment of the underlying pathology, not the pleasure.

2. The Latin word for anus, *culus,* is masculine.

3. Edward Stein reminds me that the existence of the prostate might make anal intercourse with a male partner a physically different experience from anal intercourse with a female partner. Even if these differences exist, they surely do not make a partner of one sex more desirable than the other. The same can be said when comparing sexual acts that are not analogous. A man will have a different sensory experience when penetrating a man anally than when penetrating a woman vaginally. Yet these sensory experiences are not sufficient to explain the preference most men have for a partner of one sex over the year. For most people, this preference precedes the experience. Even physically unpleasant sexual contacts, as might occur in rape or in cases of dyspareunia, do not usually lead to a change in sexual orientation.

4. Were it otherwise, we would have difficulty explaining why women who are able to achieve an orgasm more readily through masturbation than with a human partner nevertheless prefer the partner. That it is a belief about the sex of one's partner that is relevant to erotic interest, rather than the partner's actual sex, can be seen by considering the case of a man being fellated by a person of one sex who is then told that his partner is actually someone of the other sex who is cross-dressing. Though some men may be indifferent to this information or titillated by it, many will be upset by the information and lose erotic interest in the partner and the experience.

5. This circumstance has led Elliston (1992) to argue that the New Guinea initiation practices should not be called "homosexual" at all, on the grounds that they are undertaken for instrumental reasons having to do with boys' maturation, and are therefore not erotic. This reasoning, however, wrongly supposes that an erotic element is necessarily absent from a practice undertaken or legitimated by instrumental goals. It also ignores the conclusions of ethnographers that an explicitly erotic element *is* present for many of the New Guinea men and boys.

6. See also Plato, *Phaedrus* 240d. This lack of reciprocity made pederastic sex unattractive to one Roman poet:

> I detest sex that does not delight both parties:
> That is why boy-love appeals to me less.
> > (Ovid, *Ars Amatoria* 2.683–84,
> > my translation)

7. The parallel is not exact because in the Greek case the active partner sought his own pleasure; in the butch-femme relationship, she sought her partner's.

8. Because the enjoyment of anal receptivity was puzzling to the Greeks in a way that desire to penetrate was not, they attempted to explain it. Texts attributed to Aristotle maintained that it could be due to habituation in childhood, or to the diversion of seminal fluid to the rectum (*Nicomachean Ethics* Bk. VII, v.1–4, vii.6; *Problemata* iv.26).

9. For some individuals, however, it may be impossible to distinguish these. Domination may be sexually arousing for some people.

10. Of course, even when cultural and social imperatives require marriage to someone of the opposite sex, homosexual relations may still be allowed before marriage and in extramarital liaisons. Acceptance of such relations is reported for many primitive cultures (Greenberg, 1988:66–68). Another possibility is marriage between same-sex partners. In almost all instances from the primitive world, these marriages entail the gender transformation of one partner, and may not be regarded indigenously as homosexual (Williams, 1986; Greenberg, 1988:40–48, 56–62, 79).

11. Likewise, Xenophon quotes Socrates as remarking, "Surely you do not suppose that lust provokes men to beget children, when the streets are full of people who will satisfy the appetites, as also are the brothels. No, it is clear that we select for wives the women who will bear us the best children and that we marry them to raise a family" (*Memiris* 2,2.4, quoted in Davies, 1984:47).

12. This statement must be qualified. Greek women spent a great deal of time alone with their female slaves. It is conceivable that affairs with slaves could have taken place without the knowledge of their husbands.

13. The attitudes such slaves and serfs might develop toward sexual pleasure have not been systematically studied. We can imagine two possibilities. One is envy of those

who are able to enjoy such pleasures, accompanied by fantasies involving the enjoyment of sensual pleasure, if necessary in the afterlife. The sensuousness of Moslem depictions of paradise might illustrate this pattern. Another possibility is repudiation of pleasures that cannot be experienced. The radical rejection of bodily pleasure in early Christian teachings is an obvious example. The revulsion toward sexual "decadence" within European working-class movements of the late nineteenth and twentieth centuries is another. Industrial work discipline does not seem to encourage favorable attitudes toward bodily pleasure. It rather promotes an outlook in which the body is valued for what it can do, rather than for what it can feel. Bodily pleasure may even be feared for the possible damage it might inflict on the body's capacity to perform—hence the masturbation phobia and warnings against overly frequent sexual intercourse found in European and American medical writings on sex beginning in the eighteenth century and continuing into the twentieth.

14. The Roman poet Martial alludes to such handbooks in XII.43 and possibly XII.95.

15. Solon supposedly founded the first brothel in Athens, but it was only in later centuries that their numbers and importance in Greek life grew.

16. Empedocles held this view, and it is found in Plato's *Protagoras.*

17. The Theban army of male lovers stands as an example showing that this fear did not preclude intimate relationships between males, but it led to a deemphasis on the sexual aspects of those relationships.

18. Sometimes the visual appeal is only alluded to indirectly. Catullus 24 addresses the beloved as "little flower of the Iuventii." The Latin *flosculus,* "little flower," is a direct translation of the Greek word that represents the anus as a rosebud. Greek reticence regarding carnal pleasures leaves us unable to answer such simple questions as what they used as a lubricant for anal intercourse. (There can be little doubt that it was olive oil.) By contrast, some Chinese literature refers to the use of saliva for this purpose (Hinsch, 1990:113).

19. Where literature featured invective, these pleasures could be mentioned. Thus in Idyll 5 of Theocritus (1982), Comitas puts Lacon down by asking:

> Don't you remember the time I was up you, and you with a grimace
> Wiggled your bottom deliciously, holding on tight to that oak tree?

20. The Cynics were alone among the philosophical schools in seeing nothing wrong with sexual pleasure (Brundage, 1987:18).

21. Nowhere in Paul's writings does one find such an extreme position as that of Saint Jerome in *Against Jovinianus* 20: "The truth is that, in view of the purity of the body of Christ, all sexual intercourse is unclean" (Schaff, 1893:361).

22. Clement of Alexandria, *Stromateis* 3.7.57–58. There is scriptural basis for this concern with desire: "Whosoever shall look on a woman to lust after her hath already committed adultery with her in his heart" (Matthew 5:28). The same principle would surely apply to the lust for a boy or man.

23. Jerome, *To Eustochium* 17 (Schaff, 1893).

24. Jerome, *To Eustochium* 6 (Schaff, 1893).

25. When late medieval medical writers gave sexual advice, they largely concentrated on methods of achieving conception (how unlike contemporary writings offering

sexual advice!), but some did suggest techniques of enhancing physical pleasure for husband and wife (Lemay, 1982).

26. To this day it regards kissing for pleasure to be a mortal sin (Regan, 1967).

27. This lack of interest in thoughts and feelings is characteristic of the penitentials, which priests used to impose penances on sinners. Penances for sexual acts (and other sins) are prescribed for *behaviors,* largely independent of their thoughts and feelings.

28. There is some continuity between this conception of the sodomite and the ancient Greek concerns with self-control. Those who were unable to bridle their passions were unfit to rule. In seventeenth-century France, when women's sexual desires were believed to be stronger than men's, profligate male sexuality resembled female sexuality as well as animal lust. These themes were highlighted in seventeenth-century French pamphlets attacking Cardinal Mazarin (Merrick, 1992).

29. Children were thought to be especially vulnerable to these problems. However, the relevance of this belief to homosexual life was becoming limited, because adults were gradually shifting from youths to adult partners. See below.

30. For a time in the late nineteenth and early twentieth centuries, persons who would now be called homosexuals were called *Urnings* or Uranians.

31. Of course, an ideology of egalitarianism can only go so far in bringing about equality between sexual partners when social inequalities persist in the larger society. The preference of some gay men for lower-class partners ("rough trade"), and male prostitution, illustrate the survival of inegalitarian patterns.

32. Prices male prostitutes charged for performing fellatio can be found in several Latin inscriptions from Pompeii (Brundage, 1987:26 n. 77).

33. Of course, fellatio was not totally unknown. A few of the penitentials created by Roman Catholic priests in the Middle Ages mention it (McNeill and Gamer, 1938; Bieler, 1963: 264; Payer, 1984:29–30; Brundage, 1987:167).

34. Unfortunately, no comparable shifts can be documented for lesbians because so little is known about lesbian sexual practices prior to this century.

35. Thus one New York gay man who reports having had thousands of sexual partners observed, "I love the hunt. I love going out finding sex. I love cruising. I love going to the baths, cruising, prowling. I think of myself as a prowler—almost catlike in the way I would stalk someone" (Silverstein, 1981:114).

36. Stephen Murray has suggested to me that having had something done to oneself should help one to perform the same action effectively on someone else. By this reasoning, a man who has been fellated should be a better fellator than a woman. And a woman who has had cunnilingus performed on her should be better at performing it than a man. How important this is in practice is not clear: the techniques can be acquired in other ways. Masters and Johnson (1979:64–76) found that committed homosexual partners communicated more readily and more effectively with one another about their sexual preferences, and drew more on knowledge of their own sexual responses in stimulating their partners. They took more time, and were less performance-oriented. This was not true of homosexual men and women with assigned partners. Nevertheless, there were few differences in levels of sexual satisfaction among gay men, gay women, heterosexual men, and heterosexual women in Blumstein and Schwartz's (1985:222, 248) national sample. Gay levels of satisfaction were, in fact, lower than those of heterosexuals, but the differences were quite small.

37. The *Oxford English Dictionary* defines "pleasure" as "The condition of con-

sciousness or sensation induced by the enjoyment or anticipation of what is felt or viewed as good or desirable; enjoyment, delight, gratification. The opposite of pain. In an unfavourable sense: Sensuous enjoyment as a chief object or end in itself." This restricted definition of pleasure as sensuous enjoyment, even when not understood unfavorably, surely does not do justice to the range of delights or enjoyments that may be experienced in a sexual encounter, such as the happiness that comes from being wanted and from pleasing a partner. A further complication arises from the fact that some people find pleasure in pain. (Others, of course, take pleasure in inflicting it.)

38. Although the object-relations theorists have heterosexual relations in mind, Epstein (1991) notes that this restriction is not required by the theory itself.

39. Casual sex is not necessarily indiscriminate. Participants are often highly selective in their choice of casual-sex partners, on the basis of criteria that can be assessed quickly, such as bodily appearance (Ackerley, 1969: 210–11; Hoffman, 1969; Tripp, 1975:142; Symons, 1979:294–95).

40. This availability and acceptance is not exclusive to the gay community. Within the last generation it has become characteristic of the youthful heterosexual population. What differs is the extent of participation, number of partners (see below), and the like.

41. There are exceptions to this generalization. Some magazines directed to lesbians now resemble those typical of gay men, and in some ads gay men seek enduring romantic relationships.

42. Bell and Weinberg did not collect comparable data for heterosexual men and women, but there can be little doubt that apart from celebrities, few heterosexual men have had as many partners as a large fraction of the homosexual men in their sample. The discrepancy would not necessarily be as large in samples drawn from other parts of the country. There are, however, substantial differences between heterosexuals and homosexuals in Blumstein and Schwartz's (1985:273–80) national survey, as well as in Saghir and Robins' (1973:57–61) earlier study.

43. To say this is not to value one kind of experience more than the other, only to note that there is likely to be a difference. This difference may be reduced by the ability of participants in casual sexual relationships to fantasize an intimacy that does not exist, or to hope that one may develop. Though moralists have often denounced casual sex as immoral or superficial, some people may welcome freedom from irksome and hypocritical seduction routines, or value the novelty casual sex provides. As will be seen below, loss of erotic interest often accompanies long-term relationships. A new partner can bring excitement that is lacking with a partner who is familiar. In sexology, this phenomenon is known as the "Coolidge effect" (Symons, 1979).

44. Steven Epstein (1993) has shown that a culture of sexual pleasure has also developed in middle-class, white, heterosexual America in the United States, particularly in the decades following the Second World War.

45. The discussion that follows offers a sociological explanation of this difference. Symons (1979:299–300) offers a biological one. He suggests that the gay male pattern is simply the male pattern, while the lesbian pattern is the female pattern. These patterns, he argues, arose through natural selection in relation to choice of opposite-sex partners, but carry over to choice of same-sex partners.

46. Much writing on gay liberation has stressed the psychological oppression of having to keep an important component of one's identity and behavior secret to avoid grave penalties. Some older gays, however, have observed that in the days before gay libera-

tion, they could gain self-esteem by regarding themselves as members of an elite secret fraternity. Greater openness has entailed the loss of this sense of being special or superior (private communications from Laurence Senelik and Wayne R. Dynes).

47. Lionel Trilling (1974) traces the concept of sincerity and the value attached to it to the Renaissance. It depended on increased privacy and individualism, and the potential for a discrepancy between appearance and reality that thrived on urbanization and the weakening of estate society.

48. Because such institutional sources of stability as cheaper insurance, and medical and pension benefits for couples, are still largely denied to same-sex couples, the reformers' position has not been fully tested. However, the historical growth in divorce rates for married couples points to the limited power of welfare benefits to stabilize marital or quasi-marital relationships.

49. This observation is conventional, but it is open to criticism for lack of supporting evidence that the spatial metaphor implied by the use of the word "deep" is subjectively meaningful to many people.

50. Scruton (1986) has made the romantic version of this sexual philosophy the basis for his critique of homosexuality and other "perversions." His argument reminds me of an exchange that appeared some years ago in a stereo magazine. When a reader took a record reviewer to task for referring to Rimsky-Korsakov's *Sheherazade* as "second-rate music," the reviewer responded by noting that if Beethoven's Fifth Symphony were to be the standard for considering a composition to be "first-rate," then one could not avoid classifying *Sheherazade* as second-rate. He added that second-rate was not necessarily bad. In listening to music one does not always want to ascend to the heights; often one wants only to relax and enjoy a less demanding aesthetic experience. The same could be said of sex. Scruton places too large and serious a burden on every sexual encounter. Much the same can be said of those Jewish and Christian religious denominations that have moved toward an acceptance of homosexual relations. This acceptance has thus far been limited to stable, loving, monogamous relations, and thus excludes a very large proportion of the sexual experiences of gay men.

51. Careful investigation is needed to ascertain how much of this shift is due to aging of an earlier hedonistic generation, and how much to fear of disease.

52. This is a common explanation of "lesbian bed death." One author has proposed that lesbians may need to create an artificial asymmetry to stimulate sexual arousal through such means as "the use of sex toys and props, through costume, through S/M (which maximizes differences between partners), by developing sexual rituals with our partners, and by introducing tricking into our relationships" (Nichols, 1987).

53. This loss is characteristic of heterosexual couples as well as homosexual, but is less likely to be accompanied by outside affairs (Blumstein and Schwartz, 1985).

54. Marilyn Frye (1990) reports, "I once perused a large and extensively illustrated book on sexual activity by and for homosexual men. It was astounding to me for one thing in particular, namely, that its pages constituted a huge lexicon of *words:* words for acts and activities, their sub-acts, preludes and denouements, their stylistic variation, their sequences. . . . Gay male sex, I realized then, is *articulate.* It is articulate to a degree that, in my world, lesbian 'sex' does not remotely approach. . . . I have, in effect, no linguistic community, no language, and therefore, in one important sense, no knowledge."

55. Pat Califia, one of the leaders of the sex radicals, complained that lesbian-

feminists would "rather caucus than copulate or cunniligicise" (quoted in Faderman, 1991:246).

56. On the other hand, some lesbians resist this development. One lesbian, writing to a gay magazine in response to an article that featured lesbian nightwear, "I'm mad as hell to see lesbians portrayed as sexual beings, just as they are in the mainstream press. Wimmin in our community do not want or need to see wimmin in mags bare-breasted, totally naked, and draped with chains" (Frederickson, 1993). In England, where similar developments took place, some women and gay/lesbian book stores refused to carry lesbian videos and magazines. The "lesbian" archives in London rejected material relating to the lesbian S/M subculture, and the support phone line would not take calls from S/M dykes. Attempts were made to ban leather from a 1989 lesbian pride march. The lesbian separatists have also attacked lesbian pornographers (Nichols, 1987).

57. The same is true of homosexual relations. Where they are harnessed to such tasks as masculinizing boys, the role of pleasure in these relations will be given little cultural prominence. The more unequal the social status of the partners, the less the attention that will be given to the pleasure or gratification of the partner with the lower status.

58. Trilling (1974: 153) locates this ethic in the early nineteenth century, quoting a letter in which the English poet John Keats (1935:336) in 1819 asked, "Do you not see how necessary a World of Pains and troubles is to school an Intelligence and make it a soul?" [that is] "*destined to possess the sense of Identity*" (emphasis in original).

References

Abramson, Paul R. and Steven D. Pinkerton (1995). *With pleasure: thoughts on the nature of human sexuality.* New York: Oxford University Press.

Ackerley, J. R. (1969). *My Father & Myself.* New York: Coward-McCann.

Altman, Dennis (1982). *The Homosexualization of America, the Americanization of the Homosexual.* New York: St. Martin's Press.

Balint, Michael (1965). *Primary Love and Psychoanalytic Technique.* New York: Liveright.

Bell, Alan P. and Martin S. Weinberg (1978). *Homosexualities: A Study of Diversity among Men and Women.* New York: Simon and Schuster.

Bieler, Ludwig (1963). *The Irish Penitentials.* Dublin: Dublin Institute for Advanced Studies.

Blumstein, Philip and Pepper Schwartz (1985). *American Couples: Money, Work, Sex.* New York: Pocket Books.

Boswell, John (1980). *Christianity, Social Tolerance, and Homosexuality.* Chicago: University of Chicago Press.

Boyers, Robert (1980). "The Ideology of the Steam Bath," *Times Literary Supplement* (May 30): 604.

Bremmer, Jan (1988). "Greek Pederasty and Modern Homosexuality," in J. Bremmer (ed.), *From Sappho to De Sade.* London: Croom Helm.

Bronski, Michael (1984). *Culture Clash: The Making of Gay Sensibility.* Boston: South End Press.

Brown, Peter (1988). *The Body and Society: Men, Women, and Sexual Renunciation in Early Christianity.* New York: Columbia University Press.

Brundage, James A. (1987). *Law, Sex, and Christian Society in Medieval Europe*. Chicago: University of Chicago Press.

Bullough, Vern (1976). *Sexual Variance in Society and History*. New York: Wiley.

Burton, Richard (1886). "Terminal Essay." Pp. 63–302 in *The Book of the Thousand Nights and a Night*, vol. 10. New York: Burton Club.

Byne, William and Bruce Parson (1993). "Human Sexual Orientation: The Biological Theories Reappraised," *Archives of General Psychiatry* 50:228–39.

Byron, Peg (1985). "What We Talk About When We Talk About Dildos," *Village Voice* (March 5): 48–49.

Callen, Michael (1992). "Your Country Needs You!" *QW* 33 (June 14): 41–45.

Carpenter, Edward (1909). *The Intermediate Sex: A Study of Some Transitional Types of Men and Women*. London: Swan Sonnenschein.

Cicero (1958). *The Speeches*, vol. 2. Cambridge: Harvard University Press.

Davies, Nigel (1984). *The Rampant God: Eros Throughout the World*. New York: William Morrow.

D'Emilio, John (1983). *Sexual Politics, Sexual Communities: The Making of a Homosexual Minority*. Chicago: University of Chicago Press.

D'Emilio, John and Estelle B. Freedman (1988). *Intimate Matters: A History of Sexuality in America*. New York: Harper and Row.

Doell, Ruth G. and Helen E. Longino (1988). "Sex Hormones and Human Behavior: A Critique of the Linear Model," *Journal of Homosexuality* 15(3/4):55–78.

Dover, Kenneth J. (1978). *Greek Homosexuality*. Cambridge: Harvard University Press.

Ehrenreich, Barbara, Elizabeth Hess and Gloria Jacobs (1986). *Remaking Love: The Feminization of Sex*. New York: Anchor.

Ellis, Lee and M. Ashley Ames (1987). "Neurohormonal Functioning and Sexual Orientation: A Theory of Homosexuality-Heterosexuality," *Psychological Bulletin* 101:238–58.

Elliston, Deborah (1992). " 'Ritualized Homosexuality' in Anthropology: Critiquing a Concept, Re-Situating Practices." M.A. Thesis, New York University Department of Anthropology.

Epstein, Steven (1991). "Sexuality and Identity: The Contribution of Object Relations Theory to a Constructionist Sociology," *Theory and Society* 20:825–73.

———. (1993). *Romantic Longings: Love in America, 1830–1980* (New York: Routledge).

Faderman, Lillian (1981). *Surpassing the Love of Men: Romantic Friendship and Love between Women from the Renaissance to the Present*. New York: William Morrow.

———. (1991). *Odd Girls and Twilight Lovers: A History of Lesbian Life in Twentieth-Century America*. New York: Columbia University Press.

Fisher, Helen E. Fisher (1992). *Anatomy of Love: The Natural History of Monogamy, Adultery and Divorce*. New York: Norton.

Flandrin, Jean-Louis (1991). *Sex in the Western World: The Development of Attitudes and Behaviour*. Trans. S. Collins. Philadelphia: Harwood Academic.

Ford, Clellan S. and Frank A. Beach (1951). *Patterns of Sexual Behavior*. New York: Harper and Row.

Foucault, Michel (1986). *The Uses of Pleasure. The History of Sexuality*, vol. 2. New York: Vintage.

——— (1988). *The Care of the Self. The History of Sexuality*, vol. 3. New York: Vintage.

Fout, John (1994). "Working-Class Homosexual Desire in Nazi Germany." Paper presented to the Wenner-Gren Symposium, "Theorizing Sexuality," Cascais, Portugal, March 19–27, 1993.

Frederickson, DeLora (1993). "Letter to the Editor," *The Advocate* #628 (May 4): 10.

Frye, Marilyn (1990). "Lesbian 'sex'." In Jeffner Allen (ed.), *Lesbian Philosophies and Cultures*. New York: SUNY Press.

Futuyma, Douglas J. and Stephen J. Risch (1983/84). "Sexual Orientation, Sociobiology, and Evolution," *Journal of Homosexuality* 9:157–68.

Gardella, Peter (1985). *Innocent Ecstasy: How Christianity Gave America an Ethic of Sexual Pleasure*. New York: Oxford University Press.

Gordon, Michael (1978). "From Unfortunate Necessity to a Cult of Mutual Orgasm: Sex in American Marital Education Literature, 1830–1940." Pp. 53–77 in James M. Henslin and Edward Sagarin (eds.), *The Sociology of Sex*. Rev. ed. New York: Schocken.

Gorman, Michael E. (1992). "The Pursuit of the Wish," pp. 87–106 in Gilbert Herdt (ed.), *Gay Culture in America: Essays from the Field*. Boston: Beacon Press.

Gosling, J. C. B. and C. C. W. Taylor (1982). *The Greeks on Pleasure*. Oxford: Clarendon Press.

Greenberg, David F. (1988). *The Construction of Homosexuality*. Chicago: University of Chicago Press.

Gregory of Nyssa, Saint (1967). *Ascetical Works*. Trans. Virginia Woods Callahan. Washington, D.C.: Catholic University of America Press.

Harris, M. (1973). *The Dilly Boys: Male Prostitution in Piccadilly*. London: Croom Helm.

Herdt, Gilbert (1981). *Guardians of the Flutes: Idioms of Masculinity*. New York: McGraw-Hill.

———. (1984). *Ritualized Homosexuality in Melanesia*. Berkeley: University of California Press.

Hinsch, Bret (1990). *Passions of the Cut Sleeve: The Male Homosexual Tradition in China*. Berkeley: University of California Press.

Hoffman, Martin (1969). *The Gay World: Male Homosexuality and the Social Creation of Evil*. New York: Basic Books.

Hoult, T. (1983/84). "Human Sexuality in Biological Perspective: Theoretical and Methodological Considerations," *Journal of Homosexuality* 9:137–55.

Hurteau, Pierre (1993). "Catholic Moral Discourse on Male Sodomy and Masturbation in the Seventeenth and Eighteenth Centuries," *Journal of the History of Sexuality* 4:1–26.

Isocrates (1990). *Tanegyricus and To Nicocles*, ed. S. Ushers. Warminster: Aris and Phillips.

Katz (1972). "Smash Phallic Imperialism." Pp. 259–62 in Karla Jay and Allen Young (eds.), *Out of the Closets: Voices of Liberation*. New York: Douglas.

Keats, John (1935). *The Letters of John Keats,* ed. M. B. Forman. London: Oxford University Press.

Kennedy, Elizabeth Lapovsky and Madeline D. Davis (1993). *Boots of Leather, Slippers of Gold: The History of a Lesbian Community*. New York: Routledge and Kegan Paul.

Kennedy, Hubert C. (1988). *Ulrichs: The Life and Works of Karl Heinrich Ulrichs, Pioneer of the Modern Gay Movement*. Boston: Alyson.

Kernberg, Otto F. (1977). "Boundaries and Structure in Love Relations," *Journal of the American Psychoanalytic Association* 25 (1977):81–114.

Keuls, Eva C. (1985). *The Reign of the Phallus: Sexual Politics in Ancient Athens.* New York: Harper and Row.

Lasch, Christopher (1978). *The Culture of Narcissism.* New York: W. W. Norton.

Lauritsen, John (1993). "Political-Economic Construction of Gay Male Class Identity," *Journal of Homosexuality* 24:221–32.

Leites, Edmund (1986). *The Puritan Conscience and Modern Sexuality.* New Haven: Yale University Press.

Lemay, Helen Rodnite (1982). "Human Sexuality in Twelfth through Fifteenth-Century Scientific Writings." Pp. 187–205 in Vern L. Bullough and James Brundage (eds.), *Sexual Practices in the Medieval Church.* Buffalo: Prometheus.

LeVay, Simon (1993). *The Sexual Brain.* Cambridge: MIT Press.

Levine, Martin P. (1992). "The Life and Death of Gay Clones," pp. 68–86 in Gilbert Herdt (ed.), *Gay Culture in America: Essays from the Field.* Boston: Beacon Press.

Lucretius (1986). *De Rerum Natura IV.* Trans. John Godwin. Warminster: Aris and Phillips.

Lutz, Cora E. (1947). "Musonius Rufus, 'The Roman Socrates'". Pp. 3–147 in Alfred R. Bellinger (ed.), *Yale Classical Studies,* vol. 10. New Haven: Yale University Press.

Lyon, Phyllis (1980). Introduction. Pp. xi–xii in Pat Califia, *Sapphistry: The Book of Lesbian Sexuality.* Tallahassee: Naiad Press.

Marcuse, Herbert (1955). *Eros and Civilization: A Philosophical Inquiry into Freud.* Boston: Beacon Press.

Martial (1987). *Epigrams of Martial Englished by Divers Hands,* ed. J. P. Sullivan and P. Whigham. Berkeley: University of California Press.

Masters, William H. and Virginia E. Johnson (1979). *Homosexuality in Perspective.* Boston: Little, Brown.

McNeill, John J. and Helena M. Gamer (1938). *Medieval Handbooks of Penance.* New York: Columbia University Press.

McWhirter, David and Andrew W. Mattison (1984). *The Male Couple: How Relationships Develop.* Englewood Cliffs: Prentice-Hall.

Merrick, Jeffrey (1992). "Sodomy and Tyranny in Seventeenth-Century France." Paper presented to the Columbia University Seminar on Homosexualities.

Meyer-Bahlberg, Heino F. L. (1977). "Sex Hormones and Male Homosexuality in Comparative Perspective," *Archives of Sexual Behavior* 6 (1977):297–325.

———. (1979). "Sex Hormones and Female Homosexuality: A Critical Examination," *Archives of Sexual Behavior* 8:101–19.

———. (1984). "Psychoendocrine Research on Sexual Orientation: Current Status and Future Options," *Progress in Brain Research* 61:375–98.

Minkowitz, Donna (1992). "See What the Girls in the Backroom Will Have: A Dyke's Adventure," *Village Voice* (June 30):34, 38.

Morgan, Edmund S. (1942). "The Puritans and Sex," *New England Quarterly* 25:591–607.

Morgan, Robin (1977). *Going Too Far: The Personal Chronicle of a Feminist.* New York: Random House.

Mosse, George L. (1985). *Nationalism and Sexuality: Middle-Class Morality and Sexual Norms in Modern Europe.* Madison: University of Wisconsin Press.

Murray, Stephen O. (1992). "Components of Gay Community in San Francisco." Pp. 107–146 in Gilbert Herdt (ed.), *Gay Culture in America: Essays from the Field.* Boston: Beacon.

Murray, Stephen and Kent Gerard (1987). "Renaissance Sodomite Subcultures?" Pp. 65–94 in Stephen O. Murray (ed.), *Cultural Diversity and Homosexualities.* New York: Irvington.

Newton, Esther (1972). *Mother Camp: Female Impersonators in America.* Englewood Cliffs: Prentice-Hall.

Nichols, Margaret (1987). Pp. 97–125 in "Lesbian Sexuality: Issues and Developing Theory," in Boston Lesbian Psychologies Collective (eds.), *Lesbian Psychologies: Explorations and Challenges.* Urbana: University of Illinois Press.

Noonan, John Thomas (1965). *Contraception: A History of Its Treatment by the Catholic Theologians and Canonists.* Cambridge: Harvard University Press.

Parker, W. H. (1988). *Priapea: Poems for a Phallic God.* London: Croom Helm.

Pattatuci, Angela M. L. and Dean H. Hamer (1994). "The Genetics of Sexual Orientation: From Fruit Flies to Humans." This volume.

Paul, Jay P. (1993). "Childhood Cross-Gender Behavior and Adult Homosexuality: The Resurgence of Biological Models of Sexuality," *Journal of Homosexuality* 24:41–54.

Payer, Pierre (1984). *Sex and the Penitentials: The Development of a Sexual Code, 550–1150.* Toronto: University of Toronto Press.

Pittman, David J. (1971). "The Male House of Prostitution," *Transaction* 8(5–6): 21–27.

Plato (1989). *Symposium.* Trans. A. Nehemas and P. Woodruff. Indianapolis: Hackett.

Pritchard, James B. (1955). *Ancient Near Eastern Texts Relating to the Old Testament.* Princeton: Princeton University Press.

Puterbaugh, Geoff (ed.). (1990). *Twins and Homosexuality: A Casebook.* New York: Garland.

Regan, A. (1967). "Lust," *New Catholic Encyclopedia.* New York: McGraw-Hill.

Reiss, Albert, Jr. (1961). "The Social Integration of Queers and Peers." *Social Problems* 9:102–9.

Ricketts, W. (1984). "Biological Research on Homosexuality: Ansell's Cow or Occam's Razor?" *Journal of Homosexuality* 9:65–93.

Ruse, Michael (1981). "Are There Gay Genes? Sociobiology and Homosexuality," *Journal of Homosexuality* 6:5–34.

Saghir, Marcel T. and Eli Robins (1973). *Male and Female Homosexuality: A Comprehensive Investigation.* Baltimore: Williams and Wilkins.

Sahli, Nancy (1979). "Smashing: Women's Relationships before the Fall," *Chrysalis* 8 (Summer):17–27.

Schaff, P., et al. (1893). *A Select Library of Nicene and Post-Nicene Fathers.* 2d series, vol. 6. New York: Charles Scribner's Sons.

Scruton, Roger (1986). *Sexual Desire: A Moral Philosophy of the Erotic.* New York: The Free Press.

Silverstein, Charles (1981). *Man to Man: Gay Couples in America.* New York: William Morrow.

Smith, Anne Marie (1992). "Resisting the Erase of Lesbian Sexuality: A Challenge for Queer Activism," pp. 200–213 in Kenneth Plummer (ed.), *Modern Homosexualities: Fragments of Lesbian and Gay Experiences.* New York: Routledge.

Smith, Daniel Scott (1973). "The Dating of the American Sexual Revolution: Evidence and Interpretation." Pp. 321–35 in Michael Gordon (ed.), *The American Family in Social-Historical Perspective.* New York: Simon and Schuster.

Smith-Rosenberg, Carroll (1979). "The Female World of Love and Ritual: Relations between Women in Nineteenth-Century America." Pp. 311–42 in Nancy F. Cott and Elizabeth H. Pleck (eds.), *A Heritage of Her Own.* New York: Simon and Schuster.

Smyth, Cherry (1990). "The Pleasure Threshold: Looking at Lesbian Pornography on Film," *Feminist Review* 34:152–59.

Sontag, Susan (1969). *Against Interpretation.* New York: Dell.

Stein, Arlene (1992). "The Year of the Lustful Lesbian," in A. Stein (ed.), *Sisters, Sexperts, Queers: Beyond the Lesbian Nation.* New York: E. P. Dutton.

Stone, Donald, Jr. (1992). "The Sexual Outlaw in France, 1605," *Journal of the History of Sexuality* 2:597.

Sundahl, Debi (1985). "Lesbian Sex—Part 11," *Advocate* (October).

Symons, Donald (1979). *The Evolution of Human Sexuality.* New York: Oxford University Press.

Tannahill, Reay (1980). *Sex in History.* New York: Stein and Day.

Theocritus (1982). *Idylls and Epigrams.* Trans. Daryl Hine. New York: Atheneum.

Todd, Margo (1980). "Humanists, Puritans and the Spiritualized Household," *Church History* 49:18–34.

Trilling, Lionel (1974). *Sincerity and Authenticity.* New York: Harcourt Brace Jovanovich.

Tripp, Clarence A. (1975). *The Homosexual Matrix.* New York: Signet.

Verduin, Kathleen (1983). "'Our Cursed Natures': Sexuality and the Puritan Conscience," *New England Quarterly* 56:220–37.

Weinrich, James D. (1987). *Sexual Landscapes: Why We Are What We Are, Why We Love Whom We Love.* New York: Scribner's.

Whitam, Frederick L., Milton Diamond and James Martin (1993). "Homosexual Orientation in Twins: A Report on 61 Pairs and Three Triplet Sets," *Archives of Sexual Behavior* 22:187–206.

Williams, Walter L. (1986). *The Spirit and the Flesh: Sexual Diversity in American Indian Cultures.* Boston: Beacon.

Wittman, Carl (1972). "A Gay Manifesto." Pp. 330–45 in Karla Jay and Allen Young (eds.), *Out of the Closets: Voices of Gay Liberation.* New York: Douglas.

Wooden, Wayne S. and Jay Parker (1982). *Men Behind Bars: Sexual Exploitation in Prison.* New York: Plenum.

CHAPTER TWELVE

Discourse, Intercourse, and the Excluded Middle: Anthropology and the Problem of Sexual Experience

DONALD TUZIN

I

Name any behavior, and you could probably get agreement from most anthropologists that we need to know more about it. This creedal attitude inspires much research and grant-getting activity, and to say that too much is known about some topic or other, is to verge on professional disloyalty. What seems curious about sex, however—though it is perhaps not unique in this regard—is that anthropologists seem unable to decide whether they know too little or too much about it. As I intend to show, this uncertainty is part of the legacy of a sixty-year-old disciplinary tradition in which behavior, as such, has played a relatively minor rôle in the analysis and interpretation of cultural systems. By committing itself early on to a discourse based on normative and propositional statements, symbolic structures, and other such abstractions, mainstream sociocultural anthropology not only lost analytic sight of what individuals do and think, it did not deal conceptually with the serious, interactive play between phenomenal events and culturally constituted ideas. Facts? We have plenty of facts about sexuality, in the sense of descriptive reports, but few data, in the sense of facts as valorized in a context of analysis. So long as what is known remains theoretically unassimilated and conceptually undeveloped, the feeling will persist that anthropology is poorly informed on the topic.

There are signs that anthropology is beginning to undergo a significant rediscovery of sexual behavior, both as part of its own theoretical progression and in response to a wider intellectual climate that has recently become friendly to examinations in this area. Works by Gilbert H. Herdt (1981, 1984) and Thomas Gregor (1985), for example, were major breakthroughs in the anthropology of sex, models of ethnographic quality and analytic ingenuity. Spurred in large part by the AIDS crisis, recent edited collections (e.g., Lindenbaum 1991; Herdt and Lindenbaum 1992) and of course the present volume, are evidence of a rediscovery of sex as an important field of anthropological inquiry. But even in science discoveries can be undone or unappreciated in their full import. To prevent this from happening, to avoid having sex be rediscovered only to be lost again, a stock-taking is in order, beginning with the question of how sex became *terra incognita* in the first place—and why it has generally remained so.

These are large topics, about which much could be written. My approach in this chapter is to select those aspects which argue for an interactionist framework for the analysis of sexual behavior (see Introduction, this volume). It so happens that technical and methodological difficulties attending the study of sex had much to do with the rise of doctrinaire cultural determinism in American anthropology (Freeman 1983). Accordingly, if the rediscovery of sex leads to the resolution of some of those earlier difficulties, such deterministic thinking would lose an important, original source of legitimacy. The interactionist perspective which I advocate here and elsewhere (Tuzin 1984) gives prominence to the experiential domain emergent from the blending of psychobiological proclivities and cultural meanings acquired through social learning. This ought to be nothing new: the "biocultural" character of human nature has been axiomatic in anthropology for most of this century. And yet, the grooves of mind-body dualism, scored deeply into Western consciousness, continue to channel epistemological debate into positions of false opposition and unmerited determinism. Sounded against most anthropological practice, the promise of "bioculturalism" rings hollow. Part of my purpose, then, is to show that sexual behavior displays with exceptional clarity the synergism of cultural and biological effects, thereby challenging us to enter conceptually into the domain of the "excluded middle," which is experience itself.

To the extent that the interactionist perspective develops certain neglected areas of culture theory, its implications are as wide as anthropology itself. For example, medical anthropology, because it typically operates at the interface of cultural and organic processes, would be a prominent beneficiary of such theoretical developments. If one is to understand why certain kinds of disorders are successfully treatable by certain kinds of folk therapies, as when shamans, faith healers, or other magical practitioners effect the relief of physical symptoms, it is not enough to say that the mobilization of a corresponding belief system, by itself, is sufficient cause for these somatic or perceptual changes. Mechanisms must be identified, processes which effect the situational intermingling of cultural understandings and bodily states within the therapeutically accessible space of immediate experience.

One such mechanism, clearly, is the phylogenetically based capacity and appetite for sexual *pleasure*—a trait which at first might seem merely epiphenomenal to biological reproduction, but which is a profound behavior in its own right (Abramson & Pinkerton 1995; Tiger 1992). To be sure, as an inducement to coitus, genital pleasure is an essential lubricant in the evolutionary engine of humans and, perhaps, certain other species—depending on how broadly one chooses to define "pleasure." None would deny, either, that sexual pleasure is a profoundly organic phenomenon, the experienced manifestation of an astonishingly intricate combination of physiological events. Nor can it be doubted that, under certain conditions, the urge to experience sexual pleasure can have a compelling quality. The need for sex may never be an emergency in the strict medical sense; for most individuals, celibacy's effects would be mild compared with those of, say, going without food. Some people—probably fewer than are claimed by science and folklore—eschew or are denied sexual pleasure for their entire lives, without apparent ill effects. It is all the more remarkable, therefore, that millions of people through the ages have eagerly risked life, limb, property, freedom, tranquility, family, reputation, happiness, have even accepted sure and eternal damnation, all for the attainment, not of offspring, but of sexual pleasure.

The bioevolutionary character of sexual pleasure cannot be disputed; but, for humans, the quest for this experience is also governed by a battery of normative and idiosyncratic controls no less intricate and subtle than those of organic origin. Perceptions, memories, fantasies, social prescriptions, situational factors, cultural understandings—all of these guide and constrain the individual's impulse to sexual pleasure. Such sources yield a corresponding multiplicity of objects and strategies through which sexual pleasure can be realized: masturbation, sadism, masochism, fetishism, voyeurism, and bestiality; pleasures bought, sold, borrowed, and stolen; partners of all kinds, including the dead and the newly born. Such runaway eclecticism means that if sexual pleasure in *Homo sapiens* is biological, it is not only biological.[1] Hence the value of an interactionist methodology, a claim I hope to substantiate later in the chapter.

The importance of understanding sexual experience in-the-round, so to speak, is no better certified than in its potential contribution to the epidemiology of sexually transmitted diseases (STD). As Bailey and Aunger's study (this volume) reminds us, the problem has to do with risk tolerance, risk denial, and other psychocultural aspects of sexuality which go far beyond a medically defined rationality. Worse: under conditions of STD contagion, cultural collapse, and the loss of traditional social controls, dangerous sex has been seen to become positively valued, perversely, as if to aid in the fulfillment of a collective death-wish.[2]

While culture is capable of valorizing any behavior, no matter how bizarre and maladaptive (Edgerton 1992), it remains uncertain just how and to what extent collective understandings determine individual sexual conduct and experience. If, as I shall argue, sexual behavior is unusually resistant to standardization or prescription, and if as a consequence ideological or normative constructs are poor predictors of what members of a population actually do in sexual privacy, then researchers must be aware of this circumstance and adjust their methodologies accordingly. The question then arises, should we ask about sexual behavior? The answer is, yes. Obvious as this might seem, it is my clear impression that very few ethnographers approach this topic in a direct manner—if they approach it at all. Even granting that sexual behavior is peripheral or irrelevant to most researchers' main interests, it is still a fact of life in all known societies, and therefore the degree of ethnographic incuriosity on the topic is noteworthy.

Commenting on this state of affairs, Devereux (1967) suggests that unconscious anxieties, let alone simple prudishness on the ethnographer's part, may often prevent open discussion with informants and that, indeed, these resistances preclude the objective study of sex. Such pessimism is premature in the light of two prior factors which cloud the issue. As noted, even without psychological blockages there are technical difficulties in gaining access to the behavior, either by direct observation or by reliable reportings. More significant, however, because it discourages advancement on those technical problems, is the absence of a conceptual apparatus for dealing with whatever information can be obtained. These issues are the subject of this chapter, beginning with the history behind anthropology's sexual shortcomings.

II

The AIDS crisis surprised anthropologists into the realization that there is apparently much we do not know about sexual behavior: missing facts that are essential to our understanding of the epidemiology of this and other sexually transmitted diseases. And yet, how can this be? How can we be the least bit uninformed on this subject? When Alfred Kinsey died in 1956, his files contained 18,500 case histories of sexual behavior (Christenson 1971), over 10,000 of which had been the empirical foundation for his well-known studies of American sexual practices (Kinsey et al. 1948, 1953). But that is the United States, some might say, where Kinsey, Masters and Johnson, and *Playboy* magazine have brought sex into the light of social and scientific day; the knowledge deficit, one might imagine, is more severe with regard to sex in non-Western societies. This view would ignore the contributions of Westermarck, Malinowski, Mead, Devereux, Róheim, Elwin, Suggs—to name only a few—and synthetic efforts, such as Ford and Beach's *Patterns of Sexual Behavior* (1951), which used facts on sexual behavior from 190 societies contained in the Human Relations Area Files. Much earlier, Havelock Ellis, in his monumental *Studies in the Psychology of Sex* (1936; orig. 1896–1928), drew from a large body of ethnographic information that had been amassed during the nineteenth and early twentieth centuries. Indeed, studies of sex during the early decades of the present century had accumulated to such a point that, writing in 1932, Malinowski complained of a "surfeit of sex." "I alone," he confessed, "have to plead guilty to four books on the subject, two of which have the word sex on the title-page" (Malinowski 1948:x [orig. 1932]).[3]

It was no accident that the two decades preceding Malinowski's comment were a time of considerable license in the wider society, as those born during the late Victorian era came of age and found daring sexual conduct (along with such things as women's suffrage, clothing fashions, and jazz) to be an excellent form of rebellion against a parental generation that had lost the moral high ground in the slaughter of the Great War (Schmalhausen 1929). Havelock Ellis—anthropologist manqué and sometime mentor of both Westermarck and Malinowski (Grosskurth 1980:119; Firth 1981:114)—gave a scientific endorsement to these trends by detailing the enormous individual and cultural variability that occurs in sexual practices. His opening chapter, for example, entitled "The Evolution of Modesty," is a compilation of the diverse things which cultures around the world insist be hidden. As Brecher remarks (1969:4), Ellis's large book can be summed up by saying, "[E]veryone is not like you, your loved ones, and your friends and neighbors." What is more, "Even your friends and neighbors may not be as much like you as you suppose" (p. 39). For sexual reformers and sexual hygienists of the time, such knowledge (and its relativistic implications) liberated the spirit to seek and live by its own, rather than by an imposed standard of sexual conduct. Thus, in a letter written to a friend in 1916, Bertrand Russell mentions his appreciative reading of Havelock Ellis's "very scientific and objective" studies, adding, "What folly it is the way people are kept in ignorance on sexual matters, even when they think they know everything" (quoted in Grosskurth 1980:220).

These trends in science and society attracted criticism, of course—and not only from clergymen. H. L. Mencken, the otherwise irreverent social commentator from Baltimore, wrote in 1919 that "even the most serious and honest of the sex hygiene volumes are probably futile, for they are all founded upon a pedagogical error. That is to say, they are all founded upon an attempt to explain a romantic mystery in terms of an exact science" (Mencken 1919:197). Futility from a scientific or hygienic point of view did not, however, prevent this new freedom from killing innocence, which it did by destroying the mystery that is supposedly central to the sexual aesthetic. "The veriest school-girl of to-day," Mencken moaned, "fed upon Forel, Sylvanus Stall, Reginald White Kauffman and the Freud books, knows as much as the midwife of 1885, and spends a good deal more time discharging and disseminating her information. All this, of course, is highly embarrassing to the more romantic and ingenuous sort of men, of whom I have the honor to be one" (p. 199). Here we have it: not only because of the scientific satiety mentioned by Malinowski, but for the sake of the quality of civilized existence, it is possible to know too much about sex. Mencken is quite explicit on this point: "In the relations between the sexes," he states, "all beauty is founded upon romance, all romance is founded upon mystery, and all mystery is founded upon ignorance, or, failing that, upon the deliberate denial of the known truth" (pp. 199–200).

Mencken's reaction typified a large body of American public opinion, which, in various ways, was to be an impediment to sex research all the way to the present.[4] More immediately, however, what Handler (1986) calls the "sex problem in America" during the 1920s, was implicated in the formation of certain anthropological habits, specifically, the systematic abandonment of behavior, in favor of social and cultural systems, as an object of study. For Edward Sapir, the eagerness with which many of his colleagues embraced the fashionable separation of love and lust, and the "romantic glorification of sex as 'primitive' and 'natural'" (quoted in Handler 1986:144; cf. McDougall 1929:95), was a troubling measure of how spurious anthropology, itself, had become. "Such an attitude," he warned, in terms not dissimilar from Mencken's,

> was psychologically unnatural, for the emotion of love . . . is one of the oldest and most persistent of human feelings. . . . Human culture has everywhere linked sex to love in such a way that sexual love "takes the ego out of itself," and becomes the prototype for "all non-egoistic identifications". . . . Anthropologists, Sapir felt, had helped to obscure this truth, with their "excited books about pleasure-loving Samoans and Trobriand Islanders" . . . ; the reading public was all too prone to mistake the absence of Western-style taboos for "primitive freedom" and, at the same time, to overlook the coercive presence of culturally unfamiliar sex regulations. (Handler 1986: 144, quoting Sapir)

In assigning blame equally to a voyeuristic readership and a loveless anthropology willing to pander to it, Sapir's position begged the question of what an acceptably sober, constructive anthropology of sex should be. The larger issue here—glimpsed in the preceding reference to love as a primordial human emotion—has to do with what Ruth Benedict later called Sapir's "quarrel with the universe" (quoted in Handler 1986:149), namely, his criticism of an anthropology which, increasingly, reified culture as an entity autonomous from, and determinative of, individuals and psyches. Correctly, he perceived the anthropological importance of sex to lie in the fact that, more than any other field of human behavior, it is the *pons asinorum* of cultural determinism; for if culture can be shown to coerce even the private antics of the bedroom, let alone the deeper privacy of sexual fantasy, then it becomes difficult to imagine any area of social and mental life that would not be governed by it. Sapir plainly believed that certain behaviors and emotional states were antecedent to the crude cultural conditioning advocated by many of his contemporaries, and that no theory of culture should ignore this self-evident truth.[5] I will return to this issue in a moment.

Sexual liberation, on the one hand, and the closely linked doctrines of cultural relativism and cultural determinism, on the other, were decidedly odd bedfellows. The claim that many behaviors (in this case, sexual behaviors) are determined by culture and not biology was used to support the promise of enlightened social engineering (Mead 1928, 1935). But if patterned behavior is no more than cultural, it is also no less than cultural; and the idea that the knowledge of alternatives empowers us to change our own attitudes and practices, paradoxically negates the putative force of cultural conditioning, which becomes a mantle to be lightly discarded at the wearer's whim. On the contrary, then, far from underpinning a liberal or reformist social policy, cultural determinism is, logically, and no less so than biological determinism, a doctrine friendly to arrangements as they are.

An escape from this dilemma—albeit one which required bending the rules of cultural determinism—was nihilism; a special exemption, as it were, granted to those sophisticated few who grasped the significance of cultural differences and could use this knowledge to soar above the confines of their own cultural traditions. Here rises the paradox of the stereotypic anthropologist, who, despite his expert knowledge of the importance of culture, is a misfit and critic among his own people, and a scorner of their popular symbols. For Sapir, whose criticisms sprang from universalistic rather than relativistic principles, the fashionable pursuit of sex in itself was "narcissistic" (quoted in Handler 1986:145)—a particularly damaging kind of perversion which, if widely embraced, would spell the end of "authentic culture," as he defined it (Sapir 1924). To the extent that anthropologists in their studies and private lives pursued "sex in itself," they exemplified and lent scientific respectability to this unhealthy trend—something which, as *un*stereotypic moral actors, few were willing to do. Even those who were members of the avant-garde, while perhaps disputing the claim that sexual liberalism must be culturally corrosive, could not but agree that explicit sexual reportings were the chief source of an unwelcome sensationalism in the public's perception of anthropology's subject matter.

The chosen alternative was to recede from concrete depictions to conceptual levels which presuppose sexual behavior but do not deal with it directly.[6] To the extent that faraway sexual "customs" were reported in a language fully abstracted from the level of individual experience, including emotional needs and responses, to the extent that culture was conceptualized as autonomous and "superorganic" (Kroeber 1915, 1917; cf. Sapir 1917), anthropology could not and did not assimilate sexuality—sex in itself—to its theoretical program. Thus from approximately 1930 onward, sex came to be treated either anecdotally or as an appendage to normative, propositional systems such as kinship and marriage, or, more recently, gender ideology.[7] Behavior, as such, was abandoned to the psychologists, while sexual behavior, in particular, became a research specialty largely associated with reproductive physiology, sex therapy, and the Sunday supplement.

In British circles, meanwhile, the same shift occurred, but in the context of the intellectual rivalry between A. R. Radcliffe-Brown and Bronislaw Malinowski, which was decided in favor of the former's relatively abstract sociological system, structural-functionalism, as against the latter's more psychoculturally focused, unhyphenated functionalism (Richards 1957; Stocking 1984). As noted earlier, Malinowski had an intense interest in sex, which, personal motives aside (Malinowski 1967; Wayne 1984), was consistent with his methodological attention to flesh-and-blood individuals (Stocking 1984:158) and to the way in which culture functions to satisfy emotional and bodily needs. As Kaberry (1957:75) observes, "If, in Malinowski's [ethnographic monographs], the people are always with us (and, some would say, too much with us), in

Radcliffe-Brown's they are conspicuous by their absence; they are the invisible facts" (cf. Firth 1981:130ff.). Although Malinowski's theoretical enunciations were crude and sometimes clumsy, history may yet judge that he was on the right track. Be that as it may, from the early thirties British social anthropology, for its own reasons, did not seek to develop an adequate theoretical framework for the analysis of sexual behavior.[8]

III

These parallel developments in Great Britain and the United States excused anthropology from having to come to terms with a behavior which, for anyone who has tried to study it, is very difficult to observe or to obtain reliable information about. There are, of course, practical, methodological and ethical difficulties in applying "participant observation" as a technique for investigating sexually intimate conduct (Devereux 1967). But even if one could guarantee the complete candor and perfect recall[9] of one's culturally participant informants, there arises the separate problem of representativeness. Virtually every scholar of the subject has remarked on the extreme intrasocietal variability in sexual behavior. In a comment written on the occasion of Kinsey's death, the biologist J. B. S. Haldane remarked that Kinsey's

> most striking result was his complete confirmation of those who believe in the extreme diversity of human beings. [Kinsey] studied a number of healthy and fertile marriages between people of the same age, and found enormous variation in the frequency of sexual activity. It was as if some people ate thirty times as much or slept thirty times as long as others. (Quoted in Christenson 1971:229; see also Tiger 1992:124)

Kinsey, whose faith in sampling procedures dated from his early days as an insect taxonomist,[10] had set out to collect 100,000 sexual case histories. But if the achieved number of 18,500 was insufficient, surely five times that number would not have been enough, either! Leaving aside the somewhat separate issue of "deviance," what becomes of the very concept of representativeness when, even granting that respondents are telling the truth about their own practices, no two persons are alike? "So far from the facts of normal sex development, sex emotions, and sex needs being uniform and constant," observed Havelock Ellis, "the range of variation within fairly normal limits is immense, and it is impossible to meet with two individuals whose records are nearly identical" (quoted in Brecher 1969:39).

Given the possibility of such variation elsewhere, not to mention the privacy that conventionally enshrouds sexual intimacy in nearly every society known (Ford and Beach 1951:68, 83; see below), and the complex reticence often felt by both ethnographers and their subjects in discussing sexually explicit topics, it is little wonder that ethnographers have tended to approach this subject obliquely, drawing conclusions about sexual behavior from normative statements or from a generalized sense of male-female relationships in the society. There are distinct hazards, however, in assuming such a concordance between ideology and behavior, especially when the latter is so private that no one can be certain of what anyone else does (Suggs 1966:178). Let me give an example.

Among the Ilahita Arapesh of the East Sepik Province, Papua New Guinea, certain precautions are taken to protect men from the ritually polluting effects of menstrual blood. It would be a mistake to infer, however, that men are excessively averse either to this substance or, more generally, to the female genitalia.[11] In this connection I once mentioned in print (Tuzin 1982:329) that cunnilingus is a form of behavior practiced among these people. In the aftermath, several Melanesianist colleagues independently expressed wonderment at this detail. Although all but one admitted never having asked an informant whether he had ever done such a thing, or ever had it done to her, they were adamant that such behavior would be unthinkable in the society they studied, because of its flagrant inconsistency with cultural ideas concerning the risks to men associated with feminine contact.

Subsequently, upon returning to the field, I pursued the matter further and discovered that the situation was more complicated than I had originally thought. Among those with whom I spoke, three men in their early forties readily admitted to the practice. One of them, moreover, was certain that it occurred widely in Papua New Guinea, judging from the many conversations he had had in the barracks of coastal and island plantations.[12] A village official in the recently established Christian church refused to admit or deny oral sex on his own part, but did recall having heard private confessions from converts who had come forward in the belief that the Bible condemned cunnilingus as a sin. Another man, aged forty-one, a non-Christian, sharply denied ever having done it; although conceding that such behavior evidently occurs nowadays, he not only rejected the idea that previous generations might have engaged in it, he became irritated at me for even voicing this as a possibility. The same question put to a highly astute traditionalist in his sixties yielded the response that some men—himself included—enjoy cunnilingus, and that probably it has always been so.[13]

Here we see the kind of behavioral and attitudinal variation which typifies the findings of sex research in Euroamerican society. But rather than despair over ever arriving at a satisfactory general characterization of sexual behavior in a given society, we should consider the highly interesting fact of the variation itself. Not having studied the issue cross-culturally, Kinsey attributed such variation to the complexity of American society; Ellis, Freud, and Sapir had other interpretations. Doubtless each position has its merits; but the one conditioning factor that no one, to my knowledge, has noticed—perhaps because it is so obvious—is the aforementioned element of privacy. Sexual activity takes place undercover in more ways than one. Ford and Beach (1951:83) note the "widespread human desire for concealment" during copulation, such that, in most societies, "couples normally seek seclusion for sexual intercourse" (p. 68).[14] The fact that, consequently, most people have only the vaguest notion of what others actually think and actually do in this important domain of experience, has a number of sociocultural and psychological implications, one of which is that sexual activities are peculiarly resistant to cultural standardization. Cultural prescriptions and normative expectations, it appears, are not sustainable without some amount of social monitoring—which is precisely lacking when it comes to what consenting adults do together in private.[15] One should therefore hesitate before inferring sexual behavior from seemingly applicable normative constructs, for the degree of "fit" may not be nearly as great as one might suppose—and any such dissonance could entail analytic opportunities in its own right.

Just as the nearly universal privacy of sex entails support for Sapir's anti-relativist contention (argued on other grounds) that culture is not the complete governor of human behavior, and that individuals exercise considerable freedom in the way they choose to express their feelings, so the details of sexual conduct may, on occasion, afford insight into the experiential basis of certain culturally constituted ideas. Let me illustrate this with an example that I have described in greater detail elsewhere (Tuzin 1980:74–77). In Ilahita, male cult initiates in middle to late childhood are taught the technique of ritually hygienic penile blood-letting. Under conditions of orchestrated terror, the boys' penises are slashed, in order to rid their bodies of maternal and other feminine essences which, it is said, would impede their growth into fully masculine maturity. Later, and for the rest of their sexually active lives, adult males periodically administer this operation to themselves, lest the reaccumulated feminine contaminants hinder their magical activities. Men jokingly refer to this as their "menstruation."

Ideas and practices very similar to these are not all that unusual in the ethnographic world, and various interpretations have been applied to them (e.g., Bettelheim 1954; Hogbin 1970). One aspect, however, did not previously appear in the literature; and, for me at least, its recognition depended crucially on witnessing the operation. This was the unmistakably autoerotic element in the observed behavior. The operation consists of the man jabbing with a razor blade and boring with barbed vegetal catheters to extract a maximum flow of blood from the glans penis and urethra, respectively.[16] For this to be achieved, the penis must be stiff and engorged with blood, a state induced by masturbation (Hogbin 1970:88). Imagining that most men would quickly wilt under such punishment, I afterward asked the man how he had managed to sustain an erection all during the procedure.

> "By thinking about things," he said. What sorts of things? "Things that I do when I am with a woman," he replied, thus affirming that erotic fantasy is the means by which the penis is maintained at the state of engorgement necessary

for effective "cleansing." He then went on to recommend, with a sly smile, that I try it myself: "I know it must look very painful to you, and it is true that the shock of the first stem makes your insides quiver. But after that the feeling is almost pleasurable, and you definitely feel better for having done it!" (Tuzin 1980:76)

It need hardly be said that this practice of ritually hygienic penis cutting is deeply situated amongst, and prompted by, antecedent cultural understandings and prescriptions. A man does this, because this is what he was taught to do; furthermore, in his world (though not in mine) it is a reasonable thing to do. For Hogbin, who discusses a similar "cleansing" custom among the Wogeo, the presence of a motivating belief is sufficient in itself to make a tonic of the act of hacking at one's glans with a crab claw. Hogbin writes (1970:91),

> The salutary effects of penile surgery are said to be immediately observable. The man's body loses its tiredness, his muscles harden, his step quickens, his eyes grow bright, and his skin and hair develop a luster. He therefore feels lighthearted, strong, and confident.

Culture, in other words, is seen to absorb responsibility for this form of self-abuse, such that we regard neither the man as insane nor the act as a symptom of psychopathology (see Cohen, this volume, for a related issue). Culture, it appears, causes people to do strange things.

The limitation of this line of argument is that it omits consideration of the masturbatory component of the operation—previously unsuspected from verbal descriptions—and the related fact that the perpetrator, remarkably enough, takes *pleasure* in the act.[17] At some point during maturation, probably soon after the onset of sexual relations with women, a moment or process of cultural cathexis occurs, whereby the psychological significance of penile incision is transformed from being an unmitigated horror into being something subjectively positive. No longer a terrified youth suffering this as an ordeal of pain, blood, and seemingly imminent castration, the man now calmly does this to himself on a regular basis. For him, penis cutting has a tonic effect, largely because it is a reassurance of his masculine power to control, dominate, and expel agents which, owing to their feminine source, are weakening and debilitating. Importantly, this effect occurs not only because cultural understandings dictate that it should; by virtue of its independent erotic component the experience verifies and by so doing naturalizes the culturally constituted idea that penis cutting is, indeed, an effective means for ridding the body of noxious, specifically feminine, substances.[18] For,

> If the climactic release of blood is emotionally equivalent to ejaculation, and if the thoughts leading up to this are fixed on erotic feminine images, then the postclimactic drop in intensity (and the corresponding sense of well-being) would be associated with the rapid dissipation of those images—discharged, by implication, with the blood itself. (Tuzin 1980:76)

We are dealing, then, with a situation in which culturally constituted ideas interact with psychobiological proclivities to produce an irreducible experience, which, being pleasurable, motivates the actor to repeat the operation in the future—and naively to recommend it to his culturally alien friend. To assume that such operations occur and are efficacious merely because they are part of a local cultural tradition, is no better than saying "clouds cause rain." By omitting the mechanism, both statements fail to account for how clouds and cultures precipitate themselves in experience, just as they ignore the feedback processes whereby clouds and cultures are continually derived. Viewing the matter in these dynamic terms, while it is true that culture causes people to do strange things, it is equally true that people cause culture to sustain strange ideas.

IV

The preceding case illustrates how culture, far from having the autonomous locus assigned to it by leading anthropological theorists of the early twentieth century,[19] may in some situations be dependent on, and indeed shaped by, behavioral phenomena of a quite different order—even as those phenomena would not normally occur in the absence of culture. Sex may be unusually potent in this regard, by virtue of its psychobiological components and attendant resistance to ego control and, as I have suggested here, cultural governance. But rather than lapse, yet again, into fruitless debate over causal priorities, based (as it usually is) on the philosophically archaic separation of mind and body, let us focus on the excluded middle, the space in which cultural discourse and biological act meet—in this case, the zone of sexual pleasure—which is surely the domain standing in greatest need of conceptual refinement (Abramson & Pinkerton 1995).

Although my topic has been sex, these same theoretical considerations would apply to virtually any situation in which culturally-derived, therapeutic ministrations are performed on the human body. Placebo effects are merely the most obvious example; increasingly, medical science is finding instances in which disease states are significantly correlated with emotional and cognitive conditions—as, for example, in the relationship between depression and certain forms of cancer (Black 1969). Even as the validity of mind-body dualism erodes in the tide of such evidence, so the need for an interactive paradigm grows all the more insistent.

In conclusion, human sexuality is a surpassingly complex subject, from which theoretical anthropology has abstained for most of the last sixty years. If it is to be significant and lasting, if it is to contribute its full measure to the general understanding of human behavior, the rediscovery of sex must also include a rediscovery of theoretical possibilities which were glimpsed only to be forgotten, in those days when anthropology was young and innocent and not so enthralled by its own abstractions.

Notes

Portions of this chapter first appeared in 1991 in *Social Science and Medicine* (33[8]:867–74), under the title, "Sex, Culture and the Anthropologist." I am grateful to that journal and its editor-in-chief, Peter J. M. McEwan, for permission to reproduce those portions. For their criticisms of earlier versions of this chapter, some of which were not heeded, I am grateful to A. L. Epstein, Faye Ginsberg, Fitz John Poole, Gayle Rubin, Michele Stephen, and Marc J. Swartz.

1. Although *Homo sapiens* has no serious contender when it comes to the exosomatic elaboration of sexual pleasure, behavior of an apparently precursory sort has been observed in other species. Most striking in this regard are Frans de Waal's findings (this volume), which indicate remarkable virtuosity among bonobos in attaining sexual pleasures and in using sexual favors in a calculating manner to manipulate social relationships. For evidence of nonreproductive sexual behavior in a wide variety of nonhuman species, including lizards, see Weinrich (1987).

2. *The San Diego Union-Tribune,* April 27, 1993, reports that in San Antonio, Texas, girls fourteen and fifteen years old are having unprotected sex with known HIV-infected partners, in order to show how "tough" and worthy of gang membership they are. Hammar's study (n.d.) of prostitution and seemingly uncontrolled, disease-ridden sex in Daru, a provincial capital in Papua New Guinea, is startling in its display of self-destructive behavior.

3. For a collection of essays which encompasses the "state of the art" of sex studies at that time, see Calverton and Schmalhausen (1929). For an excellent study of the influences operating on Malinowski during the 1920s, and of how he came to "desexualize" the sexual problem, see Lyons and Lyons (1986).

4. An extreme case was the obloquy directed at Alfred Kinsey by numerous religious and citizens' groups, including the United States Congress. Christenson (1971:159–67) reviews the events leading up to the termination, in 1954, of Kinsey's funding from the Rockefeller Foundation, as channeled through the National Research Council.

Doubts concerning Kinsey's character, motives, and methodology are surfacing again, this time from neoconservative critics of modernist morality. In his chapter, "The Case against Kinsey," Jones (1993) portrays the Indiana sexologist as one whose science was corrupted by his desire to justify a perverse, possibly criminal (p. 111), fascination with pedophilia, homosexuality, and other forms of "sexual misbehavior." Calling Kinsey "America's original dirty old man," "a charlatan and a fraud," the conservative commentator Patrick J. Buchanan (1993) applauds Jones's exposé, using it to blast current attempts by The North American Man Boy Love Association to bring about the repeal of laws that forbid men to have sex with children (see note 10, below).

Kinsey's guilt or innocence aside, I suspect that these critics—like their liberal counterparts—would condemn *any* study of sexual behavior that did not uphold, at least by implication, the morality they espouse. Ever since the days of Havelock Ellis and Sigmund Freud, conservative critics have repeatedly held that knowledge of sexual alternatives is *inherently* subversive of public morality; that the only sex *worth knowing about* is that which occurs within wedlock and for reproductive purposes. Like Mencken, but usually with none of his mirthfulness and wit, such critics are saying—openly or in effect—that sex should remain a mystery.

5. Abramson and Mosher (1979) provide rare empirical data on this issue. Their experiments on the masturbation fantasies of UCLA undergraduate subjects reveal systematic differences between male and female respondents. For example, males tend to imagine scenarios and partners unprecedented in their experience, whereas the female fantasies tend to invoke remembered erotic encounters. A cross-cultural test of these findings would be worthwhile, to determine whether the observed differences are specific to American gender constructs or are indicative of generic sex differences.

6. This alternative resembles, outwardly if not by intention, the treatment of sexuality in publications of the Victorian era (Tuzin 1994). In an amusing passage, Malinowski (1948 [1932]:xxxii) tweaks his forebears and contemporaries for their reticence over the details of sexual behavior. Commenting on how anthropologists of the earlier period engaged in "an apparently innocent, theoretical pastime: speculations about the 'origins of marriage'," Malinowski observes that,

> One school, and a very powerful school, believes in group marriage, that is, in a state when individual marriage was unknown and instead of that human beings were sexually united into group marriage—something very immoral, terribly prurient, in fact, so unthinkable that it has never been clearly defined! Can you imagine Morgan, the respectable Puritan of New England, entering into the details of his own famous hypothesis, "group marriage," explaining how it really took place? . . . This was, perhaps, excusable, certainly comprehensible, in a man of his moral outlook and with a lack of sociological training. . . . What is really shocking to the modern sociologist is that not one of his numerous followers ever exercised his creative imagination sufficiently to give us a clear vision and definition of those imaginary modes of human mating.

7. See Lyons (1981) for a discussion of the moral dilemma which anthropology attempted to avoid by desexualizing its interpretation of ritually conducted genital mutilation, in particular, clitoridectomy and infibulation—operations usually designed to obliterate a woman's capacity and appetite for sexual pleasure. See Walker (1992) for a novelistic treatment of this subject, one which dramatizes the clash between universalist morality and cultural relativism.

8. In addition to the fate of Malinowskian functionalism, these reasons involve, *inter alia,* the rapid eclipse of scholarship in the styles of James G. Frazer and E. B. Tylor, the discrediting of evolutionism and diffusionism as adequate anthropological paradigms, and the problematic relationship between anthropology and psychoanalysis in Great Britain during this period (Birth, n.d.). As in the American case, this is a large topic. For relevant historical studies of British social anthropology, see Stocking (1984, 1986) and Langham (1981). For an account of leading figures in the British psychoanalytic movement, beginning in the teens of this century, see Hughes (1989).

9. See Berk, Abramson, and Okami (this volume) for a graphic illustration of mem-

ory distortions—some of them, interestingly, gender-inflected—which can vitiate studies dependent on informants' recall of sexual events, even in the very recent past.

10. As an entomologist, Kinsey's research passion had been the gall wasp, of which he personally collected between two and four million specimens over a twenty-year period. During a flight of what might be called entomania, Kinsey "examined and classified 150,000 specimens while preparing a single paper on a single aspect of their structure" (Brecher 1969:111). In judging that a "less likely preparation for sex research can hardly be imagined," Brecher (ibid.) was perhaps unaware that the gall wasp is one of the few creatures in the entire animal kingdom capable of reproducing parthenogenically! The younger Kinsey, it seems, like the younger Havelock Ellis (Grosskurth 1980), was sexually repressed to an unusual degree, and the caption under his picture in the high-school yearbook was the passage from Hamlet: "Man delights not me; no, nor woman neither" (Christenson 1971:19). To say the least, the motives of Kinsey the bug-and-sex scientist were complex and overdetermined.

11. The author conducted twenty-one months' fieldwork during the period 1969–72, funded by the Australian National University and the Wenner-Gren Foundation for Anthropological Research, and eleven months' fieldwork during 1985–86, funded by the National Science Foundation.

12. Until recently (e.g., Herdt 1981, 1984; Gregor 1985; but see Swartz 1958), oral sex received little treatment in the ethnographic literature. On the basis of HRAF materials, Ford and Beach report that cunnilingus is practiced "predominantly in Oceania" (1951:51), specifically, among the Alorese, Aranda, Kusaians, Marquesans, Ponapeans, and Trukese. Oral stimulation of the penis by the female reportedly occurs among the Aranda, Ponapeans, Trukese, and Wogeo (p. 52). Malinowski writes (1932:400) of the Trobrianders, that fellatio "is probably practised in the intimacy of love making. . . . Receiving my information exclusively from men, I was told that no male would touch the female genitals in this manner, but, at the same time, I was assured that penilinctus was extensively practiced. I do not feel convinced, however, of the truth of this masculine version. The expression, *ikanumwasi kalu momona*, 'lapping up the sexual discharges,' designates both forms of fellatio."

Margaret Mead reports (1940:375) that among the Mountain Arapesh—linguistic cousins of the Ilahita—having a woman's vulva put to his mouth is the "most shameful thing that can happen to a man." The somewhat beclouding context of this comment is a myth in which a group of women punish a rapist by stomping on him, piercing his penis with sago needles, and slapping his face with their aprons; the rape victim herself is the one who puts her vulva to his mouth. It is unclear whether the man's shame is due to the oral-genital contact, per se, or to its having been forcibly thrust upon him— changing him from a manly rapist into an unmanly rape victim. Less violently, an Ilahita woman may mock and shame a man by flashing her vulva at him in public; but this in no way contradicts the friendly, erotic potential of the vulva in other contexts.

13. A similar range of responses was obtained by my wife, Beverly Tuzin, who discussed the matter with married female informants.

14. The same authors report a few exceptions to this global pattern. "In the summertime some Formosan natives copulate out of doors and in public, provided there are no children around. Yapese couples, though generally alone when they engage in inter-

course, copulate almost anywhere out of doors and do not appear to mind the presence of other individuals" (Ford and Beach 1951:68). Such cases, if accurately reported, should be distinguished from instances in which public or quasi-public sex is performed in defiance of values prevalent in the wider society (see Manderson, this volume, for a discussion of public sex shows in Thailand and their sometimes mocking undertones). The latter are not counterexamples to my argument, in that their existence is created in reaction to, and therefore remains dependent on, the broader normative context; see Brecher's review (1969: chap. 9) of research into the sexual freedom movement and the "swinging scene" in the United States. All of this raises, of course, the interesting evolutionary question of why, in human societies, privacy so widely accompanies sexual intimacy. See Stoddart (1990:227, 243) for an interesting treatment of this issue as it pertains to the diminution of olfactory sensitivity in early hominids.

15. This is shown in the futility of criminal laws in the United States which have sought to prohibit certain sexual acts between consenting adults. For example, at its inception in 1872 the Penal Code of the State of California, under section 288a, stated that, "The acts technically known as fellatio and cunnilingus are hereby declared to be felonies and any person convicted of the commission of either thereof shall be punished by imprisonment in the state prison for not more than fifteen years." In 1975, after a decade of open legal debate and more than a century of weak-willed, hopeless efforts at enforcement, the law ceased to apply to such acts committed between free and consenting adults, thus removing the presumed and possibly widespread discrepancy between public words and private deeds.

16. Subsequent interviews confirm that penis-cutting is a fairly standardized procedure, which, as noted, males first acquire under the quasi-public circumstances of ritual initiation. Though a man will retire to a secluded stream bed to perform the operation, penis-bleeding is not a particularly secret activity; rather, it is private in a sense comparable to toilet functions in our own society. In view of its (auto)erotic overtones, it is noteworthy that penis-cutting is the ritual climax of a couple's honeymoon seclusion. On this, the one and only time the operation is performed in the wife's presence, the blood carries a prayer to the ancestral spirits of the stream, that their marriage will be blessed with love and fruitfulness (Tuzin 1980:21).

17. For insights pertaining to the internalization of belief, see Devereux (1980) and Spiro (1982).

18. The autoerotic (and also homoerotic) element of penis-cutting comes through very clearly in a graphic film taken of Ngadadjara (South Australia) subincision rites during Norman B. Tindale's Warburton Range Expedition of 1935 (Reel 7). In vivid contrast to the youthful initiates, who had to be forcibly restrained during their inaugural operation, the senior men reopened their old wounds with evident masturbatory glee, amidst rollicking horseplay with their fellows (Films of the Board for Anthropological Research, University of Adelaide, Adelaide, South Australia).

19. For a more recent version of this general position, see Sahlins (1976).

References

Abramson, Paul R. and Donald L. Mosher. 1979. An Empirical Investigation of Experimentally Induced Masturbatory Fantasies. *Archives of Sexual Behavior* 8(1): 27–39.

Abramson, Paul R. and Steven D. Pinkerton. 1995. *With Pleasure: Thoughts on the Nature of Human Sexuality*. New York: Oxford University Press.

Bettelheim, Bruno. 1954. *Symbolic Wounds: Puberty Rites and the Envious Male*. Glencoe: The Free Press.

Birth, Kevin K. N.d. "British Anthropology and Psychoanalysis: The Emergence of Asserted Irrelevance." Paper. Department of Anthropology, University of California, San Diego.

Black, Stephen. 1969. *Mind and Body*. London: William Kimber.

Brecher, Edward M. 1969. *The Sex Researchers*. Boston: Little, Brown.

Buchanan, Patrick J. 1993. "America's original dirty old man." *San Diego Union-Tribune*, September 8, 1993.

Calverton, V. F. and S. D. Schmalhausen, eds. 1929. *Sex in Civilization*. New York: Macaulay.

Christenson, Cornelia V. 1971. *Kinsey: A Biography*. Bloomington: University of Indiana Press.

Devereux, George. 1967. "The Irrational in Sexual Research." In G. Devereux, *From Anxiety to Method in the Behavioral Sciences*. The Hague: Mouton, pp. 103–20.

Devereux, George. 1980 (orig. 1956). "Normal and Abnormal." In G. Devereux, *Basic Problems in Ethnopsychiatry*. Chicago: University of Chicago Press, pp. 3–71.

Edgerton, Robert B. 1992. *Sick Societies: Challenging the Myth of Primitive Harmony*. New York: The Free Press.

Ellis, Havelock. 1929. "Introduction." In V. F. Calverton and S. D. Schmalhausen, eds., *Sex in Civilization*. New York: Macaulay, pp. 15–28.

Ellis, Havelock. 1936 (orig. 1896–1928). *Studies in the Psychology of Sex*. 2 volumes. New York: Modern Library.

Firth, Raymond. 1981. "Bronislaw Malinowski." In S. Silverman, ed., *Totems and Teachers: Perspectives on the History of Anthropology*. New York: Columbia University Press, pp. 100–139.

Ford, Clellan S. and Frank A. Beach. 1951. *Patterns of Sexual Behavior*. New York: Harper and Brothers.

Freeman, Derek. 1983. *Margaret Mead and Samoa: The Making and Unmaking of an Anthropological Myth*. Cambridge: Harvard University Press.

Goldenweiser, Alexander. 1929. "Sex and Primitive Society." In V. F. Calverton and S. D. Schmalhausen, eds., *Sex in Civilization*. New York: Macaulay, pp. 53–66.

Gregor, Thomas. 1985. *Anxious Pleasures: The Sexual Lives of an Amazonian People*. Chicago: University of Chicago Press.

Grosskurth, Phyllis. 1980. *Havelock Ellis: A Biography*. New York: Alfred A. Knopf.

Hammar, Lawrence. N.d. "The Three Crises on Daru: sexual exchange, ethnographer shame, and anthropological accountability." Manuscript.

Handler, Richard. 1986. "Vigorous Male and Aspiring Female: Poetry, Personality, and Culture in Edward Sapir and Ruth Benedict." In G. W. Stocking, Jr., ed., *Malinowski, Rivers, Benedict and Others: Essays on Culture and Personality*. Madison: University of Wisconsin Press, pp. 127–55.

Herdt, Gilbert H. 1981. *Guardians of the Flutes: Idioms of Masculinity*. New York: McGraw-Hill.

Herdt, Gilbert H., ed. 1984. *Ritualized Homosexuality in Melanesia*. Berkeley: University of California Press.

Herdt, Gilbert H. and Shirley Lindenbaum, eds. 1992. *The Time of AIDS.* Newbury Park, Calif.: Sage.

Hogbin, Ian. 1970. *The Island of Menstruating Men: Religion in Wogeo, New Guinea.* Scranton: Chandler.

Hughes, Judith M. 1989. *Reshaping the Psychoanalytic Domain: The Work of Melanie Klein, W. R. D. Fairbairn, and D. W. Winnicott.* Berkeley: University of California Press.

Jones, E. Michael. 1993. *Degenerate Moderns: Modernity as Rationalized Sexual Misbehavior.* San Francisco: Ignatius Press.

Kaberry, Phyllis M. 1957. "Malinowski's Contribution to Fieldwork Methods and the Writing of Ethnography." In R. Firth, ed., *Man and Culture: An Evaluation of the Work of Bronislaw Malinowski.* New York: Harper and Row, pp. 71–91.

Kinsey, Alfred C., Wardell B. Pomeroy, and Clyde E. Martin. 1948. *Sexual Behavior in the Human Male.* Philadelphia: W. B. Saunders.

Kinsey, Alfred C., Wardell B. Pomeroy, Clyde E. Martin, and Paul H. Gebhard. 1953. *Sexual Behavior in the Human Female.* Philadelphia: W. B. Saunders.

Kroeber, Alfred L. 1915. "Eighteen Professions." *American Anthropologist* 17(2): 283–88.

Kroeber, Alfred L. 1917. "The Superorganic." *American Anthropologist* 19(2): 163–213.

Langham, Ian. 1981. *The Building of British Social Anthropology: W. H. R. Rivers and His Cambridge Disciples in the Development of Kinship Studies, 1898–1931.* Dordrecht: D. Reidel.

Lindenbaum, Shirley, ed. 1991. "Anthropology Rediscovers Sex." *Social Science and Medicine* 33(8):865–907.

Lyons, Harriet. 1981. "Anthropologists, Moralities, and Relativities: The Problem of Genital Mutilations." *The Canadian Review of Sociology and Anthropology* 18(4):499–518.

Lyons, Andrew P. and Harriet D. Lyons. 1986. "Savage Sexuality and Secular Morality: Malinowski, Ellis, Russell." *Canadian Journal of Anthropology* 5(1):51–64.

Malinowski, Bronislaw. 1932 (orig. 1929). *The Sexual Life of Savages of North-Western Melanesia.* 3d edition. London: Routledge & Kegan Paul.

Malinowski, Bronislaw. 1948 (orig. 1932). "Foreword." In A. I. Richards, *Hunger and Work in a Savage Tribe: A Functional Study of Nutrition among the Southern Bantu* Glencoe: The Free Press, pp. ix–xvi.

Malinowski, Bronislaw. 1967. *A Diary in the Strict Sense of the Term.* London: Routledge & Kegan Paul.

McDougall, William. 1929. "Should All Taboos Be Abolished?" In V. F. Calverton and S. D. Schmalhausen, eds., *Sex in Civilization.* New York: Macaulay, pp. 82–96.

Mead, Margaret. 1928. *Coming of Age in Samoa.* New York: William Morrow.

Mead, Margaret. 1935. *Sex and Temperament in Three Primitive Societies.* New York: William Morrow.

Mead, Margaret. 1940. "The Mountain Arapesh: II. Supernaturalism." *Anthropological Papers of the American Museum of Natural History* 37, part 3, pp. 317–451.

Mencken, H. L. 1919. *Prejudices: First Series.* New York: Alfred A. Knopf.

Richards, Audrey I. 1957. "The Concept of Culture in Malinowski's Work." In R. Firth, ed., *Man and Culture: An Evaluation of the Work of Bronislaw Malinowski.* New York: Harper & Row, pp. 15–31.

Sahlins, Marshall. 1976. *Culture and Practical Reason.* Chicago: University of Chicago Press.

Sapir, Edward. 1917. "Do We Need a 'Superorganic' "? *American Anthropologist* 19(3): 441–47.

Sapir, Edward. 1924. "Culture, Genuine and Spurious." *American Journal of Sociology* 29:401–429.

Schmalhausen, Samuel D. 1929. "The Sexual Revolution." In V. F. Calverton and S. D. Schmalhausen, eds., *Sex in Civilization.* New York: Macaulay, pp. 349–436.

Spiro, Melford E. 1982. "Collective Representations and Mental Representations in Religious Symbol Systems." In J. Macquet, ed., *On Symbols in Anthropology: Essays in Honor of Harry Hoijer.* Malibu: Udena Publications, pp. 45–72.

Stocking, George W., Jr. 1984. "Radcliffe-Brown and British Social Anthropology." In G. W. Stocking, Jr., ed., *Functionalism Historicized: Essays on British Social Anthropology.* Madison: University of Wisconsin Press, pp. 131–91.

Stocking, George W., Jr. 1986. "Anthropology and the Science of the Irrational: Malinowski's Encounter with Freudian Psychoanalysis." In G. W. Stocking, Jr., ed., *Malinowski, Rivers, Benedict and Others.* Madison: University of Wisconsin Press, pp. 13–49.

Stoddart, D. Michael. 1990. *The Scented Ape: The Biology and Culture of Human Odour.* Cambridge: Cambridge University Press.

Suggs, Robert C. 1966. *Marquesan Sexual Behavior.* New York: Harcourt, Brace & World.

Swartz, Marc J. 1958. "Sexuality and Aggression on Romonum, Truk." *American Anthropologist* 60(3): 467–86.

Tiger, Lionel. 1992. *The Pursuit of Pleasure.* Boston: Little, Brown.

Tuzin, Donald. 1980. *The Voice of the Tambaran: Truth and Illusion in Ilahita Arapesh Religion.* Berkeley: University of California Press.

Tuzin, Donald. 1982. "Ritual Violence among the Ilahita Arapesh: The Dynamics of Moral and Religious Uncertainty." In G. H. Herdt, ed., *Rituals of Manhood: Male Initiation in Papua New Guinea.* Berkeley: University of California Press, pp. 321–55.

Tuzin, Donald. 1984. "Miraculous Voices: The Auditory Experience of Numinous Objects." *Current Anthropology* 25(5):579–89, 593–96.

Tuzin, Donald. 1994. "The Forgotten Passion: Sexuality and Anthropology in the Ages of Victoria and Bronislaw." *Journal of the History of the Behavioral Sciences* 30(2):112–35.

Walker, Alice. 1992. *Possessing the Secret of Joy: A Novel.* New York: Harcourt Brace Jovanovich.

Wayne (Malinowska), Helena. 1984. "Bronislaw Malinowski: The Influence of Various Women on His Life and Works. *Journal of the Anthropological Society of Oxford* 15(3):189–203.

Weinrich, James D. 1987. *Sexual Landscapes: Why We Are What We Are, Why We Love Whom We Love.* New York: Scribners.

CHAPTER THIRTEEN

The Pleasures of Castration: The Postoperative Status of Hijras, Jankhas and Academics

LAWRENCE COHEN

Introduction

This essay contrasts three groups who represent and reenact a castration. Two of the groups are in the city of Varanasi, in north India, and the third is more globally situated:

1. *Hijras* may undergo castration and penectomy—often while possessed by a goddess—in becoming what they and others term a third sex or third gender, "neither man nor woman," to use the expression cited by the anthropologist Serena Nanda (1990). A minority of *hijras* are congenitally third. The analgesic trance of the operation is but one strand of the dense relationship between *hijras* and their powerful goddess; through her, *hijras* bring fertility when they dance for gifts at births and weddings. *Hijras* are organized into households with a *hijra* guru as head, into territories delimiting where each household can dance and demand money from merchants, and into larger regional and supraregional associations or *pancayats* linking them to other cities across South Asia. Nanda's work on Indian *hijras*, challenging decades of sensationalist description by non-*hijras* through her close attention to *hijra* narratives, inaugurated a flood of sympathetic dissertations, documentaries, news reports, and other professional writing. *Hijras* became canonical inclusions in representations of international gay and lesbian studies (Abelove, Barale, and Halperin 1993) and in discussions of an increasingly global category of "third gender" (Herdt, 1994).

2. *Jankhas* are men who sometimes dress like women and dance like *hijras* but who do not elect castration. They are more frequently called *zenanas* in literature on *hijras;* by any name, they have not been appropriated into a metropolitan canon as have *hijras*. *Jankha* itself is a term denoting effeminancy, applied to these men by other men in their neighborhood. *Jankhas* occasionally use *jankha* or *zenana* but far more often just speak of themselves as part of a group of girlfriends, or *sahelis*. Harriet Ronken Lynton and Mohini Rajan (1987) mention a group of *zenanas* in the south central Indian city of Hyderabad; the authors speak only with *hijras,* who discuss their dislike of *zenanas* for trying to pass themselves off as *hijras* and stealing business. Nanda in her work reports a similar divide between the two groups, but documents occa-

sional alliances between some *zenanas* and the more marginal of *hijras*. But much of how *jankhas* in Varanasi live and perform and experience gender is not mimetic of *hijras*. Their training in dance and gender performance is tied to a tradition of urban low-caste burlesque performance.

3. *Academics* are persons of various genders who sometimes utilize conceptions of third gender as metaphors in social theory. But though third gender is good to think with, its theorization is often exquisitely insensitive to the bodies with which it plays. Much is at stake: some metropolitan academics have earned part of their living as gatekeepers, using their cultural capital as sex experts to decide the fate of others who would surgically transform their bodies. On the world's peripheries, much else may be at stake.

This essay is concerned with newer, more subtle forms of gatekeeping. It is about what it means to make sexual difference matter—through various surgical, sartorial, or discursive tactics—in terms of other forms of social difference: class-based, caste-based, metropolitan, and patriarchal. Following *hijra* practice, it re/members castration as a bloody act and takes the violence as central to these representations of thirdness.

Castrations are routinized as enactments of signification and of culture itself in both 1950s Culture and Personality anthropology and in contemporary psychoanalytic cultural criticism; they become signs displaced from the possibility of the act in itself. Castrations and castrati are discovered everywhere, and particularly in social settings characterized by extreme political domination and marginality. Thus a repeated metaphor in colonial and postcolonial literature on the Indian subject, by definition male, is of a castration resulting in the loss of true manhood, the latter measured against some projection of "Western" masculinity. This metaphor was naturalized by such Culture and Personality anthropologists as G. M. Carstairs (1957) and such clinical psychoanalysts as Sudhir Kakar (1978). Both these authors construct developmental schemas of culturally located psychopathology (mother too close, father too distant) to explain why the Indian (male) subject *desires* his political domination.

Though the heyday of these sorts of exegeses has passed, Ashis Nandy in *The Intimate Enemy: Loss and recovery of self under colonialism* (1983) argues that Indian (still male) subjects remain interpellated within an emasculating and now internalized colonialism. Nandy's solution is to disengage the violence of this internalized castration not by inverting it (thus the martial hypermen which now circulate through the iconography of the Hindu right in India) but by renegotiating it with a different and more empowering form of androgyne, a Gandhian figure who eschews the violence. As in *hijra* discussions of *zenana* identity, two figures circulate in Nandy's argument, one false (the colonial eunuch) and the other authentic (the Gandhian androgyne). All thirdness is not alike.

This point cannot be overemphasized. There is more at stake in castration than the maneuver of writing, dislocating, and rewriting the phallic signifier. As I began composing this essay, a disturbing account appeared in the Indian media of the forcible castration of Bishambar, a poor, low-caste man jailed for falling asleep by the roadside on a bed that was owned by a wealthy upper-caste man. Bishambar was beaten by the police and tied down; a bribe was solicited from his family. When it did not appear, he was tortured and eventually castrated. The case was leaked to the press and became a *cause célèbre*. The police contended Bishambar castrated himself (with a rusty blade he found in a garbage heap) to avoid arrest for theft (Tejpal 1992).

Against the circulation of castration and third gender as scholarly markers of both the violence and pleasure of signification, I want to locate the materiality of gender within what is differentially at stake for people. The other text I take up in juxtaposition to that of Nandy's, Marjorie Garber's *Vested Interests: Cross-dressing and cultural anxiety* (1992) offers a celebration of the possibilities of gender performativity. A disembodied notion of gendered liminality suffuses the text, linking very different sorts of bodies and ignoring questions of violence and authenticity critical to both *hijra* and postcolonial projects. By playing on the *hijra* claim that there exist both real and spurious projects of materializing gender, I would like to trouble the project of privileging gender fluidity that I read in Garber's book and hear reenacted in diverse academic fora.

There is of course a danger in writing against fluidity and appropriating a category of inauthenticity. Against the *hijra* critique of spurious gender, the narratives of *jankhas* challenge their being relegated to any position of spuriousness and their being represented as in any way exploitative. *Jankha* identity not only challenges any quick reading of India as having a three-gendered "system," it pushes us to avoid enlisting groups like *hijras* or *jankhas* in grand touristics of gender difference without challenging what is at stake for each in gender. That my own text here is implicated in the sort of writing which worries me is inevitable.

Two prefatory remarks, on terminology and location.

Terminology. I collapse the terms sex and gender here, for two reasons. First, in listening to and representing the stories of Banarsi[1] *hijras* and *jankhas,* I am confronted with narrative and language which resists any a priori divisibility into embodied sex and expressive gender. Second, I follow the concern articulated by Judith Butler in *Gender Trouble* (1990), who suggests that the move to denaturalize much of sexual difference through the creation of a category of socially and individually constructed gender difference is less liberating than it initially appears to be. By splitting biological sex from socially constructed gender, it maintains and paradoxically legitimates a residual category of indubitable and unambiguous biological difference. A critical analysis which would refuse to take the biological for granted—which would leave no intractable point beyond critique, in Butler's phrase—must in its practice resist the easy possibility of any such naturalized realm. In this reading of Butler I am not suggesting the impossibility of a biology or of the differences which constitute it. I suggest, rather, that as such differences can only be made to matter through languages, narratives, and contexts which are inextricably social, critical engagement with these representations must at every point interrogate the obvious.

Not only are the bodily facts of sex thoroughly social, however; all social constructions of sex, as they are articulated by embodied actors, are rooted in the body's corporeality (Merleau-Ponty 1962; Csordas 1990). Any theory of gender which is not rooted in this corporeality of lived experience must misrepresent it. Neither "the social" nor "the bodily" can be maintained as an independent analytic realm without a close examination of their rootedness in one another.[2]

Location. The ethnographic part of this essay comes from work in Varanasi, a city and metropolitan area of about one million people in the north Indian state of Uttar Pradesh, conducted informally while engaged in other formal research from 1988 to 1990, and formally in 1993. Much has been written on Varanasi in the past few decades, including some work on the body, gender, and gender ambiguity (Searle-Chatterjee 1981; Prasad 1987; Kumar 1988; Parry 1989; Alter 1992). This research is based in four neighborhoods in the south and west of the city, primarily in Asi but also in Sigra, Karaundi, and Nagwa.

Two dangers still lurk in a short essay on *hijras:* (1) To frame a discussion of sex and sexual difference in South Asia in terms of *hijras* works to maintain an exoticizing gaze. *Hijras*—like *sati,* sacred cows, fakirs on beds of nails, and "the caste system"—become essentialized icons of India. The *hijra* as sign of essential Indianness affirms the colonial splitting of Indian male sexuality into the despotic hypersexual pederasty and unresistant homosexual or eunuch penetrability that Nandy addresses. Thus *hijras* literally embody Carstairs's diagnosis of Indian male psychopathology (boys who lack the psychic resources to challenge too-distant fathers and who retreat into lifelong oedipal deferral) by deferring phallic privilege forever. (2) *Hijras* often stand for "the Indian homosexual" in compendia of cross-cultural sex. The relationship between *hijra* desire and male same-sex desire is complex; writing about *hijras* without locating them within such contexts further routinizes and disembodies the specificity of their sexual difference. To illustrate the problem of location, I construct a vignette expanded from field notes. The vignette also helps locate myself and a few of my own various projects and artifices in relation to what follows. I have maintained the narrative flow of the notes at the risk of derailing the project slightly.

Idyll: the Varanasi park hustle as told by men like this

Three of us are walking through Maidagin Park at night, eight-thirty or thereabouts. It was once called Company Bagh, after an earlier regime, and it still sits across from the Varanasi Town Hall and other places of authority here.

The police make periodic sweeps through the park, harassing and blackmailing loitering men, but they usually come later in the evening and right now the park feels safe, expansive. My friend Pramod is on my right, and to his right is his friend Guddu, with whom we've just hooked up.

Maidagin's my favorite of the three large city parks; it surrounds a big square tank filled with slightly algae-clotted water, and at night cool breezes blow across the tank and onto the lawns and winding paths where people stroll or sit on the grass or benches. All sorts of people, during the day: athletes from a wrestling *akhara* who each morning work out in the mud by the muscled image of Lord Hanuman; a few families; boys playing games or practicing martial arts; men playing cards, chewing *paan* betel or intoxicating *bhang,* or snoozing; women and men crossing the park on the way to and from errands and work; the gardeners and their assistants; and groups of old men, talking or sitting. In the evenings Maidagin is less crowded: the old men are still there, some of them, and the sleepers. But the men who come in the evenings to wander—the Hindi verb, *ghumna,* is more expressive of the pleasures of going nowhere with friends—are *aisa* or *aise,* "like this," "like that," or "like these," and they come to cruise for sex or for other pleasures and to talk with *aise* others.[3]

In Hindi-speaking places like Maidagin Park, many strolling men who like to have sex with men identify friends and prospective friends through the language of similitude—*aise* and *jaise,* like this, like these, this way—and shared play (being *khel main,* in the game). The language of *aise* and *khel* is not a label or a fixing of essential identity in the different but parallel ways the utterance of *khush* or *hijra* often demand. The "these" of *aise*'s "like these" is contingent, reflexive, and dialogic, pointing not to some category or class *out there* but to what is being enacted by the very encounter of speaker and listener together in the park at night. Thus language points inward—being "in the game," identifying the coherence of desires through their being located *in* the park—and is momentary. A confessional imperative—Foucault's "regulated and polymorphous incitement to discourse" (1978)—seems absent. Yet against the lack of a sexual science, in Foucault's sense, *aise* indexes no subterranean and esoteric world of pleasures, no Orientalist vision of the *ars erotica* Foucault presents as historical predecessor and structural Other to sexual science. Neither is *aise*'s obliqueness a political silencing of a love that dares not speak its name. The repressions in Maidagin lie elsewhere.

Guddu agrees that Maidagin is the best park: it has the most men. He breaks into a laugh as he tells us about parks in Calcutta where there are hundreds of men, like this. Pramod has never been to Calcutta, and when I am there it is inevitably in the company of myriad adopted aunties, so we listen in delighted half-belief. Pramod doesn't agree—about Maidagin that is; he prefers the new park in Sigra, surrounded by wealthier residential colonies. There is less trouble from unsavory types in Sigra, he argues, whether *gunda* thugs or swishy *lachak-mathak* Number Sixes.

A young man passes us, tall and well-built, his eyes resting on us summarily, not with the slight pause that usually constitutes the park glance and which signifies the identity of its pleasures as surely as locutions like *aise*. "Who is—" I begin, but Pramod cuts me off. "He's bad, a *gunda* [tough guy]-type, one of the Harischandra college boys. Leave it alone." Harischandra is an inter-college with many village guys who don't get in to more prestigious places; its students have a reputation among men like this for extorting money from them, usually after demanding and engaging in oral sex or a hand job on a darkened bench.

Pramod and I had come to the park that night to do AIDS outreach work; we split up and began canvassing other men. I ran into the *gunda,* and for all the wrong reasons unmindful of my friends' advice, I began to talk with him about AIDS. We walked around the tank talking, but when we reached the far end of the park he pushed me roughly towards a bench. *"Karte ya karwate hain?"* he demanded: Do you or are you done to? It's a frequent park question, along with other similarly paired verbs: *lagne ya lagane?*—stick it or get it stuck in?; *lete ya dete?*—take it or give it away?

It's frequent enough that for many men who *ghum* in the parks of the city, *aise*—the possibility of shared desire—initially refers to the realization of one or the other of these positions, narratively coherent through joking and insulting terms heard since boyhood which suddenly take on new meaning: one is either a *gandu*—one who is done to, up the ass—or a *londebaaz*—one who delights (*baaz*) in doing young men (*londe*). Some men, particularly infrequent park visitors, remain on one side or the other; others go more to extremes, like both the "*gunda*-type" *londebaaz* who had just sat me down and like the Number Sixes I introduce below. But for most men who are, like Pramod and Guddu, *aise,* early park encounters lead to a set of friends characterized less by what they want than by where they are: together, here, in the park, *aise.* Doing and being done to are usually distributed by relative age but renegotiated as the play of a tryst shifts into the longer-range intoxication of *pyar mohabbat* or deep love.

Guddu saw me with the *gunda;* he gave a low whistle of warning. I said to the *gunda:* "Neither," but he grabbed my thigh tightly and demanded money. With Guddu nearby, I felt safer, despite having been roughed up once by Delhi *gunda*-types for refusing to pay up. I refused again, and asked him why he tried to coerce money from men in the park. He said it wasn't coercion, but *quid pro quo:* "I'm from a small village; we don't have much money, but we have good land and air and eat right. So I'm strong. These city boys, these sons of great Seths [a merchant caste] come with their fathers' money but are weak. They take my strength [referring to his semen] and I receive something in exchange."[4] I escaped. I should have listened when earlier Pramod said "leave it." Then the three of us had kept walking, around the circular flower bed in the center of the park and towards the west gate, away from the *gunda.* At the gate, Pramod laughed. "This is where the Number Sixes come in," he said, referring to the other kind of park hustler.

Like *hijra* and *jankha, chah nambar*—number six—and *chakka*—a sixer—
are epithets in north India thrown at effeminate-seeming men, at *jankhas,* and
at *hijras;* they are also used as general insults or joking terms between close
male friends.

We leave Maidagin by the west gate, and grab some tea at one of the shops
which line the periphery of the park before Pramod and I take our leave of
Guddu and flag down a rickshaw. It is late, but along the storefronts of the
Chowk market street men are seated outside drinking tea and hot milk, talking. "There's another Number Six, a *jankha,*" Pramod says, pointing to a
young man swaying his hips and trying to catch some tea-drinker's eye. I mull
over Number Six as we head home toward Asi and home. Pramod leaves me
at the head of my lane; a shadowy figure is seated near my door. "It's your
neighbor," he snorts. "He's dirty. The *jankha.*"

I walk the rest of the way alone. Pramod was right; the figure is indeed
Kamal, my neighbor, whom I've known for several years. He sleeps outside
his family's house in the lane; he is the youngest of several brothers, who are
mostly tailors; he has held several jobs during the time I have known him; he
has been fired from a soap factory and now works on odd tailoring jobs with
his brother and several other tailors; he supplements his meager income, as
before, by cruising street corners in this part of the city, in men's clothes but
with a bend of the waist—*lachak*—and jiggle of the bottom—*mathak;* he
hangs with a group of *sahelis,* who often dance for weddings in saris, somewhat like *hijras.* "They do births; we do weddings," Kamal once said of the
difference between him and the girlfriends on the one hand and *hijras* on
the other.

"Where are you coming from?" he laughs. I evade his question, and tell
him his friend Ram Prasad, whom he sometimes calls Rita, has been both-
ering me, stopping me on busy roads in broad daylight and making passes.
With *sahelis,* Kamal calls himself Kamala. "And what am I called?" I once
pleaded somewhat pathetically, afraid to be out of the loop. "You, you're
called my husband," Kamala returned.

"But I don't want to be your husband."
"Yes, you do, of course you do. And what else could you be?"
"Your friend . . . your *saheli.*"
"You can't be my *saheli,* you're too *siddhe-sada* [straight and regular]. . . ."
I perhaps misread "straight," and responded:
"What do you know? I have a husband in America."
"Oh, that again."
"Why won't you believe me? I do."
"You really want to be a *saheli?*"
"Do I look like I want to be your husband?"
"Well. We'll see. We'll call you Anita. Anita Devi."

Rita, for her part, has never pleaded with *siddhe-sada* types, she seduces
quite brazenly. Kamala laughs again, and says about her: "that's why the *hijras*
don't want to take him. He's very bad." I am surprised: "I didn't know the *hijras*

often refused people." "The *hijras* here have gone away to a *pancayat* meeting where they will discuss whether they have to take him," Kamala confides. "Ram Prasad is always going up to men in Asi crossing and making remarks, offering to eat them; he always wants to play like that. That's not like *hijras*."

Hijras and Jankhas

What is like *hijras,* and who are *jankhas?* A household of three *hijras* lived a few lanes over from Kamal and Ram Prasad's neighborhood, on the edge of an untouchable slum. A fourth *hijra,* Ganga, lived by the slum with her husband, and came by early each morning. The four spent the day "dancing": traveling to the homes of the newborn to dance and sing and to bless them with fertility, looking for more newly born children to visit, and when all else failed making the rounds of merchants in their territory of the city, threatening to pull up their saris and reveal their postoperative genitals, the sight of which is said to make a man impotent, in a sense a *hijra* himself. A fifth *hijra* lived nearby as well, but she lived with her family of birth. Pramod first noticed her when he went up onto his landlord's roof; she lives next door. The other neighbors confirmed quietly that there was indeed a *hijra* on the lane, living with her family, but that she never went out. When I asked Pramod once whether *hijras* ever altered their bodies surgically, he deferred answering but said of this neighbor: "that one was born that way."

The multiple relationships and spaces in which *hijras* may live in one neighborhood suggests the difficulty with an overly essentialized vision of third gender. An acquaintance in Sigra, to the north of Asi, lived near another group of *hijras* and took me to meet Rani, a *hijra* guru there. Rani was out dancing, and I sat with her brother and brother-in-law awaiting her return. "Her" was for me only—for her family, she was *chachaji,* a friendly paternal uncle. Like Arjuna in the *Mahabharata,*[5] Rani was for her family gendered through her role as a famed dance instructor—the fact of her being neither man nor woman was sidelined by their lifelong sense of her as *he,* but a complex dance-teacher sort of he.

Hijras occasionally are born "neither male nor female," or within the more binary possibilities of biomedicine, intersexed. Far more frequently, *hijras* are born as phenotypic males who in adolescence or young adulthood realize that they are essentially neither male nor female and join a community of *hijras;* full adoption of *hijra* identity often involves castration, penectomy, and one's dedication to the service of the goddess. As her vehicles, they bring fertility when they come to dance and collect gifts at births and weddings. Pramod, from a poor petty-bourgeois family, once said to me that as a rule *hijras* are born third, discovered by other *hijras* when they come to see newborn babies and examine their genitals. Middle-class men and women I knew from Varanasi often said *hijras* were never born that way *nor* did they elect an operation, but were kidnapped and sold into a sexual slave trade for which purpose they were castrated and penectomized. Men across class also said *hijras* were impotent men, literally non-men, and that their thirdness was secondary to their inability to please a wife.

The question of who *hijras* are has long sparked controversy. A debate raged in the pages of the *American Anthropologist* in the late fifties between Carstairs (1957, 1960) and Morris Opler (1959, 1960) over the definition. The two agreed that *hijras* were castrated and penectomized men who dressed as women, but differed on almost everything else. Carstairs held they were prostitutes; Opler that they were ritual specialists, devotees of the goddess Bahuchara Mata, who through her conferred blessings on newborn sons and newlywed couples. *Hijras* may be both, and the debate spun around a hermeneutic circle in which the sexual marketplace and auspicious ritual were too cleanly opposed.

Another older but equally circular debate on *hijra* identity framed the essential question as that of religious etiology. In Richard Burton's famous "Terminal Essay" to the *Arabian Nights* (1885), *hijras* were signs of the licentious comradery of the Islamic world, the narrative center of his vision of a Sotadic Zone, a tropical space of blurred gender and sexual relations. In the text attributed to the Abbé Dubois (1899), the early nineteenth-century missionary and ethnographer, *hijras* were signs not of the fluidity of Islam but of the hypocritical propriety of Brahmanic Hinduism, a religion preaching celibacy but tolerating unlimited perversity. In the twentieth century, this etiologic debate has become a set of competing apologetics. The last princely ruler of the south Indian state of Hyderabad banished *hijras* from his court in a move to purify his Islamic regime from regional and Hinduized degenerate culture (Lynton and Rajan 1974). Hindu apologists, including some contemporary Indologists, in contrast see *hijras* as an Islamic importation, reading the gender play of gods and epic heroes and particularly that of Arjuna and Sikhandin as having no connection to the origins of *hijras;* popular narratives, *hijra* and non-*hijra,* which do read divine and epic androgyny in terms of a *hijra* role are seen as contemporary bricolage. In practice, *hijras* are both Hindu and Muslim, sharing joint devotional practice to the goddess as central to their identity as well as having distinct rites of passage within their respective religious communities. The debate on religion disguises a move of erasure.

A third and very current debate on *hijra* origins takes up the question of coercion. A recent article in the *Lancet* (Allahbadia and Shah 1992) documents the existence of (1) the sale (by indigent parents) of their boys, or (2) the kidnapping of boys, and their forcible castration. The authors assume—against overwhelming narrative and ethnographic evidence (Sinha 1967, Lynton and Rajan 1974, Anderson 1977, Preston 1987, Sharma 1989, Nanda 1990)—that most *hijras* are forced into castration and third-gender identity. The sale, most frequently in impoverished rural sites of endemic famine, of boys as well as girls into the sex trade certainly occurs; with the increasing corporatization and dominance by international crime cartels in the control of sectors of the Bombay sex trade it may well be growing, though this has not been documented. But as in the case of popular Indian literature on female prostitutes, stories of selling and kidnapping children disguise other far more common but less palatable reasons for sexual difference: in the case of women, escape, economic necessity, and institutionalized misogyny (Oldenberg 1992), and in the case of *hijras,* desire. *Hijras* themselves often construct a narrative of their abject origins, explicitly for the consumption of nosy outsiders.

Jankhas or *zenanas* are often represented by social scientists as incomplete or preoperative *hijras.* The *hijra* whose experience Lynton and Rajan relate in their history of Hyderabad is beaten as a young boy by his uncle because he did girls' work and dressed in saris; he runs away to the *zenanas* where he hears of the *hijras* and begins to dance with the latter group. The narrative of her move from son to *zenana* to *hijra* offers two readings of the difference between the latter two groups.[6] The first story centers on the presence of the penis and on the transformation of castration:

> When I joined the Hijras I had, just as a man has, everything. So I thought I would live like that with the Hijras, wearing a sari and going to dance, still keeping all that. But there are some women, if they call us to dance, when we dance they also dance. While they are dancing they twirl money over their heads to avert the evil eye and give it to us. So if an elderly woman is there, while we are dancing, suddenly—gup! she puts her hand there to see if one is a true Hijra. . . .
>
> With me it happened like this. . . . I used to go to the villages nearby and ask [for money or other gifts]. Now in every village there are one or two smart alecks who say, "If you are a Hijra, show us." In that village also there was one. So no one in the village would give me a single *paisa* because they said, "What kind of Hijra are you? Get out!". . . .
>
> So I got into a fury . . . I went into the jungle between the two villages and I had a knife with me. . . . (1974: 195–96)

The unnamed *hijra* castrates herself, invoking the goddess to aid her healing, and returns to the same "smart aleck" to reveal her wound dramatically.

In narratives of this sort, the castration is social (proof to the heckling crowd), symbolic (giving up the position of having "just as a man has, everything"), and often physiological. Castration is necessary physically to change internal gender. Through the bleeding, maleness flows out, femaleness flows in; mixture results. Hijras from Baroda explain to Vyas and Shingala that "maximum blood should be poured out of the body during the castration ceremony. . . . the castration ceremony carries away male blood out of the body. And fresh blood . . . is of a female body" (1987:39).

The second reading of the move from *zenana* to *hijra* precedes and encompasses the castration. Lynton and Rajan follow their *hijra* informants and Morris Opler in describing *hijras* as asexual ritualists; *zenanas* are the prostitutes:

Born as males, the Hijras rejected sexual activity of all kinds but indulged their preference for the clothing, the cosmetics, and the domestic activities of women. Without the Hijra community to shelter them, they would have no choice but to become zenanay, practicing homosexuals, who were cast off by their families, despised by society, and used by any male with a taste for pretty boys. But there was a difference, for the zenanay made up their eyes and wiggled their hips when they walked in order to advertise their availability, but the true Hijra was incapable even of desire. With one door after another closed against him, the Hijra turned the violence born of his agony against himself and cut off his external genitalia. (ibid.: 191–92)

The unnamed *hijra* contrasts *zenana* and *hijra* life:

I lived with the zenanay for some time. Having begged, I would return and it would be nighttime and some rough fellow who had been drinking would catch me and pull me about, slap me, show me a dagger or a knife. Then he would take me off and when once or twice I had been spoiled, I said to myself, "Creature, this is no good." . . . Those zenanay people also used to say: "Hijras live there. They do like this; it is like that with them. One has to live respectably with them. If one goes there they close the door like a prison. At nine o'clock the lock falls on the door; nobody can go and come there." (ibid.: 194)

In this reading, *hijra* life is ordered, respectable, asexual, and safe; *zenana* life is chaotic, indulgent, homosexual, and dangerous. Becoming a *hijra* is represented as a move through a liminal phase characterized by homosexual rape into a controlled sexuality where sartorial gender, rather than genital sex, constitutes essential difference. Here castration is a social necessity, the violent performance of *hijra* asexuality, but not a transformative moment—which long precedes castration. According to some of the Asi *hijras* with whom he had hoped to move in, Ram Prasad was unsuitable. His behavior demonstrated he was not like a *hijra*. Others concurred. "He's too forward," said Kamal in retrospect. "He's just a *jankha*," said Pramod.

Zenanas are not only represented as overly and deviantly sexed precursors to *hijras* but as competitors. Nanda underscores the concern with authenticity by the audiences for whom *hijras* and *zenanas* dance, as well as the economic concerns of *hijras* themselves:

These other people, who imitate us, they are real men, with wives and children. They come to join us only for the purpose of making a living. How do we know what a person is when he comes to join us? Just recently there was a case in our group. This man's name was Hari. He was the father of four children and he dressed up as a woman and put on a woman's hairstyle. He behaved like a hijra and danced at people's houses, disguised as a hijra. One day we caught him red-handed. We beat him up bodily and handed him over to the police. It cannot be allowed for someone to take our place as it deprives us of our right and our income. . . . I thought to myself, I am so different from them, like the earth and the sky; these people are men whereas I am neither a man nor a woman. (1990:11–12)

How the *zenana* was caught red-handed is unspecified, but whether his difference was demonstrated through the revelation of a penis or through *zenana*-type rude and oversexed behavior is unimportant. In either case, the revelation leads to an affirmation of the reality of *hijra* gendering: *zenanas* occupy a two-gender system (men "dressed up as a woman") and *hijras* occupy a three-gender system ("neither man nor woman"). Though elsewhere *hijras* may frame themselves within a binary language (we are born boys but act like girls; we castrate ourselves to let the male blood flow out so we can become female), against *zenanas, hijras* articulate themselves here as unambiguously third.[7]

In Varanasi, Kamal and Ram Prasad called each other *saheli,* girlfriend. They called themselves *hijras* sometimes, and at other times differentiated themselves from the *hijras.* Two lanes over from where Kamal and I lived was the household of *hijras* that Ram Prasad had wanted to join. When he was refused admission by the *hijras' panchayat* (council) meeting in another city, the *hijras* did not discuss his case with me. Ram Prasad himself claimed he had changed his mind: "I don't want to be with them; I want a husband." Having a husband did not seem to be a barrier to becoming a *hijra* in Asi; the *hijra* Ganga lived with a husband. But Ram Prasad now identified being a *hijra* with celibacy and, like Kamal, said he wanted a "macho-macho" and *"siddhe-sada"* man, straight and plain and not *chah nambar.* Neither of the two *jankhas* was yet married; neither had plans to get married nor—or so they claimed—were their families pressuring them to do so.

Both men were very poor and low-caste, and had grown up in communities with drama troupes which played drums and performed satiric skits with female ingenue roles often played by *lachak-mathak* young men like themselves. Dressing in saris and dancing was not only a sign of gendered difference but part and parcel of local subsistence. The two men shared a guru, a dancing teacher who had several young men he both trained and directed in performance at weddings and communal celebrations. Both in adolescence had been introduced to sex by other men, and both had become informal sex prostitutes. Ram Prasad's parents had died and he had no siblings in the city; Kamal helped his family with his tailoring work, particularly the wife and children of his eldest brother who was sick. Kamal slept on a neighbor's stone verandah, never in the house with his family.

Both men talked occasionally of joining the *hijras* or called themselves *hijras;* another *saheli,* who no longer hung out with the others in the drama troupe, lived in the Chamar untouchable colony a kilometer south. Birju denied he was either a *hijra* or wanted to become one: "I'm a man." Like Kamal, he had been introduced to *nautak*—drama—by a neighborhood drummer and guru. Pramod and Guddu called him *chah nambar* and *jankha,* but Birju resisted the labels, sometimes playfully and sometimes angrily. He seldom danced, and only turned tricks when forced to, probably by one of the senior police officers at the local station. Youngest son of a poor father in an untouchable slum, Birju had his father's welfare on his mind much of the time. At one point his father had arranged a marriage for him, around the time he had been admitted to an intercollege (two-year preparatory college). College and marriage had fallen through; Birju says there was not enough money for either, particularly after a robbery and the theft of his late mother's jewels.

After the marriage fell through, Birju continued to spend time with his lover, a married tailor with a shop near the slum, and to call himself the tailor's second wife. The tailor's son would tease Birju by calling him "uncle," at which Birju would playfully hit the boy—"what's my name, what's my name?"—until the boy would yell "stepmother, you're my stepmother."

Like Ganga, Birju wants a husband; like her, he refuses to define his desire in the manner of Kamal or Ram Prasad. But he still on occasion talks of getting married not to his tailor but to a woman. Pramod begrudgingly admits Birju is different than some of the other Number Sixes. Kamal knows him, and says that he too is a *saheli.* Birju does not deny being Kamal's *saheli,* but unlike his girlfriend he is adamant about not being a *hijra.*

Ram Prasad and Kamal cruise street corners looking very *lachakmathak* in the evenings, looking for men who will pay them for sex, and in Kamal's case looking for husbands. Other Banarsi men from slightly more well-off petty bourgeois families also play at street corners with glances and *lachakmathak* body movement, but seldom trick *quid pro quo* for cash or gifts. Halfway between the slum and Maidagin is the main crossing of Godolia. Raju is a Bihari villager who came to Varanasi for work five years earlier and got a job selling ladies' clothing at a discount store there, Bombay Sale. When Pramod got a job at Bombay Sale, he and Raju became friends. Pramod would see Raju at another of the city's parks, or sometimes in the evenings at Godolia crossing, acting slightly *lachak* and catching the eye of older men. Raju would joke with his coworkers at the Sale, making coded references to his boyfriends and sex, playing with words like *saheli.* But his friends weren't *sahelis* in the more formal sense that Ram Prasad used the word, living life with girlfriends. Raju played with words, including terms ordinarily far more violent and abusive than Number Six, such as *gandu* (someone who takes it up the ass).

Raju's lovers came and went, usually going with violent consequences: jealous Ashok, who let Raju sleep at his paint shop (his wife and children were at home) as a kept man until he heard false rumors of Raju's infidelity and threw him out; portly Khansahib, who came on sari business monthly from Bombay but liked to get drunk and finally used Raju so brutally that Pramod had to take him to the hospital for stitches; and currently Dasgupta Uncle, who took Raju in as a kept man and stepson in a flat next to his own family's house. Dasgupta was different than the others: "He loves me!" Raju exulted, avoiding the unnecessary question of whether he returned the sentiment. With Dasgupta, Raju was no longer the ubiquitous queen of the crossing; there was hardly a trace of the old *lachakmathak* when he would return to Godolia on errands.

Pankaj was a low-level government bureaucrat who rented a one-bedroom flat near Godolia. He, like Raju, used to meet men at the crossing more often than in the parks; he was more subtly *lachak-mathak* than Raju when he met younger men's gazes in the rush of the evening crowds. "I want poetry," he always lamented. "There's no poetry in this city." Pramod called Pankaj *jankha* and Number Six: "He is impotent, and can only have it done to him. He has secret [venereal] diseases from every man doing him." For Pramod, Pankaj's consistent position of being done to, places him bodily outside a framework of play: he has diseases, and is impotent. Pankaj neither sees himself as having much in common with *hijras* or *jankhas* nor with the men who are *aise,* words he would not use. "I am a gay," he used to say, "and there is nothing for me here in Varanasi." He took frequent trips to Delhi and cruised its much larger parks, looking for more poetic and educated men. Through these connections he learned of *Trikone,* a magazine for South Asian gays and lesbians produced in the United States, and through personal and pen-friend ads in *Trikone* met friends and lovers in other north Indian cities. When a group of older gay men established their own newsletter and organization in the city of Lucknow, Pankaj quickly became involved; and he took the earliest opportunity to get a transfer out of Varanasi, a city perhaps "like this" but not terribly gay.

Two Appropriations of Third Gender

> Concomitant with the dubious achievement of a diagnostic category is the inevitable blurring of boundaries as a vast heteroglossic account of difference, heretofore "invisible" to the legitimate professions, suddenly achieves canonization and simultaneously becomes homogenized to satisfy the constraints of the category. Suddenly the old morality tale of the truth of gender . . . becomes pancultural in the 1980s. . . . the *berdache* and the stripper, the tweedy housewife and the *mujerado,* the *mah'u* and the rock star, are still the same story after all, if we only try hard enough. ("A Posttranssexual Manifesto," Stone 1991)

Sandy Stone writes the above in showing how American professional authority through the medicalization of "transsexuals" comes to demand a single narrative of transsexual experience, rooted entirely in an asexual articulation of gender. Individuals must perform culturally feminine gender to assure the gatekeepers of sex of their naturally female self; personal testimonies of transsexual identity must contain a total identification with culturally readable femininity and a lack of any male genital investment. In highlighting what she terms a preoperative ritual—"wringing the turkey's neck," one last jerking off before penectomy—Stone suggests the inadequacy of the official binary logic of transsexualism and offers the possibility of myriad gendered trajectories in her "post-transsexual" manifesto against Raymond's critique of male to female transsexualism as the ultimate patriarchical appropriation.[8]

The homogenization of gender transformation is not restricted to medical authority or a certain style of radical feminist critique. "Third gender" has become a key site in several academic debates. It invokes a global semantic network (encompassing caricatures of transsexual, *berdache, xanith, hijra, mah'u,* androgynous, hermaphroditic, and often gay and lesbian experience) invoked to demonstrate the possibility of collapsing boundaries of all sorts: cultural, political, patriarchal, biological. I turn to two such debates that fail to engage what is at stake for many who articulate a gendered identity which is neither female nor male. The first debate is located primarily within American feminism and literary theory: Is transsexualism a subversion or an extension of a binary and patriarchal economy of gender? Against positions like Raymond's, Garber in *Vested Interests* argues for the necessity of liminally gendered figures in establishing and maintaining the very possibility of gender difference, a "center-out-there" argument structurally similar to the anthropological approach of Victor Turner. Rather than the villainous undercover agent of patriarchy, the cross-dressed or the transgendered body here has a more critical role in relation to patriarchal structure.

Garber's scope is encyclopedic; she explores the deployment of gender liminality not only in representations of, and by, transgendered, third-gendered, and cross-dressed persons, but also in *Peter Pan, Uncle Tom's Cabin,* the styles of Elvis, Madonna, Liberace, Josephine Baker, and Valentino, Freud's analysis of Schreber, Little Red Riding Hood's wolf, and the stories of the Chevalier d'Eon and the Chinese opera singer upon whom *M. Butterfly* is based. These last two are the sorts of narratives she handles to best effect, stories in which each successive revelation of the *real* truth of gender dissolves into a further surprise. The text has been celebrated as a validation by many—particularly middle-class—members of transsexual and transvestite communities in the United States.

One problem with the text is its unflagging functionalism, in which third-gendered desire is ultimately explained in terms of its function: maintaining a society's system of gender through the demarcation of the boundaries. Individual and socially located desire is deprived of its specificity in Garber's reading of myriad lives in terms of a single narrative. The bodies in her text lack any pleasures in and for themselves; they point only to the boundaries. Ultimately, each incarnation of gender dissolves painlessly into the next: there is no materiality or historicity to the radically regendered body, and no blood of castration auspiciously or terrifyingly marking the vestments which litter the text. Transgendered bodies signify their difference alone; there is never any there there. Thus when politics do enter the text, as in Garber's discussion of African-American cross-dressing and drag, the principal of difference invoked by the examined body shifts from one totalized conception (gender) to another: race. Again, what is at stake for individuals elides the possibility of their own located desire: black drag is primarily "the translation of a mode of oppression and stigmatization into a supple medium for social commentary and aesthetic power" (1992:303). The relationship *between* the body of a desire and a cultural politics of social difference is not engaged.

I juxtapose *Vested Interests* with a very different sort of text, Nandy's *The Intimate Enemy*. A psychologist by training who became a cultural critic and political analyst in Delhi, Nandy examines transformations of Indian and British selfhood through their colonial engagement (1983). Reminiscent of Fanon (1967) and Said (1978), Nandy focuses on the internalization and continual reification by a generalized but male- and bourgeois-inflected Indian subject of his colonial construction as both infantile and emasculate. Nandy discovers the origins of representational emasculation not only in the choreography of oppressor and oppressed but also in the hermeneutics of cultural contact. The British, Nandy suggests, misread a local Indian ethic of the good self as sexually balanced and androgynously experienced and found Indians unmanly. Given both their lack of a valorized cultural category of gender neutrality and their displacement of colonial inhumanity onto the bodies of the colonized, Nandy's British read the majority of their subjects as what he terms hypomasculine and a minority as hypermasculine martial races.

Nandy develops the figure of the hypomale at considerable length. Indians continue, he argues, to structure themselves against an internalized sense of unfulfillment, desiring wholeness as violent hypermasculinity. His response to this gendered colonization of the self is to reclaim a "precolonial" transcendant androgyne over and against the effeminate male or the hypermale. This authentic, Gandhian androgyne is offered as a bridge transcending gendered difference—here the fragments of a colonized and divided self—and freeing the self from hypomasculine identification and hypermasculine fantasy. Implying not object choice but self-construction, Nandy terms the liberatory self bisexual: it encompasses sexual difference rather than standing for it. Like Garber, Nandy offers a sexually liminal figure as a liberation from binary political structures, but as political difference is central to his project we are left with mirror figures—the true and the false androgyne—rather than a single celebratory gesture which acknowledges other forms of difference but resists acknowledging their desire.

Both Garber and Nandy downplay patriarchal difference: perhaps in response to Raymond, Garber submerges the specificity of a body marked female at birth within a narrative that focuses overwhelmingly on bodies initially marked male. Both of Nandy's androgynes—the emasculate and the encompassing—respond to the specificity of a male colonial subject. Androgynes, Wendy O'Flaherty notes, classically have offered the possibilities of plurality inscribed on an initially male body (1980). The political metaphor Nandy offers cannot easily represent the experience of women. Yet Nandy's discussion of postcolonial desire and the need to rethink the subjectivity of the Other has had an impact for elite critics, women and men, far outstripping the masculine confines of the imagery he offers.[9]

A second and subtler exclusion is class-based; the harmoniously balanced androgyne Nandy offers as political redemption draws on an elite aesthetics, not limited to India, of representing the self as lacking explicit sexual signification and the subordinate Other as hypersexual. Nandy offers a liberatory poetics of encompassment and balance. His androgynes eschew extremes. But there are multiple aesthetics of the political body. I offer the example of the moustache.

Pramod once offered another term to explain Number Six: *munchmunda*— being without a moustache. Young men in Varanasi inevitably have moustaches, which they grow marking their ascension to young manhood, much as shaving seemed to mark a parallel move where I grew up in the United States. Moustaches are an explicit sign of *mardhana,* of masculine power, and in parts of India are associated with the phallus through double entendre and codes of upturned versus downturned moustaches as status markers. In several, particularly high-caste Hindu traditions, a son cannot shave the moustache as long as his father is alive. Guddu, Pramod, and several friends experimented with shaving their moustaches only when away from the city, looking elsewhere for work.

Fathers, however, wear their patriarchal authority differently. A term like *munchmunda* has less salience. In Varanasi, men often shave moustaches in their forties and onward, marking in a less narrativized fashion than the growth of a moustache a movement into a different universe of political representation. Moustaches thus signify masculine presence doubly: young men wear moustaches, marking the bodily strength of young manhood but not the social and political domination of middle age; older men may shave a moustache without the threat of appearing *munchmunda.* Generationally, a man moves from a position of explicit phallic signification toward one of submerged, pseudo-androgynous sexuality. Yet, while Pramod would tease a *munchmunda* friend of similar age, he did not conceptualize older men without moustaches as being *munchmunda.*

Most young men in the city had moustaches; those who didn't, in my experience, were either elite middle-class young men or, in the slum, *jankhas.* Pankaj had a mustache, but many of his friends in government service did not. One young engineer, Bishwanath, spoke of shaving his mustache as a matter of hygiene: "it feels dirty." Models for advertisements appealing to the "common man" are always mustachioed, selling fertilizers or family planning. Models for advertisements for luxury products are often not mustachioed, particularly if the pitch is to the aesthetics of the male body. The advertisement for Aramusk soap in 1990 pictured a clean-shaven male model glaring moodily at the camera: the caption announced the class location of the product and its requisite body: "*extravagantly* male." A 1991 advertisement for a New Delhi luxury barber shop, Villa Appearances, shows a photograph of a clean-shaven young man staring out at the reader and resting his head on an embroidered pillow, the photo framed by the legend "Come Indulge Yourself." Against a Banarsi male aesthetic which equates *munchmunda* with being a Number Six, many elite young men can construct a sartorial style with an encompassing aesthetic, the powerful pseudo-androgyny of generational authority. Bishwanath's shave

THE PLEASURES OF CASTRATION 293

is—against Pramod's reading—no castration at all, but rather an ascension to the encompassing authority of the subtle phallus, the position of indulgence. The androgyne that Nandy imagines draws on a Gandhian vision, but overlaps uncomfortably with the aesthetics of the Aramusk body. What is or is not at stake in being *munchmunda* is different, powerfully so, across class in the city's streets.

The Reification of Third Gender

I have chosen to imagine all too briefly the pleasures of several men and *hijras* at a given time in their lives; I do so to write against the easy reading of either *hijras* or *jankhas* as just third gender. One could construct an Indian edition of *Vested Interests,* encompassing not only all that which might be conveyed by *hijra, jankha, chah nambar, saheli, londa, lachakmathak,* and *zenana,* but also mythic figures like Arjuna, Sikhandin, and countless other sex shifters and androgynes; religious festivals, performances, and sites of possession where men cross-dress, often possessed by a goddess or other female presence; the possession of women by male spirits and ghosts; the spring carnival of Holi when magazines cross-dress most major politicians and actors; the occasional news stories of girls who were school friends and run off together, one having a sex change operation to marry the other; devotional Hindu *bhakti* and Islamic Sufi religious and poetic practice through which a male devotee or poet loses himself by becoming the female lover of God as a young male; the film star Sridevi dancing as Charlie Chaplin in the film *Mr. India;* Ayurvedic medical and Jain religious texts detailing elaborate cosmologies of sexual difference; religious and political leaders who play with conventions of gender, and from Ramakrishna and Gandhi to Uma Bharati and the career of former prime minister V. P. Singh's on-again, off-again moustache.

At best, the exercise would iterate Garber's point, that of the centrality of gender liminality to cultural production. At worst, a colonial image of India as the tropical ground of gender muddle—Carstair's vision—would resurface. In either case, how speaking of *sahelis* and loitering at street corners differs for the marginally subsisting *jankhas* and their still poor but relatively more secure petty bourgeois shopkeeper and ready-made salesmen neighbors is avoided. The radically different choices and outcomes for persons who have operations to become male, *hijra,* or female are erased (Mahurkar 1990, Rodrigues 1991). To read what's at stake in projects of regendering in terms not only of something called "gender difference" but also of a more generalized recognition of the embodiment of other forms of social and economic difference is critical. The appropriation of "neither man nor woman" as a metaphoric strategy for antinomian empowerment by academics may evade precisely what is most at stake in sex—the embodied terrain of pleasure and affliction (Abramson and Pinkerton 1995).

The invocation of socioeconomic difference can become as easily reductive as that of patriarchal difference, as it did in responses to an article in the journal *Man* (an irony noted by Garber) by the anthropologist Unni Wikan. Wikan presented a description of a "transsexual" Omani gender category, the *xanith,* as part of a three-gender system: "not merely women and men, but also male transsexuals" (1977). Wikan's effort is to understand *xanith* identity not in and of itself but in terms of a *systemic* analysis of gender: "I seek to develop a role analysis which does not see the transsexual in artificial isolation, but confronts the role in the context of the reciprocal roles of man and woman."

Wikan's article led to several critiques: I focus on a debate with Gill Shepherd. Shepherd uses her fieldwork in coastal Kenya comparatively to suggest that Wikan downplays the economic roots of male prostitution and reads what is fundamentally economic as gender difference (1978a, 1978b). Wikan responds, arguing against the easy comparison of their respective data and against any reductionistic economic rationales for *xanith* roles (1978a, 1978b).

Shepherd, in suggesting the equivalence of *xanith* and male prostitute roles and the economic roots of male prostitution in unemployment, suggests that "poverty" explains the need to become a transgendered prostitute. Wikan points out that most poor men do not become *xanith* and that not all *xanith* are destitute; no simple correlation between any degree of economic marginality and becoming a *xanith* exists. Rather, she emphasizes the Omani narrative that sexual potency is the principal marker of male-*xanith* difference.

This "cultural" explanation is not much more satisfying than the crude economic one Wikan refutes. Wikan's emphasis on systemic coherence in the construction of cultural roles may have caused her to offer a narrative of *xanith* origination as an ideal "cultural" structure. Despite her insistence on approaching *xanith* identity from the inside, Wikan does not offer a very thick reading of *xanith* experience from a *xanith* perspective. Her potency narrative parallels a common South Asian narrative of *hijra* origin—*hijras* are impotent and useless as husbands, so they castrate themselves to attempt productive roles as auspicious vehicles of the Goddess—as well as the American clinical construction of legitimate transsexuality—the denial of penile pleasure that Stone challenges in mentioning "wringing the turkey's neck." Both *hijras* and transsexuals reproduce this narrative—Stone reminds us that transsexuals have little choice but to mark themselves as unambiguously third to utilize the apparatus of bodily transformation—but beyond the gatekeepers, the clients, the police, and the enthusiasts, their own lives and pleasures may offer other stories than those possible within the hegemony of a cultural system, however triune.

The Wikan-Shepherd debate maintains itself through an unhelpful distinction between sexuality and poverty: Either one is *xanith* because one is sexually different or because one is poor. That both sexual and economic difference integrally shape who and how one is *xanith* is not taken up. Shepherd's resistance to the possibility of any *xanith* desire not rooted in the direst of necessities suggests unexamined phobia; Wikan's reading of *xanith* in terms of a gender *system* assumes not only that the gender categories and narratives of the majority of Omanis are adequate glosses to the lives of sexual minorities, but that sexual identity is a distinct realm from other aspects of embodied experience. An overly harmonic and seamless vision of Omani gender relations is used by Wikan to legitimate reading *xanith* experience through dominant constructions of male and female gender. The problem is in part the notion of system. Analyses which locate the *xanith* in terms of a system of genders presume that being *xanith* is essentially about gender and preclude alternative approaches. The local pleasures and afflictions of *xanith*—the specificity of the body—is peripheral to discussion.

One must take up Shepherd's suggestion—that economic marginality is not irrelevant to the construction of sexual difference and sexual desire—without reducing desire and difference to utilitarian schemas and without erasing the pleasures of inalienable difference. My suggestion is that sexual difference is experienced and enacted through other forms of hierarchical social difference, that it gives meaning to and takes meaning from other hierarchies: patriarchal, racial, economic, generational, national, and so forth. The superimposition of multiple frames of difference upon the body creates an analytic challenge: on the one hand, the need to defer efforts to read the etiology of the sexed body in terms of the primacy of either cultural system or political economy or to reduce it to biology or psychology, in favor of an analysis which locates the body within a *multiplicity* of differences; on the other hand the need to listen to the obviousness and necessity of sexual identities and embodiments, and not to drain the corporeality of embodied experience by forcing it to stand for difference and difference alone.

The Blood of Castration

Hijras distinguish between true and false androgynes, between the pretense of claiming gender difference and the proof of being able to pull up your sari. Yet the absent phallus is an inadequate marker of authentic gender; *hijras* locate their essential difference processually, along a path of self-awareness. In interpreting this path through the rereading of *hijra* narratives, I face an interpretive dilemma. *Hijra* voices in Nanda's ethnography present themselves as having always been *essentially* Hijra; the traumas of becoming are practical—the indignities of prostitution, the danger and cost of the operation. Meera, a *hijra,* notes:

> As early as 4 or 5 years old, whenever my parents went out, I would put on *bindi* and would imitate the work of the women. I would pretend I was a girl and put a sway into my walk. Because I was an only child to my parents, they didn't object when I wore bindi and dressed up in girl's clothes. They said I could lead any life which suited me.

Desire similarly unfolds just-so:

> As I got older, sometimes boys would come and ask me out for a picture, and
> so we would go. And when we went for a picture, the boy would take me and
> kiss me. . . . At first I was scared of men, but after the first scare I started to
> get interested in them.

In its benign character, Meera's narrative parallels that of Adi, an upper-
class Parsi from Bombay who was interviewed in 1991 in the monthly magazine *Society* as "a man who's changed his sex." The article, in which Adi describes being "trapped in a wrong body," has no mention of *hijras:*

> Around the age of four, I discovered that my preferences, my thinking, and
> behavior were different from those of other boys. My physical mannerisms
> and, above all, my inner being, were womanlike. . . . When my mother went
> out, I would wear her dress and raid her cosmetics, for which acts the servants
> would get blamed. . . . Before I went in for a change, I had no choice but to
> be gay. (Rodrigues 1991:22–25)

Becoming a *hijra* is a more ambivalent and complex process in the narratives
retold by Lynton and Rajan, Vyas and Shingala, and Sharma, other ethnographers of the Hijra. Violence and exploitation are central to these testimonies,
but in very different ways than the bourgeois kidnapping stories. Thus, an unnamed Hijra in Baroda challenges Vyas and Shingala's portraying him only in
terms of essential thirdness, angrily denying the ease of transformation that the
Hijras who speak through Nanda evoke:

> Saheb, how little you know the world. A damn sodomite in the [house] in
> which I lived misused me even before I had grown a moustache. He buggered
> me by force and often. After a while I began liking it too. When I was 21, I
> was glad to get myself castrated [*sic*]. (Vyas and Shingala 1987:45)

My reading of these narratives remains one of suspicion, Hijras dialogically
constructing their experience in terms of the expected coercion narrative of
their interlocutors. This hermeneutic was reinforced for me by the authors'
generally insensitive translations; "sodomite" and "buggered" do not reflect
the very different semantic loads of the several terms they may be standing for,
and they carry a set of gratuitous nuances.

Yet violence is central in a very different way to the signs and enactments
by which *hijras* are known: the paradigmatic act of pulling up a sari. The pulling of the sari appears in two sorts of narratives: someone, often an old woman,
challenges the *jankha*'s or not-yet-castrated *hijra*'s authenticity and thus auspi-
ciousness by pulling up her sari. Or a *hijra,* either jokingly but far more often
threateningly, pulls up her sari when a merchant or other expected patron has
refused to give her money on her rounds of the market. The sight of the postoperative hole—the seal of the *hijra*'s impotence—is paradoxically potent,
causing impotence in the man who is exposed to it. The ability to threaten by

pulling their saris up differentiates *hijras* from *jankhas.* The violence of the gesture recreates the violence of castration, but—in revealing the site of the operation and in causing impotence, the simultaneous cause and effect of the operation—it displaces the violence onto the other, here the householder, the male shopkeeper.

Being a *hijra* seems rooted both in this narrative of having always been *hijra* and in a continual reenactment of the moment of becoming—the gesture of castration. *Hijras* ground who they are in both the simple and essential facticity of their gendered identity as neither men nor women and in an ambivalently understood loss of masculine identity and a socially constituted will to castration. Hijra essentiality and constructedness—the ubiquitous poles of writing on sexuality—are united in the cultural figure which constitutes their recognition: the lifting of the sari, the showing of the "hole" which simultaneously proves that they are true and not false and yet bloodily constructed androgynes.

The tactics of *hijra* survival—the relentless demand for money from shopkeepers, to the piercing rhythm of the *hijras'* clapping alerting passers-by to their presence—depend on a powerful rhetoric of entitlement. *Hijras* reiterate laments to outsiders:

> Look at me. Have a good look.
> Neither man nor woman that is my curse . . . and it is the so-called normal people, respectable people like you [who] have made us thus.
> [You] put [your] unsuspecting wives to sleep and then come to us, to embrace this bag of [shit]. (Vyas and Shingala 1987:43)

Along with the lament comes a demand for citizenship and state support. One of the Banarsi *hijras,* according to a friend of Pramod's, pointed toward her hole and laughed, "All-India pass." With the pass, some men in Asi say, *hijras* can board trains anywhere, even to Pakistan. Claims for state recognition appropriate any and all nationalist symbols; when an Indian cosmonaut went into space along with a Soviet crew in 1984, the president of a large Delhi *hijra* organization wrote to Indian and Soviet leaders, requesting that they "give parity to the sexually under-privileged and socially neglected persons of the 'Third Sex' by sending at least one of this group in to space in future ventures" ("Clapping demand" 1984).

Hijras are represented in popular Indian media in terms of a second hole, the anus penetrated by powerful men. In the best-selling Indian English novel *Delhi,* the author Khushwant Singh narrates a love affair between a semi-autobiographical character and his mistress, a *hijra* named Bhagmati (1990). The narrator relishes detailing his sexual conquests of various women; Bhagmati, repeatedly abused yet always coming back for more, is the ultimate foil to his position as sexual conquerer. The novel tells the story of Delhi over the ages, its multiple sackings and destructions; Bhagmati becomes a symbol of the city and her people, repeatedly humiliated and yet always unbowed, ever demanding, always able to turn a rape of one hole into the defiant revelation of the other.

Similarly, in the Bhojpuri film *Mai* a young village man flees his native place for the city of Patna to escape the repeated assaults on his family by their villainous and lustful feudal landlord, or *zamindar.* The young man plies a rickshaw in the city, but his conscience gets the better of him and he returns to his mother in the village, to certain destruction. He survives by disguising himself as a *hijra,* the ultimate sexual object; seeing him, the *zamindar* must have him. *Zamindars* and *hijras* are dramatic foils in oral narratives in the area: the unlimited desire of the former mirrors the unlimited availability of the latter. One is all take, the other all give—the ultimate park hustle. Once inside the landlord's apartments, the hero entraps the villain with his newfound *hijra* wiles and then kills him.

In these texts, becoming a *hijra* not only marks but transforms the hierarchy of victimization: the *hijra* is the body with nothing left to lose, and is thus capable of losing everything and surviving. Far from occupying a space betwixt and between, the representational *hijra* occupies the far edges of possibility. She is perhaps no closer to the real lives of *hijras* than are the forced castrati of the *Lancet* article; yet her offering of an utterly abject yet indestructible and ultimately triumphant body may be closer to a more marginalized male desire than is the disembodied *munchmunda* Nandy offers against colonial losses.

In Varanasi, the feudal countryside to the east in Bihar is said to be rife with the rape of men and boys by landlords and their henchmen. The *hijra* as landlord-slayer offers the impossible solution to the loss of male peasant subjectivity: impossible, as it remains a fantasy position reflecting options neither open to nor desired by most men or for that matter *hijras.* Unlike the fantasy androgynes of the academics, the fantasy-*hijra* can only be envisioned through a reenactment of the violence of everyday life. Without castration and its consequent hemorrhage—without the violent embodying of the truth that phallic power is not uniformly distributed—one has not paid the necessary price to transform gendered dominance into intergendered, auspicious, and playful thirdness. Castrations are not playful matters; any claim that the *Lancet* overstates its case must be well documented. But the blood of castration—its violence—is the point, central to the narrative structure of becoming a *hijra* long before the moment of castration.

Two Versions of a Conclusion

Hijra **conclusion**

In Varanasi, relations between *hijras* and *jankhas* vary from limited alliances to suspicion (by the former of the latter). For *hijras,* Ram Prasad and the *zenanas* or *jankhas* of the ethnographic literature are not sisters in abjection; when they pull up their saris, there is nothing at stake. They lack gender: they lack a committed body. The parallel desires, origin narratives, class positions, and adjectival styles of *hijras* and *jankhas* are not enough. *Jankha* practice challenges the possibility of *hijra* essentiality; it suggests that anyone can become a third gender without fundamentally challenging the binary and hierarchical regulation of bodies. If gender is disembodied, there need be nothing at stake in gender. Through castration, through the denial of any intractable point— anatomical or social—eluding transformation, *hijra* practice demands that all gendered and sexed positions be viewed ultimately in terms of what's at stake.

Like *jankhas* as understood by *hijras*, Nandy and Garber utilize the semantics of androgyny without renouncing a gendered superordinate position. Garber offers transgendered experience as a liminal but sexless idyll; its analytic thinness ultimately replicates the surgical gatekeeping structures that Sandy Stone challenges. Nandy's project engages political difference, splitting the androgyne, but the "bisexual" man-plus-woman he invokes to transcend the colonial gendering of Indian elite men as effeminate maintains their position vis-à-vis women and subordinate men. On some level, these authors fail to engage the body in the gender. But when they lift up their saris, what's at stake is revealed.

Jankha conclusion

Everyone in the slum where Birju lives knows that since childhood he has played with the girls and acted like them. His neighbors and cousins protect him against the slurs of outsiders. Birju's father is a widower and a well-respected teacher, and unlike his siblings Birju has devoted himself to caring for his father, feeding him and keeping house. Sitting at home, cleaning and cooking, Birju wears a worn-out shawl, its initial color indecipherable from its threadbare state. He keeps another shawl, a bright red "ladies" fabric, for special occasions. When he was a *londa*, a cross-dressed dancer for a *nautaka* troupe from the slum, his guru had lent him a sari and accessories. Birju would play the young women's parts in satirical dramas, mocking the chastity of upper-caste women and the piety of their husbands, or he would dance obscene and comic numbers, like the infamous "Chicken."

In Birju's slum, culture—the world of Brahmanical purity and temple ritual and Sanskrit text so lavishly present in Varanasi—is so much performance, or *nautaka*. Drama, dancing, and drumming troupes form a significant part of the slum economy.[10] Most men in the slum have a guru, an older man versed in three sorts of arenas: dramatic performance, Chamar ideology (Birju's untouchable caste), and *ojha* power (the undoing and casting of spells to win allies, make love, and destroy enemies). Birju was trained by his guru from boyhood in how to dance as a *londa*, a cross-dressed boy. In performance he would dance with two women, prostitutes from the city. Some of the *londas* acted in comic troupes, playing a young wife cuckolding her elderly husband with a temple Brahman. Some *londas* turned tricks themselves.

Most *londas* ceased to be *lachakmathak* as they grew older. But for Birju, the meaning of *nautaka* and the dance are central to the path of his desire and his difference: having a husband and step-son, keeping a home for his father, knowing how to dress. Being what some would call *jankha* is not a way station on the road to becoming a *hijra* but a coherence to pleasures which grow out of his community's performative traditions. Birju, for his family and neighbors, occupies a desiring position whose meaning is encompassed though never exhausted by the body of the slum.

Birju no longer dances, and no longer wears his saris and bangles. He no longer hangs out with *jankha sahelis* like Kamal. He struggles to get by, spends time with his husband the tailor when he can, and takes care of his father. He keeps his red shawl for special occasions.

When I first started learning from and reading about *hijras,* I was struck by the centrality of the rhetoric of the false *hijra,* and of the power of this *hijra* insight in writing against the appropriation and misreading of the radically regendered body by those with perhaps less at stake. A set of gestures, bound up in the reenacted violence of pulling up the sari, helped bring together a framing of sexual difference which could take on the circular debate of the *xanith* controversy.

But just as *hijras* are not the disembodied liminal markers of thirdness of academic texts on gender, *jankhas* are seldom the conniving pseudo-*hijras* that *hijras* often experience them as being. Both the *hijras* and the *jankhas* of the city were associated with their own brands of *nautaka* which in different ways ran against the grain of local constructions of patriarchal difference. Against the pulled-up sari of the *hijra,* throwing its observer into a space of sudden thirdness, is the unrelenting *nautaka* of the Asi *jankhas,* in which gender, caste, and other materializations of the lived body are mocked and again exploded.

> Another evening: I am on the road to Asi. Ram Prasad is pedalling his heavy trolley filled with coal to be delivered. Ram Prasad is heavily muscled and looks like a *gunda,* a neighborhood tough. Kamal just told me Ram Prasad didn't get accepted by the *hijras.* I ask him what happened. He smiles, and offers a husky falsetto: "I don't want to be a *hijra,* beautiful. I just need a husband, and I like to play. Husband, wife, *hijra,* macho-type, foreigner, Indian. Let's go play."
>
> But Kamala, to me: "You really want to be a *saheli?*"

Notes

I am grateful to Alissa Ayres for discussions of her own work (1992). The persons I call Guddu, Pramod, Kamal/Kamala, Ram Prasad/Rita, Birju, Raju, and Pankaj let me transgress the bounds of old friendships and acquaintance when I began the dangerous alchemy of turning life into research. Anne Ogborne has begun to challenge my working assumptions regarding transgendered politics with her trenchant and thoughtful criticism. This essay is of course endebted to the work of Serena Nanda, to Gil Herdt for suggesting that I write it, and to Paul Abramson for infinite patience.

1. I.e., from Varanasi.

2. There is a danger in this collapse of sex and gender, if it is read as turning our attention away from a systematic history of gendered violence by men against women. One strand of feminist critique challenges deconstructions of sexual difference as erasing the ubiquity of gendered violence. Catherine MacKinnon questions the historical contingency of "sexuality" and sexual politics and the chain of epistemic breaks posited by Foucault, placing against these a continuity of gendered oppression and sexual violence (1991). Janice Raymond, in *The Transsexual Empire: the making of the she-male,* challenges the claims to femaleness of male-to-female transsexuals, reading their move as the ultimate male appropriation of female space (1979). Though MacKinnon sidesteps and dramatically misreads Foucault's project and Raymond phobically refuses to engage the possibility of a transgendered subject position, much writing by academics—including aspects of the work of Garber and Nandy—on third-, cross-, inter-, or trans-sexualities or genders *does* erase political differences between male and female experience. It does so when it (1) highlights male to female or male to third shifts and downplays female to male or female to third shifts, (2) assumes that much the same is at stake for initially "male" as for initially "female" bodies, and (3) upholds an opposition of binarily gendered versus third-gendered subjectivity in which the former implicitly stands for a male (as opposed to a female or male) position. Ultimately, much writing on "third gender" by nontransgendered persons works with a two-gendered system, *male and third,* in which the female position has been erased.

To write against this sort of erasure by insisting on the fixedness of male and female subject positions substitutes a parallel erasure and reaffirms the sexist deployment of biology that Butler reminds us is sustained by such essentializing language. To confront the prevalence of both embodied and epistemic violence against women without maintaining an essentialized and ultimately violent delimiting of the category of "women" is a challenge on many fronts of contemporary feminist debate. Here I will attempt a provisional terminology, refusing to imagine gender or sex as useful binaries in the way I will deploy class, yet maintaining a category of *patriarchal* difference to represent the real and ubiquitous oppression and violence MacKinnon and others continue to point us to.

3. One will not find words like *aise* in articles or books on homosexuality or transgendering in South Asia, or more generally in the catalogues and compendia of the varieties of sexual experience globally. Two terms predominate: *hijra* and *khush.* The "India" sections of international atlases of sex exhibit the figure of the *hijra,* alternately translated as eunuch, homosexual prostitute, transsexual, gender-transformed, or third gender, along with the boy prostitute (Ellis 1921; Greenberg 1988); the implicit but unsignified third in such discussions is a presumed Oriental appetite for pederastic pleasures. In the 1980s, South Asian activists articulated another identity, *khush* (literally: pleasurable, happy, or gay) as simultaneously an appropriation of the homoerotic in South Asian traditions and a response to the political and semiotic exclusions of gay

and lesbian social movements and categories identified with the West (Parmar 1990, *Bombay Dost* 1993). *Khush*, lesbian, and gay South Asian organizing was initially located in expatriate communities and subsequently in South Asian metropolitan centers. Central to one of the most visionary of the *khush* activists, the late Siddhartha Gautam, was a politics based on an alliance between *hijras*, lesbians, and gay men; other Delhi activists have argued and still argue that class differences between *hijras* and the semi-organized gay male community and political differences between *hijras* and lesbian and feminist communities render a common agenda unlikely.

4. Unless otherwise noted, all field-note quotations are not word-for-word transcriptions but recollections two hours to a day after the conversation or interview.

5. Arjuna is the central hero of much of the *Mahabharata;* he receives a curse from a celestial damsel whose attentions he spurns because he knows her, despite her youthful beauty, to be his ancestress and the union to be incestuous. The curse would emasculate him, but its sting is softened and Arjuna is doomed only to spend a year emasculate. When he and his brothers and wife are required to spend a year in exile incognito, he disguises himself as a cross-dressed dance teacher and receives a position in the women's apartments of a king. The text is somewhat ambiguous about whether the curse has transformed Arjuna genitally as well as sartorially. Sikhandin is a brother-in-law and ally of Arjuna in the great war of the Epic; he was in a former life the princess Amba who had been spurned by Bhisma, the eldest warrior of Arjuna's lineage. Amba received a boon from the god Siva to be reborn as a man who would be responsible for killing Bhisma. She is reborn as a girl; but her father is instructed to raise her as a boy and train her as a warrior. She is married to a princess, with disastrous results. She flees to the forest where she meets a supernatural being who takes pity on her and agrees to change sex with her temporarily. Genitally a man, Sikhandin returns to his wife. Despite the complexity of Sikhandin's move from male to female, he was described by most Banarsis (who had limited familiarity with the Sanskrit version of the epic) as a *hijra*, and portrayed in the televised version of the Epic as a *lachakmathak* effeminate man.

6. I follow the usage of several Banarsis in speaking of *hijras* in the feminine and *jankhas* contextually in both the feminine and masculine; I have varied the pronominal reference to given individuals as their gendered identification shifts.

7. Ayres (1992) has noted this always located ambiguity of binary and third gender.

8. See n. 2 above.

9. I make this assertion, though it is difficult to document, based on conversations with numerous colleagues and interlocutors in India and abroad over the years since *The Intimate Enemy* was published.

10. See also Freeman (1979).

Works Cited

Abelove, Henry, Michele Aina Barale and David M. Halperin, eds. 1993. The lesbian and gay studies reader. New York: Routledge.

Abramson, Paul R. and Steven D. Pinkerton. 1995. With pleasure: thoughts on the nature of human sexuality. New York: Oxford University Press.

Allahbadia, Gautam N. and Nilesh Shah. 1992. Letter: India: begging eunuchs of Bombay. The Lancet 339 (January 4): 48–49.

Alter, Joseph S. 1992. The wrestler's body: identity and ideology in north India. Berkeley: University of California Press.

Anderson, Christopher. 1977. Gay men in India. Manuscript. University of Wisconsin, Madison.

Ayres, Alyssa Christine. 1992. "A scandalous breach of public decency": defining the decent—Indian Hijras in the 19th and 20th centuries. Senior honors thesis. Harvard University Archives.

Bombay Dost collective. 1993. Khush khat. Bombay Dost 2 (4, October–December): 12.

Burton, Richard F. 1885. A plain and literal translation of the Arabian nights entertainments, now entituled The Book of the thousand nights and a night; with introduction explanatory notes on the manners and customs of Moslem men, and a terminal essay upon the history of The Nights. Benares: The Kamashastra Society.

Butler, Judith P. 1990. Gender trouble: feminism and the subversion of identity. New York: Routledge.

Carstairs, G. Morris. 1957. The twice-born: a study of a community of high-caste Hindus. London: Hogarth Press.

———. 1960. "Mother India" of the intelligentsia: a reply to Opler's review. American Anthropologist 62:504.

Clapping demand. 1984. Hindustan Times. April 10.

Csordas, Thomas J. 1990. Embodiment as a paradigm for anthropology. Ethos 18 (March 1): 5–47.

Dubois, Jean Antoine. 1889. Hindu manners, customs and ceremonies. Henry K. Beauchamp, tr. and ed. 2nd ed. Oxford: Clarendon.

Ellis, Havelock. 1921. Sexual inversion. 3rd ed. Philadelphia: Davis.

Fanon, Frantz. 1967. Black skin, white masks. Charles Lam Markmann, tr. New York: Grove.

Foucault, Michel. 1978. The history of sexuality. Robert Hurley, tr. New York: Pantheon Books.

Freeman, James M. 1979. Untouchable: an Indian life history. Stanford: Stanford University Press.

Garber, Marjorie B. 1992. Vested interests: cross-dressing and cultural anxiety. New York: Routledge.

Greenberg, David F. 1988. The construction of homosexuality. Chicago: University of Chicago Press.

Herdt, G. 1994. Third sex, Third gender. New York: Zone Books.

Kakar, Sudhir. 1978. The inner world: a psycho-analytic study of childhood and society in India. Delhi: Oxford University Press.

Kumar, Nita. 1988. The artisans of Banaras: popular culture and identity, 1880–1986. Princeton: Princeton University Press.

Lynton, Harriet Ronken and Mohini Rajan. 1974. The days of the beloved. Berkeley: University of California Press.

MacKinnon, Catherine A. 1991. Does sexuality have a history? Michigan Quarterly Review 30 (1):1–11.

Mahurkar, Uday. 1990. Gender Jam: Case of a curious marriage. India Today. April 15: 110.

Merleau-Ponty, Maurice. 1962. Phenomenology of perception. Colin Smith, tr. New York: Humanities Press.

Nanda, Serena. 1990. Neither man nor woman: the Hijras of India. Belmont, Calif.: Wadsworth.

Nandy, Ashis. 1983. The intimate enemy: loss and recovery of self under colonialism. Delhi: Oxford University Press.

O'Flaherty, Wendy Doniger. 1980. Women, androgynes, and other mythical beasts. Chicago: University of Chicago Press.

Oldenberg, Veena Talwar. 1992. Lifestyle as resistance: the case of the courtesans of Lucknow. Contesting power: resistance and everyday social relations in South Asia. Douglas Haynes and Gyan Prakash, eds. Berkeley: University of California Press.

Opler, Morris E. 1959. Review of The twice-born: a study of a community of high-caste Hindus, by G. M. Carstairs. American Anthropologist 61:140–42.

———. 1960. The Hijara (hermaphrodites) of India and Indian national character: a rejoinder. American Anthropologist 62:205–11.

Parmar, Pratibha. 1991. Khush. Film.

Parry, Jonathan. 1989. The end of the body. Fragments for a history of the human body, part two. Michel Feher, ed. New York: Zone.

Prasad, Onkar. 1987. Folk music and folk dances of Banaras. Calcutta: Anthropological Survey of India.

Preston, Laurence W. 1987. A right to exist: eunuchs and the state in nineteenth-century India. Modern Asian Studies 21 (2):371–87.

Raymond, Janice G. 1979. The transsexual empire: the making of the she-male. Boston: Beacon Press.

Rodrigues, Pradip. 1991. Pretty Woman. Society. December: 22–29.

Said, Edward W. 1978. Orientalism. New York: Pantheon Books.

Searle-Chatterjee, Mary. 1981. Reversible sex roles: the special case of Benares sweepers. Oxford: Pergamon Press.

Sharma, Satish Kumar. 1989. Hijras, the labelled deviants. New Delhi: Gian.

Shepherd, Gill. 1978a. Correspondence: transsexualism in Oman. Man [N.S.] 13(1): 133–34.

———. 1978b. Correspondence: The Omani xanith. Man [N.S.] 13(4): 663–65.

Singh, Khushwant. 1990. Delhi. New Delhi: Viking.

Sinha, A. P. 1967. Procreation among the eunuchs. Eastern Anthropologist 20:168–76.

Stone, Sandy. 1991. The Empire strikes back: a posttranssexual manifesto. Body guards: the cultural politics of gender ambiguity, Julia Epstein and Kristina Straub, eds. New York: Routledge.

Tejpal, Tarun J. 1992. Haryana: a barbaric blow. India Today (November 30): 109–12.

Vyas, M. D. and Yogesh Shingala. 1987. The life style of the eunuchs. New Delhi: Anmol.

Wikan, Unni. 1977. Man becomes woman: transsexualism in Oman as a key to gender roles. Man [N.S.] 12(2): 304–19.

———. 1978a. Correspondence: The Omani xanith: a third gender role? Man [N.S.] 13(3): 473–75.

———. 1978b. Correspondence: The Omani xanith. Man [N.S.] 13(4): 667–71.

CHAPTER FOURTEEN

The Pursuit of Pleasure and the Sale of Sex

LENORE MANDERSON

Introduction

The rapid spread of HIV infection in Thailand has resulted, in the space of a few years, in dramatic changes: a shift from official denial to acceptance and concern with the spread of infection nationwide (Bamber, Hewison, and Underwood, 1993); the introduction of the "condom only" law for commercial sex establishments, introduced in 1991, to reduce transmission within brothels (Weniger et al., 1991); and the development of nongovernmental organization-based (NGO) projects to provide health education to reduce risk behaviors in the general population and promote employment opportunities for young women who might otherwise work as prostitutes.[1] Parallel to these public health initiatives in response to the HIV epidemic, there has been a mushrooming of research projects concerned with the epidemiology of HIV, with social-risk factors of infection, knowledge-attitude-practice (KAP) surveys, and the feasibility of interventions, of which the acceptance and use of condoms has been the most predictable (Ford and Koetsawang, 1991; Na Bangchang, 1991; Pongswatanakulsiri et al., 1991; Sittitrai et al., 1991; Thanprasertsuk and Pimyothamakorn, 1991; AIDSCAP, 1992; Havanon, Knodel, and Bennett, 1992; Muecke, 1992; Lyttleton, 1994).

Although HIV infection can no longer be regarded as a health problem of sex workers only or primarily, public attention has continued to focus on this group, both as the major vectors and victims of the virus. Such attention to the sex industry and its workers has a historical basis, given a long history of the representation of Thailand as a "paradise for Western males" (Bamber, Hewison, and Underwood, 1993, pp. 151–2).[2] As a consequence, there is a sizeable literature on prostitution by Thai and other social science researchers, novelists, and journalists, which clearly articulates the political economy of prostitution in Thailand (Cohen, 1982; Hewison, 1985; DaGrossa, 1988; Khin Thitsa, 1980; Muecke, 1984, 1992; Truong, 1990) and emphasizes women's agency in the industry (Pasuk, 1982; Sukanya, 1983, 1984, 1988).[3] Even so, within Thailand and in Western commentary, the popular emphasis has been upon the "innocents" of this industry: young children and only slightly older virgins, sold by desperately poor parents to the brothel keepers of Bangkok and Pattaya, lured to the cities by the false promises of pimps and procurers for employment in the service sector; destitute orphaned boys and girls with no options other than to sell their bodies on a market that is represented as being dependent upon and essential to the tourist industry (see, for example, ABC, 1993; Kempton, 1992; Cater 1993).

Such dramatic representations of prostitution and the associated sex industry are repeated in the print and electronic media in Thailand and overseas.[4] These journalistic texts carry a common argument. Extreme poverty forces parents to surrender their children to prostitution; foreign tourists sustain the demand for commercial sex with very young girls and boys; the Thai economy is dependent upon tourism; for this reason the government is not prepared to restrict or control prostitution and is unable to redress the economic and political problems which have resulted in rural poverty. The circle is complete.

Descriptions and analyses of the sex industry in Thailand have had much to say about prostitution as an institution, although with remarkably little variation over the past decade and with little to say about sex despite its depiction in film documentaries and documentary dramas (e.g., O'Rourke, 1991).[5] In an article on public sex performances (Manderson, 1992), I chose to focus on the sex acts in the bars of Patpong to examine the subjectification of women and women's resistance through the choreography of pornographic dance, tricks, and staged couplings. From this perspective, I then sought to link both specific acts and the institutions of the sex industry to Thai cultural practices, images, structures, and understandings of sexuality, maleness, and femaleness. The impetus for the direction of that paper was, to me, the unsatisfactory proposition that the scope and forms of Thailand's sex industry were "because of" U.S. R and R (i.e., rest and recreation for American troops stationed in Vietnam) or subsequent sex tourism. All evidence points to the long antecedent history of prostitution and its prevalence, indigenously as well as within its entrepots (Embree, 1950; Turton, 1982; Bamber, Hewison, and Underwood, 1993), and to the fact that whenever prostitution is discussed, particularly in the context of regulation, prohibition, or control, its incidence is always represented as increasing, as was the case during the 1960s when the influx of troops changed the social geography of the sex industry possibly more than the incidence of prostitution.[6]

Yet despite the case I made for women's agency and the cultural locus of commercial sex work (Manderson, 1992), it remains true that the most flamboyant and excessive aspects of the sex industry *are* in tourist centers such as Patpong (in Bangkok), Pattaya, Hat Yai, and Chiangmai; and that many Japanese, northern European, American, and Australian men do travel to Thailand precisely for commercial sex.[7] In recognition of this fact, for countries such as Australia, the primary issue has been an unsurprising self-interested concern that nationals might become infected with HIV by Thai prostitutes and then spread infection at home.[8] In this context, sex tourism has gained increasing attention, although how it is defined and who is included in any discussion of it is usually unclear, as are the health (as opposed to moral and ethical) issues implicated by its promotion and practice.

Sex tourism is the "pursuit of pleasure" in the title of this chapter. The sale of sex refers to its marketing, commodification, and representation, not to its purchase. The sex that is sold is not only prostitution but also film, theater, other forms of performance, and paintings, sculptures, and other printed representations which have explicit sexual and erotic components. I include also the sexual referents and illusions used to "package" nonsexual services; sex both sells and is sold by these marketing strategies. In this chapter I deliberately sidestep issues of the motivations and desires of the tourist-purchaser, and the structure of sex that offers an ephemeral pleasure in the explicit sex shows of Thailand.

Focusing on the entertainment industry, I first consider the nature of tourism and sex tourism, then describe the theatrical display of sex and its ironies in Bangkok, through descriptions of live sex shows and transvestite cabarets, prior to addressing more generally the production of sexual stereotypes as a means of sustaining the tourist market.

Tourism and the Tourist Gaze

Sex and tourism share marginal status within the social sciences. The disinclination of anthropologists, among others, to study the latter has been in part a wariness of the uncomplimentary analogy between tourism and anthropological practice, in part also because of tourism's association with leisure, hence the implicit triviality of its study as well as pursuit (Finney and Watson, 1979, p. 470; Leiper, 1979, p. 392; Crick, 1985, p. 77). For sex, too, uncomfortable sets of personal associations pertain (Manderson, 1982; Herdt, in press; Tuzin, this volume). In general and until relatively recently, those who have described, deciphered, and rendered problematic this "frivolous diversion" (Rubin, 1992, p. 267) have occupied peripheral places within their disciplines, and the scientific imperatives in the time of AIDS[9] have only just begun to change the politics of the production of knowledge.

A discussion of sex tourism necessitates, as a first step, a more general discussion of the nature of tourism and of what John Urry (1990a, 1990b) refers to as the "tourist gaze." Borrowing from Foucault and his notion of the "medical gaze," Urry argues that gazes are constructed through difference, varying according to society, social group, and period. At a given moment the tourist gaze is produced in relation to the opposite, the obverse; the tourist image and experience provides a mirror to everyday social experience and consciousness, an image (often enough, imaginary) that contrasts with and therefore serves to validate and legitimize routine experience, domestic and working life, and the social structure within which they are located.

Urry (1990a, pp. 2–3) sets out the characteristics of tourism, which he argues hold regardless of time and place. In the first case, as noted above, he argues that tourism "presupposes its opposite." It is a temporary, organized and contrastive experience juxtaposed against the familiar. In this respect it is "out of bounds," although in reality it is no less than routine life bounded, controlled, and defined both by the tourist and by the site and structures where the tourist activities take place. The activities undertaken by the tourist are distinctive from and contrastive to everyday "at home" life: the landscape and places subject to the "tourist gaze" are extraordinary and are unconnected with usual activities, including work, usual domestic and personal life. In the context of this chapter and its referents to sex tourism, the individual tourist journeys to and returns (often within a relatively short time-frame), with intent while away to "have fun" and to seek out novel and unusual experiences. These predisposing factors shape interactions of tourists with places and other people in various ways—in Thailand these include sex workers, "tribal villagers," mahouts and their elephants, monks, Buddhist temples, floating markets, palaces, and archaeological ruins.

Tourism involves a journey *to* and *from*. The physical relocation both defines the activity of tourism and makes possible certain behaviors and activities that would not occur "at home." Further, the journey and the stay are temporary. The tourist departs and sojourns with a clear intention to return "home"; hence the temporal as well as experiential boundaries of tourism, and consequently, too, the function of tourism in legitimating everyday life (*pace* Turner, 1973, 1974; Urry, 1990a, p. 10). The internationalization of travel and the mass character of tourism have also resulted in the reproduction of an infrastructure that circumscribes and bounds the experience. This is the "environmental bubble" to which Cohen (1972, p. 166) refers. One can travel and find "home" at the end of the journey—a Sheraton hotel, Kentucky Fried Chicken, Sanka coffee, and an American Express office, for example; "doing" tourism is limited therefore to a preselected range of activities, events, and places.

A number of characteristics identified by Urry are particularly relevant to this chapter: the mass character of tourism, the mass production of objects of the tourist gaze, the anticipation of place and experience by the tourist which is created and sustained by media representations, and the construction of the gaze through signs. In the case of Thailand, the gaze is constructed through select images taken to constitute "real Thailand" or "the Orient." Tourists depart on a journey that is anticipated and can be realized: the gaze is preselected. They can travel by boat along the *klongs* of Bangkok, see the Emerald Buddha, go to bars in Patpong, or travel north to Chiangmai. Both they and others have a clear idea of what these activities or experiences might include; they can buy postcards that document them in specific, familiar, and recognizable ways, and they can, on returning home, tell stories around these events that fit with others' preconceptions or prior experiences of the same tourist journeys (Mintz, 1977,

p. 60). Others are able to locate, associate, imagine, and replicate the experience, and to collapse the journey into singular, emblematic acts; hence "going to Bangkok" becomes a euphemism or substitution for "going to a live sex show." A "sex tour" to Thailand is a very clearly defined activity, usually physically located in Patpong or perhaps Pattaya or Chiangmai, built around images of beautiful Thai women in G-strings, and naked dancers performing a variety of explicit, gymnastic rather than erotic, tricks (in the language of the handbills distributed to tourists, "fire stick in pussy show," "egg cracking show," "pussy smoke cigarette show," and so on (e.g., O'Merry, 1990, p. 168; Dawson, 1988; Manderson, 1992). It is also, at least for some men, built around a fantasy that extends beyond the idea of a "good time" to the possibility of romance and true love that flows from a notion of "the Oriental woman" who is not only physically beautiful and sexually exciting but also caring, compliant, submissive, and *not* "Western" or modern (O'Merry, 1990; Barnes, 1993; Lehtimaki, 1993).

The commodification of sex within tourism involves a double journey. Tourism itself, as already noted, changes place and context. Likewise, a visit to a brothel is a journey, a liminal or antistructural experience (Turner and Turner, 1978) which functions as a secular pilgrimage to legitimize bourgeois domestic relations. In sex tourism, place ("Asia," "the Orient") and sex are both commoditized, setting up a dual opposition to the conventions and ideologies of contemporary industrial/Western (e.g., North American or Australian) life.

Marketing Pleasure

Sex tourism is oriented to both heterosexual and homosexual men; this chapter focuses on its heterosexual components only. It is dependent upon the marketability and marketing of "Thai sex" and Thai women as a product, and the extensiveness of sex tourism to Thailand raises questions about the basis of Western representations of Thailand whereby nation and woman, and woman as sex, are collapsed. In documentary films, novels, newspaper articles, and tourist brochures, Thailand is constantly represented as "the land of smiles," "the brothel of the East"[10] and "the world's largest sex resort"; the partial displacement of monks in saffron robes by young women in G-strings as a national synechdoche maintains the tourist market. The promotion of Thailand as sex haven has occurred with official complicity and with wider political support. In the late 1960s, for example, the then minister of the interior, General Prapas Charusathiarana, was reported to have argued that a larger sexual service industry would result in increased tourism, with attendant economic advantages. In 1980 banker Boonchu Rojanasathien similarly exhorted provincial governors to promote sex tourism to boost the economy (Bamber, Hewison, and Underwood, 1993, p. 152). The promotion of Thailand as a "pleasure periphery"[11] has proceeded despite reactions from within Thailand against its representation as a brothel (or, anthropomorphized, as a whore), seen as a slur on national integrity and nation/woman's virtue (Parker et al., 1992, pp. 1,6). In such rejections of the representation of Thailand as sex haven, foreign men (*farang*) are portrayed both as a symbol and vehicle of a neocolonialism whose rape/domination of women and the country mocks Thailand's earlier independence from the nineteenth-century colonizations of Asia.

Tourism to Asia is organized within the political economy of global relations and derives its market value from the general commodification of the "Orient" as well as the commodification of leisure and pleasure. Current constructions of "Asia" are successors to the Orient of nineteenth-century imperialism, travelers' tales, early anthropology, and their associated projects, all resulting in the collapse of the exotic and erotic to create a fetishized, imagined Other with little attention to empirical veracity (Said, 1978; Kabbani, 1986; Marcus, 1992). The "Orient" is mythic and fanciful, the named places even more so. "Thailand" is about being "anywhere" rather than "somewhere" (Crick, 1985, p. 79; Lea, 1988, pp. 23–24).[12] If the place is a mythical tourist destiny, so too are its people. Or rather, the "Oriental woman" does and does not exist: she is produced partially and variably in different times and places, a set of embodied ideas that derive from notions of liberalism, fantasy, license, fancy, and adventure, a vehicle to an imagined lawless paradise that might be anywhere (though not at home). In such fantasies, the Oriental woman—and oriental sexuality, although the term is an anachronistic one with respect to the nineteenth century—are both objects of desire and control: the licentious, uncontrolled Orient a lure (or a promise) of imperialism and the justification for its oppressions.

These mythological representations of places and women are shared; it is their pervasiveness and predictability that ensures their efficacy for marketing purposes. They are common therefore at any point where tourists might be targeted, within the region as well as beyond. For example, a Hong Kong tourist brochure, *The Pearl* (July 1992), distributed at currency exchange points in Kai Tek Airport, captures European obsession with foreign sexuality and how it is constituted (cf. Patton, 1992, p. 225); it describes Hong Kong "girlie bars" as running "the gamut from slightly sleazy dives all the way to glittering hostess clubs with wall-to-wall Oriental and Occidental femininity" and continues:

> Years ago, the main attraction (if it can be called that) in all the sleaze bars along the strip were topless Chinese bargirls. However management slowly cottoned to the fact that staring at two flea bites with nipples attached held appeal almost as limited as the girls' English vocabulary. . . . The upshot of this was "dancers" were imported from first the Philippines and more recently Thailand . . . (but an) economy class return ticket to Manila starts at around HK$1,200 (US1:HK7.3) and to Bangkok for a little bit more. . . .

Here Chinese women are represented as sexless ("flea bite" breasts) and unintelligent; elsewhere in the text as ugly, as "sluts," and as conniving, manipulative, wicked, and deviant. Thai and Filipina women are represented as sexually more alluring and prettier, nicer, even (as not Chinese) decent women, and a better deal. As commodities, the text says, the Hong Kong product (Chinese women) is flawed; Thailand offers value for money.

This is not to say that Thailand is marketed as the only sex tourist destiny; the above inclusion of Filipina women demonstrates this, of course.[13] Other poorer countries, too, eager for tourist dollars and foreign investment, use similar (if subtler) marketing strategies. A recent article in a tourist booklet on Shenzhen, China, for example, juxtaposed photographs of bars and song-and-dance halls with a photograph of women workers in crowded sleeping cubicles (Guo and Shi, 1993). The text noted that "(m)any of Shenzhen's female workers come from Sichuan and Hunan provinces. They are generally hard-working, frank and open to new ideas," and that "90% of the 1,000,000 workers who have come to Shenzhen from elsewhere are young women, between 20–30 years of age, resulting in a very unequal male-female ratio in the city" (Guo and Shi, 1993, pp. 20–21). Another article in the same journal describes the forty-two song-and-dance halls which now operate legally in Shenzhen and attract 50,000 customers a night: "(T)here is much to do at night in Shenzhen, whatever your pleasure" (Guan and Jun, 1993, p. 45).

It remains true, however, that Thailand is the premier sex tourist destination. Images of Thailand as "the land of smiles," of the specific nature of its sex industry, and of Thai women as available objects are, as the earlier discussion implies, mass-produced signs of Thailand that all tourists, women as well as men, expect to see and seek out. Hence women travelers returning by Qantas from Bangkok to Sydney joke with each other and the airline attendants of the "delights of the dart blowers of King's Castle" (Fieldnotes, June 1993) without apparent self-consciousness or embarrassment from their patronage of the shows or complicity in an industry that is also, contemporaneously, being portrayed by the Australian media as incredibly nasty, violent, and exploitative (e.g., ABC, 1992; Eddy and Walden, 1992; O'Donnell, 1992; ABC, 1993).

Patpong and the Pleasures in Looking

In the construction of images of country, people, and sexuality, individuals are stripped of agency. But in addition, they are denied personhood; they become *the sex.* As Spillers argues (with respect to black women), "sexual experience . . . is so boundlessly imagined that it loses meaning and becomes, quite simply, a medium through which *the individual is suspended*" (1992, p. 84; my emphasis). The dissolution of individuals is not unique in sex tourism, of course, nor in discourse of the sex(uality) of others. However, the structural subordination and textual silencing or muting (E. Ardener, 1975) of particular groups—women, the peasantry, the proletariat, homosexual men, and lesbians—make them equally vulnerable to the essentialist representation that has them either *as sex alone,* or *without sex.* The representations of sexuality and sexual relationships found in both printed and other texts are not only descriptive, however; they may also reinforce or critique those relations, or contribute to their determination.

Bruner argues (1984, p. 3) that such phenomena as play, games, storytelling, parades, carnivals, and so on are all means by which reshaping (of social and political formations) occurs (cf. MacAloon, 1984). Below, both live sex shows and transvestite theater in Thailand are explored in this light. In this section, I provide a brief description of sex performances, based on observations in Patpong bars in 1990 (for detail, see Manderson, 1992). The bars have a high profile and serve an important function in attracting tourists to the city; certainly they are as well known as Wat Arun (Temple of the Dawn) or the Emerald Buddha. The bars attract men in search of commercial sex (that is, those who wish to pay for sexual intercourse), but the action within the bars, is, I suggest, in its own right a means of attracting patrons, and is as much about sex as the promise (or purchase and experience) of coitus itself.

Although Dawson (1988) suggests that lewd sex in the Patpong bars is relatively recent (from the early 1980s), and that until then bars primarily employed girls who worked as go-go dancers, the depiction in *Emmanuelle* (Jaeckin, 1974) of a variety of acts now characteristic of the Patpong performances suggests a rather longer history, even if not in the same area.

Patpong consists of two lanes or *soi* (Patpong 1 and Patpong 2), which run from Silom Road to Surawong Road, and the name is connotative of both the lanes and their side alleys, their snack bars and souvenir stalls, the nightclubs, drinking bars, beer lounges, disco shows, and go-go bars. Most performance sex takes place in the bars, usually upstairs. Access may be through a cover charge or for the price of a drink only. Patrons are expected to buy "bar girls" a drink if they are joined by them, and pay the bar a "fine"—usually around 350 baht—if they wish to go off with a woman. She then negotiates directly the price of her services, and in Patpong this can be from 500 to 1000 baht.[14] In brothels, the brothel keeper takes about 50 percent of the woman's earnings, and in some cases women may work for a "tip" only, at times receiving no money for their services (as described by Aoi, in O'Rourke, 1991).

Within the bars, when not on stage, women move among bar patrons, clothed and wearing numbered identity badges to facilitate "ordering" by patrons. On stage, women work as dancers and as performers of a variety of erotic and lewd sex acts, either as single performers or with one or more partners. In general, single acts are trick acts using the vagina to explore two interrelated themes: female sex as power, and exploration of the unknown/fear of castration. Acts included the use of the vagina to smoke cigarettes, by squeezing of the perineal muscles; to insert and release Ping-Pong balls; to blow darts/burst balloons; to blow out candles on a birthday cake; to open bottles of soft-drinks; to hold liquid within the vagina from a bottle of Coke and then empty it into a second bottle; to pick up sushi with chopsticks; to write messages ("Hello, Japan"); and so on.[15] Other acts that manipulate the imagery of vagina as cavity, and play on a fear of castration, include the extraction from the vagina of metres of ribbon, of around three metres of razor blades threaded on a string (depicted in *The Good Woman of Bangkok* [O'Rourke, 1991]), of needles on a string, and of small bells. The bottle-opening trick, a display of muscularity, probably explores the same realm of fear/excitement and, in variations of this, the audience is invited to check that the bottle has not been opened already. The vagina is represented as dangerous, since by implication, insertion of the penis would occur at the risk of amputation. There is also a carpet-snake routine (the woman inserts the snake, tail up, into her vagina), which also represents the vagina as dangerous while exploring the themes of the insatiability of woman's desire and the animality of her sexuality. In these acts, women are vaginas without faces (see Spillers, 1992, p. 77); this is the imagery used also in product advertisements that carry the eyes to the space between the legs (see fig. 14.1). If Thailand had already been reduced through marketing strategies of tourism to woman/sex, now woman has been reduced to vagina, leaving us with a final bleak analogy (Thailand:Other :: vagina:penis).

The duo acts may be trick acts but may also include sexual intercourse; the trio (and larger number) acts usually replicate single routines (i.e., more than one girl performs the same trick) and include such tricks as cigarette smoking and the removal of ribbons, flowers, flags (reading "Welcome," "Thank You," and "Enjoy") and razor blades. In addition, sexual intercourse, heterosexual or lesbian, may be performed. Heterosexual sex acts work through a menu of poses that display penile length, stroke-style, and female agility, usually without ejaculation since there are often several performances in an evening. Lesbian sex involves caressing, tribadism, and cunnilingus. These live-act shows are relatively infrequent; perhaps six single acts or similar duo acts, and group dancing, might occur between them.

The bars and the voyeurism of their shows provide, I have argued, an environment of disinhibition, the necessary precondition to maximize customer potential in the world of commoditized sex. In addition, part of the point of the shows is their location, that is, sex is performed before an audience, and each patron is one among hundreds observing the same show. Urry (1990b) underlines the significance of the social experience involved in many tourist contexts; that is, the importance for the tourist of being able to consume particular commodities in the company of others: in this case, "watching sex" is the commodity. However, it is difficult to determine the effect of the acts on the bar patrons, and observer responses, reactions, and imputed meaning varies for a single individual for a number of reasons. For some patrons, the bar is simply a familiar place, the performances "background noise" to drinking (as implied at several points in O'Merry, 1990). These patrons, often longtime sojourners in Bangkok, contrast with others—tourists—for whom the bars are unfamiliar and the performances entirely extraordinary. Others affect boredom and disinterest. For others again, the desire to explore the erotic realms played out on stage is translated into a desire to return, for further viewing: the voyeur is a consumer catered for within the context of the bar and its performances. Whether or not the commoditization shifts from voyeurism to active sex, sex remains a commodity, and the bar a commercial venue for the sale of sex.

In pornographic performance, women remain objects, existing for and representing the fantasies of men (usually), as corporeal reality and erotic illusion. However, at one level, women are not simply objects, for the performances are also enactments of men's versions of women and their sexuality, staged examples of "passive female eroticism as a compliant compliment for (men's) own active desire" (Cocks, 1989, p. 9). Yet their subordination is not complete; parody, irony, and satire are possible. Although writers such as Sontag (1970: 148) have argued against the possibility of parody in pornography (it remains pornography regardless), I have argued that the performances in the bars of Patpong provide women with the opportunity to invert, caricature, tease, manipulate, and exploit those who use their bodies (see Manderson, 1992, pp. 463–66). In particular, Thai notions of pollution, and the profaneness of the genitals, allow—with or without intentionality—a nice inversion within the bars, as women, genitals displayed, literally perform over the heads of men. The fact that most bar patrons are unaware of this insult only adds to its power (cf. S. Ardener, 1975).

In the Eye of the Beholder . . .

In the Patpong bars, the irony is subtle. This is not the case in the transvestite cabarets such as Calypso in Bangkok and Simon Cabaret in Pattaya; it is to these shows that I now turn. This section describes Calypso in Bangkok, and in so doing explores the inversions, paradoxes, and parodies of sex, gender, desire, and sexuality, and also of nation and ethnicity. The following description, like that for the Patpong bars, again derives from observations (in 1989), and the intent of the performers of the emergent parodies is open to question.[16] The potentiality is there, even so.

Calypso is located off Sukhumvit Road in Bangkok, and is again patronized by tourists, primarily from Japan, northern Europe, America, and Australia.[17] The performance consists of mime and dance to English, Japanese, Chinese, and Thai songs, with specific routines using from two to thirty performers. Costuming is elaborate; sometimes, as in the "straight" rendition of Chinese opera pieces, the music would appear to be a vehicle to enable the performers to dress flamboyantly. Other songs, however, appear selected for text and style. The songs presented in English are performed with "high camp" in costumes which exaggerate body forms and features—décolleté gowns, tuxedos, waist cinches, bare buttocks, tight, ripped jeans; the dress used for Japanese songs predominantly parody various dress styles from Japan (kimono, geisha attire, frilly dresses preferred by female pop stars in television appearances). In contrast, local Thai dances are performed conventionally (cross-dressing is the only minor departure from more conventional performance), and in these numbers there is no apparent subtext concerning Thailand/the Other. Indeed, both representations of Chinese and Thai music are conveyed conventionally and without the apparent camp and parody characteristic of a drag show, and in consequence they stand in contrast with most of the songs (English and Japanese).

The English-language songs have a clear autobiographical text alluding to sexual preference, sexual identity, gender identity, and desire. These are songs that fit with contemporary (camped up) identity politics and include, for instance, "If They Could See Me Now," "I Did It My Way," and "I Love You Just the Way You Are." Other songs uphold musical comedy and "camp" favorites like "Mame" (from the musical *Mame*), "Welcome" (from *Cabaret*), and "Let Me Entertain You" (from *Gypsy*), and Marilyn Monroe numbers ("Diamonds Are a Girl's Best Friend," performed by a Monroe look-alike). The Monroe impersonations were numerous, but there were also frequent "appearances" of Japanese pop-star Matsuda Seiko, suggesting that her comic potential for parody is nearly as great as Monroe's. In addition, Japanese members of the audience were singled out for ridicule with the presentation of "Nagasaki Minatomachi," performed in a highly stylized representation of courtesan attire with heavy makeup and immense wig, which allowed the performers to direct their refrain "Baka mitai" ("You idiot!") to various Japanese men in the audience.[18]

The sex and sexual identity of each performer remains mysterious. The audience is asked to speculate upon the sex of each performer, and presumptively, any sex/gender status is possible. Actors may include gay men, transsexuals (who have had hormone therapy) and transvestites, although these terms all have primary reference to Western, not indigenous, sexual categories. The possibility, to the audience, that any man or woman on stage might fall into any of these gender categories, challenges conventional categories. The audience is teased, too, by further play with identities. For example, as noted above, throughout the show, an actor appears as Marilyn Monroe. In the finale, there are three Marilyns, and we are left to ask, who is the "real" one? Sex and gender identity are also used as themes of specific routines. In "I Did It My Way," the performer slowly strips off makeup and clothes and transforms herself before us to his "real" self. In general, the sex of the performer is not revealed; in the striptease mime to "Let Me Entertain You" the tease is sustained, and the sexual and gender identity of the performer remains a mystery. The lack of revelation sustains the possibility that the "woman" might be a man, hence any man (or woman?) might cross over the borders of gendered identity or desire. At the same time, in shows such as Calypso, Thai transvestites, cross-dressed actors, and transsexuals—all with different notions of their own sexuality and/or gender identity—perform in ways that reflect their own perceptions of the feminine or their perceptions of Western notions of feminine—or parody both. Hence a European man watches a Thai man performing/passing as a European (or other) woman, caught by illusions of both race and sex (is the woman really man, the American really Thai?). As Garber (1992) argues, this play with reality is precisely the point in transvestite (and any) theater.

While at one level the shows exploit the theatricality of drag, the inversions are a commentary on the paradoxes of sex, gender, identity, and desire. In several numbers, members of the audience are brought onto the stage, where their juxtaposition with the players makes a stark, visual contrast which itself conveys a message. The teasing of members of the audience by performers challenges conventional constructions of sex and sexuality, as the text "speaks" of possible worlds and possible ways of orientating oneself within them (Ricouer, 1971, p. 558). Even so, the inversions explored within the shows are bound spatially and temporally; the space for these is contained within the theater.

The cabarets are about sex, as well as about identity and desire. Acts of sex are depicted through the eyes of men, albeit homosexual and heterosexual; since the theater associates itself with commercialized male homosexuality, this is not surprising. Anal intercourse, masturbation, and fellatio are all depicted through explicit choreography of the songs. In "Surprise," for example, the dancers form pairs, back to front, hands on hip; the "women" are receptors, the men-as-men the active penetrative partners punctuating chorus lines with pelvic thrusts. The sex of women remains largely invisible, although implied in two numbers, when the "women" straddle the men, their crotches over the men's faces or "on top." But since in this show the women are also men, and we are constantly reminded of this, the renderings of female sexuality are doubly ambiguous. Women through their omission, by definition because of the nature of this show, are occluded or erased (cf. Garber, 1992).

An analysis of the performance draws attention to the way in which its structure and content operate as text (Bruner, 1984; Ricoeur, 1971; Geertz, 1975). Each performance provides description and commentary at both textual and subtextual levels on Thai (men) and the Other, "opening up a world which it bears within itself" (Ricoeur, 1971, p. 544). The Calypso Theater is a drag show modeled on those that one might find elsewhere (or anywhere), perhaps here reflecting the international commercialization of "the homosexual" (Altman, 1982) and the creation and reproduction of gay male identity in Bangkok and elsewhere in Asia, assembled from icons and symbols that have an international currency (*Nation,* 28 August 1990, p. A2). However, although forms of transvestism differ in rural Thailand, ambiguities of sex, gender, and sexuality are also familiar and are used in irony and play: Gray (1990), for example, refers to the transvestite buffoonery of a bawdy theatrical performance at a village wedding in northern Thailand; in northeastern Thailand, young men seek to ward off the "widow ghosts" (*phii mae mii*) by painting their nails and sleeping in women's sarongs (Fieldnotes, 1990). In addition, discordance with community norms in terms of sexuality, desire, and gender identity may be flagged through cross-dressing:[19] these are the images that Calypso appropriates.

I have noted that Calypso uses Western and Japanese musical repertoire for parody and "camp" performance; it includes few Thai numbers and these are done as fairly conventional set pieces. Calypso Theater contrasts, as a result, with other performances which draw on indigenous metaphor or mixed genres: Calypso presents a "modern" cosmopolitan show in a familiar format, by means of which to examine the elasticity of gender identity and desire and its cultural scaffolding. In contrast, in Thai live-sex shows, traditional imagery and form merge with Western music and style to exploit multiple layers of meanings (Manderson, 1992). In other clearer examples of syncretism in theater, the differences between "indigenous" and "other" are fully exploited for rhetorical purpose. The White Lion Dance Company, for example, in its AIDS education show performed in the bars of Soi Cowboy and Patpong in Bangkok, includes a number that provides a very direct commentary on sex tourism: an ugly and drunk red-haired European male leers at the dancers as they sing "I love Thailand / I love Pattaya / I love Patpong"; dressed in Thai costume, the "Thai" in the troupe rally together and destroy the foreign devil.

Sustaining the Stereotypes

Images of Thailand, and specifically Bangkok, frequently center on its particular confluence of sex and entertainment, and these images—of Patpong rather than the cabarets—are repeated in a wide range of visual and text representations of Thailand, despite often fundamental differences in their major purposes.[20]

Many of the documentaries produced over the past five years (see note 4) provide analyses of the sex industry in Thailand that are critical of the Patpong bars and their neighboring brothels, massage parlors, and tea houses while identifying the economic and cultural basis of their operation. Such commentaries are sympathetic to and repeat the arguments of a number of sociological studies of prostitution (e.g., Khin Thitsa, 1980; Muecke, 1992; Pasuk, 1982; Sukanya, 1983, 1984, 1988; Truong, 1990), which also argue the importance of the political economy in understanding the extent of sex work in Thailand. The film *Slaves of Progress* (BBC, 1984), for example, speaks of women working in the bars of Patpong from "poverty-stricken villages," picked up by men, held against their will, and sold to the highest bidder. Porteus and Cooper, in *Foreign Bodies* (1988), argue that prostitution needs to be understood in the context of a complex set of circumstances that include rural poverty and indebtedness, the importance of the tourist industry, the establishment of a foreign-oriented sex industry as a consequence of the Vietnam War and continuing, subsequent American presence, together with—they argue—the subordination of women and their lack of negotiating power within Thai society (women are "chattels under Buddhism"). Several studies emphasize, too, the cycle in which women are caught. Despite some evidence that women are able to move from prostitution back to conventional village life when their earning potential within the sex industry decreases or according to other changed circumstances (e.g., Muecke, 1992), others are skeptical of this and note the usual downward mobility of women involved in various paying liaisons (Cohen, 1982, p. 424; Gray, 1990). In *Foreign Bodies* (Porteus and Cooper, 1988), Bee asks "What can I do? I can't go back to being a virgin"; in *The Good Woman of Bangkok* (O'Rourke, 1991), Aoi's aunt says: "She is so damaged now. No man in this village would marry her."

While some of the film texts that highlight the domestic economics of sex work draw attention to the exploitation of women as a result of sex tourism, many romanticize women's recruitment into prostitution and their loyalty to their families that keeps them working. Further, explanations of the political economy of sex work in Thailand, of rural poverty and local culture, have been so well rehearsed that the arguments are repeated by those running tourist services and by tourists themselves. Tim Dragoo, an American bar owner in Pattaya, told one team of filmmakers that "the woman feels very grateful (to her client or short-term partner) that he's helping her family—getting tractors, drinking water, mosquito nettings etc." (Porteus and Cooper, 1988). In *The Good Woman of Bangkok* (O'Rourke, 1991), an Australian argues

> They are prostitutes and we feel sorry for them. They're very poor, but we love 'em. I feel sorry for them because they have to resort to what they do. I think that it's best that we do go with them because what we give them . . . it helps them . . . if it helps them, it's not so wrong. The oldest girl comes to Thailand (i.e., Bangkok), they try to get a job and this is all they can really get because they haven't got an education. So to break a vicious cycle they send the money home to get an education for the younger ones, which is good, because eventually there wont be this, they wont need to do this.

These sentimental accounts are certainly more sympathetic than the portraits of Thailand included in films such as *Shocking Thailand (a.k.a. Weird Thailand)* (Friedman and Gatewood, 1991),[21] which includes the Patpong sex shows as part of a panoply of purported exotica and other "out-of-the-ordinary" acts that include opium smoking, eating baked snake, ritual mutilation, tattoos, dirty books and postcards, and riding trishaws and pedicabs (*tuktuk*) as exemplary of "weird" Thailand. The images in this kind of material are fantastic and partly imaginary exotica, a means of marketing. The marketing of destination through sex is itself predicated upon the liminality that the journey affords: the tourist steps outside of (his own) culture; unconstrained/temporarily unenculturated, he is able to act in ways unimagined or barely imagined at home. Beyond the moral control of home/the West, *anything can happen* (cf. Manderson, 1992).

Other films offer a counter-commentary which argues that sex tourists, not the sex workers, are the innocent and exploited. The documentary *You Can't Buy a Wife, Can You?* (Lehtimaki, 1993), for example, explores the rather complex issues surrounding marriage agencies and intercultural "relationships," implicated also, of course, in *The Good Woman of Bangkok*. In *You Can't Buy a Wife, Can You?* the central English character is a romantic, naive but with some insight: he maintains that 98 percent of Thai women have a "higher morality" than Western women, but he concedes that their interest in European men is largely economic. The original evil "character" of the film is the marriage agency and its Bangkok manager. In the end, however, the Thai wife shifts from her position as a morally innocent factory worker, to a duplicitous and manipulative woman who has used marriage with *farang* to generate, through dowry payments, an irregular but lucrative flow of cash to her family. (An alternative reading here, of course, would be to give her higher moral ground, through actions that privilege filial loyalty and duty over personal affiliative ties.) A similar perspective—of women's agency *or* their exploitation of lonely men, depending on the reader's perspective—is possible at the end of *The Good Woman of Bangkok,* when Aoi accepts O'Rourke's offer to purchase a rice farm and then returns to work in Bangkok.[22]

The above version of women's duplicity is also presented by Barnes (1993), in a brief newspaper article that challenges "(t)he image of corrupt western men plucking Asian girls from a wall of vulnerable and innocent young flesh" with a counter-image of naive and lonely men whose emotional involvement in the women they partner lead them to confusion and hurt. In this account of Thai/Western encounters, men confuse the language of love and the language of work, the payments for sex and financial support for a lover/beloved; the women, in turn, are shrewd, manipulative, and willful. Here Pearce and Moscardo's (1986) concept of authenticity is useful: the conflicts that are pursuant upon men's involvement with sex workers are an outcome of their pursuit of authenticity and their failure or unwillingness to perceive the "staged" or inauthentic nature of the scene, that is, that women's declarations of love are part of their work (cf. Hochschild, 1983; Wouters, 1989). However, not all Western men are fooled, and others exploit the system to their own advantage (O'Merry, 1990).

The difficulty in interpreting these works, and other written work on Thailand, is the line between the production and representation of such stereotypes, as suggested by a film like *Shocking Thailand* (Friedman and Gatewood, 1991) or *The Good Woman of Bangkok* (O'Rourke, 1992; for discussion, see Hamilton, 1993; Manderson, 1993). Margaret Drabble's latest book, *The Gates of Ivory* (1992), provides another example: a work that hovers between novel and social history (note the bibliography)[23] and characterizes Bangkok by its red-light district and brothels—red-Indian style, geisha style, and wedding style complete with gowned brides and organ music. This may be a further ironic play at the way in which sexuality and desire transgress national boundaries and seek the erotic in the (stereotypic) other, but we must take on faith that the attitudes of racism and ignorance in the book are those of the characters, not Drabble's own; that the errors are innocent;[24] and that Bangkok is presented as a brothel because that is how tourists come to know the city. In other texts, there is less reason to assume irony or satire. An Australian magazine, targeted at middle-aged women, in an article on male impotence, refers to the possibility of learning "the internal muscular tricks of Asian girls" (Spencer-Mills, 1992, p. 61).

Earlier in this chapter, I noted some government resistance to the promotion of Thailand as a sex resort, resulting, *inter alia,* in initiatives to enforce closing hours of brothels (in the face of lack of success in suppressing them, notwithstanding their technical illegality), and to prevent the publication of material which might imply women were other than innocent before marriage and chaste thereafter.[25] To some extent, the national English-language press, whose readership includes tourists as well as longer-term visitors, has also sought to counter Thailand's stereotypic images by offering alternative images of chaste womanhood, while exposing the most excessive violent edges of the sex industry, such as the prostitution of children (e.g., Pornpimol, 1990; Pongpet, 1990). At the same time, unofficial voices also challenge this conflation of sexuality and nation, and challenge the economic and political relationships implicit in sex tourism, as the example of the White Lion Dance Company, described above, suggests.

Yet this is not complete. While images of women's bodies are used to sell Thailand to foreign tourists, the same images are also used to market a wide range of commodities within Thailand. These images are presented both in voyeuristic and invitational poses (Kuhn, 1985, p. 42). The voyeuristic images position the woman within her own activities, the male viewer of the advertising poster (or elsewhere the bar patron, the film viewer, the reader) is the voyeur; in contrast, the invitational poses position the woman to provoke and establish contact with the viewer. An example: an advertisement for a Thai film, placed over a cinema in Khon Kaen in northeast Thailand (fig. 14.1) draws upon this repertoire of woman as object: the woman's eyes are directed at the viewer in an invitational pose, her legs spread so that her hidden vagina is the central focus of the shot (and see Patra, 1990). Advertisements for products such as Kodak film and Nescafé instant coffee (fig. 14.2) also use invitational poses to seduce the viewer to buy.

Conclusions

Earlier I referred to Said's argument about the creation of "the Orient" as a cultural, political, and intellectual entity. Said, and others following his lead,

Figure 14.1   Cinema advertisement, Khon Kaen, 1991.

have argued that current constructions of "Asia" are successors to the fetishized, largely mythic, geographically proximate, and sometimes faithless
"Orient" of the nineteenth century (Said, 1978; Kabbani, 1986; Cocks, 1989;
Marcus, 1992; Suleri, 1992), such that the popular representations of Asia in
general, and countries such as Thailand in particular, are a sentimental mix of

Figure 14.2   Nescafé advertisement, Bangkok, 1991.

the erotic and exotic. European tourists to Thailand today may have little interest in or awareness of the postcolonial context in which they operate, far less
the theoretical and scholarly backdrop that has shaped it; they are influenced
primarily or solely by the popular cultural images corralled to promote tourism
and investment. As Cocks has argued, in this respect global expansion of capital has been accompanied by a cultural imperialism of a "corrosive/productive
sort" whereby poor countries are reconstituted "both in the West's own image
and . . . as its negative reflection" (1989, p. 16). Said has written of the "idea"
of the Orient (1991 [1978], p. 23); in this case, the "idea" is that of Thailand,
of Thai women, and Thai sexuality. As he notes (Said, 1991 [1978], p. 26), the
electronic media have drawn the Orient nearer, such that it is "less a myth
perhaps than a place criss-crossed by Western, especially American, interests,"

hence the advantages of marketing the place as a tourist destination, wherein the Orient becomes, not idle fancy, but a possible lived "trip of a lifetime." With contemporary tourism, the tourist travels "anywhere" and finds home— as elaborated above—and at the same time takes advantage of the "out-of-bounds" nature of this other place, with access (at least theoretically) to sexual expressions or experiences not imaginable or tolerated or possible at home.

Popular culture, in media such as film and television, cements these stereotypes. Just as industrial interests (American, Japanese, and Australian companies particularly) were lured to offshore factories through favorable concessions, the lure of cheap labor, and the pliability of the (female) labor force, collapsed within the image of the "nimble fingers" of Asian women (Elson and Pearson, 1981, p. 149), so tourists are lured to Thailand and other resort settings of Southeast Asia by low costs, friendly service, pliability of the "native women" and their purported gymnastic skills. The marketing technique, and the symbolic use of bodies, are the same: fingers and vaginas are the synechdoche of both woman and nation.

Notes

1. Government of Thailand projections estimate that by 2000, between two and four million Thais will be infected with HIV (Weniger et al., 1991); sentinel seroprevalence surveys indicate that around 50–60 percent of commercial sex workers and injecting drug users are infected (Thailand, Ministry of Public Health, 1992).

2. Note that paradise and the accessibility and availability of women and sex are the same thing.

3. Kleiber (1991: 8–9) make this same point with respect to the German-language literature. Schoepf (1992) also argues that women's participation in prostitution (and their reluctance to ensure protection from risk of HIV infection) is a rational response to their economic and social/personal situation where choice is limited and personal and economic power are both as much determined by the global economy and the fragility of the national economy as any particularly local factors. The parallel with Thailand is obvious but does not deal with the alternative arguments, including the personal (and health) costs born by individual women and their children.

4. For Thailand, see the references in Cohen, 1988; overseas, radio, and film sources include BBC, 1984; Porteus and Cooper, 1988; Molenaar, van Wijk and van Rooy, 1990; Friedman and Gatewood, 1991; ABC, 1992; Eddy and Walden, 1992; O'Donnell, 1992; and for a recent popular print story, see the article in *Time* (1993).

5. Lyttleton (1994) makes this point also.

6. See Bamber, Hewison, and Underwood (1993) for several occasions over the past century where, in the context of proposals for legislative control, prostitution was said to have been increasing at an unprecedented rate, often during times of social change. This proposition would seem readily tested in other times and places.

7. Agisra (1990, cited by Kleiber, 1991) estimates that 60 percent of travelers to Thailand in 1986 were sex tourists, three times the total number of tourists visiting the Philippines, the other sex-tourist port in Southeast Asia.

8. To the present, HIV in Australia has predominantly affected gay men, and popular

concern with sex tourism is to protect the heterosexual population. In this discourse, Australian men are represented as the innocents abroad, albeit irresponsibly so.

9. This phraseology, evocative of Gabriel Garcia Marquez, is from Herdt and Lindenbaum (1992).

10. Until around 1949, it was Shanghai that had the dubious reputation of "Whore of the Orient" (Broinowksi, 1992, p. 39).

11. See Turner and Ash (1975), also Crick (1985, p. 80) and Lea (1988, p. 1).

12. Lea (1988, p. 23) associates this with the promotion of tourism, which aims to create "an image of the destination in the mind of the potential traveller," resulting in the "growth of a mythology about some Third World destinations. . . . Imagery is thus an essential part of tourist decision-making but it can be manipulated to suggest that a destination has all the requirements of the 'bliss formula'." By way of example, he presents near identically worded advertisements for two separate countries; the marketing is so packaged that each is interchangeable for the other (1988, p. 24).

13. See Enloe (1989), Cass (1992), and Sturdevant and Stoltzfus (1992) on the Philippines, and the latter also for discussions of sex tourism associated with the U.S. military in Japan and South Korea.

14. On the street and in some other more basic brothels, sex is much cheaper, as little as 30 baht (U.S. $1.20; U.S. $1 = 25 baht at time of research and at present). O'Merry (1990) provides considerable information about income from prostitution, influenced by location of the brothel, clientele, type of services, and ethnicity of the sex worker.

15. Cass (1990, p. 18) documents similar acts in the Philippine bars, where women use their vaginas to stack coins, smoke cigarettes, cut or swallow bananas or sausages, and break eggs.

16. An earlier version of this section was included in Hardacre and Manderson (1990). I am grateful to Helen Hardacre for her translation of the Japanese used in performance and in the advertisements for this show, and for the lengthy discussions we had concerning its significance.

17. The show is advertised in Japanese at the airport as "family entertainment," and many Japanese family groups were present at the show; other groups did not take children.

18. I am grateful to Helen Hardacre for her interpretation of this piece.

19. This was, of course, common in both America and Australia prior to gay liberation.

20. A fuller discussion of film representations of Thailand and Thai sexuality is provided in Manderson (1993).

21. Although Paul Abramson (pers. comm., 1993) has suggested that Charles Gatewood's work is often closer to ethnography (e.g., *Side Tripping*, with William Burroughs; *Forbidden Photographs*), the "home-video" quality of the film and the breathy "gee whiz, guess what else they do here" nature of the commentary certainly allow this more generous reading.

22. This is underscored by the fact that Aoi had an off-screen Thai boyfriend, information that was not included in the film but became public knowledge after the film's release (Hamilton, 1993, p. 4).

23. See review by Grossman (1992).

24. For example, Ajahn ("teacher") is incorrectly used as a given name, not as an honorific (Drabble, 1992, p. 276).

25. The suppression of a research thesis written by a Thai student on the sexual strategies of "good" women, students at a regional university, was a case in point (Srirasa, 1988; *Time,* 1990).

References

ABC (Australian Broadcasting Commission). (1992). *AM* (Morning radio program) [Decreasing age of Thai prostitutes to cater for tourist tastes] (6 October).

ABC. (1993). *The Thai Sex Industry.* Foreign Correspondent (July 3, 19 mins).

AIDSCAP. (1992). *Inventory of Recent AIDS Field Research in Thailand.* Bangkok: AIDSCAP (mimeo).

Altman, D. (1982). *The Homosexualization of America and the Americanization of Homosexuality.* New York: Doubleday.

Ardener, E. (1975). Belief in the Problem of Women. In S. Ardener (ed.), *Perceiving Women,* pp. 1–17. London: Malaby Press.

Ardener, S. (1975). Sexual insult and female militancy. In S. Ardener (ed.), *Perceiving Women,* pp. 29–53. London: Malaby Press.

Bamber, S., Hewison, K. J. and Underwood, P. J. (1993). A history of sexually transmitted diseases in Thailand: policy and politics. *Genitourinary Medicine 69,* 148–57.

Barnes, B. (1993). Emotional hell of predators who fall for their exotic prey. *The Australian,* May 14, 11.

BBC (British Broadcasting Corporation). World in Action. (1984). *Slaves of Progress* (film). Series: 60 Minutes. Sydney: Channel 9 (April 15, 12 mins.)

Broinowski, A. (1992). *The Yellow Lady. Australian Impressions of Asia.* Melbourne: Oxford University Press.

Bruner, E. M. (1984). Introduction. In E. M. Bruner (ed.), *Text, Play and Story: The Construction and Reconstruction of Self and Society,* pp. 1–18. 1983 Proceedings of the American Ethnological Society. Washington: American Ethnological Society.

Bruner, E. M. and Plattner, S. (eds). (1984). *Text, Play and Story: The Construction and Reconstruction of Self and Society.* 1983 Proceedings of the American Ethnological Society. Washington: American Ethnological Society.

Cass, A.-M. (1992). "Gender and Violence in the Philippines." Ph.D. dissertation. Brisbane: University of Queensland.

Cater, N. (1993). Lost Innocents. Young faces, scarred bodies: the victims of Thailand's sex trade. *The Courier-Mail,* July 10, 29.

Cocks, J. (1989). *The Oppositional Imagination. Feminism, Critique, and Political Theory.* London: Routledge and Kegan Paul.

Cohen, E. (1972). Towards a sociology of international tourism. *Social Research 39,* 164–82.

Cohen, E. (1982). Thai girls and farang men: The edge of ambiguity. *Annals of Tourism Research,* 9, 3, 403–28.

Cohen, E. (1988). Tourism and AIDS in Thailand. *Annals of Tourism Research, 15,* 467–86.

Crick, M. (1985). Tracing the anthropological self: Quizzical reflections on field work, tourism, and the ludic. *Social Analysis, 17,* 71–92.

DaGrossa, P. S. (1987–8). "The Dirt Wall (Gam Phaeng Din). A Study of Prostitution in the All-Thai Brothels of Chiang Mai City." Ph.D. dissertation, University of Wisconsin-Madison's College Year in Thailand Program.

Dawson, A. (1988). *Patpong. Bangkok's Big Little Street.* Bangkok: Thai Watana Panich Press.

Drabble, M. (1992). *The Gates of Ivory.* New York: Viking.

Eddy, P. and Walden, S. (1992). Terror in the Land of Smiles. *The Australian Magazine,* September 19–20, 10–18.

Elson, D. and Pearson, R. (1981). The subordination of women and the internationalization of factory production. In K. Young, C. Wolkowitz and R. McCullagh (eds.), *Of Marriage and the Market. Women's Subordination in International Perspective,* pp. 144–66. London: CSE Books.

Embree, J. F. (1950). Thailand—a loosely structured society. *American Anthropologist, 52,* 181–93.

Enloe, C. (1989). *Bananas, Beaches and Bases.* London: Pandora.

Finney, B. R. and Watson, K. A. (1979). A new kind of sugar. *Annals of Tourism Research, 6,* 469–71.

Friedman, Bart and Gatewood, C. (Producer and Director) (1991). *Shocking Thailand (a.k.a. Weird Thailand).* (Released by Forbidden Planet). Woodstock, N.J.: Media Bus Inc.

Ford, N. and Koetsawang, S. (1991). The socio-cultural context of the transmission of HIV in Thailand. *Social Science and Medicine, 33,* 405–14.

Garber, M. (1992). The occidental tourist: *M. Butterfly* and the scandal of transvestism, pp. 121–46, In A. Parker, M. Russo, D. Sommer, & P. Yaeger (eds.), *Nationalisms and Sexualities,* pp. 121–46. Routledge: New York and London.

Geertz, C. (1975). On the nature of anthropological understanding. *American Scientist, 63,* 47–53.

Gray, J. (1990). "The Road to the City." Ph.D. thesis, Department of Anthropology, School of Behavioural Sciences. Sydney: Macquarie University.

Grossman, J. (1992). Good time, bad time. *The Women's Review of Books, 9,* 10–11, 30.

Guan Fei and Jun Feng (Trans. Xiong Zhenru). (1993). Shenzhen's Booming Night Life, *China Tourism, 156,* 40–45.

Guo Hongyi and Shi Bao Xiu (Trans. Wang Mingjie). (1993). China's newest melting pot, *China Tourism, 156,* 16–25.

Hamilton, A. (1993). Mistaken identities: Art, truth and dare in "The Good Woman of Bangkok." Manuscript, School of Behavioural Sciences, Macquarie University, Sydney.

Hardacre, H. and Manderson, L. (1990). The Hall of Mirrors. Paper presented to the International Workshop on the Construction of Gender and Sexuality in East and Southeast Asia. Los Angeles: University of California.

Havanon, N., Knodel, J. and Bennett, T. (1992). *Sexual Networking in a Provincial Thai Setting.* Aids Prevention Monograph Series, Paper No. 1. Bangkok: AIDSCAP.

Herdt, G. (in press [1982]). *The Guardians of the Flutes* (rev. ed.). New York: McGraw-Hill.

Herdt, G. and Lindenbaum, S. (eds.) (1992). *The Time of AIDS. Social Analysis, Theory and Method.* Newbury Park: Sage.

Hewison, K. (1985). Economic development, prostitution and tourism in Thailand. *Inside Asia, 6,* 33–35.

Hochschild, T. (1983). *The Managed Heart: Commercialization of Human Feeling.* Berkeley: University of California Press.

Jaeckin, J. (Director). (1974). *Emmanuelle* (film). Sylvie Kristel, Marika Green, Alain Cuny. Yves Rousset-Rouard, Executive Producer. Trinacra Films (86 mins).

Kabbani, R. (1986). *Europe's Myths of the Orient.* Bloomington: Indiana University Press.

Kempton, M. (1992). A new colonialism. *New York Review of Books.* November 19, 39.

Khin Thitsa. (1980). *Providence and Prostitution. Image and Reality for Women in Buddhist Thailand.* London: Change International Reports.

Kleiber, D. (1991). AIDS und (Sex-)Tourismus. In Niedersachsisches Sozialministerium (ed.), *AIDS und Tourismus,* pp. 1–28. Hannover: Edition AIDS 11.

Kuhn, A. (1985). *The Power of the Image: Essays on Representation and Sexuality.* London: Routledge and Kegan Paul.

Lea, J. (1970). *Tourism and Development in the Third World.* London: Routledge.

Lehtimaki, H. (Writer and Director) (1993). *You Can't Buy a Wife, Can You?* Finland: Forsti-Filmi Production (Screened Sydney, SBS Television, Connections, May 20, 51 mins).

Leiper, N. (1979). The framework of tourism. Towards a definition of tourism, tourist and the tourist industry. *Annals of Tourism Research, 6,* 390–407.

Lyttleton, C. (1994). Knowledge and meaning: The AIDS education campaign in rural northeast Thailand. *Social Science and Medicine, 38,* 1, 135–46.

Macaloon, J. J. (1984). *La Pitada Olimpica:* Puerto Rice, international sport, and the constitution of politics. In E. M. Bruner (ed.), *Text, Play and Story: The Construction and Reconstruction of Self and Society,* pp. 315–55. 1983 Proceedings of the American Ethnological Society. Washington: American Ethnological Society.

Manderson, L. (1982). Sexuality and the study of culture: The anthropology of homosexuality, *Gay Information, 11,* 12–17.

Manderson, L. (1992). Public sex performance in Patpong and explorations of the edges of imagination. *Journal of Sex Research, 29,* 4, 451–75.

Manderson, L. (1993). Parables of imperialism and fantasies of the exotic: Western representations of Thailand, place and sex. Paper presented to Conference on Sexuality, Reproduction and the State in Asia and the Pacific, Canberra, Australian National University, 15–17 July 1993.

Marcus, J. (1992). *A World of Difference: Islam and Gender Hierarchy in Turkey.* Women in Asia Publications Series. Sydney: Allen and Unwin.

Mintz, S. (1977). Infant, victim, and tourist: the anthropologist in the field. *Johns Hopkins Magazine, 27,* 54–60.

Molenaar, H., Van Wijk, J. and Van Rooy, H. (Directors) (1990). *Cannot Run Away* (film). Series: The Cutting Edge. Sydney; SBS (Special Broadcasting Service) (May 29, 58 mins).

Muecke, M. A. (1984). Make money not babies: Changing status markers of Northern Thai women. *Asian Survey, 24,* 4, 459–70.

Muecke, M. A. (1992). Mother sold food, daughter sells her body: the cultural continuity of prostitution. *Social Science and Medicine 35,* 7, 891–901.

Na Banchang, N. (1991). Comparison study of the knowledge about AIDS before and after health education among textile workers. In *9th National Seminar on Epidemiology: Abstracts,* August.

Nation. (1990). Thai daily apologises over "Sex Thesis." August 28, A2.

O'Donnell, M. (Producer) (1992). *The AIDS Domino.* Series: Four Corners. Sydney: ABC (Australian Broadcasting Corporation) (February 17, 42 min.)

O'Merry, R. (1990). *My Wife in Bangkok.* Berkeley: Asia Press.

O'Rourke, D. (Writer and Director). (1991). *The Good Woman of Bangkok* (film). Film Australia (O'Rourke and Associates Filmakers in association with the Australian Film Commission and Channel 4) (82 mins).

Parker, A., Russo, M., Sommer, D., and Yaeger, P. (1992). Introduction. In A. Parker, M. Russo, D. Sommer & P. Yaeger (eds.), *Nationalisms and Sexualities,* pp. 1–18. New York and London: Routledge.

Pasuk Phongpaichit. (1982). *From Peasant Girls to Bangkok Masseuses.* Women, Work and Development, 2. Geneva: International Labour Office.

Patra Danutra. (1990). When movies turn blue. *Nation* August 26, C1.

Patton, C. (1992). From nation to family: Containing "African AIDS." In A. Parker, M. Russo, D. Sommer, and P. Yaeger (eds.), *Nationalisms and Sexualities,* pp. 218–34. New York and London: Routledge.

Pearce, P. L. and Moscardo, G. M. (1986). The concept of authenticity in tourist experiences. *Australia and New Zealand Journal of Sociology, 22,* 1, 121–32.

The Pearl. (1992). July issue. Hong Kong.

Pongpet Mekloy. (1990). Finding ways to solve boy prostitution problem. *Bangkok Post* September 1, 25.

Pongswatanakulsiri, P., Sitikul, S., Kasemsook, R., et al. (1991). AIDS infection opportunity among labourers. In *9th National Seminar on Epidemiology: Abstracts,* August.

Pornpimol Kanchanalak. (1990). Thai image hampered in American TV show. *Bangkok Post,* June 9, 1, 3.

Porteus, A. and Cooper, T. (Producers) (1988). *Foreign Bodies* (film) (Reporter: Tim Cooper), London: Clarke Productions for Channel 4 (December 21, 1987, 38 mins. 30 sec.)

Ricoeur, P. (1971). The model of the text: Meaningful action considered as a text. *Social Research, 38,* 529–62.

Rubin, G. (1992 [1984]). Thinking sex: Notes for a radical theory of the politics of sexuality, In C. S. Vance, (ed.), *Pleasure and Danger. Exploring Female Sexuality,* pp. 267–319. London: Pandora Press.

Said, E. W. (1991 [1978]). *Orientalism.* London: Penguin.

Schoepf, B. G. (1992). Women at risk: Case studies from Zaire. In G. Herdt and S. Lindenbaum (eds.), *The Time of AIDS. Social Analysis, Theory and Method,* pp. 259–86. Newbury Park: Sage.

Sittitrai, W., Phanuphak, P., Barry, J., Sabaiying, M. and Brown, T. (1991). Survey of partner relations and risk of HIV infection in Thailand. *VII International Conference on AIDS.* Florence, June [abstract MD4113].

Sontag, S. (1970). The pornographic imagination. In D. A. Hughes (ed.), *Perspectives on Pornography* (pp. 131–69). New York: Mcmillan and St. Martin's Press.

Spillers, H. J. (1992). Interstices: a small drama of words. In C. S. Vance (ed.), *Pleasure and Danger. Exploring Female Sexuality,* pp. 73–100. London: Pandora Press.

Srirasa, S. (1988). ["Student Life at Khon Kaen University"]. Master's thesis, Department of Higher Education, Graduate School. Bangkok: Chulalongkorn University.

Sturdevant, S. P. and Stoltzfus, B. (1993). *Let the Good Times Roll: Prostitution and the U.S. Military in Asia.* New York: The New Press.

Sukanya Hantrakul. (1983). Prostitution in Thailand. In L. Melville (ed.), *Women, Aid and Development,* pp. 61–63. Proceedings of a Workshop Co-sponsored by Women and Development Network of Australia, Australian Council for Overseas Aid, and Development Studies Centre of the Australian National University. Canberra: Women and Development Network of Australia.

Sukanya Hantrakul. (1984). Dutiful Daughters on Society's Lower Rungs. *Far Eastern Economic Review,* January 5, 39–40.

Sukanya Hantrakul. (1988). Prostitution in Thailand, In G. Chandler, N. Sullivan and J. Branson, (eds.), *Development and Displacement: Women in Southeast Asia,* pp. 115–36. Monash Papers on Southeast Asia 18. Clayton: Centre for Southeast Asian Studies, Monash University.

Suleri, S. (1992). *The Rhetoric of English India.* Chicago: University of Chicago Press.

Thailand, Ministry of Public Health. (1992). ["Summary of the Survey on HIV Infection in Dec 1991"]. Bangkok: mimeo.

Thanprasertsuk, S. and Pimyothamakorn, S. (1991). [Epidemiology of HIV Infection in Thailand]. In [*First National Seminar on AIDS*] Bangkok: Division of Epidemiology, MOPH.

Time. (1993). Skirmish in the sex-trade war. August 2, 10.

Truong, T.-D. (1990). *Sex, Money and Morality. Prostitution and Tourism in South-East Asia.* London: Zed Books.

Turner, L. and Ash, L. (1975). *The Golden Hordes. International Tourism and the Pleasure Industry.* London: Constable.

Turner, V. (1973). The center out there: pilgrim's goal. *History of Religions, 12,* 191–230.

Turner, V. (1974). *The Ritual Process.* Harmondsworth: Penguin.

Turner, V. and Turner, E. (1978). *Image and Pilgrimage in Christian Culture.* New York: Columbia University Press.

Turton, A. (1982). Thai institutions of slavery. In J. L. Watson (ed.), *Asian and African Systems of Slavery,* pp. 251–92. Oxford: Basil Blackwell.

Urry, J. 1990a. *The Tourist Gaze, Leisure and Travel in Contemporary Societies.* London: Sage Publications.

Urry, J. (1990b). The "consumption" of tourism. *Sociology, 24,* 1, 23–35.

Weniger, B. G., Khanchit L., Kumnuan, U., et al. (1991). The epidemiology of HIV infection and AIDS in Thailand. *AIDS, 5* (Supp. 2), S71–85.

Wouters, C. (1989). The sociology of emotions and flight attendants: Hochschild's *Managed Heart. Theory, Culture and Society, 6,* 95–124.

CHAPTER FIFTEEN

Sexuality and the Experience of Love

THOMAS GREGOR

The study of sex is relatively new to the discipline of anthropology, having begun only after the liberating impact of psychoanalysis (see Tuzin, this volume). Even today, some sixty-five years after the publication of Malinowski's *Sex and Repression in Savage Society,* there is no abundance of data and theory. Detailed case studies of the sexual lives and sexual culture of non-Western peoples, which are vital to constructing a panhuman perspective on sexuality, are few and far between. Systematic studies of sexual pleasure, as opposed to sex as reproduction, or of the relationship of gender and sex, are rarer still (see, however, Abramson & Pinkerton 1995). Why is so little known, when sex is essential to procreation, the basis of kinship, the source of much joy and pain, and, universally, a subject of interest and even obsession? This ignorance, I believe, is largely due to repression, which stifles understanding and constricts knowledge.

Like sex, love is also an important topic. It is a main theme of popular culture; it is the preoccupation of the young (and not so young); and, for those who are lucky, it is the source of one of life's most meaningful and perhaps most pleasurable experiences. Conversely, the pathologies of love are responsible for much of the emotional pain of the human condition. Lying in the wake of broken relationships are discord and abuse. Dysfunctional love (strife between adults in the home) is also a root cause of many cases of child abuse and neglect (Tzeng 1992:ii).

If knowledge of sex is repressed, understanding of love is only slightly less so. Until recently, studies of love faced ridicule, as in 1976 when Senator William Proxmire mockingly awarded his "Golden Fleece Award" to a social psychologist who had applied to the National Science Foundation for a research grant on love:

> I'm against it because I don't want the answer. I believe that two hundred million Americans want to leave some things in life a mystery. And right at the top of the list of things we don't want to know is why a man falls in love with a woman and vice versa. . . . So, National Science Foundation, get out of the love racket. Leave that to Elizabeth Barrett Browning and Irving Berlin.

The questioning of love as a serious scholarly topic also pervades the social sciences. In sociology, for example, love has been interpreted as a device to maintain class stratification through endogamous marriage. That is, what one obtains in marriage is more or less their market worth in money, looks, and personality. Thus, after experiencing many painful rejections, lovers presumably settle for "resource homogeneous coupling." From this perspective, love is little more than the relief that comes from escaping a punishing marriage market.

Although there is nothing inherent in feminism that would reject love, some feminists have also been disdainful of it. Love, according to several writers, is a sham reward for conforming to traditional roles; it is a trap designed to lure women into punishing and unequal relationships (Safilios-Rothschild 1977).

The mental hygiene movement has also been wary of love (see Person 1989:17), regarding passion as an immature experience that might, if lovers are fortunate, be a prelude to a committed relationship. M. Scott Peck, a psychiatrist and the author of a perennial best-seller, *The Road Less Traveled,* writes ". . . the myth of romantic love is a dreadful lie. . . . Its ultimate purpose? . . . falling in love is a trick that our genes pull on our otherwise perceptive mind to hoodwink or trap us into marriage" (1978:90–92). Some view love even more negatively. For example, love has been identified as a newly discovered addiction, every bit as damaging as chemical dependencies and eating disorders: "love addiction . . . is just about the most common, yet least recognized, form of addiction" (Peel 1975:17).

Psychoanalysis may well offer the greatest potential for understanding love. Traditionally, however, analysis has been reluctant "to explore love in any rigorous fashion" (Gaylin & Person 1988). Typically, love is seen as a kind of regression. In its most intense form, the beloved is "overvalued," and the love partners are in a state, that for Freud, resembled hypnosis or even a psychotic break:

> From being in love to hypnosis is evidently only a short step. The respects in which the two agree are obvious. There is the same humble subjection, the same compliance, the same absence of criticism towards the hypnotist as towards the love object. . . . There is the same sapping of the subject's own initiative. (Freud 1965)

However, recently analysts have begun to take a deeper look at love (e.g., Kristeva, 1987). Perhaps the best effort by an analyst to fully understand and honor the experience of love is Ethel Person's *Dreams of Love and Fateful Encounters.* Significantly, much of her insight comes from poets and novelists rather than from members of her own profession or the other social sciences. She remarks that, with respect to the understanding of love, "What is unique about our century . . . is the extent to which love is no longer even deemed worthy of intellectual analysis" (1989:18). While this conclusion has much heuristic value, I want to also note that in the last few years social psychology, among other fields, has paid increasing attention to love as a topic meriting research. There is now a journal partly devoted to the subject of love (*The Journal of Social and Personal Relationships*) and a good deal of vigorous investigation. In a recent book Oliver Tzeng (1992) looks systematically at no less than twenty-one theories of love, all generated by social psychologists.[1]

Despite this recent work, however, there continue to be gaps in our knowledge of love, and distortions in how we think about the relevant issues. For example, do people in other cultures experience love as we do? Is sexual love a universal human phenomenon? What is the relationship of love and sex? In thinking about love, as in thinking about sex, we often lack basic data and theory. My intention in this paper, therefore, is to link sex and love theoretically, and explore the opposition of repression and sexual love in the context of a small tribal society, the Mehinaku of Brazil.

Sex and Love

Sex without Love

One of the least explored areas in love and sexuality is the connection between the two. This is striking because intuitively we feel they are joined. Certainly our popular culture says that they are. In fact, lovingness, ideally in the state of marriage, is the only completely sanctioned context for sexual relations. Love *justifies* sex. Yet, scientifically, the two are considered apart. Moreover, the study of sex seldom does justice to the emotional connection between those who participate in the sexual act. Rather, sex is often described ethologically, producing a list of behaviors and practices rather than explicating their emotional meanings. For example, Kinsey's studies, *Sexual Behavior in the Human Male* and *Sexual Behavior in the Human Female,* are made up, in considerable part, of lists and tables of sexual behavior. A typical table is titled "Utilization of Petting Techniques at Three Educational Levels," in which we learn that the technique "kissing, deep, marital" is performed by 77.3 percent of individuals of all ages with more than thirteen years of education (1948:368). The accompanying text explains that:

> Deep kissing is utilized as a prime source of erotic arousal by many persons in the better educated and top social levels. A deep kiss may involve considerable tongue contact, deep lip contact and extended explorations of the partner's mouth. . . . Such behavior is a regular concomitant of coital activity among many of the vertebrates. (1948:368)

The behavioralized approach to sex characteristic of Kinsey's path-breaking work has found its way into other areas of the social sciences, including anthropology. Hence, in Ford and Beach's (1951) classic study, *Patterns of Sexual Behavior,* data on sex are taken from 190 societies, stripped from any cultural or psychological context, and presented in summarized form: "Most of the societies in our sample prefer women who have a broad pelvis and wide hips. The Yakut are an exception in that they specifically dislike a woman with these characteristics" (1951:86). Often, the emphasis is on the exotic: On "returning from a head-hunting raid the Lhota Naga hang up the hearts, fingers and toes of their victims and then sleep apart from their wives for six nights" (1951:77). As for love, most anthropological works on sex give it scant attention. In Ford and Beach, love receives only passing reference under "love magic." More recently, Suzanne Frayser's *Varieties of Sexual Experience* (1985), which emerges from the same comparative tradition, gives only slight attention to the topic.

Current anthropological case studies now examine the cultural symbolism of sex even if its emotional meaning to individuals is not investigated. Sex is seen as "culturally constructed" and linked to ideas about kinship, power, and religion. Placing the study of sex within the context of culture is a step forward. Nonetheless, culture is often a mask that conceals or misrepresents our deepest feelings. Sexual culture is as likely to be the first line of repression as it is to be an accurate guide to individual experience. Biographical, "person-centered" data are therefore also essential. The only fields that collect this kind of material in abundance are psychiatry, psychology, and psychoanalysis, which often explore sexuality in a profound manner. The focus, however, is usually not on the positive dimensions of sex, but on its darker side, as in the study of paraphilia and pathology.

What are we to make of the extent to which sex is described as if it were disconnected from emotion, especially from positive emotion? I suggest that the antiseptic, clinical approach to sex is, in many regards, both a defensive reaction to the repressive atmosphere in our culture, and a manifestation of it. The ethology of sex, and even the cultural symbolism of sex, are far easier to describe and contemplate than are the deeper emotional experiences that lie beneath them. It is, perhaps, no accident that Kinsey, one of the great pioneers in the study of sex, was originally a professor of zoology.

Love without Sex

In the scientific literature, sex is often cut off from the spirit. Love, in contrast, is treated too ethereally, as though separate from the body. Freud, for instance, argued that love could not coexist with sex. Love, he maintained, was equivalent to "goal-inhibited" libido. Once sexual relations occurred, there was no longer a need to invest sexual energy in romantic fantasy. Love, in its intense form, would therefore dissipate (1965). This position may have had an impact on subsequent research. Hence, affection, regard, commitment, and even longing are seen as part of love, but sex is seldom seen as its cornerstone. In the anthropological literature love is so disembodied that it is seldom described at all, much less linked to sex. So rare are accounts of love and so vaporous are its descriptions, that Robert Endleman (1989), in a work that I will return to further on, maintains that it may not exist outside of cultures such as our own.

Love Mirrors Sex

The separation of love and sex is, I believe, an error. Love is an erotic relationship involving passion, intimacy, commitment, and idealization of another. Like sex, its aim is union: "The aim of love is nothing less than to overcome separateness and achieve union or merger with the beloved" (Person 1989:82). Person describes the merging qualities of love in terms that would apply equally to sex:

> feelings of union will be interspersed with ecstatic moments of merger. These magic moments are experienced as epiphanies. At such times, there is, if not a loss of ego boundaries, at least a permeability of ego boundaries. During these moments, the lovers experience a sense of timelessness, bliss, and transcendence . . . (yet) the self is preserved, the spirit exalted. (1989:127)

Moreover, in the context of the loving relationship, the pleasure of the sexual act is intensified: "It is in love that one is granted the most compelling sexual experiences of one's life" (1989:64).

Sex is often linked to love because it achieves the physical union that love seeks emotionally and spiritually. In this view, the act of intercourse models and embodies the risk-taking, the gratifications, and the sense of merger of the love experience. As such, it is the most intense expression of lovingness and, in all likelihood, is a universal concomitant of love. We can easily imagine sex without love; in fact it is probably the most common experience. But it is more difficult to imagine romantic love between adults without sex, or at least the yearning for sex (Person 1989:81). I believe it is helpful to be as specific as possible about the parallels between love and the sexual act.

Sex Mirrors Love: Parallels between the Physical Act of Sexual Relations and Love

Sex, Love, Risk, and Trust

Falling in love, like the act of sex, is an act of risk and an act of trust. As in any merger, one must be sure of one's partner. At risk are substantial material and emotional resources. Can your beloved be trusted with confidences and secrets? Will he (or she) kiss and tell? Will you be forsaken for another? These fears are substantial enough, but deeper fears lie beneath the surface. According to psychoanalytic theory, loving relationships are evocative of Oedipal conflicts and taboos. The beloved may be attractive precisely because he or she resembles the opposite sex parent. The resemblance, however, evokes the barriers associated with incest. Thus, at the deepest level, the experience of love may tap profound anxieties. The sense of merging, which is love's most heady intoxicant, can also awaken preoedipal fears of fragmenting, disorganization, and dissolution of the self. Consequently, "falling in love," writes Ethel Person, "is, by its nature, predicated on risk-taking" (1989:44).

Like love, the physical act of sex requires trust. Will one be injured while having intercourse? The female is particularly vulnerable, due to greater male strength, but, in fact, both male and female are almost without defense against a lover bent on mayhem. In many nonhuman species sex and violence are potentially linked, but adaptive mechanisms limit the possibility of harm. The most basic adaptations are those that limit the sexual act to the minimum that is required for reproduction. These include demarcated breeding seasons and periods of heat (estrus), extremely brief acts of intercourse and rapid ejaculation, and rapid separation after the act of sex (see Pavelka, this volume). A second set of adaptations directly reduces violence. These include stereotyped courtship rituals that precede the sexual act; female submission and passivity that reduce the potentially high costs of confronting a stronger male; and, sexual positions (dorsal mounting) that minimize the trauma that can be done by teeth and claws.

The more advanced the species in the primate order, the fewer the mechanisms that limit sexual interaction and the greater the potential for bonding. At one extreme, rhesus macaques take only 3 to 5 seconds to copulate, while the great apes may precede the act with partners manually stimulating one another and taking from 3 to 17 minutes to complete intercourse (Frayser 1985:38). Pygmy chimpanzees (bonobos), who have many similarities with humans, also engage in frequent sexual behavior (apparently well beyond the need to reproduce), utilize ventral sexual positions, and express preference for specific sexual partners (see de Waal, this volume).

Humans forgo many of the protective devices employed by other mammals for reducing the risks of sexual relations. By prolonging sex and prefacing it with foreplay, humans entrust sensitive, usually defended regions of the body to a partner. The risks are real, since the act of sex can be an intensely regressive experience that awakens latent and primitive forms of aggression. Furthermore, there is an unquestionable liability to sexual access, as is evidenced by the frequency of rapes, physical coercion, and beatings associated with sexual relations in our own culture. Unlike animals who rely more on behavioral and physical adaptation, we must trust our partners within the sexual act. Trust is essential to sex, and, through association, to love as well.

Trust also has a second, more symbolic dimension. In sexual relations we expose ourselves to the other's gaze, and possibly to their negative judgments. Due to codes of modesty and sexual repression (which, in different forms, are cultural universals), the sexual anatomy is heavily defended territory. Our sexual partners confirm or disconfirm the worth of our sexual selves. Just as lovers share intimacies and bare their souls, sexual partners expose their bodies, contingent upon trust.

The Sexual Act and Ego Boundaries: Body Fluids

Love is ultimately about union and the overcoming of separateness. The sexual act models the transcendence of boundaries at both physical and psychological levels. Sex is an act of crossing and blurring the boundaries of self. At the simplest level, sexual partners share sweat, semen, saliva, vaginal secretions, and perhaps tears, blood, hair, urine, excrement and (unfortunately) microorganisms as well. In all cultures, substances that go across the boundaries of self are endowed with more than ordinary significance (see Leach 1964). They are believed to have magical power to heal or inflict harm, and are often utilized as fetishes in witchcraft. In our own culture, boundary-crossing substances are powerful contaminators (see Rozin & Nemeroff 1991; Goffman 1959). They are shared in the context of ritualized interactions, such as those with service personnel (doctors, dentists, barbers), deliberate defilements (for example, with saliva or excrement), and in the act of sex itself. Only in sex do we, as adults, totally open ourselves and welcome the experience of crossing boundaries. Psychologically, therefore, the sexual act is very much like the experience of love. Both require the surrender of the self and a willingness to merge with the partner at a very profound and magical level.

Sexual Feeling

Demeanor and comportment define the social self (Goffman 1956). The full experience of sexual feeling is such that the individual must give up the behaviors that construct that self. In "bed" there is a fundamental democracy. Partners face one another in a unique personal communitas, during which, posture, facial expression, and vocalizations are no longer monitored:

> The person in the grip of sexual excitement appears tense from head to toe. The activities of the muscles, though dramatic, are by no means the only sexual response of the body. The skin becomes flushed; salivation increases; the nostrils may flare; the heart pounds; breathing grows heavy; the face is contorted and flushed; the person feels, looks and acts quite unlike his or her ordinary self. (Katchadourian & Lunde 1980:64)

Giving up on self-boundaries and self-control facilitates the sense of merging. Lovers appear to one another as open, spontaneous, and sharing the same experience. The mutuality of pleasure promotes even greater permeability of ego boundaries, so that the two partners feel as one.

Plateau and Orgasm

Based on laboratory measurements of 694 individuals experiencing more than 10,000 orgasms, Masters and Johnson divided the human sexual response into the phases of excitement, plateau, orgasm, and resolution. The timing of these events is highly variable. The plateau phase, which is essentially a continuation of a high level of myotonia and vascular congestion, may be deliberately pro-longed for up to an hour or more.[3] The subjective experience may be that of a dreamlike state of intense connectedness, isolation of the couple within the relationship, and physical gratification. There is evidence that the last phases of the sexual plateau and orgasm provide an experiential basis for the feelings associated with love. Hence individuals report that in these circumstances the most undesirable and unappealing partners appear, albeit very briefly, as in-tensely attractive and wonderful. Orgasm, especially simultaneous orgasm, confirms the sexual partners' sense of having merged, and models what is to many people the ultimate goal of love—the union of lovers: "The ultimately biological roots of human attachment . . . are realized through intense double identification during orgasm" (Kernberg 1976). The lovers sense of mutual gratification is thereby further generalized, so that the benefits of sex enhance the nonsexual attributes of the relationship.

Love, Sex, and Love Repression

Love Repression

The act of sex is often a lesson in love. It models and rewards the trust, the lowering of ego boundaries and the sense of merging that constitutes the loving relationship. If sex is universal, should not love also be? Unfortunately, the literature tends to be skeptical, limiting love to Western traditions and finite historical periods. Typical of this perspective is the following statement: "Only in a society with an enormously powerful ideology of the individual, in which the 'alienation' of the individual from the larger society is not only tolerated but even encouraged and celebrated, can the phenomenon of romantic love even be conceivable" (Solomon 1981:136).

William Goode argues that love appears primarily in cultures that facilitate it. He lists a number of characteristics of such cultures, including the autonomy of the nuclear family, emphasis on the conjugal bond, and freedom of adoles-cents (1959:54). Western societies offer prime examples of love-facilitating cultures. They not only have the correct institutional base, but they also make love the predominant theme of popular and classical culture.[4] Furthermore, love is often the only acceptable basis for marriage. In such societies a person must offer a good rationalization for marriage without being in love.

The anthropological literature appears to support Goode. The number of reports of well-documented love relationships from tribal societies are astoundingly few (see Shostack [1981] for an exceptional description). Impres-sed by this paucity of data, Robert Endleman wondered whether love (in the sense of an intense sexual relationship involving commitment and idealization) exists at all in tribal societies. To find out, he chose twelve tribal cultures where the ethnography was unusually rich and was written from a psychological per-spective. He concludes in *Love and Sex in Twelve Cultures,* that "something like our Western conception of love, though not entirely absent, seems to be rare in . . . tribal or transitional societies" (1989:83).

Certainly the *expectation* of love is unusual in many cultures. It is seldom institutionalized or a normative requirement for marriage, as is the case in our own society. The question, however, is why don't *all* cultures institutionalize love? The answer, I believe, is that, if sexual repression is a universal, the inhibition of love is almost as ubiquitous. Significantly, many of the same kinds of devices that repress sex also repress love. Collins (1993:15–17) notes that these devices are of two kinds, those that create external institutional barriers to love, and those that erect psychological barriers within the individual. Among the most widespread of the institutional barriers are arranged marriage, harem polygyny, gender inequality, unequal age at marriage, seclusion of women and chaperonage, obsession with virginity, descent systems that create primary allegiances to parents rather than spouses, clitoridectomy, the men's-house complex, association of women with impurity and contamination, totalitarianism that subverts family loyalties, and patterns of sexual promiscuity that undermine enduring relationships.

Operating within the individual, psychological barriers also prevent the formation of loving relationships. Endleman (1989), with a focus on love in tribal societies, suggests that idealization of the love partner depends on warm, consistent, and enduring bonds between children and their parents. Unfortunately such relationships are rare. In a pattern typical of many small-scale cultures, children are a focus of intense parental attention only until a new sibling is born, at which point they are abruptly separated from the mother, often to be "farmed out to other, possibly unreliable and uncaring kin" (1989:117). The physical realities of life in many societies also disrupt the relationships of parents and children. Warfare, malnutrition, disease, and infanticide create an environment that is unpredictable and potentially lethal. In such a setting it makes sense to withhold emotional investment in children, who, after all, may never survive (see Scheper-Hughes 1985).

The repression of love is thus undoubtedly real and widespread. This finding, I believe, is striking. It also raises the question of whether love is a culture-bound emotional experience. For example, if Endleman had claimed that anger, jealousy, envy, or sexual longing were absent from a sample of cultures, we might have been skeptical. Yet, love seems easier to dismiss as being neither fundamentally human nor universal. Thus I raise the question of whether love is really absent, or whether it is simply not reported. Anthropologists are mainly concerned with official culture rather than actual experience, and as a consequence, they often miss the nuances of relationships (see Tuzin, this volume, on normative concerns, and Cohen, this volume, as they relate to the Hijra). Nonetheless, there is evidence that love may be experienced by at least some individuals in *every* culture. In a recent cross-cultural study, William Jankowiak and Edward Fischer (1992) examined a sample of 166 societies for evidence of love relationships. The authors coded romantic love as existing if any one of the following were present: descriptions of longing and anguish; presence of love songs; elopement due to affection; or, informants' or the ethnographer's statement that romantic love exists. The authors were able to demonstrate the occurrence of love in 88.5 percent of the cultures in their sample, a finding that is "in direct contradiction to the popular idea that romantic love is essentially limited to or the product of Western culture." Further, they concluded that love "constitutes a human universal or at the least a near universal." [5]

It is no surprise that people fall in love in our society. Cultural scripts guide us towards the experience. But in the absence of these scripts how do love partners find one another? Quoting La Rochefoucauld, Endleman asks "Who would ever fall in love / Had they never heard of love?" The fact that love partners find each other, apparently even in the most unpromising environments, suggests the power of the need to love, and the ability of individuals to transcend their "official" cultures.

Sex, Love and The Mehinaku

I now propose to examine the dialectic of repression and sexual love in the context of a small Amazonian society, that of the Mehinaku Indians of Brazil.[6] I do so in part to provide rare documentation of loving relationships in tribal societies, but also because the Mehinaku are an interesting test case. The villagers are at once extremely active sexually, yet in many ways they are repressed. The opposition of repression and emotional need is an everyday Mehinaku reality that finds expression in individual behavior and in the villagers' culture.

Mehinaku Sexual Freedom and Sexual Repression

The Mehinaku are a tribe of some 135 Arawakan-speaking tropical-forest Indians who live in Brazil's Xingu National Park. Like all of the Xingu Indians who have been described in the literature, the villagers claim our attention because they are sexually free in ways that we are not. For example, the Mehinaku have ordinary and honorable words for basic sexual anatomy.[7] Adults freely discuss sexual matters in their children's presence and even incorporate children in their sexual intrigues as bearers of messages or gifts. What is especially surprising from our perspective is the network of sexual affairs that involves nearly all of the adults in the village. The number of such relationships is extraordinary. When I conducted a survey in 1972, one energetic and extraverted young man of about twenty was carrying on affairs with ten women. The average number of affairs was 4.4 per individual.[8]

Liaisons take place in the woods and brush that surround the village. A network of pathways, called "alligator paths" (*yaka apui*), in humorous reference to this animal's sexual role in Mehinaku myth, encircles the village. A man wishing to conduct an assignation takes a path to the back door of his love partner's house and lays in wait, "just as the alligator waits for his prey." When she appears, he calls to her, and they go to an "alligator place," a small cleared spot where they can have sexual relations. Normally, there is only a small amount of time for talk and the exchange of gifts (so-called *yamala;* a term that refers specifically to gifts exchanged by lovers).

It would be difficult to overestimate the importance of these relationships for village life. A woman who is sexually active receives a regular supply of fish (the main source of protein) from her lovers, since fish are quintessential *yamala.* Affairs also have implications for kinship. Since the villagers believe that many acts of intercourse are necessary to make a child, a mother may recognize her lover as one of a number of fathers of the child, which may widen the scope of the incest taboo. Understandably, the village churns with gossip and intrigue. Sex is said to be "pepper" that gives life interest and verve.

By our standards, spouses are tolerant of discreetly conducted affairs. They have a live-and-let-live attitude, which comes across in an interview I taped with a middle-aged married couple who jointly reminisce about past indiscretions and jealousy. The discussion is also noteworthy because it reveals the playfulness and evident affection they have for one another.

> Anthropologist: Have you had sex with other women?
>
> Husband: I have had sex with them.
>
> Wife: Yes he does, he still has sex with them, he does not listen to me! "Don't have sex with others!" I tell you and you don't listen to me.
>
> Husband: (Laughingly) Oh, she is jealous about me, she holds me dear.
>
> Wife: I do, I do. I burned him with a brand from the fire in the past (laughter between them).
>
> Husband: It is over now. I am older, my penis has "died" now. My wife, she also had sex with other men in the past.
>
> Wife: No, That's a little lie! (mutual laughter).
>
> Anthropologist: If a man had sex with your wife would you be jealous?
>
> Husband: Oh yes! I would be very angry! Very angry! For five days! I would not get fish for her, I would not get her food. That is the way we are. But then we would talk together. I would go fishing for her. We would have sex together.
>
> Wife: So it is with the woman. Yes. I would be a little jealous if my husband had sex with other women. In the past he had sex with all of them. Oh, he gave many lover's gifts to all of the Mehinaku women in the past. Even the old women. Oh, that one was a shameless joker! Go ask him if that wasn't so. Ask him "Were you not a shameless joker?"
>
> Anthropologist: Were you a shameless joker?
>
> Husband: Just a little. Yes. I was, just a little!

Mehinaku Sexual Repression and Love Repression

The dialogue gives the impression that the Mehinaku are sexually very free. They seem so to us because they are free in areas where we may feel confined.

In truth, sex brings a profound ambivalence to Mehinaku life, for repression exists alongside freedom and delight. As in other cultures, repression has an institutional and psychological basis.

The Mehinaku men's house with its attendant rituals, is at the center of a set of ideas that link sex with violence and danger. Within the men's house are three sacred flutes that are taboo to women. A woman who sees the flutes, even inadvertently (they are often brought out of the men's house for rituals) is ritually raped by all of the villagers other than her immediate kin. This happens rarely among the Mehinaku, the last incident being more than forty years in the past. Yet it has occurred more recently in neighboring tribes, and the threat is real.

Gang rape is a terribly frightening and personally defiling experience for the women. Typically, a child born of such an act would be put to death at birth. Less frightening, but far more common, is individual rape, which is called "dragging off." A woman alone outside the village is a potential target for rape or coerced sex. In practice, the line between consent and rape is somewhat difficult to draw, since a woman may consent only to avoid a more aggressive assault or the possibility of becoming a victim of witchcraft.

Male sexual antagonism also has an informal component in aggressive jokes and jeers and a general sense that women are not men's intellectual and moral equals. When I approached a woman for a myth, the men would say: "they won't get it right; the words do not stay in their stomachs." The women are therefore the targets of both sexual aggression and disparagement. In addition, their feelings about sex are tinged with fears of pregnancy and childbirth in a culture with neither contraception nor adequate medical care. It is no wonder that the women are less positive about sex than the men, and some are disdained as "rejecting women."

Behind the men's sexual antagonism lies fear. The men fear that sex can stunt growth, cause disease,[9] break bones and induce weakness, prevent a man from catching fish, cause him to lose at wrestling, and, in general, subvert his ability to perform the masculine role. Even sexual wishes are dangerous, as they may attract a dangerous spirit, Japujaneju (Angry Woman Spirit), who lures men to their demise. Menstrual blood is a special focus of male anxiety, since it is believed to magically contaminate food and cause illness.[10]

Aggressive and fearful ideas about sex are in conflict with the institutionalization of romantic love. In fact, our own concept of love appears as slightly ridiculous to the Mehinaku. One of the young man, who listened to Portuguese love songs on his transistor shortwave radio, asked me "What is this 'I love you, I love you'? I don't understand it. I don't like it. Why does the white man make himself a fool?"

Male fear and antagonism towards women may be the result of early socialization. Infants are engaged in an intense maternal relationship. Mother and infant are in constant physical contact. Nursing is frequent (and may continue, intermittently, until age five or more), the child is carried about on the mother's hip, and mother and infant sleep in the same hammock. This "lush" period of child-rearing comes to an abrupt end with the appearance of a new sibling, who displaces the infant at his mother's breast and in her hammock. Many boys respond with an anger that is focused by the culture of the men's house and is subsequently generalized towards all women.[11]

The pattern of gender relationships among the Mehinaku is similar to that reported in other parts of Amazonia and Melanesia. It would seem, however, that especially in Melanesia the overall intensity of sexual antagonism and fear exceeds that among the Mehinaku. I believe, speculatively, that the difference may be in the relationship of father and son, which appears to be far more positive among the Mehinaku than in many other societies with a men's-house culture. But in any case, the trauma of maternal separation among the Mehinaku is consonant with the pattern of aggression and fear of women that is built into the villagers' institutions.

Mehinaku Lovingness

Institutionalized gang rape, informal sexual violence, sexual fear, and Oedipal trauma do not look like fertile ground for cultivating either sex or love. Yet, this appearance may be a matter of our focus. After reading a book on plant disease, we might erroneously conclude that it is impossible to grow plants at all. Like plants, Mehinaku lovingness survives, albeit in an occasionally harsh environment. We shall find it in relatively isolated areas of the villagers' culture, and more abundantly, in their feelings and behavior.

A Mehinaku Love Story: The Myth of Pahikyawalu

According to one of the Mehinaku, "a myth is a dream that many have begun to tell." Like a dream, a myth is fantasy reflecting desires and conflicts. Significantly, love has only a small role in Mehinaku mythology. Myths that deal directly with sexual matters are, for the most part, cautionary tales about the dangers of sex (see Gregor 1985). The most notable exception is the myth of Pahikyawalu (see Gregor 1988), which better than any other, reflects the dialectic of loving human emotion and the repressiveness of culture.

The myth is set in "Ancient Times," a period when cultural heroes created the institutions of Mehinaku society. Pahikyawalu was a woman who violated the most heavily sanctioned taboo of Mehinaku society. She dressed as a man, entered the men's house at night, and played the sacred flutes. Her husband discovered what she had done and denounced her to the rest of the men. They decided that the standard punishment of rape was too good for her. In the words of the narrator: "They wanted to see her die in the grave. They wanted to bury her. They wanted her to suffer." The men took Pahikyawalu and interred her, still alive, in a pit in front of the men's house. There she lived for ten days, drinking her own urine, and eating her own feces. Translated literally, "Pahi-kyawalu" means "she who is covered with feces."

Thus far the myth conforms to the complex of fear and antagonism that shapes the culture of Mehinaku gender. Women who confront the system as boldly as Pahikyawalu pay a heavy price. But can men and women who are also united by kinship, by the division of labor, and by the pleasures of sexuality, be so at war with one another? The myth answers that they cannot.

After ten days, Pahikyawalu is rescued by her lover, who comes to dig her up. The narrator explains: "He was *really* her lover. She was dear to him, and that is why he wanted to help." In what is surely the most poignant scene in the myth, her lover holds her tenderly and bathes her, even though she is covered with excrement:

> She was smeared with feces all over her body. But he was not disgusted. He was her lover. In the middle of the night he carried her in his arms to the stream. He washed her with soap. He rinsed her with water.

The lover took Pahikyawalu to another tribe, where she prospered and became beautiful, so much so that no one recognized her:

> She grew fat, and several months later she was very beautiful, with broad strong thighs and her hair down her back. . . . Her legs were bound in cotton, she wore a twine belt, she was beautiful. "Ah, who is that beautiful one," said the men . . .

Ultimately, after exacting revenge on the husband who denounced her, she re-joined her lover in marriage.

Pahikyawalu is an unusual myth among the Mehinaku. Other myth fragments deal with the love of men and women, but none so vividly confronts the most repressive sector of the Mehinaku culture of gender. Lovers not only defy the system, they triumph. The myth, as a fantasy of loving relationships, is evidence of the power of idealization (represented by the newly emergent and beautiful Pahikyawalu) and attraction in an unpromising setting.

The Relationship of Lovers

The village men maintain that the best sex is with a lover. This sex is *kaki* (salty, spicy), while sex between husbands and wives is *mana* (without taste, like water). Kaki sex is voluptuous (*weiyupei*, a term that also means "itch-ing"), and delicious (*awirintyapai*). Despite the pleasure, many affairs occur with little emotional commitment. Women may enter sexual relationships for the gifts they receive, for the protection afforded by powerful men, and for sexual adventure. Lovers from different tribes may not even speak the same language. As one of the young men explained to me, "When you Americans have sex with your girlfriends you spend a lot of time. You drink sugary coffee together. We are different. We just have sex." Sex without love is thus common.

Ideally, however, the lovers' relationship is one of mutual caring which is (hopefully) separate and hidden from their spouses. On occasion, lovers feel deeply for one another. They are said to "hold one another dear." They exchange gifts of greater value than is customary. They are likely to link the male partner to the woman's children in paternal relationships, and after death they mourn one another's passing.

When the relationship is new, lovers, young and old, may be joyful. These individuals can be recognized in the village. One young woman, noting that her grandfather had smiled at her (a rare event), commented: "He is a sour old man, but now that he has a girlfriend he is as jolly as can be." A young man, in the midst of a new relationship, asked me to take a photograph of his girlfriend, so that he would have a memento of her: "I hold her dear," he said.

The villagers' willingness to defy the limitations and sanctions *against* intense relationships is also evidence of the power of love. One of the villagers was ridiculed for having given his girlfriend a shell belt, an expensive, high-prestige item that must be obtained in trade from another tribe. Another, who had become ill, was said to be sick from "thinking too much" about his love partner, which attracted Angry Woman Spirit. A third was teased for rushing back from a fishing expedition so that he could see his girlfriend.

Marriage, Sex and Love

Marriage may begin with intense mutual attraction. The spouses are called "a new couple" (*autsapalui*). They take joy in one another's company, so much so that, unlike any other villagers, they sleep together in the same hammock. This is an astonishing feat, as both my wife and I can testify from finding ourselves in a Xingu village for ten (sleepless) nights with only one hammock.

In time, sexual interest within marriage diminishes. The young men claim that they have sex with their wives far less frequently than with their lovers. Nonetheless, sex is expected and valued in marriage. Moreover, it is the only opportunity for sex that takes place without anxiety or time pressure. Most sex and marital intimacy occur in the gardens around the village when husband and wife go to work together. The relationship that develops, especially after the birth of a child, is generally enduring and often affectionate and warm. Here a villager in his early forties recalls the beginning of his marriage, some twenty-five years before:

> Yes, she was beautiful to me. Beautiful to me. Therefore I asked for her in marriage. . . . I have grown up with her; we were young together. Together we have grown older. The children, our family, have grown up. You don't leave such a person. She is dear to me!

There are many other ways in which husbands and wives express their mutual concern. One of the more touching of these occurs when the men go on fishing expeditions prior to major ceremonies. Away for as much as two weeks at a time, their wives await their return in concern about their safety. Prior to departure, a husband takes two pieces of string and makes an equal number of knots in each. One string will hang next to his wife's hammock. Each morning, she unties one knot, knowing that he is doing the same thing at his encampment at a distant lake. When the last knot is untied, she can expect that her husband will return.

The most poignant cultural evidence of love between spouses is mourning. A widow or a widower enters seclusion and becomes "an owner of sadness" for a full year. The bereaved individual speaks in a low voice, remains indoors, and cries. The Mehinaku explain that the purpose of seclusion is to direct all of one's thoughts to the deceased spouse. A bereaved husband imagines his wife's voice and her form, and visualizes the places they have been together. Above all, he cries. After the year is over, he emerges, is bathed, and reenters the life of the community. From that point on he is not expected to feel sadness or loss. Hirikya, a widower recently in seclusion, speaks of his deceased wife:

> I cried a lot, for my former wife, I cried, I cried, I cried. I missed her a great deal. Oh there were tears, so many tears. "I see you, I see you," I said. "Alas for you, my wife!" [When she died] anutto dye was rubbed on her body, beads were placed about her, cotton bands were put on her legs. I felt such sadness! Such sadness! There was so much crying. So much crying. . . .
>
> Now her shadow [soul] is in the Sky Place. She is happy now. She has gone to her mother, to her people, to her kin and others, to her sisters. I did miss her; I did miss her. I did not speak with others. "Hello," "Hello," "Hello," others said to me. I did not respond. I was really missing her. Now it is over.

Love Versus Love Repression

The relationship of lovers and spouses and the myth-fantasy of Pahikyawalu, demonstrate the desire, the intensity, the idealization of the other, the self-sacrifice, and the sense of union that characterize the love experience. How can love and repression coexist? There are a number of ways by which the Mehinaku balance the two.[12] Among these is the villagers' ability to *encapsulate* sexual fears. By following ritual precautions and sporadic sexual abstinence, it is possible to avoid the diseases and the dangers magically associated with sex. In a variant form of encapsulation, the men split the image of women into good and bad, as in the familiar instance in our own culture of madonna and prostitute. In the Mehinaku case, the prostitute is replaced by Angry Woman Spirit, a seductive female who destroys men, and who, in mythic accounts, has herself been assailed by the men.[13] To a degree, sexual fears and antagonism are thereby diverted so that ordinary women need not be the focus of extreme anxiety and hostility.

The most significant reason that love survives among the Mehinaku is that individual personalities are not simply reflections of culture. There is variation in the extent to which sexual fear and aggression are internalized and built into the motivational structure of individuals. For some, especially the young, sexual fears and aggression are acute. Those who are more mature and confident take risks and will confront the prevailing culture. A few, almost like Pahikyawalu and her lover, have dared to break stringent taboos (such as that against having sex during the menstrual period) and have lived to tell the tale. Others, though they are few in number, separate themselves from the culture of the men's house. One man in his early thirties was bitterly critical of gang rape and those who would perform it:

> No! I don't think (rape) is good. . . . It was those headless, faceless idiots of long ago, of mythic times, that did this. . . . I feel sympathy for a woman who has seen the flutes. A man who is a good man does not participate in raping her. . . . A man who does not feel pity is a sex fiend, an unbathed, headless, fool.

This is very much a minority opinion. But the fact that it exists at all is a reminder to us that, although the villagers have created their culture, not all of them are creatures of it. Just as among ourselves, they can stand apart and form their own beliefs and their own (loving) relationships.

Love is thus possible among the Mehinaku. Sex, and especially the villagers' enthusiastic sex, brings men and women together in gratifying relationships and models the possibility of something more. Sex *embodies* the trust, intensity, lowering of ego boundaries, and sense of union that define love. Sex, which is available in abundance in Mehinaku society, is the natural teacher of love.

Conclusion: The Balance of Cultural Repression and Personal Freedom

Sigmund Freud's view of culture and the individual was one of opposition. He saw our sexual and aggressive nature as a threat to social life. However, the creation of the superego, the cultural arm of the personality, made social life possible. In order to exist, Freud taught us, culture necessarily trades heavily in guilt and repression.

The material on Mehinaku culture is in accord with this formulation in that there is ample evidence of repression and its effects. The men's house, gang rape, sexual fears, and Angry Woman Spirit are real enough to the villagers. Love is not idealized as it is in our own culture, or modeled as an especially desirable experience. The achievement of love in this repressive environment is therefore far greater than the simple capacity to act in ways that defy the rules. As Kinsey's research established nearly a half century ago, it is a truism that individual sexual behavior goes beyond "official" cultural restrictions. What the Mehinaku have done, however, is not just a self-gratifying act. Without benefit of cultural scripts, each generation reinvents an entire relationship

and way of feeling. It is therefore significant to discover that in this environment men and women find one another and create lovingness.

The tension between culture and the individual exists in all societies, but the
balance between the two and the outcome may be different than they are
among the Mehinaku. In our own Victorian era, sex was often associated with
many of the same fears as among the villagers. Semen was believed to be
the source of physical and especially spiritual strength. Its depletion, through
masturbation or "excess," caused disease and death. Mechanical devices of
metal and leather designed to prevent erections and enforce chastity were in-
vented and marketed. The sexual culture of the time was one of massive denial
and repression. Sexual terms were deleted from the language, and the Bible
and Shakespeare were cleansed of erotic images. Women were regarded as
free of defiling sexual needs. The overall picture was one of the intense sexual
fear, although for them, unlike the Mehinaku, *nonerotic* love survived as an
ideal. For many Victorians, the perfect marriage was a loving *spiritual,* but not
physical, relationship.

In recent years Carl Degler (1974, 1980) and Peter Gay (1986) have presented a revisionist interpretation of Victorian sexuality. Without denying the
repressive aspects of the culture, they have offered diaries, letters, and an extraordinary survey of the actual sexual behavior of forty-five Victorian women
that was compiled at the turn of the century and published in 1980 (see Mosher
1980). These documents show that Victorian women and men, very much like
their Mehinaku counterparts, enjoyed and participated in sexual relations despite a repressive culture. But it is also clear, as is surely true among the Mehinaku, that "official" culture had an impact. A recent reexamination of the
Mosher survey by Steven Seidman (1991) shows that the women surveyed after
1900 were more sexually active and positive about sex than those surveyed
before, when the culture was more repressive.

Culture and individual needs are thus in constant tension. As Ethel Person
has noted, "Love" (and I would add "sex") is "a loose cannon on the deck of
human affairs" (1989:14). Everywhere, love and sex are to a degree repressed,
usually far more so than is needed. Though individual lovers may nonetheless
find one another and even triumph, they often do not. Those that succeed may
pay a heavy price in terms of guilt, anxiety, and social opprobrium. However,
with much struggle, as Freud taught us, it is possible to push back the darkness.
Repression can be replaced with enlightenment and personal freedom. And
with enlightenment is created a liberated, intense, human sexuality and the
capacity to love.

Notes

I gratefully acknowledge the assistance of the National Science Foundation, the Harry
Frank Guggenheim Foundation and the United States Institute of Peace in support of
the field research for this paper. This paper was originally prepared for the Wenner-

Gren symposium, "Theorizing Sexuality: Evolution, Culture and Development," held March 19–27, 1993, at Cascais, Portugal.

1. One writer now quips "How do I love thee? . . . Let me count the articles."

2. In this atmosphere our knowledge of love is necessarily preliminary. Note, for example, an outstanding researcher's conclusion as to the nature of love: "'What is love?' . . . I don't really know" (Berscheid 1988:373).

3. This is admittedly exceptional. In Kinsey's survey, three-quarters of the males reached orgasm less than two minutes after beginning intercourse (1948:580).

4. In a recent study of the norms underlying romantic love in adolescent girls, the authors report that a fundamental rule is that "one should always be in love." One of the researchers observed that "a girl had 'I love' written on her hand and asked her about it. Although this girl's romantic feelings had no particular target, she explained that she was ready to add the name of a boys as soon as a suitable target was found" (Simon, Eder, and Evans 1992:42).

5. Jankowiak and Fischer's work is supported by an earlier cross-cultural study by Paul Rosenblatt (1966).

6. A full treatment of Mehinaku sexuality is available in Gregor (1979, 1985, 1988, 1990).

7. The terms for penis, vagina, and sexual intercourse are examples. Other terms, however, such as clitoris (*itskikiri*), evoke anxious tittering or amusement, depending on the situation.

8. I counted a couple as having an affair if they had an ongoing sexual relationship. This does not mean that they had sex frequently. Hence some of these relationships were relatively dormant, while others were far more active.

9. One of these diseases is a paralytic illness called *makatsiki* (literally, without legs), an illness (probably caused by toxicity of root medicines) that occurs in adolescent seclusion and is said to be occasioned by sexual relations in violation of a taboo. Paralysis at the time in which a boy is moving towards manhood is a powerful symbolic expression of the threat that women and sexuality pose to emerging masculinity.

10. The images associated with these ideas are redolent with themes suggesting castration anxiety, the *vagina dentata* motif, and other fears linked to physical harm that may come from association with women (see Gregor 1985).

11. Although girls also experience separation from the mother, they do not have a development that parallels that of little boys. As girls, they remain closely identified with the mother, they are encouraged to remain close to her, and they are rapidly incorporated in caretaking roles. Boys are not only separated from the mother, they are encouraged to spend time outside of the house away from her side.

12. See Gregor (1985:149–51) for a more extended discussion.

13. Most of the men have had personal experiences with Angry Woman Spirit, who is typically encountered in areas distant from the village or in dreams. Her eyes (seen in dreams) and her voice (usually heard from afar) are said to paralyze her victims and cause disease. On several occasions, according to myth, the men have killed Angry Woman Spirits. The body parts were appropriated by village witches as fetishes; they used them to make people sick, and eventually passed them along to their sons, who also became witches.

References

Abramson, Paul R. and Steven D. Pinkerton. 1995. *With pleasure: thoughts on the nature of human sexuality.* New York: Oxford University Press.

Berscheid, Ellen. 1988. "Some Comments on Love's Anatomy: Or, Whatever Happened to Old-Fashioned Lust?" In *The Psychology of Love,* ed. Robert J. Sternberg and Michael L. Barnes. New Haven: Yale University Press.

Collins, Jan Clanton. 1993. "Narratives of Positive Gender Relationships." Ph.D. Dissertation. Ann Arbor: University Microfilms.

Degler, Carl. 1974. "What Ought to Be and What Was: Women Sexuality in the Nineteenth Century." *American Historical Review* 79:1467–90.

Degler, Carl N. 1980. *At Odds: Women and the Family in America from the Revolution to the Present.* New York: Oxford University Press.

Endleman, Robert. 1989. *Love and Sex in Twelve Cultures.* New York: Psyche Press.

Ford, Clellan S. and Frank A. Beach. 1951. *Patterns of Sexual Behavior.* New York: Harper.

Frayser, Suzanne G. 1985. *Varieties of Sexual Experience: An Anthropological Perspective on Human Sexuality.* New Haven: HRAF Press.

Freud, Sigmund. 1965. "Being in Love and Hypnosis" (1921). In *Group Psychology and the Analysis of the Ego,* pp. 54–61. New York: Bantam Books.

Gay, Peter. 1986. *The Bourgeois Experience,* Vols. 1 and 2. New York: Oxford University Press.

Gaylin, William and Ethel S. Person. 1988. *Passionate Attachments. Thinking About Love.* New York: The Free Press.

Goffman, Erving. 1956. "The Nature of Deference and Demeanor." *American Anthropologist* 58:473.

Goffman, Erving. 1959. *The Presentation of Self in Everyday Life.* New York: Anchor.

Goode, William J. 1959. "The Theoretical Importance of Love." *American Sociological Review* 24:38–47.

Gregor, Thomas. 1979. "Secrets, Exclusion and the Dramatization of Men's Roles." Pp. 250–69 in *Brazil: Anthropological Perspectives,* Maxine Margolis, ed. Columbia University Press.

Gregor, Thomas. 1985. *Anxious Pleasures: The Sexual Lives of an Amazonian People.* Chicago: The University of Chicago Press.

Gregor, Thomas. 1988. "Pahikyawalu: She Who Is Covered With Feces." *The Dialectics of Gender: Essays in Honor of Robert F. and Yolanda Murphy,* ed. Richard Randolph. Boulder: Westview Press.

Gregor, Thomas. 1990. "Male Dominance and Sexual Coercion." In *Cultural Psychology,* James Stigler, R. Shweder and G. Herdt, eds. Chicago: University of Chicago Press.

Jankowiak, William and Edward Fischer. 1992. "A Cross-Cultural Perspective on Romantic Love." *Ethnology* 1:149–55.

Katchadourian, Herant A. and Donald T. Lunde. 1980. *Fundamentals of Human Sexuality,* Third Edition. New York: Holt, Rinehart and Winston.

Kernberg, Otto. 1976. *Object Relations Theory and Clinical Psychoanalysis.* New York: J. Aronson.

Kinsey, Alfred C. and Wardell B. Pomeroy and Clyde E. Martin. 1948. *Sexual Behavior in the Human Male*. Philadelphia: W. B. Saunders.

Kristeva, J. (1987). *Tales of Love*. New York: Columbia University Press.

Leach, Edmund. 1964. "Animal Categories and Terms of Verbal Abuse." *New Directions in the Study of Language*, Eric H. Lennenberg, ed., 23–63. Cambridge, Mass.: MIT Press.

Mosher, Clelia Duel. 1980. *The Mosher Survey: Sexual Attitudes of 45 Victorian Women*, ed. James MaHood and Kristien Wenberg. New York: Amo Press.

Peck, M. Scott. 1978. *The Road Less Traveled: A New Psychology of Love, Traditional Values and Spiritual Growth*. New York: Simon and Schuster.

Peel, Stanton. 1975. *Love and Addiction*. New York: Taplinger.

Person, Ethel S. 1989. *Dreams of Love and Fateful Encounters: The Power of Romantic Passion*. New York: Penguin.

Rosenblatt, Paul. 1966. "A Cross-Cultural Study of Child Rearing and Romantic Love." *Journal of Personality and Social Psychology* 4:336–38.

Rozin, Paul and Carol Nemeroff. 1990. "The Laws of Sympathetic Magic: A Psychological Analysis of Similarity and Contagion." In *Cultural Psychology*, James Stigler, R. Shweder, and G. Herdt, eds., Chicago: University of Chicago Press, pp. 205–32.

Safilios-Rothschild, Constantina. 1977. *Love, Sex, & Sex Roles*. Englewood Cliffs, N.J.: Prentice-Hall.

Scheper-Hughes, Nancy. 1985. "Culture, Scarcity, and Maternal Thinking: Maternal Detachment and Infant Survival in a Brazilian Shantytown." *Ethos* 13:291–317.

Seidman, Steven. 1991. "The Power of Desire and the Danger of Pleasure: Victorian Sexuality Reconsidered." *Journal of Social History* 1:47–67.

Shostak, Marjorie. 1981. *Nisa: The Life and Words of a !Kung Woman*. New York: Vintage.

Simon, Robin W. and Donna Eder and Cathy Evans. 1992. "The Development of Feeling Norms Underlying Romantic Love Among Adolescent Females." *Social Psychology Quarterly* 55, no. 1:29–46.

Solomon, R. C. 1981. *Love, Emotion, Myth and Metaphor*. Garden City, N.Y.: Anchor.

Trawick, Margaret. 1990. *Notes on Love in a Tamil Family*. Berkeley: University of California Press.

Tzeng, Oliver C. S. 1992. *Theories of Love Development, Maintenance and Dissolution*. New York: Praeger.

PART FOUR

Quantitative Models and Measurement

CHAPTER SIXTEEN

Model-Based Representations of Human Sexual Behavior

Edward H. Kaplan

Worldwide epidemics of sexually transmitted diseases, notably AIDS, have sparked renewed interest in human sexual behavior and its role in disease transmission. As part of an enormous research effort to understand disease transmission dynamics, forecast the spread of HIV and AIDS, and evaluate proposed policies for slowing these epidemics, epidemiologists and policy modelers have developed mathematical models that describe the spread of sexually transmitted diseases in differing epidemiological environments. Implicit in these models are representations of human sexual behavior that are of interest in their own right. This chapter reviews mathematical descriptions of human sexual behavior as expressed in disease transmission models with an eye towards quantifying key features of sexual activity.

Quantifying sexual behavior is probably not the first item on the social scientist's agenda when attempting to theorize human sexuality (though, of course, a number of important issues arise; see Berk et al., this volume). Given the nature of human sexual behavior, sex researchers might balk at the idea of reducing sex to necessarily simplified mathematical models. This is doubly true for those seeking a pleasure-based theory of human sexuality (see, e.g., Abramson and Pinkerton, 1995), for the majority of models created to date describe *what* people do rather than *why*. As such, most models of sexual behavior might best be thought of as describing the *consequences* of the search for pleasure without explicitly acknowledging how pleasure leads to such outcomes (though there are some exceptions noted below).

It is perhaps not surprising, then, that much of the mathematical description of sexual behavior has *not* been developed by sex researchers, but rather by mathematical epidemiologists for whom sex is merely a means of transmitting disease. This somewhat detached epidemiological viewpoint has produced quantitative depictions of sexual behavior that are somewhat striking when viewed independently of disease transmission.

In this chapter, I will provide a tour of implicit models of sexual behavior as gleaned from the mathematical modeling literature surrounding sexually transmitted diseases. Given such a tour, my hope is that sex researchers will be able to build on the existing technical base and construct their own models which better reflect ideas in good currency in the field of sex research. I plead guilty at the outset to *not* being a sex researcher myself, but given this limitation, I hope my attempt at distilling the modeling literature kindles the reader's interest at a minimum, and perhaps even stimulates some thought regarding how models of the form discussed might play a useful role in new research initiatives.

I will begin with the simplest of sexual behaviors prevalent in epidemic models, the *homosexual homogeneous* model. Following this, various *heterogeneities* in sexual activity rates will be described, though still within the confines of a homosexual model. *Random mixing models* are useful devices for highlighting counterintuitive principles of sexual behavior at the population level, though *nonrandom mixing models* are more accurate in the descriptive sense. *Role separation models* incorporate a different sort of heterogeneity, namely, sorting by sexual role. Mathematically, the simplest models of *heterosexual* behavior turn out to be special cases of homosexual role separation. The introduction of sexual roles enables the concept of *role switching*, where people play different sexual roles at different times. A different phenomenon is *serial monogamy*, which is addressed using *pair formation models*. The generalization of serial monogamy is the occurrence of *concurrent partnerships* over time. Finally, *age dependence, duration dependence,* and *information dependence* are three different ways sexual activity rates can change for a *single* individual over time, either within a single relationship or when confronting a new sexual partner. Information models in particular emphasize the role of decision-making in sexual behavior. As it is not unreasonable to postulate that sexual decision-making is informed by pleasure in many circumstances, these decision models do explicitly ascribe pleasure a role in determining observed sexual outcomes. I emphasize that the concepts to be introduced are not exhaustive, but rather reflect a large and rapidly growing literature on mathematical models of sexually transmitted diseases (most notably HIV and AIDS). While I hope this chapter succeeds as a tour, for the reader interested in technical details there is no substitute for exploring the original sources.

The Homogeneous Model

The simplest model describes a homosexual population where all members behave identically over time. To be concrete, imagine a community of gay men whose members average c different sex partners per person per unit time. The homogeneous model imagines that *each* man in the population acquired sex partners with rate c per unit time. The quantity c is referred to as the contact rate. In the homogeneous model, each man in the population remains sexually active for some duration d on average, so the lifetime number of sexual partners per man is given simply by the product cd.

Set aside are a number of concerns to the sex researcher. First, what is meant by *sex partner?* Behaviors ranging from kissing to mutual masturbation to oral sex to anal sex could qualify. Epidemiologists focus on *risky sex,* so in models of HIV/AIDS, one attempts to make the quantity c refer to some specific sex act such as unprotected anal sex that risks HIV transmission. Second, what is meant by averaging c partners per unit time? One must be careful to distinguish between new partners and long-term partners, for example. Thus, in administering surveys, questions such as "How many sex partners did you have in the last year" should be augmented with questions like "Of all of your sex partners in the last year, how many were *first-time* partners?" Third, c is assumed to be unchanging across persons and across time, clearly a crude approximation. Fourth, even if all in the population had the same *average* number of partners in a given year, there will be natural statistical variation in the *actual* numbers of partners people experience. A man who averages two different partners per year over several years could have no new partners in one year, four new partners in some other year, and so forth. Finally, people remain sexually active for different lengths of time in real life. The homogeneous model gives everyone's sex life the same average duration.

What is the purpose behind such a simple model? As is well known among epidemiologists, it is possible to derive simple expressions for the fraction of the population that is infected with whatever sexually transmitted disease is being studied under the homogeneous assumptions (Anderson and May, 1991; Bailey, 1975). And, while the resulting *epidemic* model is far from exact in describing true transmission dynamics, it does suggest the main qualitative features epidemiologists care about. For example, if the contact rate c is made sufficiently small, ultimately the infection will be removed from the population. In the case of risky sex, reducing c (viewed as the number of risky partners per unit time) can be achieved through the distribution and utilization of condoms, for example. Or, barring any intervention, where will the prevalence of infection level off? So, though the model may seem artificial to the sex researcher, it has the ability to produce key epidemiological results that are, at least qualitatively, in accord with what one observes in reality.

Heterogeneity: Random Mixing Models

Sexual behavior is heterogeneous, however, so it is important to relax the assumptions of the homogeneous model in several key ways. Perhaps the simplest relaxation is to assume that the population of gay men in question can be subdivided in accordance with the frequency of sexual partnerships. To accomplish this, imagine a population consisting of n groups. Within each group, assume a constant mean contact rate, so c_i is the average number of distinct sexual partners per man per unit time for men in group i, $i=1,2,\ldots,n$. The random mixing model results when all men select sex partners according solely to *availability*. Thus, the chance that a partner selected is from group i will depend both on the number of men in group i, and the mean contact rate c_i for men in group i (Anderson and May, 1991).

This selection by availability leads to a result that may seem counterintuitive to some. Imagine a neighborhood where there are two kinds of men: those who average one sex partner per year, and those who average ten sex partners per year. Further, suppose that 50% of all of the sexually active men in the neighborhood are of the first type, with the remaining 50% of the men of the second type. A new arrival enters the neighborhood's lone bar in search of a sex partner, and before long strikes up a conversation with one of the locals. What is the chance that this prospective sex partner averages ten distinct partners per year? In spite of the fact that only 50% of the men average ten partners per year, the assumption of random mixing assigns a probability of 10/11, or 91% to this event. Why? *Those averaging ten partners per year must be searching for partners ten times as often as those who average only one partner per year.* Thus, random mixing increases the chance of encountering those who average many partners per unit time beyond the proportion of such men in the population (Anderson and May, 1991; Kaplan, 1989).

The epidemiological consequences of random mixing are not pleasant, for broadly speaking the likelihood of contracting a sexually transmitted disease increases with the mean number of sex partners one has per unit time. As a consequence, the likelihood that a partner selected via random mixing is infected with some sexually transmitted disease such as HIV is *higher* than the *proportion* of the sexually active population that is infected with the disease. Worded differently, the chance that a partner selected at random is infected exceeds the prevalence of infection in the population. This should not be taken lightly. As an illustration, epidemiological surveys of gay men residing in San Francisco's Castro district have produced HIV prevalence estimates near 50%. Adjusting for random mixing, however, I have calculated that the chance a partner selected in accordance with his availability is infected increases to 67% (Kaplan, 1989).

While the random mixing model is an improvement over the homogeneous model in that heterogeneity in sexual activity has been considered, one may reasonably question the degree to which random mixing matches reality. After all, sex partners are not exactly "selected" at all, and in any event, do matchings really occur at random in real populations? Actually, in some settings such as sex clubs, bars, and bathhouses, random mixing may not be that far removed from the actual mixing patterns that occur. However, outside of such settings, it is difficult to believe in random mixing patterns. Thus, the next step is to consider nonrandom models of sexual mixing.

Before doing so, however, let me formalize the random mixing model of sexual partner selection. If in subgroup j there are m_j men, each averaging c_j

sex partners per unit time, then the probability that *any* selected sex partner is a member of group j is given by

$$\Pr\{\text{Selected Partner from Group j}\} = \frac{c_j m_j}{\sum\limits_{k=1}^{n} c_k m_k}. \tag{1}$$

The impact of both the abundance of men in group j and their rates of sexual partner acquisition on the selection probability resulting from random mixing is clear. Now let us see how nonrandom mixing differs from the above.

Heterogeneity: Nonrandom Mixing Models

Nonrandom mixing models also stratify the population of men into n subgroups. The characteristics leading to this stratification can be completely arbitrary, including as examples age, race, location, preferred sexual practice, and so forth. It will still be the case that regardless of how the population is stratified, men in subgroup i will average c_i distinct partners per unit of time. Within the bounds of what is possible, however, mixing between different subgroups can be completely arbitrary.

The nonrandom mixing pattern is completely characterized by the *mixing probabilities* ρ_{ij}, which dictate the probability that a partner selected by a member of group i comes from group j. Equation (1) above for random mixing is only one possible formulation for the ρ_{ij}'s; note that under random mixing, the likelihood that a partner selected is from group j is the same without regard to the subgroup of the man searching for a partner. How can one characterize which patterns are possible and which are not?

There are three physical constraints that must be satisfied by any proposed mixing pattern (Blythe et al., 1991; Jacquez et al., 1988; Kaplan and Lee, 1990). These are:

$$\rho_{ij} \geq 0, \qquad i=1,2,\ldots,n; \, j=1,2,\ldots,n. \tag{2}$$

$$\sum_{j=1}^{n} \rho_{ij} = 1 \qquad i=1,2,\ldots,n. \tag{3}$$

$$m_i \, c_i \, \rho_{ij} = m_j \, c_j \, \rho_{ji} \qquad i=1,2,\ldots,n; \, j=i,i+1,\ldots,n. \tag{4}$$

The first of these constraints simply states that the probability a partner selected by a group i man is from subgroup j must be nonnegative. The second of these constraints says that whenever someone from subgroup i selects a partner, that partner must come from *some* subgroup. The third and by far the most interesting constraint expresses the *law of conservation of sex partners:* the rate with which partners selected by men in group i originate from group j must equal the rate with which partners selected by men in group j originate from group i. Given that it takes two to tango, as it were, equation (4) is a necessary condition for any possible mixing pattern.

The essence of nonrandom mixing models reduces to the specification of the mixing probabilities. There are endless possibilities here, so I will mention only a few models considered in the literature. First, there is the model of *segregation,* where men only have sex with other members of their subgroup (Jacquez et al., 1988; Kaplan and Lee, 1990). The mixing probabilities that yield this pattern are easy to understand: $\rho_{ij}=1$ if and only if $i=j;$ otherwise $\rho_{ij}=0$. The segregation model is appealing for its simplicity: within any population subgroup, the homogeneous model applies, thus the assumption of segregation enables independent analysis of the subgroups of interest. When one considers the epidemiological implications of segregation, what one discovers are "wavy" epidemics at the overall population level, where successive waves of infection result from the epidemics that occur in the individual subgroups. This representation can be extended beyond sexual contacts. In New York City, for example, it appears that there are only very weak links between the HIV epidemics among gay men and injecting drug users respectively, so it is not unreasonable to consider these epidemics separately when devising AIDS interventions (Hethcote and Van Ark, 1992).

The usual development of the segregation model assumes that those in different subgroups *prefer* sex with others similar to themselves. However, as an illustration of how completely different behavioral postulates at the individual level can lead to the same patterns at the population level, consider the following model of *risk averse* men in possession of *perfect information* regarding sexual behavior in the population (Kaplan, Cramton, and Paltiel, 1989). If the only issue for men seeking sex partners is the avoidance of sexually transmitted disease, and as it is known that the likelihood of infection increases with the mean number of sex partners one has, *all* men in the population would prefer to have sex with those having very low contact rates. Of course, men with low contact rates would *also* prefer each other (for they also wish to avoid disease), and as a consequence, those men in the subgroup with the lowest contact rates would mix exclusively with themselves. Once this happens, the men in the subgroup with the second lowest contact rates become the objects of desire (except, of course, for the men in the already segregated group with the lowest contact rates). However, history repeats itself, and the men with the second lowest contact rates segregate themselves. Though these men would prefer sex partners from the safest group, they cannot obtain such partners, for those with the lowest contact rates have already segregated! This process repeats until *all* of the subgroups have segregated. My point in introducing this example is really quite simple: given that many different behavioral patterns at the individual level can produce the same pattern at the population level, it is extremely difficult (if not impossible) to reconstruct what must be happening at the individual level when confronted with only population mixing patterns.

Returning to our more general discussion, the segregation model is perhaps a useful first cut at categorizing what sexually active populations are up to, for the most important part of formulating such a model is deciding what the different subgroups are. However, that segregation implies *no* contact between the members of different subgroups is clearly a shortcoming. There are various ways to address this issue; let's consider some of them.

One appealing relaxation of the segregation model is to imagine a situation where several defined subgroups exist, and where most sexual mixing takes place within subgroups. However, there are various *bridges* connecting different subgroups; a bridge is just a metaphor for people who have sex with members of different subgroups (that the usefulness of such metaphors is model-dependent becomes clear when one realizes that in random mixing models everyone is a bridge). Such bridges are important epidemiologically, for they serve to connect subgroups in a chain of disease transmission, facilitating the spread of disease. *Why* such bridges form relates in part to what persons find sexually attractive ("opposites attract") or convenient (sex workers) in each other, and this in turn relates to pleasure.

The simplest bridge-type model assumes that when a person has sex with someone outside of his subgroup, he picks a sex partner at random from the population at large (Hethcote and Van Ark, 1987; Jacquez et al., 1988; Kaplan, Cramton, and Paltiel, 1989; May and Anderson, 1984; Nold, 1980). Suppose that for all in the population, with probability θ a selected sex partner is selected from within one's own group, while with probability $1-\theta$ a partner is selected according to the random mixing model, $0 \leq \theta \leq 1$. The resulting mixing probabilities will take on the mathematical form

$$\rho_{ij} = \theta \cdot 1_{(if\ i=j)} + (1-\theta) \cdot \rho_j \tag{5}$$

where ρ_j is given by equation (1). As an exercise, the reader may wish to verify that the mixing probabilities expressed in equation (5) satisfy the mixing constraints (2)–(4) listed earlier. Note that if $\theta = 1$ above, one achieves the model of segregation, while if $\theta = 0$, the random mixing model results.

A simple extension of the above model allows the members of different subgroups to possess different probabilities of choosing sex partners outside of their own grouping (Jacquez et al., 1988). Suppose that a man in subgroup i selects partners from his own group with probability θ_i, and with probability $1-\theta_i$ chooses a partner from the outside. Define

$$q_j = \frac{c_j m_j (1-\theta_j)}{\sum_{k=1}^{n} c_k m_k (1-\theta_k)}. \tag{6}$$

A valid mixing pattern is defined by

$$\rho_{ij} = \theta_i \cdot 1_{(if\ i=j)} + (1-\theta_i)\, q_j. \tag{7}$$

The interpretation here is that men either mix within their own group or select at random from all men willing to select (or be selected) at random. Of all men willing to mix outside of their home groups (these are the bridges), q_j is the relative availability of men from subgroup j. Again, the reader is invited to verify that the mixing pattern described in equation (7) satisfies the mixing constraints (2)–(4).

One interesting epidemiological implication of models like those of equation (5) or equation (7) is that relatively small bridge populations (i.e. relatively large values of θ) can lead to epidemics of sexually transmitted diseases that are extremely similar to what one would expect as a consequence of random mixing (Kaplan, Cramton, and Paltiel, 1989). Thus, from an epidemiological point of view, one does not need to observe random mixing in a population to obtain epidemics that look like they were caused by random mixing. This is an important point, for random mixing models are much easier to formulate (one does not need to estimate the values of the θ's).

The models described above show one way to relax the restrictive assumptions of random mixing or segregation. There are of course other nonrandom mixing models available (Abramson and Rothschild, 1988; Anderson, Gupta, and Ng, 1990; Blower and McLean, 1991; Blythe and Castillo-Chavez, 1989; Hethcote and Yorke, 1984; Hyman and Stanley, 1988; Kaplan and Lee, 1990; Sattenspiel and Simon, 1988). Imagine that there are L distinct locations (e.g., bars, parks, bathhouses, dances, etc.) where men search for sex partners. Let $s_{i\ell}$ denote the probability that a man from group i chooses to visit location ℓ to search for a partner, $\ell = 1, 2, \ldots, L$. Within each of these different locations, matching occurs at random among those in attendance. Define

$$q_{\ell j} = \frac{c_j \, m_j \, s_{j\ell}}{\sum_{k=1}^{n} c_k \, m_k \, s_{k\ell}}.$$ (8)

The quantity $q_{\ell j}$ represents the fraction of available men in location ℓ who are from subgroup j. The mixing function defined by

$$\rho_{ij} = \sum_{\ell=1}^{L} s_{i\ell} \, q_{\ell j}$$ (9)

satisfies the mixing constraints (2)–(4) and is thus a valid mixing pattern. This mixing formulation has been named *structured mixing,* for it assumes a structural partner-selection process whereby one can think separately about *where* people go to find partners (the $s_{i\ell}$'s) and *how* people select partners within locations (Jacquez, Simon, and Koopman, 1989). If one cleverly selects the mixing locations, the selection process within any location can reasonably be treated as random. Structural mixing is interesting in that it proposes a natural decomposition of the partner selection process. Indeed, it may be easier to obtain data from which to estimate the $s_{i\ell}$'s than it is to gather information directly corresponding to the ρ_{ij}'s.

Characterizing mixing patterns is a reasonably complicated mathematical problem. Nonetheless, a complete theory has been developed that provides a representation for *any* possible mixing pattern (Blythe et al., 1991). Recently, advances have been made that enable the estimation of nonrandom mixing patterns from sample surveys (Castillo-Chavez et al., 1992; Granath et al., 1991; Morris et al., 1991). These estimations are tricky, for while mixing patterns must obey the fundamental constraints (2)–(4), there is no guarantee that responses from surveys regarding partner selection will also observe these conditions. The mathematics of the most general mixing models are beyond the scope of this survey, so the interested reader should consult the original papers (Blythe and Castillo-Chavez, 1991; Jacquez et al., 1988; Kaplan and Lee, 1990).

Role Separation

Thus far, I have focused exclusively on sexual activity, assuming tacitly that "sex" is completely reciprocal in nature. This is not necessarily the case at all. In the case of anal intercourse, for example, in any single act there is an insertive partner and a receptive partner. It has been documented that in some populations where men have sex with men, there are those who play exclusively the insertive role, those who play exclusively the receptive role, and those who "go both ways" (AC/DC) (Carrier, 1976; Carrier, 1989; Van Druten, Hendriks, and Van Griensven, 1992). Indeed, role separation is required for the simplest model of *heterosexual* intercourse.

Consideration of role separation places constraints on the kind of sexual mixing that can occur. Men who are exclusively insertive cannot by definition have anal sex with other men who are exclusively insertive. The same holds for men who are exclusively receptive. Role separation thus places additional constraints on the mixing formulation, for by definition there is *no* mixing between certain subgroups in the population.

The simplest heterosexual model is one where all men are treated equally, as are all women. In the absence of bisexuals, this model yields a single balance equation (Le Pont and Blower, 1991), namely,

$$m_{MEN} \, c_{MEN} = m_{WOMEN} \, c_{WOMEN}. \tag{10}$$

This of course explains why men and women need not average the same number of sex partners in a sexually active population. Suppose there are many more sexually active men than women. It then must be the case that those women who are sexually active have many more partners on average than the men (as is the case with female sex workers and their clients).

Consider now a role separation model involving gay men who prefer exclusively insertive, exclusively receptive, or are willing to play dual roles in anal intercourse. There are seven mixing probabilities that must be found. In an obvious notation, these are: ρ_{IR}, ρ_{RI}, ρ_{ID}, ρ_{DI}, ρ_{RD}, ρ_{DR} and ρ_{DD}. In addition to

(2), equations (3) and (4) impose six constraints on these quantities. These are (Van Druten, Hendriks, and Van Griensven, 1992):

$$m_I \, c_I \, \rho_{IR} = m_R \, c_R \, \rho_{RI}. \tag{11}$$

$$m_I \, c_I \, \rho_{ID} = m_D \, c_D \, \rho_{DI}. \tag{12}$$

$$m_R \, c_R \, \rho_{RD} = m_D \, c_D \, \rho_{DR}. \tag{13}$$

$$\rho_{IR} + \rho_{ID} = 1. \tag{14}$$

$$\rho_{RI} + \rho_{RD} = 1. \tag{15}$$

$$\rho_{DI} + \rho_{DR} + \rho_{DD} = 1. \tag{16}$$

Proper formulation of role separation models involves determining mixing patterns that satisfy the above six constraints. Clever methods for automatically satisfying these constraints have been developed and explored in the literature (Wiley and Herschkorn, 1989).

Again, it pays to mention the epidemiological impact of role separation. If the probability of becoming infected is much greater for receptive partners than for insertive partners, then it is clear that those willing to play dual roles are crucial to the spread of an epidemic. Initially infected insertive partners would infect receptive partners, but these receptive partners would not be capable of generating large numbers of new infections owing to the inefficiency of transmission from receptive to insertive partners. Similarly, initially infected receptive partners would also be incapable of infecting large numbers of insertive partners. Now, as it appears that the infectivity of the human immunodeficiency virus is much greater from insertive to receptive partners than vice versa, it appears that men willing to play both roles were an unwitting but crucial vector for the spread of HIV in the gay community (Wiley and Herschkorn, 1989).

Role Switching

Once role separation is allowed into models of sexual behavior, it is also possible to consider role switching. Thus, over time one may observe sexual behavioral changes among roles. The simplest model is one where, in any given time period, a man playing role i stands a probability p_{ij} of switching to role j in the next time period. This is a *Markov model* of role switching, and enables one to predict the fraction of men in the population who will be playing any given role at some time in the future. If there are $m_j(t)$ men in subgroup j at time t, then the number of men expected in subgroup j at time $t+1$ is given by

$$m_j(t+1) = \sum_{i=1}^{n} m_i(t) \, p_{ij} \tag{17}$$

assuming that the population is closed to immigration and emigration (assumptions that can be relaxed easily). Over time, the expected sizes of the population subgroups approach a steady state which can be easily calculated. It is interesting to note that a cohort study of gay men in Amsterdam has discovered role switching behavior that is almost perfectly consistent with the simple Markov model described above. Such behavior is perhaps surprising given the AIDS epidemic among sexually active gay men; one would surely have expected the role switching probabilities p_{ij} *themselves* to be time dependent. Role switching models are a relatively new development in mathematical models of sexual behavior that seem especially well suited for more detailed study by sexual scientists (Van Druten, Van Griensven, and Hendriks, 1992).

Pair Formation: Serial Monogamy

A different family of models developed to describe sexually transmitted disease transmission among heterosexual populations incorporates the idea of *pair formation*. In these models, men and women pair off, and are unavailable for sex with other partners outside of their pair. The new variable of interest becomes the *duration* of any given relationship. The simplest pair formation model is that of *serial monogamy*. Conceptually, individuals in such models are always in one of two states: paired or unpaired. In the unpaired state, one is searching for a sex partner, while in the paired state, one has a sex partner for the duration of the relationship (Dietz and Hadeler, 1988).

Pairing models require conservation laws similar to those described earlier for nonrandom mixing models. For example, in a simple heterosexual model, the aggregate rate with which men enter pairs must equal the aggregate rate with which women enter pairs. Similarly, the aggregate rates with which men and women enter the unpaired population as a result of pair dissolution must balance. In the case where a relationship ends due to the death of one partner, these models assume an equal likelihood of survival for the man and the woman (though this need not be the case in general). If a relationship ends for other reasons, then both the man and the woman return to single status. All of these status flows must seem obvious to the reader, but the point is that one must be careful in formulating these flows *mathematically* so that everything works out as intended.

There is no inherent reason for restricting pair formation models to heterosexuals only, and indeed such models have been extended to consider the formation and dissolution of relationships among homosexuals (Dietz, 1988). Of course, as these models were developed for epidemiological investigations, pair formation has been emphasized more as a heterosexual phenomenon with respect to disease transmission. Serially monogamous pair formation tends to slow epidemics down, for infectious persons spend more time with *fewer* partners as the duration of relationships expands. The majority of epidemic models considering sexually active gay men have ignored pure pair formation, because of the large numbers of distinct sexual partners involved.

Pair Formation: Concurrent Partnerships

Of course, concurrent partnerships are a common feature of sexual behavior, whether in the form of secretive affairs or multiple regular sex partners. It is possible to extend the pair formation ideas just discussed to consider the formation and dissolution of triads, quartets, and so on, and one recent paper has in fact formulated a model for HIV transmission involving heterosexual triangles.

A very different approach merely distinguishes between first-time and former sex partners. Anytime one has sex, the partner involved is a new partner (found in accordance with our old friend the *contact rate*), or a former partner. Former partners are treated essentially as inventory in these models, and the length of time a former partner is available for sex (the shelf life as it were) is determined by the typical duration of a partnership (May and Anderson, undated).

A useful model enabling the determination of average partnership durations from survey data is as follows. Imagine that in a sexual behavior survey, one asks respondents the following two questions among others: how many different sex partners have you had in some specified time interval; and of these, how many are first-time partners. From the survey data, one obtains both the total number of sex partners and the number of first-time sex partners in the period of interest. The model of concurrent partnerships enables one to estimate the typical *duration* of a relationship as follows. As before, let c reflect the number of new sex partners acquired per unit time. For any given respondent, this can be estimated as the reported number of new partners divided by the length of the time period in question. Also, let random variable D denote the duration of any partnership.

The expected number of sex partners one would expect to observe in some time interval, say from t_0 to t_1, would be given by the equation

$$\text{Expected Number of Partners} = \int_0^{t_0} c \, \Pr\{D > t_0 - x\} \, dx + c(t_1 - t_0) \qquad (18)$$

The integral on the right-hand side of equation (18) calculates the expected number of former partners with whom a physical relationship is still ongoing during the time period of observation, while the second term calculates the expected number of new partners acquired during the period of observation. Now, the integral can be approximated closely by $c \cdot E(D)$, where $E(D)$ is the expected duration of a partnership. As a consequence, the average duration of a sexual partnership can be evaluated from survey data in surprisingly simple fashion: subtract the number of first-time partners reported from the total number of partners reported, and divide by the contact rate c. What is interesting about this model is that *no questions were asked regarding the duration of sexual partnerships!* Thus, in addition to demonstrating how one can formulate models involving concurrent partnerships, this example demonstrates how models can help one obtain estimates of interesting quantities in the absence of directly observable data describing those quantities.

Age Dependence

One unrealistic feature of all of the partner selection models we have considered is that the contact rates c remain constant over time (though they can vary across subgroups). Of course, this is patently false. Until one becomes sexually active, for example, one's contact rate is zero! More generally, one would expect that the rate with which sex partners are acquired depends upon how long one has been sexually active. It is natural to incorporate this possibility by formulating models with *age dependent contact rates*. One can measure age either biologically (years from birth) or sexually (years from initiation of sexual activity) in formulating such models. In principle, one can augment the models discussed earlier by replacing c with $c(a)$, where the variable a represents the age of the person in question (Anderson, Gupta, and Ng, 1990; Anderson and May, 1991). The same augmentation is possible for models involving population subgroups as well.

A different use of age in modeling sexual behavior is recognizing the strong role age often plays in mixing patterns. For example, it has been observed in certain societies that heterosexual partnerships often involve couples with roughly constant age separation. In other societies, partnerships are most often formed by couples of similar age. The role of age mixing has epidemiological implications. For example, the most obvious case involves mixing among those of similar age; when infection is introduced to the population, only those in the age bracket of the initially infected are at immediate risk, while those in older age groupings are at very low risk of infection. Of course, as discussed earlier, only minimal bridges out of this "age segregated" model are needed to place virtually all those sexually active at risk of infection (Anderson, Gupta, and Ng, 1990; May and Anderson, 1991).

The mathematics of age dependent modeling, familiar to mathematical demographers, become complicated when applied to sexual mixing models. One simplification essentially borrows from the role switching model discussed earlier, where the roles are replaced by different age groupings such as newly sexually active, active for five to ten years, active for ten to fifteen years, and so forth. The probabilities of role switching are such that one might move from age group i to age group $i+1$ with a given probability in any time period, or that one might remain in group i with a complementary probability. One never goes backwards (from i to some class $j<i$), nor does one ever skip a class (from i to some class $j>i+1$). Though not strictly an age progression model in the usual sense, the approximation suggested here would certainly simplify matters.

Duration Dependence

A different model worth exploring investigates sexual behavior *within* a relationship. Suppose that $\lambda(x)$ represents the rate with which a couple actually has sex at time x in a relationship. How does $\lambda(x)$ behave as x progresses? For example, one plausible model is that the frequency of sex declines with the age of a relationship. Initially, the thrill of a new encounter could lead to many exploratory sexual episodes, but the frequency of sex would decline as the novelty of the new partner wore off. Whatever model one proposes for $\lambda(x)$, the expected total number of sex acts one would find from a relationship would be given by

$$E(\text{Total Number of Sex Acts}) = \int_0^\infty \lambda(x)\, f_D(x)\, dx \qquad (19)$$

where $f_D(x) \cdot dx$ is the probability that a relationship ends between x and $x+\mathrm{d}x$ time units after it started.

The ideas of this section have not been explored by epidemiologists. Generally speaking, sex is modeled as though there was a budget constraint on the number of sex acts any person has over some time period such as one year. Let B be this budget. Then, among those with contact rates equal to c partners annually, the number of sex acts per partner is automatically set equal to B/c; thus there is a built-in negative correlation between the number of sex partners a person has on the one hand and the number of sex acts *per partner* on the other. Is this really true? Perhaps those with higher contact rates are more active in general, perhaps reflecting a proclivity for "pleasure drives," and thus have higher sex budgets. It may be that the number of sex acts per partner is the relevant variable to consider. After all, the number of sex acts per partner must *at least* equal 1. If we believe in fixed sex budgets, the number of sex acts per partner can shrink below 1 on average, which is clearly unrealistic. On the other hand, it does seem unreasonable to believe that the number of sex acts per partner remains constant, for then the *total* number of sex acts could increase without bound. The model suggested by equation (19) could be useful here, as those with many partners probably have shorter partner durations on average, and as a consequence the average number of sex acts per partner will decline, but in a natural way as filtered through equation (19). To my knowledge, nothing is known empirically in this regard.

Information Dependence

Finally, as a last paradigm for modeling sexual behavior, it may well be that contact rates (and the frequency of sexual acts) change in accordance with *information* acquired about specific sex partners, or the "market" for sex partners in general. Suppose that in a given geographical location, α represents the cumulative incidence of AIDS in that location. One model of *information dependence* would be to model the contact rates c as functions of α, that is, the contact rates in this model would be denoted by $c(\alpha)$. Presumably, $c(\alpha)$ would be a decreasing function of α, indicating that as the AIDS epidemic becomes more severe, contact rates decline (Philipson and Posner, 1992).

A different formalization operating at the individual level would consider one's *perceptions* regarding others. If, for example, an individual perceives that a prospective partner is infected with HIV with probability h, then the likelihood of actually pursuing sex with that prospective partner could be modeled as decreasing in h. Note that the perceptions need not be accurate; there are those who believe erroneously that they "know" who is infected and who is not (Philipson and Posner, 1992).

A similar model of this form has been proposed by Pinkerton and Abramson (1992), who consider an individual faced with a choice between three decisions: abstain from risky behavior, engage in safer sex, or engage in risky sex. Given the probabilities of getting infected from each option on the one hand, versus the *pleasure* derived from each option on the other, what is the "rational" decision?

To simplify matters, consider the following reduced version of the Pinkerton-Abramson scenario: a person may either abstain from all risky behavior, a decision which carries zero risk of becoming infected, but delivers utility (i.e., pleasure) equal to u, $0 \leq u \leq 1$. Alternatively, the person may engage in risky sex. If risky sex results in infection, an event that occurs with some probability π, the resulting utility to our "decision-maker" equals 0 (the worst case). Risky sex that does not result in infection, however, yields the best case utility of 1 (and happens with probability $1-\pi$).

As a "rational" decision-maker acts to maximize expected utility (or pleasure), we see that the decision to engage in risky sex may be viewed as rational whenever $\pi \cdot 0 + (1-\pi) \cdot 1 = 1-\pi > u$. Worded differently, risky sex may result from rational decision-making if the perceived risk of infection π is less than the threshold value $1-u$. This has an interesting interpretation, for as the *highest* utility achievable is that from risky sex that does not result in infection (and numerically equals 1), we see that if the risk of infection is less than the incremental pleasure available from risky sex in the best case, then risky sex is the preferred course of action for this decision-maker!

Moving this last example from the individual to the population level, one can imagine nonrandom mixing models where people actually form subgroups on the basis of perceived information. This is not merely a matter of conjecture; singles clubs requiring repeated negative HIV tests for membership have been reported in the popular media. As a different example, some infected men have been reported as seeking other infected men for sex. One interpretation of such behavior is that it lessens the psychological risk of being rejected as a sex partner due to infection. A different interpretation follows from the assumption that no further damage can ensue from unprotected sex following infection, an assumption that is also sadly wrong.

Within the world of our earlier mixing models, one can imagine replacing the mixing probabilities ρ_{ij} by a more complete function $\rho(h_i,h_j)$ which reflects the information status of the different groups (here measured as perceived HIV prevalence levels within subgroups). Or, one might consider the structured mixing model described earlier, and ascribe levels of risk to the different mixing locations (*so* uninfected sexually active individuals might have a high proclivity to seek out singles clubs of the sort mentioned above).

While the examples discussed above all use perceived HIV status as an information variable, models of information dependence are not restricted to this parameter. Other attributes such as wealth, education, or perceived social attitude could function just as well. The point is that such models provide a more dynamic approach to the study of sexual behavior at the population level, in that group membership and preferences for one individual can change over time in accordance with the acquisition and updating of information (real or perceived) about others.

Conclusion

This brings us to the end of the tour. Looking over the models developed by those with epidemiology as their main interest, it is striking how rich with potential these modeling frameworks are for the description of sexual behavior. Indeed, as one way to define sexual behavior is simply to carefully state what people are doing, the descriptive models reviewed should prove capable of contributing to the empirical analysis of sexual behavior. While it seems that the existing models do a pretty fair job of describing *how* people behave, with few exceptions the models say very little regarding *why* people do what they do. For the sex researcher, then, a useful next step might be the incorporation of individual decision-making processes into models of sexual behavior (as suggested by Pinkerton and Abramson, for example). It may well be that this latter domain is where sex researchers stand to make their greatest contribution to model-based representations of human sexual behavior.

References

Abramson, P. R. and Pinkerton, S. D. (1995). *With pleasure: Thoughts on the nature of human sexuality.* New York: Oxford University Press.

Abramson, P. R. and Rothschild, B. (1988). Sex, drugs and matrices: mathematical prediction of HIV infection. *Journal of Sex Research,* 25:323–46.

Anderson, R. M., Gupta, S. and Ng, W. (1990). The significance of sexual partner contact networks for the transmission dynamics of HIV. *Journal of Acquired Immune Deficiency Syndromes,* 3:417–29.

Anderson, R. M. and May, R. M. (1991). *Infectious Diseases of Humans: Dynamics and Control.* Oxford: Oxford University Press.

Bailey, N. J. T. (1975). *The Mathematical Theory of Infectious Diseases and Its Application.* London: Griffin.

Blower, S. M. and McLean, A. R. (1991). Mixing ecology and epidemiology. *Proc. Royal Society of London B,* 245:187–92.

Blythe, S. P. and Castillo-Chavez, C. (1989). Like-with-like preference and sexual mixing models. *Mathematical Biosciences,* 96:221–38.

Blythe, S. P., Castillo-Chavez, C., Palmer, J. S. and Cheng, M. (1991). Toward a unified theory of sexual mixing and pair formation. *Mathematical Biosciences,* 107: 379–405.

Carrier, J. (1976). Cultural factors affecting urban Mexican male homosexual behavior. *Archives of Sexual Behavior,* 5:103–24.

Carrier, J. (1989). Sexual behavior and the spread of AIDS in Mexico. *Medical Anthropology,* 10:129–42.

Castillo-Chavez, C., Shyu, S-F., Rubin, G. and Umbach, D. (1992). On the estimation problem of mixing/pair formation matrices with applications to models for sexually-transmitted diseases. In *AIDS Epidemiology: Methodological Issues* (N. P. Jewell, K. Dietz and V. T. Farewell, editors), Boston: Birkhäuser, pp. 384–402.

Dietz, K. (1988). The dynamics of spread of HIV in the heterosexual population. In *Statistical Analysis and Mathematical Modelling of AIDS* (J. C. Jager and E. J. Ruitenberg, editors), Oxford: Oxford University Press, pp. 77–105.

Dietz, K. and Hadeler, K. P. (1988). Epidemiological models for sexually transmitted diseases. *Journal of Mathematical Biology,* 26:1–25.

Granath, E., Giesecke, J., Scalia-Tomba, G., Ramstedt, K. and Forssman, L. (1991). Estimation of a preference matrix for women's choice of male sexual partner according to rate of partner change, using partner notification data. *Mathematical Biosciences,* 107:341–48.

Hethcote, H. W. and Yorke, J. A. (1984). *Gonorrhea, Transmission Dynamics, and Control.* Berlin: Springer-Verlag (published as Volume 56 of *Lecture Notes in Biomathematics*).

Hethcote, H. W. and Van Ark, J. W. (1987). Epidemiological models for heterogeneous populations: proportionate mixing, parameter estimation, and immunization programs. *Mathematical Biosciences,* 84:85–118.

Hethcote, H. W. and Van Ark, J. W. (1992). Weak linkage between HIV epidemics in homosexual men and intravenous drug users in New York City. In *AIDS Epidemiology: Methodological Issues* (N. P. Jewell, K. Dietz and V. T. Farewell, editors), Boston: Birkhäuser, pp. 174–208.

Hyman, J. M. and Stanley, E. A. (1988). Using mathematical models to understand the AIDS epidemic. *Mathematical Biosciences,* 90:415–73.

Jacquez, J. A., Simon, C. P., Koopman, J., Sattenspiel, L. and Perry, T. (1988). Modeling and analyzing HIV transmission: the effect of contact patterns. *Mathematical Biosciences,* 92:119–99.

Jacquez, J. A., Simon, C. P. and Koopman, J. (1989). Structured mixing: Heterogeneous mixing by the definition of activity groups. In *Mathematical and Statistical Approaches to AIDS Epidemiology* (C. Castillo-Chavez, editor). Berlin: Springer-Verlag (published as Volume 83 of *Lecture Notes in Biomathematics*), pp. 301–15.

Kaplan, E. H. (1989). What are the risks of risky sex? Modeling the AIDS epidemic. *Operations Research,* 37:198–209.

Kaplan, E. H. and Lee, Y. S. (1990). How bad can it get? Bounding worst case endemic heterogeneous mixing models of HIV/AIDS. *Mathematical Biosciences,* 99:157–80.

Kaplan, E. H., Cramton, P. C. and Paltiel, A. D. (1989). Nonrandom mixing models of HIV transmission. In *Mathematical and Statistical Approaches to AIDS Epidemiology* (C. Castillo-Chavez, editor), Berlin: Springer-Verlag (published as Volume 83 of *Lecture Notes in Biomathematics*), pp. 218–39.

Le Pont, F. and Blower, S. M. (1991). The supply and demand dynamics of sexual behavior: Implications for heterosexual HIV epidemics. *Journal of Acquired Immune Deficiency Syndromes,* 4:987–99.

May, R. M. and Anderson, R. M. (1984). Spatial heterogeneity and the design of immunization programs. *Mathematical Biosciences,* 72: 83–111.

May, R. M. and Anderson, R. M. (undated). Heterogeneities, cofactors, and other aspects of the transmission dynamics of HIV/AIDS. Draft book chapter for *Current Topics in AIDS: Volume 2.*

Morris, M. (1991). A log-linear modeling framework for selective mixing. *Mathematical Biosciences,* 107:349–77.

Nold, A. (1980). Heterogeneity in diseases-transmission modeling. *Mathematical Biosciences,* 52:227–40.

Philipson, T. J. and Posner, R. A. (1992). *Private Choices and Public Health: The AIDS Epidemic in an Economic Perspective,* manuscript.

Pinkerton, S. D. and Abramson, P. R. (1992). Is risky sex rational? *Journal of Sex Research,* 29:561–68.

Van Druten, H. A. M., Hendriks, J. C. M. and Van Griensven, G. J. P. (1992). Homosexual role separation and the spread of HIV. *VIII International Conference on AIDS,* Amsterdam, The Netherlands, July 19–24, 1992, abstract ThC 1518.

Van Druten, H. A. M., Van Griensven, G. J. P. and Hendriks, J. C. M. (1992). Homosexual role separation and modelling the spread of HIV. *IVth EC Workshop on Quantitative Analysis of AIDS: Modelling, Impact Assessment, Forecasting and Scenario-analysis,* Netherlands National Institute of Public Health and Environmental Protection (RIVM), Bilthoven, The Netherlands, July 16–18, 1992.

Wiley, J. A. and Herschkorn, S. J. (1989). Homosexual role separation and AIDS epidemics: Insights from elementary models. *Journal of Sex Research,* 26:434–49.

CHAPTER SEVENTEEN

Sexual Activities as Told in Surveys

RICHARD BERK, PAUL R. ABRAMSON, AND PAUL OKAMI

Introduction

All theories of human sexuality ultimately depend upon data. Data are instrumental for creating theories and essential for testing theories. Yet, it is difficult to obtain accurate data on human sexual behavior. Sex, at least among humans, is generally a private activity and, as such, is not easily observed. Human sexuality is also socially constructed in ways that vary substantially by time and place. One cannot assume that a given act has the same causes, meanings, or consequences in different settings. Finally, as a practical matter, propriety, discretion—and institutional review boards—make it exceedingly difficult to do empirical research on human sexuality.

Given these constraints, the retrospective sexual survey has emerged as a popular data collection method. If one cannot directly observe human sexual behavior, one can at least elicit peoples' recollections about it. The Kinsey studies (Kinsey et al., 1948, 1953) and the current Laumann et al. study (1994) are, of course, the obvious illustrations, but other examples include research on AIDS-related risk factors (Catania et al., 1992), on sexual behavior among runaways (Rotherman-Borus et al., 1992), on contraceptive use among college students (Baldwin et al., 1992), and on alcohol consumption and unsafe sex (Temple and Leigh, 1992).

Whether the survey instrument is used in face-to-face interviews, delivered by telephone, or self-administered by respondents, a common format is employed. Some recall period is defined, such as the last six months, and then the respondents are asked to state the number of times a particular kind of sexual behavior (e.g., vaginal intercourse, anal intercourse) occurred.[1]

Our reading of the literature using sexual surveys suggests that, by and large, sexual behavior recall-data are treated uncritically, or are legitimated with broad assertions that all is well. An instructive illustration can be found in the recent paper by Catania and his colleagues (1992, p. 1102), published in *Science*.

> Two measures of condom use were constructed, one based on the proportion of condom use during all acts of vaginal intercourse in the past 6 months (aggregated across partners) and one based on all acts of anal intercourse

(6-month report). Six-month estimates of sexual behavior have reasonably good reliability, and the six-month time frame is broad enough to sample behavior patterns that may not be apparent with assessments based on shorter time intervals (such as one month). Current evidence from comparisons of self-reported condom use and infection rates of HIV and STDs in a variety of sample populations suggests that self-reports of condom use are valid.

Catania and his colleagues are far more careful than most researchers employing this methodology. They explicitly raise the issue of measurement quality and cite several studies to support their conclusions that all is well. However, in none of the studies cited is there any external validation of the measures used. Measurement is assessed by looking for sensible patterns between the measures and other variables with which they should covary. As a result, the validation is at best indirect.

There are also a priori reasons to be uneasy. It is inconceivable that any reconstruction of a sexual history for a number of months will be error-free, unless there is very little sexual activity to report. It is also inconceivable that recall measures of sexual activity will be immune to well-known survey response biases (Abramson, 1992; Abramson et al., 1975; Groves, 1989). So, the key questions involve the sizes and kinds of distortions that are likely.

Finally, the results of sexual surveys are generally divorced from their contextual domains. In particular, it seems equally important, at least to us, to consider the process of recalling—or failing to recall—sexual behavior, since such information may be particularly relevant to the manner in which sex is experienced and encoded. This concern is forcefully expressed by Shweder (1990:7), who notes that responses to surveys (and other traditional social science experiments) are presumed to have been obtained from a "transcendent realm where the effects of context, and meaning can be eliminated, standardized, or kept under control." With this in mind, we wish to emphasize that our concern is not just with errors in recall data, but with understanding the meaning of such errors and what they convey about human sexual behavior.

In this chapter, therefore, we report the initial results from a study of how accurately college students are able to reconstruct their sexual behavior through a conventional survey instrument. The focus of this paper is heterosexual activity, including vaginal intercourse and oral sex. The research design, described below, was consciously conservative in that the recall tasks presented to subjects were far less demanding than the recall tasks presented to most survey respondents (e.g., Laumann et al., 1994). Consequently, if there is evidence that recall is seriously flawed, it raises significant questions about conventional surveys of sexual behavior in which the recall task is far more demanding. This concern is of particular significance to this volume because such recall data often serve as the foundation for theories about human sexual behavior, including both pleasure and reproduction.

Research Methods

The research was designed to examine several issues. While our primary concern was recollections of sexual behavior, other methodological issues were also considered. For example, does writing a daily sexual diary enhance the recall of past sexual experiences? Or similarly, can recall be improved by utilizing a mnemonic device? These questions were particularly important because we were not merely attempting to document errors. We assumed a priori that such errors occur, though their extent and direction are certainly nontrivial considerations. Yet, since the sexual survey is not likely to disappear, regardless of the errors we detect, we also wanted to examine factors which might facilitate recall in sexual surveys. Thus, broadly speaking, this study was designed to: (1) provide an estimate of error in the recall of sexual behavior over a short time period; (2) examine factors that might facilitate recall on a sexual survey; and (3) consider the meaning of such findings for how we experience and encode human sexual behavior.

A randomized 3×2 factorial design was employed. The treatment factor was composed of three levels: (1) a memory enhancement procedure adopted from the Cognitive Interview Technique (Geiselman et al., 1986);[2] (2) an atheoretical "placebo" memory enhancement procedure that relied completely on an instructional set designed to increase subjects' motivation and provide an environment conducive to subjects' focusing attention on the recall task; and (3) a control treatment consisting of no instructional set. Additionally, a condition factor was used and separated into two levels: (1) keeping a daily sexual diary for two weeks, and (2) not keeping a diary at all.

Regardless of treatment or condition, all subjects completed the same experimental outcome measure: a self-administered questionnaire that asked about particular sexual activities experienced during the two weeks covered by the diaries (or "no diary" control time). The specific reproducibility of students' sexual accounts can be addressed by examining the empirical relationships found between the diary accounts and the follow-up questionnaires. Similarly, ways to enhance reproducibility can be addressed in an analysis of the impact of the treatment interventions.

Subjects were recruited from a pool of UCLA undergraduates who receive course credit for participating in psychological studies. Sexually active college students were deemed relevant because they have generally not altered their sexual behavior in response to safe-sex interventions (Baldwin et al., 1992).

The study was initially explained to subjects as examining "different methods of reporting sexual experiences and different statistical methods of analyzing data. You will be asked to keep a diary of your sexual experiences for two weeks. We'll go over the details of the diary in a minute. You'll be asked to fill out two questionnaires about yourself."[3]

The study was repeated twice, and ultimately a total 217 students partici-pated. As implied in the instructions given to students, there were three collec-tion instruments: a diary and two questionnaires. For reasons that will become clear shortly, a random half of the subjects was asked to fill out a sexual diary for the subsequent two-week period. The diary entries were to be written in standard prose, but considerable time was spent explaining to subjects the kind of detail desired and the need to report as accurately as possible what occurred (including nothing at all). Examples of clear and unclear writing were re-viewed. Entries like "Well, then we, you know, got it on" were unacceptable.

It was also explained to subjects who had been randomly assigned to the no-diary condition that they would begin keeping diaries at a later date, follow-ing completion of the second questionnaire. In fact, because this group essen-tially served as a control for the effects of keeping diaries, diary data collected from this group were irrelevant to the study. They were collected only to avoid any disappointment about having been deceived.[4]

Before the blank diary forms (one for each of two seven-day periods) were distributed, all of the students filled out a short questionnaire, which included some standard biological questions and the Mosher Sex Guilt Scale (Mosher, 1966). The diaries were collected two weeks later and then, after two weeks had elapsed, all of the subjects were asked to fill out a second questionnaire addressing any sexual activity that had occurred during the two-week diary period (whether or not a diary had been filled out). In other words, the recall period was only two weeks, and the time elapsed until the recall questionnaire was administered was only two weeks.

The self-administered recall questionnaire was worded in a conventional manner. Definitions of various sexual activity were given as needed (e.g., for vaginal intercourse), and a two-question format was employed. For example:

> Over the two week period indicated, did you engage in vaginal inter-course?
>
>   YES_____ NO_____
>
> If the answer is yes, on how many separate occasions did you engage in vaginal intercourse?[5]

Each follow-up questionnaire was packaged with one of two experimental interventions, or the control condition. The first intervention was meant to en-hance recall using an instructional set modified from the Geiselman Cognitive Interview. As an aid in recall for eyewitnesses to crimes, the Cognitive Inter-view has demonstrated utility and appears to be based on sound principles of human information processing (Geiselman et al., 1984). Because the recall task at hand involved summing a number of events over a two-week period rather than recalling the details of one salient event, and because the sensitive nature of the data being collected among undergraduate students precluded the use of interactive face-to-face interviews, as required by the procedure of

Geiselman and colleagues, considerable modification of the mechanics of the Cognitive Interview was necessary. The ultimate focus was on the provision of instructional and material aids (calendars, scratch pads, and posterboards) that would assist subjects in mental reinstatement of the total environmental and personal context of each sexual event. In addition, an effort was made to put subjects at ease and provide as much time as necessary to complete the task.

The second intervention was intended as a placebo. Subjects were offered an instructional set emphasizing the importance of the project and, as in the first treatment condition, an effort was made to put subjects at ease and allow sufficient time. Scratch pads and calendars were again offered, but no information was given about specific mnemonics of the mental reinstatement of context. Subjects were largely on their own in developing any mnemonic techniques.

Subjects in the control condition were simply given the recall questionnaire and asked to fill it out, with the two-week recall period specified by date. While these subjects were also made to feel comfortable, and given as much time as necessary, no further instructions were given and no recall aids were provided.

For all subjects, the recall session was the first indication that the study in fact was concerned with memory of their sexual experiences. Upon entrance to the experimental room, all subjects were told: "We can now tell you a little bit more about the study. We are looking at how accurately people can remember and report their sexual experiences. . . ."

Findings

Of the many kinds of sexual behavior addressed in the diaries and questionnaires, we focus here on vaginal intercourse, cunnilingus, and fellatio. The first issue is reproducibility: how well the diary accounts and the questionnaire accounts correspond. We use the term "reproducibility" since there is no way to definitively determine which dataset captures more of the truth. The diary accounts, written once a day, probably suffer from relatively fewer memory defects. Yet, some respondents certainly failed to remember all that transpired or did not bother to write it down. The questionnaire had the advantage of asking explicitly about various kinds of sexual activity, but at least two weeks had elapsed since the sexual activity occurred. And for both, there was some inevitable ambiguity in the sexual activity itself. For example, one wonders how accurately male respondents could report the number of orgasms their female partner achieved.[6] On the other hand, there are some kinds of sexual activity for which it is reasonable to conclude that the diaries are quite accurate. For example, vaginal intercourse is probably sufficiently salient for both men and women to be properly captured in the diary accounts. If the questionnaire data do not reproduce the diary data, there is reason to be suspicious of the questionnaire data.

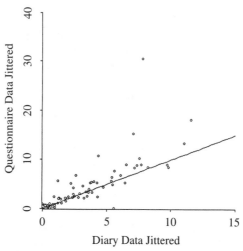

Figure 17.1   Occurrences of Vaginal Intercourse

To begin, for the number of different sexual partners during the two-week diary period, the questionnaire data reproduced the diary data almost perfectly. In retrospect, this is not surprising, since the majority of subjects had one partner, and the vast majority had one or none. Clearly, remembering the number of partners for the two-week period was not a taxing assignment.

The story is quite different for the reproducibility of the reported amount of vaginal intercourse. Figure 17.1 shows a jittered scatterplot in which the number of acts of vaginal intercourse reported in the diary is arrayed on the horizontal axis and the number of acts of vaginal intercourse reported in the questionnaires is arrayed on the vertical axis.[7] If the diary were perfectly reproducible, all of the points would fall on a straight line with a slope of 1.0 and an intercept of 0 (i.e., x = y). That line is displayed in figure 17.1. Clearly the questionnaire data are on the average greater in value than the diary data; the points tend to fall above the line.

A useful way to summarize the apparent difference between the diary and questionnaire data shown in figure 17.1 is to compare the means. The mean for the diary data is 2.5 acts of vaginal intercourse and the mean for the questionnaire data is 3.3 acts of vaginal intercourse. There is, however, one substantial outlier in the questionnaire data (i.e., 30 reported acts of vaginal intercourse). If that point is removed, the questionnaire mean falls to 3.0. The disparity is substantial, and it is not clear that the outlier should be removed. Distributions of sexual behavior often have long tails that are of particular interest (e.g., in research on AIDS).

One can get another perspective on the data reproducibility by fitting the summary line to the scatter plot in figure 17.1 (without jittering the data). We

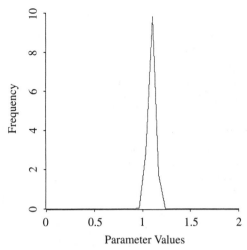

Figure 17.2 Posterior for Vaginal Intercourse
Slope (Tight Prior)

used a linear regression formulation with a Poisson error term.[8] The estimated y-intercept was .10, and the estimated slope was 1.29.[9] One cannot reject a null hypothesis of 0 for the intercept at conventional levels. However, one can reject the null hypothesis of 1.0 for the slope (t-value = 3.6) at conventional levels. In combination, the two tests imply that for every act of vaginal intercourse reported in the diaries there are nearly 1.3 acts of vaginal intercourse reported in the questionnaires. But the disparity comes primarily from the subjects who report at least one act of vaginal intercourse in the diaries. The vast majority of subjects who report no acts of vaginal intercourse in the diaries report no acts of sexual intercourse in the questionnaire.

Are these findings sufficient to shake conventional assumptions of reproducibility? One can address this issue by employing Bayesian inference. If a diffuse prior is used for the intercept and slope, the posterior distribution for the slope is massed well above 1.0. This is consistent with our conventional regression results.

Suppose, however, that one began the analysis quite confident that the intercept was 0 and the slope was 1.0. One can represent those views by assuming a normal prior distribution on the intercept with a mean of 0 and a standard deviation of .05, and by assuming a prior distribution on the slope with a mean of 1.0 and a standard deviation of .05. These parameter values imply that the researcher is 95% sure (before looking at the data) that the true intercept falls between .1 and −.1, and that the true slope falls between 1.1 and .90. In other words, this is a very confident researcher, who would need very strong evidence to question the assumed reproducibility.

Figure 17.2 shows the new posterior distribution for the slope. The added information has reduced the posterior's spread, but virtually all the mass is still substantially above 1.0. In other words, the researcher should now believe that the slope is greater than 1.0; the data are sufficient, even with a very tight prior around 1.0, to alter the researcher's beliefs. Thus, the weight of evidence now indicates that questionnaire accounts from college students of the amount of vaginal intercourse tend to be overestimates.

But one can go further. Stereotypes of how men talk about their sexual prowess imply that men may be more likely than women to overreport in their recollections of vaginal intercourse. Estimates of different regression lines for men and women seem to support this view. The slope for the Poisson regression is 1.21 for women, and the mass of the posterior, assuming a diffuse prior, is well above 1.0. The slope of the Poisson regression for men is 1.61, and the mass of the posterior, assuming a diffuse prior, is well above 1.21.[10] In short, the women overreport a bit, and the men overreport a lot.

However, the greater slope for the men depends substantially on a single leverage point (7 in the diary data and 30 in the questionnaire data). If that point is removed, the slopes for men and women are very similar. But, as noted above, it is not clear that the single leverage point should be removed. On the one hand, much research on human sexuality quite properly includes individuals who are statistically unusual. On the other hand, the data point may reflect a serious reporting error.

To summarize, it is apparent that the questionnaire data are unable to fully reproduce the diary data. In addition, the disparities are systematic: respondents who report at least some vaginal intercourse in the diaries tend to report greater amounts of vaginal intercourse in the questionnaires. This tendency may be especially pronounced for certain male subjects. Since vaginal intercourse is likely to be very salient for both men and women, the diary accounts may well be accurate. Consequently, it may be proper to conceptualize the disparities between the diaries and questionnaires as errors in the questionnaire data. Finally, given the conditions under which the recall data were elicited, the usual errors in recall surveys may be substantially worse.

Do similar problems surface for oral sex? Figure 17.3 shows the relationship between the diary data and the questionnaire data for giving oral sex. We include here only those acts leading to orgasm, since we are interested in especially salient events that are likely to be reproduced in the diaries. Figure 17.4 shows the relationship between the diary data and the questionnaire for getting oral sex. Again, and for the same reasons, only acts leading to orgasm are included.

For both figures, we again find that the questionnaire data do not reproduce the diary data, and that there is a general tendency for the number of acts reported in the questionnaires to be larger than the number of acts reported in the diaries. Regression analyses, much like those reported above, revealed slopes of well above 1.0, comparable to the slope for vaginal intercourse. But what of the differences between male and female subjects?

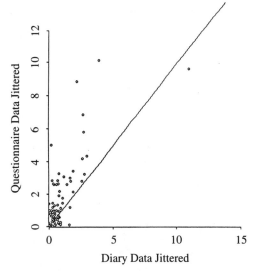

Figure 17.3   "Gives" Oral Sex

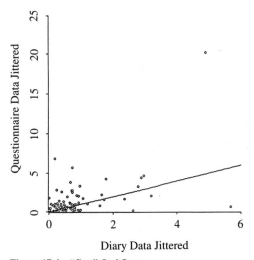

Figure 17.4   "Gets" Oral Sex

Efforts to estimate different slopes for male and female subjects failed. An examination of tables 17.1–4 will show why and raises some new substantive issues.

There are at least three implications of the tables. First, many more reports of oral sex are elicited by the questionnaires than the diaries. This is, of course, consistent with the data on vaginal intercourse. Second, both men and women report more oral sex in the questionnaires than in the diaries, but the pattern is

Table 17.1   Gender by the Number of Times "Giving" Oral Sex Reported in the Diaries

	0	1	2	3	10
Female	37	10	7	1	1
Male	29	0	0	0	0

Table 17.2   Gender by Number of Times "Giving" Oral Sex Reported in the Questionnaires

	0	1	2	3	4	5	6	8	9	10
Female	29	8	8	4	2	1	1	1	1	1
Male	21	3	4	0	0	0	0	0	0	0

Table 17.3   Gender by Number of Times "Getting" Oral Sex Reported in the Diaries

	0	1	2	3	4	5
Female	43	6	4	1	1	1
Male	27	1	1	0	0	0

Table 17.4   Gender by Number of Times "Getting" Oral Sex Reported in the Questionnaires

	0	1	2	3	4	5	6	20
Female	33	6	8	4	3	0	1	1
Male	23	4	1	0	0	1	0	0

a bit more pronounced for women. Finally, there is an apparent inconsistency when the data for women and men are compared. Note that in both the diaries and questionnaires, women are substantially more likely to report giving and getting oral sex than men. Since the vast number of the respondents were active in heterosexual sex, the comparisons do not add up.

Consider, for example, the questionnaire data. About 50% of the women report giving oral sex. Yet, only about 20% of the men report getting oral sex. Likewise, about 40% of the women report getting oral sex, and only about 25% of the men report giving oral sex. The story is similar for the diary data. The reported lack of involvement in oral sex by men explains why separate slopes cannot be effectively estimated; for men the amount of oral sex too often approaches the constant of 0.

More interesting, however, is that perhaps the samples of men and women differ in some fundamental ways. That is, *these* women engage in more oral sex with their male partners than *these* men do with their female partners. We certainly cannot rule out this possibility, but it is difficult to think of a reason why such large differences between the men and women would surface by differential self-selection into the study.

On the other hand, the differences apparent in tables 17.1–4 could be real (i.e., not a self-selection artifact) in the sense that men and women may store, recall, and/or report their experiences with oral sex differently. A number of possible mechanisms come to mind. For example, our reading of the diaries suggests that men and women tend to write rather different kinds of sexual narratives. In a rather stereotypic fashion, women write about intimacy, with sexuality being a part of the whole experience. Men write about discrete sexual acts with very little text about the relationship.[11] Perhaps for women, the narrative itself helps them to more thoroughly reconstruct their sexual activities— particularly as it relates to oral sex. For example, if oral sex is more salient to women than to men, conceivably the narrative minimizes the extent of distortion and memory decay associated with less salient sexual activities. Since women are more likely to achieve orgasm during oral sex (as opposed to sexual intercourse) by virtue of the direct clitoral stimulation, it is perhaps a more salient experience (in a mnemonic sense). In contrast, men are easily orgasmic during intercourse and oral sex, which may diminish the mnemonic uniqueness of the latter.

Other interpretations seem equally viable. A man's orgasm during oral sex is more obvious, for a woman, than is a woman's for a man. In this case, a woman would be more likely to mention this fact. A man, on the other hand, may not recognize whether a woman reached orgasm during oral sex and, for this reason, may fail to report it.

More broadly, the salience of sexual behavior, in general, may also have been overestimated in survey methodology—and perhaps more importantly, in theories of human sexual behavior. For example, it is implicit in sex research that sexual experiences are uniquely significant. This conclusion is reasonable, since sexual experiences are highly pleasurable, have many emotional and status correlates, and are critical to reproduction, kinship, and inheritance (Abramson and Pinkerton, 1995). Thus, the measurement of sexual behavior, whether in a survey, interview, or ethnographic report, often asks individuals to recall behaviors over a long "personal history." Certainly, in our culture, one would not presume to ask people how often they shook hands over the past ten years. But, we would not hesitate to ask about their sexual behavior over the same time period.

Yet, if the findings of the present study are instructive, especially as they relate to the relatively short period of two weeks, perhaps the salience of sex is more important in terms of cultural meaning than in underlying cognitive processes. Emotion influences memory, particularly in these types of real-world behaviors (Linton, 1978). But perhaps only particularly emotional events (e.g., first sexual intercourse) are remembered vividly (though, as Linton demonstrates, not necessarily accurately). Sex, if it is repeated often, may not be particularly salient or vivid, resembling in a mnemonic sense, eating. Eating is pleasurable, satisfies a basic survival need, and is repeated very often. Presumably, unusual eating experiences would be remembered (or distorted less); perhaps the same is true of sex.

If subjects cannot accurately remember their sexual behavior over a two-week period, especially after having been primed by the diary and other relevant cues and incentives, it tells us something about the significance of routine sexual activity. Possibly, as Foucault (1980) has suggested, the salience of sex is that we talk about it all the time. And the talking, debating, moralizing about sex makes us presume that it is uniquely significant at all levels of consciousness. Although we are not implying that sex is trivial in personal or cultural dynamics, it does seem conceivable that sex is, at some level, merely one of the pleasures of life, one that has particular relevance to reproduction.

The finding that subjects had difficulty recalling a supposedly salient behavior in the recent past is also consistent with the literature on married (and dating) couples. Christensen (Christensen and King, 1982; Christensen, Margolin, and Sullaway, 1992; Christensen, Sullaway, and King, 1983; Sullaway and Christensen, 1983), for example, has demonstrated that married/dating couples are not particularly accurate reporters of their own behavior if questioned about recent, specific events, and are only in moderate agreement with each other on the occurrence of specific events in the recent past (e.g., the previous 24 hours and the preceding 3–5 days). This was true for interparental agreement on child behavior problems, dyadic interaction (e.g., we took a shower or a bath together), and time spent talking. Although the correlations vary by activity and perspective (Kashy and Kenny, 1990), it is clear that recency is no assurance of accurate remembering. Of course, since it appears that memory itself is fractionalized (Desimone, 1992), it is not apparent to what extent this finding can be generalized to all memory systems. Perhaps this is specific to working, or short-term, memory for specific behavioral domains (Baddeley, 1992). The kinds of behavior that we have examined in the present study (i.e., sexual) are not the kinds of behaviors or stimuli routinely used in memory experiments. Therefore, it is unclear what memory processes and what memory domains we have tapped. Certainly, we have utilized naturalistic (or "everyday") memory (Neisser, 1978; 1982), but even this process is not universally accepted in the literature (Klatzky, 1991). Thus, it is perhaps best to conclude that we have demonstrated that recent sexual behaviors are often difficult to recall, and that this difficulty may have implications for how sexual experience is organized and encoded.

Finally, there is the issue of experimental effects. Remember that our experimental design included two factors: (1) diary versus no diary, and (2) memory enhancement versus a placebo versus nothing. If the lack of reproducibility was the result of recall errors, we anticipated that subjects who filled out the diaries would report more or less sexual activity, but that subjects exposed to the memory enhancement condition would report more sexual activity.

The treatments did not work as expected. For vaginal intercourse, subjects reported an average of about .5 more events when they filled out the diary and also when they were exposed to either memory enhancement or to the placebo. In other words, all of the interventions, compared to doing nothing, led to a greater amount of vaginal intercourse reported in the questionnaires. In contrast, the amount of oral sex reported was unaffected by any of the interventions. Overall, therefore, one possible inference is that the lack of reproducibility was not the result of memory errors after all. Another possible inference is that the factors we anticipated as improving recall did not function in that way.

As it turns out, the latter inference is quite plausible. Because of institutional review-board restrictions about face-to-face interviews, we had to make substantial changes in the Cognitive Interview Technique. Thus, this technique may not be applicable to summary recall under self-administered conditions but may be dependent upon recall of one salient event in an interactive context. As employed in the present study, it may have simply served as a variant of the placebo by enhancing motivation and providing direction to think carefully about the two-week period under study. And in this regard, both the placebo and the Cognitive Interview Technique had small enhancing effects.

Since the enhancing effects were small, another possibility exists. Introductory psychology students are notorious for their disinterest in psychology experiments. In general, they want to get out of the experimental situation and to do each task as fast as possible. While a sex experiment is inherently interesting, the intro-psych student effect may still be operating. Thus, it may have been that although the Cognitive Interview Technique and placebo were helpful for those subjects who were seriously interested in the study, the remainder of subjects viewed them as delays and distractions. Consequently, the intervention did not "take."

Finally, as suggested previously, perhaps sex is not nearly as salient as we think it is, at least at the memory level. From this perspective, diary keeping and the treatments we employed were not powerful enough to offset the blending, distortion, and memory decay that occur for routine behaviors.

Conclusions

There is no disputing that on the average our subjects could not reproduce in their questionnaires what they reported in their diaries. This failure is especially compelling since the recall period was only two weeks, and the interval between the diary and questionnaire was only about two weeks. Moreover, students were placed in an experimental setting where the need to accurately represent their sexual activities was continually emphasized.

The errors in reproducibility were often systematic. There was a general tendency for all subjects to report more sexual activities in the questionnaires than in the diaries. For vaginal intercourse, the tendency was perhaps more pronounced in men than women. For oral sex, overreporting was clearly more pronounced in women than in men. But the data on oral sex raised more fundamental issues. Women were far more likely to report both giving and getting oral sex than men. Since the vast majority of respondents were heterosexual, these patterns did not add up, and they suggest that men and women store, recall, and/or report oral sex rather differently.

We also failed to find the anticipated effects for our experimental interventions. One conclusion may be that the lack of reproducibility was less about recall than about systematic distortions. Another conclusion may be that our interventions simply did not work to improve recall.

Finally, and most important, we believe our findings raise important questions about conventional surveys of sexual behavior. Self-reports about the amount of sexual activity may well be subject to more than relatively friendly random errors. The errors are perhaps systematic and related to important explanatory variables. Consequently, when different amounts of sexual activity are reported for different kinds of people, the patterns risk seriously confounding lifestyle explanations with significant measurement error.

Notes

The authors wish to thank the following individuals for their assistance with the research project: Denis Bozulich, Amy Engerman, Joann Gonzalez, and Lea Shim.

1. In other words, the respondent is asked to reconstruct a sexual history and then extract various kinds of summary information.

2. This technique was originally developed as an aid for recall in eyewitness reports of crime. It is grounded in Tulving's (1974) research on retrieval cues and is predicated in part on the assumption that retrieval may be enhanced through mental reinstatement of the environmental and personal context of an event.

3. Before those details were presented, the procedures to ensure confidentiality were explained.

4. The study was advertised as a *diary* study of sexual experiences.

5. Similar questions were asked for a variety of possible sexual activities.

6. It is doubtful that any of the respondents participated in sexual activity with each other, so there is no way to get two accounts of the same sexual encounter.

7. Figure 17.1 contains 85 observations from an initial sample of 217. Most of the missing data result from the random assignment; approximately half of the 217 subjects were not assigned to the diary condition. Then, an additional 10 percent failed to answer the questionnaire items on vaginal intercourse.

8. The linear form was chosen because the theory of perfect reproducibility is linear. We chose a Poisson disturbance because the response variable was a count.

9. If the outlier is removed, the slope drops to 1.20 and the t-value drops to 2.4. That is, overall conclusions do not change very much.

10. Multicolinearity precluded stable estimation of the different intercepts for men and women as well as different slopes.

11. This finding, incidentally, is consistent with gender differences in reported sexual fantasies (Ellis and Symons, 1990), as well as in gender differences in fantasies created to accompany sexually explicit films (Abramson and Mosher, 1979).

References

Abramson, P. R. (1992). Sex, lies, and ethnography. In G. Herdt and S. Lindenbaum (eds.), *The Time of AIDS*. Newbury Park, Calif.: Sage.

Abramson, P. R., Goldberg, P. A., Mosher, D. L., Abramson, L. M., and Gottesdiener, M. (1975). Experimenter effects on responses to explicitly sexual stimuli. *Journal of Research in Personality, 9,* 133–46.

Abramson, P. R., and Mosher, D. L. (1979). An empirical investigation of experimentally induced masturbatory fantasies. *Archives of Sexual Behavior,* 8, 27–39.

Abramson, P. R., and Pinkerton, S. D. (1995). *With Pleasure: Thoughts on the Nature of Human Sexuality.* New York: Oxford University Press.

Baddeley, A. (1992). Working memory. *Science, 255,* 556–59.

Baldwin, J. D., Whiteley, S., and Baldwin, J. I. (1992). The effect of ethnic group on sexual attitudes related to contraception and STDs. *Journal of Sex Research,* 29, 189–206.

Catania, J. A., Coates, T. J., Stall, R., Turner, H., Gagnon, J., Wiley, J., and Groves, R. (1992). Prevalence of AIDS-related risk factors and condom use in the United States. *Science*, 258, 1101–6.

Christensen, A., and King, C. E. (1982). Telephone survey of daily marital behavior. *Behavioral Assessment,* 4, 327–38.

Christensen, A., Margolin, G., and Sullaway, M. (1992). Interparental agreement on child behavior problems. *Psychological Assessment,* 4, 419–25.

Christensen, A., Sullaway, M., and King, C. E. (1983). Systematic error in behavioral reports of dyadic interaction: Egocentric bias and content effects. *Behavioral Assessment,* 5, 129–40.

Desimone, R. (1992). The physiology of memory: Recordings of things past. *Science,* 258, 245–46.

Ellis, B. J., and Symons, D. (1990). Sex differences in sexual fantasy: An evolutionary psychological approach. *Journal of Sex Research,* 27, 527–56.

Foucault, M. (1980). *The History of Sexuality.* New York: Vintage.

Geiselman, E. R., Fisher, R. P., Firstenberg, I., Hutton, L. A., Sullivan, S., Avetissian, I., and Prosk, A. (1984). Enhancement of eyewitness memory: An empirical evaluation of the cognitive interview. *Journal of Police Science and Administration,* 12, 74–80.

Geiselman, E. R., Fisher, R. P., MacKinnon, D., and Holland, H. L. (1986). Enhancement of eyewitness memory and cognitive review. *American Journal of Psychology,* 99, 385–401.

Groves, R. M. (1989). *Survey Errors and Survey Costs.* New York: John Wiley.

Kashy, D. A., and Kenny, D. A. (1990). Do you know whom you were with a week ago Friday? A re-analysis of the Bernard, Killworth, and Sailer studies. *Social Psychology Quarterly,* 53, 55–61.

Kinsey, A. C., Pomeroy, W. B., and Martin, C. E. (1948). *Sexual Behavior in the Human Male.* Philadelphia: Saunders.

Kinsey, A. C., Pomeroy, W. B., Martin, C. E., and Gebhard, P. H. (1953). *Sexual Behavior in the Human Female.* Philadelphia: Saunders.

Klatzky, R. L. (1991). Let's be friends. *American Psychologist,* 46, 43–45.

Laumann, E. O., Gagnon, J. H., Michael, R. T., and Michaels, S. (1994). *The Social Organization of Sexuality.* Chicago: University of Chicago Press.

Linton, M. (1978). Real-world memory after six years: An in vivo study of very long-term memory. In M. M. Gruenberg, P. E. Morris, and R. N. Sykes (eds.), *Practical Aspects of Memory.* London: Academic Press.

Mosher, D. L. (1966). The development and multitrait-multimethod matrix analysis of three measures of three aspects of guilt. *Journal of Consulting Psychology,* 30, 25–29.

Neisser, U. (1978). Memory: What are the important questions? In M. M. Gruenberg, P. E. Morris, & R. N. Sykes (eds.), *Practical Aspects of Memory.* London: Academic Press.

Neisser, U. (1982). *Memory Observed: Remembering in Natural Contexts.* San Francisco: Freeman.

Rotheram-Borus, M. J., Meyer-Bahlburg, H. F. L., Koopman, C., Rosario, M., Exner, T. M., Henderson, R., Mattheieu, M., and Gruen, R. S. (1992). Lifeline sexual behaviors among runaway males and females. *Journal of Sex Research,* 29, 15–30.

Shweder, R. A. (1990). Cultural Psychology—what is it? In J. W. Stigler, R. A. Shweder, and G. Herdt (eds.), *Cultural Psychology.* Cambridge: Cambridge University Press.

Sullaway, M., and Christensen, A. (1983). Couples and families as participant observers of their interaction. *Advances in Family Intervention, Assessment and Theory,* 3, 119–60.

Symons, D. (1990). Sex differences in sexual fantasy: An evolutionary psychological approach. *Journal of Sex Research,* 27, 527–56.

Tanur, J. M. (ed.). (1992). *Questions about Questions.* New York: Russell Sage Foundation.

Temple, M. T., and Leigh, B. C. (1992). Alcohol consumption and unsafe sexual behavior in discrete events. *Journal of Sex Research,* 29, 207–20.

Tulving, E. (1974). Cue-dependent forgetting. *American Scientist,* 62, 74–82.

APPENDIX

Theorizing Sexuality: Seeds of a
Transdisciplinary Paradigm Shift

PAUL OKAMI AND LAURA PENDLETON

The topic of human sexuality remains conceptually undeveloped. In anthropology, in particular, sexuality is typically ascribed the status of illegitimate child in the study of marriage, reproduction, and kinship relations (Frayser 1993, Tuzin 1991). Perhaps this is not surprising. There are many pressures and obstacles facing serious researchers in the field of human sexuality (Abramson 1990, Vance 1991). Professors specializing in such topics remain untenured, unfunded, and held suspect by their colleagues, while few adequate training programs in human sexuality exist at the graduate level. Indeed, graduate students are urged to avoid the subject as a career liability. Sexuality is, however, a pervasive factor in human motivation and behavior. With the emergence of AIDS, new reproductive technologies, changing roles for men and women, and recognition of the magnitude of sexual diversity, it has become imperative that the study of sexuality achieve the status of a legitimate social and biological science. Toward this end, Paul Abramson and Gilbert Herdt coorganized a symposium sponsored by the Wenner-Gren Foundation for Anthropological Research and attended by twenty-three scholars. The symposium, titled "Theorizing Sexuality: Evolution, Culture, and Development," was held March 19–27, 1993, in Cascais, Portugal. It represented what was probably the first major attempt in almost thirty years to combine anthropological perspectives on sexuality with those emerging from other social and biological sciences.

The symposium originated in a cooperative "dream" that had preoccupied Abramson and Herdt throughout the late 1980s: to create "a disciplinary matrix, a gestalt, that would fashion paradigmatic change in how we look at sexuality." They noted that the focus of sexuality-related discourse has always been reproduction. This focus makes sense at lower levels of the phylogenetic ladder, where sex invariably is linked to procreation. Higher on the ladder, however, the relationship between sex and reproduction becomes more complex. Even among nonhuman primates, for example, sex has functions other than reproduction, such as peace-keeping or pair-bonding. Higher still, the major portion of human sexual behavior (e.g., masturbation, intercourse with contraception, homosexuality, etc.) appears unrelated to procreation. Indeed, the more closely one looks at human sexual motivation the larger looms the concept of *pleasure* (Abramson and Pinkerton 1995).

Because evidence for the plasticity of human sexual behavior emerges primarily from the anthropological record, Abramson and Herdt sought assistance from the Wenner-Gren Foundation for Anthropological Research. In 1991, the organizers met with representatives of the foundation in Los Angeles to finalize details of a conference that would unite the cross-cultural perspective on sexuality with other social and biological sciences. Attending the conference were nine anthropologists, two psychologists and one evolutionary psychologist, four sociologists, two primatologists, a philosopher, a developmental geneticist, a historian, an operations researcher, and an endocrinologist. (Jeffrey Weeks, a social historian, had been scheduled to attend but was unable to do so.) All papers had been distributed in advance to facilitate a more intensive and heuristic discussion.[1]

In her opening statement, Sydel Silverman, president of the Wenner-Gren Foundation, noted that it had never before convened a symposium on human sexuality and in fact had never held a symposium representing so wide a range of disciplines and perspectives. She emphasized the inevitable lack of exchange between disciplines and stated that the goal of the conference was to reshape research agendas rather than achieve consensus.

Sketching the contours of his "dream," Abramson stressed that whereas paradigmatic shift was an ultimate goal, the more proximate goals of the conference were illumination, discovery, and the generation of interest in the scientific and scholarly study of sexuality. Reflecting on the history of investigations of human sexuality, Herdt argued that the paradigm developed by early contributors such as Freud and Darwin and later researchers such as Mead and Kinsey was based on self-limiting assumptions. He noted the conceptual split that emerged during the 1960s between "sex" (biology) and "gender" (culture), with gender predominating as a focus of inquiry over the past several decades, and observed that throughout this work, inquiry into the nature of desire and pleasure was inexplicably absent. Thus, the critical questions for Abramson and Herdt for this conference were: (1) What are the received assumptions within each field, and how can we incorporate nonreproductive sex into our paradigms? (2) How can we move past the influence of constricting dichotomies of sex/gender (biology/culture) and essentialism/constructionism? and (3) How can we create a dialog that asks new questions across disciplines?

The first session was dedicated to the history and state of sex research in general. Abramson began by noting that, whereas "oxymoron" might be an appropriate term to characterize the notion of "sexual science," there were, in fact, many competent scholars and scientists producing important work in this field, either by circumventing entrenched academic prejudice or by establishing themselves in fields other than "human sexuality."

Meyer-Bahlberg expressed some of the contradictions between researchers trained in the biological sciences and those trained in the social sciences when he admitted that most of his associates (physicians) gave little thought to "theory," being concerned primarily with biological "facts" and the needs of patients. He reviewed some of the startling advances made over the past two decades in genetics, endocrinology, and neuroscience and detailed concerns emerging from his clinical work on sexual and reproductive dysfunctions such as ejaculatory disorders, infertility, and complications arising from the fashioning of sexual organs for intersex surgery.

Vance offered a social constructionist view of the history of anthropological involvement in the study of sexuality. She noted that even as anthropologists rebelled against essentialist biomedical models and created what she termed the "cultural influence model," they failed to question assumptions such as that sex equals reproduction, that males and females differ in behavior and desire, and that homosexuality and heterosexuality are discrete categories. She argued that their attempts to escape ethnocentrism tended to further it by treating culture-specific categories as though they were shared cross-culturally. She described social constructionism as not simply a focus on "nurture" but a method of inquiry that locates beliefs within their historical, social, and cultural circumstances. Supporting Abramson's comments about pleasure, she suggested that all large social movements are ultimately about pleasure whereas the accompanying rhetoric is *never* about pleasure.

De Waal countered that reproduction precedes pleasure and that the function of sex cannot be said to be pleasure. Abramson and Herdt replied that sex is multifunctional and focusing on pleasure is necessary simply to offset the prevailing view that procreation is primary. This objection and clarification inaugurated a pattern that was to pervade the conference. It became clear that the multiple disciplines represented ideological gulfs and substantial discrepancies in the usages and understandings of language. Historians and social constructionists such as Fout and Vance emphasized the importance of terminology and located the oppression of women and sexual minorities within the heterosexist ideology propagated by the scientific community—particularly by the "pseudoscientific" discourse related to sexuality. Scientists involved in primatology, genetics, and endocrinology retorted that the constructionists seemed more interested in dismantling "texts" than in attempting to understand problems or advance useful scientific endeavors.

Meanings and uses of terms such as "sex," "gender," "science," "biomedical," "homosexual," "adaptation," "intersex," "function," and "reproduction" became points of heated contention. Even the notion of "sexual pleasure" was questioned: was it a socially constructed category, or did it exist autonomously within human biology and experience? In response to this challenge, Abramson—invoking Mark Twain's admonition that "the difference between the right word and the almost right word is the difference between lightning and a lightning bug"—outlined a definition admittedly imperfect and imprecise: "Sexual pleasure refers to functionally specific positive sensations evoked in the genitals and other relevant body parts when these body parts are stimulated. Sexual pleasure also includes the subjective experience of the positive sensations evoked by such stimulation." He contended that such experience is hard-wired at birth, innate and intrinsic to human capability, but may be moderated by the physical and cultural milieu. He saw the capacity for sexual pleasure as an evolutionary adaptation serving as an incentive to sexual exploration—exploration that may lead to, among other things, conception. He emphasized, however, that the value of sexual pleasure itself is recognized in both humans and other primates in the absence of awareness of its connection to conception and that sex is therefore pursued, traded, regulated, and commoditized in human and nonhuman communities.

In attempting to manage the objections to position statements such as Abramson's, conference participants were suddenly faced with Hekma's sobering question: "Is it worthwhile to try to develop a sexual science that incorporates so many disciplines?" Berk wondered "Why save disciplines?" and Symons argued that one characteristic of good science is that it is not inconsistent with the products of other sciences, and therefore what is critical is the development of a body of knowledge that meets this criterion. Pavelka asked, "Well, then, what do we know for sure?" There was little subsequent agreement.

The next morning's session, devoted to the study of primate diversity and its relation to sex and human nature, was dominated by de Waal's overview of his work with bonobos. While acknowledging data on the link between sex and aggression in primates, de Waal described his interest in the link between sex and reconciliation. He presented data on increases in sexual cues and behaviors among bonobos at food-sharing time and hypothesized that sex may serve a peace-keeping function for some primates. Indeed, he suggested that such behavior may reflect the evolutionary origins of the mated, bonded pair. These primates' clear expression of nonreproductive sexual behavior, including frequent same-sex behavior, particularly between females, and apparent experience of "pleasure" during these acts seemed to him to make comparisons with humans tempting—a temptation Silverman later took pains to warn against.

Participants such as Pavelka and Symons were careful to distinguish sociobiology, which dominated evolutionary theorizing during the 1980s and was characterized in part by a potential for reductionism, from the newer approaches to evolutionary psychology and primatology that attempt to avoid throwing out the sociobiological baby with its reductionist bathwater. Pavelka emphasized that the study of primates includes the study of humans and that anthropology might best be characterized as a subdivision of primatology. In response, Symons suggested that a clearer rationale than is typically offered is needed to justify the study of primate behavior as an adjunct to the study of human behavior. For example, simply because it could be demonstrated that prosimians were evolutionary ancestors of gorillas, would we study them for clues to gorilla behavior, or would we simply study gorillas themselves? He located a coherent rationale for primate study in the realm of hypothesis generation and noted that different animals are differentially useful for these purposes depending on the hypotheses being explored.

Taking a more pessimistic view, Gregor argued that the history of primate study is the history of projective anthropomorphic identification. He wryly noted that the original objects of study were baboons, but because their behavior was unpalatable to social scientists seeking clues to human evolution they were abandoned in favor of chimpanzees—which in turn seem to have been discarded in favor of the still more attractive "peace-keeping" bonobos. Symons recalled the anxiety and surprise evoked among Jane Goodall's associates by the revelation of the unpleasant nature of the chimpanzee, to which they had looked as a model for human nature and evolution. Gregor went on to suggest that the differences between subhuman primates and humans—in language and family organization, for example—are so substantial as to make findings among primates of limited utility for understanding human behavior. This point of view was expressed more vehemently by Fout, who, following Pattatucci's observation that similarity between humans and bonobos does not necessarily imply an evolutionary link between the two species, asked rhetorically,"What does primate sexuality have to do with human sexuality?" To this de Waal answered, "Everything—there is no difference" (i.e., human sexuality *is* primate sexuality).

The afternoon was devoted to historical and constructionist views of ideas on desire and pleasure. Feher summarized his work on historical conditions related to the "arts of love," focusing on Foucault's preconditions for the emergence of love: freedom and some type of intrinsic difficulty or obstacle to be overcome. Greenberg, proposing that the "reproduction vs. pleasure" dichotomy is too simplistic, pointed to multiple motives and goals of sexuality including aggression and punishment (e.g., rape)—goals which may themselves incorporate or lead to pleasure in a broader context. Tuzin reviewed recent "revisionist" scholarship on Victorian sexuality, locating the rise of structural-functionalism as coincident with the response to late Victorian obsession with sexuality. According to Tuzin, structural-functionalism served to "reinstate sublimation" and to foster abstraction and inhibit consideration of the phenomenology of sex, particularly its pleasurable aspects. He observed that our own end-of-century preoccupation with homosexuality, pornography, women's rights, urban blight, and international migration strikingly paralleled *fin de siècle* Victorian obsessions.

According to Manderson, the primary difficulty facing conference participants was the operationalization of "slippery" ideas such as "sex." Did nocturnal emissions count as "sex"? Did "masturbation"? Manderson contended that sexuality is primarily a linguistic problem, the very notion of sexuality having emerged only during the nineteenth century. All of our nouns are problematic, she continued, pointing to the centrality of consideration of how the nouns are used and by whom in judging their meaning and effects. She argued that the body is both a vehicle and a "text" that should be interpreted in the context of social relations of production and reproduction.

It was comments such as these that prompted Berk to compare historical constructionism with historical fiction. His experience working with police documents and newspaper reports of crime—which he characterized as "essentially fiction"—had led him to conclude that scientific evidence cannot be obtained from historical sources because these data are of highly questionable reliability and validity. Indeed, he suggested that the enterprise being reflected in the day's proceedings was not science. Silverman countered that the proceedings were intended to explore the history of ideas, not test theory, and that such exploration had "everything to do with the scientific enterprise."

Issues related to human biological development were next on the conference agenda. Wilson explained the fundamentals of hormonal influences on the developing fetus and person, focusing on the relationship of hormones to what he termed "sex drive" and "sexual [gender] identity." He emphasized that the bulk of the evidence still supported John Money's contention that "whether you feel male or female" is most dependent upon having been raised as male or female. He concluded, however, that the impact of hormones is still not well understood. This theme was picked up by Meyer-Bahlberg, who discussed the relationship in rats and humans between hormones and what he termed "arousability" (what Wilson had earlier termed "sex drive" and others had called "libido"). He pointed to the significant (but not sufficient) role of hormones in human sexual desire and motivation and noted that this role is somewhat clearer and less complicated in the case of males. The critical unanswered question for him was the role of hormones in selectivity of human sexual desire—that is, how hormones influence arousability to a particular type of person or to a particular gender.

Pattatucci, who (with her colleague Dean Hamer) had recently reported startling findings regarding the role of genetics in the sexual orientation of fruit flies and male humans, rejected the idea that such investigations exemplified any "harder" a scientific enterprise than work in the other disciplines represented at the conference. She referred to genes as "abstract constructs of reality" and admitted to being "ashamed" to have used the word "homosexual" in reporting on her fruit-fly work. In an impassioned plea for responsibility in the sciences, she wondered exactly what was problematic about homosexuality that it needed to be studied at all, given that same-gender sexual behavior constituted "one of many adaptive behaviors for our species." She concluded rhetorically, "If we find a gene [that determines homosexuality], what have we found?"

Symons presented a clarification of the rationale for and methods of evolutionary psychology. He emphasized that the simplistic biological determinism often ascribed to evolutionary theorizing misrepresents an approach in which interactions between organisms and their environments are of intrinsic con-

cern. He explained that, according to evolutionary theory, the organism interacts with an environment it chooses and with which it has been adapted to
interact over long periods of evolutionary time. If some aspect of the environment is changed in a novel way, some aspect of an adaptation may be perturbed. For example, evidence suggests a species-wide taste preference for
foods high in sugar, fat, and salt. Such taste preferences may have been adaptive when foods containing these elements were in short supply, but now that
they are overwhelmingly part of our environment this once adaptive taste preference "is killing us." Thus, there is no mysterious inner drive promoting reproductive success. Instead, there is merely a bundle of adaptations acquired over
tens of thousands of years that may or may not promote reproductive success
in novel environments.

Schlegel reviewed the findings from her exploratory cross-cultural study of
adolescent sexuality in 186 societies. In all these societies, adolescence is
clearly delineated as a discrete social stage, although in one society girls' experience of this stage is somewhat ambiguous. Contrary to commonsense expectations, differences in the treatment of boys and girls are remarkably constant
across societies—a finding consistent with evolutionary models. Schlegel emphasized the universality of strong social constraints on the sexual behavior of
adolescents, noting that these constraints typically entail a longer waiting period for boys between the onset of puberty and the age at which socially sanctioned heterosexual behaviors are permitted (girls typically marrying soon
after menarche while boys marry in young adulthood).

While acknowledging the compelling and internally coherent nature of the
"just-so stories" told by evolutionary theorists, Berk expressed concern over
what he considered to be the deterministic implications of evolutionary psychology. Drawing on his own model of uncertainty in the social sciences, he
questioned whether we have any way of determining whether an observed behavior represents an adaptation or "noise" (accidental or haphazard variation).
He argued for the development of statistical buffers to prevent the investigator
from being seduced by such "noise" and suggested that stories need to be told
in terms of distributions rather than point estimates (something that had not
been attempted in papers such as Symons's). At the same time, he stressed that
statistics cannot solve the problem of uncertainty. Inferential statistics represent little more than a language for talking about uncertainty—a language that
is often ill-spoken because data are typically not drawn in such a manner as to
warrant the claims made for them. He asserted that uncertainty is everywhere,
cannot be avoided, and needs to be built into the design and analysis of research. Finally, he challenged the concept—seemingly necessary to the scientific enterprise—that every phenomenon has an explanation or at least an explanation that can be found. He expressed concern that many of the questions
being asked during the conference may fall into the category "interesting but
unanswerable."

A critical portion of the symposium involved the comparative ethnographic record. It is in comparative ethnography that questions of sexual nature vs. sexual culture have traditionally been addressed. Gregor began this portion of the proceedings by reviewing what is known about sexual universals, among which he counted mother-son incest avoidance, sexual jealousy, shame, and fear, the correlation of love and sex, the social use of sex as metaphor to express a portion of cultural world view, and the absence of "neutrality" toward sex (the one seeming exception to this last being the sexually "indifferent" Dani studied by Heider [1976]). He went on to point to the ubiquity of sexual or "romantic" love in non-Western societies, a finding contrary to the often re-peated contention that "love" as a construct is specific to Western societies. He argued that, like sexuality, love may be socially repressed. He offered a poi-gnant and effective evocation of the ecstatic experience of passionate love and then reviewed psychological and sociological theories related to this emotion. These theories ranged from the pragmatic economics of Randall Collins's "wine-press" theory through Freud to Sternberg's (1986) and Lee's (1973) clas-sification schemes for love styles and Bowlby's (1958) work on attachment—work that Shaver, Hazen, and Bradshaw (1988) have extended to explore the notion that infant attachment styles are templates for adult love relationships.

The case-study method Gregor used for portions of his work came under challenge from Berk, who again wondered exactly what enterprise was being represented. In response, Herdt and Abramson defended case studies from an anthropological viewpoint, and, when used inductively, from the point of view of a traditional Baconian model of science. Schlegel suggested that methods such as the case study may help to identify patterns that can be correlated with known statistical facts.

Herdt reviewed his groundbreaking work on ritualized same-sex behaviors among the Sambia of New Guinea (cf. Herdt 1987). He explained why he had dropped the use of the term "homosexual" for the ritualized fellating of older Sambian men by boys. Because this behavior, founded as it is on the belief that insemination is essential for the boy's sexual growth and passage into adult-hood and heterosexual marriage, emphasizes symbolic or biological reproduc-tion, use of the term "homosexual" to describe it may distort the meaning of the term as a categorical construct. Nevertheless, he pointed out, pleasure, lewdness, and lasciviousness are also involved in this ritual. In attempting to explain this apparent paradox, he identified the "extremist" positions typically taken to explain it—on the one hand as a universal experience of same-sex desire couched in ritual and on the other as a culture-specific practice that cannot be compared in any way to Western notions of homosexuality—and argued that neither position is adequate. Consistent with the former position are bonding and fantasizing about one's ritual partner, gift giving, protection of the boy by the older male, and frequent continuance of a "special" friend-ship—minus the fellatio—after the boy has achieved manhood and marriage.

Consistent with the latter position are the absence of same-sex behaviors among equal-age-paired partners, the fact that the sexual aspect of the "relationship" is never continuous throughout life (indeed, boys are discouraged from maintaining the same insemination partner for too long), the absence of a "gay" category in Sambian culture, the limitation of same-sex behaviors to males, and the fact that the acts of oral sex are strongly linked to the growth of the boys and only relatively weakly linked to pleasure. Thus, Herdt concluded that what occurs among the Sambia is the fusing of a set of desires with an emphasis on growth and socialization of the young, a practice distinct to time and place; whereas comparisons with other cultures and practices may be made, it is important to be aware of the limitations of such comparisons.

Issues of data measurement and modeling were explored by Berk and Kaplan. Berk reported the findings of a study coauthored by Abramson and Okami that attempted to measure error in self-reports of sexual behavior. Undergraduate students were asked to keep diaries of their sexual experiences and then subsequently asked to recall the number of times they had engaged in various activities during the diary period. The emergence of specific clusters of recall problems called into question the reliability of sexual "histories" that survey researchers generally take for granted.

Kaplan explained to the uninitiated the difference between statistical models, which try to construct unbiased estimates, and policy models, which attempt to "build in" every known bias. Uses of policy modeling in AIDS research and sexual behavior in general were delineated. Kaplan explained how policy modeling reduces the amount of evidence that needs to be collected in attempting to structure questions regarding sexually active populations and briefly reviewed some newer uses of modeling in exploring issues of pleasure—for example, Pinkerton and Abramson's (1992) use of such techniques to explore the notion of "rationality" in "risky" sexual behaviors.

The remainder of the conference was devoted to attempts at synthesis, with the critical question being whether theoretical integration was possible or even desirable. The discussion centered once again on the opposition between empirical data gathering and hypothesis testing and postmodern, postpositivist constructionist scholarship/science. Whereas several participants attempted to resist such dichotomies, they were generally unsuccessful, as the fundamental contradictions between the two approaches resurfaced repeatedly. The more extreme view of them was articulated by Fout, who considered communication across this opposition almost impossible. Tuzin, in contrast, painted an optimistic picture—one that was probably not shared by a majority of participants. He identified a "family of generic categories of problems" emerging from the conference: (1) measurement, (2) biomedical issues related to the existence or nonexistence of "sexuality" as an entity suitable for study, (3) evolutionary mechanisms in reproductive and nonreproductive sex, (4) regulative dimensions of sexuality such as how state societies regulate, control, and dominate in spheres of sexual life, and (5) humanistic concerns for human beings' "deep and abiding interest in sexuality as a topic." He contended that a "meta-problem" emerged from the synergism of the five "problems" just mentioned: What are our choices for the future?

Ultimately, Abramson reflected, we would either grow closer together or become more cognizant of our differences. Herdt noted that whereas we had not gone beyond the categories that dominated the conference chaired in the mid-1960s by Frank Beach—probably the last major attempt to convene a symposium integrating multidisciplinary approaches to the study of sexuality—at least we had looked at categories that had not been on the table since that time. He echoed Abramson in wondering if we could simply accept our differences or at least live with them.

Note

1. The conference participants, their affiliations, and (where appropriate) their paper titles were as follows: Paul R. Abramson (Department of Psychology, University of California at Los Angeles), coorganizer; Robert C. Bailey (Department of Anthropology, University of California at Los Angeles), "Sexuality, Infertility, and Sexually Transmitted Disease among Farmers and Foragers in Central Africa"; Richard Berk (Department of Sociology, University of California at Los Angeles), "Sexual Activity as Told in Surveys" (coauthored by Paul Abramson and Paul Okami); Lawrence Cohen (Department of Anthropology, University of California at Berkeley), "The Mustache Paper"; Franz de Waal (Department of Psychology, Emory University), "Sex as an Alternative to Aggression in the Bonobo"; Michel Feher, "Enamored Pedagogues, Interpreters of the Flesh, and Artists of Desire"; John C. Fout (Department of History, Bard College), "Working-Class Homosexual Desire in Nazi Germany"; David Greenberg (Department of Sociology, New York University), "The Pleasures of Homosexuality"; Thomas Gregor (Department of Anthropology, Vanderbilt University), "Sexuality and the Experience of Love"; Gert Hekma (Department of Sociology, University of Amsterdam), "Modern History of Homosexuality: Theories and Practice"; Gilbert Herdt (Committee on Human Development, University of Chicago), coorganizer; Edward Kaplan (Department of Operations research, Yale University), "Model-Based Representations of Human Sexual Behavior"; Igor Kon (Department of Sociology, Wellesley College), "We Have No Sex! Rediscovery of Sexual Pleasure in Russia"; Lenore Manderson (Tropical Health Program, University of Queensland), "Introspection: Western Representations of Thailand and the Commodification of Sex and Race"; Heino F. L. Meyer-Bahlburg (Department of Psychiatry, Columbia University); Paul Okami (Department of Psychology, University of California at Los Angeles), conference monitor; Angela Pattatucci (National Institute of Health), "The Genetics of Sexual Orientation: From Fruit Flies to Humans"; Mary S. M. Pavelka (Department of Anthropology, University of Calgary), "Aspects of Human Sexuality in a Cross-Species and Evolutionary Perspective"; Alice Schlegel (Department of Anthropology, University of Arizona), "Lusty Children: The Cultural Management of Adolescent Sexuality"; Donald Symons (Department of Anthropology, University of California at Santa Barbara), "Beauty Is in the Adaptations of the Beholder: The Evolutionary Psychology of Facial Attrac-

tiveness"; Donald Tuzin (Department of Anthropology, University of California at San Diego), "The Forgotten Passion: Sexuality and Anthropology in the Age of Victoria"; Carole S. Vance, "Anthropology Rediscovers Sexuality: A Theoretical Comment"; Jeffrey Weeks, "The Pleasures of Intimacy"; and Jean Wilson (Department of Internal Medicine, University of Texas), "Gonadal Hormones in Sexual Behavior." Representing the Wenner-Gren Foundation were Sydel Silverman (President), Laurie Obbink (Conference Program Associate), Ann Berg (Grants Curator), and Fatima da Silva Lopez (Consultant).

References

Abramson, P. R. 1990. Sexual science: Emerging discipline or oxymoron? *Journal of Sex Research* 29:147–66.

Abramson, P. R., and S. D. Pinkerton. 1995. *With pleasure: Thoughts on the nature of human sexuality.* New York: Oxford University Press.

Bowlby, J. 1958. *Attachment and love.* New York: Basic Books.

Frayser, S. 1993. Childhood sexuality from an anthropological perspective. Paper presented at the Western Region meeting of the Society for the Scientific Study of Sex, Seattle, Wash.

Heider, K. G. 1976. Dani sexuality: A low-energy system. *Man* 2:188–201.

Herdt, G. H. 1987. *Guardians of the flutes.* New York: Columbia University Press Morningside Edition.

Lee, J. A. 1973. *The colors of love.* New York: Bantam Books.

Pinkerton, S. D., and P. R. Abramson. 1992. Is risky sex rational? *Journal of Sex Research* 29:561–68.

Shaver, P., C. Hazen, and D. Bradshaw. 1988. "Love as attachment," in *The psychology of love.* Edited by R. J. Sternberg and M. L. Barma. New Haven: Yale University Press.

Sternberg, R. J. 1986. A triangular theory of love. *Psychological Review* 93:119–35.

Tuzin, D. 1991. Sex, culture, and the anthropologist. *Social Science and Medicine* 33:867–74.

Vance, C. S. 1991. Anthropology rediscovers sexuality: A theoretical comment. *Social Science and Medicine* 33:875–84.

Contributors

Paul R. Abramson, Ph.D.
Department of Psychology, University of California, Los Angeles

Robert V. Aunger, Ph.D.
Committee on Human Development, University of Chicago

Robert C. Bailey, Ph.D.
Department of Anthropology, University of California, Los Angeles

Richard Berk, Ph.D.
Department of Sociology, University of California, Los Angeles

Lawrence Cohen, M.D., Ph.D.
Department of Anthropology, University of California, Berkeley

Frans B. M. de Waal, Ph.D.
Yerkes Regional Primate Research Center and Department of Psychology, Emory University

David F. Greenberg, Ph.D.
Department of Sociology, New York University

Thomas Gregor, Ph.D.
Department of Anthropology, Vanderbilt University

Dean H. Hamer, Ph.D.
National Cancer Institute, National Institutes of Health

Edward H. Kaplan, Ph.D.
Yale School of Organization and Management, and Department of Internal Medicine, Yale School of Medicine

Lenore Manderson, Ph.D.
Tropical Health Program, University of Queensland Medical School

Heino F. L. Meyer-Bahlburg, Dr. rer. nat.
New York State Psychiatric Institute, and Department of Psychiatry, College of Physicians and Surgeons of Columbia University

Paul Okami, Ph.D.
Department of Psychology, University of California, Los Angeles

Angela M. L. Pattatucci, Ph.D.
National Cancer Institute, National Institutes of Health

Mary S. McDonald Pavelka, Ph.D.
Department of Anthropology, University of Calgary

Laura Pendleton, B.A.
Department of Psychology, University of California, Los Angeles

Steven D. Pinkerton, Ph.D.
Department of Psychology, University of California, Los Angeles

Alice Schlegel, Ph.D.
Department of Anthropology, University of Arizona

Donald Symons, Ph.D.
Department of Anthropology, University of California, Santa Barbara

Donald Tuzin, Ph.D.
Department of Anthropology, University of California, San Diego

Kim Wallen, Ph.D.
Department of Psychology and Yerkes Regional Primate Research Center, Emory University

Jean D. Wilson, M.D.
Department of Internal Medicine, University of Texas

Index

Abnormal sexual development, 125–30
Abramson, Paul R., 24, 270n.5, 367, 387, 388, 389, 394, 395, 396
Absent testis syndrome, 126
Acne, 96
Activational effects, 139
Adaptationism, 23, 24, 81–87, 103
Adaptations, complex, 83–84
Adolescence, 177–94, 393; adolescent sexuality as nature constrained, 189, 393; adult power over adolescent sexuality, 185–88; avoidance of sibling incest, 184–85; defined, 177; differences in boys and girls, 393; homosexual activity in, 182–84, 190–91; love for adolescent girls, 348n.4; love and freedom in, 337; in primates, 178; promiscuity in, 189; puberty, 130, 177; value of virginity in, 179–82
Adolescent dormitories, 187–88, 192n.4
Adolescent sub-fecundity, 180
Adrenal androgen, 124
Adrenalectomy, 124
Adrenal hyperplasia, congenital (CAH), 126, 127, 128, 140, 142, 145
Africa, 195–222; African sexuality and sexually transmitted diseases, 197–98; attitudes about premarital sex, 213–14; Cameroon, 195, 196; fertility rate in, 195; frequency of sexually transmitted disease in, 196; infertility belt, 195, 215; Ituri Forest, 198, 200–207; Kikuyu, 188; Lesotho, 183; marriage in, 197, 208; medical treatment for sexually transmitted diseases, 211–13; Nigeria, 195; Nyakyusa, 183, 186; procreative ethos in, 197, 215; promiscuity in, 208–9; prostitution in, 197; sexual histories of men in, 207–9; sexually transmitted disease in men, 209–11; Uganda, 195, 196; Zaire, 195, 196, 197

Age: and female sexual attractiveness, 88–90, 106; as a morph, 84; waist-to-hip ratio as index of, 92
Age dependence, 354, 365
Age dependent contact rates, 365
Aggression, 27–31; and biological determinism, 30–31; explanations of male, 28–30; and feeding, 50; in female rhesus monkeys, 67; and immobilization of females, 62; infanticide, 29; in male primates, 28; parental investment explanation of, 28–30; and sex, 27–31, 390; sex as alternative to in the bonobo, 37–56; violence, 335. *See also* Rape
AIDS: and distributions of sexual behavior, 376; effect on homosexual practices, 241; effect on sexual practices, 236; mathematical models for transmission of, 353, 355, 358, 367. *See also* HIV infection
Aise, 280, 281, 301n.2
Alexander, R. D., 218
Allen, L. S., 146
Alligator paths, 339–40
Ambiguous genitalia, 126, 127, 130, 131, 140
Amenorrhea, 96, 214, 215
Amsterdam, 363
Anal intercourse: anal rape, 227; as form of homosexual contact, 236; lubricants for, 247n.18; male versus female anus, 224, 245n.3; role separation model of, 361–62; sodomy, 234, 238; in Thai transvestite cabaret, 316
Androgen action, abnormalities of, 126, 127
Androgen insensitivity, 140, 141, 142
Androgen receptors, defects of the, 126, 127, 141, 144
Androgen replacement therapy, 124
Androgen resistance, 128–29
Androgens: in abnormal sexual development, 127; adrenal androgen, 124; hormonal regu-